NAZISM
1919-1945
A History in Documents and
Eyewitness Accounts

VOLUME I

NAZISM
1919-1945

A History in Documents and
Eyewitness Accounts

VOLUME I

The Nazi Party, State and Society   1919-1939

J. Noakes and G. Pridham, Editors

Schocken Books New York

All rights reserved under International and Pan-American Copyright
Conventions. Published in the United States by Schocken Books Inc.,
New York. Distributed by Pantheon Books, a division of Random
House, Inc., New York. Originally published in Great Britain as *Nazism
1919–1945,* Vols. I and II, by the Department of History and
Archaeology, University of Exeter, in 1983 and 1984.

Library of Congress Cataloging-in-Publication Data

Nazism: A History in Documents and Eyewitness Accounts, 1919–1945
  J. Noakes and G. Pridham, editors.
      p.   cm.
    Reprint. Originally published in 3 v.: Exeter : University of Exeter,
  1983–1988. Originally published in series: Exeter studies in history.
  Includes bibliographical references.
    Contents: v. 1. The Nazi party, state, and society, 1919–1939 —
  v. 2. Foreign policy, war, and racial extermination.
    ISBN 0-8052-0973-5 (v. 1).—ISBN 0-8052-0972-7 (v. 2)
    1. National socialism—History—Sources.   2. Germany—Politics
  and government—1918–1933—Sources.   3. Germany—Politics
  and government—1933–1945—Sources.   I. Noakes, Jeremy.
  II. Pridham, Geoffrey, 1942–
  DD256.5.N365   1990
  943.085—dc20   89-16096

Manufactured in the United States of America

First American Edition

Contents

Preface

This is the first volume of what will be a three-volume collection of documents on Nazism. The second volume covers foreign policy from 1933 to 1939, the waging of war and the practice of genocide. The third volume will cover the German home front from 1933 to 1945, i.e., the political system, economy, society and the Resistance. This first volume is very loosely based on the first four parts of the authors' *Documents on Nazism* (Viking Press 1975), now out of print. However, the commentary has been drastically revised and much of the documentation is new, reflecting the research of the past fifteen years. It contains material from a wide range of sources both published and unpublished: State and Party documents, newspapers, speeches, memoirs, letters and diaries. Since these volumes are aimed primarily at non-specialists, we have felt justified in largely dispensing with a scholarly apparatus. However, in a work such as this the authors are bound to be heavily indebted to fellow scholars. Where this is particularly true we have given an explicit acknowledgement, but we also wish to express our gratitude to those from whose work we have drawn without explicit acknowledgement. Colleagues in the field will in any case be aware of our sources.

We are particularly grateful to Professor Ian Kershaw for useful comments on the manuscripts and his general encouragement of the project, to Dr. Lesley Sharpe for valuable assistance with the burden of translation, and to Mrs. Barbara Mennell, whose role in first bringing these books to press went far beyond the call of duty.

J. Noakes and G. Pridham

Introduction

Nazism was as a political movement essentially a product of the First World War, of defeat and of the revolutionary upheaval which followed. Its ideological roots, however, go back to pre-war Germany. They lay, firstly, in the new wave of antisemitism which began with the 'great depression' of 1873–1896; and secondly, in the emergence of a new radical form of right-wing movement which began in the 1890s and found expression in imperialist pressure groups and anti-democratic organisations such as the Pan-German League. Both of these developments were, in turn, responses to the social dislocation produced by the rapid and uneven industrialisation and urbanisation which followed national unification.

Pre-war German antisemitism appealed to those social and economic groups whose lives were being most seriously disrupted by economic and social change. There were peasant farmers who found it difficult both to adjust to the rapid price fluctuations of a full market economy and to adapt their crops to the changing demand patterns created by urban growth; there were artisans under pressure from the cheap mass produced goods pouring from the new factories; and finally, there were small shopkeepers who were confronted with growing competition from new developments in retailing—the growth of chain and department stores and consumer cooperatives. All these groups, who had traditionally regarded themselves as the backbone of society, the healthy 'middle estate' (*Mittelstand*), now found their economic existence threatened by forces which they could not really understand. Moreover, these economic forces confronted them in the human guise of cattle dealers, corn brokers, department store owners, and money lenders, many of whom—for historical reasons—were Jewish. Furthermore, as the local economy became more and more integrated into the national and international economies, the whole issue acquired a new dimension. For, behind the local dealer or money lender who, at least would be a familiar figure, perhaps resented but difficult to regard as a demon, there appeared to lurk the anonymous forces of high finance—the banks and the stock exchange in which the Jewish presence was well-known to be strong. Against this background, theories of a Jewish conspiracy to destroy the German *Mittelstand* could acquire a certain plausibility. An important aspect of pre-war German antisemitism then represented a revolt by traditional economic and social groups against the economic forces of the modern world, which the Jew came to symbolise and provide a focus of hostility for.

Not only the traditional German *Mittelstand* felt under pressure during the pre-war decades. The German professional classes and intelligentsia were also faced with disturbing changes. The numerical expansion of the traditional professions as well as the creation of new professions or quasi-professions to meet new needs associated with the modernisation process—architects, surveyors, accountants etc.—was often interpreted by traditional professional families as a threat to their professional and social status. Simultaneously, there occurred an influx of Jews into the professions. They took advantage of the process of emancipation associated with the Liberal era of the 1860s to move into occupations hitherto barred to them. Many of these Jewish doctors, lawyers and so on were not only able but also highly motivated to succeed in their new careers and, therefore, were liable to pose strong competition for the established professional community.

Unfortunately, however, the Jews achieved their emancipation just at the moment when the liberal values to which they owed it were about to go into eclipse. Liberalism was discredited firstly, by the fact that national unification had been achieved through the diplomacy and the military power of the conservative Prussian establishment rather than through the pious aspirations of Liberal politicians; secondly, by the economic crisis of the 1870s, which undermined confidence in the basic tenets of Liberal economic theory, and finally, by the failure of Liberalism to respond adequately to the demands of a modern industrial society. The political culture of the new German nation state was to be shaped not by the relatively enlightened liberalism of the years of unification but by a hybrid combination of traditional authoritarian values with a strong militarist flavour and an increasingly influential form of integral nationalism. This integral nationalism had no place for the Jews in its conception of German national identity; indeed, to some extent it defined itself in opposition to them and what they were conceived to represent. But, before looking at this new form of nationalism, there is one other aspect of pre-war antisemitism which needs to be considered—a particularly ominous one.

Towards the end of the nineteenth century, a new pseudo-biological form of antisemitism began to appear which defined Jews not in terms of religion, culture, or ethnicity but as a distinct, biologically determined, and inferior race. Attempts to divide human beings into distinct races and to assign to each a particular rank in a scale of quality have a long history. The first influential modern racial theory was that of the Frenchman, Count Joseph Arthur de Gobineau (1816–1882). Gobineau transformed the term 'Aryan', used by philologists to describe the Indo-Germanic peoples whose languages had been discovered to have a common root, into a racial term. He attributed superior physical and cultural qualities to this 'Aryan race' which he associated with the Germanic as opposed to the Latin or Semitic peoples. Later in the century Gobineau's theory was taken up by influential intellectuals such as Houston Stewart Chamberlain who claimed the Germans were the purest form of Aryans.

Racist theories received encouragement from new advances in biology during the second half of the century which encouraged the attempt to understand human beings and their behaviour primarily in biological terms. Such biological theories did not necessarily imply an antisemitic attitude, just as antisemitism was not necessarily racially motivated. But, by the end of the century, the racist form of antisemitism was becoming an increasingly influential strain within the movement. There was a growing literature, mostly in pamphlet form, which described the Jews as a parasitic race, acting as an element of decomposition within their host nations, and engaged in a conspiracy to achieve world domination.

This theory had important implications for the position of the individual Jew. For since, according to this theory, the Jews were a biologically distinct race, their evil was inherent in each individual Jew. Just as it was impossible for a leopard to change his spots, so it was impossible for a Jew to cease being a Jew i.e. evil. By definition, there could be no such a thing as a good Jew. When, as in the past, antisemitism had been motivated by religious or economic factors, it had been possible for Jews to escape persecution by religious conversion or, at any rate after emancipation, by changing their occupations. But, if racist antisemitism had its way, there could be no possibility of escape. Indeed, racist antisemites were already beginning to draw the logical conclusions from their own premises. Thus, the Hamburg programme of the 'Union of Antisemitic parties', formed in 1899, stated that 'since the Jewish question in the course of the twentieth century will become a question of world significance, it must be finally solved by the separation and finally by the extermination of the Jewish people.'

Before 1914, antisemitism as an organised movement was by no means unique to Germany. Indeed, by comparison with Austria-Hungary and even France, it was relatively insignificant. Its organisations were divided and their membership comparatively small and this was reflected in their

tiny political representation in the Reichstag. Nevertheless, in the form of
a basic dislike of the Jews and of what they were felt to represent, it had
succeeded in permeating broad sections of German society from the Kaiser
down to the lower middle class. Ominously, it was particularly strongly
entrenched within the academic community, thereby influencing the next
generation.

Above all, antisemitism had become accepted as an essential component
of a new definition of German nationalism which had become dominant by
1914. This new populist (*völkisch*) form of nationalism emerged during the
1890s and radicalised German right-wing politics. It reflected the increasing politicisation of the mass of the population as a result of rapid
industrialisation and urbanisation. On the one hand, this politicisation
found expression in the rise of the Social Democratic Party on the Left,
representing industrial workers. On the other hand — partly in response —
it also saw the political mobilisation of petty bourgeois groups and the
consequent emergence of a basis for a mass politics of the Right.

This 'new Right'—like its French counterpart—developed outside the
political parties in pressure group-type organisations known as 'leagues'—
the Pan-German League, the Navy League etc. Its ideology reflected the
ideas and political aspirations of the middle-class generation which had
grown up in the immediate aftermath of German unification and came to
maturity in the 1890s and 1900s. These men had discarded the remnants of
the enlightened 1848 Liberalism of their fathers and grandfathers. According to Heinrich Class, who became chairman of the Pan-German League,
three ideals had characterised the liberalism of his father's generation:
'patriotism, tolerance, humanity'. However, 'we youngsters had moved
on: we were nationalist pure and simple. We wanted nothing to do with
tolerance if it sheltered the enemies of the *Volk* and the state. Humanity in
the sense of that liberal idea we spurned, for our *Volk* was bound to come
off worse.'[1] For men like Class the fortunes of the new German state had
acquired paramount importance; their own self-esteem came to be bound
up with the prestige of the new Reich.

The populist flavour of this new nationalism derived from their sense of
exclusion from the traditional Prusso-German establishment. As successful
businessmen, professionals and bureaucrats who had benefited from the
rapid economic development following unification, they resented the
patronising attitudes of the traditional elites who tended to regard them as
parvenus. Moreover, they felt that the elitist nature of the political
establishment weakened Germany by alienating the masses, encouraging
the growth of class spirit and dividing the nation. In their view, this
fragmentation of the nation was also encouraged by the existing political

---

[1] Quoted in G. Eley, 'Reshaping the Right: Radical Nationalism and the German Navy
League 1898–1908' in *Historical Journal* 21.2.1978 p.348. This section owes much to the work
of this author.

system of parliamentary and party government. This, it was felt, simply reinforced the divisions between Germans and led to the sacrifice of national interests for the benefit of sectional advantage. They rejected the idea central to liberal democracy that the national interest could only emerge out of the free interplay of differing interests and groups. Instead, they proclaimed a mythical concept of the *Volk*—an equivalent to the *pays reél* of pre-1914 French integral nationalism—as the real source of legitimacy and claimed that current political institutions (the Reichstag, parties etc.) were distorting the true expression of national will. In their view, the key to uniting the nation was the indoctrination of an ideology of extreme nationalism; above all, the goal of imperial expansion would rally and unite the nation.

For the *völkisch* movement the Jews represented the 'golden international' of high finance and Western liberalism which, together with the 'black international' of the Roman Catholic Church and the 'red international' of Socialism, threatened to undermine German national unity and the German cultural identity. In other words, they saw behind their domestic opponents—the left Liberals, the Catholic Centre party, and the Social Democrats—a foreign threat; domestic opposition was a form of treason. This way of thinking had been prepared to some extent by Bismarck's habit of labelling his same political opponents 'enemies of the Reich'. It was also to bedevil the Weimar Republic when the Versailles settlement instead of uniting the nation fatally divided it.

By 1914, the *völkisch* Right had begun to impose their radical intolerant stamp on German right-wing politics. Faced with the apparently inexorable rise of the Social Democratic Party, which in the 1912 election had become the largest single party in the Reichstag, and faced with a government which not only appeared weak in foreign affairs but, above all, seemed increasingly willing to seek an accommodation with the moderate Left, the old traditional, conservative Right began to make common cause with the new radical Right.

It was, however, during the course of the First World War that this new Right seized the initiative. The main focus of their efforts was a campaign to commit the Government to a so-called *Siegfrieden* in which Germany would use her expected victory to demand large-scale territorial annexations in both East and West and in the form of overseas colonies. This was regarded as vital not simply in order to reestablish Germany as a world power, but also as a means of diverting pressure for democratic reform at home. As the pressure for a compromise peace and for constitutional reform increased after 1916, the Right responded with even more vigorous agitation. The main emphasis of this campaign was on trying to reach a mass audience. On 24 September 1917, in a direct response to the Reichstag Peace Resolution of 17 July, a new party was founded—the Fatherland Party. Financed by heavy industry, and organised by the

Pan-German League and similar bodies, its aim was to mobilise mass support for a *Siegfrieden* and to resist moves towards parliamentary democracy. The party soon acquired over a million members, mainly among the middle class.

The Pan-Germans were, however, particularly anxious to reach the working class. Already, in the summer of 1917, a 'Free Committee for a German Workers' Peace' had been established in Bremen by the leader of a 'yellow' i.e. pro-employer workers' association in the Krupp dockyards, which carried out imperialist propaganda suported by the Army authorities. Among its claimed 290,000 members was a skilled worker in the railway workshops in Munich named Anton Drexler, who established a Munich branch of the organisation on 7 March 1918 and who soon was to become a co-founder of the Nazi Party. Its success, however, was limited; it only acquired forty members. Drexler's failure to mobilise the working class for Pan-German policies reflected a general pattern and this lack of success prompted the Pan-German leadership to seek more effective propaganda themes.

From the autumn of 1917 onwards, antisemitism came to play an increasing role in Pan-German propaganda until, by the spring of 1918, it had become a key factor. On 13 April 1918, at a meeting of the executive committee of the Pan-German League, Heinrich Class noted 'a satisfactory growth in the antisemitic mood which had already reached an enormous extent...Our task will be to bring this movement out on to the national political arena...for the Jews the struggle for existence has begun.' This trend increased as Germany moved towards defeat and as the threat of democratic reforms increased. At another meeting on 20 October, Class argued that 'if the political goal of the war can be achieved through a dictatorship then it will be unnecessary to bring up the Jewish question.' But, if it could not be, he went on, then it would be vital to do so. For, in a struggle with the parliamentary system 'one of the most effective means of influencing people is through fear of the Jews'. In which case it should 'not be treated simply in an academic-political fashion but also in a demagogic-practical one'. They should exploit the 'situation for fanfares against the Jews and use the Jews as a lightning conductor for all injustices'. In short the Jews were to be made the scapegoat for the national humiliation of defeat, a defeat for which in reality the German establishment bore full responsibility. Class concluded: 'I will not be afraid to use any means and, in this connexion, will follow Heinrich von Kleist's dictum [which referred to the French]: 'Strike them dead; at the last Judgment you will not be asked for your reasons'.[2]

---

[2] Quoted in W. Jochmann, 'Die Ausbreitung des Antisemitismus' in W. E. Mosse and A. Paucker, eds. *Deutsches Judentum in Krieg und Revolution 1916–1923* (Tübingen 1971) pp. 438–440.

PART I
THE RISE TO POWER
1919–1934

CHAPTER 1

From the Founding of the Party to the Putsch 1919–1923

(i) The Founding of the Party

The German military collapse in the Autumn of 1918 was followed by a revolution at the beginning of November, forcing the Kaiser to abdicate. The semi-autocratic regime of the Second Reich was replaced in 1919 by a constitution accepted by a National Assembly meeting at Weimar, establishing a parliamentary democracy similar to those of Germany's enemies in the West. This represented a victory for the opposition forces of the Empire—Social Democrats, Catholics, and left-wing Liberals. They benefited from the fact that the majority of the population associated the Kaiser and his government with defeat and felt Germany needed a new start. Many hoped democratic reforms would conciliate the Allies and produce more favourable peace terms.

The *völkisch* movement, however, refused to accept the triumph of the Left and determined to reverse it. They saw the key to this in the mobilisation of the masses against the Left through a campaign of antisemitism. The Pan-German League had already established a special committee in September to coordinate antisemitic propaganda, including representatives from the various antisemitic organisations. From December 1918 onwards, a flood of antisemitic propaganda in the form of leaflets, pamphlets, speeches, and lectures—all paid for by sections of heavy industry—poured over Germany. Its main theme was that the Jews had conspired to defeat Germany and promote revolution as a stage on the path towards their goal of world domination.

Although the working class remained largely resistant to this propaganda, it did achieve some resonance among the middle class. Defeat had come as a great shock to the German people; until the last moment they had been lulled into believing all was well. The revolution had alarmed and dismayed the middle class. Since the German establishment had lost its credibility and was paralysed by the events of November 1918 there were no satisfactory explanations for what had happened from traditional opinion leaders. So, for a time at least, the antisemitic agitators were operating in a political vacuum. In this chaotic situation, ideas of a conspiracy by Jewish international capital in league with the West, and of a 'stab in the back' by Jewish-Bolshevik agitators could seem plausible to desperate and bewildered middle class people, particularly since latent antisemitic feelings were already widespread and deep-rooted.

During 1919, as the population became increasingly disillusioned with the moderate Left government, the political mood in Germany shifted further and further to the extremes. The Peace Settlement of Versailles had imposed severe conditions on Germany and had met with a wave of protest. In particular, the 'war-guilt clause' by which Germany was obliged to accept full blame for the war stuck in the throats of the German people. Some of the unpopularity of the treaty was transferred to the Government, which had been obliged to sign it and to the new democratic system itself, which had been expected to pacify the Allies but was now associated with national humiliation.

Particular foci of Pan-German antisemitic agitation were the Army, which was particularly anxious to counter left-wing or even democratic subversion in its ranks, and also the Free Corps. The Free Corps were paramilitary formations composed of ex-army officers and volunteers, mostly young men from the middle- and lower-middle classes. They were recruited by the government to suppress left-wing revolutionary activity, to defend the eastern borders against Polish incursions, and to retain German influence in the Baltic states. The Free Corps proved extremely fertile soil for *völkisch* propaganda. It was not surprising, therefore, that the first major challenge to the new democratic order—in March 1920—came from an attempted coup carried out by a Free Corps, resisting its disbandment under the terms of the Versailles settlement. It operated in collaboration with high-ranking army officers and Conservative politicians and, significantly, the coup or 'putsch' was led by a prominent Pan-German, the Prussian civil servant, Friedrich Kapp. The putsch proved unsuccessful, partly as a result of a general strike called by the deposed Socialist government and the Trade Unions, partly because of the refusal of cooperation by key civil servants and Army leaders, and partly because of the incompetence of its leaders. But, though it failed to establish its authority at national level, the Right was far more successful in the state of Bavaria.

The Founding of the Nazi Party

The Nazi Party was merely one of a number of similar *völkisch* groups which sprang up all over Germany during 1919. It had, however, the particular advantage of being based in Bavaria, where events had been especially turbulent. The swing to the Left had been more marked than elsewhere; the swing to the Right was correspondingly strong. From the beginning of November 1918, there were four different left-wing regimes within a period of six months. But, on 1 May 1919, all revolutionary activity was crushed by troops sent by the Socialist central government, including the Free Corps. This force put down the revolution with considerable ferocity and restored the previous moderate Socialist government in Bavaria. In the meantime, however, the revolutionary events of these months had alienated the traditionally conservative population, many of whom were Catholic peasants. They also resented the removal of some of Bavaria's constitutional privileges by the Weimar Constitution. In March 1920, a right-wing group exploited the disorder caused by the Kapp putsch to carry out their own coup in Bavaria and replaced the Socialist government by a right-wing regime under a Conservative, Gustav von Kahr. Under the Weimar Constitution the police were responsible to the federal states rather than to the central or Reich government. So, for the next few years, Bavaria became a haven for right-wing extremists from all over Germany. In many other states and particularly in Prussia (which covered three-fifths of Germany), they were harried by the police at the orders of Socialist-dominated state governments. But in Bavaria the state authorities regarded their activities with benevolence. The early months of left-wing extremism had produced an excessive preoccupation with the threat of Bolshevism and an atmosphere in which the Nazi Party could flourish.

The defeat and revolution of November 1918 created favourable conditions for the birth of Nazism; the *völkisch* movement and the Army were to act as midwives. As elsewhere, the Army in Bavaria held indoctrination courses for its personnel, addressed by Pan-Germans and other supporters of the *völkisch* Right. Among the soldiers who attended such a course in Munich was a thirty year old private, Adolf Hitler. The son of an Austrian customs official, Hitler had been influenced by the Pan-German nationalism current among much of the German-speaking population of pre-war Austria-Hungary and of which his history teacher in Linz had been an ardent supporter. He despised the multi-national Habsburg empire as an ethnic mishmash and his consciousness of his German cultural identity was no doubt reinforced by his years spent among the rootless in the men's hostels of pre-war Vienna after failing his entry examination to the Art Academy. It was presumably comforting to feel that, although he was living among the socially deprived, he was at least a member of the master race of the empire. He had also acquired the Pan-German dislike for Catholic politics and, above all, their hostility to the Social Democrats. His dislike of the 'reds' was no doubt reinforced by his desperate struggle to maintain his petty bourgeois status above the ranks of the workers. During his Vienna years, Hitler also appears to have adopted the racist form of antisemitism which was to form the core of his future ideology. Various forms of antisemitism were virulent in pre-war Vienna including its racist version which was popularised in numerous pamphlets which Hitler eagerly devoured. It evidently provided him with an answer to the problems of identity and purpose which had troubled him.

After moving to Munich in 1913 to try and improve his prospects as an artist and also to escape National Service for the despised Habsburg Empire, he eked out a precarious existence selling his paintings. His artistic ambitions had been frustrated; his petty bourgeois social pride was being constantly humiliated through the circumstances of his daily life; like many a young man in his position, his only refuge from his colourless existence lay in day-dreaming about grandiose future achievements, in his case in the field of architecture. In this situation the outbreak of war came as a godsend. He immediately volunteered for the Bavarian Army in which he was to prove a loyal, brave, and efficient soldier. At last he had found a purpose and order in his life. Ironically, however, his C.O. did not recommend the future Führer for promotion on the grounds that 'he lacked leadership qualities'! Wounded by a gas attack in the Spring of 1918, he emerged from hospital to find his world in ruins: Germany had been defeated and the old order overthrown. He was still in the Army, but was not likely to be kept on for long and what then? The prospect of a return to his aimless, hand-to-mouth pre-war existence must have seemed bleak. In fact, however, the chaos produced by defeat and revolution was to offer opportunities to a man of Hitler's background and qualities which would have been inconceivable in the stable order of the pre-war world. In the historical conjuncture of Hitler's return to Munich after the war the man, the place, and the moment were made for one another.

Soon after his arrival in Munich Hitler was assigned by the Army to one of the political indoctrination courses being run with the assistance of the Pan-German League. Here he flourished. His endless arguments with fellow inmates of the men's hostels in pre-war Vienna had laid the foundations of his abilities as a mass orator; and now he found in lectures to other members of the course that he had a real talent for public speaking. His oratorical abilities drew him to the attention of Captain Mayr, head of the Press and Propaganda section in the Bavarian section of the Army. Mayr decided to use Hitler as an agent to keep an eye on the various political activities going on in Munich.

As part of this activity, Hitler was assigned to report on the German Workers' Party (DAP), led by the railway mechanic, Anton Drexler, and a journalist, Karl Harrer. The party had been founded on 9 January 1919 on Drexler's initiative and under the auspices of the so-called Thule Society, a cover name for the headquarters of the *völkisch* movement in Munich, of whom Harrer was effectively the representative on the Party's executive committee. Drexler later described what happened at the meeting which Hitler attended:

1

On 12 September 1919, the German Workers' Party held a monthly meeting in the Veterans' Hall of the Sterneckerbräu, in the so-called 'Leiber Room'. Gottfried Feder spoke on the 'Breaking of Interest Slavery'. The first National Socialist pamphlet, *My Political Awakening: From the Diary of a German Socialist Worker*, had just appeared. I had collected a few proof copies from the publisher, Dr Boepple, and was standing with five copies in my hand at the bar of the pub, listening with growing enthusiasm to the second speaker in the evening's discussion, who was a guest. He was dealing with the first speaker in the discussion, a Professor Baumann, who had urged the secession of Bavaria from Germany, and he was tackling the Professor in a way which it was a joy to watch. He gave a short but trenchant speech in favour of a greater Germany which thrilled me and all who could hear him. When the speaker had finished I rushed towards him, thanked him for what he had said and asked him to take the pamphlet I had away with him to read. It contained, I said, the rules and basic ideas of the new movement; if he was in agreement with them, he could come again in a week's time and work in a smaller circle, because we could do with people like him.

This was Hitler. He was persuaded to join the Party, whose membership was still very small and, by the end of the year, had become its propaganda chief. The DAP provided him with an outlet for his political energies and it was small enough to enable him to make his influence felt immediately. It attracted him because of its emphasis on antisemitism and on the need to win over the masses. His experience as a soldier had taught him the importance of morale and of the part played by propaganda in influencing morale. He believed the Allies had been more successful at mobilising the energy and enthusiasm of their own people and that the Germans had lost because of Socialist propaganda which had undermined their morale in the interests of international Jewry. He believed that Germany must learn from the Allies and that the first task must be to win the masses for nationalism and antisemitism. Only when this had been achieved would she be able to assert herself abroad.

His military superiors were happy to encourage his political activity and it was at their request that, on 16 September 1919, he wrote his first major political statement in reply to a letter asking for information on the Jewish problem from one of his fellow-participants in the Army indoctrination course, Adolf Gemlich. It expressed a number of ideas which were to remain basic to his thought for the rest of his life. Important, for example, was his emphasis on the fact that the Jews were a racial community rather than a religious group. Secondly, there was the emphasis on the need for the 'rebirth of the moral and spiritual energies of the nation...through the ruthless action of personalitics with a capacity for national leadership', though there is no evidence that he yet saw himself in such a role.

2

If the danger represented by the Jews today finds expression in the undeniable dislike of them felt by a large section of our people, the cause of this dislike is on the whole not to be found in the clear recognition of the corrupting activity of the Jews generally among our people, whether conscious or unconscious; it originates mainly through personal relationship, and from the impression left behind him by the individual Jew which is almost invariably unfavourable. Antisemitism thereby acquires only too easily the character of being a manifestation of emotion. But this is wrong. Antisemitism as a political movement must not be, cannot be, determined by emotional criteria, but only through the recognition of facts. The facts are as follows: First, the Jews are definitely a race and not a religious community. The Jew himself never calls himself a Jewish German, a Jewish Pole, a Jewish American, but only a German, a Polish, an American Jew. From the foreign nations in whose midst he lives the Jew has adopted very little more than their language. A German who is compelled to use French in France, Italian in Italy, Chinese in China, does not thereby become a Frenchman, an Italian, or a Chinese; similarly a Jew who happens to live among us and is thereby compelled to use the German language cannot be called a German. Even the Mosaic faith, however important for the maintenance of this race, cannot be considered as absolutely decisive in the question of whether or not someone is a Jew. There is hardly a single race whose members belong exclusively to one particular religion.

Through a thousand years of inbreeding, often practised within a very narrow circle, the Jew has in general preserved his race and character much more rigorously than many of the peoples among whom he lives. And as a result, there is living amongst us a non-German, foreign race, unwilling and unable to sacrifice its racial characteristics, to deny its own feeling, thinking and striving, and which none the less possesses all the political rights that we ourselves have. The feelings of the Jew are concerned with purely material things; his thoughts and desires even more so. The dance round the golden calf becomes a ruthless struggle for all those goods which, according to our innermost feelings, should not be the highest and most desirable things on this earth.

The value of the individual is no longer determined by his character, by the importance of his achievements for all, but solely by the amount of his possessions, by his money.

The value of the nation is no longer to be measured in terms of the sum of its moral and spiritual forces, but solely on the basis of the wealth of its material goods.

From this feeling emerges that concern and striving for money and for the power which can protect it which makes the Jew unscrupulous in his choice of means, ruthless in his use of them to achieve this aim.

In an autocratically governed state he whines for the favour of the 'Majesty' of the prince and abuses it to batten on his subjects like a leech. In a democracy he courts the favour of the masses, crawls before the 'majesty of the people' and yet knows only the majesty of money.

He destroys the character of the prince with byzantine flattery, and national pride, which is the strength of a nation, with mockery and shameless training in vice. His weapon is that public opinion which is never given utterance by the press, but is always led by it and falsified by it. His power is the power of money which in the form of interest effortlessly and interminably multiplies itself in his hands and forces upon nations that most dangerous of yokes, the sad consequences of which are so difficult to perceive because of the initial gleam of gold. Everything which makes men strive for higher things, whether religion, socialism or democracy, is for him only a means to an end, to the satisfaction of a lust for money and domination. His activities produce a racial tuberculosis among nations.

And this has the following result: Antisemitism stemming from purely emotive reasons will always find its expression in the form of programs [sic]. But antisemitism based on reason must lead to the systematic legal combating and removal of the rights of the Jew, which he alone of the foreigners living among us possesses (legislation to make them aliens). Its final aim, however, must be the uncompromising removal of the Jews altogether. Both are possible only under a government of national strength, never under a government of national impotence.

The Republic in Germany owes its birth not to the united national will of our people but to the cunning exploitation of a series of circumstances which combined to produce a deep general discontent. But these circumstances were independent of the form of the State, and are still active today; more active, indeed, today than before. And a large section of our people is aware that no mere change in the form of the State as such can alter or improve our position, but only the rebirth of the moral and spiritual energies of the nation.

This rebirth will be set in motion not by the political leadership of irresponsible majorities under the influence of party dogmas or of an irresponsible press, nor by catchwords and slogans of international coinage, but only through the ruthless action of personalities with a capacity for national leadership and an inner sense of responsibility.

But this fact robs the Republic of the internal support of the spiritual forces of the nation which are so necessary. And so the present leaders of the State are compelled to seek support from those who alone benefited from the changed situation in Germany and do so now, and who for this reason have been the driving forces of the revolution, namely, the Jews. Taking no account of the Jewish peril, which has certainly been recognised by present-day leaders—proof of this is the various statements of present leading figures—they are compelled to accept the support readily offered by the Jews for their own benefit, and therefore to pay the required price. And this price consists not only in giving the Jews every possible encouragement, but above all in hampering the struggle of the duped nation against their brother Jews—in the neutralising of the antisemitic movement.

Apart from antisemitism, extreme nationalism and a form of anti-capitalism predominated in the Party's propaganda at this stage. All these elements were present in the Party programme which was presented on 24 February 1920 to a public meeting in the Hofbräuhaus, a big Munich beer cellar. The programme, often erroneously ascribed to Gottfried Feder who played an influential role in the early years of the Party, was in fact almost certainly composed by Drexler and Hitler and only Point 11 derives from Feder.

3

The Programme of the German Workers' Party is designed to be of limited duration. The leaders have no intention, once the aims announced in it have been achieved, of establishing fresh ones, merely in order to increase, artificially, the discontent of the masses and so ensure the continued existence of the Party.

1. We demand the union of all Germans in a Greater Germany on the basis of the right of national self-determination.

2. We demand equality of rights for the German people in its dealings with other nations, and the revocation of the peace treaties of Versailles and Saint-Germain.

3. We demand land and territory (colonies) to feed our people and to settle our surplus population.

4. Only members of the nation may be citizens of the State. Only those of German blood, whatever their creed, may be members of the nation. Accordingly, no Jew may be a member of the nation.

5. Non-citizens may live in Germany only as guests and must be subject to laws for aliens.

6. The right to vote on the State's government and legislation shall be enjoyed by the citizens of the State alone. We demand therefore that all official appointments, of whatever kind, whether in the Reich, in the states or in the smaller localities, shall be held by none but citizens.

We oppose the corrupting parliamentary custom of filling posts merely in accordance with party considerations, and without reference to character or abilities.

7. We demand that the State shall make it its primary duty to provide a livelihood for its citizens. If it should prove impossible to feed the entire population, foreign nationals (non-citizens) must be deported from the Reich.

8. All non-German immigration must be prevented. We demand that all non-Germans who entered Germany after 2 August 1914 shall be required to leave the Reich forthwith.
9. All citizens shall have equal rights and duties.
10. It must be the first duty of every citizen to perform physical or mental work. The activities of the individual must not clash with the general interest, but must proceed within the framework of the community and be for the general good.
We demand therefore:
11. The abolition of incomes unearned by work.
The breaking of the slavery of interest
12. In view of the enormous sacrifices of life and property demanded of a nation by any war, personal enrichment from war must be regarded as a crime against the nation. We demand therefore the ruthless confiscation of all war profits.
13. We demand the nationalisation of all businesses which have been formed into corporations (trusts).
14. We demand profit-sharing in large industrial enterprises.
15. We demand the extensive development of insurance for old age.
16. We demand the creation and maintenance of a healthy middle class, the immediate communalising of big department stores, and their lease at a cheap rate to small traders, and that the utmost consideration shall be shown to all small traders in the placing of State and municipal orders.
17. We demand a land reform suitable to our national requirements, the passing of a law for the expropriation of land for communal purposes without compensation; the abolition of ground rent, and the prohibition of all speculation in land.
18. We demand the ruthless prosecution of those whose activities are injurious to the common interest. Common criminals, usurers, profiteers, etc., must be punished with death, whatever their creed or race.
19. We demand that Roman Law, which serves a materialistic world order, be replaced by a German common law.
20. The State must consider a thorough reconstruction of our national system of education (with the aim of opening up to every able and hard-working German the possibility of higher education and of thus obtaining advancement). The curricula of all educational establishments must be brought into line with the requirements of practical life. The aim of the school must be to give the pupil, beginning with the first sign of intelligence, a grasp of the notion of the State (through the study of civic affairs). We demand the education of gifted children of poor parents, whatever their class or occupation, at the expense of the State.
21. The State must ensure that the nation's health standards are raised by protecting mothers and infants, by prohibiting child labour, by promoting physical strength through legislation providing for compulsory gymnastics and sports, and by the extensive support of clubs engaged in the physical training of youth.
22. We demand the abolition of the mercenary [i.e. professional] army and the formation of a people's army.
23. We demand legal warfare on deliberate political mendacity and its dissemination in the press. To facilitate the creation of a German national press we demand:
(a) that all editors of, and contributors to newspapers appearing in the German language must be members of the nation;

(b) that no non-German newspapers may appear without the express permission of the State. They must not be printed in the German language;

(c) that non-Germans shall be prohibited by law from participating financially in or influencing German newspapers, and that the penalty for contravening such a law shall be the suppression of any such newspaper, and the immediate deportation of the non-Germans involved.

The publishing of papers which are not conducive to the national welfare must be forbidden. We demand the legal prosecution of all those tendencies in art and literature which corrupt our national life, and the suppression of cultural events which violate this demand.

24. We demand freedom for all religious denominations in the State, provided they do not threaten its existence nor offend the moral feelings of the German race.

The Party, as such, stands for positive Christianity, but does not commit itself to any particular denomination. It combats the Jewish-materialist spirit within and without us, and is convinced that our nation can achieve permanent health only from within on the basis of the principle: *The common interest before self-interest.*

25. To put the whole of this programme into effect, we demand the creation of a strong central state power for the Reich; the unconditional authority of the political central Parliament over the entire Reich and its organisations; and the formation of Corporations based on estate and occupation for the purpose of carrying out the general legislation passed by the Reich in the various German states.

The leaders of the Party promise to work ruthlessly—if need be to sacrifice their very lives—to translate this programme into action.

When Hitler joined the DAP the Party was small and insignificant. No doubt he later exaggerated its weakness in order to emphasise his own impact upon it, but the following description, written in a newspaper article in 1929, is probably fairly accurate, at least for the very early period up to about October 1919:

4

Our little committee, which with its seven members in reality represented the whole party, was nothing but the managing committee of a small whist [*Skat*] club. The procedure was very simple. Every Wednesday a committee meeting took place. To start with, we met in a pathetic little room in a small pub, 'Rosenbad', in the Herrenstrasse... . In 1919, Munich was still in a bad way. Not much light, a good deal of dirt, refuse, shabby people, down-at-heel soldiers, in short the sort of picture which could be expected after four-and-a-half years of war, especially if, as in the case of Germany, the war had been followed by a shocking revolution. So it was a very poor 'committee room' in which we met... . The committee's proceedings consisted in reading out letters received, discussing replies to them, and registering the letters that were sent off following this discussion, i.e., reading them out also. Since that time I have developed a deadly hatred of writing letters and of letter writers.

It was always the same people, probably the chairmen of associations similar in size. We were sent comradely greetings, we were told that in their particular place the seed had been sown or had even sprouted. We were asked if we could say the same of ourselves and the necessity of joint action was stressed. We had also 'association funds'. These consisted of material goods and cash. The cash fluctuated around 5 marks, and when times were good it rose to 12, 13, 15, and once, I remember, even to 17 marks. The material goods consisted of a cigar box in which the money was kept, notepaper, envelopes, a few stamps and the 'statutes' of the association.

Hitler's main contribution to the Party in this early period was his ability as a political speaker and his drive and energy. The following excerpt from a speech by Hitler on 26 October 1920, based on notes taken by a member of the Bavarian political police, indicates some of the main themes which he emphasised during this period. The speech, entitled 'National Welfare and Nationalist Idea' was given in the Kindlkeller, a Munich beer cellar:

5

We need some national pride again. But who can the nation be proud of these days? Of Ebert[3] perhaps? (*laughter*) Of the Government? We need a national will just as much. We must not always say: We can't do that. We must be able to do it. In order to smash this disgraceful peace treaty, we must regard every means as justified (*loud applause*). First, there must be a nationalist mood and then will come the economic prosperity of the nation. We must have blind faith in our future, in our recovery.

Now Hitler turned to deal with the Right and the Left. The Nationalists on the Right lack a social sense, the Socialists on the Left a nationalist one. He appeals to the parties on the Right: If you want to be nationalist then come down among your people and put away all your class pride. To the Left he appeals: You who proclaim your solidarity with the whole world, first show your solidarity with your own compatriots, be Germans first and foremost. Do they look like heroes who want to smash the world and yet crawl before foreigners for fear they might not like something they see here? (*applause*) You who are real revolutionaries, come over to us and fight with us for our whole nation (*loud applause*). Your place is not over there with the procurers of international capital, but with us, with your own people!! (*stormy applause*).

Then Hitler turned to the future of Germany, to the youth of Germany, and, in particular, with warm words for their intellectual leaders, the German students. Your place is with us, with the people. You who are still young and still have the fire of enthusiasm in your veins, come over to us, join our fighting party, which pursues its aims ruthlessly, with every means, even with force! (*loud applause*) We are not a class party, but the party of honest producers (*Schaffenden*). Our strength does not lie in the International but in our own strength, that is to say in our people! (*long and stormy applause*)

---

[3] Friedrich Ebert, Social Democrat President of the Weimar Republic, 1919–25.

Hitler succeeded in establishing a notable *rapport* with the Munich masses whose economic plight was worsening owing to progressive inflation. He showed remarkable intuition in sensing and articulating their hopes and fears. He succeeded in projecting himself as a representative figure—an ex-soldier now drifting without a regular job, filled with hatred and resentment against those he considered responsible for the plight of Germany, which he in turn identified with the personal plight of his audience. He not only showed that he understood his hearers' mood and their predicament and gave them an emotionally convincing explanation for their problems; he also conveyed his own willpower and determination to change things, to restore Germany to her former greatness and to destroy those who were responsible for the present situation. Kurt Ludecke, one of Hitler's early associates, later recorded his impressions on first hearing him speak in 1922:

6

My critical faculty was swept away. Leaning from the rostrum as if he were trying to impel his inner self into the consciousness of all these thousands, he was holding the masses, and me with them, under an hypnotic spell by the sheer force of his conviction... . I do not know how to describe the emotions that swept over me as I heard this man. His words were like a scourge. When he spoke of the disgrace of Germany, I felt ready to spring on any enemy. His appeal to German manhood was like a call to arms; the gospel he preached, a sacred truth. He seemed another Luther. I forgot everything but the man; then glancing around, I saw that his magnetism was holding these thousands as one. Of course I was ripe for this experience. I was a man of thirty-two, weary with disgust and disillusionment, a wanderer seeking a cause, a patriot without a channel for his patriotism, a yearner after the heroic without a hero. The intense will of the man, the passion of his sincerity, seemed to flow from him into me. I experienced an exaltation that could be likened only to religious conversion.

In February 1920 the Party had changed its name to 'National Socialist German Workers' Party' (NSDAP), thereby emphasising its attempt to combine both a nationalist and a socialist appeal. An early membership list of some 200 names showed a fair cross-section of the city's population: tradesmen, craftsmen, shopkeepers, bank and post-office employees, and a few doctors and engineers as well as a number of soldiers and workers. Largely as a result of Hitler's successful oratory, membership gradually increased to 2,000 at the end of 1920, 3,300 by August 1921 and branches were beginning to be founded outside Munich. The first was established in Rosenheim, forty miles from Munich, as early as April 1920. In July 1921 a branch was founded in Hanover and one or two others followed elsewhere. In November 1922, however, the Party was banned in Prussia and in some other states; Bavaria, and Munich in particular, remained the main centre. The success of the Party drew the attention of military circles. At the end of 1920, with the assistance of funds from the Reichswehr, the Party purchased a newspaper. Having appeared since 1887 as the *Münchener Beobachter*, a racialist weekly, the *Völkischer Beobachter* (*VB*), as it had been renamed on 9 August 1919, was now published twice a week as the organ of the NSDAP. It did not become a daily until 8 February 1923. The state of the Party's finances was at the moment precarious. Funds were derived from membership dues, very small, collections at meetings and occasional contributions from wealthy sympathisers. Nearly all the staff were unpaid.

(ii) Hitler takes over the Party leadership, August 1921

By mid-1921 Hitler had clearly established himself as the key figure in the Party. It owed its rise in membership to his abilities as a speaker, and he also possessed extremely useful connexions with the Army, which he had left on 31 March 1920, through Captain Ernst Röhm, who acted as a political liaison officer for the Army HQ and was a member of the NSDAP. Yet Hitler was still officially only the propaganda chief. In January 1920 Harrer had been obliged to resign as chairman of the Party. He had disagreed with Hitler and Drexler about the intensive propaganda activities of the Party, wishing it to remain a select group on the lines of a Masonic lodge. Harrer had been replaced as chairman by Drexler, who recognised Hitler's ability and, as he told Feder on 13 February 1921, wanted him to assume more responsibility in the organisation, 'though without my being pushed into the background in consequence'. Hitler himself, however, rightly regarded his propaganda activities as the most important function in the Party, particularly since he still saw his objective as the winning of 'the masses' for more important nationalist figures. He was not tempted by the routine work of chairman and declined Drexler's offer of the post. Shortly after, however, the question of the Party organisation and Hitler's position within it was brought to a head when the committee began to pursue a course of action to which Hitler strongly objected. This brought home to him for the first time the importance of the formal distribution of power within the organisation and forced him not only to take over the chairmanship but to establish a new structure of authority in which the chairman was no longer merely *primus inter pares* within a committee, but a leader, superior to the committee. The crisis persuaded him that only in this way could he ensure that the Party pursued the policies which he believed were the right ones. And then, having established his position as leader, he rationalised this development with a theory of political leadership which condemned the traditional form of committee organisation and insisted on the need for a dominant leader.

The fusion of the NSDAP with other National Socialist parties, discussed at conferences in August 1920 at Salzburg and in March 1921 at Zeitz brought the conflict to a head. Other parties involved were the German Socialist Party (DSP), whose organisation was more widespread throughout Germany than that of the NSDAP, and National Socialist groups from Austria and Bohemia such as the German National Socialist Party. Drexler and other NSDAP leaders favoured a union, believing a unified *völkisch* movement would be more effective than various groups operating on their own. Hitler, however, was contemptuous of the other racist groups which he regarded as too bourgeois in their political style and too academic in their antisemitism. A merger would dilute the energy and drive of the Nazi Party and threaten the position which he had built up for himself as the indispensable motor of the Nazi Party, a role where at last he had found personal fulfilment.

During a long absence of Hitler in Berlin in the early summer of 1921, Drexler was persuaded by a Dr Dickel, the leader of a *völkisch* group in Augsburg, to merge the NSDAP with Dickel's own group, the *Abendländischer Bund* (Western League). Informed of this, Hitler returned at once from Berlin and tried to persuade the committee to change their minds. When they refused, he resigned on 11 July and threatened to set up his own party, three days later issuing an ultimatum stating his conditions for rejoining. These included a stipulation that the headquarters of the Party should remain in Munich and not be moved to Augsburg or Berlin, thereby depriving him of much of his influence since his main personal following was in Munich. The terms of his ultimatum were as follows:

7

---

1. That an extraordinary membership meeting be immediately summoned within eight days from today with the following agenda: The present committee of the Party to resign their offices. At the new election I demand the post of chairman with dictatorial powers for the immediate establishment of an action committee which must ruthlessly purge the Party of foreign elements which have now penetrated it. The action committee to consist of three people.
2. That the unalterable rule be laid down that the headquarters of the movement is and always shall be Munich. Finally, that the Party leadership shall be vested in the Munich local branch until the movement has reached a size sufficient to enable it as a whole to finance its own Party leadership.
3. That any further alteration of the name or programme of the Party shall be absolutely avoided for the next six years. Members working in this direction or to this end shall be excluded from the movement.

4. All further attempts at such a fusion between the National Socialist German Workers' Party and the movement which unjustifiably calls itself the German National Socialist Party must in the future cease. The Party can never agree to a fusion with those who wish to make contact with us; they must join the Party. Reciprocal gestures on our part are out of the question... .

I do not make these demands because I am hungry for power, but rather because recent events have convinced me now more than ever that without iron leadership the Party will in a very short time cease to be what it ought to be: a National Socialist German Workers' Party and not an *Abendländischer Bund*.

A sharp struggle followed, during which Drexler attempted to defeat Hitler by expelling some of his colleagues from the Party. Hitler's victory was swift for Drexler changed his mind and threw in his lot with Hitler. He had long agreed with Hitler on the need for vigorous mass propaganda and he realised that the Party could not dispense with Hitler's superior talent as a public speaker. Hitler had also the backing of the younger and more activist element in the Party, attracted by his drive. The dispute had already been settled when a special meeting of the Party was called on 29 July. Hitler dominated the meeting and was elected chairman of the Party. According to the minutes:

8

The chairman of the meeting was the previous chairman of the association, Herr Anton Drexler...
1. Report on recent events.
2. Amendments or additions to the statutes.
3. A new election of the committee.
He then read out the draft of the new statutes. Comrade Hitler as chairman of the meeting then proceeded to take the vote on the new statutes. The statutes were with one exception (Comrade Posch) unanimously adopted (*enthusiastic applause*). Comrade Drexler then began to speak and proposed the election of Comrade Hitler as Chairman of the Party. The election is unanimously confirmed with loud applause.

Drexler was made honorary president. The statutes adopted at this meeting formalised the dictatorial powers of the Party chairman. The committee of Party officers created by the first statutes of 1920 was retained merely for the purposes of registration of the NSDAP as a legal organisation, while Hitler's responsibility to the membership meeting was a formality. Article 5 read as follows:

9

The headquarters of the National Socialist German Workers' Association is in Munich. The leadership of the Party as such will be combined with the leadership of the Munich branch so long as the Association does not have sufficient funds flowing in from the individual branches to finance a leadership for the Party itself.

Since the Munich branch is the mother group of the whole movement, generous use will be made of its income as before in order to promote the movement as a whole.

The association is subdivided into local branches which are subordinate to the main headquarters.

These will be combined to form *Gau* organisations and the *Gaue* to form state organisations as required.

In order to facilitate a decisive leadership of the movement, the I. Chairman is made responsible for the leadership of the movement as a whole. The leadership of the individual branches is the responsibility of the chairmen of the local branches.

The I. Chairman of the movement as a whole is its legal representative. In his absence the II. Chairman will deputise for him.

The Party headquarters section

The Party headquarters section consists of: (1) the committee to be legally elected by the membership meeting and composed of the first and second chairmen, the first and second treasurers, and the first and second secretaries; (2) the subordinate committees. Since the real responsibility for the leadership of the association lies in the hands of the first chairman, his position must be regarded as standing above the committee. He is responsible solely to the membership meeting.

Hitler placed his leading supporters in positions of authority. Hermann Esser was put in charge of propaganda, and Max Amann, Hitler's former army sergeant, became business manager.

(iii) The development of the Party, 1921-23

In a memorandum of 7 January 1922 Hitler emphasised the fundamental differences of character between the traditional parties and the NSDAP. The NSDAP had not the limited appeal of the bourgeois parties of prewar Germany—it was a new kind of party, a party of action, a movement of the people:

10

The ninth of November[4] meant above all the complete collapse, not of the party life in itself but of bourgeois party life, of that mixture of goodwill, harmless naïvety, theoretical knowledge and utter lack of instinct. The racialist movement also, just like the bourgeois national parties, utterly failed in its main task of winning the broad masses for the national cause. Responsibility for the collapse lies with the bourgeoisie. The racialists [*Völkisch*] were not capable of drawing the practical conclusions from correct theoretical judgements, especially in the Jewish question. In this way the German racialist movement developed a pattern similar to that of the 1880s and 1890s. As in those days, its leadership gradually fell into the hands of highly honourable but fantastically naïve men of learning, professors, district councillors, schoolmasters and barristers—in short a bourgeois, idealistic and refined class. It lacked the warm breath of the nation's youthful vigour. The impetuous force of headstrong fire-eaters was rejected as demagogy. The new movement was therefore a nationalist movement but no longer a movement of the people... . There reappeared in the new movement the distressing characteristics of our bourgeois parties, lacking any uniform discipline or form...

This utter failure in all the matters mentioned led to the founding of the NSDAP. The new movement aimed at providing what the others did not: a racialist movement with a firm social base, a hold over the broad masses, welded together in an iron-hard organisation, instilled with blind obedience and inspired by a brutal will, a party of struggle and action... . If this new kind of movement is to become great and important, its aims must be propagated with fanatical ardour and the total energy of its few supporters must be placed at the service of its propaganda as there is nothing there yet to organise.

With power in Munich, Hitler determined to consolidate his authority by abolishing the autonomy enjoyed by the local branches under Drexler. By May 1922 there was a total of forty-five branches, though most of them in Bavaria. At a meeting of branch leaders in January 1922 Hitler insisted on their subordination to the Munich headquarters. In fact he found it impossible to exercise effective control over the Party outside Bavaria because the situation in the racialist movement elsewhere was so confused. Nevertheless, his authority over the Party in Munich was now absolute.

In the summer of 1921, the armed squads employed to protect Party meetings from disruption by opponents were formally organised in a special unit under the cover name of 'Gymnastic and Sports Section', renamed in October the 'Storm Detachments' (SA). It appealed to the considerable number of ex-soldiers and ex-Free Corps men who had no use for conventional political activity, but were looking for the type of violent action not possible since the dissolution of the Free Corps by the Government. The SA, paramilitary in both organisation and appearance,

---

[4] 9 November 1918—the date of the declaration of the Republic.

had military ranks, wore uniforms and marched in formation. The founding of the unit was formally announced in the *Völkischer Beobachter* on 3 August 1921.

11

The NSDAP has created its own gymnastic and sports section within the framework of its organisation. It is intended to bind our young party members together to form an organisation of iron, so that it may put its strength at the disposal of the whole movement to act as a battering ram. It is intended to uphold the idea of the importance of the military for a free people. It is intended to provide protection for the propaganda activity of the leaders. But above all it is intended to develop in the hearts of our young supporters a tremendous desire for action, to drive home to them and burn into them the fact that history does not make men, but men history, and that he who allows himself to be put in the chains of slavery without any resistance deserves the yoke of slavery. But it [the SA] will also encourage mutual loyalty and cheerful obedience to the leader.

A good indication of the nature of the organisation is provided by the pledge which every stormtrooper was obliged to make on joining:

12

As a member of the storm troop of the NSDAP I pledge myself by its storm flag [*Sturmfahne*]: to be always ready to stake life and limb in the struggle for the aims of the movement; to give absolute military obedience to my military superiors and leaders; to bear myself honourably in and out of service; to be always companionable towards other comrades!

The SA protected Nazi meetings from disruption, assisted in propaganda activities, and disrupted the meetings of other parties. On 14 September 1921, for example, a meeting of the federalist Bavarian League was disrupted, as described by a correspondent of the *Münchner Neueste Nachrichten*:

13

The meeting, which was well attended, came to a premature end owing to an attack systematically planned by the National Socialists. National Socialist youths had early on taken the seats near the speakers' platform, and numerous National Socialists were distributed as well throughout the hall. When Hitler, the leader of the National Socialists, appeared in the hall, he was greeted by his followers with demonstrative applause. His arrival gave the cue for the violence that followed.

The former editor of the *Völkischer Beobachter*, Esser, climbed on a chair and declared that Bavaria owed the situation it was in to the Jews. Ballerstedt had always avoided the Jewish question. The National Socialists therefore saw themselves 'forced' to stop Ballerstedt from speaking and let Hitler speak instead. Hitler's followers, bent on making it a National Socialist meeting, thereupon occupied the platform. But a large section of the meeting protested and demanded that Ballerstedt should speak. He had pushed his way through to the platform, but could not begin because the National Socialists were all the time shouting, 'Hitler!' The uproar grew even worse when someone tried to prevent the fight which was feared by switching off the electricity. When the lights came on again, Ballerstedt declared that anybody who tried to disturb the meeting would be charged with disturbing the peace. After this the young people on the platform, many of them hardly in their teens, surrounded him, beat him up and pushed him down the platform steps. Ballerstedt received a head injury which bled badly. As the audience were naturally growing more and more excited, three members of the state police appeared in the hall. A [plain-clothes] detective declared the meeting dissolved. A fairly strong group of state police then cleared the hall; this operation went smoothly without further incident after an announcement that the charge for admission would be refunded.

Regular SA intimidation of political opponents involved especially members of left-wing parties—as with the vicious brawl with Social Democrats in the Hofbräuhaus in November 1921. Opponents who demanded the right to speak in the so-called 'discussion' at Nazi meetings were often given rough treatment.

Jews were banned from Nazi functions. Political violence, whatever its outcome, gave Hitler and his party publicity, and the Bavarian authorities were remarkably tolerant of such disorder. After the assassination of the Jewish German Foreign Minister, Walther Rathenau, by right-wing fanatics in June 1922, the NSDAP was prohibited in almost every state in Germany. Yet no action was taken by the Government in Bavaria, where the Party's activities continued unabated. In the autumn of 1922, Julius Streicher a notorious antisemite from Nuremberg, declared his allegiance to Hitler. Streicher, who controlled the DSP in northern Bavaria, was an important acquisition and became one of the Party's most popular speakers.

The NSDAP arranged for its first Party rally in Munich in January 1923. The Bavarian Government took fright at the possible consequences and declared martial law in the city. The rally was banned, but on Röhm's intercession and a last-minute assurance by Hitler that he would not attempt a 'putsch', the meetings went ahead as planned. Karl Alexander von Müller, a Munich professor of history, was present at the rally.

14

On the 28th, 6,000 SA men instead of 5,000 lined up on the Marsfeld. The previous evening Hitler had dashed in his car from one meeting to another. In the 'Löwenbräu' I heard him speak in public for the first time. How often I had attended public meetings in this hall! But neither during the war nor during the revolution had I been met on entering by so hot a breath of hypnotic mass excitement. It was not only the special tension of these weeks, of this day. 'Their own battle songs, their own flags, their own symbols, their own salute', I noted down, 'military-like stewards, a forest of bright red flags with black swastika on white ground, a strange mixture of the military and the revolutionary, of nationalist and socialist—in the audience also: mainly of the depressed middle class of every level—will it be welded together again here?' For hours, endless booming military music; for hours, short speeches by subordinate leaders. When was he coming? Had something unexpected happened? Nobody can describe the fever that spread in this atmosphere. Suddenly there was a movement at the back entrance. Words of command. The speaker on the platform stopped in mid-sentence. Everybody jumped up, saluting. And right through the shouting crowds and the streaming flags the one they were waiting for came with his followers, walking quickly to the platform, his right arm raised stiffly. He passed by me quite close and I saw. This was a different person from the one I had met now and then in private houses; his gaunt, pale features contorted as if by inward rage, cold flames darting from his protruding eyes, which seemed to be searching out foes to be conquered. Did the crowd give him this mysterious power? Did it emanate from him to them? 'Fanatical, hysterical romanticism with a brutal core of willpower', I noted down. 'The declining middle class may be carrying this man, but he is not of them; he assuredly comes from totally different depths of darkness. Is he simply using them as a jumping-off point....?

(iv) The Hitler–Putsch 8–9 November 1923

The French and Belgian occupation of the Ruhr in January 1923 alarmed the Army authorities, who became increasingly concerned lest France or other states on Germany's borders try to annex parts of German territory. In an attempt to mobilise all available German forces to meet this threat the Army secretly took under its wing many extreme right-wing paramilitary leagues to form a so-called 'Black Reichswehr'. Among these was the SA, which became increasingly militarised during 1923, a tendency to which it had been prone from the beginning. Hitler himself did not approve, believing the Ruhr occupation and soaring inflation were polarising public opinion in Germany and that civil war was imminent. Consequently, he now felt obliged to work with other nationalist groups without wishing to be forced into a position of cooperating with the Government against the French. He wished the nationalist forces to be used to defeat any coup from the Left and to replace the Republican regime with a right-wing dictatorship.

By August 1923, it had become clear that the policy of passive resistance to the French had failed and the rather conservative government of Wilhelm Cuno resigned, being replaced by a government under a right-wing Liberal, Gustav Stresemann, which included the Social Democrats. On 26 September, it announced the ending of passive resistance in the Ruhr. Hitler believed these developments represented the first stage in the establishment of a Communist regime, as Communists had already allied with Socialist state governments in Thuringia and Saxony to form proletarian paramilitary units. In the meantime, Hitler had become political head of the *Kampfbund*, which coordinated the activities of the NSDAP and other paramilitary groups in Bavaria. Under its pressure the Bavarian Government declared a state of emergency and appointed Kahr State Commissioner with dictatorial powers. There now developed an uneasy relationship between the Bavarian authorities and the *Kampfbund*. Both groups shared a determination to bring down the national government in Berlin, through a march on Berlin along the lines of Mussolini's 'March on Rome' of October 1922. They would use the excuse of the need to crush the left-wing governments in Thuringia and Saxony which lay between Bavaria and Berlin. They hoped to coordinate action with right-wing groups in north Germany and in particular the Army.

The attitude of the Army authorities in Bavaria, vitally important to the success of such an enterprise, was soon tested. The national government in Berlin had replied to the declaration of a state of emergency in Bavaria by declaring a state of emergency in the Reich as a whole, handing over emergency powers to the Army Commander General von Seeckt. Acting under these emergency powers, the Reich authorities now attempted to get the Bavarian authorities to ban the *Völkischer Beobachter* for its bitter and mendacious attacks on Stresemann. Kahr refused to comply and persuaded General von Lossow, Commander of the Bavarian military district, to support him. After refusing point blank an order from Berlin to ban the paper, Lossow was dismissed. However, after swearing an oath of loyalty to the Bavarian government, he was promptly reinstated by them. Berlin and Munich appeared to be on a collision course.

Although Kahr and the *Kampfbund* basically agreed on objectives—the overthrow of the Weimar constitution, they differed on the necessary tactics. In October 1923, the Reich government's preemptive stroke, ordering the Army to crush the left wing governments in Saxony and Thuringia, caused the authorities in Bavaria to hesitate since they no longer had an excuse to march on Berlin. The right-wing groups in north Germany were also hesitant. In particular, the Army commander, von

Seeckt, although sympathetic to the idea of a right-wing coup, was ultra-cautious—the example of Kapp was not exactly encouraging. Kahr, therefore, decided to warn the leaders of the Kampfbund against independent and precipitate action, at a meeting with them held on 6 November:

15

To introduce the discussion, Kahr said the first priority is the creation of a nationalist government. We agree on that. Now we have to divide the work between us. The Stresemann Government is not nationalist and therefore must be fought from the start. Kahr then dealt with the fact that various leagues—the *Kampfbund* was not mentioned by name—had acted somewhat independently during the last few days and it was rumoured that the leagues would start the attack independently. He warned them against this, for he counted on the support of the leagues if the abnormal path was chosen. For, in the present situation, it was doubtful whether the normal path could be followed. The abnormal path would have to be prepared. Preparations had already been made. But if this abnormal path was to be followed everybody must stand together. A uniform well-prepared and well-thought-out plan must be followed...

While Kahr could afford to wait, Hitler could not, having worked the enthusiasm and expectations of his followers up to fever pitch. Furthermore, the crisis would not last for ever; there were signs that the national government was getting a grip on the situation. Once conditions had returned to normal, Hitler would have lost his opportunity possibly for ever. He decided, therefore, to take the initiative himself by creating a situation in which Kahr and Lossow would be forced to join him. He used the opportunity of a public meeting in the Bürgerbräukeller, a big Munich beer cellar, on the evening of 8 November. At the meeting, held to protest against the growth of Bolshevism in Germany, Kahr was to speak and General von Lossow, Colonel von Seisser (the head of the Bavarian Landespolizei or paramilitary police) and other leading citizens of Munich were to be present. Some six hundred armed SA men were posted outside the meeting hall as Hitler burst in and interrupted Kahr's speech to announce that 'the national revolution' had begun. The historian von Müller, who later on was a witness at Hitler's trial, gave the following account:

16

Herr von Kahr had spoken for half an hour. Then there was movement at the entrance as if people were wanting to push their way in. Despite several warnings, the disturbance did not die down. Herr von Kahr had to break off speaking.

Eventually, steel helmets came into sight. From this moment on, the view from my seat was rather obscured. People stood on chairs so that I didn't see Hitler until he had come fairly near along the main gangway; just before he turned to the platform, I saw him emerge between two armed soldiers in steel helmets who carried pistols next to their heads, pointing at the ceiling. They turned towards the platform, Hitler climbed on to a chair on my left. The hall was still restless, and then Hitler made a sign to the man on his right, who fired a shot at the ceiling. Thereupon Hitler called out (I cannot recollect the exact order of his words): 'The national revolution has broken out. The hall is surrounded.' May be he mentioned the exact number, I am not sure. He asked the gentlemen Kahr, Lossow, Seisser to come out and guaranteed their personal freedom. The gentlemen did not move. The General State Commissioner [Kahr] had stepped back and stood opposite Hitler, looking at him calmly. Then Hitler went towards the platform. What happened I could not see exactly. I heard him talk to the gentlemen and I heard the words: Everything would be over in ten minutes if the gentlemen would go out with him. To my surprise the three gentlemen went out with him immediately... .

Hitler took Kahr, Lossow and Seisser into a side room to persuade them to throw in their lot with him. His excited behaviour contributed to the melodramatic atmosphere of the evening, but Kahr refused to be browbeaten when Hitler threatened violence. The whole affair was very much improvised. General Ludendorff, who was to play a major part in Hitler's plans for a national government, had not yet arrived. According to the official account prepared by the Bavarian police:

17

After the three gentlemen had entered the room, Adolf Hitler called out: 'No one leaves the room alive without my permission'. At the door a member of the bodyguard walked up and down continually, holding a pistol.

Then Hitler turned to Excellency von Kahr with the statement: 'The Reich Government has been formed, the Bavarian Government has been overthrown. Bavaria is the springboard for the Reich Government. There must be a Reich governor in Bavaria. Pöhner[5] is to become Minister-President with dictatorial powers. You will be Reich governors. Reich Government—Hitler; national army—Ludendorff; Lossow—army minister; Seisser—police minister.

'I know this step is a difficult one for you, gentlemen, but the step must be taken, it must be made easier for the gentlemen to make the leap. Everybody must take up the post which he is allotted. If he does not, then he has no right to exist. You must fight with me, achieve victory with me, or die with me. If things go wrong, I have four bullets in my pistol, three for my colleagues if they desert me, the last bullet for myself.' While saying this, he put the pistol which he had been holding all the time to his head. While he was speaking to Excellency von Kahr, he noticed Major

---

[5] Ernst Pöhner, the Munich police chief was sympathetic to the Nazis.

Hunglinger[6] in the room and motioned with his hand for him to leave. Kahr declared to Herr Hitler: 'You can arrest me, you can have me shot, you can shoot me yourself. Whether I live or die is unimportant.' Whereupon Hitler turned to Colonel von Seisser who accused him of not keeping his promise [not to attempt a putsch]. Hitler replied: 'Yes, that's true, but I did it in the interests of the fatherland. Forgive me.'

Herr von Lossow tried to say something to the other two gentlemen. But this was prevented by a shout: 'You gentlemen are not allowed to talk to one another.'

Lossow then stepped back to the window, disgusted with the proceedings. While looking out between the curtains, he noticed in front of every window a group of armed men, some of whom looked into the room with their guns at the ready. Hitler, who clearly saw the unpleasant impression made, waved them away with his hand. Excellency von Lossow asked: 'What is Ludendorff's attitude to the affair?' Hitler replied: 'Ludendorff is ready and will soon be fetched.' Hitler then left the room. He got no answer during this time, either from Herr von Kahr or from the other gentlemen... .

The crowd in the hall was becoming impatient. Hitler could not go back on his plans as he had staked his prestige on success and his supporters expected much of him. He returned to the hall and, in an effort to put pressure on Kahr and his colleagues, announced that they had agreed to his plans. The effect of Hitler's speech was electric. According to von Müller, the crowd was not entirely on Hitler's side and was aware of his clever tactics:

18

...The general mood—I can of course only judge from my surroundings, but I think that this represented the general feeling in the hall—was still against the whole business. One heard: 'Theatrical!' 'South America!' 'Mexico!' That was the prevailing mood. The change came only during Hitler's second speech when he entered about ten minutes later, went to the platform and made a short speech. It was a rhetorical masterpiece. In fact, in a few sentences it totally transformed the mood of the audience. I have rarely experienced anything like it. When he stepped on to the platform the disturbance was so great that he could not be heard, and he fired a shot. I can still see the gesture. He got the Browning out of his back pocket and I think it was on this occasion that the remark about the machine gun was made. When things did not become quiet, he shouted angrily at the audience: 'If you are not quiet, I shall have a machine gun put up on the gallery.' In fact he had come in to say that his prediction of everything being over in ten minutes had not come true. But he said it in such a way that he finally went out with the permission of the audience to say to Kahr that the whole assembly would be behind him if he were to join. It was a complete reversal. One could hear it being said that the whole thing had been arranged, that it was a phoney performance. I did not share this

[6] Major Franz Hunglinger, Seisser's adjutant.

opinion because Kahr's attitude seemed to contradict it. Seeing him at close quarters, one got the impression of confusion, of great dismay... .

Ludendorff arrived, pretended to be surprised by the affair and joined him in persuading Kahr, who, after much hesitation finally agreed. The official police account continues:

19

...Ludendorff then entered the room in a hat and coat and, without asking any questions, with obvious excitement and with a trembling voice, declared: 'Gentlemen, I am just as surprised as you are. But the step has been taken, it is a question of the fatherland and the great national and racial cause, and I can only advise you, go with us and do the same.'

With the appearance of Ludendorff the character of the proceedings in the adjoining room changed completely. The pistols had disappeared. It took the form of friendly persuasion. (Because of this, Ludendorff, who was not a witness of the initial attack in the hall, may have got the impression that no force had been used, whereas Kahr, Lossow, and Seisser had no doubt that Ludendorff was accessory to the enterprise which had been essentially arranged for him.)

Shortly after Ludendorff, Pöhner entered the room. Hitler, Ludendorff and Weber[7] now began a process of urgent persuasion. Excellency von Kahr, in particular, was besieged on all sides. Moved by the feelings previously described, Lossow at last gave Ludendorff the consent he wanted with the dry comment, 'All right'. After some hesitation, Colonel von Seisser also nodded his agreement. Then Hitler, Ludendorff, and Dr Weber, with Pöhner also, worked on Excellency von Kahr with coaxing and pleading. Lossow and Seisser were asked to take part in the coaxing, but neither replied. Ludendorff took Major Hunglinger on one side and asked him to persuade Herr von Kahr. But still no discussion with Ludendorff or discussion between the three gentlemen was allowed; they only wanted to hear 'Yes' from them. Hitler could no longer go back, whatever the position of Kahr, Lossow, and Seisser might prove to be. Hitler kept bringing this out with statements like: 'The deed has been done, there is no going back. It has already passed into history.'

After long urging, Kahr declared: 'I am ready to take over the destiny of Bavaria as the representative of the monarchy.' Hitler insisted that this statement should be made in the hall. Herr von Kahr replied that after the way in which he had been led out of the hall he refused to go back into the hall. He wanted to avoid any public fraternising. But Hitler insisted with the words: 'You will be carried shoulder high, you will see what jubilation will greet you: the people will kneel before you.' Kahr replied: 'I can do without that.' They then went into the hall.

The leaders of the putsch returned to the hall and put on a show of

---

[7] Dr Friedrich Weber, leader of the paramilitary league, Bund Oberland, was also taking part in the putsch.

solidarity, but von Müller noticed the difference in behaviour between them:

20

...An hour after Hitler's first appearance the three gentlemen came back into the hall with Hitler and Ludendorff. They were enthusiastically received. On the platform Kahr began to speak first without being requested to and gave the speech which was printed word for word in the papers. Ludendorff too in my opinion spoke without being requested to, whereas Lossow and Seisser only spoke after repeated requests—I can't remember the words, but only the gestures—on Hitler's part. If I am to depict the impression made by the gentlemen on the platform, I would say that Kahr was completely unmoved. His face was like a mask all evening. He was not pale or agitated, he was very serious, but spoke very composedly. I got the impression that there was a melancholy look about his eyes. But that is perhaps being subjective. Hitler, on the other hand, during this scene was radiant with joy. One had the feeling that he was delighted to have succeeded in persuading Kahr to collaborate. There was in his demeanour, I would say, a kind of childlike joy, a very frank expression which I shall never forget. Excellency Ludendorff by comparison was extremely grave; when he came in he was pale with suppressed emotion. His appearance as well as his words were those of a man who knew it was a matter of life and death, probably death rather than life. I shall never forget his expression. It was such that when I heard in town on the following day the rumour that he had been killed, I said to myself: That's what he looked like last night. Lossow's expression was very different; there was something detached, relaxed about his whole attitude. I don't want to make a party point but, if I am to describe it, it struck me that he made a slightly ironical fox face. A certain impenetrable smile never left his features. Seisser was pale and upset. He was the only one who gave the impression of personal agitation, of external agitation. His words were merely a variant of Lossow's. The report in the papers of the words of these two gentlemen was not correct: it was somewhat touched up. .

Hitler's apparent triumph was short-lived. The situation changed completely overnight. Ernst Röhm had occupied Army headquarters in Munich and there was sympathy for the putsch among junior officers, but the attitude of the Reichswehr as a whole never remained in doubt and when Lossow returned to his headquarters reinforcements were ordered to the Bavarian capital. Kahr followed suit by revoking the agreement he had been forced to make at gunpoint. In spite of these setbacks, arrangements went ahead for a march into the city centre of a few thousand supporters of Hitler in the forlorn hope of winning sufficient support among the population to force Kahr, Lossow and Seisser to join them. Hitler and Ludendorff led the procession. An official report prepared for the subsequent committee of inquiry related what happened:

21

...The column of National Socialists about 2,000 strong, nearly all armed, moved on through the Zweibrückenstrasse across the Marienplatz towards the Theatinerstrasse. Here it split up, the majority going down the Perusastrasse to the Residenz, the rest going on along the Theatinerstrasse. The police stationed in the Residenz tried to cordon it off as well as the Theatinerstrasse by the Preysingstrasse. Numerous civilians hurried on ahead of the actual column in Residenzstrasse and pushed the police barricade. The ceaseless shouts of 'Stop! Don't go on!' by the state police were not obeyed. Since there was the danger of a breakthrough here, a police section, originally in the Theatinerstrasse, hurried round the Feldherrnhalle to give support. They were received with fixed bayonets, guns with the safety catches off, and raised pistols. Several police officers were spat upon, and pistols with the safety catches off were stuck in their chests. The police used rubber truncheons and rifle butts and tried to push back the crowd with rifles held horizontally. Their barricade had already been broken several times. Suddenly, a National Socialist fired a pistol at a police officer from close quarters. The shot went past his head and killed Sergeant Hollweg standing behind him. Even before it was possible to give an order, the comrades of the sergeant who had been shot opened fire as the Hitler lot did, and a short gun battle ensued during which the police were also shot at from the Preysingpalais and from the house which contains the Café Rottenhöfer. After no more than thirty seconds the Hitler lot fled, some back to the Maximilienstrasse, some to the Odeonsplatz. General Ludendorff apparently went on towards the Odeonsplatz. There he was seen in the company of a Hitler officer by a police officer barring the Briennerstrasse, who went up to General Ludendorff and said to him: 'Excellency, I must take you into custody.' General Ludendorff replied: 'You have your orders. I'll come with you.' Both gentlemen were then accompanied into the Residenz.

The putsch had failed. Its leaders were arrested and the Nazi Party, its membership grown to 55,000, was banned. Hitler, a prisoner of the public enthusiasm which he had encouraged, had not succeeded in gaining control over events. The attempt failed because of the lack of support from the Army and the police.

On 26 February 1924, Hitler, Ludendorff, Pöhner and the leaders of the Kampfbund were put on trial for high treason in Munich, with the conservative nationalist leaders, Kahr, Lossow and Seisser, as the chief witnesses for the prosecution. The trial received enormous publicity and Hitler's bravado enabled him to turn the ignominious failure of the putsch into a considerable propaganda victory. For, while asserting that Kahr and the others had pursued a similar goal, he did not deny his own part—but claimed it was a patriotic act. He blamed the failure of the enterprise on the pusillanimity of the nationalist leaders. As a result of this stand, Hitler now became a hero to many antisemites in other parts of Germany who before had never heard of him. They saw him as the one man who had had the courage and energy to act. This ensured that when the Party was refounded after his release, numerous new branches could be established outside Bavaria.

22

...Lossow said here that he had spoken with me in the spring and had not noticed then that I was trying to get something for myself and had thought that I only wanted to be a propagandist and a man who would rouse people.

How petty are the thoughts of small men! You can take my word for it, that I do not consider a ministerial post worth striving for...

From the very first I have aimed at something more than becoming a Minister. I have resolved to be the destroyer of Marxism. This I shall achieve and once I've achieved that, I should find the title of 'Minister' ridiculous. When I first stood in front of Wagner's grave, my heart overflowed with pride that here lay a man who had forbidden any such inscription as 'Here lies State Councillor, Musical Director, His Excellency Richard von Wagner'. I was proud that this man and so many others in German history have been content to leave their names to posterity and not their titles. It was not through modesty that I was willing to be a 'drummer' at that time for that is the highest task [*das Höchste*]: the rest is nothing.

Mr Public Prosecutor! You emphasise in the indictment that we had to wait with clenched teeth until the seed ripened. Well, we did wait and when the man came, we cried: 'The seed is ripe, the hour has come.' Only then, after long hesitation, did I put myself forward. I demanded for myself the leadership in the political struggle; and secondly, I demanded that the leadership of the organisation for which we all longed and for which you inwardly long just as much should go to the hero who, in the eyes of the whole of German youth, is called to it. The witness Seisser declared cynically that we had to have Ludendorff so that the Reichswehr would not shoot. Is that a crime? Was it treason that I said to Lossow, 'The way you are beginning it must come to a conflict; as I see it, there need be no conflict'?...

...What did we want on the evening of 8 November? All these gentlemen wanted a Directory in the Reich. If one has striven for something in the Reich, one cannot condemn it in Bavaria. The Directory already existed in Bavaria, it consisted of Messrs Kahr, Lossow and Seisser. We no longer knew anything of a legal government, we only feared that there might be scruples over the final decision.

I am no monarchist, but ultimately a Republican. Pöhner is a monarchist, Ludendorff is devoted to the House of Hohenzollern [Prussia-Germany]. Despite our different attitudes we all stood together. The fate of Germany does not lie in the choice between a Republic or a Monarchy, but in the content of the Republic and the Monarchy. What I am contending against is not the form of a state as such, but its ignominious content. We wanted to create in Germany the precondition which alone will make it possible for the iron grip of our enemies to be removed from us. We wanted to create order in the state, throw out the drones, take up the fight against international stock exchange slavery, against our whole economy being cornered by trusts, against the politicising of the trade unions, and above all, for the highest honourable duty which we, as Germans, know should be once more introduced—the duty of bearing arms, military service. And now I ask you: Is what we wanted high treason?...

Now people say: But His Excellency von Kahr, von Lossow and von Seisser did not want the events of the evening of 8 November. The bill of indictment says that we pushed these gentlemen into an embarrassing situation. But it was through these gentlemen that we ourselves had got into an embarrassing situation; *they* had pushed *us* into it. Herr von Kahr should have said honourably: Herr Hitler, we understand something different by a *coup d'état*, we mean something different by a march on Berlin. He had a duty to say to us: In what we are doing here we mean something different from what you think. He did not say that, and the consequences should be borne solely by these three gentlemen...

...The army which we have formed grows from day to day; it grows more rapidly from hour to hour. Even now I have the proud hope that one day the hour will come when these untrained [*wild*] bands will grow to battalions, the battalions to regiments and the regiments to divisions, when the old cockade will be raised from the mire, when the old banners will once again wave before us: and the reconciliation will come in that eternal last Court of Judgement, the Court of God, before which we are ready to take our stand. Then from our bones, from our graves, will sound the voice of that tribunal which alone has the right to sit in judgement upon us. For, gentlemen, it is not you who pronounce judgement upon us, it is the external Court of History which will make its pronouncement upon the charge which is brought against us. The verdict that you will pass I know. But that Court will not ask of us, 'Did you commit high treason or did you not?' That Court will judge us...as Germans who wanted the best for their people and their fatherland, who wished to fight and to die. You may pronounce us guilty a thousand times, but the Goddess who presides over the Eternal Court of History will with a smile tear in pieces the charge of the Public Prosecutor and the verdict of this court. For she acquits us.

The judges, right-wing and sympathisers with the motives of the conspirators, acquitted Ludendorff and gave Hitler the minimum sentence of five years' imprisonment, with the clear understanding that he would be released early on probation.

CHAPTER 2

The Creation of a Nationwide Party Organisation 1924–28

During Hitler's imprisonment the banned Nazi Party disintegrated into rival factions. Hitler had nominated Alfred Rosenberg, editor of the *Völkischer Beobachter*, to act as his deputy during his imprisonment. Rosenberg, however, was unable to assert his authority and was soon challenged by rivals, notably Esser and Streicher. Outside Bavaria the dominant racialist party was the German Racialist Freedom Party, or DVFP, founded in 1922 by three Reichstag deputies, former members of the main extreme right-wing party, the German National People's Party (DNVP). Although during elections, the DVFP worked with former Nazis in an electoral alliance, the so-called *Völkisch*-Social Block, its ambitions were bitterly resisted by many other former Nazis, particularly young people, who considered the party too bourgeois in its social composition and political style. For a time they worked with Esser and Streicher until personal differences caused a bitter row. These opponents of the DVFP looked to Hitler as their leader and appealed to him for support. But Hitler, finding that he could not control events from prison and unwilling to compromise himself with any commitments, decided to withdraw from active politics until his release. The confusion in the *völkisch* movement strengthened his own position.

In Landsberg Prison, Hitler was working out his plans for the Party after his release. The coalition of antisemitic groups formed for the Reichstag election of May 1924 won 9 per cent of the vote and thirty-two deputies, although of these only ten were former Nazis. In the spring election to the Bavarian state diet the racialists became the second largest party in the diet. This impressed Hitler. The putsch had proved unsuccessful because the Army did not cooperate and the end of the political and economic crisis made an attempt to seize power by force look less and less feasible. A new policy was necessary as Hitler told Ludecke when he received a visit from him in Landsberg:

23

...I noticed that he barred in particular any reminder of the putsch and any question concerning his policy towards the Party schism...I gladly eschewed the subject as too delicate. But the lesson it taught was another matter, which Hitler himself took up.

'From now on,' he said, 'we must follow a new line of action. It is best to attempt no large reorganisation until I am freed, which may be a matter of months rather than years.'

I must have looked at him somewhat incredulously. 'Oh yes', he continued, 'I am not going to stay here much longer. When I resume active work it will be necessary to pursue a new policy. Instead of working to achieve power by armed conspiracy, we shall have to hold our noses and enter the Reichstag against the Catholic and Marxist deputies. If outvoting them takes longer than outshooting them, at least the results will be guaranteed by their own Constitution! Any lawful process is slow. But already, as you know, we have thirty-two Reichstag deputies under this new programme, and are the second largest party in the Bavarian Landtag diet. Sooner or later we shall have a majority and after that we shall have Germany. I am convinced that this is our best line of action now that conditions in the country have changed so radically...

Although now ready to participate in elections and to enter Parliament, Hitler did not in any way give up his hostility to it. The putsch attempt made it much easier for him to pursue a constitutional course since he could never be accused of weakness. This was important. For it was the extremism of the Nazis which distinguished them from similar groups and contributed so much to their success.

(i) The Refounding of the Party, 27 February 1925

Hitler was released in December 1924 and, after promising to work within the Constitution, was permitted to refound the Nazi Party at a meeting in the same Bürgerbräu beer cellar in Munich on 27 February 1925. Hitler made it clear in the *Völkischer Beobachter* of 26 February that he was interested only in what the individual could offer him in terms of abilities and in whether he was prepared to obey the leader without preconditions. He justified this demand for absolute control with a promise to render an account in a year's time and take the responsibility whatever the outcome. Finally, unlike other antisemitic groups, particularly in north Germany, he was not interested in fighting Roman Catholicism. This would only limit the potential support of the Party particularly in Bavaria itself and it would antagonise the Bavarian Government, now dominated by the Catholic Bavarian People's Party, which he was trying to conciliate in order to secure freedom for the Party to operate effectively:

24

National Socialists! Party Comrades!

...In this hour we do not only want to remember again those who in November 1923 became blood witnesses of our political beliefs and aims; we also want to thank all those who in this past year did not despair of the movement and what it stands for, but laboured in its service regardless of whatever camp they felt drawn to.

Above all, we want to remember the one man who had nothing to gain but rather stood to lose the fame of being the undying leader of the heroic German armies in the greatest war on earth, and who despite all this decided to make the great sacrifice of giving his name and his energy to a movement which had no leader.

In General Ludendorff the National Socialist movement will for ever honour its most faithful and unselfish friend. The movement will be bound to him not by the memory of friendship given in happy times but by loyalty maintained in persecution and misery.

My task as leader of the movement is not to look for the causes of a previous quarrel or to assess who was right, but to mould the movement into a unified weapon regardless of the interests of individuals. Thus I shall not inquire into the past of those comrades who rejoin, but only work to ensure that the past will not repeat itself in the future. From our supporters I demand that if they are willing to join the new movement they should feel themselves once more to be brothers in a great fighting community and stand together loyally shoulder to shoulder as before.

But I expect the leaders, in so far as they come from the old camp, to give me the same obedience as we all give to the common idea.

Those who cannot forget the past are not worthy of serving a better future.

I myself promise to render an account to the comrades in a year's time as to whether the Party has become a movement or whether the movement has suffocated by being a party.

In either case I shall take the responsibility.

Long live the National Socialist German Workers' Party!

Long live our German fatherland!

25

'*On the revival of our movement*'
...I do not consider it to be the task of a political leader to try and improve, let alone make uniform the human material which he has at hand. The temperaments, characters, and talents of individual people are so various that it is impossible to unify a large number of completely similar people. It is also not the task of a political leader to try and remove these deficiencies by 'training' people to be united. All such attempts are condemned to failure. Human nature is a given quantity which does not lend itself to alteration in particulars, but can only transform itself through a process of development lasting for centuries. But even then the prerequisite for such a change is generally alterations in the basic racial elements...

If a political leader departs from this awareness and if instead he attempts only to seek people who come up to his ideal, he will not only wreck his plans, but also in a very short time leave behind him chaos instead of an organisation. The guilt which he then attributes to individual supporters or subordinates is in reality only his own lack of awareness and ability.

For this very reason, if I try today to revive the old NSDAP, I cannot recognise commitments which derive from past events. I am not prepared to accept conditions, whose fulfilment would only represent that lack of psychological awareness and ability which I described above.

I shall, therefore, see it as my particular task to direct the various temperaments, talents and qualities of character in the movement into those channels in which by supplementing one another they benefit everybody.

In the future, the movement's struggle must once more take the form which we intended at its foundation. With all its forces concentrated together it must be turned against that power to which above all we owe the collapse of our fatherland and the destruction of our people. This does not mean an alteration in or a 'postponement' of the old and main aim of our struggle, but simply its reassertion.

At this point, I must object particularly to the attempt to drag religious quarrels into the movement, or even to go so far as to equate the movement with such things. I have always opposed the collective description 'racialist' [*völkisch*], because the extremely vague definition of this term has opened the way to damaging activities. For this reason, earlier on, the movement placed more emphasis on its clearly defined programme as well as on the unified trend of its struggle than on a term which was incapable of being clearly defined and which was conducive to a more or less verbose interpretation.

I see in the attempt by various people to turn the racialist movement into a struggle about religion the beginning of the end of that movement.

Religious reformations cannot be carried out by political infants and these people are rarely anything but that.

I am quite clear about the possibility of beginning such a struggle, but I doubt if the gentlemen involved are clear about its probable end result.

In any case, it will be my main task to make sure that in the newly awakened NSDAP members of both confessions can live peacefully side by side and can stand together in the common struggle against that power which is the deadly enemy of every form of Christianity, no matter what confession.

No movement has fought harder against the Centre Party and its supporting groups than our own, not for religious reasons but solely from political considerations. And so from now onwards we must fight the Centre not because it claims to be 'Christian' or 'Catholic' but solely because a party which has allied itself with atheistic Marxism for the suppression of its own people is neither Christian nor Catholic.

We do not declare war on the Centre for religious reasons, but solely for national-political ones.

History will pass judgement on who will be successful, we or the advocates of a cultural struggle.

Finally, I demand of the movement's supporters that from now onwards they direct all their energies outwards and do not weaken themselves in a fratricidal struggle.

The best local branch leadership is not the one which 'unites' the other nationalist organisations or 'wins them over' to the movement, but the one which wins antinationalists back to the German people.

The success of our movement must be measured not by the number of Reichstag or Landtag seats we win, but by the extent to which Marxism is destroyed and by the degree of enlightenment about its originator, the Jews.

Let those who wish to join in this struggle do so; let those who do not, stay away.

(ii) The assertion of the primacy of the 'Führer'

After the refounding of the Party, Hitler, soon banned from public speaking in Bavaria and many other states, concentrated on writing the second volume of *Mein Kampf*. During the summer of 1925, the Munich branch of the Party became involved in bitter factional squabbles in which personalities played a major part. Hitler had left the day-to-day running of the Party in the hands of the Party officials—Bouhler (the secretary), Schwarz (the treasurer), Amann (the head of the publishing house) and Esser (the propaganda chief). In addition, Julius Streicher, the branch leader of Nuremberg, and Artur Dinter, Gauleiter or regional leader of Thuringia, were influential. This group had fought a bitter feud with other Bavarian antisemites and former Nazis during 1924 and this feud now broke out again. But Esser, Streicher and Dinter were also extremely unpopular among many Party members throughout Germany and particularly in the north and west. Some of the Gauleiters here, where the Party was now growing more rapidly than in Bavaria, resented the authority of what they regarded as an unsavoury Munich clique. This conflict dated back to the previous year when Esser's abrasive personality had alienated many Nazis, particularly when he committed the cardinal sin of washing the Party's dirty linen in the pages of the influential 'Jewish' newspaper, the *Frankfurter Zeitung*. But apart from questions of personality, important issues of principle now emerged. Some leading members of the Party outside Bavaria disagreed on aspects of Party policy. In the first place, the Party leaders in Göttingen and Hanover disagreed with participation in elections. This represented a challenge to the new parliamentary tactics now being followed by the Party. Secondly, Gregor Strasser, the Gauleiter of Lower Bavaria, who had met many of the north and west German Party leaders while acting as Hitler's deputy in the refounding of the Party there, felt that the Party programme was too vague and should be defined more concretely in a 'Socialist' direction. He was supported by some of the local Party leaders in the industrial areas of north and west Germany who wanted to compete with the Left for the support of the workers.

The 'Socialism' of Gregor Strasser was in fact typical of that of most racialists—a determination to try to win the workers for nationalism by giving them a greater sense of belonging to the nation. It sprang from his experience in the trenches during the war, as he told a meeting in 1927:

26

...How did all those tens of thousands in all parts of Germany become National Socialist? Perhaps I may be allowed to recall how I became one...because I am a test case here! Before the war we did not bother with politics. I grew up the son of a low-ranking civil servant. I had no ambition other than to get on through hard work. In the war we became Nationalists, that is to say, out of that vague feeling that the fatherland had to be defended, that it was something great and sacred, the protector of the existence of the individual, out of this vague notion which for many of us was not clear, we became nationalists on the battlefield. When I saw all the nations of the earth rushing against the German trenches with bloodthirsty destruction, when the international stock exchange armed one country after another and set them going against the single German nation in the trenches— Americans, Portuguese, Blacks, Yellows, against the little group of Germans fighting for their existence, it became clear to me: if Germany wants to survive, every German must *know what it means to be a German and must defend this idea to the limits of self-sacrifice*. Companies and batteries reduced from 250 to 60 men did not have to be told about the *community of need*; they knew: if we do not stand together the Blacks will be on us. We knew that the first priority of manhood is to defend oneself, and the second, all who speak the same language must stick together, must organise themselves to be strong by being united!

And why did we become Socialists?

This notion was still as far from many who today stand in our ranks as the notion of nationalism in terms of its real significance. We learnt all sorts of things at school. But nobody told us that half the German people were hostile to the nation *because they had been denied the most basic needs of life by the other half.* Not a word were we told about that tragic hour for the German people *when the growing German workers' movement was nothing but the cry of millions of German fellow countrymen for acceptance into the nation on equal terms (loud applause).* So these millions of people were left to the Jew Marx who created Marxism out of the German workers' movement, who intended to do nothing but *destroy the German nation* with the strength of these millions *and to make it a colony of world capital.*

We must always regard *one* principle as fundamental: to be ready to recognise mistakes, to see that when a nation goes under, it is mainly the *fault of the rulers* of that nation. They had the power to prevent everything which in the long run forced people to become hostile to the nation and state.

This person, whom the Jew Marx had perverted into a 'Social Democrat', a Marxist, was suddenly found standing next one in the platoon, in the battery, by the guns. During the long hours of sentry duty there would be discussion: What are you? A mechanic. Politically? A red, a Marxist. And we who came from the bourgeoisie, we who had been told nothing, were surprised.

Why am I a Marxist? Because you have never bothered with us! Then one started thinking, then came the great realisation how brave the man is, and how well he does his duty! It was my experience that the best soldiers were frequently those who had least to defend at home *(applause).* He cooperated, he did his duty unfailingly, and from conversations with him we understood *the mistakes of our great-grandfathers. Because we had become nationalists in the trenches we could not help becoming Socialists in the trenches,* we could not help coming home with the brutal intention of gathering the whole nation round us and teaching them that the greatness of a nation depends on the willingness of the individual to stand up for this nation and say to it: Your fate is indissolubly linked with the fate of your people, with the fate and greatness of your nation. We could not help coming home from this war with this resolve: *Those who have fought together with us and who are hostile towards the nation because it has not bothered with them must be emancipated so that Germany will in future be strong and the master of her enemies! (loud applause).*

In order to further his attempt to change the programme and as a counterweight to the Party bureaucracy in Munich, Strasser now took the initiative in establishing a so-called 'working group' (*Arbeitsgemeinschaft*) of the Gauleiters in north and west Germany. In fact, however, as is clear from the following report, written by Fobke, a Göttingen leader, of the first meeting, held at Hagen in Westphalia on 10 September, there were deep disagreements between these Gauleiters over the various points at issue, particularly over the question of elections which was the main issue for the Göttingen leaders. The only aim on which most of them were agreed was cooperation in matters of organisation among regions with similar problems and the development of new ideas appropriate to their needs which the bureaucrats in the Munich headquarters 'Esser & Co' were apparently incapable of doing. These would, it was hoped, meet with Hitler's approval and it is significant that Point 4 of the statutes of the

working group shows that they had been careful to gain Hitler's general
approval for the organisation:

27

...The movement is at the moment undergoing a crisis associated mainly with the
name of Hermann Esser. This extremely dubious character, of obscure political as
well as moral background, is at the moment absolute boss in the Party leadership.
The result is a continual diminution of all the good elements in the movement,
which today, for example, in the city of Munich only comprises 700 members.
Thousands stand aside without joining any group, others—the smaller part—have
joined together in the National Socialist People's League [*Nationalsozialistische
Volksbund*] under the leadership of Dörfler and Anton Drechsler [*sic*], which
parted from the NSDAP some time ago under the slogan 'With Hitler but without
Esser!' when Hitler did *not* do without Esser. In the last few days, an open conflict
has developed between Alfred Rosenberg, editor of the *Völkischer Beobachter* and
publisher of the *Weltkampf*, and Adolf Hitler, the origin of which must be sought in
the prominent position in the Party of Esser, Amann and Streicher. Of my personal
acquaintances with me in the prison in Landsberg, the best are standing aside in
convinced opposition.

Hitler himself, whom I met on 26 and 27 August, adopts a completely passive
attitude towards the business; this, under the circumstances, is equivalent to
supporting Esser. At the moment his activity is entirely confined to the completion
of the second volume of his book, *Mein Kampf*. Any suggestion of getting rid at last
of Esser & Co., including above all Streicher and Dinter, he counters with the
insubstantial objection that for him their usefulness is the decisive factor. He
overlooks the fact that the total rejection of them throughout the Reich is being
outweighed by their theoretical usefulness within a limited area. Outside Bavaria
too the movement is in my opinion in a stagnant condition, which, apart from the
general political indifference, has its origin in the sorry state of things at the Munich
headquarters.

Opposition to the Esser dictatorship is naturally making itself evident. To create
a counterbalance to this dictatorship was the purpose of a meeting which Gregor
Strasser, Hitler's honest and extremely hard-working, even if not exactly inspired
colleague, summoned for 10 September at Hagen in Westphalia. Strasser himself
was prevented from attending, with the result that the discussion was perhaps not
as far-reaching as it would have been had he been there... .

As convener, Herr Strasser originally intended to use the negotiations at the
meeting to play off the block formed by those invited against the pernicious Munich
line. Of this plan, apart from Haase [Gauleiter] of Göttingen, only Dr Goebbels[8]
and a man unknown to us by name who chaired the meeting,[9] were aware. Since
Strasser did not attend, the real purpose of the meeting was not touched on;
instead, to begin with, the only decision reached was the setting up of a close

---

[8] A party activist in Elberfeld.
[9] Dr Hellmuth Elbrechter, a Nazi from Elberfeld.

association between the *Gaue* mentioned above, with the name 'Working Group of the north and west German Gauleiters of the NSDAP'. Cooperation was planned through an exchange of speakers, and organisational help of every kind was arranged by setting up a headquarters and by the publication of the 'National Socialist Letters' [*NS Briefe*]. These are intended for the leadership and are meant to effect a uniform clarification of basic questions, to be achieved by a free exchange of views. At the head of this working group is Strasser.

When it looked as if in Strasser's absence the question of Esser would not be mentioned, I brought it up with the agreement of Herr Haase. This produced a general reaction of horror. Some people strongly opposed such a 'palace revolution', and the representative from Rhineland-North, who was chairing the meeting, suggested postponing discussion of the matter. Haase and I agreed to this postponement intentionally because by pressing the point we had sown a seed which could be cultivated at the monthly meetings which were planned to follow. Consultation with the chairman who was deputising for Strasser and with Dr Goebbels produced unanimity on this point.

Haase had travelled to Hagen with the firm intention of bringing about at all events a clarification of the question of participation in any elections, whether local council, county council, regional diet or Reichstag, in view of the Prussian elections which were coming up. A preliminary sounding produced the situation that at the moment Telschow (Hanover-East) and Lohse (Schleswig-Holstein) were supporting us in opposing, whereas Vahlen (Pomerania) and Haake (Cologne) were against us and in favour of electoral participation. Already some time back we had had Rust's (Hanover-Brunswick) pledge to support non-participation.

Haase therefore made a short statement to the effect that we and those gentlemen who agreed with our position *would under no circumstances participate in any elections, no matter what directives had been given by Munich headquarters. The other Gaue would have to adapt themselves to our attitude.* This declaration produced a shocked and embarrassed pause. But the discussion produced a majority agreement on a resolution to Hitler which this time was unanimously approved. This stated that *all* the Gauleiters meeting in Hagen absolutely rejected participation in elections and demanded a clear statement from the Party leadership, which so far had sent three different sets of instructions to three different places... .

To conclude, the newly founded working group offers the possibility of securing further recognition for our position in the National Socialist movement. Haase is determined to exploit this possibility to the limit and, next to the question of Parliament, to try also to settle the case of Esser, that is the purging of the movement in accordance with our views...

28

Statutes of the working group
1. The Working Group of the North and West German *Gaue* of the NSDAP comprises the *Gaue*: Rhineland-North, Rhineland-South, Westphalia, Hanover, Hanover-South, Hesse-Nassau, Lüneberg-Stade, Schleswig-Holstein, Grea-

ter-Hamburg, Greater-Berlin and Pomerania.

2. The aim and purpose of the Working Group is: the greatest possible uniformity among the affiliated *Gaue* in organisation and propaganda; the creation of uniform propaganda methods, the swapping of speakers; the good-neighbourly encouragement of friendly personal relations among the Gauleiters; the exchange of ideas on questions of politics and organisation by letter and by regular meetings; when necessary, joint statements on current political issues.
3. The journal of the Working Group is the bi-monthly *NS Briefe*, to be published by Comrade Gregor Strasser and edited by Comrade Dr Goebbels.
4. Both Working Group and *NS Briefe* exist with the express approval of Adolf Hitler.
5. The director of the Working Group is Comrade Gregor Strasser, Landshut.
6. The secretary of the Working Group is Comrade Dr Goebbels, Elberfeld.
7. The office of the Working Group is until further notice at Elberfeld, Holzerstrasse 4. Tel. 6526.
8. The Gauleiters affiliated to the Working Group meet for joint discussions, when necessary, in a city in one or another of the above-mentioned *Gaue*... .

The meeting of the Working Group in Hanover on 22 November 1925 invited Gregor Strasser to draft a new Party programme. Two months later, however, on 24 January 1926, a second meeting in Hanover set up a sub-committee to consider a new programme after rejecting Strasser's draft as too vague and verbose. He had clearly proved unable to reconcile the differing views on such questions as the structure of the future National Socialist state and foreign policy. A number of members, including Goebbels, favoured an alliance with Russia against the 'Jewish-capitalist' West, regarding Russia under Stalin as a 'nationalist' power. The Göttingen group, on the other hand, regarded Russia as a field for German expansion.

Another important issue discussed was the need to decide whether or not to support a referendum organised by the Left to demand the expropriation of the royal princes. The Party's attitude on this question would be regarded as a test of Nazi claims to be considered a genuinely workers' and Socialist party. The meeting passed the following resolution which, despite its equivocation, went some way towards committing the Party to the principle of expropriation. This did not prove sufficient to persuade many workers to support the Nazi Party but it does indicate that the Working Group, led by Strasser, Goebbels and the other Elberfeld leaders, were serious in their intention of winning working class support.

29

The study group holds the view, without in any way wishing to anticipate the decision of Party headquarters, that the so-called question of compensation for the princes is not a question of fundamental importance for the Party as such.

It is guided by the view that the question of so-called compensation for the princes is not only a legal but also a social matter. In a state in which law and justice prevailed, one would obviously regard it only from the legal standpoint. This state of Weimar, however, which has perpetrated upon pensioners, war-loan recipients and state creditors the enormous injustice of confiscating their property and calling it revaluation, has violated the very basis of law and property, and this not in the interests of the community, but, on the contrary, in the service of speculative, immoral stock exchange capital which is in the hands of only a few.

The distressing circumstances in which the German people find themselves, owing to the criminal policy of the government parties of all shades, do not permit, simply with reference to formal law, the granting of hundreds of millions of Reichsmarks to former princes, the majority of whom did not understand or further the racial tasks of Germany.

But this attitude makes it doubly necessary to point out the crude mendacity of the parties of the Left, who want to exploit this question for sordid party purposes...

For such wealth, which is immoral in view of the present distress of the German people, is not only in the hands of former princes, but above all is in the possession of Jewish financiers great and small. Therefore, if the Marxist petition for the expropriation of the Royal Houses without compensation is accepted, we demand also the expropriation without compensation of all Eastern Jews who have entered Germany as immigrants since 1 August 1914, as well as the confiscation of all increases in property after 1 August 1914, paying particular attention to bank and stock exchange profits.

We ask all Party members in public discussions to adopt on this question a position in accordance with this point of view.

Hitler's representative, Gottfried Feder, regarded himself as the leading ideologist of the Party and resented the criticism levelled at the programme by the Working Group. His report on the support given by the meeting to the referendum, on their determination to rewrite the programme, and above all on their critical attitude towards the Munich headquarters, which may or may not have included the leader himself, forced Hitler to act. His attempts to win the approval of businessmen, a tactic which would be undermined by Party support for the expropriation of the princes, would be threatened. Furthermore, while Hitler regarded the details of the Party programme as of relatively minor significance, he was not prepared to have the programme itself discussed since this would give it undue importance. If the programme could be altered as a result of discussion and pressure from the membership, the Party would be liable to endless doctrinal disputes such as those that bedevilled the parties of the Left. This would detract from the main aim of winning power. Above all, if the programme was made to appear so important and was subject to alteration by the membership, then it would inevitably restrict the freedom of the leader to act as he thought fit in any given circumstances. Instead of the party line being defined by the leader, he would be bound by a party programme whose interpretation would be in the hands of the party membership. The issue at stake was whether the party was to be a 'Führer party' in which the leader was the source of all authority, or whether authority was to be ultimately derived from the programme as interpreted by the membership. Finally, Hitler feared the growth of the Working Group into a regional organisation which might challenge the authority of Munich headquarters. To meet this challenge, therefore, he summoned a conference of Party leaders on 14 February at Bamberg in Bavaria at which, without actually attacking the Working Group, he made it clear that their policies were unacceptable. Goebbels described the occasion in his diary:

30

Leaving Saturday morning. In Bamberg we shall have to act the part of the bashful maiden and lure Hitler on to our territory. I am glad to notice that our [i.e. the Socialist] spirit is on the march in all towns. Not a soul has faith in Munich. Elberfeld must become the Mecca of German Socialism... .
...Sunday morning. Strasser comes to fetch me in the morning. He is hopeful. Plan for action ready. With Rust and Vahlen. Then tour of Bamberg. Charming town. Old, Jesuit. Hitler's car tears past us. A handshake. Well, well, Schlange-Berlin,[10] Streicher, Esser, Feder. Then to work. Hitler speaks for two hours. This pretty nearly finishes me. What kind of Hitler? A reactionary? Amazingly clumsy and uncertain. Russian question: altogether beside the point. Italy and Britain the natural allies. Horrible! It is our job to smash Bolshevism. Bolshevism is a Jewish creation! We must become Russia's heirs! A hundred and eighty millions!!! Compensation for princes! Law is law. Also for the princes. Question of not weakening private property [sic]. Horrible! Programme will do! Happy with it. Feder nods. Ley[11] nods. Streicher nods. Esser nods. It hurts me deeply to see you in that company!!! Short discussion. Strasser speaks. Hesitant, trembling, clumsy, good, honest Strasser; Lord, what a poor match we are for those pigs down there! Half an hour's disussion after a four-hour speech! Nonsense, you will win! I cannot say a word! I am stunned! By car to the station. Strasser is quite beside himself! Waving and *Heil*. My heart aches! Farewell from Strasser. We meet again in Berlin the day after tomorrow. I want to cry! Journey home. Sad journey home. With Haake and Dr. Ley. I say hardly a word. A horrible night! Probably one of my greatest disappointments. I can no longer wholly believe in Hitler. This is terrible. I have lost my inner support. I am only half myself. Grey dawn appears. Elberfeld. A few hours' sleep. Kaufmann.[12] I want to embrace him. We all say all there is to be

---

[10] Dr Schlange, Gauleiter of Berlin 1925–26.

[11] Dr Robert Ley, Gauleiter of Rhineland-South 1925–31; 1931–33, posts in Munich headquarters; after 1933, head of the German Labour Front and of Party organisation.

[12] Karl Kaufmann, Gauleiter of the Ruhr 1926–28, Gauleiter of Hamburg 1929–45.

said. Schmitz and Toni join us. The result: we are Socialists. We don't want to have been it in vain! Telegram from Lohse, Strasser, Vahlen. Do nothing hasty. Tomorrow discussion in Göttingen. Then Wednesday to Strasser. Proposal: Kaufmann, Strasser and I go to Hitler to impress on him: he must not allow those rogues down there to tie him hand and foot. Well then, train again tomorrow. Into battle. I despair! Sleep! Sleep! Sleep!

Although for a few weeks Goebbels and some other members of the Working Group still hoped that they would win over Hitler, this proved impossible. The Party Congress in May 1926 declared the programme once again immutable and in July working groups within the Party were forbidden. In the meantime Goebbels had made his peace with Hitler and in November was appointed Gauleiter in Berlin.

(iii) The creation of the Party cadre

The importance of the period 1925–29 in the history of the Nazi Party lies in the creation of a cadre of dedicated activists scattered in towns and villages throughout Germany. The basic framework had been laid before 1925 for the Party began with a number of supporters already involved in the *völkisch* movement either in the Nazi Party before its ban or in the German *Völkisch* Freedom Party (DVFP). These, rather than join the new DVFP, joined the refounded Nazi Party largely because of its reputation for activism and of the prestige won by Hitler during his trial. Significantly, those who joined the Nazi Party tended to be younger than those joining its rival. The basic pattern of Nazi organisation was regional. Germany was divided into *Gaue* or regions, and regional Party leaders or Gauleiters were appointed, usually men already successful in establishing their leadership in the area who were in effect confirmed by Party headquarters in Munich. Until 1928, the boundaries of the *Gaue* had been arranged on a largely *ad hoc* basis depending partly on the existing political and administrative divisions, partly on the extent of the area over which respective Gauleiters had established their authority. In 1928, however, the *Gaue* were reorganised to correspond with the thirty-five Reichstag electoral districts. Below the *Gaue* came the local branches and 'strongpoints' varying from a few hundred members down to one or two, who, not forming a branch, carried out propaganda in their area as best they could. In time, a district (*Kreis*) organisation developed between the *Gau* headquarters and the local branches but this only became fully effective after 1929. The main burden of Party work during this period fell on the *Gau* headquarters, in touch with both Munich and the local branches. In the early period the main correspondence with Munich concerned membership forms and subscriptions. As for propaganda, the *Gaue* could expect only an occasional speaker from headquarters. Most propaganda work was carried out by the Gauleiters and a few leading local activists, speaking at meetings arranged by the local branches, often in neighbouring towns and villages as yet without a branch. Such meetings might produce enough new members to found a branch—usually a minimum of fifteen. Once a branch had been founded it would canvass support in neighbouring villages by holding periodic meetings and distributing pamphlets.

A typical example was the village of Affinghausen in the district of Diepholz in Lower Saxony. The history of the local branch written in 1937 records the founding as follows:

31

In the year 1928-29 the National Socialist speaker, Jan Blankemeyer [a peasant] from Oldenburg came and talked to us about Adolf Hitler and his movement. Comrade Blankemeyer then came every two months and in winter even more frequently. He was living then in Uenzen, Kreis Grafschaft Hoya [a neighbouring district]. Comrades from the Uenzen branch ran the meetings here. Then Dincklage, the deputy Gauleiter, came. In October 1929, after a Blankemeyer meeting, eleven people joined the Party. Then in November 1929 the SA from Borstel near Nienburg [in a neighbouring district] held a propaganda march, which was followed by a meeting with Comrade Leister from Nienburg, and a branch was founded with farmer Hermann Menke as branch leader. Then we carried out propaganda in the surrounding villages.

Before 1928-29 it was a slow process, characterised by much conflict within the various local Party organisations. But a cadre organisation was being created, which provided the organisational framework essential if the Party was to be capable of successfully exploiting the economic and social discontent of 1929-33. The character of these men, who were to form the political leadership of the Third Reich, helped shape the future development of National Socialism. Their youth, radicalism, and sense of commitment, helped to determine the charismatic nature of the Party organisation, expressed in the emphasis on the absolute authority of Hitler as leader. This had ensured the failure of the Working Group, whose members themselves and notably its most dynamic leader, Joseph Goebbels, shared this commitment to Hitler's leadership. They wanted a leader and they recognised that Hitler was by far the most effective leader in the *völkisch* movement. He offered them the type of political action which they enjoyed. Politics for them was not a matter of discussion, bargaining and compromise within established bodies and procedures, but the thrill of physical action in the streets and beer halls or of inspiring an audience with a speech; the sense of comradeship induced by the struggle against an enemy; the glow of self-righteousness springing from a comparison of one's own self-sacrifice for the sake of the nation with the 'philistinism' of the citizen going about his ordinary daily life.

This style of politics appealed to many young people and to many uprooted during the post-war crisis from normal ties of family and job whose alienation now became a source of pride rationalised by an ideology which condemned the established order and glorified them as an elite. These men ousted the older generation of *völkisch* leaders whose political style had been shaped by the pre-war years, as the young Dr. Albert Krebs, who became for a short time Gauleiter in Hamburg, later recalled:

32

Characteristic of this period was the steady disappearance of all leaders and subordinate leaders (with the exception of a few parliamentary deputies) whose views and methods of struggle were still rooted in prewar days. Their places were taken by the young men of what was known as the front generation of 25–35 years old.

The importance of this changing of the guard can hardly be overemphasised. The openness of the feeling and judgement of these young men, their unweakened power of faith, their sheer physical energy and pugnacity lent the Party an impetus which the bourgeois parties above all could not match. Only rarely can the attack of youth be parried with the wire entanglement of grey-haired experience or the barbed-wire barricades of bitter scepticism. For the youth of the twenties these were nothing but a new provocation to their defiance and revolutionary enthusiasm. The quickest to feel it were those racialist groups and parties whose leadership represented conservative, or rather reactionary, views taken over from the past. Within only two short years they no longer had any political role whatsoever, even though such of them as the 'German Racialist League of Defence and Defiance'[13] had at one time several hundred thousand followers. Even in Hamburg, where the development of the NSDAP progressed rather slowly, the Racialist Freedom Party was already after one year in total disintegration. 'Without young people', one of their representatives confessed to me, 'nothing can be organised, not even the distribution of leaflets'.

A young member from Bad Harzburg who joined the SA during this period described his 'conversion' as follows:

33

For me this was the start of a completely new life. There was only one thing in the world for me and that was service in the movement. All my thoughts were centred

---

[13] A large antisemitic organisation established by the Pan-German League in 1919.

on the movement. I could talk only politics. I was no longer aware of anything else. At the time I was a promising athlete; I was very keen on sport, and it was going to be my career. But I had to give this up too. My only interest was agitation and propaganda.

This created problems of discipline. Indeed the structure of the local Party organisations during these early years bore in some ways a closer resemblance to a street gang than to a conventional political party. The post of leader was fiercely competitive, the incumbent being constantly required to prove himself in the eyes of his followers by his drive and radicalism. When things were going well this competition contributed to the dynamic of the Party. When things went badly, it could cause serious internal conflict as the following account by Ludolf Haase, Gauleiter of Göttingen, indicates:

34

When in the year 1914 our magnificent army went to war, leadership was conferred by rank.... . But as the years went by, and the period of the great *Materialschlachten* arrived with their incredible spiritual and physical demands, the only real leader, so far as his troops were concerned, was the man who proved himself in a crisis. The thing that now counted in an officer was not his uniform but the example he set people and his readiness to die for them. Here in blood, pain and mud, was born National Socialism, to which similar laws later applied, though under apparently quite different conditions. But basically in the movement it is only the true man, not the official, who is leader.

This explains why there was very often tension in the Party. The movement wanted to see men at the top who understood how to master conflict and opposition and who would yield to no one. If the leadership appeared to fall short, they were soon discontented and, because their obedience had been voluntarily given, there was risk of serious disturbance. The falling short might not even be real, only suspected; but still, if some individual had personal designs and spread accusations in the attempt to secure a following, serious damage could be done.

The quieter things were, the greater was this continual threat of internal unrest in the still immature party; the revolutionary spirits wanted to find an outlet, and as soon as the external enemy was less active or less under attack they turned their energy inwards. This hidden process, constantly at work within the movement, was the death of many a local branch in the early period and more than one Gauleiter fell victim to it. The leader of an area grew in the struggle and learned his lessons both from his opponents and from his own troop.

This reflection of his own Social Darwinist view of life won Hitler's approval. Indeed, he himself encouraged the emergence of leaders through a type of natural selection. Gustav Seifert, a Party member who had founded the Hanover branch in 1921 and who asked to be reappointed

leader in 1925, was told by Max Amann from Munich headquarters in a
letter dated 27 October 1925:

35

You know from your earlier activity as a branch leader of the National Socialist
German Workers' Party that Herr Hitler takes the view on principle that it is not
the job of the Party leadership to 'appoint' Party leaders. Herr Hitler is today more
than ever convinced that the most effective fighter in the National Socialist
movement is the man who wins respect for himself as leader through his own
achievements. You yourself say in your letter that almost all the members follow
you. Then why don't you take over the leadership of the branch?

Hitler did not like intervening personally in such conflicts, preferring to
leave one or other combatant to come out on top. He believed leaders
would prove themselves by the success with which they maintained and
extended their position and he particularly admired ruthlessness in the
pursuit of power. On the other hand, he qualified this approach by a
tendency to show loyalty to those associated with him from an early stage
even if later they had shown themselves not entirely competent.

Sometimes, for the sake of the stability of the organisation, it became
necessary for Party headquarters to intervene to uphold the authority of a
local leader who was being threatened with faction, and very occasionally
Hitler would have to intervene personally and appoint someone from
outside to restore order. This occurred, for example, in 1926 with the
Berlin branch. Hitler appointed Joseph Goebbels as the new Gauleiter of
Berlin. He recognised Goebbels's ability and was anxious to conciliate him
after the affair of the Working Group. Goebbels, who had soon become
reconciled to the failure of the Working Group and whose admiration for
Hitler was unbounded, accepted with alacrity. The following reports
written by Reinhold Muchow, a leading member of the Berlin organisation, describe the impact of Goebbels's appointment. The first is for
October 1926:

36

The internal party situation has not been good this month. The state of affairs
which has developed in our *Gau* reached such a climax this time that a complete
disruption of the Berlin organisation seemed likely. The tragedy of the *Gau* has
been that it has never had a proper leader, particularly necessary in this city of
millions. With all respect to the first Gauleiter, Comrade Dr Schlange, who has
worn himself out, he never succeeded in establishing a clear line in the *Gau*. He
lacked the gift of oratory and his work was paralysed by much unjust

hostility...There began slowly to develop in the *Gau* an opposition which strongly criticised the bad state of affairs.... This opposition was partly justified, but it was unruly rather than positive or objective, and when Comrade Dr Schlange transferred the management of the *Gau* to the deputy Gauleiter, Comrade Schmiedicke, it spread further and further. This comrade was even less capable of the determination required to master the confused situation. The result was that the opposition gathered fresh strength...The fighting efficiency of the Party sank to nil. Only a very few branches in the *Gau*—Neukölln and Spandau—looked at things dispassionately and persevered patiently, partly on their own responsibility. The unity of both these branches was preserved by the complete isolation of their membership from the details of the personal intrigues which went on in the meetings of the branch leaders. These two branches have an especial significance in that both, particularly Neukölln, are situated in the largest centres of Marxism.

When it proved impossible to establish order in the general chaos and when the local opposition groups went so far as to ignore all the decisions of the deputy Gauleiter, negotiations were started with the Reich party leadership in Munich with the request for a new Gauleiter. We received at length the news that Comrade Dr Goebbels would probably become the future Gauleiter of Berlin. A genuine sigh of relief went up from the disorganised *Gau*, proving how much all the comrades had felt the lack of a real leader. An official statement has not yet been made, but all Berlin comrades confidently hope that Comrade Dr Goebbels will definitely come... .

Goebbels diverted the energy and violence of the Party activists against the Party's political opponents in Berlin, of whom the Communists were the most active. It was an uphill struggle, but the important fact was that the members were now engaged against the enemy under a leader whose energy and radicalism they could admire. This is clear from the following report dated 'February 1927':

37

On the 11th of this month the Party held a public mass meeting in the Pharus [Beer] Halls' in Wedding, the real working class quarter, with the subject: 'The Collapse of the Bourgeois Class State'. Comrade Dr Goebbels was the speaker. It was quite clear to us what that meant. It had to be visibly shown that National Socialism is determined to reach the workers. We succeeded once before in getting a foothold in Wedding. There were huge crowds at the meeting. More than 1,000 people filled the hall whose political composition was four-fifths SA to one-fifth KPD. But the latter had gathered their main forces in the street. When the meeting was opened by Comrade Daluege, the SA leader, there were, as was expected, provocative shouts of 'On a point of order!'. After the KPD members had been told that *we*, not they, decided points of order, and that they would have the right to ask questions after the talk by Comrade Dr Goebbels, the first scuffling broke out. Peace seemed to be restored until there was renewed heckling. When the chairman announced that the hecklers would be sent out if the interruptions continued, the KPD worked themselves into a frenzy. Meanwhile, the SA had gradually surrounded the centre of the disturbance, and the Communists, sensing the danger, suddenly became aggressive. What followed all happened within three or four minutes. Within seconds both sides had picked up chairs, beer mugs, even tables, and a savage fight began. The Communists were gradually pushed under the gallery which we had taken care to occupy and soon chairs and glasses came hurtling down from there also. The fight was quickly decided: the KPD left with 85 wounded, more or less: that is to say, they could not get down the stairs as fast as they had calmly and 'innocently' climbed them. On our side we counted 3 badly wounded and about 10–12 slightly. When the police appeared the fight was already over. Marxist terrorism had been bloodily suppressed… .

As a result of his success in reviving the Berlin *Gau*, Goebbels was later appointed head of the Party's propaganda organisation on 27 April 1930.

The following document written, significantly by Gregor Strasser, on 9 January 1927 for his paper *Der Nationale Sozialist für Sachsen* indicates the progress already made by the cult of the Führer. Despite the frequent tensions within local Party organisations, Hitler had now succeeded in establishing for himself an unchallenged position, and the respect of the rank and file for his leadership now provided the main cohesive force within the Party:

38

…The tremendous superiority which the NSDAP has as a fighting instrument compared with all the other formations which instinctively pursue the same aim of German liberty and the rebirth of the German people, is due to the fact that we have the outstanding leader, who holds not only supreme power but also the love of his followers—a much stronger binding force.

'Duke and vassal!' In this ancient German relationship of leader and follower, fully comprehensible only to the German mentality and spirit, lies the essence of the structure of the NSDAP, the driving force of this aggressive power, the conviction of victory!

Heil Hitler! This is our first salute in the new year as it was the last one in the old year: Heil Hitler! In this salute lies the pride in the success of the past year which in all the *Gaue* of our beloved fatherland saw the powerful, irresistible progress of the National Socialist idea! In thousands of public meetings, members' evenings, in many hundreds of mass meetings the idea of National Socialism, the name of Adolf Hitler, was hurled among the masses of the German people and a hush fell on the ranks of this enslaved, exploited, starved people. An awareness of this glowing will for the struggle, the struggle to preserve the German people, the struggle for that people's freedom, freedom both within and without—for the one is worthless and impossible without the other—an awareness of those metallic accents of a brutal harshness which call things by their real names and challenges those things to a

struggle, a relentless struggle giving no quarter... .
Friends, a new year lies before us. Let us join hands in a silent vow to struggle in the new year with redoubled, with threefold vigour, each one at his post, for the victory of National Socialism, that is for the inward and outward freeing of the German people, to struggle without wavering, without flinching, in selfless devotion and true comradeship. And then, friends, raise your right arm and cry out with me proudly, eager for the struggle, and loyal unto death, 'Heil Hitler'.

The Annual General Meeting on 2–3 September 1928 illustrated the Party's pride in its rejection of democratic procedures in favour of the acclamation of a leader:

39

...Above all, Hitler notes the gradual penetration of the whole movement with the basic concepts of our ideas. He stresses primarily the gradual consolidation of the leadership principle [*Führer prinzip*]. The movement can be proud of the fact that it is the only one based on a logical foundation. This was necessary in order to make up for our numerical minority by a maximum degree of inner discipline, stability, fighting power, in short, energy... .
...The disintegration spreads slowly but surely; there is hardly any serious resistance. But antisemitism grows as an idea. What was hardly there ten years ago is there today: the Jewish question has been brought to people's notice, it will not disappear any more and we shall make sure that it becomes an international world question; we shall not let it rest until the question has been solved. We think we shall live to see that day (*enthusiastic applause*)... .
The chairman of the meeting, Gregor Strasser, expresses the mood of the meeting very well by remarking that any other party would now say that they had heard the reports of the chairman, whereas we National Socialists have heard the speech of the leader. And there is the same difference between the chairman of the old parties and the leader of the movement as there is between the report of a chairman of a party and the speech we have just heard.
The party business is now quickly dealt with according to the regulations. First, 'the election of the statutory executive committee'. To the amusement of the audience, Strasser proposes NSDAP member Hitler as Chairman. He notes that he has been unanimously elected by a show of hands (*laughter*). In the place of Comrade Schneider, who has been transferred by his employer away from the city, Comrade City Councillor Fiehler is elected Secretary in the same way. Also Reich treasurer Comrade Schwarz, who had 'resigned', is elected as first Treasurer, whereupon Strasser declares the acceptance of the election by the person nominated.

The main burden of Party activity fell on the SA to which at this period nearly all fit and active members of the Party belonged. Hitler took his time about its refounding, which officially took place in the autumn of 1926 under a former Free Corps leader, von Pfeffer. He wanted to ensure it did not become either a military-style formation, as had happened during 1923, or a group of revolutionary conspirators, since in either event the Government might use this as an excuse to ban the Party. In his first orders to the new SA, therefore, on 1 November 1926, he made it clear it was to be purely a propaganda weapon and strong-arm squad:

40

Letter from Adolf Hitler to Captain von Pfeffer (SA Order I)
To conclude our discussions about the programme of your reorganisation, I would like to sum up briefly my main instructions.

The training of the SA must be carried out, not on a military basis, but in accordance with the needs of the Party.

In so far as the members undergo physical training, the main emphasis must be, not on military drill, but far more on sports activities. Boxing and Jiu-Jitsu have always seemed to me far more important than any ineffective, because only incomplete, shooting practice. Physical training must implant in the individual the conviction of his superiority and give him that self-assurance which lies only in confidence in one's own strength; furthermore, it should give him those athletic skills which serve as a weapon for the defence of the movement.

The organisation of the SA as well as its clothing and equipment must accordingly be carried out, not on the model of the old army, but in a way appropriate to its task.

In order right from the start to prevent the SA acquiring any secretive character, quite apart from the fact that its clothing is recognisable to everybody, the size of its membership must define the path which assists the movement, one which is known to the public. It must not meet in secret but should march in the open air and thereby be channelled into activities which conclusively destroy all legends of a 'secret organisation'. To provide a mental diversion from any temptation to satisfy its activism by petty conspiracies, it must from the very beginning be initiated into the great idea of the movement and be trained in the task of representing this idea to such a degree that the horizon is widened right from the start and the individual SA man does not see his mission in the elimination of some crook or other whether big or small, but in helping to build a new National Socialist racialist state. Thereby the struggle against the present state will be raised above the atmosphere of petty acts of revenge and conspiracy to the greatness of an ideological war of extermination against Marxism, its constructions and its string pullers.

What we need is not a hundred or two hundred daring conspirators, but a hundred thousand and hundreds of thousands more fanatical fighters for our *Weltanschauung*. We must not work in secret conventicles but in huge mass marches, and neither by dagger nor poison nor pistol can the path be cleared for the movement, but only by conquering the street. We have to teach Marxism that National Socialism is the future master of the streets, just as it will one day be master of the State.

[signed] ADOLF HITLER

I hereby bring this letter to the notice of the SA leaders as a directive.

CHAPTER 3

The Emergence of Nazism as a Mass Movement 1928–1933

By 1928, the Weimar Republic had superficially acquired a degree of political stability and economic prosperity. Yet, although these years 1928–29 are often seen as the high point of economic prosperity before the Wall Street crash and ensuing slump, this view requires qualification. Firstly, this economic prosperity was based on very insecure foundations. During the years 1924–28 German industry, agriculture, and local government had borrowed extensively on the American market at high rates of interest and largely on a short-term basis. If economic difficulties occurred in the United States, many of these loans were liable to recall at short notice.

Secondly, by the end of 1927, agriculture and the *Mittelstand*—artisans and small retailers—were already in economic difficulties. The years 1924–29 saw something of a shift in the economic balance of power towards big business on the one hand and organised labour on the other and against agriculture and the *Mittelstand*. It was a period of rationalisation in German industry, involving an acceleration of the historical trend towards the concentration of firms into big trusts and cartels against which small businesses found themselves competing at a disadvantage. At the same time, organised labour in the shape of the Trade Unions and the Social Democrats had some success in pressing demands for higher wages and improved welfare measures. Thus, a major new unemployment insurance scheme was introduced at the end of 1927, financed by contributions from employers and employees. *Mittelstand* groups found that, in addition to the burden of high interest rates on their loans, they had to pay high taxes and social security contributions for their employees.

Finally, at the end of 1927, a world-wide agricultural depression began, whose effects were exacerbated by trade treaties with countries such as Poland, by which Germany agreed to import agricultural produce in return for German industrial goods. These treaties were a response to pressure both from the dominant export-oriented sections of industry—chemicals, electrical goods, and machinery—and also from organised labour which wanted cheap food. Inevitably, this agricultural crisis soon involved groups dependent on agriculture such as artisans and small traders in rural areas.

The economic difficulties of peasants and *Mittelstand* groups, which had already suffered the effects of hyperinflation in 1923, imposed increasing strains on the political system. The Protestant middle class electorate, already divided between several major parties began to fragment still further as new parties emerged offering to provide more determined representation of their specific interests—a process facilitated by the extreme form of proportional representation enshrined in the Weimar Constitution. The problem was that, although these special interest parties—for peasants, landlords, tenants, etc.—could sometimes play a pivotal role in Parliament, ultimately this fragmentation was bound to weaken the political weight of these groups. The growing awareness of this led to further disillusionment with the whole political system, a disillusionment which the Nazis were quick to exploit.

(i) The Breakthrough 1928–30

The relative prosperity and political stability of 1924–28 had created a climate unconducive to the growth of Nazism. The tactics followed by the Party in concentrating on trying to win over the industrial workers made things worse. By the end of 1927 this policy had manifestly failed to achieve results. Workers remained loyal to the Social Democrats and the Communists. Moreover, the majority of the middle class suspected the Party's working class, 'Socialist' image. It had built up a nucleus of diehard supporters but they were still fewer than 75,000 in the whole of Germany. Its seven deputies made the Party a negligible quantity in Parliament. The Nazi Party was a fringe group on the far right of German politics and without influence.

A new tactic was clearly necessary if the energies of the Party were not to turn inwards in self-destructive internal conflict. In fact, a change of emphasis by the beginning of 1928 led the Party, while continuing to try to attract workers, to concentrate increasingly on the middle class, now recognised as more responsive. In December 1927 the deputy Gauleiter of

Hanover-North, Karl Dincklage, wrote to Franz Stöhr, a Nazi Reichstag deputy, and referred to the line which Hitler had taken at a conference of Party leaders in Weimar on 27 November:

41

...In full agreement with the remarks of our leader in Weimar we too believe that we shall not yet succeed in winning much ground from the Marxists in the coming election. We shall receive most sympathy from the small businessman as the strongest opponent of department stores and consumer cooperatives. Further, from the white-collar worker, who being in the DHV,[14] is already an antisemite...

In the winter of 1927–28 discontent began among the rural population of north-west Germany and soon spread. It was sparked off by an increase in the salaries of civil servants on 16 December 1927. This infuriated the rural population which regarded itself as grossly overtaxed. The Nazis were quick to exploit the possibilities and in December 1927 Hitler made a major speech to a protest meeting of farmers from Schleswig-Holstein.

The following police report of a mass demonstration on 26 January 1928, in the city of Oldenburg, in the middle of a big livestock farming area in north-west Germany, describes these grievances. It also shows how the Nazis exploited them by trying to discredit the professional organisations which had organised the meeting, and to convince their members that the whole parliamentary system was at fault and that only a political movement dedicated to the overthrow of that system could bring relief:

42

...In meetings of the rural population which were held in many places in the state of Oldenburg during the past weeks, the majority of those participating demanded again and again that an open-air protest meeting should be held in the state capital of Oldenburg, in order to give weight to the demands of the rural population, outlined below, which emerged in the meetings and were in the meantime formulated by a committee. It would also open the eyes of the state government to the masses of discontented who stand behind these demands. The Rural League [Landbund], the Farmers' Association [Bauernverein], the League of Smallhold-ings, the Artisans' League, the Settlers' Association, and the Shopkeepers' Guild had therefore called their members to a combined mass demonstration which took place in the Horsefair on 26 January. According to fairly accurate estimates, approximately 20,000 country people had assembled in the Horsefair by 12 noon...
      After the speeches of the representatives of various trade associations, the

---

[14] Deutschnationaler Handlungsgehilfenverband: the German Nationalist Commercial Employees' Association, a white collar workers' union with völkisch sympathies.

general secretary of the Oldenburg Farmers' Association, a farmer named Brende-
bach, announced the following fourteen demands of the rural population and said
that during the next few days a delegation was to go to Berlin to convey these
demands to the Reich Government and to demand radical measures for improving
the situation of the rural population:
1. An embargo on all superfluous foreign imports.
2. Protection of agriculture through tariffs equivalent to those already applied to
   industry.
3. Simplification of the tax system; replacement of current direct taxes by income
   tax and property tax after suitable alterations; furthermore, the right for states
   and parishes to impose surcharges on these taxes.
4. Tax remission for farmers, craftsmen, and shopkeepers who are in distress.
5. Speedy radical reduction of government activity and expenditure.
6. Economical management in all branches of public administration, and reduction in the number of officials.
7. Temporary suspension of the pay regulations for civil servants of 16 December
   1927.
8. We do not see in the incorporation of Oldenburg into Prussia a measure
   making for cheaper administration.
9. Reduction of social insurance contributions to a level which business can stand.
10. Permission for voluntary overtime work after the 8-hour working period. Loyal
    application of the Reich regulations on contracts. Radical measures against
    non-guild work.
11. Planned reduction of controlled housing policy and promotion of building
    programmes.
12. The prerequisite for any settlement activity must be its profitability.
13. Availability of long-term cheap credit for improvement of the debt situation
    with the aim of wiping out debts.
14. The privileged treatment of civil servants in Parliament who receive a salary in
    addition to allowances and a substitute must cease.
   The reading out of the demands drew loud and prolonged applause from the
   majority of the participants... .
   A certain Münchmeyer,[15] formerly pastor of Borkum, as well as the National
Socialists, had used the assembly of large numbers of the rural population for
propaganda purposes for their parties. After ineffective appeals to the leadership of
the protest meeting to be allowed to speak at the Horsefair, Münchmeyer called a
public meeting at the Lindenhof for 10 a.m., which was attended by approximately
800 people... .
   The NSDAP had scheduled two public meetings at the Lindenhof and the
Ziegelhof at 3 p.m. At the meeting at the Lindenhof which was attended by over
1,000 people, Reichstag Deputy Kube[16] of Berlin was the speaker; Reichstag
Deputy Gottfried Feder of Munich spoke at the meeting at the Ziegelhof which was
attended by about 500 people... .

[15] A leading antisemite who was to join the Nazis in April.

[16] Wilhelm Kube, Gauleiter of Kurmark 1928–1936, General Commissioner of White Russia
1941–43.

All the speakers at the Kube meeting expressed the view that the rural population could not be satisfied with the form and outcome of the demonstration. At the end the following resolution was read out and adopted unanimously:

'The thousands of Oldenburg farmers and middle-class people assembled today in the Lindenhof, together with the tens of thousands of their fellow-countrymen, who have come here in the most bitter distress to give visible expression of their despair, having listened to the speech of the National Socialist Reichstag Deputy Wilhelm Kube of Berlin, declare their absolute determination not to be deceived, misled, exploited and expropriated.

'We have recognised that the distress of agriculture is inseparably bound up with the *political* misery of the whole German people; that parliamentarism which is corrupt through and through and a weak government are unable to overcome the German political and economic emergency.

'Let us do away with this Marxist-capitalist extortion system that has made Germany, our homeland, powerless, without honour, defenceless, and that has turned us free German farmers and middle-class people into poor, misused slaves of the world stock exchange.

'But let us also do away with the professional federations who only throw dust in our eyes and neutralise any vigorous action because politically they stand in the camps of those parties who have caused all this misery by accepting the Dawes Plan. The middle class and the farmers of Oldenburg see in the German National Socialist Hitler movement the only salvation from the parliamentary morass, from the pathetic and cowardly fulfilment policy.

'Only when Germany is reborn in power, freedom and honour, led by unselfish German men who are not burdened by the contemptible policy of the last few years, only then will the German farmer stand as a free man on free soil serving the great German community as the backbone of our people.'

It was noted that after the meeting several farmers approached Reichstag Deputy Kube to secure him for talks in the countryside.

The Nazis' opponents stigmatised them as a radical, socialistic, working class party, the image it had tried to convey hitherto. Efforts to frighten the peasants with Point 17 of the Nazi programme led Hitler to 'clarify' it on 13 April 1928. This alteration indicates the significance attached by Hitler to the reorientation of the Party:

43

In view of the false interpretations on the part of our opponents of Point 17 of the Programme of the NSDAP, it is necessary to make the following statement:

Since the NSDAP accepts the principle of private property, it is self-evident that the phrase 'confiscation without compensation' refers simply to the creation of possible legal means for confiscation, when necessary, of land acquired illegally or not managed in the public interest. It is, therefore, aimed primarily against Jewish companies which speculate in land.

This new orientation had insufficient time to have much effect before the Reichstag election in May 1928. The results appeared to reflect the improved situation. The extreme Right suffered a serious defeat compared with December 1924. The Nazis lost 100,000 votes and polled 2.6 per cent of the vote. The ultra-conservative German Nationalists with 78 seats had lost 25 seats. The Left increased their vote to over 40 per cent of the total. The Social Democrats gained 21 seats and had 152; the Communists with 54 gained 9 seats. Although greeted at home and abroad as a victory for Weimar democracy, the results in fact indicated the situation was by no means as satisfactory as appeared at first sight. Not only the Right lost support; the parties of the Centre—the Democrats or left-wing Liberals, the German People's Party or right-wing Liberals, and the Catholic Centre Party—all lost seats. Their voters had either stayed away—the percentage of those voting declined sharply—or supported the new economic interest parties established between 1924–28. The Business Party which catered for artisans and small shopkeepers increased its seats from 17 to 23.

This was an ominous result. For the past four years Germany had been ruled by a coalition of the Right and Centre—German Nationalists, German People's Party, Democrats, and Catholic Centre Party. The vote for the Left and against the Centre and Right, was not a vote of confidence in the existing government. If anything, it was a vote against or at least an abstention. Unfortunately, the conclusions which the Right and Centre parties drew led them to interpret the result to mean that participation in the Government would alienate their own supporters.

This reaction reflected the nature of the German party system. Parties tended to represent specific interests: the German Nationalists—agriculture, particularly the big arable landowners of the east, the Junkers; the German People's Party—industry, and particularly heavy industry; the Centre Party—the Catholics; the Social Democrats—the trade unions. At the same time, the parties competed with one another within a broad segment of the population—the German Nationalists, the People's Party and the Democrats competed for the support of the Protestant upper and middle classes; the Social Democrats and Communists competed for the support of the workers. Parties committed to specific interests and competing against rivals for support within the same segment of the population, made the formation of coalitions difficult at the best of times. The result of the election of 1928 made the position even worse. The parties were convinced that by participating in government they would damage their electoral prospects by compromising the interests of their voters and members to maintain a coalition with parties which represented other and often conflicting interests. This would play into the hands of rivals who were not members of the Government, as the growth of the economic interest parties, regarded as dangerous new competitors, showed. The party bureaucracies, primarily concerned about retaining the backing of interests and voters, applied increasing pressure on the parliamentary groups to stay in opposition to enable the party to assert without compromise the interests of their supporters. The parliamentary party groups in turn put pressure on their colleagues in the Government coalition to leave the Government rather than compromise.

These considerations determined the future trend of politics. The German Nationalists had previously compromised their hostility to the Republic, participating in government to protect the interests of their mainly agrarian supporters in the formulation of tariff legislation. From now onwards, they began to move to the Right, back to the uncompromisingly anti-Republican position they had adopted in the first years of the Republic. The People's Party did not follow this trend to the Right immediately. Indeed, it now entered a coalition with the Social Democrats, largely because of Gustav Stresemann, who was aware that the democratic system depended on a strong Centre and on a willingness to compromise with the moderate Left. Pressure, however, continued to build up within the party against this coalition, particularly in view of the competition from the intransigent Nationalists on the Right. When Stresemann died on 3 October 1929, it was to be only a matter of time before the coalition broke down under the strain of the rightward drift of the People's Party under the influence of its strong industrial wing.

Finally, even the Catholic Centre Party began to move Right, particularly under its new and more conservative leader, Ludwig Kaas, from the end of 1928. This drift of the parties of the Centre towards the Right was paralleled by a leftward trend of the Social Democrats, the result of increasing competition from the Communists, evident from their election gains in 1928. In short, after the election of 1928 a polarisation of politics began which threatened to paralyse the parliamentary system by making coalition governments impossible. Whether or not it would continue would depend on future economic developments; a deterioration in the economic situation would force the parties to uphold, even more rigidly, the particular interests of their members and voters.

Although the new middle-class campaign had not had time to take effect before the election, the low average Nazi vote of 2 per cent disguises district variations. In some north-west rural districts where the protest movement had been strong, they gained over 10 per cent. The Party summed up the lessons of the election in the *Völkischer Beobachter* on 31 May 1928:

44

...The election results from the rural areas in particular have proved that with a smaller expenditure of energy, money and time, better results can be achieved there than in the big cities. In small towns and villages mass meetings with good speakers are events and are often talked about for weeks, while in the big cities the effects of meetings with even three of four thousand people soon disappear. Local successes in which the National Socialists are running first or second are, surprisingly, almost invariably the result of the activity of the branch leader or of a few energetic members...

Nazi Party membership steadily increased from 100,000 to 150,000 between October 1928 and 1 September 1929. The next turning-point came in the autumn of 1929. With the Wall Street crash, the economic situation in Germany rapidly deteriorated. American financiers, under pressure, called in the numerous short-term loans made to Germany since 1924. Bankruptcies followed. Moreover, since the crisis was international, export markets disappeared and businesses were forced to shed labour or close down. This reduced home demand, making the situation even worse. Unemployment figures began to soar. At this point, an issue emerged which was ideally adapted for a right-wing attack on the Republic.

Under the chairmanship of the American banker, Owen Young, the Allied Reparations Commission had devised a plan finally to settle German war reparations. Germany would pay less than originally intended but would still make substantial annual payments until 1988, a total of 34,500 million goldmarks. This was seen by the extreme Right as an excellent opportunity to exploit the growing discontent and regain the support lost in the 1928 election. They claimed Germany's children were being sold in slavery to the Allies. The German Nationalists had a new leader, the press and film magnate Alfred Hugenberg, a co-founder of the Pan German League. Hugenberg had used the Party's electoral failure and subsequent financial difficulties to impose himself and his extreme anti-Republican views on the Party. In the Autumn of 1929, he organised a referendum for a law rejecting the Young Plan and making any politican who agreed to the plan face trial:

45

§1. The Reich Government will solemnly inform the foreign powers without delay that the compulsory recognition of war guilt in the Versailles Treaty contradicts historical truth, is based on false preconceptions, and is not binding under international law.

§2. The Reich Government will endeavour to secure abrogation of the recognition of war guilt in Article 231 as well as of Articles 429 and 430 of the Versailles Treaty. It will also endeavour to secure the immediate and unconditional evacuation of the occupied territories and the removal of all controls over German territory, irrespective of the acceptance or rejection of the Hague Conference.

§3. New burdens and obligations vis-à-vis foreign powers on the basis of the recognition of war guilt may not be undertaken.
This also includes the burdens and obligations which are to be undertaken by Germany on the basis of the proposals of the Paris experts and the agreements deriving therefrom. [i.e. the Young Plan.]

§4. Reich Chancellors, Reich Ministers and their plenipotentiaries who sign treaties contrary to the regulation contained in §3.1 will be subject to the penalties contained in §92, No.3 of the Penal Code. [i.e. Penal servitude for not less than two years.]

To win maximum support for this draft law, Hugenberg invited the help of all willing to cooperate including the Nazis.

Hitler saw this as an ideal opportunity for his party, giving him access to the funds of the Right and national publicity in the Hugenberg press. More important, the association of the Nazis with the conservative and upper-class Nationalists would remove the stigma of being radical and working class and make it more acceptable to the middle class. Finally, the Nazis as the most active of all the groups participating in the campaign gave the impression of being the most dynamic of the anti-Republican groups on the Right. They appeared more attractive than their conservative rivals to the growing number of those discontented with the Republican parties owing to the deteriorating economic situation. The fact that the subsequent plebiscite failed to win anything like sufficient support—5.8 million instead of the necessary 21 million votes—did not detract from these advantages. Indeed, the Young Plan campaign coincided with the state and local government elections of November–December 1929, in which the Nazis made significant gains. In the election in the state of Thuringia, for example, they won 11.3% of the vote and participation in the Government. Nazi local government propaganda used rumour and scandal to discredit opponents. Whether the scandal was true or not did not matter; they hoped to benefit from the belief that 'there's no smoke without fire'. They aimed to discredit the local establishment whether Conservative or Social Democrat.

There were, however, some within the Party who resented this reorientation of its propaganda towards the middle class and rural areas. They continued to press for a more definite 'socialist' commitment; they also objected to the subordination of the Party and its ideology to the leader. A leading spokesman for this group was Otto Strasser, the brother of Gregor Strasser. The newspapers of the Kampfverlag, the Strasser publishing house, continued to adopt a comparatively 'left wing' line, complicating Hitler's appeal to the middle class. The issue was finally fought out at an interview between Hitler and Otto Strasser in 1930. First, Hitler challenged the claim of Strasser's associates that the 'idea', i.e. the ideology, of the Party was distinct from and superior to the leader, then the argument turned to the question of the definition of Socialism about which Hitler and Strasser had very different views:

46

How do you justify Blank's[17] theories?' Hitler demanded. 'His conception of loyalty, the distinction he makes between the Leader and the Idea, are incitements to Party members to rebel.'

'No,' I said, 'it is not a question of diminishing the Leader's prestige. But for the free and Protestant German the service of the Idea first and foremost is an ingrained necessity. The Idea is divine in origin, while men are only its vehicles, the body in which the Word is made flesh. The Leader is made to serve the Idea, and it is to the Idea alone that we owe absolute allegiance. The Leader is human, and it is human to err.'

'You are talking monumental idiocy. You wish to give Party members the right to decide whether or not the Führer has remained faithful to the so-called Idea. It's the lowest kind of democracy, and we want nothing to do with it! For us the Idea is the Führer, and each Party member has only to obey the Führer...'

'What you say would lead to the dissolution of our organisation, which is based on discipline. I have no intention of allowing our organisation to be disrupted by a crazy scribbler. You have been an officer; you see that your brother accepts my discipline, even if he doesn't always see eye to eye with me. Take a lesson from him; he's a fine man.'

He seized my hands, as he had done two years before. His voice was choked with sobs, and tears ran down his cheeks... .

'All that is very simple for you, Herr Hitler', Strasser continued, 'but it only serves to emphasise the profound difference in our revolutionary and Socialist ideas. The reasons you give for destroying the Kampfverlag I take to be only pretexts. The real reason is that you want to strangle the social revolution for the sake of legality and your new collaboration with the bourgeois parties of the Right.'

At this Hitler grew violent.

'I am a Socialist, and a very different kind of Socialist from your rich friend Reventlow.[18] I was once an ordinary working-man. I would not allow my chauffeur to eat worse than I eat myself. But your kind of Socialism is nothing but Marxism. The mass of the working classes want nothing but bread and games. They will never understand the meaning of an ideal, and we cannot hope to win them over to one. What we have to do is to select from a new master-class men who will not allow themselves to be guided, like you, by the morality of pity. Those who rule must know they have the right to rule because they belong to a superior race. They must maintain that right and ruthlessly consolidate it... .

'What you preach is liberalism, nothing but liberalism. There is only one possible kind of revolution, and it is not economic or political or social, but racial, and it will

---

[17] Herbert Blank was a friend of Otto Strasser.
[18] Count von Reventlow, a leading *völkisch* activist.

always be the same: the struggle of inferior classes and inferior races against the superior races who are in the saddle. On the day the superior race forgets this law, it is lost. All revolutions—and I have studied them carefully—have been racial... .'

'Let us assume, Herr Hitler, that you came into power tomorrow. What would you do about Krupp's? Would you leave it alone or not?'

'Of course I should leave it alone', cried Hitler. 'Do you think me so crazy as to want to ruin Germany's great industry?'

'If you wish to preserve the capitalist regime, Herr Hitler, you have no right to talk of Socialism. For our supporters are Socialists, and your programme demands the socialisation of private enterprise.'

'That word "socialism" is the trouble', said Hitler. He shrugged his shoulders, appeared to reflect for a moment and then went on:

'I have never said that all enterprises should be socialised. On the contrary, I have maintained that we might socialise enterprises prejudicial to the interests of the nation. Unless they were so guilty, I should consider it a crime to destroy essential elements in our economic life. Take Italian Fascism. Our National Socialist state, like the Fascist state, will safeguard both employers' and workers' interests while reserving the right of arbitration in case of dispute.'

Hitler, exasperated by my answers, continued: 'there is only one economic system, and that is responsibility and authority on the part of directors and executives. I ask Herr Amann to be responsible to me for the work of his subordinates and to exercise authority over them. Herr Amann asks his office manager to be responsible for his typists and to exercise his authority over them; and so on to the lowest rung of the ladder. That is how it has been for thousands of years, and that is how it will always be.'

'Yes, Herr Hitler, the administrative structure will be the same whether the state is capitalist or socialist. But the spirit of labour depends on the regime under which it lives. If it was possible a few years ago for a handful of men not appreciably different from the average to throw a quarter of a million Ruhr workers on the streets, if this act was legal and in conformity with the morality of our economic system, then it is not the men but the system that is criminal.'

'But that—' Hitler replied, looking at his watch and showing signs of acute impatience 'that is no reason for granting the workers a share in the profits of the enterprises that employ them, and more particularly for giving them the right to be consulted. A strong state will see that production is carried on in the national interest, and, if these interests are contravened, can proceed to expropriate the enterprise concerned and take over its administration.'

On 27 March 1930, the polarisation within the Reichstag finally brought the breakdown of the coalition government of the right-wing Liberal People's Party and the Social Democrats which had ruled Germany since 1928. The Government split on financing the deficit in the unemployment benefit fund, becoming daily larger as the numbers of unemployed rose. The interest groups behind the two parties made their weight felt. The People's Party under the influence of the industrialists wished to reduce the benefits, thereby putting the whole burden on the unemployed. The Social Democrats, on the other hand, under the pressure of the trade unions insisted on an increase in the social insurance contributions, of which the employers would have to pay half. After months of negotiation compromise proved impossible and the Government was forced to resign.

This was to mark the end of parliamentary government in Germany for nearly twenty years. The issue at stake in the conflict was: who would bear the main burden of the economic crisis—capital or labour? The trade unions regarded a cut in unemployment benefits as the thin end of the wedge. Were it accepted it would begin the erosion of the whole structure of wage and welfare concessions laboriously built up since 1918. It would discredit them in the eyes of their members and be grist to the mill of the Communists. The industrialists, on the other hand, saw the unemployment insurance issue as a classic demonstration of labour's success in exploiting the democratic system of Weimar to increase its share of the nation's wealth. Industry wanted a government that would cut back public expenditure and encourage profits. To achieve this would require the removal of the Social Democrats from the Government as a minimum goal. Many went further and wished to curb the power of the Reichstag.

Although the issue of unemployment insurance was the overt cause of the collapse of the coalition, behind the scenes negotiations had been going on since at least December 1929 for the removal of the Social Democrats. The Army had become increasingly disillusioned with the way the parliamentary system operated. It had drawn the lesson from the First World War that modern war required the total mobilisation of the nation's resources. It was vital, therefore, for the Army to have political support not simply for rearmament but also to create a climate of public opinion favourable to national mobilisation. The Weimar political system, already associated in their eyes with defeat and revolution, had discredited itself above all because of its failure to provide such a climate. Democracy enabled the Left with its strong pacifist sentiments to exert too much influence.

The Army's political expert, General Kurt von Schleicher, found sympathy for its view within the entourage of Reich President von Hindenburg. The weakness of coalition governments had been producing growing disillusionment with the system for several years. For some time the President's State Secretary, Otto Meissner, had been contemplating schemes to reduce the influence of the legislature. Hindenburg needed little persuading of the need to seize the opportunity of the anticipated breakdown of the coalition to remove the Social Democrats and establish a strong government of the moderate Right, which would be able to remain largely independent of the Reichstag by using the emergency powers contained in Article 48 of the Constitution.

Schleicher's candidate for the Chancellorship was the leader of the parliamentary group of the Catholic Centre Party, Heinrich Brüning, who had a reputation as a financial expert. Brüning's background as a volunteer machine-gun officer in the war had given him a great respect for the Army and he regarded Hindenburg, the old war hero, with considerable awe. He too was disillusioned with the operation of the parliamentary system and believed in strengthening the executive at the expense of the legislature, ideally culminating in a restoration of the monarchy. Initially he hoped to achieve this by a Right/Centre coalition with a majority in the Reichstag, excluding the Social Democrats from influence. The key, however, lay with the German Nationalists, split into those who supported Hugenberg in his intransigent opposition to the Republic and a more moderate rebel group. Brüning hoped to strengthen the moderates, thereby acquiring a majority. If he did not succeed, he could always use the emergency powers in paragraph 2 of Article 48 of the Weimar Constitution to issue legislation by Presidential decree:

47

§2. If a *Land* fails to fulfil the responsibilities assigned to it under the Constitution or the Reich Laws, the Reich President can take the measures necessary to restore law and order with the help of the armed forces.

In the event of a serious disturbance of or threat to law and order, the Reich President can take the measures necessary to restore law and order, intervening if necessary with armed force. For this purpose he may provisionally abrogate either partially or completely the basic rights contained in Articles 114, 115, 117, 118, 123, 124, and 153.

§3. The Reich President is obliged to inform the Reichstag immediately of all measures taken under paragraphs 1 or 2 of this Article. The measures are to be revoked on the request of the Reichstag.

In the event of an emergency a Land Government may provisionally implement the measures in paragraph 2 in its own area. The measures are to be revoked on the request of the Reich President or the Reichstag.

Further details will be defined by a Reich Law.

Since the law mentioned in paragraph 3 was never passed, interpretation of when a threat to law and order existed was left to the Reich President himself.

The new Government's policy for solving the economic crisis reflected the emphasis of traditional economic theory on the need to balance the budget, particularly after the experience of hyperinflation in 1923. It was, however, also determined by Brüning's desire to demonstrate to the Allies that even with the best will in the world Germany was incapable of coping with the burden of reparations. He hoped to secure the ending of reparations and thereby free Germany's hands to pursue a more aggressive foreign policy both for its own sake and to take the wind out of the sails of the radical Right.

When, on 16 July 1930, part of the Government's tough budget was rejected by the Reichstag, the Nationalists voting against, Brüning implemented it by Presidential decree. When the Reichstag responded by demanding its revocation, it was dissolved and elections fixed for 14 September. Brüning hoped for a reduction in the Socialist vote, since they would probably be blamed for the economic crisis which had occurred under an SPD Chancellor. He also hoped the German Nationalist Party rebels would be strengthened and it would then be possible to form a Right/Centre coalition with a majority in Parliament. This disastrous miscalculation had far-reaching consequences.

At the Reichstag election on 14 September 1930 the most striking result was the increase in votes for the Nazi Party from 810,000 to 6½ million. Some of the increase came from new voters who had not voted in the previous election because they were disaffected or too young to qualify. Much, however, came from those who had previously voted for the middle class Liberal and Conservative parties (People's Party, Democrats, and Nationalists), who lost 67 seats between them. The Catholic parties (Centre and Bavarian People's Party) increased their support slightly, while the Social Democrats lost support mainly to the Communists who gained 23 seats. But there could be no doubt about the main significance of the result—the Nazi Party with 107 seats had become the second largest party in the Reichstag. The breakthrough for which the Party had been working for so long had at last been achieved.

(ii) Propaganda 1930–1932

An important factor in the Nazis' electoral success between 1930–33 was the Party's propaganda. Although there was not always a direct correlation between the areas of Nazis success and those of maximum propaganda activity, and although the propaganda effect was often indirect—for example through the recruitment of opinion leaders—rather than direct, there can be no doubt that the Party's propaganda made a major contribution to its success.

By 1930 Nazi propaganda was controlled by a special propaganda department represented at all levels of the Party. At the top was the Reich propaganda department headed by Goebbels after 27 April 1930. Each *Gau* or Party regional headquarters had its propaganda department with its own chief and, below that, each branch had an official in charge of propaganda. Although this propaganda department was subject to the overall authority of the political leadership at the various levels, it also had its own separate chain of command. Directives from the Reich propaganda department to the propaganda departments of the *Gaue* were relayed to the propaganda officials in the local branches in their region. Reports of propaganda activity, information on political opponents, and suggestions were passed up the chain in the reverse direction. The Reich propaganda headquarters exercised a tight control over all aspects of propaganda, particularly at election times.

As the following memorandum of the Prussian Ministry of the Interior of May 1930 indicates, Nazi propaganda was already geared to a high pitch of efficiency and the campaign had merely to be intensified for the September Reichstag election among a population now acutely anxious about their economic situation and disillusioned with the failure of their professional and political representatives. The rest of the parties, on the other hand, were obliged to turn from their legislative activities and face a hostile electorate which had little sympathy for their political manoeuvrings:

48

Hardly a day passes on which there are not several meetings even in narrowly restricted local areas. Carefully organised propaganda headquarters in the individual *Gaue* ensure that the speaker and subject are adapted to the local and economic circumstances. The Reichstag and Landtag deputies of the Party and many other Party speakers travel about every day to undertake and build up this agitation. Through systematic training courses, through correspondence courses and recently through a school for NSDAP speakers established on 1 July 1929, such agitators are trained for this task over a period of months, even years. If they prove themselves, they receive official recognition from the Party and are put under contract to give at least thirty speeches over a period of eight months and receive as an incentive a fee of 20 Reichsmarks or more per evening in addition to their expenses. Rhetorical skill combined with subjects carefully chosen to suit the particular audience, which in the countryside and in the small towns is mainly interested in economic matters, ensure, according to our observations, halls which are almost invariably overcrowded with enthusiastic listeners. Meetings with an audience of between 1000 and 5000 people are a daily occurrence in the bigger towns. Frequently a second or several parallel meetings have to be held because the halls provided cannot hold the numbers who attend... . On such occasions the network of local branches is extended as far as possible or at all events contact men are recruited who are intended to prepare the ground through intensive propaganda by word of mouth for the spread of the movement which can be observed everywhere. Frequently such propaganda squads stay in a certain place for several days and try to win the local population for the movement through the most varied sorts of entertainment such as concerts, sports days, tattoos in suitable places and even church parades. In other places an outside propaganda speaker is stationed for a certain time; with a car at his disposal, he travels systematically through the surrounding district. National Socialist theatre groups travelling from place to place serve the same purpose.

On 10 September 1930 the Party issued the following manifesto:

49

The victory of the national socialist movement will mean the overcoming of the old class and caste spirit. It will allow a nation once more to rise up out of status mania and class madness.

It will train this nation to have an iron determination.

It will overcome democracy and reassert the authority of personality.

It will restore justice to the German people through the brutal assertion of the principle that one has no right to hang the little ones so long as the biggest criminals go unpunished and untouched.

The other parties may have come to terms with the thievery of the inflation, may recognise the fraudulent revolution. National socialism will bring the thieves and traitors to justice. National socialism fights for the German worker by getting him out of the hands of his swindlers and destroying the protectors of international bank and stock exchange capital.

With its victory the national socialist movement will purge the German administration of the parasites who, though with no right to belong and without qualifications, have got in simply on the basis of their party card and are a burden on the nation. Anyone who talks of new taxes should first free the administration of the revolutionary parasites who have streamed in during the past twelve years. One protects the honest civil servant only by opening the way for his efficiency and honest labour and by removing the parliamentary profiteers from the civil service.

With its victory the national socialist movement will also seek to guarantee the economic protection of German people. As long as stock exchanges and department stores are inadequately taxed any further tax increases on the little man are a crime.

With its victory the national socialist movement will protect the peasant through the ruthless education of our people to consume our own products.

Our upper ten thousand will have to learn to eat black bread too, otherwise our rye will rot and wheat will have to be imported.

We will emphasise our national honour and national pride by avoiding all that is foreign as far as possible and giving preference to the results of our own hard work.

We will ensure that the reform of our attitude to defence and a change in our foreign policy will be at the top of the list of reforms.

After its victory the national socialist movement will no longer continue the policy of continually currying France's favours. Every hand which is offered to us in Europe which is in a similar plight and shares our way of thinking will be thankfully grasped.

We want to ensure that in future the importance of our nation once again corresponds to its natural worth rather than the pathetic representation of the past fifteen years.

The national socialist movement is not fighting a campaign on a short term basis. The path on which it has embarked may be a long one but victory will lie at the end... .

During the following three years, the party propaganda machine became increasingly sophisticated. The most modern techniques were used: highly coordinated press campaigns, whirlwind campaigns by air, film shows and so on. During election campaigns, a stream of directives specified precise details of what themes were to be emphasised and slogans to be used at different stages. Furthermore, a selection of standard leaflets and posters were produced which the *Gaue* were expected to order. The use of important speakers was centrally controlled and they were deployed where headquarters felt they would be most effective. The high degree of efficiency and attention to detail characteristic of the Nazi propaganda machine during these years is shown in the following excerpts from Reich Propaganda Department directives for the Presidential elections of March–April 1932 signed by Goebbels:

50

(a) Reich Propaganda Department to all *Gaue* and all *Gau* Propaganda Departments.
...A striking slogan:
Those who want everything to stay as it is vote for Hindenburg. Those who want everything changed vote for Hitler.
...
(b) Reich Propaganda Department to all *Gaue* and all *Gau* Propaganda Departments.
...Hitler Poster. The Hitler poster depicts a fascinating Hitler head on a completely black background. Subtitle: white on black—'Hitler'. In accordance with the Führer's wish this poster is to be put up only during the final days [of the campaign]. Since experience shows that during the final days there is a variety of coloured posters, this poster with its completely black background will contrast with all the others and wil produce a tremendous effect on the masses... .
(c) Reich Propaganda Department
Instructions for the National Socialist Press for the election of the Reich President
1. From Easter Tuesday 29 March until Sunday 10 April inclusive, all National Socialist papers, both daily and weekly, must appear in an enlarged edition with a tripled circulation. Two-thirds of this tripled circulation must be made available, without charge, to the *Gau* leadership responsible for its area of distribution for propaganda purposes... .
2. From Easter Tuesday 29 March until Sunday 3 April inclusive, a special topic must be dealt with every day on the first page of all our papers in a big spread. Tuesday 29 March: Hitler as a man. Wednesday 30 March: Hitler as a fighter

(gigantic achievements through his willpower, etc.). Friday 1 April: Hitler as a statesman—plenty of photos... .

3. On Sunday 3 April, at noon (end of an Easter truce), the great propaganda journey of the Führer through Germany will start, through which about a million people are to be reached directly through our Führer's speeches... . The press organisation is planned so that four press centres will be set up in Germany, which in turn will pass on immediately any telephone calls to the other papers of their area, whose names have been given them... .

The Party surpassed itself in the stage-management of mass rallies, particularly when Hitler himself was speaking. In the following account written at the time Frau Luise Solmitz, a Hamburg school teacher married to a former army officer, gives her impression of such a meeting in 1932:

51

...The April sun shone hot like in summer and turned everything into a picture of gay expectation. There was immaculate order and discipline, although the police left the whole square to the stewards and stood on the sidelines. Nobody spoke of 'Hitler', always just 'the Führer', 'the Führer says', 'the Führer wants', and what he said and wanted seemed right and good. The hours passed, the sun shone, expectations rose. In the background, at the edge of the track there were columns of carriers like ammunition carriers. What they carried were crates of beer. Aeroplanes above us. Testing of the loudspeakers, buzzing of the cine-cameras. It was nearly 3 p.m. 'The Führer is coming!' A ripple went through the crowds. Around the speaker's platform one could see hands raised in the Hitler salute. A speaker opened the meeting, abused the 'system', nobody listened to him. A second speaker welcomed Hitler and made way for the man who had drawn 120,000 people of all classes and ages. There stood Hitler in a simple black coat and looked over the crowd, waiting—a forest of swastika pennants swished up, the jubilation of this moment was given vent in a roaring salute. Main theme: Out of parties shall grow a nation, the German nation. He censured the 'system' ('I want to know what there is left to be ruined in this state!'). 'On the way here Socialists confronted me with a poster, "Turn back, Adolf Hitler". Thirteen years ago I was a simple unknown soldier. I went my way. I never turned back. Nor shall I turn back now.' Otherwise he made no personal attacks, nor any promises, vague or definite. His voice was hoarse after all his speaking during the previous days. When the speech was over, there was roaring enthusiasm and applause. Hitler saluted, gave his thanks, the Horst Wessel song sounded out across the course. Hitler was helped into his coat. Then he went.—How many look up to him with touching faith! as their helper, their saviour, their deliverer from unbearable distress—to him who rescues the Prussian prince, the scholar, the clergyman, the farmer, the worker, the unemployed, who rescues them from the parties back into the nation.

Although he spared no effort in his personal campaigning, particularly at the time of the Presidential elections in 1932, the main burden of propaganda lay on the *Gaue* and local Party organisations. Their energy and resourcefulness kept the Party firmly in the public eye. Numerous speakers from all classes, graded according to ability were deployed at local, regional or national level. Beside expenses they were paid a graded fee for their pains, and, since many were unemployed, they had an incentive to speak as often as possible.

An indication of the care devoted to local propaganda is provided by the instructions for the organisation of rural propaganda contained in the July 1931 issue of *Wille und Weg*, the monthly magazine of the Reich Propaganda Department:

52

The first meeting in a village must be prepared in such a way that it is well attended. A prerequisite is that the speaker should be fairly well informed about specifically rural questions. Then, it is most advisable to go to a neighbouring village some time after, but to advertise the meeting in the first village as well, then many people will certainly come over for it. After this, one holds a big German Evening in a central hall for a number of villages with the cooperation of the SA and the SA band... . The German Evening, provided it is skilfully and generously geared to producing a big public impact, has the primary task of making the audience enthusiastic for our cause; secondly, it is intended to raise the money necessary for the further build-up of propaganda. The preparation of the village meetings is best carried out in the following way: most effectively through written personal invitations to every farmer or inhabitant; in the bigger villages through a circular carried from farm to farm by Party comrades. For the meeting itself the question of finance has to be considered. Our movement is so poor that every penny counts. Collections must therefore be held during all discussion evenings and also in the big mass meetings if permitted by the police, either in the interval or at the end, even when an entrance fee has been taken at the beginning of the meeting. In this way, especially when plates and not caps are used, surprising amounts can sometimes be got out of a meeting.

One key to the Nazis' success in acquiring mass support was awareness of the extent to which German society had disintegrated into its sectional components, a process accelerated by postwar economic crises of inflation and then depression. By developing separate departments to organise the various economic interests and social groups, they successfully combined the pose of effectively representing individual interests and of a party of integration creating a unified national community of which they claimed the Party was already a microcosm. Thus, there were Party organisations for, among others, doctors, lawyers, teachers, war-disabled and war-pensioners, and civil servants. Perhaps the most successful were the

Agrarian Office and the *Mittelstand* Office (for artisans and retail traders), later known as the Combat League of Middle Class Tradespeople. Networks of specialists, often leading farmers or leading representatives of particular trades canvassed their colleagues and through the very fact of their own support for the movement provided invaluable propaganda.

The *Mittelstand* Office emphasised the Nazis' determination to preserve small businesses in face of the competition from the large department stores which had become intense during the depression. They were particularly astute at exploiting local issues:

53

Draft pamphlet [undated: c. *April 1932]*
Attention! Gravediggers at work!
Middle-class citizens! Retailers! Craftsmen! Tradesmen!
A new blow aimed at your ruin is being prepared and carried out in Hanover! The present system enables the gigantic concern
WOOLWORTH (America)
supported by finance capital, to build a new vampire business in the centre of the city in the Georgstrasse to expose you to complete ruin. This is the wish and aim of the black-red[19] system as expressed in the following remarks of Marxist leaders.

The Marxist Engels declared in May 1890: 'If capital destroys the small artisans and retailers it does a good thing... .'

That is the black-red system of today!

Put an end to this system and its abettors! Defend yourself, middle-class citizen! Join the mighty organisation that alone is in a position to conquer your arch-enemies. Fight with us in the Section for Craftsmen and Retail Traders within the great freedom movement of Adolf Hitler!

Put an end to the system!

Mittelstand, vote for List 8!

These departments also encouraged the infiltration of the main professional organisations and purged their leadership by pressure from below. The agrarian office very successfully took over the main professional organisation of agriculture, the *Landbund*. An example of the tactics used is provided by the Party's take-over of the North-West German Artisans' Association in 1932:

---

[19] Black for the Catholic Centre Party and red for the Social Democrats, who together formed the coalition government in the state of Prussia.

54

Urgent circular to the District Leaders and District Representatives of the Mittelstand *Office in* Gau *Hanover-South-Brunswick*

The Gauleiter   *Hanover, 11 January 1932*
CONFIDENTIAL!
A discussion between the Gauleiter and the executive committee of the North-West German Artisans' Association resulted in a decision to arrange the entry of NSDAP members into the executive committee and Association leadership. Since the general meeting of the representatives of the Association is to be held in three weeks' time, the following must be clarified immediately:
1. The political attitude and personal qualities of the chairman and secretary of your particular district Artisans' Association.
2. Which Party members, or, if there aren't any available, which artisans of the National Socialist persuasion are eligible for membership of the executive committee and Association leadership.
3. Which members of the NSDAP are organised in the North-West German Artisans' Association and therefore what influence can be thrown into the scales. The situation requires an immediate meeting of the district leaders and district experts with the *Gau* leadership on 14 January 1932 in Hanover.

Three weeks later Gauleiter Rust reported to Party headquarters in Munich that his attempt to penetrate the Artisans' Association from below had succeeded and that its leaders would be replaced by National Socialists or Nazi sympathisers:

55

Gau *Hanover–South-Brunswick*   *1 February 1932*

The Gauleiter

Dear Herr Wagener,[20]
    I take note with interest of your acceptance of the invitation to Brunswick. I hope to be able to introduce to you a mainly National Socialist executive committee of the North-West German Artisans' Association. For about ten weeks we have had a major fight to win control of the Association. On 8 amd 9 February an extraordinary meeting of delegates will take place in Hanover at which I have demanded the removal of the present president, Freidel of the Business Party, his replacement by a president who, though not a member of the NSDAP, is working completely along our lines, and two vice-presidential posts for members of the NSDAP. Meetings of

---

[20] Otto Wagener was head of the NSDAP's Economics Section in the Nazi Reich Headquarters.

artisans, usually overcrowded, have taken place in all the county towns [*Kreis-städte*] of the *Gau* which set things in motion. Furthermore, two meetings of all district experts of the *Mittelstand* Office have made this subject an issue in the *Gau*.

I take this opportunity of telling you that the executive committee of the Chamber of Industry and Commerce—a rare selection of first-rate economic reactionaries—have applied to me to arrange for the Führer to have a personal discussion with them. Here too the reason for this is pressure from below.

Heil!   BERNHARD RUST

The penetration and politicising of economic associations by the Nazi Party was a most effective way of winning new supporters and helped prepare the way for the 'coordination' of these groups after the Nazi takeover of power in Germany.

The Nazi appeal to youth proved particularly strong. Its dynamic and colourful style of politics, its proclaimed aim of breaking down class barriers, its leader-follower relationship, and its remarkably young membership and leadership offered young people the type of commitment in politics which they were seeking and which the other parties' traditional parliamentary methods did not offer. Only the Communists offered anything similar and they, because of their class commitment, remained largely confined to the working class, particularly the young unemployed. Young people, particularly from the middle class, saw the Nazi movement both as a means to destroy the hidebound conventions and social and occupational barriers associated with the older generation and as a national crusade to restore Germany to greatness. The basically emotional appeal to this group is shown by the following report from 1931 on the problems of containing the growth of Nazism in the Protestant youth movement:

56

The cause which at the moment is most closely associated with the name of National Socialism and with which, at a moderate estimate, certainly 70 per cent of our young people, often lacking knowledge of the facts, are in ardent sympathy, must be regarded, as far as our ranks are concerned, more as an ethical than a political matter. Our young people show little political interest. Fifth-formers are not really much concerned with the study of Hitler's thoughts; it is simply something irrational, something infectious that makes the blood pulse through one's veins and conveys an impression that something great is under way, the roaring of a stream which one does not wish to escape: 'If you can't feel it you will never grasp it... .'

To exploit this appeal to youth the Nazis developed the Hitler Youth movement for those under 18, a pupils league for boys in grammar schools, and a students' league. The activities of these organisations increasingly politicised schools and universities. In the state of Oldenburg, for example, there were complaints that the children of Republicans were being harassed by the fellow pupils:

57

To the Oldenburg Ministry for Churches and Schools:　　　21 November 1930

The Committee of the Oldenburg branch of the Reichsbanner Black-Red-Gold[21] submits the following matter to the State Ministry with a request for a prompt comment:

Leaflets have recently been distributed in the playgrounds of the schools of the city of Oldenburg and its vicinity, inviting people to join a National Socialist Pupils' Association. We enclose one of these leaflets.

A number of pupils have already followed the appeal to join this pupils' association. These consider themselves pledged, in the spirit of the leaflet, to bully those who disagree with them. In the playground these pupils join together and sing National Socialist combat songs. Children of Republicans are called names, their satchels are smeared with swastikas, and they are given leaflets with swastikas or 'Heil Hitler' or 'Germany awake' written on them. In the school in Metjendorf the son of a Republican was beaten up during the break by members of the pupils' association so badly that he had to stay at home for over a week. Grown-ups who are known to be members of a Republican party are called names by the pupils when they pass by the school. In one case this even happened out of the window of a classroom.

Since the children of Republicans are unfortunately in a minority in secondary schools they cannot defend themselves against these combined attacks. With an effort they preserve their self-control, but as soon as the child gets home, this too collapses. He then seeks refuge in tears and complaints. The parents find that lessons following breaks in which their child has been molested by his classmates are useless because he is too preoccupied with the events of the break. Sometimes teachers, not knowing the reason for the child's inattention, punish him as well. The same state of mind influences his homework, which therefore cannot be of a standard which a child in a good, cheerful mood would normally achieve. Again this has its effects at school.

It might be answered that parents and children have the right to make a complaint. This is true and yet at the same time not true. It must unfortunately be said that apart from a group of teachers who would treat such a complaint objectively, there are a number from whom this cannot be counted on and to whom one does not turn because they too are National Socialists or are active in other right-wing associations. The relationship of trust necessary between teachers and parents and their children has completely gone.

Since we have heard that some headmasters have already declared that they are

[21] The *Reichsbanner* Black-Red-Gold was a pro-Republican paramilitary organisation set up in 1924 by Social Democrats and Democrats to defend the Republic against the right-wing paramilitary organisations.

not in a position to deal with these incidents as required, since they have still received no instructions from the Ministry, we request that such instructions should be issued as soon as possible. We can presumably be sure that the State Ministry will adopt an attitude which does justice to all concerned and will decree that pupils' associations of political organisations are forbidden.

Yours faithfully,
The Committee of the Oldenburg Branch of the Reichsbanner Black-Red-Gold.

Although the Nazis concentrated much of their propaganda on specific groups, one of their main themes was a general appeal to nationalism and a claim that they, alone of all the parties, had succeeded in bridging the barriers between class and occupation. An example of such propaganda was the way they used the Kaiser's fourth son, Prince August-Wilhelm of Hohenzollern, as a speaker. He was always paired with an 'ordinary citizen', usually a farmer or a worker. At a meeting in Öttingen in central Bavaria in June 1931 such a meeting drew a crowd of between 900 and 1000 people, according to the police report:

58

The speakers were:
    Prince August-Wilhelm of Prussia
    Farmer Stegmann from Schillingsfürst
    Julius Streicher—NSDAP Gauleiter of Franconia

The speech of Prince August-Wilhelm, which was kept short and matter-of-fact, was followed by the national anthem which was sung standing up in the hall, whereas the Streicher speech had been followed by the Hitler song. The meeting did not have the character of a political but rather of a patriotic meeting or rally. The audience had arrived in large numbers from far and wide on motor cycles and by car.

The effect of such propaganda is clear from an entry in the diary of the upper middle class Hamburg lady already referred to:

59

I. vi. 32

...I myself also know that not only the desperate but also those who purposely contract debts in our neighbourhood are enthusiastic Hitler people—as are all those who hope for something from a swing to the Left or the Right or anywhere.

Nevertheless, every person who thinks and feels as a German, the bourgeois, the farmer, the aristocrat, the prince, and the intelligentsia, stands by Hitler. It is the nationalist movement.

(iii) Statistics on the Social and Geographical Bases of Nazism

Between 1928 and 1930 the Nazi Party had concentrated largely on trying to win over sections of the middle class, notably the peasantry, the artisans, and the small retailers. After 1930, while still continuing much of their propaganda for these groups, they revived their pre-1928 efforts to win over the workers. In January 1931, for example, they established a Factory Cell Organisation (NSBO) in an attempt to challenge the Left in their factory strongholds. This organisation, however, had little success. Apart from white collar workers, the majority of workers remained loyal to the Social Democrats and Communists and, if under the pressure of unemployment they became more extreme, they tended to move to the Communists rather than the Nazis. Those blue collar workers who did support the Nazis tended to fall into one or more of the following categories: young, unorganised, employed in small workshops, in small towns or semi-rural areas, or in municipal or state enterprises e.g. gas works, railways. The middle classes proved much more vulnerable. They felt their economic position and their social status threatened by the Left, and the Social Democrats often appeared a more immediate threat than the Communists.

The statistics on party membership also show workers much under-represented in relation to their proportion of the population as a whole, while the middle-class occupations were correspondingly over-represented, though more peasants seem to have voted Nazi than become members. Between 1930 and 1933, the workers increased their proportion of the Party, while that of most other groups correspondingly declined. But this shift was marginal and workers continued to be heavily under-represented—32.5 per cent of the Party compared with 46 per cent of the population, although of course in terms of sheer numbers the workers formed a sizeable group within the Party. The statistics on age show the predominance of youth within the Party membership.

Electoral statistics confirm that while the Party drew support from all classes the middle class was significantly over-represented. They also show the significance both of religion and of the rural/urban division. The main strength of Nazism lay in the Protestant and predominantly rural areas of the north German plain stretching from East Prussia to Schleswig-Holstein. Eight out of the ten districts with the largest Nazi vote in July 1932 are in this area; the exceptions are Liegnitz (Silesia) and Chemnitz-Zwickau. Nazism was weakest in the big cities (e.g. Berlin and Leipzig) and in industrial areas generally, particularly in predominantly Catholic ones (e.g. Düsseldorf East and West). In the cities it tended to draw most support from upper middle class districts. It was also weakest in overwhelmingly Catholic rural areas (e.g. Koblenz-Trier). The religious factor is most evident in Bavaria, where the north (Franconia) contained many Protestants who tended to vote Nazi, while in the overwhelmingly Catholic south (Upper and Lower Bavaria) the Nazi vote was among the lowest in Germany, although the Party had originated and was still based there.

Exceptions to this general pattern were the high Nazi vote in much of Silesia (Liegnitz and Breslau), a predominantly Catholic area with industry, and in the Palatinate, mainly Catholic and rural. The border issue may have played a part here. Silesia had been hotly contested with Poland and, after a plebiscite ordered under the Versailles treaty, much of Upper Silesia was awarded to Poland. The Nazis probably benefited from the intense nationalism generated by this conflict. In the Palatinate, France's attempt to establish a separatist regime in the early 1920s had also generated nationalist feelings which may help to account for the vote. In mixed Protestant and Catholic areas such as Franconia Nazism tended to unify the Protestants, long resentful of the dominance of the Catholic Centre/Bavarian People's Party but whose vote, split among several parties, had been less able to influence events.

Electoral Map for 31 July 1932

60

Percentage of votes cast in favour of the NDSAP

Reichstag elections:	4.v.24	7.xii.24	20.v.28	14.ix.30	31.vii.32	6.xi.32	5.iii.33
Number of seats:	32	14	12	107	230	196	288
National vote:	6.5	3.0	2.6	18.3	37.3	33.1	43.9

District							
1 East Prussia	8.6	6.2	0.8	22.5	47.1	39.7	56.5
2 Berlin	3.6	1.6	1.4	12.8	24.6	22.5	31.3
3 Potsdam II	6.5	2.9	1.8	16.7	33.0	29.1	38.2
4 Potsdam I	5.8	2.8	1.6	18.8	38.2	34.1	44.4
5 Frankfurt a.d. Oder	5.0	3.2	1.0	22.7	48.1	42.6	55.2
6 Pomerania	7.3	4.2	1.5	24.3	48.0	43.1	56.3
7 Breslau	4.0	1.4	1.0	24.2	43.5	40.4	50.2
8 Liegnitz	1.5	1.5	1.2	20.9	48.0	42.1	54.0
9 Oppeln	2.6	1.5	1.0	9.5	29.2	26.8	43.2
10 Magdeburg	4.9	3.0	1.7	19.5	43.8	39.0	47.3
11 Merseburg	8.7	4.3	2.7	20.5	42.6	34.5	46.4
12 Thuringia	9.9	5.4	3.7	19.3	43.4	37.1	47.2
13 Schleswig-Holstein	7.4	2.7	4.0	27.0	51.0	45.7	53.2
14 Weser-Ems	7.4	4.8	5.2	20.5	38.4	31.9	41.4
15 East Hanover	8.6	4.4	2.6	20.6	49.5	42.9	54.3
16 South-Hanover-Brunswick	7.6	3.4	4.4	24.3	46.1	40.6	48.7
17 Westphalia-North	3.5	1.3	1.0	12.2	25.7	22.3	34.9
18 Westphalia-South	1.5	1.1	1.6	13.9	27.2	24.8	33.8
19 Hesse-Nassau	5.6	2.5	3.6	20.8	43.6	41.2	49.4
20 Cologne-Aachen	1.5	0.6	1.1	14.5	20.2	17.4	30.1
21 Koblenz-Trier	1.3	—	2.1	14.9	28.8	26.1	38.4
22 Düsseldorf-East	3.9	1.6	1.8	17.0	31.6	27.0	37.4
23 Düsseldorf-West	2.6	0.9	1.2	16.8	27.0	24.2	35.2
24 Upper Bavaria-Swabia	17.0	4.8	6.2	16.3	27.1	24.6	40.9
25 Lower Bavaria	10.2	3.0	3.5	12.0	20.4	18.5	39.2
26 Franconia	20.7	7.5	8.1	20.5	39.9	36.4	45.7
27 Palatinate	5.7	1.9	5.6	22.8	43.7	42.6	46.5
28 Dresden-Bautzen	4.5	1.5	1.8	16.1	39.3	34.0	43.6
29 Leipzig	7.9	1.8	1.9	14.0	36.1	31.0	40.0
30 Chemnitz-Zwickau	7.7	4.2	4.3	23.8	47.0	43.4	50.0
31 Württemburg	4.1	2.1	1.9	9.4	30.3	26.2	42.0
32 Baden	4.8	1.9	2.9	19.2	36.9	34.1	45.4
33 Hesse-Darmstadt	2.9	1.3	1.9	18.5	43.1	40.2	47.4
34 Hamburg	6.0	2.3	2.6	19.2	33.7	27.2	38.9
35 Mecklenburg	20.8	11.9	2.0	20.1	44.8	37.0	48.0

61

Age of Nazi Party membership as of 1 January 1935, divided according to date of joining

		Date of Party membership										
		Before seizure of power						After seizure of power				
		Before 14.ix.30		From 14.ix.30 to 30.i.33		Total		After 30.i.33		Total		Percentage of total population
Date of birth	Age	Number	Per cent	Number	Per cent	Number	Per cent	Number	Per cent	Number	Per cent	
1916–1914	18–20	468	0.5 / 0.4	14,972	17.0 / 2.1	15,440	17.5 / 1.8	72,648	82.5 / 4.4	88.088	100.0 / 3.5	5.8
1913–1904	21–30	47,167	5.5 / 36.4	296,438	34.8 / 41.3	343,605	40.3 / 40.4	508,869	59.7 / 31.0	852,474	100.0 / 34.1	25.3

		No.	%	No.	%	No.	%	No.	%	No.	%	
1903–1894	31–40	40,700	5.9 / 31.4	193,937	28.0 / 26.9	234,637	33.9 / 27.8	459,780	66.1 / 27.9	694,417	100.0 / 27.9	22.0
1893–1884	41–50	22,835	4.7 / 17.6	122,884	25.2 / 17.1	145,719	29.9 / 20.8	342,338	70.1 / 19.6	488,057	100.0 / 17.1	
1883–1874	51–60	12,546	4.5 / 9.7	66,454	23.9 / 9.2	79,000	28.4 / 9.3	199,491	71.6 / 12.1	278,491	100.0 / 11.2	14.5
1873 and earlier	61 and over	5,847	6.3 / 4.5	24,761	26.8 / 3.4	30,608	33.1 / 3.6	61,755	66.9 / 3.8	92,363	100.0 / 3.7	15.3
Total		129,563	5.2 / 100.0	719,446	28.9 / 100.0	849,009	34.1 / 100.0	1,644,881	65.9 / 100.0	2,493,890	100.0 / 100.0	

NOTE. In the percentage columns, the upper of the two figures shows the percentage of Party membership on 1 January 1935; the lower figure shows the percentage of Party membership within the period of time covered by each pair of vertical columns.

62

Party members as of 1 January 1935, divided according to jobs and date of membership

Job	Date of Party membership										Society June 1933
	Before seizure of power						After seizure of power		Total		
	Before 14.ix.30		From 14.ix.30 until 30.i.33		Up to 30.i.33		After 30.i.33				
	No.	%	No.	%	No.	%	No.	%	No.	%	%
I Persons in employment	121,151	5.1	669,678	28.4	790,829	33.5	1,567,055	66.5	2,357,884	100.0	
		93.5		93.1		93.1		95.3		94.5	
I Workers	33,944	4.5	233,479	30.8	267,423	35.3	488,544	64.7	755,967	100.0	46.3
		26.3		32.5		31.5		29.7		30.3	
2 White-collar employees	31,067	6.4	147,855	30.6	178,922	37.0	305,132	63.0	484,054	100.0	12.4
		24.0		20.6		21.0		18.6		19.4	
3 Self-employed	24,563	5.2	124,579	26.2	149,142	31.4	326,081	68.6	475,223	100.0	9.6
		18.9		17.3		17.6		19.8		19.0	
Artisans	11,059	5.3	55,814	26.8	66,873	32.1	141,309	67.9	208,182	100.0	
		8.5		7.7		7.9		8.6		8.3	
Tradesmen	9,918	5.3	48,920	26.0	58,838	31.1	128,776	68.7	187,614	100.0	
		7.6		6.8		6.9		7.8		7.5	
Professions	3,586	4.5	19,845	25.0	23,431	29.5	55,996	70.5	79,427	100.0	
		2.8		2.8		2.8		1.4		3.2	

4 Civil servants	10,015	3.3	7.7	46,967	15.3	6.5	56,982	18.6	6.7	250,223	81.4	15.2	307,205	100.0	12.4	4.8
Civil servants	7,992	3.6	6.2	36,088	16.2	5.0	44,080	19.8	5.2	179,033	80.2	10.9	223,113	100.0	9.0	
Teachers	2,023	2.4	1.5	10,879	12.9	1.5	12,902	15.3	1.5	71,190	84.7	4.3	84,092	100.0	3.4	
5 Peasants	17,181	6.7	13.2	89,800	35.2	12.5	106,981	41.9	12.6	148,310	58.1	9.0	255,291	100.0	10.2	20.7
6 Others	4,381	5.5	3.4	26,998	33.7	3.7	31,379	39.2	3.7	48,765	60.8	3.0	80,144	100.0	3.2	6.2
II Persons not in employment 7 Pensioners	2,453	6.5	1.9	11,684	30.7	1.6	14,137	37.2	1.7	23,736	62.8	1.4	37,873	100.0	1.5	
III Family dependents without a full-time job	5,959	6.1	4.6	38,084	38.8	5.3	44,043	44.9	5.2	54,090	55.1	3.3	98,113	100.0	4.0	
8 Housewives	4,706	7.3	3.6	29,304	45.3	4.1	34,010	52.6	4.0	30,617	47.4	1.9	64,627	100.0	2.6	
9 Students and school children	1,253	3.7	1.0	8,780	26.2	1.2	10,033	2.9	1.2	23,473	70.1	1.4	33,506	100.0	1.4	
Total	129,563	5.2	100.0	719,446	28.8	100.0	849,009	34.0	100.0	1,644,881	66.0	100.0	2,493,890	100.0	100.0	

NOTE. In the percentage columns, the upper of the two figures shows the percentage of Party membership on 1 January 1935; the lower figure shows the percentage of Party membership within the period of time covered by each pair of vertical columns.

CHAPTER 4

The Struggle for Power, 1930–33

Electoral success, a prerequisite for the acquisition of power, by itself was not enough in view of the Party's failure to achieve an absolute majority. Now that parliamentary government had broken down and power lay with the President under Article 48 of the Weimar Constitution, it was just as important to win the approval of the conservative elites whose influence increased in proportion to the decline of that of Parliament. The Army, senior members of the bureaucracy, big landowners and particularly the Junkers of east Germany (among whom the President could now count himself after industry's gift to him of his old family estate), industry itself—all these groups, had retained their economic and social power. They now found a sympathetic hearing from the President and from the camarilla which surrounded him, notably his State Secretary, Otto Meissner, and his son, Oskar. These groups saw an opportunity to replace Weimar democracy with a more authoritarian regime, to undo the results of the revolution. On what form such a regime should take there were different views. Some toyed with the idea of restoring the monarchy; others wished to restore the political system of the Second Reich but with a president in place of the emperor. But common to most of these views was the determination to reduce Parliament to a subordinate role and thereby to exclude the Left from effective political influence. In these plans the Nazi movement came to have an important function.

Initially, it had been hoped to secure a majority for a presidential regime with the moderate Right and Centre—this was Brüning's plan. But as the regime based on Article 48 established itself more and more firmly, and as political opinion became increasingly polarised, it became clear that it would be impossible to achieve a majority on such a basis. Instead the Brüning Government was sustained in a negative fashion by the unwillingness of the Social Democrats and all groups to the left of the German Nationalists to bring down the Government for fear of the election that would follow. But to permit the Social Democrats to wield influence had now become anathema to the German Right. The presidential regime, run by the bureaucracy, open to the influence of conservative pressure groups and largely independent of Parliament, had become congenial. It fitted in with the German tradition of the State ruling above the parties, though of course in practice the State invariably represented the conservatives. They wanted to give it a permanent basis, no longer dependent on the toleration of the moderate Left.

Yet it was realised that an authoritarian government seeking to secure a permanent basis would need mass support. When it became clear that the Brüning experiment had failed, and that its policies were beginning to threaten conservative interests, as with a plan to break up bankrupt Junker estates and settle them with peasants, the Right began to base their hopes on the Nazi movement as the means of acquiring mass support. Brüning himself had tried to use the Nazis and tame them by securing their participation in government; now the Right decided that Brüning had become an obstacle to this policy. There were many aspects of the Nazi movement of which the Right disapproved. It was too radical, too violent, its economic policies smacked too much of Socialism, and the characters of some of its leaders were dubious, to say the least. It was, however, a nationalist movement and a movement hostile to the 'Marxist' Left. It offered the chance of 'conquering the streets' and wresting them from the Left. It contained many young people with the right ideas about the need to restore German greatness and who, apart from anything else, would provide excellent recruits for the Army. It was essential therefore to harness this movement for a new regime of the Right. If Hitler were brought into the Government in a subordinate capacity, he would be forced to become more 'responsible'. While power would continue to lie in the hands of the conservative establishment, Hitler would use his gifts as a propagandist to sell the policies of the Government to the masses. There was also another factor. If Hitler were not brought into the Government, there was a danger that the Nazis might attempt to come to power by force. This would lead to a civil war between Right and Left which would destroy the social order and ruin Germany's chances of regaining her military strength. The radical elements in the Nazi movement might get the upper hand and make common cause with the Communists against the conservative Right, and the Army might well find it impossible to deal with such a combined front. Such considerations lay behind attempts to persuade Hitler to join the Government or at least give it his support.

Hitler, on the other hand, was determined to avoid being harnessed in this way. He was not prepared to come into a Conservative Government in a subordinate capacity—if he was to bear the responsibility he wanted to have the power as well. Initially, he insisted on a government dominated by Nazis. By the end of 1932, however, the crisis in the Party caused largely by the failure to achieve office persuaded him to settle for less. Provided he had the Chancellorship and one or two key ministries, he was prepared for a government dominated by the Conservatives. Banking on their majority in the Cabinet, on their influence with the President, and on their greater political experience, the Conservatives assumed that they had managed to harness him to their cause. Hitler was content with the compromise, confident that it would not take him long to break out of the frame within which they had tried to fetter him.

(i) The Path of Legality and the Problem of the SA

Success in the 1930 election apparently justified the policy of 'legality' followed since 1925. Yet the Party's substantial representation in the Reichstag raised the question of its revolutionary aims and the reconciliation of its contempt for parliamentary democracy with participation in the parliamentary process.

In September 1930, three Army lieutenants accused of working for the Nazi Party were tried before the Supreme Court at Leipzig on a charge of subversion. Hitler, called as a witness, made the following statement in which he carefully distinguished between means and ends:

63

The National Socialist movement will try to achieve its aim with constitutional means in this state. The constitution prescribes only the methods, not the aim. In this constitutional way we shall try to gain decisive majorities in the legislative bodies so that the moment we succeed we can give the state the form that corresponds to our ideas.

The chairman of the court summed up the statement to the effect that the setting up of the Third Reich was being worked for in a constitutional way...

This important statement helped forestall a possible prohibition of the Party, enabled the State authorities and the Army to rationalise their unwillingness to take action against the movement, however wild its excesses, and convinced them that cooperation with the Party was possible.

There were, however, those in the Party, particularly in the SA, who resented the limitations imposed by the tactics of legality. Before 1930, most Party members were in the SA and the Party and SA had formed a fringe group of zealots whose isolation in a hostile environment welded them together in comradeship. They were crudely anti-capitalist in their hostility to big business and banks and suspicious of and hostile towards 'bosses' of all kinds. They despised conventional parliamentary politics and politicians seeing the Reichstag as a sink of corruption. It was an aggressively male world, formed through service in the military and the Free Corps, whose supreme values were physical courage, comradeship and loyalty to a leader who had won their respect. After September 1930, the SA was faced with the need to move within the world of conventional politics, where a new kind of party—no longer a collection of like-minded individuals but a huge organisation in which bureaucracy proliferated—would give them orders through Party officials whose sole claim to importance seemed to be ability at paper work. Many bitterly resented these changes. They resented doing all the dirty work, risking injury or even their lives fighting political opponents, spending long hours in arduous marches and parades while the political wing of the Party monopolised influence and even the 'perks' such as a majority of the Reichstag seats in the 1930 elections. For their contempt for Parliament did not stop them wanting seats in it and the salaries that went with them.

Hitler was obliged to move carefully between alienating the conservative pressure groups by appearing to conciliate the military and revolutionary ambitions of the SA and alienating the SA by appearing to renege upon the revolutionary goals of the movement through a compromise with the conservative establishment. The former danger had been dealt with temporarily by the Leipzig oath. This was given official recognition, in January 1931, when the Army removed the ban on the employment of Nazis in Army installations and on Nazi enlistment. But the other danger remained. Just before the elections in September 1930, the Berlin SA had mutinied and it had required all Hitler's powers of persuasion and a promise of a higher subsidy to pacify them. After the elections the danger recurred. On 20 February 1931, as an earnest of the sincerity of his policy of legality, Hitler forbade the SA to take part in street fighting. But, for many this was a typical instance of the way in which the ideals of the movement were being compromised. In April 1931, the leader of the SA in east Germany, Walter Stennes, who wished Hitler to return to the revolutionary path, was dismissed. Some SA units, however, remained loyal to him and tried to resist, including the one in Berlin which distributed the following pamphlet:

64

National Socialists of Berlin!
The Munich party leadership of the NSDAP yesterday ordered the dissolution of the Berlin SA and dismissed the supreme SA leader, Captain Stennes, whom Hitler

had repeatedly assured of his trust.

The news has provoked indignation, embitterment and a deep feeling of shock in the Berlin SA and beyond that in SA sections throughout the Reich.

What is at stake?

Is it only a conflict of personalities, a leadership struggle?

No, the cause of National Socialism is at stake!

In the person of Captain Stennes the whole SA is being attacked. Munich has forgotten that readiness for sacrifice and simplicity once created the Party and made it strong. Today they build the 'Brown House' in Munich at a cost of millions whereas the individual SA men have not a penny with which to repair their torn boots.

In the face of the emergency decree, in the face of daily sacrifices of blood by the SA, while the fight against the movement and the terror have reached their peak, a Munich clique brings fratricidal warfare into the ranks of the Party.

The SA has helped the Party in its struggle to gain thousands of seats in the Reich, states and communes

Now the SA have done their duty, they can go. They are now a cumbersome conscience, reminding people of the betrayed Party programme and demanding the fight for the old ideals of National Socialism, in contrast to the opportunistic policy of interests in Munich.

This is not illegal putschism, as the Jewish press wants to represent it, but only in order to prevent the Party's betrayal of the SA and of National Socialism.

The SA leadership has no intention of letting their SA comrades be misused for the financing of the Brown House and as a pawn in political bargains. With a sense of deep responsibility towards every single SA man and towards the whole German people, it acts according to the great fundamental law of National Socialism:

The common welfare comes before individual welfare and according to the deepest law of comradeship, loyalty for loyalty.

'With our flag held high and our ranks tightly closed'.

The SA marches.

Stennes takes over command.

Significantly in their appeal to the SA in Silesia the rebels insisted that 'our struggle is not directed against Adolf Hitler but against those round him whom he has not yet recognised for what they are'. Hitler moved quickly and made a strong personal appeal to the SA, demanding declarations of loyalty from each of its leaders. The affair brought a decisive victory for the political leadership and some important reforms in organisation, including tighter control over the membership and activities of local branches, the introduction of training schools for SA leaders, and the further centralising of administration in the SA, begun after Röhm's appointment as SA chief of staff at the beginning of 1931.

Conflict between the political organisation and the SA, however, remained endemic at all levels of the Party, and was most commonly expressed in rivalry over finance.

(ii) Relations between Nazis and Nationalists in 1931–32

During 1931 the Brüning Government appeared to be firmly established as a result of its toleration by the moderate Left and Right in the Reichstag. Hitler had the difficult task of maintaining some contact with the reactionary Nationalists and of cultivating powerful interest groups such as industry—all of whom had growing political influence in the vacuum left by the breakdown of the parliamentary system—without at the same time alienating his activist and radical followers and without allowing himself to be used as a pawn by reactionaries bent on counter-revolution.

In the summer of 1931 Hitler and Hugenberg, the leader of the Nationalists, made tentative moves towards reviving the cooperation begun with the Young Plan campaign of 1929. In July they announced their decision to work together to overthrow the existing 'system'. This led to a big demonstration of the extreme Right at Bad Harzburg on 11 October, dominated however by the reactionaries, with whom Hitler basically had little sympathy. He demonstrated the · Nazi Party's determination to preserve its independence by leaving the rostrum after the SA march past and before the nationalist ex-servicemen's association, the Stahlhelm, had arrived. Sir Horace Rumbold, the British ambassador in Berlin, commented on the Harzburg meeting in his report of 14 October:

65

The Harzburg meeting, which has been a theme of conversation in political circles for many weeks, was expected to mark a turning-point in the political history of Germany. For the first time all the parties of the Right were to join forces, and it was expected that the outcome would be a spectacular reconciliation between the Nazis and Nationalists, followed by the issue of a joint programme on which all the parties of the Right had agreed to unite. This was counted upon to win over the small wavering parties of Right tendency. So far, however, as one can gather from the reports of the meeting, little in the way of unity was achieved beyond the outward show, and it remains to be seen whether any real working agreement can be established between the two main Opposition parties. It is true that a joint resolution was passed to the effect that the parties of the Right were ready to take over the responsibility of governing the Reich and Prussia and the other federal states. Implacable opposition to the present Brüning Government constituted, so far as one can ascertain, the main plank of the political platform on which the groups and parties present agreed to unite. The National Socialist press publishes the speeches of the Nazi leaders as well as the text of the joint resolution in many columns, but devotes only half a column to Herr Hugenberg's speech, while the Stahlhelm are scarcely mentioned as participating. The Nationalist press returns the compliment, and is at pains to emphasise the leading part played by Hugenberg.

There is nothing in Herr Hitler's speech to suggest that he has sacrificed any part of the Socialist section of his programme in order to fall into line with Herr Hugenberg and the big industrialists.

There appears to have been no settled programme at Harzburg. Hitler issued the address summarised above to a gathering of his own followers before noon. It was prefaced by a cynical speech on the part of Herr Frick, who sought to allay 'the very comprehensible misgivings of his party friends' by assuring them that the Nazi leaders were merely using the Nationalists as a convenient ladder to office. Mussolini, he asserted, had done the same thing before assuming sole control of the Government of Italy.

Although Hitler insisted on retaining his Party's independence from the other sections of the Right, he was also anxious to win the sympathy of powerful interests, necessary to acquire finance for the elaborate Party organisation and propaganda. Hitler cultivated relations with industrialists and financiers in the Rhineland in an endeavour to remove the radical image of the Party. Most notable was the speech he made to the influential Industry Club in Düsseldorf in January 1932, on an invitation by Fritz Thyssen, a major Ruhr industrialist and keen Nazi supporter:

66

...People say to me so often: 'You are only the drummer of national Germany'. And supposing that I were only the dummer? It would today be a far more statesmanlike achievement to drum once more into this German people a new faith than gradually to squander the only faith they have... . The more you bring a people back into the sphere of faith, of ideals, the more will it cease to regard material distress as the one and only thing that counts. And the weightiest evidence for the truth of that statement is our own German people. We will never forget that the German people waged wars of religion for 150 years with prodigious devotion, that hundreds of thousands of men once left their plot of land, their property, and their belongings simply for an ideal, simply for a conviction. We will never forget that during those 150 years there was no trace of even an ounce of material interest. Then you will understand how mighty is the force of an idea, of an ideal. Only so can you comprehend how it is that in our movement today hundreds of thousands of young men are prepared to risk their lives to withstand our opponents. I know quite well, gentlemen, that when National Socialists march through the streets and suddenly in the evening there arises a tumult and a commotion, then the bourgeois draws back the window-curtain, looks out, and says: 'Once again my night's rest is disturbed: no more sleep for me. Why must these Nazis always be so provocative and run about the place at night?' Gentlemen, if everyone thought like that, then, true enough, no one's sleep at night would be disturbed, but then also the bourgeois today would not be able to venture into the street. If everyone thought in that way, if these young folk had no ideal to move them and drive them forward, then certainly they would gladly be rid of these nightly fights. But remember that it means sacrifice when today many hundreds of thousands of SA and SS men of the National Socialist movement have every day to mount on their lorries, protect meetings, undertake marches, sacrifice themselves night after night and then come back in the grey dawn to workshop and factory, or as unemployed to take the pittance of the dole: it means sacrifice when from the little they possess they have further to buy their uniforms, their shirts, their badges, yes and even pay their own fares. Believe me, there is already in all this the force of an ideal—a great ideal! And if the whole German nation today had the same faith in its vocation as these hundreds of thousands, if the whole nation possessed this idealism, Germany would stand in the eyes of the world otherwise than she stands now! (*loud applause*). For our situation in the world in its fatal effects is but the result of our own underestimate of German strength. (*'Very true!'*) Only when we have once more changed this fatal undervaluation of ourselves can Germany take advantage of the political possibilities which, if we look far enough into the future, can place German life once more upon a natural and secure basis—and that means either new living space [*Lebensraum*] and the development of a great internal market or protection of German economic life against the world without and utilisation of all the concentrated strength of Germany. The labour resources of our people, the capacities, we have them already: no one can deny that we are industrious. But we must first refashion the political preconditions: without that, industry and capacity, diligence and economy are in the last resort of no avail; an oppressed nation will not be able to spend on its own welfare even the fruits of its own economy but must sacrifice them on the altar of exactions and of tribute.

And so in contrast to our own official Government I see no hope for the resurrection of Germany if we regard the foreign politics of Germany as the primary factor: our primary need is the restoration of a sound national German body politic armed to strike. In order to realise this end I founded thirteen years ago the National Socialist movement: that movement I have led during the last twelve years and I hope that one day it will accomplish this task and that, as the fairest result of its struggle, it will leave behind it a German body politic completely renewed internally, intolerant of anyone who sins against the nation and its interests, intolerant of anyone who will not acknowledge its vital interests or who opposes them, intolerant of and pitiless towards anyone who shall attempt once more to destroy or undermine this body politic, and yet ready for friendship and peace with anyone who has a wish for peace and friendship (*long and tumultuous applause*).

In fact the response to Hitler's speech was disappointing. And, although the Party acquired some finance from big business, the sums were smaller than those provided for other bourgeois parties. Before 1933, only a minority of major industrialists actively supported them; more important were contributions from smaller businessmen at local level. The Party was, however, largely self-financing from membership dues, entry fees, etc.

The main task remained convincing the President. Hindenburg was persuaded to see Hitler in October 1931 but the interview was not a success. Earlier, in a meeting with the Nationalists' leader, Hugenberg, on 1 August 1931, Hindenburg had expressed his scepticism about the Nazis:

67

The Reich President referred to the cooperation of the German Nationalists with the National Socialists who, he feared, were more socialist than nationalist and whose behaviour in the country he could not approve. He, the Field-Marshal and liberator of East Prussia, had during his East Prussian journey, particularly on the drive across the battlefield of Tannenberg, been repeatedly insulted by scandalous demonstrations of National Socialists and had had to comment very unfavourably on these young people who had been misled. He did not regard them as a reliable national party.

To this Privy Councillor Dr Hugenberg replied that it was for this very reason—to bind the National Socialists to the nationalist side and prevent their slipping towards socialism or communism—that he had decided to work with the Nazis over the past one-and-a-half years and he took credit for this. He believed also that the National Socialists had been politically educated thereby. The demonstrations which the Reich President deplored had probably not been meant so badly. Meetings held by him, Hugenberg, were also often accompanied by National Socialist demonstrations and the shout of 'Germany, awake!' He could not stop these demonstrations either. To a suggestion by the Reich President that Hugenberg should use his press to oppose these demonstrations which were particularly embarrassing in view of the age and standing of the Reich President, he gave us no definite reply.

In the spring of 1932 Hindenburg's seven-year term as President came to an end. Brüning and the parties of the Centre and moderate Left wished to extend it for a year or two to keep Hitler from the presidency and provide more time to solve the crisis and thereby undermine the Nazi Party. Under the Constitution an extension required a two-thirds majority in the Reichstag and for this the agreement of the Nazis would be necessary. It was hoped to persuade Hitler by a hint that he could replace Brüning as Chancellor in a year or two and by the difficulty of defeating Hindenburg in an election. The Nazi leadership was divided on the issue. Röhm, and Goebbels wanted to reject the plan and try and defeat Hindenburg in the election, while Gregor Strasser, the head of the Party's organisation, argued that Hitler would not be able to defeat Hindenburg and that they should therefore accept the plan. Hitler hesitated and negotiated with General Groener who was both Minister of the Interior and Minister of Defence. But when Hugenberg rejected the idea in the name of the Nationalists, Hitler felt obliged to follow suit in order not to be outflanked. He counterattacked, however, by offering to support Hindenburg if he would replace Brüning with a right-wing government comprising Nazis and Nationalists and to hold new elections for the Reichstag and Prussian Landtag. When Hindenburg refused, Hitler had to decide whether or not to enter the election, knowing that he would almost certainly lose.

Although he hesitated for a month, in fact he had little choice. Refusal would have been widely interpreted as cowardice, something Hitler could afford even less than defeat.

In the Presidential elections of March–April 1932 Goebbels surpassed all previous Nazi propaganda campaigns, to no avail. In the first ballot on 13 March Hindenburg polled 18,661,736 votes (49.45 per cent) against Hitler's 11,338,571 votes (30.23 per cent). The remaining votes were divided between the Stahlhelm leader, Düsterberg, the candidate of the Nationalists (6.81 per cent), and Thälmann, the Communist leader (13.23 per cent). Since Hindenburg had just failed to win the absolute majority needed, a second ballot was held on 10 April in which Hindenburg gained 52.9 per cent and Hitler 36.6 per cent. Düsterberg did not run and his votes were divided between Hitler and Hindenburg, the majority of them going to Hitler. Thälmann too appears to have lost votes to Hitler, slipping back to 10.1 per cent.

(iii) From Brüning to Papen

With their direct assault on the citadel of power thwarted by Hindenburg's re-election, the Nazis concentrated on Brüning. Brüning and his supporters had reason to believe that for the time being their position was secure. Brüning's entire dependence on the President's support was, however, to prove fatal. For Hindenburg, though relieved at his re-election, had resented its being achieved by Social Democrats, Catholic Centre, and Democrats who had opposed his first election in 1925, while the Right, to which he had first owed his election and with whom he had far more in common, had opposed his re-election. Instead of being grateful to Brüning, he tended to blame him and increasingly lent his ear to conservative pressure groups urging the replacement of Brüning by an uncompromisingly right-wing government not reliant on the toleration of the Centre and moderate Left, but counting on the support of the Nazis.

The Government's decision to ban the SA opened the breach between Hindenburg and Brüning. Pressure from the state governments for action against the SA had been mounting. After the first ballot in the Reich presidential election, Prussian police, acting on instructions from Severing, the Social Democrat Prussian Minister of the Interior, had raided Nazi headquarters throughout the state and found evidence that the SA had planned to carry out a coup in the event of Hitler's securing a majority. The evidence was forwarded to the Supreme Court in Leipzig and as a result pressure on the Reich Government increased. The decision whether or not to impose such a ban lay with General Wilhelm Groener, Reich Minister of the Interior, with overall responsibility for internal security in the Reich. Groener, however, relied heavily upon the advice of his chief political adviser, General von Schleicher. Schleicher had played a significant part in the appointment of Brüning, but had become increasingly disillusioned with the Chancellor's dependence on the Left. He had already established contact with the Nazis and in particular with the SA, which he was anxious to harness by integrating it into a new state organisation for pre-military training. He also believed it possible to win the support of the Nazis for a more right-wing government which would then be able to dispense with the Left. Schleicher, therefore, was furious at Severing's move against the SA, which, as he told Groener on 23 March, he saw as an attempt to force the Reich Government to come out against the Right in the Prussian elections fixed for 24 April:

68

...Basically their aim is to win Your Excellency for the struggle against the Right in the Prussian elections so that you will be branded as a faithful ally of the Socialists. To achieve this end they regard any means as permissible, such as mysterious hints about the Border Guard to French correspondents [i.e. that Germany was evading the Versailles restrictions] and naked threats by the SPD party headquarters and by the Prussian Ministry of the Interior that they will not vote for Hindenburg on 10 April if your Excellency does not take up the struggle against the SA... After the events of the past few days, I am quite glad that a counterweight exists in the shape of the Nazis though they too are naughty boys and must be handled with extreme care. If they did not exist one would really have to invent them. The course which your Excellency is following—no one's friend and no one's enemy—is, I believe, in these circumstances the only correct one...

Groener however, feared if he did not act, the states would go ahead with their own separate bans. Moreover, he envisaged a ban on the SA as a means of taming the Nazi Party as he explained in a letter to a friend, Alarich von Gleich, on 2 April 1932:

69

On Monday or Tuesday, the Ministers of the Interior of the states are coming to a meeting about the SA. I have no doubt that we will master it—one way or the other. I think we have already drawn its poisonous fangs. One can made good tactical use of the endless declarations of legality made by the SA leaders, which they have handed to me in thick volumes. The SA is thereby undermining its credibility. But there are still difficult weeks of political manoeuvring until the various Landtag elections are over. Then, one will have to start working towards making the Nazis acceptable as participants in a government because the movement, which will certainly grow, can no longer be suppressed by force. Of course the Nazis must not be allowed to form a government of their own anywhere, let alone in the Reich. But in the states an attempt wil have to be made here and there to harness them in a coalition and to cure them of their utopias by constructive government work. I can see no better way, for the idea of trying to destroy the Party through an anti-Nazi law on the lines of the old anti-Socialist law I would regard as a very unfortunate undertaking. With the SA of course it is different. They must be eliminated in any event, and ideally the so-called Iron Front[22] as well... .

The conference with the Ministers of the states on 5 April finally persuaded Groener to go ahead with a ban. He now came up against opposition from Schleicher, however, anxious to avoid a confrontation with the Nazi Party. Schleicher suggested the idea of first sending an ultimatum to demand changes in the SA; only if these were rejected would it be necessary to go ahead with the ban. When Hindenburg rejected this idea and accepted an immediate ban, Schleicher intrigued to have the decision reversed. Groener noted down at the time what followed:

70

In the afternoon of the 10th, State Secretary Zweigert rang me up to inform me that State Secretary Meissner of the Reich President's Office had told him while at breakfast with Reich Minister of Transport Treviranus that the President had changed his mind under the influence of General von Schleicher brought to bear on him by his own son... .
12 April.... I met Col. von Hindenburg who was in a state of great agitation about the fact that once again his father was expected to sign a decree, although he had only just been appointed Reich President. His father would only have dirt thrown at him again by the Right. They might at least wait a little. He did not bring up any objective reasons, in fact he emphasised that he was not interested in the SA. In view of his excitement, it was impossible to have an objective discussion with him. But I was in no doubt about the fact that his opinion was based purely on naïve and sentimental feelings... .
At five o'clock in the afternoon, the Reich Chancellor and I went to see the Reich President. State Secretary Meissner was present at the interview. The Chancellor gave a lengthy explanation of why the ban was necessary. I supplemented it by slowly reading out the official explanation which was later released. The Reich President made no substantial objections; in fact his attitude was in no way one of fundamental opposition... . At the end, the Reich President stated that it should not be held against his son if he tried to protect his father. He was prepared to sign the decree if the Chancellor and the Reich Minister of the Interior considered it necessary.

---

[22] The Iron Front was a propaganda organisation formed by the Social Democrats and the Reichsbanner at the end of 1931.

The decree banning the SA and the SS was issued on 13 April. The intrigue, however, continued; as Groener later reflected:

71

My hands were tied as regards these manoeuvres because any attempt to get the Reich President to take action against these officers would have met with such resistance that there would have been nothing left but immediate resignation. But this would have also brought about the fall of the Brüning Government even before the Prussian elections, before the Reichstag had convened, and in the middle of the Geneva negotiations on disarmament.... I knew very well that the intention was to bring down the Chancellor. In the course of the winter, the Reich President had twice mentioned to me that Dr Brüning did not quite represent his ideal as Reich Chancellor. He did not accept my comment that at the moment he would not find a better one. General von Schleicher had also made no bones about the fact that he was thinking in terms of a change of Chancellor. In view of his connexions with the Reich President's entourage, it can be assumed that he took part in the removal of Dr Brüning as Chancellor. During the absence of the Reich President in Neudeck, his country estate, where Brüning's fall was decided upon, General von Schleicher was in continual contact by telephone with Hindenburg's son.

Schleicher succeeded in bringing about Groener's fall on 13 May. It was only a preliminary move towards the main objective, the dismissal of Brüning, particularly vulnerable because of his total dependence on the President. He had failed to win popular support because he had consistently subordinated domestic politics to foreign affairs. Although initially under pressure to fulfil reparations obligations, Brüning's position was relieved by the moratorium declared on 20 June 1931 by President Hoover. Nevertheless, Brüning continued his rigid deflationary policies because of his determination to secure the complete ending of reparations by demonstrating Germany's inability to pay. This would then free Germany's hands for a more aggressive foreign policy, in particular challenging French and British influence in South East Europe. He assumed such diplomatic gains would secure his position with public opinion at home and, in particular, against his right-wing critics. In fact, however, his deflationary economic policies only resulted in the growing alienation of many not only from his own government but from the political system itself, while the fruits of his foreign policy were to be garnered by his successors. In addition, after his failure in 1930 to secure a new right-wing majority he had neglected the Reichstag. The increasingly presidential regime associated with rule by decree accorded with his own sympathy for the pre-war system of a government ruling 'above the parties' under the direction of the emperor.

By the spring of 1932, however, he had lost the support of the President.

In addition to the elements of intrigue a final factor emerged. Junker landowners were bitterly hostile to the Government's plans to take over bankrupt Junker estates and divide them up among landless peasants. The Junkers could now claim Hindenburg's particular sympathy because they had recently presented him with his old family estate, bought with funds subscribed by industrialists. But before Hindenburg could be persuaded to dismiss Brüning an acceptable alternative had to be provided. Schleicher proposed Franz von Papen, a Catholic aristocrat from Westphalia who had been a member of the same regiment as Hindenburg's son. Although a member of the Centre Party on account of his Catholicism, his political views had far more in common with those of the Nationalists than with even the right wing of his own party. Papen's aristocratic manner appealed to Hindenburg, while Schleicher assumed he would be pliable.

Before engineering the replacement of Brüning by Papen, Schleicher had conducted extensive negotiations with the Nazis in an attempt to secure their toleration of the new government. In return he had promised Papen would lift the ban on the SA and call an election. Without committing himself on paper, Hitler succeeded in conveying the impression he would be sympathetic to such a bargain. Goebbels's diary provides an insight into the atmosphere of intrigue which preceded Brüning's fall:

72

8 May 1932. On Saturday the delegates come and give us some information. The Führer has an important interview with Schleicher in the presence of a few gentlemen of the President's immediate circle.

All goes well. The Führer has spoken decisively. Brüning's fall is expected shortly. The President of the Reich will withdraw his confidence from him.

The plan is to constitute a Presidential Cabinet. The Reichstag will be dissolved. Repressive enactments are to be cancelled. We shall be free to go ahead as we like, and mean to outdo ourselves in propaganda.

11 May 1932. The Reichstag drags on. Groener's position is shaken; the Army no longer supports him. Even those with most to do with him urge his downfall.

This is the beginning; once one of these men falls, the whole Cabinet, and with it the system, will crash. Brüning is trying to salvage what he can. He speaks in the Reichstag, and cleverly beats a retreat on foreign politics. There he becomes aggressive. He believes himself within sight of the goal. He does not mention Groener at all. So he too has given him up!

The whole debate turns on the lifting of the ban on the SA. Groener strongly objects to this. It will be his undoing. I proceed as if the Reichstag were already dissolved. Our preparations are being made on quite a large scale... .

The ban on the SA has suddenly become the pivot upon which home affairs would seem to turn... .

24 May 1932. The Prussian Diet is convened. Through our confidential agents we are assured that we stand a good chance. Saturday will see the end of Brüning.

Secretary of State Meissner leaves for Neudeck. Now we must hope for the best. The list of Ministers is more or less settled: von Papen, Chancellor; von Neurath, Minister of Foreign Affairs, and then a list of unfamiliar names. The main point as far as we are concerned is to ensure that the Reichstag is dissolved. Everything else can be arranged. The Prussian question can only be solved in this way... .

30 May 1932. The bomb has exploded. Brüning has presented the resignation of the entire Cabinet to the President, at noon. The system has begun to crumble. The President has accepted the resignation. I at once ring up the Führer. Now he must return to Berlin at once... .

Meet the Führer at Nauen. The President wishes to see him in the course of the afternoon. I get into his car and give him a good all-round summary. We are tremendously delighted... . Pay our SA at Wilmersdorf a short visit. The Führer is already waiting for me at home. The conference with the President went off well. The SA prohibition is going to be cancelled. Uniforms are to be allowed again. The Reichstag is going to be dissolved. That is of the first importance.

Von Papen is likely to be appointed Chancellor, but that is neither here nor there. The Poll! the Poll! It's the people we want. We are all entirely satisfied.

2 June 1932. All through the morning and afternoon we wait for news from Berlin. It arrives at four. The Opposition demands a written undertaking from the Führer that he will work smoothly with von Papen even after the election. Such a statement cannot be made... .

After the meetings we have long consultations with the Führer. He has no intention of writing either letter or memorandum. The main things is dissolution and re-election.

If the election is not to miscarry, we must contest it unhampered by any such pledges.

On the opposite side also there are men who need to be tackled with circumspection. Intrigues are everywhere afoot. We are playing a risky game. So much the more must the dissolution of the Reichstag be a *sine qua non.*

The Führer estimates his opponents very exactly. He is very logical and an amazingly quick worker.

4 June 1932. Friday. The Führer has nevertheless dictated a memorandum on the question of dissolution of the Reichstag. Résumé: it must come off, otherwise further development is impossible. The Führer meets Schleicher on a neighbouring estate. He wants me to go through the note again. It is then sent after him by express. The motor-cyclist gets there too late. The conference is already over, so that it is impossible to deliver it.

When the Führer gets back, he is beaming with contentment. Everything went off well. The Reichstag is going to be dissolved and the SA prohibition cancelled. (But not until 16th.)

New Reichstag elections were called for 31 July and Hitler's confidence in success was confirmed by results in the June state elections. For Goebbels, the new Papen Cabinet, with its strong aristocratic image, presented a new quandary—how to campaign as a party of opposition without losing support from conservative bourgeois circles and alienating the President and his entourage. His answer was to ignore the new Government and concentrate on attacking the political system in general:

73

Reich Propaganda Department   4 June 1932
To all Party Offices for their confidential information

During this Reichstag election no judgement is to be passed on the actions of the von Papen Cabinet but instead on the acts of those governments and parties responsible for the crime of November 1918 [i.e. the revolution] and who from then until now have as a system to bear the responsibility for the greatest historical collapse of recent centuries. This election will be the moment for dealing with the people responsible for the thirteen years behind us, but not, as the propaganda of our opponents wants to pretend, for the few bridging weeks of the von Papen Cabinet. All our party offices must refrain from any discussion of the von Papen Cabinet during this campaign and any attempt by our opponents to discuss it must be rejected right from the start.

Papen was bent on replacing the democratic system of Weimar with an authoritarian dictatorship as soon as possible. On 20 July 1932, he took the first major step by using the President's emergency powers to depose the Prussian Government, a coalition of Social Democrats and Catholic Centre and long a target of right-wing hostility. He appointed himself as Reich Commissioner for Prussia, and Bracht, the Mayor of Essen and a Nationalist, as his deputy and Prussian Minister of the Interior. A purge of the Prussian administration replaced civil servants who were loyal to the Republic with Nationalists. Since Prussia formed three-fifths of the Reich, this devastating blow to the Republic helped to prepare the way for the Nazi take-over of power in 1933.

Its extremely narrow basis of support made Papen's Government vulnerable. The Cabinet contained so many aristocrats that it was dubbed by its opponents 'the Cabinet of the Barons'. Papen hoped, as did his mentor Schleicher, the Nazis would provide a basis of mass support for the regime. They were to be disappointed. Initially the Nazis did exercise some restraint towards the Government. But after the SA ban had been lifted and the election held on 31 July, the Party refused to become lobby fodder for Papen. The election brought a big advance. The Nazis won 37 per cent of the vote as against 18 per cent in September 1930. With 230 seats as against 107 they were now by far the largest party in the Reichstag, but still did not possess an overall majority. Could this increased vote be turned into concrete political power? Hitler felt in a strong position, particularly as the parties supporting the Government—the Nationalists and some of the People's Party—had lost heavily to the Nazis and now held only 44 seats beteen them out of 608. At a meeting with Schleicher on 5 August he demanded the Chancellorship for himself and other key posts for Nazis. Papen, however, failed to react. Once again because Hitler could not form a government with a majority in the Reichstag power still lay with the

President who had the use of Article 48 and the right to appoint the Chancellor. At an interview in the morning of 13 August, Papen rejected Hitler's demands and Hindenburg confirmed this in the afternoon. Unlike Brüning in the last months of his Chancellorship, Papen still had the full confidence of the President. On 13 August, Hindenburg listened calmly to Hitler's case for forming a government but refused to be swayed. Hitler's hope that his large popular following would convince the President proved incorrect. The meeting was a personal disaster for Hitler and ended with his threatening more uncompromising opposition to the Papen Government. Otto Meissner, head of the Presidential Chancellery, took minutes of the second meeting between Hitler and Hindenburg:

74

The President of the Reich opened the discussion by declaring to Hitler that he was ready to let the National Socialist Party and their leader Hitler participate in the Reich Government and would welcome their cooperation. He then put the question to Hitler whether he was prepared to participate in the present government of von Papen. Herr Hitler declared that, for reasons which he had explained in detail to the Reich President that morning, his taking any part in cooperation with the existing government was out of the question. Considering the importance of the National Socialist movement he must demand the full and complete leadership of government and state for himself and his party.

The Reich President in reply said firmly that he must answer this demand with a clear, unyielding No. He could not justify before God, before his conscience or before the fatherland the transfer of the whole authority of government to a single party, especially to a party that was biased against people who had different views from their own. There were a number of other reasons against it upon which he did not wish to enlarge in detail, such as fear of increased unrest, the effect on foreign countries, etc.

Herr Hitler repeated that any other solution was unacceptable to him.

To this the Reich President replied: 'So you will go into opposition?'

Hitler: ' I have now no alternative.'

The Reich President: 'In that case the only advice I can give you is to engage in this opposition in a chivalrous way and to remain conscious of your responsibility and duty towards the fatherland. I have had no doubts about your love for the fatherland. I shall intervene sharply against any acts of terrorism or violence such as have been committed by members of the SA sections. We are both old comrades and we want to remain so, since the course of events may bring us together again later on. Therefore, I shall shake hands with you now in a comradely way.'

This discussion was followed by a short conversation in the corridor between the Reich Chancellor and me, and Herr Hitler and his companions, in which Herr Hitler expressed the view that future developments would lead to the solution suggested by him and to the overthrow of the Reich President. The Government

would get into a difficult position; the opposition would become very sharp and he could assume no responsibility for the consequences.
The conversation lasted for about twenty minutes.

Goebbels commented in his diary:

75

...The Führer is back in under half an hour. So it has ended in failure. He has gained nothing. Papen is to remain Chancellor and the Führer has to content himself with the position of Vice-Chancellor!
A solution leading to no result! It is out of the question to accept such a proposal. There is no alternative but to refuse. The Führer did so immediately. Like the rest of us, he is fully aware of the consequences. It will mean a hard struggle, but we shall triumph in the end... .
In the back room the SA leaders assemble at the command of the Chief of Staff. The Führer and he give them a fairly full outline of events. Their task is the most difficult of all. Who knows if their units will be able to hold together? Nothing is harder than to tell a troop with victory already in their grasp that their assignment has come to nothing!
A grim task, but we have to go through with it. There is no other way. The idea of the Führer as Vice-Chancellor of a bourgeois Cabinet is too ludicrous to be treated seriously. Rather go on struggling for another ten years than accept that offer.
The Führer maintains an admirable calm. He stands above all vacillations, hopes, vague ideas, and conjectures; a point of rest in a world of unrest.
The first game is lost.
Well, the fight goes on! In the end the Wilhelmstrasse will give in. There is no Cromwell in the Cabinet, and in the long run, despite everything, strength and tenacity will win the day... .

(iv) The crisis months, August–December 1932

Hindenburg's refusal to appoint Hitler Chancellor was, as Goebbels recognised, a serious blow to the Party. After waging an incessant and exhausting propaganda campaign for nearly three years, the whole movement had assumed they had at last reached their goal. The shock of disappointment had very damaging effects on Party morale and particularly on its most active members in the SA. It appeared the policy of legality, pursued since 1925 had led to a cul-de-sac. Gregor Strasser advocated a coalition with the Catholic Centre Party, some of whose members believed that the Nazi Party should be brought into the government either to make it 'responsible' or to discredit it with the masses. Hitler agreed to negotiations but primarily to put pressure on Papen. These contacts bore fruit in the election of Göring to the Reichstag presidency with Centre support. Meanwhile, Papen, aware of the decline in Nazi morale, decided to apply pressure by calling another election. He hoped they would lose votes and would then be in a mood for cooperation. On 12 September, therefore, he dissolved Parliament. The Nazis could only retaliate rather futilely by holding up the dissolution until a motion of 'no confidence' proposed by the Communists had been passed by 513 votes to 32.

Since Papen had captured the conservative ground, Goebbels decided to launch a radical campaign against the reactionary nature of the Papen regime, a line to which he himself was most sympathetic. On the day of the dissolution, therefore, he issued the following instructions:

76

Reich Propaganda Department   *12 September 1932*
To all Gauleiters and Gau Propaganda Directors:

As we have already stated in our express circular, dated 3 September, the struggle against the Papen Cabinet and the reactionary circles behind it must now begin all along the line... . We have no reason to defend ourselves against Herr von Papen and his policy. On the contrary, in accordance with old National Socialist tactics we are now going over to the attack... , The aim is to isolate the Papen regime from the people and prove to the world that it is only a small feudal clique with no other aim than to isolate the National Socialist movement and thereby make its impact ineffectual. The struggle which is now beginning must be carried out ruthlessly and is restricted only by the existing laws and not by any tactical considerations. The NSDAP has no reason whatsoever to spare the Papen regime in any way... .

There were dangers that this would alienate the middle class, hitherto the Party's main support, without capturing the working class. It might also alienate the influential elites who held part of the key to the appointment of Hitler as Chancellor. Hess, possibly acting for Hitler, pointed out some of these dangers in a memorandum:

77

*It is inexpedient to gear the campaign to the slogan: 'Against the rule of the barons',
as has already happened in some cases in the Party's propaganda and press.* This slogan is welcome ammunition to the Government, the German Nationalists, and other opponents who can, with some appearance of justification, maintain that the NSDAP, having already 'given up the fight against the Centre', having 'stood by

parliamentary methods',[23] is now 'showing class war tendencies'... .
The electoral damage produced by this would be greater than any advantage
gained. A large number of voters on the Right will undoubtedly be impressed by
the partly justified claim that the NSDAP is going over to class-war slogans. We
cannot expect to make up for this by extra votes from the Left. For the majority of
those who are impressed by this slogan will gravitate towards or stay with the party
which expresses it in the most radical way. And that means now, as before, the
Marxist parties, for class war is one of the basic points in their programme... .
The [Nazi] movement has now won over just about all the voters it can by the
methods of propaganda pursued hitherto, that is to say, by means of its general
ideological line and propaganda based on general aims. In addition, in this election
campaign we are confronted by a government that has succeeded in creating the
impression among part of the electorate, and no doubt among some of our former
supporters, that it is they who are now putting into practice, or in some cases have
already carried out, the things which the National Socialists aimed for but were not
themselves in a position to carry out. They claim that the National Socialists have
no clear and practical goals and that in so far as their aims are known, they
represent dangerous experiments; the Nazis can certainly damn the measures taken
by the Government but they do not explain how they propose to do better... .
Criticism of the Government, therefore, must above all not be phrased in too
general terms such as 'Government of the Barons', 'reactionary legacy hunters',
but must always be supported with concrete examples... .

Whether or not as a result of this memorandum, Goebbels was obliged
to tone down the radical campaign slightly:

78

Reich Propaganda Department

Strictly Confidential Information No. 8, valid 12–14 October

IMPORTANT!

Through the attempt of the Papen Government to exclude Adolf Hitler from
power, we have come into sharp conflict with a certain kind of anti-social and
therefore capitalistic concept of economics. This opposition is justified and must be
carried out with all our strength.

But it must not lead to a complete condemnation of all employers as such and
thereby get into the deep waters of Marxist class war. For instance, it is wrong to
equate, as Marxism does, employers with exploiters, just as it is wrong to spread
details of the unjustifiable salaries of leading industrial figures... .

It is also wrong to make industry as a whole responsible for the deficiency of the
Papen agrarian programme, as has happened now and then... .

In every political situation we must adhere to the old, tried guidelines of National

---

[23] This refers to the Nazis' cooperation with the Centre Party in the Reichstag against the
Papen Government.

Socialism; not treating all business alike in the Marxist way, but distinguishing strictly between healthy business leadership, which is indispensable to the economy, and exploiters. To talk of the expropriation of all industrial concerns is, of course, a direct contravention of National Socialist principles.

Moreover, the fight against the Papen Cabinet must not develop into a fight against the aristocracy as such. We must always be aware of the fact that the best part of the German aristocracy fights in our own ranks and therefore does not deserve to be demoted from the German front just because of a few black sheep.

Nevertheless, during the last few weeks of the campaign, the radical line culminated in cooperation with the Communists in support of the Berlin transport workers' strike, which had broken out in protest against the wages policy of the Government.

The extent to which the radical campaign against Papen had alienated the upper and lower middle classes, who had hitherto supported or at least been sympathetic to the Nazis, is apparent in the following document. In her diary Frau Luise Solmitz gives an insight into the attitude of many of the upper middle class during the autumn of 1932:

79

13.viii.32.....Goebbels in the National Socialist *Angriff!*[24] We know this language only too well from Socialist and Communist papers; we don't want to hear it from Goebbels! This is just what deters many; these are the objections which bourgeois-orientated Hitler supporters have to fight again and again. Perhaps this language is necessary to bring in the masses who tend to the Left, but it alienates the valuable bourgeois element; to embrace them all becomes impossible. Hitler, remain master in your own house!

29.ix.32. The trade unions are no longer Marxist enough for the Nazis; they demand that the trade unions should call a strike against the underbidding of wage agreements—and thus against the re-employment of the unemployed. And they want to expel every employer from their ranks who lowers wages in order to enlarge the number of employees. Can an employer remain a Nazi at all?!....

3.xi.32. E.M. said, shaking his head, 'One can't possibly vote for Hitler.' He met a Herr von S., whom he knows from the war: 'I voted for Hitler twice; it's no longer the thing to do.' Our old carrier: 'Hitler? He is far to the Left! I have always voted for Hugenberg.' Old Professor H. persists in voting for his stale old *Volkspartei*,[25] his daughter is fanatically pro-Hitler....

If only one could summon up some enthusiasm for the German Nationalist Party and Hugenberg! With the National Socialist Party we had a love match. The German Nationalist marriage which we are about to enter is a marriage of convenience and without passion [*Schwung*].

---

[24] *Der Angriff*, the daily paper of Goebbels's *Gau*, Berlin.

[25] The *Deutsche Volkspartei* (German People's Party), the right-wing liberal party.

31.xii.32. This year has robbed us of a great hope—this *year*, not death. Adolf Hitler. Our reviver and great leader towards national unity...and the man who in the end turns out to be the leader of a party sliding more and more into a dubious future. I still cannot come to terms with this bitter disappointment... .

Hampered by the decline in morale and by shortage of money now that the Party had alienated the upper classes with its radical line, the Party's propaganda machine found the going hard. In October, Goebbels noted in his diary that 'the organisation has naturally become a bit on edge through these everlasting elections. It is as jaded as a battalion which has been too long in the front trenches, and just as nervy'. The election held on 6 November was indeed a setback for the Nazis. Their vote fell from 37 per cent to 33 per cent and their seats from 230 to 196. Even more important than the number of votes lost was that for the first time they had actually lost votes. The myth of invincibility, projected so successfully hitherto, which had played a substantial part in their appeal had been broken. Nothing could disguise the fact that they were in trouble.

Yet although his gamble had paid off, Papen had not really solved his problems. While the Nationalists had gained slightly, the Government still rested on an extremely narrow basis. Moreover, contrary to Papen's hopes, Hitler was still not prepared to join the Government in a subordinate capacity nor was he prepared to become Chancellor except with a Cabinet dominated by his party and with full freedom to use the powers contained in Article 48. This, however, was unacceptable to President Hindenburg.

Frustrated in his attempt to acquire a mass base, Papen contemplated a coup, replacing the Weimar Constitution by an authoritarian presidential dictatorship. This plan, however, would require the elimination of both the Nazis and the Communists, both bound to resist this development by force. President Hindenburg, wishing to retain Papen for whom he had developed considerable affection, was prepared to acquiesce. General von Schleicher, however, now Minister of Defence, did not believe the Army capable of dealing with the SA and the Communists simultaneously, particularly as the junior officer corps was permeated with Nazi ideas. Furthermore, he was not a simple reactionary like Papen. He was aware that in an advanced industrial society it is impossible to rule without some degree of mass support, however acquired. This was essential if Germany's armed strength was to be fully restored. Schleicher was influenced by a group of young right-wing intellectuals associated with the journal, *Die Tat*, who attacked both liberal capitalism and Marxist socialism. They advocated an organic authoritarian state based on *Stände* (estates) which, by combining social and nationalist principles, would offer Germany a 'third way' between the capitalist West and the Communist East. Schleicher believed mass support could be won for a rightist regime sympathetic to rearmament if such a regime pursued social and economic policies more attractive to the masses than those of the reactionary Papen Government, such as a more vigorous attempt to solve the unemployment problem, if necessary by public expenditure. He also believed he could acquire support by splitting the mass movement of the Right, winning over elements within the Nazi Party, most notably Gregor Strasser, primarily interested in a practical contribution to solving the economic and political crises, especially unemployment. They feared the opportunity to make it might be jeopardised by Hitler's stubborn insistence on all or nothing. He also thought he could split the Left, winning over the Trade Unions and the Reichsbanner for whom the solution of the unemployment problem would be more important than doctrinaire principles. That his government would be more socially concerned than that of either Papen or Hitler and would avoid the danger of either Papen or Hitler establishing a dictatorship would be sufficient to commend it to these groups.

Of the alternatives offered by Papen and Schleicher, Hindenburg preferred the former and, after Papen had formally resigned following the election, the President asked him to form another government. Schleicher now intervened and declared the Army could not support the *coup* envisaged by Papen. Regretfully, the President was forced to accept Papen's resignation and to appoint Schleicher to see if his solution would work. Schleicher at once tried to put his plan into operation. In a broadcast on 15 December he announced that his government's programme would concentrate above all on 'creating work' and he appointed a special Reich Commissioner for Employment to carry it out. He also announced that he was not a dogmatic supporter of either capitalism or Socialism. He then repealed the deflationary measures such as wage and benefit cuts introduced by Papen on 4 September.

Schleicher's attempts to win support from a section of the Left and to split the Nazis were, however, both abortive. The trade unions were forced to end the negotiations under pressure from Social Democrats suspicious of Schleicher. His previous role as an intriguer made this understandable, but nonetheless short-sighted. On 3 December, Schleicher offered Strasser the Vice-Chancellorship which he was anxious to accept, enjoying the sympathy of some of the Nazi deputies including their leader Frick. Göring and Goebbels, however, were strongly opposed and Hitler, though agreeing to continue negotiations with Schleicher, took them out of Strasser's hands. After a stormy interview on 7 December, Strasser wrote Hitler a letter of resignation and, on the morning of the 8th, called a meeting of the Party's regional inspectors—the senior Gauleiters—in the Reichstag building. To this group Strasser announced his resignation and, according to a post-war account by Hinrich Lohse, Gauleiter of Schleswig-Holstein, gave the following explanation of his action:

80

For some time I have been aware of a development which affects not so much the programme or the final goal but rather the way of achieving this goal, and which I can no longer go along with. At least since August, since the time of his first meeting with Papen, Schleicher and Hindenburg, the Führer has not been following a clear line of policy in his endeavour to achieve power. He is only clear about one thing—he wishes to become Reich Chancellor. He should, however, have become aware of the fact that he is being consistently refused this post by everybody and that in the foreseeable future there is no prospect of his attaining this goal. As a result of this situation, the movement is being put under considerable stress which is undermining its unity and may expose it to splits and disintegration. In view of the appalling distress of our supporters, we cannot let our SA men and our ordinary Party comrades wait for ever or they will become impatient and in the end leave the movement in a mood of disappointment. There is no doubt that our enemies have been waiting for this moment, not just recently but for a long time. The Party must, therefore, come to a decision one way or the other.

There are two paths which can lead to a solution of this serious crisis and if the collapse of the movement is to be avoided one of them must be followed: the legal or the illegal path. I would be prepared to follow either path. But I refuse to wait until the Führer is made Reich Chancellor, for by then the collapse will have occurred. If the legal path was to be followed, the Führer should have accepted Hindenburg's offer in August to make him Vice-Chancellor. From this basis the attempt should have been made to secure new positions. The Vice-Chancellor should have made it clear to the coalition Cabinet in which the National Socialists were participating that without the carrying out of National Socialist ideas there could be no recovery for Germany. The same thing should have happened in a Prussian coalition government and in other state governments.

Had Vice-Chancellor Hitler not succeeded in this task, he would have been weighed and found wanting; his departure from the political stage and the collapse of the government would have been deserved. History does not concern itself with methods but only with success.

The second method is the illegal path. I would have been prepared to follow this path as well. The National Socialist stormtroops of the SA and SS are still intact; they are prepared for the final march and will be at the ready the moment the order comes. This conquest of power by force would also have had a chance of success even if it had been bloody and confronted by serious resistance from the State. For who could withstand this well-organised army which has a firm ideological commitment, which has already passed the half-million mark, and the whole of which is under the leadership of front-line officers and soldiers? But this path has also been rejected and for my part I no longer see any possibility of future activity.

So far as the personal aspect of the problem is concerned, I am aware of an increasingly prevalent game of intrigue within the entourage of the Führer and of personal insults and slights which I am simply no longer able to put up with. I also naturally want to see and speak with the Füher occasionally—both for personal and for official reasons. If I go to the Kaiserhof or to the Brown House in Munich, I always find the same people there. During such visits I usually learn little, at any rate nothing detailed about the current issues of the day, about political meetings or the current state of discussions being carried on with individuals or with groups and parties.

I have no desire to take second place to Göring, Goebbels, Röhm, and others. If they are invited, I expect also to be honoured with an invitation. This the Führer has never done. I regard this as a slight, as a personal humiliation which I have not deserved and which I am no longer prepared to tolerate. Apart from this, I am at the end of my strength and nerves. I have resigned from the Party and am now going to the mountains to recuperate. I ask you all not to draw any conclusions for yourselves from my action but rather to continue to carry out your duties.

Strasser's speech caused consternation among his audience. Gauleiter Rust, the regional inspector of Lower Saxony, reported to Hitler what had happened. Hitler immediately called a meeting in the Kaiserhof at twelve o'clock for those who had been present at the Strasser meeting.

Dr Ley gave an account of what Strasser had said to the Regional Inspectors and Hitler made the following comments:

81

'I thought Gregor Strasser was much cleverer than that; I am shocked by the position he adopts and even more by the fact that, after twelve years' acquaintanceship and comradeship in the Party, he did not consider it necessary to let me know about these things and discuss them with me. I find it very difficult to accept this account as an adequate explanation for his momentous decision.

'I will answer you point by point:

'1. The path to the conquest of power depends upon imponderables which Strasser, according to his own account, either completely ignores or does not wish to see, or is simply not aware of. With a man of his calibre one would have thought that was impossible. He spoke to you about the legal path to the conquest of power and declared that it was my duty in August to accept the office of Vice-Chancellor. Herr Strasser knows quite well that Herr von Papen and Herr von Schleicher are not National Socialists and therefore are not willing to follow National Socialist policies. Judging by the measures introduced by and the results of the policy of Reich Chancellor von Papen, as Vice-Chancellor I would have had serious differences with him within the first week. If I did not want to abdicate all influence, betray my movement and make my position in the eyes of the public impossible, I would have had to protest against his policies. I would have had to make demands concerning a whole range of burning issues in economics and the administration, in social, labour and financial policies, demands which would have been turned down flat. Herr von Papen would have declared to me with a smile, "Forgive me, Herr Hitler, but I am Chancellor and head of the Cabinet. If my political course and the measures which result from it do not suit you, I am not forcing you to stay. You can resign your office. But in any case I reject your demands and proposals."

Gentlemen, can you imagine the effect of such a conclusion to my Vice-Chancellorship on the Party and on public opinion? Herr von Papen and his backers, on the other hand, would have achieved their goal—the proof of the incapacity of Hitler and his subordinates would have apparently been provided. The Party comrades and the electorate would have turned their backs on me in fury, the movement would have collapsed, and in the end over its body not Herr von Papen but, as the last elections show, Bolshevism would have triumphed. I reject this path and intend to wait until I am offered the post of Chancellor. That day will come—it is probably nearer than we think.

'Whether or not the movement disintegrates does not depend on the Party comrades and is not encouraged by them. It lies entirely in our own hands; it depends on our unity and on our unshakeable faith in victory; it depends on our leadership.

'2. The illegal path to the conquest of power is even more dangerous and more fatal. It cannot be said that I do not have the courage to carry out a *coup* by force and, if necessary, by a bloody revolution. I tried it once in Munich in 1923. Herr Strasser knows that; he was there.

'But what was the result and what would the result be now? Our formations are without weapons and, if there are some which have been kept hidden here and there against my wishes and without my knowledge, they would have no effect against the united action of the police and the Reichswehr which are armed with the most modern weapons. You surely do not believe that they would stand by. The police will shoot at the command of Herr von Papen and the Reichswehr at the command of its Supreme Commander, Reich President Hindenburg, for they have taken their oath to him and not to me.

'In the past the police have invariably obeyed the existing political power in the State completely irrespective of the political tendency within the State.

'General [sic] von Reichenau[26] said to me recently: "Herr Hitler, you have wonderful troops whose discipline is voluntary. The fact that it is not based on the law and that the leaders do not possess any State authority makes it even more worthy of recognition. The Reichswehr is different. It is under oath and is subordinate to the Field-Marshal as Reich President. If your columns march against the law, the Reichswehr would be compelled to shoot and would carry out the order even though its heart would bleed to do so. If you were Reich President and the Reichwehr was under oath to you, we would obey your orders in just the same way and shoot at the enemies of your State if you gave the order. We are unpolitical, obey the law, obey orders and keep the oath we have given. I urge you to keep within the law. One day power will inevitably fall into your lap."

'Gentlemen, I am not irresponsible enough to drive German youth and the generation of front-line soldiers who are the best representatives of the nation's manhood into the machine guns of the police and the Reichswehr. Gregor Strasser will not see that happening!

'3. I distribute political tasks to my closest colleagues according to specific

[26] Colonel von Reichenau was Chief of Staff of the Wehrkreis I (East Prussia). An ambitious man, he was already pro-Nazi, and with the appointment of his Commanding Officer, General von Blomberg, as Minister of Defence in Hitler's Cabinet he came to play an influential role in politics, notably in the so-called Röhm 'putsch' of June 1934.

principles. The nearer we come to the decision, the more attempts are made by our opponents to create divisions within our own camp and to break us. Whether or not they have already succeeded with Gregor Strasser is a subject I will not go into.

'If I am here in the Reich capital I carry out the most important discussions with ministers, generals, and party and pressure group [*Verband*] leaders myself. If I am not here, we cannot have a situation in which one moment Strasser is negotiating with the Centre in a certain direction, while tomorrow Goebbels is negotiating with Hindenburg in another direction, and the day after Göring is negotiating with the Reichswehr in a completely opposite direction. During my absence from Berlin, my authorised representative is Reichstag President Göring, who knows my intentions, who knows where I am, who can therefore inform me at once about any important discussions and to whom I can if necessary give an immediate counter-order... .

'Furthermore, I do not like the reorganisation of the Party leadership and their spheres of operation put forward by Strasser, although I approved it in order to avoid a dispute.[27] It is completely wrong that you as Regional Inspectors have given up your office as Gauleiters and are left hanging completely in the air. You are the oldest and most experienced Gauleiters. You must remain rooted in the soil in which you have grown and developed through the fulfilment of your assignment. I shall cancel the order in order to avoid upheaval and damage to the movement... .

'4. ...I do not issue invitations to any particular Party comrades. Anyone who visits me is welcome. I receive, as soon as I am available, anyone who wishes to and has to speak to me. Naturally I feel closer to some than to others. But is this not normal in human life?

'For some time I have noticed that Gregor Strasser has been avoiding me and when we see each other he is reserved, serious and uncommunicative. Is that my fault? Am I to blame for the fact that Göring and Goebbels visit me uninvited more often that Strasser? Did I not receive you when you wanted to speak to me? Did I not ask you to dine with me if you were with me and I had time for you? Is that sufficient reason for one of my closest and oldest colleagues to turn his back on the movement?'

Hitler became quieter and more personal, more amiable and appealing. At the end of the two-hour-long interview he had found that comradely tone which those present knew and found completely convincing. Now he was their friend, their comrade, their leader, who had shown them the way out of the hopeless situation which Strasser had portrayed, who had won them over both emotionally and intellectually....He, Hitler, triumphed and proved to his indispensable comrades, who in the most serious crisis of the movement first wavered and then recovered their nerve, that he was the master and Strasser the journeyman... . Those present once more sealed their old bond with him with a handshake... .

Strasser's unwillingness to lead a revolt against Hitler together with the total commitment of the Party leadership to Hitler as Führer ensured that the crisis was contained. The loss of confidence throughout the Party continued, however, and on 15 December Goebbels noted in his diary that

---

[27] Strasser had recently appointed some of the more senior Gauleiters to new posts as 'Regional Inspectors' who were intended to supervise the *Gaue* in their regions.

it was 'very difficult to hold the stormtroopers and the departmental officials on a straight course. It is high time we attained power and at the moment there is no sign of it.'

(v) The appointment of Hitler as Chancellor, 30 January 1933

At the lowest point in the Party's fortunes the tide turned. Papen had not overcome his resentment at being elbowed aside by Schleicher. He was determined to bring down Schleicher and return to office himself, even if not as Chancellor. To achieve this he would have to prove to the President that he could secure the mass support his previous government had lacked and which Schleicher had promised but failed to get. Without support from the Left or from the Catholic Centre Party, the only possibility was the Nazis. Their decline implied both the danger that the crisis would pass without having been used to change the regime and the likelihood of the Nazis' now proving more cooperative and amenable. During December, therefore, Papen opened negotiations with Hitler through various contacts, including Wilhelm Keppler, Hitler's economic adviser and a liaison with industry, Schacht, the former President of the Reichsbank, and Kurt von Schroeder, a Cologne banker and member of the Party.

As a result of these contacts, Hitler agreed to meet Papen on 4 January at Schroeder's house in Cologne. After the war Schroeder gave an account to the Nuremberg Tribunal of the background to the meeting and of what transpired at it:

82

On 4 January 1933 Hitler, von Papen, Hess, Himmler and Keppler arrived at my house in Cologne. Hitler, von Papen and I went into my study where a two-hour discussion took place. Hess, Himmler and Keppler did not take part but were in the adjoining room...The negotiations took place exclusively between Hitler and Papen. ...Papen went on to say that he thought it best to form a government in which the conservative and nationalist elements that had supported him were represented together with the Nazis. He suggested that this new government should, if possible, be led by Hitler and himself together Then Hitler made a long speech in which he said that, if he were to be elected Chancellor, Papen's followers could participate in his (Hitler's) Government as Ministers if they were willing to support his policy which was planning many alterations in the existing state of affairs. He outlined these alterations, including the removal of all Social Democrats, Communists and Jews from leading positions in Germany and the restoration of order in public life. Von Papen and Hitler reached agreement in principle whereby many of the disagreements between them could be removed and cooperation might be possible. It was agreed that further details could be worked out later either in Berlin or some other suitable place. This happened, as I learned later, at a meeting with Ribbentrop.

This meeting between Hitler and Papen on 4 January 1933 in my house in Cologne was arranged by me after Papen had asked me for it on about 10 December 1932. Before I took this step I talked to a number of businessmen and informed myself generally on how the business world viewed a collaboration between the two men. The general desire of businessmen was to see a strong man come to power in Germany who would form a government that would stay in power for a long time...

Business was in fact divided in its attitude to the political possibilities. Although Schleicher's policies evoked sympathy from sections of export- and consumer-oriented industries, they met with bitter opposition from heavy industry and, in general, industry was suspicious of his wooing of the trade unions. In their concern to replace Schleicher Hitler now appeared a more attractive ally, although Papen remained their first choice.

To demonstrate that his party was not yet finished Hitler decided to stake his prestige on the outcome of the state elections in Lippe-Detmold on 15 January. Although the electorate was only 90,000, Hitler needed an election victory to dispel the defeatist mood which still affected the Party and to convince the President and his advisers it was not a spent force. He, therefore, concentrated all his propaganda resources there during the week before polling and his efforts brought an increase in the vote for the NSDAP (39,000 votes compared with 33,000 in November). This result deprived his opponents of an excuse to block his ambition.

Papen now concentrated on trying to win over the President to a Hitler Government of which he himself would be Vice-Chancellor. In order to achieve this, the President's camarilla and, in particular, his son Oskar had to be persuaded to work on Hindenburg. One important factor influencing Hindenburg against Schleicher was the pressure from agriculture organised in the Nazi-influenced *Reichslandbund*. Agriculture had long been demanding a moratorium on debt repayments and protective tariffs. On 11 January 1933, the *Reichslandbund* publicly accused Schleicher's Government of discriminating against agriculture and in favour of export industries: 'the plundering of agriculture in favour of the all-powerful money-bags interests of the internationally-oriented export industry and its satellites continues'. The Junker landowners of East Elbia also feared Schleicher's plans to settle agricultural workers on bankrupt estates in the East. As a Junker himself, Hindenburg was particularly sensitive to this kind of pressure. Moreover, this sensitivity must have become particularly acute when the Centre Party and SPD Reichstag deputies succeeded in setting up an enquiry by the Public Accounts Office into the misuse of government money provided for the Eastern Aid Programme to bail out bankrupt Junker estates. There were even rumours that Oskar von Hindenburg was involved in the corruption. It has been suggested that Hitler offered to prevent such an investigation in the event of his becoming Chancellor. Certainly these events formed the background to the fall of Schleicher and Hitler's appointment as Chancellor. Otto Meissner, the State Secretary in the Reich President's office gave the Nuremberg Tribunal an account of the developments leading to Hitler's appointment:

83

...Papen was dismissed because he wanted to fight the National Socialists and did not find in the Reichswehr the necessary support for such a policy, and...Schleicher came to power because he believed he could form a government which would have the support of the National Socialists. When it became clear that Hitler was not willing to enter Schleicher's Cabinet and that Schleicher on his part was unable to split the National Socialist Party, as he had hoped to do with the help of Gregor Strasser, the policy for which Schleicher had been appointed Chancellor was shipwrecked. Schleicher was aware that Hitler was particularly embittered against him because of his attempt to break up the Party, and would never agree to cooperate with him. So he now changed his mind and decided to fight against the Nazis—which meant that he now wanted to pursue the policy which he had sharply opposed when Papen had suggested it a few weeks before. Schleicher came to Hindeburg therefore with a demand for emergency powers as a prerequisite of action against the Nazis. Furthermore, he believed it to be necessary to dissolve, and even temporarily eliminate, the Reichstag, and this was to be done by Presidential decrees on the basis of Article 48—the transformation of his government into a military dictatorship, and government to be carried on generally on the basis of Article 48.

Schleicher first made these suggestions to Hindenburg in the middle of January 1933, but Hindenburg at once evinced grave doubts as to its constitutionality. In the meantime Papen had returned to Berlin, and by an arrangement with Hindenburg's son had had several interviews with the President. When Schleicher renewed his demand for emergency powers, Hindenburg declared that he was unable to give him such a blank cheque and must reserve to himself decisions on every individual case. Schleicher for his part said that under these circumstances he was unable to stay in office and tendered his resignation on 28 January.

In the middle of January, when Schleicher was first asking for emergency powers, Hindenburg was not aware of the contact between Papen and Hitler—particularly, of the meeting which had taken place in the house of the Cologne banker, Kurt von Schroeder. In the latter part of January, Papen played an increasingly important role in the house of the Reich President, but despite Papen's persuasions, Hindenburg was extremely hesitant, until the end of January, to make Hitler Chancellor. He wanted to have Papen again as Chancellor. Papen finally won him over to Hitler with the argument that the representatives of the other right-wing parties which would belong to the Government would restrict Hitler's freedom of action. In addition Papen expressed his misgivings that, if the present opportunity were again missed, a revolt of the National Socialists and civil war were likely. Many of Hindenburg's personal friends, such as Oldenburg-Januschau,[28] worked in the same direction as Papen, also General von Blomberg.[29] The President's son and adjutant, Oskar von Hindenburg, was opposed to the Nazis up to the last moment. The turning-point at which his views changed came at the end of January. At Papen's suggestion, a meeting had been arranged between Hitler and Oskar von Hindenburg in the house of Ribbentrop. Oskar von Hindenburg asked me to accompany him; we took a taxi, in order to keep the appointment secret, and drove out to Ribbentrop's home. On our arrival we found a large company assembled; among those present were Göring and Frick.

Oskar von Hindenburg was told that Hitler wanted to talk to him *tête à tête*; as Hindeburg had asked me to accompany him, I was somewhat surprised at his accepting this suggestion and vanishing into another room for a talk which lasted quite a while—about an hour. What Hitler and Oskar von Hindenburg discussed during this talk I do not know.

In the taxi on the way back Oskar von Hindenburg was very silent; the only remark he made was that there was no help for it, the Nazis had to be taken into the Government. My impression was that Hitler had succeeded in getting him under his spell...

Joachim von Ribbentrop, who had married into a large German champagne business, had become a member of the Party in 1931. It was in his villa in Dahlem, a fashionable Berlin suburb, that many of the crucial negotiations were held. His wife dictated the following notes of these meetings at the time:

84

Wednesday, 18th January: In Dahlem at noon: Hitler, Röhm, Himmler, Papen. Hitler insists on being Chancellor. Papen again considers this impossible. His influence with Hindenburg was not strong enough to effect this. Hitler makes no further arrangements for talks. Joachim tentatively suggests a meeting between Hitler and Hindenburg's son.
Thursday, 19th January: Long talk between Joachim and Papen.
Friday, 20th January: In the evening long talk at Papen's house. He says that young Hindenburg and Meissner will come to Dahlem on Sunday.
Saturday, 21st January: Joachim reports to Hitler, who explains why he will not invite Schleicher. Hitler wants to bring Göring and Epp.
Sunday, 22nd January: Meeting at Dahlem at 10 p.m. Papen arrives alone at nine o'clock. Present: Hitler, Frick, Göring, Körner, Meissner, young Hindenburg,

---

[28] A leading and ultra-reactionary Prussian Junker.
[29] The district commander in East Prussia, who had come into contact with Hitler during 1932 through the Protestant Chaplain Müller, who was an ardent Nazi. As a result, Blomberg had become very sympathetic to Nazism.

Papen and Joachim. Hitler talks alone to young Hindenburg for two hours, followed by Hitler-Papen talk. Papen will now press for Hitler as Chancellor, but tells Hitler that he will withdraw from these negotiations forthwith if Hitler has no confidence in him.
Monday, 23rd January: In the morning Papen saw Hindenburg, who refused everything. Joachim goes to Hitler to explain this. Long talk about the possibility of a Schacht Cabinet. Hitler rejects everything.
Tuesday, 24th January: Tea in Dahlem: Frick, Göring, Papen, Joachim. Resolved to form national front which is to support Papen *vis-à-vis* old Hindenburg.
Wednesday, 25th January: Again tea in Dahlem: Joachim sees young Hindenburg alone. Hitler's Chancellorship under the auspices of a national front does not appear quite hopeless. Young Hindenburg promises to talk to Joachim again before his father makes final decision.
Thursday, 26th January: Long talk with Frick and Göring in the Reichstag. Negotiations with German Nationals. In the evening at Prince [*sic*] Oskar's house in Potsdam, letter to Hugenburg.
Friday, 27th January: Hitler back in Berlin. Long talk with him at Göring's flat. Hitler wants to leave Berlin forthwith. Joachim proposes link-up with Hugenberg for a national front. New meeting with old Hindenburg arranged. Hitler declares that he has said all there is to say to the Field Marshal, and does not know what to add. Joachim persuades Hitler that this last attempt should be made, and that the situation is by no means hopeless. Joachim suggests that the national front should be formed as soon as possible and that Hitler should meet Papen in Dahlem at 10 p.m. Hitler agrees to negotiate with Papen and Hugenberg in the evening. Followed long talk with Göring to discuss further tactics. Late in the afternoon Göring telephones to say that Joachim should go to the Reichstag President's house immediately. There talk with Hugenberg, Hitler and Göring (two names illegible), broken off because of impossible demands by German Nationals. Hitler very indignant, wants to leave for Munich immediately. Göring persuades him to stay or at least to go only as far as Weimar. Gradually Göring and Joachim calm Hitler down, but all his suspicions are revived. Situation very critical. Hitler declares he cannot meet Papen in Dahlem that evening, because he is not in a position to talk freely.'

The remainder of the notes were dictated by Ribbentrop personally:

'I have never seen Hitler in such a state; I proposed to him and Göring that I should see Papen alone that evening and explain the whole situation to him. In the evening I saw Papen and convinced him eventually that the only thing that made sense was Hitler's Chancellorship, and that he must do what he can to bring this about. Papen declared that the matter of Hugenberg was of secondary importance, and that he was now absolutely in favour of Hitler becoming Chancellor; this was the decisive change in Papen's attitude. Papen has become conscious of his responsibility—three possibilities: a Presidential Cabinet, followed by (illegible), return of Marxism under Schleicher, or Hindenburg's resignation. As opposed to these the one and only clear solution: Hitler's Chancellorship. Papen is now absolutely certain that he must achieve Hitler's Chancellorship at all costs, and that he must abandon his belief that it is his duty to remain at Hindenburg's disposal.

This recognition by Papen is, I believe, the turning point. Papen has an appointment with Hindenburg for Saturday at 10 a.m.

Saturday, 28th January: About 11 a.m. I went to see Papen who received me with the question: 'Where is Hitler?' I told him that he had probably left, but could perhaps be contacted in Weimar. Papen said that he had to be got back without delay, because a turning point had been reached; after a long talk with Hindenburg he, Papen, considered Hitler's Chancellorship possible. I went to see Göring immediately and heard that Hitler was still at the Kaiserhof. Göring telephoned him, Hitler will remain in Berlin. Then a new difficulty arose: the question of Prussia. Long argument with Göring. I declared that I would withdraw from the negotiations immediately if suspicions of Papen were revived. Göring gave in and expressed his complete agreement with me; he promised to do what he could to bring the matter to a satisfactory conclusion together with Hitler. Göring promised to persuade Hitler to accept the Prussian settlement proposed by Papen. Göring and I then went to see Hitler. Long talk with Hitler alone, explaining that a solution depended entirely on trust and that his Chancellorship did not now appear to be impossible. I asked Hitler to see Papen that very afternoon. But Hitler first wanted to think over the question of Prussia, and see Papen on Sunday morning. This I reported to Papen, who was again very worried. He said: "I know the Prussians." Then we arranged a Hitler-Papen meeting for 11 a.m. on Sunday morning.

Sunday, 29th January: At 11 a.m. long Hitler-Papen talk. Hitler declared that on the whole everything was clear. But there would have to be general elections and an Enabling Law. Papen saw Hindenburg immediately. I lunched with Hitler at the Kaiserhof. We discussed the elections. As Hindenburg does not want these, Hitler asked me to tell the President that these would be the last elections. In the afternoon Göring and I went to Papen. Papen declared that all obstacles are removed and that Hindenburg expects Hitler to-morrow at 11 a.m.

Monday, 30th January: Hitler appointed Chancellor.'

To sum up, the following factors were involved in the winning over of the President: firstly, Schleicher's economic policies, geared to winning mass support, were alienating powerful interests. Industry, in particular heavy industry, objected to his labour policies as inflationary and too favourable to the workers; the Junkers resented his policy of encouraging export industry—as they saw it at their expense—and bitterly opposed his attempt to revive Brüning's plan of breaking up bankrupt Junker estates and settling them with peasants. These interests pressed their views vigorously with the President. Secondly, Hindenburg had never really forgiven Schleicher for forcing Papen's resignation. He wanted 'Fränzchen' back in the Government. Finally, Schleicher had patently failed in his objective of acquiring a mass base for his government. He had no alternative to offer other than another election, action against the Nazis and a dictatorship through Article 48. This had been not far from the policy he had prevented Papen from carrying out and the President did not see why he should allow Schleicher to do what Papen had been prevented from doing. Hindenburg's refusal to grant a dissolution of the Reichstag forced Schleicher to resign on 28 January.

Yet, despite his growing disenchantment with Schleicher, Hindenburg was still not happy about the idea of Hitler as Chancellor. As late as 26 January, he told the Army generals that they surely did not believe he would make this 'Austrian corporal' Reich Chancellor. Hindenburg was finally persuaded by the structure of the proposed government and by the fact that it promised to secure a parliamentary majority and so relieve him of the responsibility of governing. In the first place, Papen had persuaded Hitler that the Nazis should have only two ministries in the Cabinet apart from the Chancellorship—the Reich Ministry of the Interior (Frick) and a Minister without Portfolio (Göring) who was also Prussian Minister of the Interior; secondly, Papen became Reich Commissioner in Prussia, i.e. Göring's superior, and had the right of being present at Hitler's audiences with the President; thirdly, the Ministry of Defence was given to a general acceptable to Hindenburg (Blomberg); and finally, Papen persuaded both the Nationalists and the right-wing ex-servicemen's organisation, the Stahlhelm, of which Hindenburg was the honorary head, to cooperate in forming the Government. The Nationalist leader, Hugenberg, was won over by the offer of the Ministries of Economics and Agriculture, refused him by Schleicher and which he though would make him virtually economic dictator; the Stahlhelm leader, Seldte, was made Minister of Labour. In short, Hindenburg believed that, as Papen put it, Hitler would be 'framed' within the Cabinet by Conservatives who would be able to control the policies which Hitler would 'sell' to the country through his Party and propaganda machine. To a doubter, Papen remarked: 'Don't worry, we've hired him.'

Hitler, however, was content with this solution. He himself, as Chancellor, had the supreme position in the Government; Göring, as Prussian Minister of the Interior, controlled the police in three-fifths of the Reich; and General von Blomberg, unbeknown to Hindenburg, was a pro-Nazi. Finally, as one of his conditions for taking office, he had insisted that the new Cabinet and the President should agree to an immediate dissolution. These were, he believed, adequate weapons for the consolidation of power. Time was to prove him right.

The composition of Hitler's first Reich Cabinet was as follows:

Reich Chancellor	Adolf Hitler (NSDAP)
Vice-Chancellor and Reich Commissioner for Prussia	Franz von Papen (DNVP)
*†Reich Foreign Minister	Constantin von Neurath

Reich Minister of the Interior	Dr Wilhelm Frick (NSDAP)
Reich Minister of Defence	General Werner von Blomberg
*†Reich Finance Minister	Count Schwerin von Krosigk
Reich Minister of Economics Food and Agriculture	Dr Alfred Hugenberg (DNVP)
Reich Minister of Labour	Franz Seldte
*†Reich Minister of Posts and Transport	Paul von Eltz-Rübenach
Reich Minister without Portfolio, Reich Air Commissioner, and acting Prussian Minister of the Interior	Hermann Göring (NSDAP)
*†Reich Commissioner of Employment	Dr Günther Gereke
*†Reich Minister of Justice	Dr Franz Gürtner (DNVP)

*Member of the previous administration.
†Conservative civil servant.

NOTE. Goebbels became a Cabinet Minister as Minister of Propaganda on 13 March 1933. Hess was named Deputy Führer on 21 April, and as such was given the power of independent decision on all Party questions; but neither he nor Röhm was nominated to the Cabinet, as Reich Minister, until 1 December. Hugenberg resigned on 27 June 1933 and was replaced by Walter Darré as Minister of Agriculture and Kurt Schmitt as Minister of Economics. Gereke was taken over from the Schleicher government as Reich Commissioner for Work Creation but was arrested on corruption charges on 24 March 1933 and dismissed from state service on the 27th. Gürtner's appointment as Justice Minister, though agreed on 29 January, was postponed until 1 February to create the illusion of a vacancy for a Centre Party member in the context of the coalition negotiations with the Centre.

CHAPTER 5

The 'Seizure of Power' 1933–1934

Though now Chancellor, Hitler had not yet achieved absolute power. Only three Cabinet members were Nazis, his Party had not a majority in the Reichstag, and he could be dismissed at any time by the Reich President. On the other hand, he had a number of important advantages. Göring as Prussian Minister of the Interior controlled the internal administration, including the police, in three-fifths of the Reich; Frick as Reich Minister of the Interior had certain limited powers of supervision over the remainder. With General von Blomberg as Minister of Defence he had little to fear from the Amy. But, above all, there was no obvious alternative candidate to represent the forces of the Right. The years 1930–32 had seen several attempts by it to establish a government at once effective, amenable to the right-wing pressure groups—the Army, the Junkers, and Industry—and able to command a degree of mass support. None had managed to fulfil all these requirements, certainly not the last. That Hitler could provide the Right with mass support had led to his appointment; and the other right-wing politicians' awareness of their lack of a popular following gave them a sense of inferiority in regard to the Nazis which helped to paralyse their will. The alternative to Hitler would be a right-wing dictatorship against both the NSDAP and the Left—an unattractive prospect. Moreover, Hitler offered the German establishment not only a way out of the political impasse but also the possibility of reviving the economy without having to make concessions to labour. Profits rather than wages would reap the main benefits of the recovery.

Hitler had no blueprint or timetable for the take-over of power. It took the form of a complex and dynamic process involving both initiatives from above as well as pressures from below, some of which were orchestrated but many of which were spontaneous and uncoordinated. There was a struggle for power among the various elements within the regime itself as well as against the previous incumbents. Hitler, however, had certain broad objectives. During his first weeks in office he sought to build up his mass support in the country in order to legitimise his own position with direct democratic sanction independent of the indirect form provided by the Constitution. This would increase his leverage not only against the right-wing politicians and pressure groups, who could command no such popular support, but against the President himself. Since Hitler's electoral support had consistently been shown to be less than 40 per cent, he now used the propaganda machine provided by his Party, assisted by the resources of the State, to project the idea that the new Government represented a 'national uprising' in which the nation was united behind a Government determined to end the crisis and to lead Germany towards a new and glorious future. In this way, he could create the myth of overwhelming support for the new regime even in the face of hard fact.

Once this myth was established, opposition to the regime wore the appearance of treason. Added weight was given to this impression by Governmental exploitation of the alleged threat of Bolshevism. To many this appeared real. The Nazis, however, used the 'Marxists' and the Jews as 'outgroups' in order to solidify the 'national community'. Here the Nazis were building on a tradition which went back fifty years to Bismarck's division of Germans into 'friends' and 'enemies' of the Reich, the latter including Left-Liberals, Catholics and Socialists, and later the Jews. The Weimar Republic, born out of defeat and revolution, had represented in the eyes of the Right the triumph of Bismarck's *Reichsfeinde* (enemies of the Reich). Thus to many it appeared as if Hitler was now restoring the situation which obtained before November 1918.

The psychological pressure on individuals created by this myth of a 'national uprising', particularly in the context of a desperate national crisis, was considerable: individuals and groups tended to 'coordinate' themselves, sometimes with enthusiasm, sometimes with a sense of resignation. This pressure towards conformity was increased by the knowledge that overt opposition would be mercilessly crushed. Those whom their political background marked out as unlikely to conform were intimidated into silence by the strong-arm methods of the SA and SS.

The degree of violence and intimidation exercised by the Nazi organisations has sometimes been underestimated in those accounts of the Nazi seizure of power which have stressed its pseudo-legality. The maintenance of an appearance of legality was undoubtedly an important element in Hitler's strategy. However, it was only one aspect of the situation; it was not always the one most evident at the time. The 'seizure of power' was in fact anything but peaceful. There was of course no fighting in the streets because the Left offered no resistance. During March, however, there began a 'revolution from below' on the part of the local Nazi organisations who interfered in a totally arbitrary manner with the State administration, with the course of justice and with commercial life; and this interference continued to a lesser extent throughout 1933.

It is as contrasted with the violence against individuals and the arbitrary interference on the part of the local Party organisations that the importance of this aspect of legality is most clearly seen. Hitler, appointed Chancellor by the President acting under Article 48 of the Weimar Constitution, headed a government which was legal in the narrow definition of that word. Once in office, he used the power to issue emergency decrees vested in the Reich President under Article 48 to strip the Constitution of its guarantees for civil liberties. In doing so he could claim to be merely taking a stage further the emergency powers used by his three predecessors. He was keeping to the letter of the Constitution even if he flouted its spirit. Moreover, maintaining the appearance of legality, he removed any qualms which might otherwise have been felt by the State officials obliged to carry out his policies. Indeed, for the civil servants and businessmen, faced with the 'revolution from below', the fact that Hitler was keeping to the letter of the law was an incentive to cooperate with the regime in the hope that this would encourage the 'moderate' Hitler to keep his local militants in check.

The fact that Hitler moved first against the Left lulled the Right into a sense of security. In the myth of the 'national uprising' Nationalists saw a reassertion of the conservative and nationalist values to which they adhered. By the time they became fully aware that Nazism was a totalitarian not a conservative movement, it was too late. In cooperating with the Nazis in projecting the image of a 'national uprising' and in identifying it with Hitler's rule, they had fatally undermined their own position and became now isolated. The only centres of power to which they could look for help were the President and the Army. The President by now senile was unwilling to face the upheaval which would be caused by dismissing Hitler. In any case, he appears to have been fed carefully selected information by his entourage. The Army was under a Minister of Defence who sympathised with the Nazi movement, its numbers were too small in comparison to those of the SA to guarantee success, and its younger officers were increasingly falling under Nazi influence.

Nevertheless, although Hitler was not prepared to tolerate a rival political organisation representing the conservative nationalists, he appreciated that he could not do without the traditional elites such as the Civil Service, Industry and the Army if he was to achieve his major goal of territorial expansion. He was therefore obliged to allow them to remain largely intact for the time being. Some of his rank-and-file followers in the SA and the Party, however, having provided the mass support and the drive to bring him to power and having then helped him to consolidate his power by terrorising their opponents, now wished to depose these elites, take over or destroy their organisations and introduce economic policies reflecting their hostility to big business. This would clearly jeopardise Hitler's major goal of rearmament, and he was prepared, if necessary, to use drastic methods to prevent such a development.

Instead of producing a thorough-going social and economic revolution, therefore, the Nazi take-over represented a compromise between the Nazi leadership who had acquired political power, and the traditional elites who retained their positions but put themselves at the service of the new regime. They were encouraged to do so by the fact that Hitler's initial objectives—the repression of the Left, rearmament, and the revision of various parts of the Versailles treaties—reflected their own wishes. But by assisting Hitler during these early years they increased his power and prestige and rendered themselves progressively superfluous. As the regime later moved towards its final goals of unbridled conquest and racial extermination, the Conservatives were replaced by technocrats or racialist fanatics who did not share their qualms at such revolutionary policies. The bravest of the Conservatives tried to make amends for their previous collaboration by going into active opposition, but once again it was too late.

(i) The 'National Uprising' — The Election Campaign of February–March 1933

On his appointment as Chancellor, Hitler's first objective was the elimination of the Reichstag as an effective organ either of legislation or of opposition, achievable only by passing an Enabling Act requiring a two-thirds majority. The first Cabinet meetings, therefore, were concerned with securing this majority. One possibility was an alliance with the Catholic Centre Party. Though negotiations were begun, neither Nazis nor Nationalists wanted success because the Centre would demand concessions limiting their freedom of action. Hitler, therefore, soon broke off negotiations arguing that the Centre's demands were too high. Other possibilities were the suppression of the Communist Party and the confiscation of their seats, or new elections. A condition for Hitler's acceptance of the Chancellorship had been the dissolution of the Reichstag. He favoured new elections, for an increased Nazi vote would add an aura of democratic legitimacy to his gradual assumption of power, and would correspondingly undermine the position of the Nationalists. Hugenberg, the Nationalist leader, conscious that the Nazis now had the full power of the state behind them, demurred, but on receiving Hitler's promise not to alter the composition of the Cabinet after the election irrespective of the outcome, acquiesced. Indeed, he went further. According to the Cabinet minutes of 31 January 1933, the initiative for the abolition of the parliamentary system and for the deposition of the Social Democratic Government of Otto Braun in Prussia came from the non-Nazis Papen and Hugenberg. The Nazis, far from being restrained by their 'conservative' colleagues, merely had to acquiesce in their requests. The election was scheduled for 5 March. It was made clear that the coalition would continue after the election but Nazis and Nationalists fought as separate groups:

85

...(2) Political Situation

The Reich Chancellor reported on his conversation held on the morning of 31 January with representatives of the Centre Party, Dr Kaas and Dr Perlitius. The representatives had told him that they did not wish to join the Government at this time, although the Centre Party might abstain from opposition to the Cabinet.

The Reich Chancellor had immediately asked them whether they would consent to an extended adjournment of the Reichstag, perhaps for a year. He had received the reply that the Centre Party could not immediately consent to an adjournment for a whole year, but at the most for two months at a time. In any event, it was not inconceivable that in this way an adjournment for a whole year might be obtainable. But such an attitude on the part of the Centre Party would depend on the replies to a series of questions which Mgr Kaas wanted to send the Reich Chancellor today in writing. As Dr Kaas further stated, the Centre Party would consider a coalition only if this would include Prussia. The Centre Party representatives had been unable to deny during the conversation that a very large part of the German people stood behind the present Government.

He would sum up the result of the conversation with the representatives of the Centre Party to the effect that a year's adjournment could not be obtained with certainty. Perhaps he could talk again about the course of the conversation and the further development of the political situation with Reich Minister Dr Hugenberg, personally.

The Reich Minister of Economics, Food and Agriculture stated he would be very glad to have such a talk.

The Reich Chancellor further stated that if a new election were held he thought that 51 per cent of the Reichstag might be found backing the present Government. He had talked on the morning of 31 January with a number of Gauleiters of the NSDAP, who had confirmed this. In his opinion, further negotiations with the Centre Party were useless; there was no alternative to a new election.

The Vice-Chancellor and Reich Commissioner of Prussia stated that it would be best to decide now that the coming election of the Reichstag would be the last one and that a return to the parliamentary system was to be avoided permanently.

The Reich Chancellor declared that he would make the following binding promises:

(a) The outcome of the new election of the Reichstag is to have no influence on the composition of the present Government;

(b) The forthcoming election of the Reichstag is to be the last election. Any return to the parliamentary system is to be absolutely avoided.

The Reich Minister of Finance pointed out that the votes in the committees of the Reichstag were gradually bringing the Reich Government into some impossible situations. The Government parties must immediately declare that, in view of the political situation, they demanded the adjournment of the committees. If an adjournment could not be obtained, the representatives of the Government parties must dissolve the committees of the Reichstag and in this way prevent them from passing resolutions.

No objections were made to this proposal of the Reich Minister of Finance.

The Reich Chancellor then read a letter received in the meantime from Dr Kaas, containing the questions to the Reich Government promised by him. The Reich Chancellor declared that it was not possible to go into the details at this time. To deal with the individual questions satisfactorily, if it was really desirable, would mean several weeks' work. In his opinion, a detailed substantive reply could not be given.

The Reich Minister of Economics, Food and Agriculture pointed out that it was urgently necessary to depose the so-called sovereign Braun Government[30] in Prussia as soon as possible. Otherwise, the civil servants in Prussia would get into an intolerable situation.

The Chancellor agreed in principle to this point of view. He then turned to the future work of the Reich Government and stated that an extension of the protection against distraint was urgently needed in the interest of the German farmer.[31] In his view, distraint proceedings against farming property must be suspended, with great respect to all claims that had arisen prior to the appointment of the present Cabinet... .

State Secretary Meissner pointed out that it was possible to dissolve the Prussian Diet by a decree based on Article 48 of the Reich Constitution. Such a decree will have to be based on the decision of the Supreme Court for Constitutional Questions that unity in the leadership of the State, the Reich, and Prussia, was required.

The Vice-Chancellor and Reich Commissioner of Prussia stated that in his opinion it would be best if the President were to appoint himself State President in Prussia.

State Secretary Meissner expressed certain objections to this proposal and said it would be best to obtain a voluntary dissolution of the Prussian Diet. If such a voluntary dissolution could not be obtained, a dissolution on the basis of Article 48 of the Reich Constitution could then be considered. In any case it would be

---

[30] The German Supreme Court had ruled on 25 October 1932 that the Presidential Decree of 20 July 1932, appointing a Reich Commissioner for Prussia and removing Prussian Minister-President Otto Braun and his Cabinet from office, was constitutional, but that the Decree could not deprive the Prussian Cabinet of the power to represent Prussia in her relations with the Reich, the Prussian Diet and other German States.

[31] As a result of the depression large numbers of farmers were being foreclosed for debt.

necessary for the so-called Braun Government to disappear soon. The Cabinet approved these statements.

The attitude of many of the upper middle class to Hitler's appointment is well summed up in the following extracts from the diary of Frau Solmitz:

86

30.i.33
And what did Dr H. bring us? The news that his double, Hitler, is Chancellor of the Reich! And what a Cabinet!!! One we didn't dare dream of in July. Hitler, Hugenberg, Seldte, Papen!!!

On each one of them depends part of Germany's hopes. National Socialist drive, German National reason, the non-political Stahlhelm, not to forget Papen. It is so incredibly marvellous that I am writing it down quickly before the first discordant note comes, for when has Germany ever experienced a blessed summer after a wonderful spring? Probably only under Bismarck. What a great thing Hindenburg has achieved! How well he neutralised Hammerstein[32] who was presumptuous enough to bring politics into the Reichswehr!

Huge torchlight procession in the presence of Hindenburg and Hitler by National Socialists and Stahlhelm, who at long last are collaborating again. This is a memorable 30 January!
6.ii.33
Torchlight procession of National Socialists and Stahlhelm! A wonderfully elevating experience for all of us. Göring says the day of Hitler's and the nationalist Cabinet's appointment was something like 1914, and this too was something like 1914; after Dr H. had only recently remarked that damned little of this spirit had survived on the way from Berlin to Hamburg between 30 January and 3 February.

On Sunday, the Reds waded through relentless rain—Gisela saw them—with wives and children to make the procession longer. The Socialists and Reds will inevitably have to give in now.

But now the weather was beautiful. Dry and calm, a few degrees above freezing. At 9.30 p.m. we took up our position, Gisela with us. I said she should stay till the end for the sake of the children. So far the impressions they had had of politics had been so deplorable that they should now have a really strong impression of nationhood, as we had once, and store it in their memories. And so they did. It was 10 p.m. by the time the first torchlights came, and then 20,000 brown shirts followed one another like waves in the sea, their faces shone with enthusiasm in the light of the torches. 'Three cheers for our Führer, our Chancellor Adolf Hitler....' They sang 'The Republic is shit' and called the colours 'black-red-mustard'[33] and 'The murderous reds have bloody hands and we won't forget the murder at the

---

[32] It had been rumoured (erroneously) that General von Hammerstein had been preparing to use the Army to avert a Nazi take-over.
[33] Black-red gold were the colours of the Republican flag. 'Mustard' is particularly derogatory since the German word can be used colloquially to mean 'nonsense'.

Sternschanz.' Dreckmann was murdered there and I happened to spot his name on one of the flags, probably the one of the section he had belonged to. The military standards are much too Roman in appearance.

Now came the Stahlhelm, a grey stream; quieter, more spiritual perhaps. On their beautiful flags they carried our old colours black-white-red,[34] with mourning crêpe at the top... How wonderful and uplifting it is that the quarrels between brothers that once so depressed us have been settled! It should always be like tonight. But between the SA and the Stahlhelm there was marching a delegation of nationalist students. And they won the hearts of Hamburg. The women at the greengrocery stalls and their customers, all the women there were saying the same thing: 'Those students! Simply charming. They were the best, weren't they?'

And it was a magnificent picture, the snow-white, scarlet, moss-green and black colours, the fantastic berets, boots and gauntlets in the dancing light of the torches, the swords, the flags. They were followed by the Stahlhelm with shining *Schellenbaum*,[35] playing the old Prussian army marches.

The SS brought up the rear of the procession.

We were drunk with enthusiasm, blinded by the light of the torches right in our faces, and always enveloped in their vapour as in a cloud of sweet incense. And in front of us men, men, men, brightly coloured, grey, brown, a torrent lasting an hour and 20 minutes. In the wavering light of the torches one seemed to see only a few types recurring again and again, but there were between twenty-two and twenty-five thousand different faces!

Nest to us a little boy of three kept raising his tiny hand: 'Heil Hitler, Heil Hitlerman!'

An SA man said to Gisela that morning: 'One doesn't say Heil Hitler any more, one says Heil Germany.' 'Death to the Jews' was also sometimes called out and they sang of the blood of the Jews which would squirt from their knives. (*subsequent addition*: Who took that seriously then?)

Opposite the Eimsbüttel Sports Hall (what a pity we could not see it) stood the leader of the Hamburg National Socialists—and beside him with his hand touching his hat, the leader of the Hamburg Stahlhelm, Lieutenant-Commander Lauenstein, who a few months before had been stabbed by SA men (ten minutes from where he now stood) and now saluted the procession of the SA, just as the SA leader saluted that of the Stahlhelm. What moments! What a marvellous thought

The National Socialists have much more new blood and young people than the Stahlhelm. Good looking, fresh, gay youths in the procession.

When everyting was over, it was actually not yet over, for the last SS men were joined by a crowd of gay people with left-over torches, who made their own procession, happy to join in the occasion.

Finally, the torches were thrown together at the Kaiser Frederich embankment, after a march from the Lübeck Gate. It was 11.30 p.m. before all was over.

Unity at last, at long last, but for how long? We are after all Germans.

What must Hitler feel when he sees the hundred thousand people whom he

---

[34] The colours of the old imperial flag.
[35] A musical instrument.

summoned, to whom he gave a national soul, people who are ready to die for him. Not only metaphorically speaking but in bitter earnest...

And these floods of people in Hamburg are only a small fraction of Hitler's support in the whole Reich... .

The following 'Appeal to the German People' of 31 January 1933 formed part of this attempt to project the image of a 'national uprising' by creating the impression of national unity and a determined Government and by describing the previous epoch as one of unmitigated disaster. By sticking to vague generalities the Government avoided specific commitments which might have alienated certain sections of the population and limited its freedom of manoeuvre. It also disguised the fact that at this stage the Government had few specific plans.

87

Over fourteen years have passed since that unhappy day when the German people, blinded by promises made by those at home and abroad, forgot the highest values of our past, of the Reich, of its honour and its freedom, and thereby lost everything. Since those days of treason, the Almighty has withdrawn his blessing from our nation. Discord and hatred have moved in. Filled with the deepest distress, millions of the best German men and women from all walks of life see the unity of the nation disintegrating in a welter of egoistical political opinions, economic interests, and ideological conflicts.

As so often in our history, Germany, since the day the revolution broke out, presents a picture of heartbreaking disunity. We did not receive the equality and fraternity which was promised us; instead we lost our freedom. The breakdown of the unity of mind and will of our nation at home was followed by the collapse of its political position abroad.

We have a burning conviction that the German people in 1914 went into the great battle without any thought of personal guilt and weighed down only by the burden of having to defend the Reich from attack, to defend the freedom and material existence of the German people. In the appalling fate that has dogged us since November 1918 we see only the consequence of our inward collapse. But the rest of the world is no less shaken by great crises. The historical balance of power, which at one time contributed not a little to the understanding of the necessity for solidarity among the nations, with all the economic advantages resulting therefrom, has been destroyed.

The delusion that some are the conquerors and others the conquered destroys the trust between nations and thereby also destroys the world economy. But the misery of our people is terrible! The starving industrial proletariat have become unemployed in their millions, while the whole middle and artisan class have been made paupers. If the German farmer also is involved in this collapse we shall be faced with a catastrophe of vast proportions. For in that case, there will collapse not only a Reich, but also a 2000-year-old inheritance of the highest works of human culture and civilisation.

All around us are symptoms portending this breakdown. With an unparalleled effort of will and of brute force the Communist method of madness is trying as a last resort to poison and undermine an inwardly shaken and uprooted nation. They seek to drive it towards an epoch which would correspond even less to the promises of the Communist speakers of today than did the epoch now drawing to a close to the promises of the same emissaries in November 1918.

Starting with the family, and including all notions of honour and loyalty, nation and fatherland, culture and economy, even the eternal foundations of our morals and our faith—nothing is spared by this negative, totally destructive ideology. Fourteen years of Marxism have undermined Germany. One year of Bolshevism would destroy Germany. The richest and most beautiful areas of world civilisation would be transformed into chaos and a heap of ruins. Even the misery of the past decade and a half could not be compared with the affliction of a Europe in whose heart the red flag of destruction had been planted. The thousands of injured, the countless dead which this battle has already cost Germany may stand as a presage of the disaster.

In these hours of overwhelming concern for the existence and the future of the German nation, the venerable World War leader [Hindenburg] appealed to us men of the nationalist parties and associations to fight under him again as once we did at the front, but now loyally united for the salvation of the Reich at home. The revered President of the Reich having with such generosity joined hands with us in a common pledge, we nationalist leaders would vow before God, our conscience and our people that we shall doggedly and with determination fulfil the mission entrusted to us as the National Government.

It is an appalling inheritance which we are taking over.

The task before us is the most difficult which has faced German statesmen in living memory. But we all have unbounded confidence, for we believe in our nation and in its eternal values. Farmers, workers, and the middle class must unite to contribute the bricks wherewith to build the new Reich.

The National Government will therefore regard it as its first and supreme task to restore to the German people unity of mind and will. It will preserve and defend the foundations on which the strength of our nation rests. It will take under its firm protection Christianity as the basis of our morality, and the family as the nucleus of our nation and our state. Standing above estates and classes, it will bring back to our people the consciousness of its racial and political unity and the obligations arising therefrom. It wishes to base the education of German youth on respect for our great past and pride in our old traditions. It will therefore declare merciless war on spiritual, political and cultural nihilism. Germany must not and will not sink into Communist anarchy.

In place of our turbulent instincts, it will make national discipline govern our life. In the process it will take into account all the institutions which are the true safeguards of the strength and power of our nation.

The National Government will carry out the great task of reorganising our national economy with two big Four-Year Plans:

saving the German farmer so that the nation's food supply and thus the life of the nation shall be secured.

saving the German worker by a massive and comprehensive attack on unemployment.

In fourteen years the November parties have ruined the German farmer.
In fourteen years they created an army of millions of unemployed.
The National Government will carry out the following plan with iron resolution and dogged perseverance.
Within four years the German farmer must be saved from pauperism.
Within four years unemployment must be completely overcome.
Parallel with this, there emerge the prerequisites for the recovery of the economy.
The National Government will combine this gigantic project of restoring our economy with the task of putting the administration and the finances of the Reich, the states, and the communes on a sound basis.
Only by doing this can the idea of preserving the Reich as a federation acquire flesh and blood.
The idea of labour service and of settlement policy are among the main pillars of this programme.
Our concern to provide daily bread will be equally a concern for the fulfilment of the responsibilities of society to those who are old and sick.
The best safeguard against any experiment which might endanger the currency lies in economical administration, the promotion of work, and the preservation of agriculture, as well as in the use of individual initiative.
In foreign policy, the National Government will see its highest mission in the preservation of our people's right to an independent life and in the regaining thereby of their freedom. The determination of this Government to put an end to the chaotic conditions in Germany is a step towards the integration into the community of nations of a state having equal status and therefore equal rights with the rest. In so doing, the Government is aware of its great obligation to support, as the Government of a free and equal nation, that maintenance and consolidation of peace which the world needs today more than ever before.
May all others understand our position and so help to ensure that this sincere desire for the welfare of Europe and of the whole world shall find fulfilment.
Despite our love for our Army as the bearer of our arms and the symbol of our great past, we should be happy if the world, by restricting its armaments, made unnecessary any increase in our own weapons.
But if Germany is to experience this political and economic revival and conscientiously to fulfil its duties towards other nations, a decisive act is required: *We must overcome the demoralisation of Germany by the Communists.*
We, men of this Government, feel responsible to German history for the reconstitution of a proper national body so that we may finally overcome the insanity of class and class warfare. We do not recognise classes, but only the German people, its millions of farmers, citizens and workers who together will either overcome this time of distress or succumb to it.
With resolution and fidelity to our oath, seeing the powerlessness of the present Reichstag to shoulder the task we advocate, we wish to commit it to the whole German people.
We therefore appeal now to the German people to sign this act of mutual reconciliation.
The Government of the National Uprising wishes to set to work, and it will work.
It has not for fourteen years brought ruin to the German nation; it wants to lead

it to the summit.

It is determined to make amends in four years for the liabilities of fourteen years.

But it cannot subject the work of reconstruction to the will of those who were responsible for the breakdown.

The Marxist parties and their followers had fourteen years to prove their abilities.

The result is a heap of ruins.

Now, German people, give us four years and then judge us.

Let us begin, loyal to the command of the Field-Marshal. May Almighty God favour our work, shape our will in the right way, bless our vision and bless us with the trust of our people. We have no desire to fight for ourselves; only for Germany.

The patronizing reaction of Frau Solmitz is probably typical of many of the educated middle class:

88

7.ii.33

...His [Hitler's] appeal, signed by the whole Government, contains too many words of foreign derivation used in an uneducated way. But I say: let him act first, and then later we shall teach Hitler good, pure German.

19.ii.33

Unfortunately, I must say that the political scales do not come to rest....I see Hitler exchanging bureaucrats [*Bonzen*] for bureaucrats, party book for party book. I hear him talk of Socialism....

The black-white-red battle front represents responsibility, represents the solid citizens, morality, protection of individuality, property, free enterprise, without experiments, without the use of force—it is a powerless little group outside Hitler's mighty shadow. What can be done?

Although the Nazis could command the radio and the police for their campaign, to avoid accusations of corruption, Hitler insisted the election campaign be not financed by the State. Instead, industry was requested to subsidise it. On 20 February 1933, Hitler addressed a small gathering of some twenty industrialists as follows:

89

...Private enterprise cannot be maintained in the age of democracy; it is conceivable only if the people have a sound idea of authority and personality. Everything positive, good and valuable, which has been achieved in the world in the field of economics and culture, is solely attributable to the importance of personality. When, however, the defence of the existing order, its political administration, is left to a majority, it will go under irretrievably. All the worldly goods which we possess we owe to the struggle of the chosen. Had we had the present conditions in the Middle Ages, the foundations of our German Reich would never have been laid. The same mentality that was the basis for obtaining these values must be used to preserve these values....It is, however, not enough to say: We do not want Communism in our economy. If we continue on our old political course, then we shall perish. We have fully experienced in the past years that economics and politics cannot be separated. The political conduct of the struggle is the primary, decisive factor. Therefore, politically clear conditions must be reached. As economics alone has not made the German Reich, so politics did not make economics. But each one built steadily higher upon the other. Just as politics and economics working hand in hand brought us to the top, so the working of one against the other, as we experienced it after the revolution, meant our continuous decline. As I lay in hospital in 1918, I went through the revolution in Bavaria. From the very beginning I saw it as a crisis in the development of the German people, as a period of transition. Life always tears humanity apart. It is, therefore, the noblest task of a leader to find ideals that are stronger than the factors which pull people apart. I recognised, even while in hospital, that new ideas must be sought conducive to reconstruction. I found them in Nationalism, in the value of personality, in the denial of reconciliation between nations, in the strength and power of individual personality... .

Now we are facing the last election. No matter what the outcome, there will be no retreat, even if the coming election does not bring about a decision. If the election does not decide, the decision must be brought about in one way or another by other means. I have intervened in order to give the people once more the chance of deciding their fate for themselves. This determination is a strong asset for whatever may happen later. If the election brings no result, well, Germany will not be ruined. Today, as never before, everyone is under an obligation to pledge themselves to success. The need to make sacrifices has never been greater than now. As for the economy, I have only one wish—that together with the internal political structure it may look forward to a calm future. The question of the restoration of the armed forces will not be decided at Geneva but in Germany, when we have gained internal strength through internal peace. There will, however, be no internal peace until Marxism is eliminated. Here lies the decision which we must face up to, hard as the struggle may be. I put my life into this struggle day after day as do all those who have joined me in it. There are only two possibilities: either to resist the opponent by constitutional means, and for this purpose, once again, the election is necessary; or the struggle will be conducted with other weapons, which may demand greater sacrifices. I would like to see them avoided. I hope therefore that the German people recognize the greatness of the hour. It will be decisive for the next ten or probably even the next hundred years. It will prove a turning-point in German history, to which I pledge myself with burning energy.

Göring concluded the meeting by pointing out that 'the sacrifices asked for would be the easier for industry to bear if it was realised that the election of 5 March would certainly be the last for the next ten years, probably even for the next hundred years'. Industry responded generously.

In the meantime, Göring through his control of the Prussian administration and police, had taken the initiative against the Nazis' opponents. A purge was carried out among the numerous SPD, Centre and Liberal police chiefs, and in the provincial administration in general. Even those who were not immediately affected were clearly intimidated. Moreover, on 17 February Göring issued the following order to the police throughout Prussia:

90

I assume that it is unnecessary to point out especially that the police must in all circumstances avoid giving even the appearance of a hostile attitude, still less the impression of persecuting the patriotic associations [the Nazi Storm Detachments and the Stahlhelm]. I expect all police authorities to maintain the best relations with these organisations which comprise the most important constructive forces of the State. Patriotic activities and propaganda are to be supported by every means. Police restrictions and impositions must be used only in the most urgent cases.

The activities of subversive organisations are on the contrary to be combated with the most drastic methods. Communist terrorist acts and attacks are to be proceeded against with all severity, and weapons must be used ruthlessly when necessary. Police officers who in the execution of this duty use their firearms will be supported by me without regard to the effect of their shots; on the other hand, officers who fail from a false sense of consideration may expect disciplinary measures.

The protection of the patriotic population, which has been continually hampered in its activities, demands the most drastic application of the legal regulations against banned demonstrations, illegal assemblies, looting, instigation to treason and sedition, mass strikes, risings, press offences, and the other punishable acts of the disturbers of order. Every official must constantly bear in mind that failure to act is more serious than errors committed in acting. I expect and hope that all officers feel themselves at one with me in the aim of saving our fatherland from the ruin which threatens it by strengthening and unifying the patriotic forces.

On 22 February, he authorised the employment of SA and SS men and Stahlhelmers as auxiliary police, to give them official status, to put pressure on the police, and also as a means of controlling them. They were issued with armbands and firearms and were officially placed under the authority of the police. But since they were employed as units rather than individuals, they were in fact able to act to a large extent independently, particularly since they could claim to be the true representatives of the new regime.

The Left was uncertain how to respond to the new developments. It was bedevilled by the split between Communists and Social Democrats. The Trade Unions had been undermined by three or more years of mass unemployment so that the prospects for a general strike along the lines of that which had helped defeat the Kapp putsch in 1920 were not encouraging. The Left had no previous experience of a totalitarian dictatorship and many underestimated the repression it would involve; they assumed the party would survive as it had during Bismarck's anti-Socialist Law of 1878–1890. Many believed that the regime would be dominated by Hugenberg and the reactionaries rather than the Nazis and saw it as a sign of the death throes of the capitalist system. They thought it would not last long and by sharpening class tension would bring forward the revolution. Also, there was the problem of choosing the right moment to resist. The Government had, after all, been installed according to the letter of the Constitution and, during its first phase, it operated under the appearance of legality. The SPD leadership were anxious not to be provoked into unconstitutional actions which would give the Government the excuse to crush the movement. Finally, although some among the rank and file were keen to resist the regime by violence if necessary, the SPD leadership had long become accustomed to working along peaceful and constitutional lines. They were temperamentally unsuited to lead a campaign of violent resistance, particularly after the demoralising political experience of the previous three years, a campaign which was in any case unlikely to succeed and would spill much blood.

Some of these considerations emerged in the discussions of a meeting of the SPD Executive Committee and representatives of the Free Trade Unions held on 5 February:

91

Wels [SPD] declares that he summoned the meeting with representatives of the Trade Unions to discuss what measures of defence should be taken. There were repeated enquiries from the factories as to when they should stop work. The comrades had been calmed down but there had been a lot of discussion in the factories about a united front [with the Communists]. Arrests and newspaper bans were increasing and there was the danger that some particular incident might start the ball rolling...We knew that we were far from being anxious and from acting rashly, but we had to come to an agreement about what might have to be done. If there was a general strike then there would be no question of elections. If the avalanche starts we must try and guide it into our channels...

Leipart [Trade Union leader]...He had to raise the question of what our aim would be in a general strike. Those workers who were now in employment would be afraid of losing their jobs. There would, therefore, not be much enthusiasm for a general strike. They would probably follow our call.

Then one should bear in mind that the Nazis were in a strong position with their SA which would probably occupy the factories in the event of a strike. If the only goal we could proclaim was: We're calling a general strike to re-establish constitutional conditions that would probably not be enough and it is questionable whether we would have any other slogans.

And even if the Communist workers joined in, there would still be a certain split in the movement because we would be fighting for the Constitution and the Communists against it...He came...to the conclusion that we should still wait until an open breach of the Constitution has occurred.

Stampfer [SPD]...He is not so opposed to a limited general strike of about a day. But that will only be possible if there is a prior agreement with the Communists. We will then have to tell them straight out that our aim is not the establishment of a Soviet Germany.

Grassmann [SPD] considers that if we were to follow Stampfer's advice we might as well pack up. Nothing at all would come of a discussion with the Communists...

Wels: The discussion has shown that our views are in complete agreement and that everyone is of the opinion that we must put ourselves at the head of the movement.

The Nazis' increasing intimidation of their opponents, particularly of the Left had its effects:

92

24.ii.33: Grzesinski (former SPD Police-President in Berlin)
to the SPD Secretaries Franz Klupsch (Dortmund),
Paul Röhle (Frankfurt am Main), Paul Bugdahn (Altona)
and Richard Hansen (Kiel) on the need to cancel meetings.

Dear Comrade,

The incidents of the past few days in the meetings of those comrades who might be called prominent have prompted the Party committee this morning to examine the question whether, in the interests of our audiences, it would not be better to withdraw these speakers, of which I am one, for the time being. Several of my meetings have been disrupted and a considerable section of the audience had to be taken away badly injured. In agreement with the Party committee, I therefore request the cancellation of meetings with me as speaker. As things are, there is obviously no longer any police protection sufficient to check the aggressive actions of the SA and SS at my meetings... .

The following letters were from members of the SPD in Hanover:
17 February 1933

93

I hereby return my membership card and signify my resignation from the Party.

I am and remain a 'religious socialist'. Under the pressure of circumstances the SPD, even against its will, will be pushed aside and into the methods of left-wing radicalism. On the other hand, pressure from the opposite side will grow. The only thing left for me to do in all conscience as a teacher, a Christian, and a German is to try to evade the double pressure and, as ten years ago, try to live for my job, my family and my books, without being a member of a party.

Yours faithfully, GEORGE M.

9 March 1933

In accordance with Paragraph 9 of the organisation statutes, I hereby signify my resignation and that of my wife with immediate effect.... .

As a civil servant I have to make a choice. On the one hand, I see how the tendency is growing on the part of my employer, the Reich, not to tolerate those employees belonging to anti-Government associations. On the other hand, there is my loyalty to the Party. Unfortunately, I see no other solution but my resignation. The existence of my family is at stake. If the fate of unemployment, which in my experience can be *very, very* hard, is unavoidable, I need not reproach myself for not have done everything in the interests of my wife and child.

HANS J.

Then, on 27 February, a week before the election, the Reichstag building was set on fire and a young Dutch Communist named van der Lubbe was caught apparently red-handed in the building. The fire came very conveniently for the Nazis who could use it to claim the Communists were plotting revolution and so justify wholesale arrests. So convenient was it that many have thought it probable that the Nazis themselves started the fire and blamed it on the Communist van der Lubbe whom they used as a dupe. Other historians, however, have denied this and argued that van der Lubbe acted alone. The controversy continues and will probably never be satisfactorily resolved. One contemporary witness was the police chief in charge of the investigation, Rudolf Diels, the head of the Prussian political police soon to become known as the Gestapo. Looking back after the war he wrote:

94

...When I pushed my way into the burning building with Schneider, we had to climb over the bulging hoses of the Berlin fire brigade, although, as yet, there were few onlookers. A few officers of my department were already engaged in interrogating Marinus van der Lubbe. Naked from the waist upwards, smeared with dirt and sweating, he sat in front of them, breathing heavily. He panted as if he had completed a tremendous task. There was a wild triumphant gleam in the burning eyes of his pale, haggard young face. I sat opposite him in the police headquarters several times that night and listened to his confused stories. I read the Communist pamphlets he carried in his trouser pockets. They were of the kind which in those days were publicly distributed everywhere. And from the primitive hieroglyphics of his diary I tried to follow his trips down to the Balkans.

The voluntary confessions of Marinus van der Lubbe prevented me from thinking that an arsonist who was such an expert in his folly needed any helpers. Why should not a single match be enough to set fire to the cold yet inflammable splendour of the Chamber, the old upholstered furniture, the heavy curtains, and the bone-dry wooden panelling! But this specialist had used a whole knapsack full of inflammable material. He had been so active that he had laid several dozen fires. With a firelighter, the 'Industrious Housewife', he had set the Chamber aflame. Then he had rushed through the big corridors with his burning shirt which he brandished in his right hand like a torch to lay more fires under the old leather sofas. During this hectic activity he was overpowered by Reichstag officials.

He also confessed to several smaller arson attacks in Berlin, the mysterious cause of which had aroused the attention of the Criminal Investigation Department. Several details suggested that Communist arsonists who had helped him in Neukölln and the Berlin Town Hall might have helped him with the Reichstag. The interrogating officers had pointed their investigations in this direction. But meanwhile things of a quite different nature had happened.

Shortly after my arrival in the burning Reichstag, the National Socialist elite had arrived. Hitler and Goebbels had driven up in their large cars; Göring, Frick and Helldorf[36] arrived; Daluege, the police chief, was not there.

One of Hitler's chief adjutants came to look for me in the maze of corridors, now alive with the fire brigade and the police. He passed me Göring's order to appear in the select circle. On a balcony jutting out into the Chamber, Hitler and his trusty followers were assembled. Hitler stood leaning his arms on the stone parapet of the balcony and stared silently into the red sea of flames. The first hysterics were already over. As I entered, Göring came towards me. His voice was heavy with the emotion of the dramatic moment: 'This is the beginning of the Communist revolt, they will start their attack now! Not a moment must be lost!'

Göring could not continue. Hitler turned to the assembled company. Now I saw that his face was purple with agitation and with the heat gathering in the dome. He shouted uncontrollably, as I had never seen him do before, as if he was going to burst: 'There will be no mercy now. Anyone who stands in our way will be cut down. The German people will not tolerate leniency. Every Communist official will be shot where he is found. The Communist deputies must be hanged this very night. Everybody in league with the Communists must be arrested. There will no longer by any leniency for Social Democrats either.'

I reported on the results of the first interrogations of Marinus van der Lubbe—that in my opinion he was a maniac. But with this opinion I had come to the wrong man; Hitler ridiculed my childish view: 'That is something really cunning, prepared a long time ago. The criminals have thought all this out beautifully; but they've miscalculated, haven't they, Comrades! These gangsters have no idea to what extent the people are on our side. They don't hear the rejoicing of the crowds in their rat holes, from which they now want to emerge', and so it went on.

I pulled Göring aside; but he did not let me start. 'Police on an emergency footing; shoot to kill; and any other emergency regulations which might be

---

[36] Count Wolf von Helldorf, the Berlin SA Chief.

appropriate in such a case.' I said again that a police radio message would be sent to all police stations in his name, putting the police in a state of alert and ordering the arrest of those Communist officials whose imprisonment had been intended for some time in the event of a ban on the Party. Göring was not listening: 'No Communist and no Social Democrat traitor must be allowed to escape us' were his last words. When I met Schneider again I tried to collect my thoughts:

'This is a mad-house, Schneider, but apart from that the time has come: all Communist and Social Democrat officials are to be arrested, big raids, a state of alert and all that goes with it!'

Schneider forgot the Social Democrats when he passed on Göring's order as a radio message. When I returned to the 'Alex'[37] after midnight it was buzzing like a beehive. The alerted operational battalions of the police stood lined up in long rows in the entrance drives with steel helmets and rifles. While squad vans arrived and whole troops of detectives with registers prepared many years before jumped on the ramps, joined by uniformed officers, the first cars were arriving back at the entrance of the building with dazed prisoners who had been woken up from their sleep...

Whoever was responsible, the Nazis exploited their opportunity to the full. Yet it appears the measures which followed were not carefully planned and coordinated but were rather spontaneous and largely irrational responses to an imagined threat of a Communist uprising. The arrests of the Communists, for example, were carried out on the basis of lists drawn up by the political police before 1933 and they were not as successful as was subsequently claimed. In fact, the Nazis had hoped to postpone the elimination of the Communists until after the election when they would be in a stronger position to deal with them. But their fear of an uprising prompted them to take precipitate and drastic action which resulted not only in these arrests, but in the most important single legislative act of the Third Reich, the Decree of the Reich President for the Protection of People and State, of 28 February 1933.

The origins of this decree are not entirely clear. It appears the original impulse came from a German Nationalist, Ludwig Grauert, a top official in the Prussian Ministry of the Interior. During the night of the 27th, wishing to legalise the arrests, Grauert suggested an 'emergency decree against arson and terrorist acts'. Hitler accepted and put it on the agenda of the Reich Cabinet meeting to be held the following day. Both Grauert and Hitler probably conceived the decree as a purely defensive measure directed specifically against the Communists. Before the Cabinet meeting, however, the Reich Minister of the Interior, Frick, redrafted the measure. Under the Weimar Constitution the powers of the Reich Minister of the Interior were restricted as the state governments had direct authority over the police and internal administration. Frick decided to use the opportun-

---

[37] The police headquarters in the Alexanderplatz.

ity presented by this decree to strengthen his control over the states, basing the new decree on the Prussian decree of 20 July 1932 which had legalised the *coup* against the Social Democrat/Centre Party Government and thereby giving it a far wider scope than originally intended. Article 2 enabled Frick, as Reich Minister of the Interior, to take over power in the states and, unlike Papen's Prussian decree of July 1932, the Reich Government, not the Reich President decided when Article 2 should be applied. This Article was to be of crucial importance in the seizure of power in the states during the first half of March. No less important was Article 1. This represented 'a kind of *coup d'état*' (Mommsen) and the suspension of civil rights which it contained provided a quasi-legal foundation for the regime of terror and intimidation which was to follow. In particular, it provided the legal warrant for the expedient of 'protective custody' used by the Gestapo to imprison without trial:

95

By the authority of Section 48 (2) of the German Constitution the following is decreed as a defensive measure against Communist acts of violence endangering the State:
1. Sections 114, 115, 117, 118, 123, 124 and 153 of the Constitution of the German Reich are suspended until further notice. Thus restrictions on personal liberty, on the right of free expression of opinion, including freedom of the press, on the right of assembly and association, and violations of the privacy of postal, telegraphic and telephonic communications, and warrants for house-searches, orders for confiscations as well as restrictions on property rights are permissible beyond the legal limits otherwise prescribed.
2. If in any German state the measures necessary for the restoration of public security and order are not taken, the Reich Government may temporarily take over the powers of the supreme authority in such a state in order to restore security.
3. States and local authorities have to comply to the limits of their responsibilities with the orders issued by the Government of the Reich under the powers conferred on it by Paragraph 2... .

Although the Government failed to produce any concrete evidence of a Communist plot, its propaganda had a receptive audience among the middle class. Frau Solmitz recorded in her diary:

96

1.iii.33
...The Reich Government spoke....Göring, like an old greying civil servant, reported dryly and very gravely the dreadful murder plans of the Communists—

who have withdrawn into the stronghold of Hamburg. It started with the going over of the Karl Liebknecht House, where a whole system of underground tunnels was discovered, as well as galleries above ground....Proof was brought to light by the hundredweight. Hostages from bourgeois circles, wives and children of police officers were to be taken and used as shields, all cultural monuments were to be destroyed as in Russia: palaces, museums, churches. They started with the Reichstag. Fire broke out in twenty-eight places. All the Communist Party leaders have been taken into custody. Thälmann has fled to Copenhagen. They wanted to send armed gangs to murder and start fires in the villages; in the meantime terrorism was to take over the big cities stripped of their police forces. Poison, boiling water, every tool from the most refined to the most primitive, were to be used as weapons. It would sound like a fairy tale of robbers—if it wasn't for Russia having experienced methods and orgies of torture which a German mind, even when sick, is incapable of devising, and, when healthy, is unable to believe.

If Italy, America and England were wise, they should send us money to fight Bolshevism—our ruin will be their ruin!

Göring said he had not lost his nerve nor would he lose it. I hope the voters won't lose their nerve and stay away from the polling booths out of fright. The streets really are dangerous these days.

In the Reichstag election on 5 March 1933 the Nazis won 288 seats compared with 196 in the November 1932 election and increased their percentage of the vote from 33.1 to 43.9. They had still failed to win an absolute majority. The Nationalists had gained only one seat, winning 52, and their percentage of the heavy poll of 88 per cent had declined slightly. Although the Government coalition between Nazis and Nationalists had a bare overall majority of 51.7 per cent, this was insufficient to pass an Enabling Act for which a two-thirds majority was necessary.

The opposition parties maintained their position remarkably well, particularly in view of such difficult circumstances. The Catholic Centre actually gained three seats, winning 73, and its percentage of the larger poll declined only slightly. The SPD lost only one seat, still retaining 120, and their proportion of the poll declined by only 2 per cent. It was significant that in Prussia, where the impact of the new regime had had most effect as a result of Göring's ruthless measures, Nazi success was more limited. In the State Diet election which took place on the same day as the Reichstag election the Nazis only managed to increase their vote from 36.3 per cent to 43.2 per cent and to win 49 additional seats. Here the Nationalists managed to win 12 more seats, which suggests that some people hoped to strengthen the Conservative wing of the coalition in the light of their experience with Göring and the Nazis. In the south German states Nazi electoral success was most striking notably in Bavaria. Here the anti-Bolshevist campaign paid dividends with conservative rural voters. This breakthrough allowed the Nazis to demand that the south German states adjust their politics to the new regime.

(ii) The Seizure of Power in the States and the SA/Party 'Revolution from Below' of March 1933

On 21 February 1933, while covering the election campaign, *The Times* correspondent in Germany had remarked on 'the starkness of the contrast between conditions in Prussia and in states where the Reich Government have not yet taken charge of the State affairs, or where the Nazis have not yet obtained local control'. The majority of the federal states were not yet controlled by the Nazis, and here the authorities which had responsibility for the police and for public order in general endeavoured to maintain an attitude of neutrality towards the various conflicting forces and to preserve the basic liberties.

The Nazis, determined to remove this contrast between Prussia and the other states, proceeded to exploit the momentum created by the election campaign to seize power in the states. They combined intimidation from below by mass action on the part of the Party and the SA with pressure from above by Frick and the Reich Ministry of the Interior. The SA created disorder, usually culminating in the hoisting of the swastika on the town hall. The local Party leadership then requested the Reich Ministry of the Interior to intervene as the existing state authorities were incapable of maintaining order and showed insufficient sympathy with the new Reich Government. The Reich Minister of the Interior then appointed a leading local Nazi as a Reich Police Commissioner as explicitly provided for in the Presidential Decree of 28 February and local Nazis could then intimidate the state governments into resignation and form Nazi governments.

The first state to experience this technique was Hamburg, where it occurred just before the election. The process began with Frick's demand for a ban on the SPD newspaper, the *Hamburg Echo*. A Nationalist senator, Paul de Chapeaurouge, wrote in complaint to Papen on 9 March:

97

...On the morning of 3 March, the Social Democrat senators resigned from the Senate because they did not want to consent to the ban on the *Echo* contemplated by the Reich Government. The remaining bourgeois senators pronounced this ban, which was undoubtedly permissible by law, as their first official act.

After the resignation of the Social Democrat senators, I, as the previous deputy police chief, had to take over the police. I knew that I had taken on a very difficult office. But I had no idea that my administration would prove as difficult as it at once became owing to the activities of the Reich Ministry of the Interior....

After the resignation of the Social Democrat senators, the Senate's first duty was to continue to carry out its functions in accordance with a strict observance of the Constitution and the laws until the new election, and to try its best to achieve an early election [of the senate]. This I was determined to do. The Reich Government had the clear duty of supporting the Senate as the official organ of legal power. In my opinion, the Reich Ministry of the Interior, which is mainly responsible for relations with the states, failed in its task. To a large extent it bears the responsibility for the developments in Hamburg. The city was quite calm; according to absolutely reliable information given to the police, no serious disturbance of public order was to be expected from the Left. The course of events has proved the correctness of this opinion held by the police authorities.

Unrest occurred in Hamburg only because a few authorities, especially the *Gau* leadership of the NSDAP, sent alarmist reports to Berlin and caused the Reich Minister of the Interior to ask the Senate officially to transfer the command of the police to the former police lieutenant, Richter.[38] This suggestion was apparently passed on from Berlin simultaneously to the NSDAP and the press. In Hamburg it was underlined by wild press articles and by pressure on the members of the Senate in personal discussions in a most questionable way, and thus the situation was aggravated.

The course which the Senate should have followed was laid down in the Constitution. According to the Constitution and the law, it was unable to meet the request which had been made. In my opinion, since the election to the Senate was obviously to take place shortly, it was the Reich Minister's duty to urge the *Gau* leadership of the NSDAP, which prided itself on its constant contact with the Ministry, to maintain law and order so that the Constitution and the law would not be broken before the forthcoming election. But, so far as I could observe events, there were no such attempts at persuasion. Despite the alarmist press articles, Hamburg remained completely peaceful; only the police, among whom the NSDAP had begun an active propaganda campaign some time before, began to waver.[39]...

...The Hamburg events were, in my opinion, determined by the NSDAP's intention, known to me since 3 March, of gaining control of the police before the election of the Senate. This aim could not be achieved owing to the present legal position in Hamburg. Therefore, the NSDAP tried to reach their goal via the Reich. Owing to the fact that the NSDAP did not want to wait over the police question, circumstances have developed in Hamburg which are very regrettable from the point of view of police discipline and public order in the future.

The fact was noted that the final order of the Reich Minister of the Interior to the Senate to give the command of the police to Police Lieutenant Richter apparently reached the *Gau* headquarters of the NSDAP before it reached the Senate. Furthermore, the way in which Gauleiter Kaufman and Harry Hennigsen, [NSDAP] member of the city council, conveyed the order of the Reich Ministry of the Interior to the Senate was in no way appropriate to the importance and gravity of the moment.

It is my firm conviction that, if the Reich Ministry of the Interior had used its full authority to persuade the NSDAP to keep the peace, Hamburg would have been spared the events of 5 March, so constitutionally and politically unsatisfactory. The

---

[38] An SA leader.
[39] A section of the police sympathetic to the Nazis hoisted the swastika on the town hall.

situation now is that, contrary to the solemn promises of the Reich Government, an interference in Hamburg's sovereignty has taken place which could have been avoided and is undesirable from the point of view of the initial work on the Reich reform... .

I must add a few personal remarks: I regard the procedure of the Reich Ministry of the Interior towards Hamburg as at the same time an injustice towards myself. The Reich Ministry knows who I am and where I stand politically and as a soldier. I met State Secretary Pfundtner only a few weeks ago at a dinner of the local Nationalist Club, of which I have been a member since its foundation, given in honour of the presence of His Royal Highness the Duke of Coburg-Gotha. In former times there was a way by which a German officer, a German graduate could take the law into his own hands. Today, unfortunately, I have to confine myself to asking you, Vice-Chancellor, to inform the Reich Government of my letter in the hope that they will then adopt the correct attitude towards me... .

During the next few days, all the other states were taken over in a similar fashion. The most important state, Prussia, was already effectively under the control of the new regime. The administration had already been purged of Social Democrats and Democrats after Papen's *coup* in July 1932. Although Papen as Reich Commissioner for Prussia was theoretically superior to Göring as Minister of the Interior, in practice Papen did not interfere because at this stage Göring's activities were directed against the Left. Furthermore, immediately after the appointment of Hitler as Chancellor, on 6 February, all the representative bodies within Prussia were dissolved and new elections were ordered; on 5 March for the Landtag, on 13 March for the provincial and local councils.

The 'coordination' completed, the Nazis proceeded to provide more solid legal foundations for their power in the states. They ensured themselves a majority in the other state assemblies through a law of 31 March and, by a law of 7 April, appointed special Reich Governors (*Reichsstatthalter*) to the states, nearly all chosen from the senior Gauleiters in the area.

The pressure from below erupted into an orgy of violence against the Party's opponents, particularly those on the Left. This violence may have been initiated from above or largely spontaneous, but it rapidly began to get out of control. It represented the unleashing of all the frustration of the SA and local Party organisations during the pre-1933 period caused by the need to follow a policy of strict legality. The Party's rank and file saw at last the possibility of taking revenge on their opponents and of acquiring the prizes of power. As far as they were concerned, it was now their state and they were not in a mood for compromise or half measures. During the following weeks trade union offices were smashed and Social Democrat officials were 'arrested' by SA men, cruelly beaten up and dragged off to hastily improvised concentration camps. The SA and local Party officials also seized the opportunity to exploit their position by intimidating Business into giving them employment in one form or another. A kind of protection racket developed. The following account by the first head of the Gestapo, Rudolf Diels, gives a good impression of the confusion and violence which characterised the first months of the allegedly peaceful national uprising:

98

The uprising of the Berlin SA electrified the remotest parts of the country. Around many big cities in which the authority of the police had been transferred to the local SA leaders, revolutionary activities took place beyond the periphery of these cities throughout the whole area of their regiments [*Standarten*] and groups. The higher the rank of these police-presidents, the farther afield extended the noisy abuses of these parhelions of the revolution. In Lower Silesia, the SA Gruppenführer [Edmund Heines] carried on a regime of violence from Breslau. In the North Rhineland, SS Gruppenführer Weitzel, the newly appointed police president of Düsseldorf, displayed violent radicalism together with the SA leader Lobck; in Essen and the cities of the Ruhr area, the SA of Terboven[40] held sway.

In East Prussia, Gauleiter Koch had allowed neither the SA nor the SS to come to power. Here the political leaders ruled. They were opposed to the 'reactionary' elements. The country was in a sort of state of war in which the aristocracy, as the imagined enemy, had to put up with a flood of arrests. From Stettin, the example of the SS Standartenführer, Engel, encouraged the Pomeranian SA to terrorise the country. From the cities of Rostock, Stargard and Greifswald, cases of beatings up were reported in which Communists and Social Democrats had been subjected to mock drownings and hangings. The torments had cost some victims their lives. In Silesia, the Rhineland, Westphalia and the Ruhr area unauthorised arrests, insubordination to the police, forcible entry into public buildings, disturbance of the work of the authorities, the smashing up of dwellings and nightly raids had begun before the Reichstag fire at the end of February... .

It was no longer possible to tell which public or private spheres had been penetrated by the SA, and scarcely possible to guess the purposes for which it allowed itself to be hired and employed. There was hardly a single business undertaking which had not employed an 'old fighter' of the SA for protection against the dangers of coordination, denunciation and threats. They were present everywhere as self-appointed directors, special commissars and SA delegates... .

...No order and no instruction exists for the establishment of the concentration camps; they were not established, one day they were simply there. The SA leaders put up 'their' camps because they did not want to trust the police with their prisoners or because the prisons were overcrowded. No information about many of these *ad hoc* camps ever got as far as Berlin. Years after my departure from Berlin I heard of the existence of some camps of which I had no knowledge in 1933. We first heard of a camp in Kemma in the Ruhr area through the foreign press. It was the

[40] Josef Terboven, Gauleiter of Essen 1928–45.

American journalist Lochner who informed the state police office that the [SA] group leader Heines had established a concentration camp near Dürrgoy in Silesia... .

In the state of Brunswick, where the Nazis had formed a coalition government with the Nationalists since 1930, relations between the Nazis and their opponents had always been particularly bad. The Nazis now took their revenge, as the following account published by the SPD in exile indicates:

99

From 3 March 1933 the atmosphere in the town and the countryside became unbearable. One brawl after another. There were growing rumours that the *Volksfreund*—the [SPD] Party, trade union and publishing house building of the workers—was to be raided by National Socialists. All demonstrations were banned. On 9 March at 11 a.m. a fight started between an SS member, obviously sent out for the purpose of provocation, and a member of the *Reichsbanner*. At about 12 noon a small police car appeared in front of the *Volksfreund* building with about ten policemen and the SS man who was alleged to have been beaten up. They searched the *Volksfreund* for the member of the *Reichsbanner* who had taken part in the fight and who, according to them, was in the building. The search of course was fruitless.

At about 3 p.m. the [SPD] parliamentary group of the provincial diet held a meeting. Meanwhile the SA and the SS continued their activities of the previous day; under the eyes of the authorities they hoisted swastika flags on public buildings. The Nazis also tore a large poster off the boathouse of the *Reichsbanner* in the presence of the police and carried it through the town, heading for the *Volksfreund*.

There, lorries with SA and SS had driven up at 4.05 p.m. The porter promptly closed the doors. But the Nazis broke the big display windows and pushed into the building through the holes. They opened fire inside the building with a number of rifles and revolvers. During this, the 28-year-old salesman, Hans Saile, the advertising manager of the Advertising Union, Berlin, was killed by a shot in the stomach. He had received an order from his superiors to leave the threatened district of Brunswick and to travel to Saarbrücken on the same day... .

The intruders rushed up the stairs and smashed in the locked doors with their rifle butts. Union secretaries, employees, typists, Co-op salesgirls were all driven together with cudgels, rifles, revolvers and daggers. Then, with the order 'Hands up!', they were locked up for hours, before being released with kicks and slaps.

Although the leadership of the organisation had endeavoured for weeks to remove important and valuable material and funds from the building, they did not succeed in securing all the money, books and documents in time. So several thousand Reichsmarks were confiscated by the intruders on their own authority. The whole building was searched for valuables. Then the swastika flag was hoisted. A certain worker, A.P., had hidden behind a cupboard as the Nazis broke in. He had seen from there how the account books had been destroyed in childish vandalism. He had heard the men grumbling that their booty of money and valuables had been far too small. A.P. was discovered, badly beaten up and then thrown out of the building.

The former police lieutenant, Richard Neuenfeldt, now a driver with the *Volksfreund*, who lived in the *Volksfreund* apartment building, Oelschlägern 27 in Brunswick, was busy doing car repairs in the yard at the outset of the occupation. He was recognised and beaten on his head and face with cudgels, steel pipes, revolver butts and metal tools until he collapsed unconscious. Even then he was kicked, dragged across the yard and thrown out. Neuenfeldt is an ex-serviceman, who served at the front and fought right through the war. Those who beat him up—a typical case that was repeated countless times—were 20-year-old boys. As a result of this beating up, Neuenfeldt is a broken man, physically and mentally.

During the course of the action, the private tenants of the *Volksfreund* building were raided in their flats, abused, threatened with weapons and beaten up.

The regular police had meanwhile blocked off the surrounding streets with a strong force. The Nazis looted the building in front of their very eyes. They destroyed the furniture and equipment. Anything that was movable they dragged out into the yard. Documents, pieces of furniture, valuable administrative material, the book supplies of the *Volksfreund* bookshop, many hundredweight of expensive propaganda film, records, account books, and flags were heaped up on a pyre and set alight. The fire burned for three days and nights.

Immediately after the raid on the building, Comrade Dr Heinrich Jasper, the former Minister-President of Brunswick, rang up the Police-President from the diet and informed him of what had happened. He accused the solicitor and deputy, Alpers, leader of the SS in Brunswick, of armed riot, unlawful assembly, housebreaking and disturbance of public order.

Police-President Lieff replied that these actions were completely legal. Deputy Alpers had been provided with a police warrant for this action.

After this phone call, the regular police units were withdrawn from the *Volksfreund*, so Alpers's hordes had a free hand.

After that, Comrade Dr Jasper got in touch with Nazi Minister Klagges and sought redress. Klagges replied that he knew nothing of these events. Jasper should file a written complaint in the usual way. He refused to intervene before the complaint had been dealt with.

There was of course no redress. On the contrary, Alpers became Minister of Justice [in Brunswick] under the Hitler regime.[41]

In the evening of this eventful day the city of Brunswick resembled a military camp. Hundreds of heavily armed Nazi patrols marched through the town, chased passers-by and beat up members of the public. In the course of this a member of the National Air Association was shot dead. The young man had allegedly raised only one hand on being told to put his hands up... .

The bourgeois papers in Brunswick reported the occupation the following morning. According to them it had been carried out quite legally, for the building had been a centre of unrest for a long time. Moreover, it was alleged that masses of

---

[41]Dr Jasper was soon afterwards arrested and sent to Dachau concentration camp where he later died of ill-treatment.

treasonable material and ammunition had been found. Not one of these statements is true... .

Such violence was not peculiar to Brunswick. It occurred throughout Germany, thogh not uniformly. Many towns escaped it. State violence in the form of police arrests and party violence in the form of SA thuggery directed largely at the Left proved a lethal combination, destroying its organisations, intimidating its members and thereby undermining both the ability and the will to resist.

In the course of this violence, a number of foreigners, particular Jews, were molested, producing protests from their diplomatic representatives. The Government became concerned about the excesses of the 'revolution from below' over which they appeared to have little control. Hitler in particular seemed torn between loyalty to his followers, with whose actions against their opponents he entirely sympathised, and the need not to alienate the conservative elites and in particular the President. On 10 March he appealed for an end to the violence, distinguishing between 'legitimate' and 'illegitimate' violence, as a gesture to demonstrate to conservative opinion at home and to foreign opinion the good intentions of the Government.

100

Comrades, SA and SS men! A revolution has taken place in Germany. It is the result of hard struggles, the greatest tenacity, but also the tightest discipline. Unscrupulous characters, mainly Communist spies, are trying to compromise the Party by individual actions which have no relation to the great work of the national uprising, but could discredit and detract from the achievements of our movement. In particular, they try to bring the Party or Germany into conflict with foreign countries by molesting foreigners and cars with foreign flags. SA and SS men, you yourselves must immediately stop such creatures and take them to task. Furthermore, you must hand them over to the police, whoever they may be.

From this day onwards the National Government has executive power throughout Germany. The further progress of the national uprising will therefore be guided and planned from the top. Only where these orders are resisted or where individuals or marching columns are ambushed must this resistance be crushed, as before, thoroughly and immediately. The molesting of individuals, the obstruction or disturbance of business life, must cease on principle. You, Comrades, must see to it that the national revolution of 1933 cannot be compared in history with the revolution of the knapsack Spartacists in 1918. Apart from this, do not be deterred for a second from our watchword. It is: The extermination of Marxism.

Its effect was to a large extent neutralised by a speech made by Göring on the same day in Essen in which he declared: 'For years past we have told the people: 'You can settle accounts with the traitors.' We stand by our word. Accounts are being settled'. Hitler was obliged to reaffirm his appeal in a broadcast on the 12th which appears to have had some effect. The situation remained confused. As Rudolf Diels indicates, the SA and SS continued to act as independent powers with complete disregard for the police and the administration under Göring, confident that in the last resort the Führer would protect them against proceedings:

101

At the beginning of October we heard that in Esterwegen and Papenburg prisoners had been shot while escaping....I was refused access to the Esterwegen camp by the SS. I had announced my visit to the camp a week before. But Göring's order, which I had to show, had not impressed the SS. When I appeared at the entrance of the camp, as far as they were concerned I was a civilian without position or rank in their mighty organisation. Only when Weitzel, the SS group leader in Düsseldorf, had given the commandant permission by telephone was I allowed to enter the camp.

The Papenburg camp granted me admission. But what can an 'inspection' of such an institution reveal? The prisoners' replies to the questions put by the inspector are determined by the fear of displeasing their tormentors in whose power the prisoners remain. The food is always adequate and the shining cleanliness of floors and barracks and the scrupulous tidiness of the beds do not tell that they are a means of tormenting the inmates. Nobody can see in the ridiculous straightness of the freshly raked expanses of sand that a violation of such orderliness means 'bunker' and corporal punishment. In Papenburg the unusual happened; a few of the prisoners' spokesmen 'let themselves go'. They not only complained of the food, but they made it clear that they had been subjected to ill-treatment.

In Papenburg, the mayor too had told me of the excesses of the SS towards the population. SS men roamed through the district pillaging like the Swedes in the Thirty Years War. They 'confiscated' arrested people who had incurred their displeasure and started brawls with the youths of the surrounding villages.

My visit had also encouraged the *Regierungspräsident*[42] in Osnabrück to inform me of the misdeeds of the SS in the camp.

Then, just at the right time, came a serious complaint by a Cologne lawyer, Dr Pünder, made to the Reich Minister of the Interior, Frick, on behalf of his brother, State Secretary Pünder, who was in the hands of the SS thugs in Papenburg. Frick had Pünder's complaint passed on to me and Gürtner[43] by *Oberregierungsrat* Erbe. Erbe promised me his support and Hanfstaengl[44] promised to work on Hitler. At the same time, the Chief Prosecutor Halm of Osnabrück had reported that investigations in the camps which he had wanted to undertake because of the ill-treatment of the innkeeper, Hillig, by SS men in Papenburg had been refused

---

[42]The senior government official for the area.
[43]The Minister of Justice.
[44]A German–American friend of Hitler's.

with severe threats. By-passing SS and Police Chief Daluege, I went with Joel, the public prosecutor, to Göring's representative, State Secretary Grauert. He gave us fifty Berlin police officers armed with carbines with whom Joel set off for Papenburg. A delegate sent by Joel was told that if the police approached the camp they would be received with machine guns. When Joel attempted to get into the camp, bullets flew round his ears. On his informing Grauert of this state of affairs, he was told to wait for further instructions. Meanwhile, Himmler had protested to Göring against the use of the police against the SS. Göring would have given in, had Joel not informed him that the SS were fraternising with the prisoners in the camp and were going to arm them. This brought a new element into the revolutionary situation. Mention of the mutinous SS put all other arguments in the shade. Göring asked me to report to Hitler in his presence on what had happened. Hitler ordered the 'take-over' of the camps by the police. When I had informed Grauert, he sent 200 Osnabrück police off to the Dutch border. But they had to make ready to lay siege, as it were, to the camps, especially as a representative of SS Group Leader Weitzel appeared on the scene and tried to intimidate the police officers with threats from Himmler. I now went to ask Hitler straight whether the police could not use force of arms against the SS. Hitler let me see him and after my renewed account of the excesses in the camps, he interrupted me in a military voice of command and ordered me to ask the Reich Defence Minister for army artillery, and to shoot up the camps, the SS and their prisoners without mercy. My colleagues were horrified when I arrived with this order from the Führer. It was clear to me that I could not take it seriously.

I asked my superior, *Ministerialdirektor* Fischer in the Ministry of the Interior, to negotiate with the mutinous SS about their 'demands' which, like freebooters, they had made the conditions of their departure. They had demanded coats, blankets, and back pay. After he had informed the SS, through an SS leader of Weitzel's, of the fulfilment of their demands, Joel took possession of the camps without bloodshed. He then spent some time in Papenburg to begin investigations into the violence of the SS guards.

...At this time Joel also went to Kemma near Wuppertal at Grauert's and my instigation. The SA had tortured the Communists there in a particularly 'original' way. They were forced to drink salty herring solution and then left to pant in vain for a sip of water throughout the hot summer days. One of my officers who had accompanied Joel reported that the SA there had also played the 'joke' of getting their prisoners to climb trees; they had to hang on in the treetops for hours on end and at certain intervals cry 'cuckoo'. The public prosecutor Winckler in Wuppertal, who proposed to act against the SA, had to flee with his wife and child from their threats. The *Regierungspräsident* Schmidt in Düsseldorf poured out his heart to me about the atrocities. With Joel, I succeeded in getting Göring to have the 'responsible' SA Group Leader relieved of his office, to ensure that Joel had a free hand in the prosecution of the SA guards. After a few months, Joel succeeded, despite the opposition of the Gauleiter Florian, in starting proceedings against the guilty SA men. But the struggle against Hitler, who finally terminated the proceedings, he was bound to lose... In reality, there were neither commands nor prohibitions. Before or after my reports to Göring and Hitler on acts of violence in the country, SA and SS leaders talked about the bravery of their men on the field of revolution. These acts were approved of and laughed over just as they were disapproved of when I represented them as excesses against the authority of the new state.... Already, the SA were breaking into the police prisons, to get hold of the Communist leaders who had been arrested after the Reichstag fire, and who, they intended, should be the victims of their special revenge. From the police headquarters they took the files which could incriminate their leaders; the frightened officials handed over what they were asked for.

This violence, directed primarily against the Left and mostly behind closed doors, was overlooked or rationalised by the middle class which referred to the crisis of the moment. Many were prepared to accept Göring's explanation that 'Where planing is going on there are bound to be shavings', the German equivalent of 'You can't make an omelette without breaking eggs'. Many felt the Left had it coming to them anyway. Even so, the official version of the take-over contrasted the 'bloodless national uprising' of 1933 with the allegedly 'bloody revolution' of November 1918.

The image of a glorious and bloodless national revolution was reinforced by the spectacle staged on 21 March in the garrison church at Potsdam, a Prussian shrine, to celebrate the opening of the new Reichstag session. Erich Ebermeyer, a dramatist and the son of the former chief public prosecutor at the Supreme Court in Leipzig, describes the scene and its impact on himself and his family. Their response is particularly significant because their general outlook was liberal and unsympathetic to Nazism:

102

The 'Day of Potsdam'. A sea of flags in all the streets. We too couldn't opt out. So I get the old black-white-red flag from the World War down from the loft and hoist it. The black-red-gold one, the good old disgraced, betrayed, and never properly respected thing has to go up to the loft in its place...

In the morning a broadcast of the ceremonies in Potsdam. All cleverly done, impressive, spell-binding even, at any rate for the masses. But we too cannot and must not shut our eyes in the face of what is going on. Today and here, the marriage took place, if not for ever then at least for a time, between the masses led by Hitler and the 'Spirit of Potsdam', Prussian values, represented by Hindenburg.

How marvellously it's been staged by that master producer Goebbels. The procession of Hindenburg, the Government, and the deputies goes from Berlin to Potsdam past a solid line of cheering millions. The whole of Berlin seems to be on the streets. Government and deputies walk from St Nicholas' Church to the Garrison Church together. The radio announcer almost weeps with emotion.

Then Hindenburg reads his speech. Plain, strong, coming from a simple heart and so presumably speaking to simple hearts. The very fact that there stands a man, who unites in himself generations of German history, who fought in 66, who was there at the Imperial Coronation in 71 in Versailles, who became a national hero between 14 and 18, from whom no lost battle and no lost world war can reduce his popularity among our peculiar people, whom, on the contrary, the defeat itself raised to a mythical state of glorification, who then as an old man once more took over the leadership of the Reich and even did so for a second time, and not out of vanity or a hunger for power but undoubtedly from a Prussian sense of duty—he now, soon to die, presides over the marriage of his world with the new rising one which the Austrian corporal, Hitler, represents.

Then Hitler speaks. It cannot be denied. He has grown in stature. Out of the demagogue and party leader, the fanatic and agitator—for his opponents surprisingly enough—a true statesman seems to be developing. So he is a genius in whose enigmatic soul lie unsuspected and unprecedented possibilities? The Government's declaration is marked by notable moderation. Not a word of hatred for the opposition, not a word of racial ideology, no threat aimed at home or abroad. Hitler says only what they want: the maintenance of the great traditions of our nation, firmness of government instead of eternal wavering, consideration for all the experiences of individual and human life which have proved useful for the welfare of mankind over thousands of years.

Hindenburg lays wreaths on the graves of the Prussian kings. The old Field Marshal shakes hands with the World War corporal. The corporal makes a deep bow over the hand of the Field Marshal. Cannons thunder over Potsdam—over Germany.

No-one can escape the emotion of the moment. Father too is deeply impressed. Mother has tears in her eyes... .

In the evening a quiet hour with M. He is completely unmoved by the day's events as if he was surrounded by a thick protective skin. He considers the whole thing simply a put up job, doesn't waver for one moment from his instinctive dislike. 'You've got it coming to you', says the 21 year old.

I remain silent, ashamed and torn.

(iii) The 'Coordination' of the Reichstag and of the Political Parties, March–June 1933

After coordinating the states, Hitler returned to his initial objectives of the destruction of the Reichstag as an effective institution, and the elimination of rival political parties. An Enabling Law would enable the Government to introduce legislative measures independently of the legislature, including alterations to the Constitution. This was not an entirely new concept in German politics. Enabling Laws had been introduced during the Weimar Republic, notably those of 13 October and 8 December 1923 which dealt with the crisis caused by the inflation and the Ruhr invasion. Moreover, during the years 1930–33 laws passed by the Reichstag had increasingly been replaced by Government decrees issued by the Reich President under Article 48 of the Weimar Constitution. In 1932, for example, there were sixty emergency decrees compared with only five Reichstag laws, and an increasing number of these emergency decrees empowered the Government to issue supplementary regulations with the force of law.

Initially, the Enabling Law was drawn up along the lines of the Weimar laws and was intended to permit the issuing of Government decrees with the force of law without the need for prior approval from the Reichstag or the Reich President. Some time between 15 and 20 March, however, the draft was modified to empower the Government to issue not merely 'decrees' (*Verordnungen*) but also 'laws' (*Gesetze*), and even laws which deviated from the 1919 Constitution and had therefore hitherto required a two-thirds Reichstag majority. The distinction between a 'law' and a 'decree' was not clear-cut, but the Weimar Constitution had imputed somewhat greater significance to laws than to decrees by restricting certain legislation (e.g. the taking up of loans by the Government) to laws. In the final draft of the Enabling Law the Reichstag surrendered its powers over the budget and over the taking up of loans.

Since this Enabling Law involved a change in the Constitution, a two-thirds majority in the Reichstag was necessary. After the election of 5 March, the two largest parties after the NSDAP—the Social Democrats (SPD) and the Centre Party—still possessed between them over one-third of the seats. If the SPD and the Centre had boycotted the debate this would have represented an effective veto, since a quorum of two-thirds of the Reichstag membership was necessary for changes in the Constitution. This danger was averted by a change in the Reichstag standing orders suggested by Frick. The new regulation, accepted by all save the SPD, provided that those members absent without leave or excluded would count as being present, the decision lying with the President of the Reichstag (Göring).

At the Cabinet meeting of 7 March 1933, the Government, reconciled to the opposition of the Social Democrats, concentrated on trying to win over the Centre:

103

(1) *Political Situation*
The Reich Chancellor opened the meeting and stated that...he regarded the events of 5 March as a revolution. Ultimately Marxism would no longer exist in Germany.

What was needed was an Enabling Law passed by a two-thirds majority. He, the Reich Chancellor, was firmly convinced that the Reichstag would pass such a law. The deputies of the German Communist Party would not appear at the opening of the Reichstag because they were in jail... .

The Vice-Chancellor and Reich Commissioner of Prussia [Papen] expressed to the Reich Chancellor and the National Socialist Organisation the thanks of the Reich Cabinet for their admirable performance in the election... .

With regard to the internal political situation, the Vice-Chancellor stated that yesterday (6 March) Dr Kaas had been to see him. He had stated that he had come without previously consulting his party and was now prepared to let bygones be bygones. He had, moreover, offered the cooperation of the Centre Party... .

Reich Minister Göring stated that the Communist deputies would not take part in the sessions of the Reichstag because they were in jail. Serious charges were also to be made against a number of Marxist deputies. Forty persons of the Iron Front had carried out united action with the German Communist Party.

He was firmly convinced that the two-thirds majority in the Reichstag would be obtained for an Enabling Law. Deputies who left the session in order to make it impossible for the two-thirds majority to be present would have to forfeit their free travel passes and allowances for the duration of the legislative period. He wished to make a change in the rules to this effect. In his opinion, the duty of the Deputy to exercise his mandate also entailed that he must not absent himself from sessions without being excused.

Grass, the chairman of the parliamentary group of the Prussian Centre Party, had been to see him even before the election. Grass had made the offer that if no further changes in personnel were made before the election, then the Centre Party would be prepared to cooperate. According to the statements made by Grass, the collaboration of the German Nationalists could then be dispensed with. It was best to tell the Centre Party that all its civil servants would be removed from office if the Centre Party did not agree to the enabling law. For the rest, the tactics to be employed towards the Centre Party would have to consist in courteously ignoring it... .

The Catholic Church authorities, however, were still hostile to the Nazi Party and their influence with the Centre Party was considerable. On 19 March, Cardinal Bertram, the senior German Catholic bishop, issued a confidential statement to the Catholic bishops that 'as a result of biased announcements to the effect that the Church will revise its attitude to the National Socialists, Vice-Chancellor von Papen brought up this question during his visit yesterday. I replied that it is for the leader of the National Socialists to revise his attitude.'

To win over the Catholics and the Centre Party, Hitler promised in his Reichstag speech on 23 March to respect the rights of the Catholic Church and stressed the Government's recognition of the importance of the Churches:

104

...By its determination to carry through the political and moral purging of our public life, the Government is creating and ensuring the preconditions for a truly deep and inward religious life. The political advantages derivable from compromises with atheistic organisations come nowhere near outweighting the consequences to be seen in the destruction of our common religious and moral values. The National Government sees in both Christian denominations the most important factors for the maintenance of our society. It will respect the agreements concluded between them and the states; their rights will not be touched. It expects, however, that its task of the national and moral renewal of our people will meet with similar appreciation from their side. The Government will treat all other denominations with objective justice. It can never, however, condone the idea that membership of a given denomination or race can be regarded as absolving any person from common legal obligations or as a licence to commit or tolerate crimes without punishment. The National Government will permit and guarantee to the Christian denominations the enjoyment of their due influence in schools and education.[45] Its concern will be for the sincere cooperation of Church and State. The struggle against the materialist ideology and for the establishment of a real national community is in the interests of the German nation as much as of our Christian faith... .

Besides being wooed by promises, the Centre were also intimidated by the fear of what would happen, particularly to Catholic civil servants, if they refused. The distinguished historian of the Centre Party, Karl Bachem, summed up their uncertainty after the Party had supported the Bill. Particularly interesting is his hope that it would be possible to cooperate with and influence the NSDAP.

105

Was this vote right? This may be doubted, though only future developments will make a definite judgement possible. It was certainly in the spirit of the call for unity which Kaas had sent out weeks ago on 17 October 1932 in Münster. It may also be said that the law would have been passed even if the Centre had voted against it or abstained. If the Centre had voted against it, it would, given the current mood of the National Socialists, probably have been smashed at once just like the Social Democratic Party and the Italian Partito Popolare.[46] All civil servants belonging to the Centre would probably have been dismissed. There would have been a great fracas in the Reichstag, and the Centrists would probably have been beaten up and thrown out. The parliamentary group would have made an heroic exit, but with no benefit to the Catholic cause or to the cause of the Centre Party. The links between the Centre and National Socialism would have been completely cut, all collaboration with the National Socialists and every possibility of influencing their policy would have been out of the question. Perhaps, then, it was right to make the attempt to come to an understanding and cooperate with the National Socialists, in order to be able to participate in a practical way in the reshaping of the future.

---

[45]Significantly this sentence was omitted from the report of the speech in the *Völkischer Beobachter* and most other publications.
[46]The Catholic party in Italy.

Certainly all this can be said. But what if this attempt fails? What if the National Socialist wave, true to its basic ideological beliefs, wants to engulf our Catholic organisations, our Catholic youth clubs etc., as in Italy? Will not people then say that it was the fault of the Centre for giving the Hitler Government a blank cheque for four years? Will not the Centre be so discredited with its followers that it will lose all influence on them and be unable to achieve anything?

Then again, can it be morally and politically justifiable to grant the Government, whose instincts are so completely different from what we stand for, such far-reaching, unique authority? The Centre has always been the party of the law, of the Constitution, and also of freedom. What has now happened has nothing to do with law, freedom, and the Constitution. It is true that parliamentarism and with it the democratic idea have come to a dead end. Brüning tried up to the last minute to save parliamentarism as it was part of the Constitution; but in vain. It is Hugenberg's fault. But it has really proved impossible. So was it justified to try a new way? Certainly, Hitler has inserted several points in his speech which meet our wishes, to a far greater extent than would have been thought possible, and give us a certain security. But will he be able to stick to this line since many of his colleagues—Hugenberg, Göring—are strongly opposed to Catholicism?

In any case: as in 1919 we climbed calmly and deliberately into the Social Democrat boat, so, in the same way, we were able to enter the boat of the National Socialists in 1933 and to try to lend a hand with the steering. Between 1919 and 1933 this proved quite satisfactory: the Social Democrats, since they were not able to govern without the Centre, were unable to do anything particularly antireligious or dubiously socialistic. Will it be possible to exercise a similarly sobering influence on the National Socialists now?

Quod Deus bene vertat![47] It would indeed be a great thing, and if it turns out like that, everyone in our party will praise the present attitude of the parliamentary group. Just as after 1919, when the association with the Social Democrats saved us from Bolshevism. It is enough if cooperation with the National Socialists can protect us against Communists, Bolshevism and anarchy! The latter is very important now. One may say: *Prius vivere, deinde philosophari.*[48] First remove the danger of Communism; then everything will sort itself out.

In short: in this question too there is no obvious solution. As so often in politics. And in life too! The risk is great, but if one had not run it the danger would have been even greater.

Ergo: for the time being we go along with the new direction of the Centre. Whether it is right nobody can say yet. *Qui vivra, verra!*[49] All splits are dangerous now. As they were before.

Hitler's Reichstag speech had satisfied not only lay Catholics but also the Church authorities, above all concerned to protect their various organisations, as the Fulda Conference of Bishops stated on 28 March 1933:

---

[47]'May God turn this to good effect!'
[48]'Live first, then philosophise.'
[49]'He who lives will see!'

106

During the last few years, the Bishops of the German dioceses, in their dutiful concern for the party of the Catholic faith and the protection of the tasks and rights of the Catholic Church, have adopted, for good reasons, towards the National Socialist movement a negative attitude, expressed through prohibitions and warnings, which were to remain in force for as long as and as far as those reasons remained valid.

It must now be recognised that public and solemn declarations have been issued by the highest representative of the Reich Government, who is simultaneously the authoritarian leader of that movement, which acknowledge the inviolability of the teachings of the Catholic faith and the immutable tasks and rights of the Church. Similarly, the full validity of the treaties concluded between the various German states and the Church is guaranteed.

Without revoking the condemnation contained in our previous statements of certain religious and ethical errors, the Episcopate nevertheless believes it can cherish the hope that those general warnings and prohibitions need no longer be regarded as necessary.

Catholic Christians, for whom the opinion of their Church is sacred, need no particular admonition to be loyal to the legally constituted authorities, to fulfil their civic duties conscientiously, and to reject absolutely any illegal or revolutionary activity.

The admonition which has so often been solemnly addressed to all Catholics, namely to stand up for peace and the social welfare of the nation, for the protection of Christian religion and morality, for the freedom and rights of the Catholic Church and the protection of the denominational school and the Catholic youth organisations, is still valid...

Only the SPD voted against the Bill. The courage this required can be judged from the following account of the atmosphere of the debate by a Bavarian SPD deputy:

107

...The wide square in front of the Kroll Opera House was crowded with dark masses of people. We were received with wild choruses: 'We want the Enabling Act!' Youths with swastikas on their chests eyed us insolently, blocked our way, in fact made us run the gauntlet, calling us names like 'Centre pig', 'Marxist sow'. The Kroll Opera House was crawling with armed SA and SS men. In the cloakroom we learned that Severing[50] had been arrested on entering the building. The assembly hall was decorated with swastikas and similar ornaments. The diplomats' boxes and the rows of seats for the audience were overcrowded. When we Social Democrats had taken our seats on the extreme left, SA and SS men lined up at the exits and

---

[50]An SPD Party leader and former Prussian Minister of the Interior.

along the walls behind us in a semicircle. Their expressions boded no good. Hitler read out his government declaration in a surprisingly calm voice. Only in a few places did he raise it to a fanatical frenzy: when he demanded the public execution of van der Lubbe and when, at the end of his speech, he uttered dark threats of what would happen if the Reichstag did not vote the Enabling Act he was demanding. I had not seen him for a long time. He did not resemble the ideal of the Germanic hero in any way. Instead of fair curls, a black strand of hair hung down over his sallow face. His voice gushed out of his throat in dark gurgling sounds. I have never understood how this speaker could carry away thousands of people with enthusiasm.

After the government declaration, there was an interval. The former Reich Chancellor, Dr Wirth, came over and said bitterly that in his group the only question had been whether they should also give Hitler the rope to hang them with. The majority of the Centre was willing to obey Monseigneur Dr Kaas and let Hitler have his Enabling Act. If they refused, they feared the outbreak of the Nazi revolution and bloody anarchy. Only a few, among them Dr Brüning, were against any concession to Hitler.

Otto Wels read out our reply to the government declaration. It was a masterpiece in form and content, a farewell to the fading epoch of human rights and humanity.[51] In concluding, Otto Wels, with his voice half choking, gave our good wishes to the persecuted and oppressed in the country who, though innocent, were already filling the prisons and concentration camps simply on account of their political creed.

This speech made a terrifying impression on all of us. Only a few hours before, we had heard that members of the SA had taken away the 45-year-old welfare worker, Maria Janovska of Köpenick, to a National Socialist barracks, stripped her completely, bound her on a table and flogged her body with leather whips. The female members of our group were in tears, some sobbed uncontrollably.

But Hitler jumped up furiously and launched into a passionate reply. When the Social Democrats were in power the National Socialists had been outlawed. Anyone who bowed down before an International could not criticise the National Socialists. If the National Socialists had not a sense of justice, the Social Democrats would not be here in the hall. But the National Socialists had resisted the temptation to turn against those who had tormented them for fourteen years. 'You are oversensitive, gentlemen, if you talk of persecution already. By God, the National Socialists would have had the courage to deal with the Social Democrats in a different way.... You, gentlemen, are no longer needed. I do not even want you to vote for the Enabling Act. Germany shall become free, but not through you.'

There was no question of the National Socialists having been persecuted in the German Republic. On the contrary, the movement had frequently been furthered

---

[51]'At this historic hour, we German Social Democrats pledge ourselves to the principles of humanity and justice, of freedom and Socialism. No Enabling Law can give you the power to destroy ideas which are eternal and indestructible. You yourself have declared your commitment to Socialism. The Socialist Law [of 1878] did not succeed in destroying Social Democracy. From this new persecution too German Social Democracy can draw new strength. We send greetings to the persecuted and the oppressed. We greet our friends in the Reich. Their steadfastness and loyalty deserve admiration. The courage with which they maintain their convictions and their unbroken confidence guarantee a brighter future.

by the State authorities. Only when its members broke the existing laws were they punished, in most cases very mildly. The Communists were made to feel the strong arm of the law in a very different way. We tried to dam the flood of Hitler's unjust accusations with interruptions of 'No!', 'An error!', 'False!' But that did us no good. The SA and SS people, who surrounded us in a semicircle along the walls of the hall, hissed loudly and murmured: 'Shut up!', 'Traitors!', 'You'll be strung up today.'

The Enabling Law, passed by 444 votes to the 94 votes of the Social Democrats, was published on 24 March. It gave the destruction of parliamentary democracy an appearance of legality. This was important for the prestige of the regime abroad, among the middle class at home, and particularly with the Civil Service. The Reichstag became merely a sounding board for Hitler's major speeches. Only seven more laws were passed by the Reichstag. Moreover, despite the statement in Article 2 that 'the powers of the President remain unaffected', in fact the signature of the President was no longer necessary for legislation or decrees. Only three more presidential decrees were issued and they had already been prepared before the passage of the Enabling Law. From now onwards the legislation of the Third Reich took the form of 'government laws' and, increasingly, of Führer edicts (*Erlasse*).

108

The Reichstag has passed the following law, which is, with the approval of the Reichsrat,[52] herewith promulgated, after it has been established that it satisfies the requirements for legislation altering the Constitution.
Article 1. In addition to the procedure for the passage of legislation outlined in the Constitution, the Reich Cabinet is also authorised to enact Laws. This applies equally to the laws referred to in Article 85, paragraph 2, and Article 87 of the Constitution.[53] Article 2. The national laws enacted by the Reich Cabinet may deviate from the Constitution provided they do not affect the position of the Reichstag and the Reichsrat. The powers of the President remain unaffected.
Article 3. The national laws enacted by the Reich Cabinet shall be prepared by the Chancellor and published in the official gazette. They come into effect, unless otherwise specified, upon the day following their publication. Articles 68–77 of the Constitution[54] do not apply to the laws enacted by the Reich Cabinet.
Article 4. Treaties of the Reich with foreign states which concern matters of domestic legislation do not require the consent of the bodies participating in

---

[52]The upper house, containing the representatives of the federal states which had now all been coordinated.
[53]These concerned the authority of Parliament over taxation.
[54]These concerned the provisions for enacting new legislation.

legislation. The Reich Cabinet is empowered to issue the necessary provisions for the implementing of these treaties.
Article 5. This law comes into effect on the day of its publication. It ceases to be valid on 1 April 1937: it also ceases to be valid if the present Reich Cabinet is replaced by another.[55]

The demise of the political parties followed. Even the partners in the coalition, the Nationalists, came under increasing pressure, particularly since after the Enabling Law their votes were no longer necessary for legislation. Protests by their leader, Hugenberg, even at Cabinet level were treated with scarcely concealed contempt:

109

7 4 April 1933 (4.0 p.m.): Session of the Reich Cabinet
3. Outside the agenda: information from the Reich Minister of Economics, Food, and Agriculture (Dr Hugenberg):
The Reich Minister of Economics, Food, and Agriculture pointed out that recently SA men had arrested chairmen and members of Chambers of Commerce who were listed members of the German National People's Party. These persons were removed from their positions in an unlawful way. He would no longer tolerate this state of affairs and urgently requested redress.
Reich Minister Göring explained that frequently arrests had been made solely at the request of the competent public prosecutor. Moreover, it was urgently necessary to have new elections for the Chambers of Commerce and the Chambers of Farmers as soon as possible. The structure of the Chambers no longer accorded in any way with the present political situation. It was therefore impossible for Reich Minister Göring himself to hold back the SA.
The Reich Minister of Economics, Food and Agriculture reported that he had already prepared the reorganisation of the provisional Reich Economic Council and that he also wished to order the dissolution of, and new elections for, the Chambers of Commerce and of Farmers. But he had to be allowed a little time to prepare all these things... .

After this Goebbels had good reason to note the following in his diary:

---

[55]In fact the Act was renewed in 1937 for a further four years and the second part of the clause, included to reassure the German Nationalists, was ignored after Hugenberg's resignation on 27 June 1933. This was facilitated by the fact that the pressure for Hugenberg's resignation had come from the Conservatives in the Cabinet led by Neurath, who had objected to his aggressive tactics at the World Economic Conference in London earlier in June.

110

22 April 1933
The Führer's authority is now completely in the ascendant in the Cabinet. There will be no more voting. the Führer's personality decides. All this has been achieved much more quickly than we had dared to hope... .

The anti-Nazi activities of SPD *émigrés* in Prague were used as an excuse to ban the SPD officially on 22 June. By the end of June, the two Liberal parties and the Nationalists recognised the inevitable and disbanded themselves. Their membership had by now virtually disappeared, either to join the Nazis or into what was termed 'inner emigration'.[56] They were followed on 5 July by the most powerful non-Socialist opposition party, the Catholic Centre.

The Centre had been still faced with the dilemma of whether or not to cooperate with the Nazi regime. Many of its members had already been swept away by the spirit of the 'national uprising' to which Catholics, traditionally a minority group, could be particularly vulnerable as the following pronouncement of the Catholic Teachers' Association of the German Reich, 1 April 1933, indicates:

111

As in the August days of 1914, a feeling of national and German emotion has seized our people. The *status quo* has been overthrown and new objectives have been set for a new, developing German nation and a new German state. Regrettably, the Catholic leadership and Catholic elements have been as little involved in this change as they were in the foundation of Bismarck's Reich. Thanks to the warning summons of Adolf Hitler and his movement, and to his work, we have succeeded in breaking through the un-German spirit which prevailed in the revolution of 1918.

Now the whole German nation in all its various parts, including the Catholics, has been summoned to cooperate and to build a new order. At this critical moment, Catholicism must not once again stand aside, adopting a wait-and-see attitude. We will lend a hand to help with the construction of a new Reich and a new nation, putting our trust in the leader of the German and *völkisch* movement. If an appeal is made to the natural and true impulses and groups of our historic nationality in its totality, the Catholic element cannot be dispensed with. Over the past centuries, it has become our destiny for the nature of the German character to grow out of Catholicism and the national characteristics of the German race. After a period of decline, we now have the duty of participating in the reorientation towards a rise and a renaissance. We must—and here we agree completely with the leader of the national movement—we must first become an internally unified nation of German

---

[56] i.c. while refraining from overt opposition to the regime. they witheld from it any cooperation as far as possible. in an attempt to keep their hands clean.

men and women. We must put aside everthing which divides us and shake hands across the barriers which have hitherto been overemphasised, in order once more to become a nation which believes in honour, cleanliness, and loyalty. The essence of the practising Catholic population, as it has emerged in associations, status groups, and modes of life, is coming to the fore in order to consider what specific Catholic contribution can be made to the national task.

The dilemma facing the Centre was outlined at the time by Karl Bachem. His feeling of impotence in the face of the crisis and his sense of the inevitability of the Nazi take-over since they alone were sufficiently ruthless and determined stand out. Remarkable also is his belief that in the fight against Bolshevism there is 'no point in being fussy about legal subtleties'. The attitude revealed by this statement, made in the context of the Enabling Act and all that had happened since 30 January, helps explain the comparative ease with which the Nazis carried out their policy of 'coordination':

112

So the Centre has been formally dissolved. The Centre has been dissolved by its own resolution! It is said that Brüning was strongly against. But concern for the Catholic civil servants was decisive. Brüning had wanted to wait for the Government to dissolve the Centre, which in that case would not itself have borne any responsibility. The same with the Bavarian People's Party. All political activity in the spirit of the old Centre Party is from now on impossible and 'forbidden'. It has been quite openly declared that any further attempts at such activities will be crushed by brute force.

This is indeed a terrible fate, hardly conceivable for a party with such an honourable record of more than sixty years' achievement. One can do nothing but succumb patiently and meekly to this decision of Divine Providence; even if this time it seems hard, very hard. 'Quam incomprehensibilia sunt judicia ejus, et investigabiles viae ejus', as it says in the Epistle to the Romans.[57] No wonder that particularly the younger, lively members of the Party are terribly upset and use harsh words accusing Brüning, Kaas and all the other leaders of having helped to bring about the downfall of the party through their inactivity and cowardice. But what in practical terms could Brüning and Kaas have done? Would it have been of any use to call on the Catholic population and the whole Centre Party to offer united resistance? Such resistance would have at once shown up the physical powerlessness of the party and would have been brutally suppressed; the leaders would have immediately been taken into 'protective custody', and thereby have been rendered harmless. The bishops having voted unanimously for the recognition of the new government, such resistance, no longer morally defensible, would have been impossible for us. There is nothing left to do but to follow the example of the

---

[57]Romans 11:33: 'How unsearchable are his judgments, and his ways past finding out!'

bishops and, in spite of everything, continue to try and remain concerned for the protection of our religious interests within the National Socialist Party and in cooperation with it. Nothing else is now possible. All our large organisations have been destroyed. Even the apprentices' associations have been deprived of their independence and coordinated with the 'National Socialist workers' front'. What will happen now no one can say. In the meantime, the future before us remains extremely black. In practice, we can do nothing but continue to try and work for our religious principles within the National Socialist Party and through quiet cooperation in its organisations. National Socialists, particularly Hitler, have often declared that they want 'positive Christianity' as the basis of the State, that they regard the Catholic as well as the Protestant Confessions as 'the most important factors for the preservation of our national character'. That is something, even if it is not yet clear what this 'positive Christianity' will be like and what its effects will be. So our people must now act as 'leaven', as the 'salt of the earth', in order to help the right principles to predominate... .

After describing the chronic state of crisis under the Weimar Republic he concludes:

In short, no more headway could be made with the democratic form of government; there could no longer be any illusions about this. Nor with the Centre's old principle of seeking an improvement in conditions only in a constitutional way, observing the regulations and the existing law. If the nation was not to sink into poverty and the life of the state be completely ruined, a different way had to be found to get out of this appalling situation. It was clear that if this was to be done it would not always be possible to observe the letter of the law... .

So one could only be grateful to the new men who, with determination, took into their hands the task of saving Germany. It really was not possible to go on any further without force, without using the principle of force, and since the Centre, because of its past, could not subscribe to this principle, it could not complain if it was pushed aside. Therefore, it is right to let the new men, particularly the leaders of the National Socialists, go ahead and not put unnecessary obstacles in their way. There are a lot of dubious things in the National Socialist movement, particularly so far as principles are concerned. But that has to be put up with for the time being. Today there is no point in being fussy about legal subtleties. What matters is first to let a strong, efficient government grow and then to support it wholeheartedly in order to suppress Bolshevism. It does seem as if Communism had already become so strong in Germany, so presumptuous, and so self-confident that it was high time to counter it with determination if it was not to result in a new Communist revolution and a terrible civil war.

But despite all this, it is hard for the Centre Party to disappear without trace after such long and honourable activity. In days to come they may say: It had fulfilled its task and could leave the stage of history. But has that task been fulfilled for the future as well? Who from now on will look after the interests of religion, the freedom and welfare of the Church? Are we not now dependent solely on the goodwill of the National Socialist Party? Will the Church keep its rights when no real political power exists to defend them? It is certain that even Catholics loyal to the Church will now join the National Socialist formations in great numbers, just as in Italy. But will their influence there become strong enough to check new animosities against the Catholic Church, especially attacks on our Catholic denominational schools and the schools of our orders etc.? There is to be a concordat with the Vatican. If the Pope concludes it, he will take the vital interests of the Church into account. But will such a Concordat remain permanently valid if there is no political power to support its validity? It is different in Italy. The whole country is Catholic and even the Liberals think of Catholicism as part of the national greatness. In Germany, on the other hand, denominational divisions go deep, and anything that has seemed to favour the Catholic Church has always been offensive to the Protestant section of the people. At the moment there is no evidence of any particularly hostile Protestant agitation against Catholicism. The Protestant Association has obviously lost much of its impetus. But will that remain so? Who knows?...

In fact, the position of the Centre had been further undermined by the negotiations between the Government, the Catholic hierarchy in Germany, and the Vatican over a Concordat. The Catholic authorities proved willing to abandon their political party in return for a Concordat guaranteeing their religious activities. Hitler, however, had no doubt that in the Concordat signed on 8 July 1933 he had a bargain as he told the Cabinet on 14 July 1933:

113

...The Reich Chancellor saw three great advantages in the conclusion of the Reich Concordat:
1. that the Vatican had negotiated at all, considering that they operated, especially in Austria, on the assumption that National Socialism was un-Christian and inimical to the Church;
2. that the Vatican should have been persuaded to bring about good relations with this purely national German State. He, the Reich Chancellor, would even a short time ago have thought it impossible that the Church would be willing to commit the bishops to the support of this State. The fact that this had now been done was certainly an unreserved recognition of the present regime;
3. that, with the Concordat, the Church should have withdrawn from activity in associations and parties, and, for instance, have abandoned even the Christian labour unions. This also he, the Reich Chancellor, would, even a few months ago, have thought impossible. Even the dissolution of the Centre could be termed final only with the conclusion of the Concordat, now that the Vatican had ordered the permanent exclusion of the clergy from party politics.
That the objective which he, the Reich Chancellor, had always been striving for, namely an agreement with the Curia, had been attained so much faster than he had imagined even on 30 January—this was such an indescribable success that, in the face of it, all critical misgivings should be withdrawn.

After all the parties had dissolved themselves, the one-Party State was formally proclaimed by the Law against the Establishment of Parties, 14 July 1933.

114

Art I. The National Socialist German Workers' Party constitutes the only political party in Germany.

Art II. Whoever undertakes to maintain the organisation of another political party or to form a new political party shall be punished with penal servitude of up to three years or with imprisonment of between six months and three years, unless the act is subject to a heavier penalty under other regulations.

(iv) The Revolution Stabilised: Conflict with the SA

Meanwhile, the SA was becoming dissatisfied with the compromises the regime had made with established institutions. It contained a large number of impoverished members of the lower middle class and a number of unemployed. Some were hostile to the Establishment, taking seriously the anti-capitalist aspects of the Party programme. The majority simply felt disgruntled at their failure to turn the Nazi take-over into the kind of concrete material benefits for themselves which they had anticipated. In fact, the Government went some way towards conciliating the Party rank and file by insisting that old Party fighters have priority in employment, a measure which led to some SA men acquiring jobs.

Nevertheless, the leader of the SA, Ernst Röhm, at least was not conciliated and in a newspaper article in June 1933 he expressed disillusionment at the inadequate fruits of the seizure of power and determination to continue the revolution:

115

...A tremendous victory has been won. But not *absolute* victory!

The new State did not have to disown the bearers of the will to revolution as the November men[58] had to with the red hordes who were the followers of their revolution, born of cowardice and high treason. In the new Germany the disciplined brown storm battalions of the German revolution stand side by side with the armed forces.

---

[58]i.e. the Social Democrats.

Not as part of them.

The Reichswehr has its own undisputed task: it is committed to defend the borders of the Reich, so far as its small numbers and completely inadequate armament enables it to do so.

The police have to keep down the law-breakers.

Beside these stand the SA and the SS as the third power factor of the new State with special tasks.

The Leader and Chancellor of the German people needs them for the tremendous work of German revival which still lies before him.

For the SA and the SS are the foundation pillars of the coming National Socialist State—*Their* State for which they have fought and which they will defend. The SA and SS are militant-spiritual [*kämpferisch-geistig*] bearers of the will of the German revolution.

Already here and there philistines and grumblers are daring to ask in astonishment what the SA and SS are still there for, since Hitler is now in power. We are after all, they point out, nationalist again. Swastika flags fly over the streets. There is law and order everywhere. And if it is disturbed, the police will take care that it is restored as quickly as possible. So why the SA and SS?

The philistines and grumblers, whether they stand in the ranks of our eternal and irreconcilable adversaries, or are 'coordinated', or even wear the swastika, have not understood the meaning of the German revolution and never will understand it.

The course of events between 30 January and 21 March 1933 does not represent the sense and meaning of the German National Socialist revolution.

Anyone who wanted to be a fellow-traveller only during shining torchlight processions and impressive parades with rumbling drums and booming kettledrums, with blaring trumpets and under waving flags, and now believes he has 'taken part' in the German revolution—can go home! He has confused the 'national uprising' with the German revolution! He has intoxicated himself with outward appearances; perhaps he has got carried away by the unheard-of mood of 'Potsdam Day', perhaps he was delighted to see millions and millions of workers march for Germany at the Festival of German Labour,[59] and for a few hours felt a breath of our spirit—*but he is not one of us*!! For the coming years of struggle he can creep back to the hearth or the desk or the pub from whence he came. The fighters in the simple brown service shirt of the SA and SS will not miss him on their path forwards to the German revolution, just as they did not meet him when, in long years marked by sacrifices and blood, they fought their passionate fight for a new Germany.

…The SA and SS will not tolerate the German revolution going to sleep or being betrayed at the half-way stage by non-combatants. Not for their own sake, but for Germany's sake. For the brown army is the last levy of the nation, the last bastion against Communism.

If the German revolution is wrecked by reactionary opposition, incompetence, or indolence, the German people will fall into despair and will be an easy prey for the bloodstained frenzy coming from the depths of Asia.

For this reason the fantasy in the minds of some 'coordinated' people and even some low-level dignitaries calling themselves National Socialists, that to keep calm

---

[59]On 1 May 1933, see below, pp. 423–4.

is the first duty of a citizen, is a betrayal of the German revolution. The people who are now everywhere 'involved' and murmur—still softly as yet—their upright-bourgeois little maxim of 'law and order' were nowhere to be seen during our long pilgrimage in search of the new Germany for which we longed. At the most they stood aside and looked on as we fought and bled for Germany. We were too undistinguished for them, too loud, too radical. We still are, as far as they are concerned. It is enough for them that the black-white-and-red colours of the Bismarck empire are flying over Germany and, as a concession to the revolution, the swastika flag. For them the degree of outward power so far acquired, in which they are allowed a share, is enough. They would have even been contented with considerably less, because they did not have to struggle; they were only the beneficiaries of our victory.

...If those bourgeois simpletons think it is enough that the State apparatus has received a new sign, that the 'national' revolution has already lasted too long, for once we agree with them. It is in fact high time the national revolution stopped and became the National Socialist one. Whether they like it or not, we will continue our struggle—if they understand at last what it is about—*with* them; if they are unwilling—*without* them; and if necessary—*against* them!

The SA were not alone at fault. All sections of the Party were guilty of arbitrary interference both in the State administration and in the business community, as the following account by an unusually responsible SA leader indicates:

116

The authority of the State is in danger through constant unjustified interference by political officials in the machinery of normal administration.

Every NSBO[60] functionary, NSBO local branch leader, NSBO district leader..., every political cell leader, political local branch leader, political district leader is giving orders which interfere with the exercise of the authority of the ministries at the lower levels, that is to say, the authority of the regional governments, the district offices, down to the smallest police station.

Everyone is arresting everyone else, avoiding the prescribed official channels, everyone is threatening everyone else with protective custody, everyone is threatening everyone else with Dachau.[61]

Businesses are being forced to dismiss any number of employees, and businesses are being compelled to take on employees without checking on their qualifications... .

Right down to the smallest police station, the best and most reliable officials have become uncertain about the hierarchy of authority; this clearly must have a devastating and destructive effect on the State.

---

[60]*Nationalsozialistische Betriebszellenorganisation*: the National Socialist Factory Cell Organisation.

[61]The notorious concentration camp near Munich.

I really cannot be counted among the pussyfooters, and for that very reason I must see that if the revolution is to be turned into an ordered relationship between State and people, the State apparatus must be made completely safe from all revolutionary interference from the street.

It must be left to the responsibility of the State ministries alone, both in the spheres of policy and of personnel, to embody revolutionary ideas in a form which is suitable to the community... .

Every little street cleaner today feels he is responsible for matters which he has never understood... .

No one can dispute that fact that, at the moment, two-thirds of the daily work in my area, and in all other areas I know, has to be wasted on trifles arising from Party officials' lack of discipline... .

The leadership principle is in grave danger from these conditions.... I do not mind if my giving this warning makes me appear a grumbler. I can only state that these present circumstances must inevitably lead to chaos.

Hitler had little sympathy for the disillusionment of the SA. He was concerned lest constant interference by the Party and the SA at the lower levels might alienate important groups such as the Army, industry, and the Civil Service. It could jeopardise economic recovery and so prevent the regime from gaining the popular support it needed. It could delay his main objective of mobilising the economic resources and will of the nation for diplomatic and strategic purposes. For this a period of stability was essential. On 6 July 1933, therefore, in a speech to the Reich Governors (*Reichsstatthalter*), he formally ended the revolution which, he insisted, must from now on take the form of evolution. This did not mean that there were to be no more fundamental changes but that such changes must in future be initiated from above and not from below, and that tactical compromises would be necessary to ensure the stability of the regime:

117

The political parties have now been finally abolished. This is an historic event, the meaning and significance of which many people have not yet understood. We must now abolish the last remnants of democracy, especially the methods of election and the majority decisions still employed today in local government, in economic organisations and works committees, and the responsibility of the individual must be stressed.

The achievement of outward power must be followed by the inward education of man. We must beware of making doctrinaire decisions from one day to the next and of expecting a final solution from them. People are easily capable of bending outward form to suit their own intellectual stamp. The switch-over must not be made until suitable people have been found to carry out the switching. More revolutions have succeeded in their first assault than, once successful, have been brought to a standstill and held there. Revolution is not a permanent state, it must not develop into a lasting state. The full spate of revolution must be guided into the secure bed of evolution. In this the most important part is played by the education of the people. The present state of affairs must be improved and the people embodying it must be educated in the National Socialist conception of the State. A businessman must not therefore be dismissed if he is a good businessman even if he is not yet a good National Socialist; especially not if the National Socialist put in his place knows nothing about business. In business, ability alone must be decisive. The task of National Socialism is the safeguarding of the development of our people. But we must not keep looking round to see what next to revolutionise; rather we have the task of securing one position after another in order to hold them, and occupy them gradually in model fashion. In this we must gear our actions to a period of many years, and plan in terms of long periods of time. We do not provide bread for any worker by theoretically coordinating people. History will not judge us by the number of businessmen we dismissed or locked up, but by whether we knew how to provide work. Today we have the absolute power to succeed. But we must be able to replace those we dismiss by their betters. The businessman must be judged first on his business abilities; we must keep the economic apparatus in order. We shall not abolish unemployment with economic commissions, or with theories and blueprints of organisations. The main thing now is not programmes and ideas but the daily bread of five million people. The economy is a living organism which cannot be changed at a blow; it is constructed according to primitive laws bound up with human nature. The carriers of intellectual poison now seeking to penetrate the economy are a menace to both State and people. Practical experience must not be rejected simply because it is opposed to a particular idea.

In confronting the nation with reforms, we must show that we understand things and can cope with them. Our task is work, work, and again work! Our success in providing work will be our most powerful source of authority. Our programme is not a matter of fine gestures, but of maintaining the life of the German people.

The ideas of the programme do not demand that we act like fools and overturn everything, but that we realise our concepts wisely and carefully. In the long run, the more successful the economic underpinning of our programme, the more secure will be our political power. Reich Governors must ensure, and are responsible for seeing, that no organisations or party authorities shall claim governmental rights, dismiss people, or fill offices for which only the Reich Government and, in the field of economics, only the Reich Minister of Econmics is responsible.

The Party has now become the State. All power comes under the authority of the Reich. The emphasis of German life must be prevented from shifting back into particular areas or even organisations. No longer does authority stem from any part of the Reich but only from the concept of the Germans as a nation.

This statement, however, had only a limited effect on the Party activists, and above all, on the SA men, who felt disgruntled at the fact that the Nazi take-over had made so little difference to their lives, apart from giving them the satisfaction of revenge on their political opponents. This is clear from the fact that only three months later on 6 October 1933 Frick felt obliged to send out the following circular:

118

Despite repeated announcements by the Reich Chancellor and despite my numerous circulars new infringements by subordinate leaders and members of the SA have been reported again and again during the past weeks. Above all, SA leaders and SA men have independently carried out police actions either for which they had no authority whatever or which they carried out in a way that cannot be reconciled with the existing laws and regulations of the National Socialist Government. In this way even the extra-territorial status of the ambassador of a foreign power has recently been seriously violated by unauthorised SA men, thereby involving the foreign policy of the Government.

These infringements and excesses must now cease once and for all. I make it the duty of Reich Governors, State Governments and all subordinate institutions to intervene sharply against such infringements or any attempt at unauthorised interference. Unless members of the SA are employed as auxiliary police officers or as auxiliary officials in the frontier service by the proper authorities, they have no police jurisdiction whatsoever. In future, therefore, all police activities of the SA in all circumstances must cease. Where it becomes necessary in exceptional circumstances to employ members of the SA to assist the police in particular actions, they must never act independently but only in the *presence* and *under the supervision* of the police and only in accordance with the orders of the police officer. The leader of the police force carries full responsibility for the employment and the conduct of such auxiliary SA men. Furthermore, auxiliary police officers and auxiliary border customs officers are not to carry out their work except in the company of an *official*. Only if these orders are minutely observed can *agents provocateurs* be effectively prevented from damaging the SA and the National Socialist State...

During the autumn and winter of 1933, the SA was becoming more and more a law unto itself. In addition to the interference of the SA commissars in the Government offices at various levels, the SA was also intervening in the judicial process, forcing the prosecuting authorities to drop charges against SA men and successfully asserting its right to discipline SA men who broke the law. It had even established its own police force, the *Feldjäger*, who claimed sole jurisdiction in matters involving the SA. The monthly reports prepared by the Gestapo on the political and economic situation referred to the discontent of the population at the undisciplined behaviour of the SA and their concern at the obvious inability of the authorities to do anything about it.

This resentment was not restricted to the State authorities, including the Gestapo, or the population at large; it was even shared to some extent by the Party authorities. The SA did not disguise its contempt for the political leadership at local and district level. According to the Gestapo, the SA men mocked the local Party officials as 'Christmas tree men' and 'Lametta stallions' because of their uniforms which the SA felt were undeserved by these Party bureaucrats. 'Political earthworms' was another current epithet.

But much more serious from Hitler's point of view were the military ambitions of the SA. Apart from its rather vague social revolutionary aims, the SA under Röhm had a more concrete objective: it aspired to become *the* armed force of the State into which the Regular Army would be integrated. To this plan the Army leadership was totally opposed. Under the new Minister of Defence, General von Blomberg, who was a pro-Nazi, the Army had adopted a benevolent attitude towards the new regime. This was also partly dictated by the belief in the need to win Hitler's support in resisting the ambitions of the SA—a good instance of the way in which Hitler could use the Nazi organisations to put pressure on other bodies so that in effect they 'coordinated' themselves.

But by the beginning of 1934, the Army authorities were becoming increasingly concerned about the military ambitions of the SA, which by absorbing other paramilitary organisations had grown to over 2,500,000 men compared with the 100,000 or slightly more of the Army. Hitler could not afford to antagonise the Army, the one organisation which had the power to remove him from office. An efficient and contented Army was also essential if he was to achieve the aims of his foreign policy. The riff-raff of the SA would be no substitute.

At a conference on 28 February 1934, attended by the Army, SA and SS leaders, Hitler rejected Röhm's idea of a militia. He made Blomberg and Röhm sign an agreement by which the SA would be responsible for pre- and post-military training under the direction of the Army. Two days later, Blomberg drew Hitler's attention to an instance of the growing military activity of the SA, particularly serious as it involved the region demilitarised by the Versailles Treaty. This could cause diplomatic complications which would in turn complicate the process of rearmament:

119

I feel obliged to refer again to the significance of the armed staff guards of the SA. According to an order of the Chief of Staff [of the SA] every *Obergruppe* and group is to set up its own armed staff guards with a heavy machine gun company. This has already begun in certain areas. According to a report by the Commander of Military District VI, leaders of SA brigades are planning the formation of such a staff guard as well and are swearing in SA people for 1–1½ years for that purpose. Selection and training are being carried out with the aim of appearing in public. In terms of numbers this would amount to 6000–8000 men permanently armed with guns and machine guns in that military district alone. It is particularly unfortunate that the formation of these staff guards is taking place in connexion with so-called SA auxiliary labour camps which are mostly situated in the big cities. Today I received a report that a staff guard armed like this is being formed in Höchst am Main, that is to say, in the neutral zone...

Tension between the Army and the SA continued to build up in the early summer. But on 7 June, following a long interview with Hitler, Röhm published the following announcement. Though it showed distinct signs of belligerence, it nevertheless seems to indicate that, despite Hitler's later allegations, Röhm had no plans for a putsch during this period.

120

I have decided to follow the advice of my doctors and take a cure in order to restore my energies which have been severely strained by a painful nervous complaint. My place will be taken by the Chief of the Leadership Office, Obergruppenführer von Krausser.

1934 will require all the energies of every SA fighter. I recommend, therefore, to all SA leaders to begin organising leave already in June.

Therefore, for a limited number of SA leaders and men, June, and for the majority of the SA, July, will be a period of complete relaxation in which they can recover their strength.

I expect the SA to return on 1 August completely rested and refreshed in order to serve in those honourable capacities which nation and fatherland expect of it. If the enemies of the SA live in hope that the SA will not return, or will return only in part, from its leave, we will allow them this brief pleasurable anticipation. They will receive the appropriate reply at the time and in the manner appearing most suitable.

The SA is and remains Germany's destiny.

During June, the crisis was deepened by two further developments. It became clear the Reich President, Hindenburg, had not long to live, which raised the matter of the succession. If Hitler wished to combine the offices of Chancellor and President and avoid a new Conservative President being imposed on him, he would need the approval of the Army.

Secondly, Papen became the spokesman of conservative circles in the bureaucracy and business who were discontented at the excesses of the SA and concerned about talk of a second revolution. On 17 June, Papen articulated this discontent in a speech at the University of Marburg, the reporting of which Goebbels promptly banned:

121

...It is certainly obvious that the bearers of the revolutionary principle should initially occupy also the positions of power. But once the revolution has taken place, the Government must represent the people as a whole, and must on no account be the exponent only of particular groups; otherwise it would fail in its attempt to construct the national community. We must also get away from false romantic notions which are not appropriate to the twentieth century. We cannot, for example, consider dividing the nation after the manner of the ancient Greeks into Spartans and helots. The final outcome of that development was that the Spartans had to concentrate on repressing the helots, thereby weakening the diplomatic strength of Sparta. In a state where there is a true national community, the domestic political war-cries must finally cease. There must certainly be a process of selection. But the natural criterion for the selection of people for appointments cannot be replaced by that of membership of a particular organisation, so long as the motives for such membership cannot be analysed.... .

I have defined the problems of the German revolution and my attitude towards them particularly sharply because there appears to be endless talk of a second wave which will complete the revolution. Anyone who irresponsibly toys with such ideas should not deceive himself about the fact that a second wave can easily be followed by a third, that he who threatens the guillotine is the first to come under the knife. Nor is it clear in what direction this second wave is meant to lead. It is true that there is much talk about future socialisation. Have we experienced an anti-Marxist revolution in order to carry out the programme of Marxism? For any attempt to solve the social question by collectivising property is Marxism. Will the German people become richer, will its national income grow bigger, will anybody be better off, except possibly those who smell the possibility of plunder in such a raid? There is certainly a social problem caused by economic and demographic processes. But these can be mastered only if property is once more made aware of its responsibilities, not by raising collective irresponsibility to a principle. A form of economic planning which moves further and further away from personal initiative and responsibility must not be made into a principle. For anyone who has not observed that every form of collectivism leads to ineradicable corruption has been going about the world with his eyes shut.

No nation that would survive before history can afford a permanent uprising from below. At some stage the movement must come to an end; at some point there must emerge a firm social structure held together by a legal system secure against pressure and by a State power that is unchallenged. A ceaseless dynamic creates nothing. Germany cannot be allowed to become a train hurtling into the blue with no one knowing where it will stop. History flows of its own accord, it does not need to be constantly driven forward. If, therefore, a second wave of new life is to sweep through the German revolution, then it must do so not as social revolution, but as the creative completion of work already begun. The statesman is there to create forms, his sole concern is for State and people. The State is the sole power and the final guarantee of that which every citizen can claim—iron justice. In the long run, therefore, the State cannot tolerate any dualism, and the success of the German revolution and the future of our nation will depend on the discovery of a satisfactory solution for the dualism between Party and State.

The Government is well aware of the selfishness, the lack of principle, the insincerity, the unchivalrous behaviour, the arrogance which is on the increase under the guise of the German revolution. Nor has it any illusions as to the threat to that reserve of public confidence on which the Government can draw. If it is desired to achieve an intimate and friendly relationship with the people, then their intelligence must not be underestimated, their trust must be reciprocated and there must be no continual attempt to browbeat them. The German people recognise the gravity of the situation, they feel the economic crisis, they have a keen awareness of the weak points in some of the laws that this crisis has produced, they are acutely sensitive to violence and injustice, clumsy attempts at deceiving them with false optimism merely make them smile. In the long run, no organisation, no propaganda, however good, can alone retain their confidence. My interpretation, therefore, of the propaganda campaign against 'carpers' is different from that of others.[62] Confidence and willingness to cooperate will not be furthered by incitement, particularly incitement of the young, nor by threats against the defenceless classes of the community, but only by discussion based upon mutual confidence. The people know that great sacrifices are expected of them. They will shoulder them and follow the Führer with unshakeable loyalty, provided they are allowed to have a share in the making and carrying out of decisions, provided every word of criticism is not immediately interpreted as malicious, and provided that despairing patriots are not branded as traitors.

It is time to come together in brotherly love and respect for every citizen, to cease obstructing the work of those who are in earnest, and to silence doctrinaire fanatics... .

There was clearly a danger that the Army would combine with the conservative elements in the bureaucracy and business to veto Hitler's succession to Hindenburg, either by persuading Hindenburg before he died to nominate someone else, or by carrying out a *coup* on his death. Hitler might be able to counter such a *coup* with the aid of the SA, but this would make him prisoner of the SA, force him into a revolution, thereby jeopardising all his diplomatic and military objectives, to which the collaboration of business and the professional Army were essential. A period of peace and quiet was needed in order to restore the economic situation dominated by a foreign exchange crisis, and to avoid diplomatic complications in view of the weakness of Germany's diplomatic situation in 1934. All this was threatened by the SA with its demands for a second revolution, its ambition to usurp the role of the Army, and its flagrant contempt for the disarmament provisions of the Versailles Treaty. The SA, which had been very helpful in the acquisition of power, was now a grave embarrassment under the leadership of the ambitious Röhm and his associates.

In the meantime, another organisation had come to play an independent role in the crisis—the SS. During 1933–34, Himmler, the head of the SS, had taken over the political police departments in every state in the Reich, including the Prussian Gestapo. Nominally, the SS was still a part of the SA, and the SA with its huge membership and ambitious leadership was now the main obstacle to the ambitions of the SS. The SS therefore began

---

[62]On 11 May, Goebbels had launched a campaign against 'grumblers and carpers', aimed primarily at Conservatives.

to warn Hitler and the Army of the intentions of the SA. These rumours prompted the Army to take action which antagonised the SA and this in turn gave rise to more suspicion on the part of Hitler and the Army. This encouragement by the SS of mutual suspicion between Army and SA was described after the war by Field-Marshal von Kleist, from whose testimony it appears that General Reichenau, the right-hand man of Blomberg, the Minister of Defence, was also involved:

122

Round about 24 June 1934, I as the army commander in Silesia was warned by the Chief of the General Staff [*Heeresleitung*] that an attack by the SA on the Army was imminent and that I should unobtrusively keep my troops on the alert.

During the tense days following, I received a flood of reports and information which gave a picture of feverish preparations on the part of the SA. This information came from the most varied sources (the troops, the SA, old Stahlhelm types, SS, civilians and government authorities). Despite the very reserved attitude adopted by the troops, a dangerous state of tension developed in the garrisons between them and the local SA. Only a spark was needed to touch off the explosion.

In this situation, I considered that bloodshed could only be avoided by a man-to-man talk.

On the afternoon of 28 June, therefore, I asked SA Obergruppenführer Heines[63] to come and see me; I told him to his face that I knew of his preparations and I gave him a warning.

He replied that he knew all about my measures and had thought that they were preparations for an attack on the SA. He had only put the SA on the alert in order to resist an attack. He gave me his word as an officer and SA leader that he had not planned or prepared any surprise attack upon the Army.

During the night of 28–29 June, he rang me up again. He said more or less that as far as he was concerned the situation had changed. He had just learned that not only the Army in Silesia, but from 28 June the Army throughout the Reich, was on the alert for an SA putsch. He was going to fly to Munich early on the 29th to see Röhm. Whereupon I also flew on 29 June to Berlin and reported to Colonel-General Freiherr von Fritsch and General Beck about my conversation with Heines. I added: 'I have the impression that we—Army and SA—are being egged on against each other by a third party.' By that I meant Himmler and that much of the information came from him. Thereupon, Colonel-General Freiherr von Fritsch summoned General von Reichenau and asked me to repeat to him what I had just said. Reichenau replied, 'That may be true, but it's too late now.'

As tension built, Hitler decided to act. On 29 June he summoned a meeting of SA leaders for the following day at Wiessee in Bavaria. The Army and

---

[63]Police-President of Breslau.

SS were put on the alert and Göring was given the responsibility of carrying out the action in Berlin. Then, on learning that the SA in Munich had been put on the alert, Hitler flew to Munich in the early hours of the 30th. After the war, Kempka, his chauffeur, described the events of 30 June:

123

...It is already dawn when we land at the Munich airport, Oberwiesenfeld. During the flight, there had been a light shower and the grass at the airport is sparkling in the morning light. When Hitler jumps out of the machine, two officers of the Reichswehr report to him. He takes them aside and gives them their orders.

Outside the reception building three cars are waiting which have been ordered by wireless from the garage of the Reich Party headquarters in Munich. Some old friends of Hitler's from the early days of the Party are standing by them. Hitler goes up to the cars and orders the hoods to be raised. I am struck by the harshness of his voice. His face is even more serious than during the flight. I am already at the wheel when he sits down beside me: 'Kempka, we're going to the Ministry of the Interior first.'...

[At the Ministry Hitler arrested the Police-President of Munich, SA Obergruppenführer August Schneidhuber.]

Hitler sits down beside me and gives the order: 'To Wiessee, as fast as possible!'

It must have been about 4.30 a.m., the sky has cleared up, it is nearly bright daylight. We meet watering carts and people on their way to work....Hitler sits beside me in silence. From time to time, I hear Goebbels and Lutze talking in the back.

Just before Wiessee, Hitler suddenly breaks his silence: 'Kempka,' he says, 'drive carefully when we come to the Hotel Hanselbauer. You must drive up without making any noise. If you see an SA guard in the front of the hotel, don't wait for them to report to me; drive on and stop at the hotel entrance.' Then, after a moment of deathly silence: 'Röhm wants to carry out a *coup*.'

An icy shiver runs down my back. I could have believed anything, but not a *coup* by Röhm!

I drive up carefully to the hotel entrance as Hitler had ordered. Hitler jumps out of the car, and after him Goebbels, Lutze and the adjutants. Right behind us another car stops with a squad of detectives which had been raised in Munich.

As soon as I have turned the car so that it is ready to leave in a moment, I rush into the hotel with my gun at the ready. In the hall I meet Standartenführer Uhl, the leader of Röhm's staff guard. Hitler's chauffeur, Schreck, is taking him at gunpoint down to the laundry room which for the next hour serves as the first prison for the arrested SA leaders. In passing, Schreck calls out to me: 'Quickly! Run up to the boss! He needs you!'

I run quickly up the stairs to the first floor where Hitler is just coming out of Röhm's bedroom. Two detectives come out of the room opposite. One of them reports to Hitler: 'My Führer...the Police-President of Breslau is refusing to get dressed!'

Taking no notice of me, Hitler enters the room where Obergruppenführer Heines is remaining. I hear him shout: 'Heines, if you are not dressed in five minutes I'll have you shot on the spot!'

I withdraw a few steps and a police officer whispers to me that Heines had been in bed with an 18-year-old SA Obertruppführer. At last Heines comes out of the room with an 18-year-old fair-haired boy mincing in front of him.

'Into the laundry room with them!' cries Schreck.

Meanwhile, Röhm comes out of his room in a blue suit and with a cigar in the corner of his mouth. Hitler glares at him but says nothing. Two detectives take Röhm to the vestibule of the hotel where he throws himself into an armchair and orders coffee from the waiter.

I stay in the corridor a little to one side and a detective tells me about Röhm's arrest.

Hitler entered Röhm's bedroom alone with a whip in his hand. Behind him were two detectives with pistols at the ready. He spat out the words: 'Röhm, you are under arrest.' Röhm looked up sleepily from his pillow: 'Heil, my Führer.' 'You are under arrest' bawled Hitler for the second time, turned on his heel and left the room.

Meanwhile, upstairs in the corridor things are getting quite lively. SA leaders are coming out of their rooms and being arrested. Hitler shouts at each one: 'Have you had anything to do with Röhm's schemes?' naturally, they all deny it, but that doesn't help them in the least. Hitler usually knows about the individual; occasionally, he asks Goebbels or Lutze a question. And then comes the decision: 'Arrested!'

But there are others whom he lets go. Röhm's doctor SA Gruppenführer Ketterer comes out of a room and to our surprise he has his wife with him. I hear Lutze putting in a good word for him with Hitler. Then Hitler walks up to him, greets him, shakes hands with his wife and asks them to leave the hotel; it isn't a pleasant place for them to stay in, that day.

We follow Hitler into the yard and here he tells his chauffeur, Schreck, to charter a bus as quickly as possible to take the SA leaders who are in the laundry room to Munich. How slowly the minutes pass! More and more SA leaders arrive from outside and are brought into the laundry room. I stand at the hotel entrance and hear Röhm order coffee from the hotel manager for the third time.

Suddenly...there is the sound of a car arriving! At first I thought it was the bus chartered by Schreck but instead, to my horror, a lorry full of heavily armed SA men rattles into the yard. Now there'll be some shooting, I think to myself. I can see Brückner negotiating with the Sturmführer of the SA. The man seems to be refusing. Walking backwards, he tries to get to his lorry....At this moment Hitler goes up to him: 'Drive back to Munich immediately!' he tells the puzzled fellow. 'If you are stopped by SS on the way, you must let yourselves be disarmed without resistance.'

The Sturmführer salutes and jumps into the lorry, and the SA men leave again. No shot, no sign of resistance. All this time, Röhm is sitting unsuspectingly drinking his third cup of coffee. Only a single word from him, and the whole thing

would have worked out differently...
Now the bus arrives which has been fetched by Schreck. Quickly, the SA leaders are collected from the laundry room and walk past Röhm under police guard. Röhm looks up from his coffee sadly and waves to them in a melancholy way... . At last Röhm too is led from the hotel. He walks past Hitler with his head bowed, completely apathetic. Now Hitler gives the order to leave. I sit at the wheel of the first car with Hitler beside me and our column, which in the meantime has grown to about twenty cars, starts moving...

After the war, the governor of the Stadelheim[64] prison recorded:

124

...Nobody was allowed to leave the prison that night either. Next morning (Sunday 1 July 1934) two SS men asked at the reception desk to be taken to Röhm. Zink, who was at the entrance, in view of the strict instructions he had been given, refused. It was about 9.30 a.m. When the two tried to force their way in, Zink alerted the prison governor and the green police [state police], who at once occupied the corridors and prevented any intrusion. The governor ascertained that neither of the SS men had proper authorisation. It therefore took hours of telephoning to check their papers; even the Reich Chancellery was rung up. When at last it became clear that they had an order from Hitler, the two murderers had to be taken to Röhm in the new building.
There they handed over a Browning to Röhm, who once again asked to speak to Hitler. They ordered him to shoot himself. If he did not comply, they would come back in ten minutes and kill him.... When the time was up, the two SS men re-entered the cell, and found Röhm standing with his chest bared. Immediately one of them from the door shot him in the throat, and Röhm collapsed on the floor. Since he was still alive, he was killed with a shot point-blank through the temple. The bullet not only penetrated his skull, but also the ceiling of the cell below... .

Six of the other SA leaders arrested at Wiessee, were executed by an SS firing squad at Stadelheim Prison. The rest of the executions were carried out in the Berlin barracks of Hitler's bodyguard. In Berlin the purge was under Göring's direction. The following description by a police official gives a sense of the atmosphere of the occasion:

125

...Suddenly there are loud shouts in the large room next door. It is Göring's study, where the executive committee is meeting. From time to time Gestapo messengers come rushing in bringing small white pieces of paper. Through the door one can see

---

[64]The prison in Munich.

Göring, Himmler, Heydrich and little Pilli Körner, Göring's State Secretary in the Minister-Presidency, putting their heads together. Of course it is impossible to hear what they are talking about. But things are happening devilish fast. Occasionally we hear an inarticulate sound like 'Off!' or 'Aha!' or 'Shoot!' or simply raucous laughter. In any case they don't seem in a bad mood.

Göring even exudes an air of well-fed comfort. He gives the impression of being in his element. He strides round his room. He struts to and fro, an unforgettable picture: with his flowing head of hair, his white tunic, his grey-blue military trousers, his white boots with their high flaps reaching up over the knees of this unwieldy pot-belly. A comparison springs to my mind: there goes Puss in Boots!...

But, as I said, things suddenly begin to get very noisy within. Police Major Jakobi rushes out of the room in great haste with his helmet on and his chinstrap under his red face. Göring's hoarse voice booms after him: 'Shoot them down...Fetch a whole company...Shoot them down...Shoot...Shoot at once...Just shoot them down...Shoot...!' One can't begin to describe the blatant bloodthirstiness, the savage fury, the hideous vindictiveness, and yet at the same time the terror, the craven terror shown in this scene. Everyone senses, Someone has escaped who must not be allowed to escape, someone whose escape will undo the whole day's work... .

The man thought to have got away was Gregor Strasser, Hitler's old colleague and rival. The rumour was untrue; Strasser was murdered all right. The purge was used by the Nazis to pay off a number of old scores. The former Bavarian State Commissioner, Gustav von Kahr, who had thwarted Hitler at the 1923 putsch, was murdered; so was General von Schleicher, who had tried to split the Nazi Party with the help of Strasser in 1932. Hitler also struck at his conservative and Catholic opponents. Papen himself was only placed under house arrest, but the author of his Marburg speech, the writer Edgar Jung, was murdered and so was his press officer, von Bose. The exact number of those murdered was probably not less than a hundred, and may have run into hundreds. It included Wilhelm Schmidt, the music critic of the Munich paper, *Münchener Neueste Nachrichten*, mistaken by the SS assassins for someone else.

The Army played a significant role in the affair. Not content to look on benevolently, it had actually provided arms and transport for the SS squads and had made preparations to counter any SA resistance. When it was all over, Blomberg, the Defence Minister, on 1 July publicly thanked Hitler in the name of the Army:

126

The Führer with soldierly decision and exemplary courage has himself attacked and crushed the traitors and murderers. The Army, as the bearer of arms of the entire people, far removed from the conflicts of domestic politics, will show its gratitude through devotion and loyalty. The good relationship towards the new SA demanded by the Führer will be gladly fostered by the Army in the consciousness that the ideals of both are held in common. The state of emergency has come to an end everywhere.

The President also sent his good wishes by telegram on 2 July with a similar telegram to Göring. He was no longer capable of making an independent assessment of the situation. That he was prepared to lend his prestige to the purge was of considerable help to Hitler who had the task or persuading public opinion that it had been essential for the security of the State:

127

I note from the reports I have received that through your decisive intervention and your courageous personal commitment you have nipped all the treasonable intrigues in the bud. You have saved the German nation from serious danger and for this I express to you my deeply felt gratitude and my sincere appreciation.

The Cabinet then retroactively legalised the purge:

128

At the meeting of the Reich Cabinet on Tuesday 3 July, the Reich Chancellor, Adolf Hitler, began by giving a detailed account of the origin and suppression of the high treason plot. The Reich Chancellor stressed that lightning action had been necessary, otherwise many thousands of people would have been in danger of being wiped out.

Defence Minister General von Blomberg thanked the Führer in the name of the Reich Cabinet and the army for his determined and courageous action, by which he had saved the German people from civil war. The Führer had shown greatness as a statesman and soldier. This had aroused in the hearts of the members of the Cabinet and of the whole German people a vow of service, devotion, and loyalty in this grave hour.

The Reich Cabinet then approved a law on measures for the self-defence of the State. Its single paragraph reads:

'The measures taken on 30 June and 1 and 2 July to suppress the acts of high treason are legal, being necessary for the self-defence of the State.'

Reich Minister of Justice Dr Gürtner commented that measures of self-defence taken before the imminent occurrence of a treasonable action should be considered not only legal but the duty of a statesman.

On 13 July 1934 Hitler justified his action in the Reichstag with a fictitious story of a plot:

129

...Without once informing me and at a moment when I had no thought of any such action, Chief of Staff Röhm entered into relations with General Schleicher through an utterly corrupt and dishonest go-between, a certain Herr von A.[65] It was General Schleicher who spelt out the secret aims of Chief of Staff Röhm. It was he who gave concrete form to the ideas of the latter and maintained that:

1. The present regime in Germany is not to be tolerated.
2. Above all, the Army and all national associations must be united in a single band.
3. The only man to be considered for such a position is Chief of Staff Röhm.
4. Herr von Papen must be removed and he himself would be ready to take the position of Vice-Chancellor; moreover, further important changes must be made in the Cabinet of the Reich.

As usual in such cases, there began then the search for the men to form the new Government, always with the understanding that I myself should, at least for the time being, be left in the position which I now hold.

The carrying out of these proposals of General von Schleicher was bound, as soon as Point 2 was reached, to come up against my unalterable opposition. Considering either the facts or his personal character, I could never have consented to a change in the Reich Ministry of War or to the appointment of Chief of Staff Röhm to that Ministry.

Firstly: consider the facts. For fourteen years I have stated consistently that the fighting organisations of the Party are political institutions and have nothing to do with the Army. On the facts of the case I should consider it a disavowal of my own convictions and of my fourteen years of political life if I were now to summon the leader of the SA to the command of the Army. In November 1923 I proposed as the head of the Army not the man who was then leader of my SA, Captain Göring, but an officer.

Secondly: consider the question of human character. On this matter I could never have concurred in General von Schleicher's proposal. When these plans became known to me my view of Chief of Staff Röhm's personal worth was already such that as a man of conscience and for the sake of the Army I could then under no circumstances even think of admitting him to that post: the supreme head of the Army is none other than the Field-Marshal and President of the Reich. As Chancellor I have given my oath into his keeping. For all of us his person is inviolate. The promise I gave him that I would preserve the Army as a non-political instrument of the Reich I hold as binding, both from my innermost conviction and also from my pledged word. Furthermore, considering my personal relations with the Defence Minister of the Reich, any such act would have been impossible. Not only I myself but all of us are happy to recognise in him a man of honour from the crown of his head to the soles of his feet. He reconciled the Army with those who were once revolutionaries and has linked it up with their Government today and he has done this from his own deepest convictions. In the most genuine loyalty he has made his own the principle for which I myself will stand to my last breath.

---

[65] Werner von Alvensleben, an associate of Schleicher's.

In the State there is only one bearer of arms—the Army; there is only one bearer of the political will—the National Socialist Party... .

In the meantime, Frick, the Reich Minister of the Interior, had seized his opportunity to eliminate the influence of the SA on the administration. This had been exercised officially through the special SA delegates (*Sonderbevollmächtigte*) appointed to supervise the various levels of administration under an order issued by Röhm on 12 May 1933. On 4 July 1934 Frick wrote to the new SA Chief of Staff, Viktor Lutze:

130

Some time ago, the previous Chief of Staff ordered the appointment of special SA delegates and representatives to the State Governments and their subordinate offices. This institution has not proved in the least beneficial. The delegates and representatives have in many cases claimed powers to which they were not entitled and have interfered with and impeded the orderly conduct of business by the State apparatus. I therefore request that you recall the special delegates and representatives at once.

The State Governments have received a copy of this letter.

Less than a week later, on 10 July, Lutze abolished the institution of SA delegates to the State administration.

However, this victory of the State authorities in their battle to retain their authority and independence was to prove only temporary. A far greater threat to their power had emerged out of the Röhm 'putsch'—the SS. On 20 July 1934 Hitler repaid his debt to the SS for their role in the affair by separating them from the now emasculated SA and granting them the status of an independent organisation. The SS were to provide the regime with a much more effective weapon for social control. Whereas the SA terror had been spontaneous, arbitrary, crude and disruptive, the SS were to make use of techniques which were far more coordinated, systematic and sophisticated; in the service of the regime they were to make terror a bureaucratic weapon. Furthermore, whereas the SA had embarked on a fruitless attempt to control the State administration (from a position outside the bureaucracy) through the SA delegates, the SS had from the start adopted a policy of infiltrating the bureaucracy and taking over segments of the State apparatus, beginning with the political police. This tactic was to prove itself infinitely more successful:

131

In view of highly meritorious service on the part of the SS, especially in connexion with the events of 30 June 1934, I elevate it to the status of an independent organisation within the NSDAP. The Reichsführer SS is therefore, like the Chief of Staff [of the SA], directly subordinate to the Supreme SS Führer. The Chief of Staff and the Reichsführer SS are both invested with the Party rank of Reichsleiter.

On 2 August 1934 President Hindenburg died. Immediately, the following law dated 1 August was promulgated. The Army and the Conservatives had repaid their debt to Hitler, who had saved them from the SA. Hitler had sacrificed the 'old fighters' to his major objective—internal mobilisation, to which political stability and economic recovery were essential. He was now officially Führer not only of the Party but also of the German people.

132

The Reich Government has enacted the following law which is hereby promulgated.

Section 1. The office of Reich President will be combined with that of Reich Chancellor. The existing authority of the Reich President will consequently be transferred to the Führer and Reich Chancellor, Adolf Hitler. He will select his deputy.

Section 2. This law is effective as of the time of the death of Reich President von Hindeburg.

The absolute control which Hitler now exercised over the State was reflected in the following oaths, introduced on 20 August. Significantly, they were taken to Hitler not as Head of the State, but as 'Führer of the German Reich and people', a totally new form of authority. The first stage in the 'seizure of power' was complete.

133

Article 1. The public officials and the soldiers of the armed forces must take an oath of loyalty on entering service.

Article 2.

1. The oath of loyalty of public officials will be:
    'I swear: I shall be loyal and obedient to Adolf Hitler, the Führer of the German Reich and people, respect the laws, and fulfil my official duties conscientiously, so help me God.'

2. The oath of loyalty of the soldiers of the armed forces will be:
'I swear by God this sacred oath: I will render unconditional obedience to Adolf Hitler, the Führer of the German nation and people, Supreme Commander of the Armed Forces, and will be ready as a brave soldier to risk my life at any time for this oath.'
Article 3. Officials already in service must swear the oath without delay according to Art. 2, number 1.

Hitler sent von Blomberg a message of thanks dated 20 August 1934:

134

Now, after the confirmation of the Law of 2 August by the German people, I wish to express my gratitude to you and through you to the Wehrmacht for your oath of loyalty to me as your leader and Commander-in-Chief. Just as the officers and men of the Wehrmacht pledge themselves to the new State in my person, so shall I always regard it as my highest duty to support the continued existence and inviolability of the armed forces in compliance with the testament of the late Field-Marshal [Hindenburg] and faithful to my own will to establish the Army firmly as the sole bearer of arms in the nation.

The attitude of the population to the Röhm affair varied. Some of the more educated people, particularly those with foreign sources of information, were horrified at what had happened. The propaganda of the Left in exile also made capital out of the crushing of the 'revolutionary' wing of the Nazi movement, though Nazi propaganda cleverly emphasised the involvement of 'reactionary elements' and made it appear as if it was these which had been crushed. The majority of people seem to have been relieved by what they saw as a timely lesson to the most undisciplined section of the Nazi movement. Hitherto they had comforted themselves with the belief that the Führer was not aware of the actions of these local Nazis and would not have approved if he had been. Now Hitler's measures over the Röhm affair seemed to confirm this judgement and they hoped that he would continue the purge through other Party organisations.

The following report of the Harburg-Wilhelmsburg Gestapo office of 5 July 1934 throws light on the attitude of the population to the purge:

135

In the month covered by this report the 30th of June naturally has pride of place. The measures proceeded smoothly in this area....Among the population at large, confidence in the Führer has been consolidated by his energetic action. There are, however, increasing requests for further energetic measures to be taken in the various Party organisations right down to the lowest levels, and in particular there are demands for liberation from 'the local Mussolinis'. If all the [Party] formations restricted themselves to the tasks delegated to them by the Führer instead of giving orders to the governmental authorities, the whole population could long ago have been filled with the spirit of National Socialism—in particular, with a sense of responsibility, cleanliness and discipline. It is essential that the Führer's announcement regarding the purging of the SA[66] should be acted upon by all Party organisations... .

One hard core SA man later reflected on his post-January 1933 experience of the events as follows:

136

That was not an SA any more. All those with money or a degree went into the SS and all the rest came into the SA on the basis of the motto: I must join otherwise...This dilution was terrible. Ernst Röhm was stupid in thinking after 1933 that he now had a tremendous power base. The SA had swollen enormously and he relied on that—but it could not be effective...

We were only waiting for Röhm to carry on the revolution, the social revolution...We thought: *we* created that, *we* prepared the way, why shouldn't we carry on with it. We were strong enough in those days to influence the party. We simply laughed at the party members running around in their uniforms after 1933. The 'officials' or whatever they called themselves—we didn't take them seriously. The politicians, these party functionaries were not at all popular with us. Party politics were suspect. And they made such a big thing of themselves: 'We define the political objectives'. We couldn't take that. A twit running around in a brown uniform and he is to define our political objectives and we are to carry out *his* political will!

We were the *fighting troop*. And we didn't want anyone to take over from us. In May, six weeks before the 'Röhm putsch' Röhm was here in Hamburg—there was a big parade—he made a very clever speech: 'They shouldn't imagine they will escape the night of the long knives', he said.

After the disgusting events at Wiessee that was the end of it for me. And not only for me. It had become pointless. Earlier on we had the Strassers, in Berlin we had Stennes and at the end we put our faith in Röhm...

What I can't understand is that after the murders in Wiessee the SA let itself be stripped of power so easily. Simply fizzled out. But by then most of the SA had got jobs. The hunt for jobs was on: an SA man could becomes a gas man, a state employee. One got a job with the Welfare Office, another with the Job Centre. Many had been unemployed and now they had work...Most of them lost much of their revolutionary elan. The real revolutionaries drew the consequences and got out. Resigned to it...

---

[66] This announcement of 2 July 1934 consisted of twelve points laid down by Hitler for the reorganisation of the SA.

List of Sources for Part I

1. Ernst Deuerlein (ed.), *Der Aufstieg der NSDAP 1919–1933 in Augenzeugenberichten* (Düsseldorf 1968), p. 60.
2. Ernst Deuerlein, 'Hitlers Eintritt in die Politik und die Reichswehr' In *Vierteljahrshefte für Zeitgeschichte* 7 (1959), pp.203ff.
3. E. Deuerlein, *Aufstieg* pp.108–112.
4. *Ibid.* pp.100–1.
5. R.G. Phelps, 'Hitler als Parteiredner: Dokument Nr. 17'. In *Vierteljahrshefte für Zeitgeschichte* 11 (1963), p.325.
6. Kurt Ludecke, *I Knew Hitler* (London 1938), pp.699–702.
7. Georg Franz-Willing, *Die Hitlerbewegung. Bd. I: Der Ursprung 1919 bis 1922* (Hamburg and Berlin 1962), pp.110ff.
8. Deuerlein, *Aufstieg*, p.144.
9. Albrecht Tyrell (ed.), *Führer befiehl...Selbstzeugnisse aus der'Kampfzeit' der NSDAP. Dokumentation und Analyse* (Düsseldorf 1969), pp.33–4.
10. Werner Jochmann (ed.), *Nationalsozialismus und Revolution: Dokumente* (Frankfurt 1963), pp.88–9.
11. Deuerlein, *Aufstieg*, p.144.
12. Tyrell, *Führer befiehl*, p.58.
13. Deuerlein, *Aufstieg*, pp.145–6.
14. ibid., pp.164–6.
15. ibid., p.192.
16. ibid., p.192–3.
17. Ernst Deuerlein, *Der Hitler-Putsch: Bayerische Dokumente zum 8/9 November 1923* (Stuttgart 1962), p.496.
18. Deuerlein, *Aufstieg*, pp.193–5.
19. Deuerlein, *Der Hitler-Putsch*, p.497.
20. Deuerlein, *Aufstieg*, pp.195–6.
21. Deuerlein, *Der Hitler-Putsch*, pp.511–12.
22. Tyrell, *Führer befiehl*, pp.65ff.
23. Ludecke, *I Knew Hitler*, pp.217–18.
24. *Völkischer Beobachter*, 26.ii.1925.
25. ibid.
26. Tyrell, *Führer befiehl*, pp.281–3.

27. Jochmann, *Nationalsozialismus und Revolution* pp.207ff.
28. ibid., pp.212–13.
29. *Nationalsozialistische Briefe* 15.x.1925.
30. *The Early Goebbels Diaries: 1925–1926* (London 1962), pp.66–7.
31. 'Geschichte der Ortsgruppe Affinghausen/Diepholz', Niedersächsisches Hauptstaatsarchiv, Hanover, Hann.Des. 310 I A Nr. 60.
32. Albert Krebs, *Tendenzen und Gestalten der NSDAP: Erinnerungen an die Frühzeit der Partei* (Stuttgart 1959), pp.42–3.
33. Geschichte der Ortsgruppe Harlingerode/Bad Harzburg, Niedersächsisches Hauptstaatsarchiv, Hann. Des. 310 I A Nr.69.
34. Ludolf Haase, *Aufstand in Niedersachsen: Der Kampf der NSDAP 1921–1924* (mimeo 1972) pp.192–3.
35. Hoover Institution Microfilms. NSDAP Hauptarchiv Reel 6 Folder 17.
36. Martin Broszat, 'Die Anfänge der Berliner NSDAP 1926–7' in *Vierteljahrshefte für Zeitgeschichte* 8 (1960), pp.102–3.
37. ibid.
38. Jochmann, *Nationalsozialismus und Revolution*, pp.241–2.
39. Tyrell, *Führer befiehl*, pp.235–6.
40. ibid., pp.163–4.
41. Niedersächsisches Hauptstaatsarchiv Hanover Hann. Des. 310 I A Nr.17.
42. Niedersächsisches Staatsarchiv Oldenburg 136 Nr.2860.
43. *Das Programm der NSDAP und seine weltanschaulichen Grundgedanken von Dipl. Ing. Gottfried Feder* (Munich 1932), pp.4–6.
44. *Völkischer Beobachter*, 31.v.1928.
45. W. Michalka and Gottfried Niedhart, *Die Ungeliebte Republik. Dokumente zur Innen-und Aussenpolitik Weimars 1918–1933* (Munich 1980), p.262.
46. Otto Strasser, *Hitler and I* (London 1940), pp.114ff.
47. Michalka and Niedhart, *Die Ungeliebte Republik*, p.62.
48. Deuerlein, *Aufstieg*, pp.306–7.
49. Michalka and Niedhart, *Die ungeliebte Republik*, pp.283–5.
50. a) Niedersächsisches Hauptstaatsarchiv, Hann. Des. 310 I B Nr.1.
    b) ibid.
    c) ibid.
51. Jochmann, Nationalsozialismus und Revolution pp.404–5.
52. Bayerisches Hauptstaatsarchiv, Munich, MA 101238.
53. Niedersächsisches Hauptstaatsarchiv Hanover, Hann. Des. 310 I A, Nr.35.
54. ibid.
55. ibid.
56. Hans Christian Brandenburg, *Die Geschichte der HJ* (Cologne 1968), p.100.
57. Niederšachsisches Staatsarchiv, Oldenburg 131 Nr.1207.
58. Bayerisches Staatsarchiv (Neuburg a.d. Donau), Bezirksamt Nördlingen, 1315.
59. Jochmann, *Nationalsozialismus und Revolution*, p.405.
60. E. Matthias and R. Morsey, (eds.), *Das Ende der Parteien 1933* (Düsseldorf 1960), p.782.
61. *Partei-Statistik 1 January 1935*. Herausgeber: Der Reichsorganisationsleiter der NSDAP (Munich 1935) Bd. I. p.162.
62. Ibid., p.70.
63. Nuremberg Document (ND) 2512–PS.
64. Hans-Adolf Jacobsen und Werner Jochmann (eds), *Ausgewählte Dokumente zur Geschichte des Nationalsozialismus 1933–1945* (Bielefeld 1961) Bd.I.
65. *Documents on British Foreign Policy, 1919–1939*, Second Series, vol.II, pp.296–8.
66. N.H. Baynes (ed.), *The Speeches of Adolf Hitler 1922–1939* (Oxford 1942), Vol.I, pp.826–9.

67. Deuerlein, *Aufstieg*, pp.353–4.
68. Gordon A. Craig, 'Briefe Schleichers an Groener', *Die Welt als Geschichte* II (1951), pp.130ff.
69. R.G. Phelps, 'Aus den Groener Dokumenten', *Deutsche Rundschau* 76 (1950), pp.1019ff.
70. R.G. Phelps, 'Aus den Groener Dokumenten', *Deutsche Rundschau* 77 (1951), pp.23ff.
71. ibid.
72. Joseph Goebbels, *My Part in Germany's Fight* (London 1938), pp.77ff.
73. Niedersächsisches Hauptstaatsarchiv, Hanover, Hann.Des.310 I A Nr.37.
74. Walther Hubatsch, *Hindenburg und der Staat* (Göttingen 1966), p.388.
75. Goebbels, *My Part*, p.122. (modified translation).
76. Niedersächsisches Hauptstaatsarchiv, Hanover Hann.Des.310 I B Nr.15.
77. National Archives, T-81, roll 1, frames 11427–11432.
78. Niedersächsisches Hauptstaatsarchiv, Hanover.Des.310 I A Nr.37.
79. Jochmann, *Nationalsozialismus und Revolution*, pp.407ff.
80. Hinrich Lohse, 'Der Fall Strasser', Forschungsstelle für die Geschichte des Nationalsozialismus in Hamburg.
81. ibid.
82. Deuerlein, *Aufstieg*, pp.411–14.
83. ND 3309-PS.
84. *The Ribbentrop Memoirs* (London 1954) pp.23–26.
85. *Documents on German Foreign Policy (DGFP)*, series C, vol.I, pp.5–8 (modified translation).
86. Jochmann, *Nationalsozialismus und Revolution*, p.421.
87. Jacobsen and Jochmann, *Ausgewählte Dokumente*, Bd II.
88. Jochmann, *Nationalsozialismus und Revolution*, pp.424ff.
89. ND 203-D.
90. *The Times* 21.ii.1933.
91. Hagen Schulze, ed., *Anpassung oder Widerstand? Aus den Akten des Parteivorstandes der deutschen Sozialdemokratie 1932/33* (Bonn 1975) pp.161–65.
92. Matthias and Morsey, *Das Ende der Parteien*, pp.234.
93. ibid., p.239.
94. Rudolf Diels, *Lucifer ante portas* (Stuttgart 1950), pp.142–4.
95. Reichsgesetzblatt (RGBL), Jg.1933, Teil I, Nr.17, p.83.
96. Jochmann, *Nationalsozialismus und Revolution*, p.427.
97. Henning Timpke ed. *Dokumente zur Gleichschaltung des Landes Hamburg* (Frankfurt 1964), pp.56–61.
98. Diels, *Lucifer ante portas*, p.200.
99. *Braunschweig unter dem Hakenkreuz* (Zurich 1933).
100. Walther Hofer, *Der Nationalsozialismus: Dokumente 1933–1945* (Frankfurt 1957), p.55.
101. Diels, *Lucifer ante portas*, pp.192–4, 199.
102. Erich Ebermayer, *Denn heute gehört uns Deutschland...Persönliches und politisches Von der Machtergreifung bis zum 31. December 1935* (Hamburg–Vienna 1959) p.47.
103. DGFP, Series C, Vol.I, pp.113–16.
104. Max Domarus, *Hitler: Reden und Proklamationen, 1932–1945*, Bd.I (Würzburg 1962), pp.232–3.
105. Matthias and Morsey, *Das Ende der Parteien 1933*, pp.431–2.
106. Hans Müller, *Katholische Kirche und Nationalsozialismus* (Munich 1963), pp.73–4.
107. Wilhelm Hoegner, *Der Schwierige Aussenseiter* (Munich 1963), pp. 92–3.
108. RGBl., Jg.1933, Teil I Nr.25, p.141.
109. Matthias and Morsey, *Das Ende der Parteien 1933*, p.643.
110. Goebbels, *My Part in Germany's Fight*, p.248.

111. Müller, *Katholische Kirche*, p.86.
112. Matthias and Morsey, *Das Ende der Parteien*, pp.443–4, 451–2.
113. DGFP, series C, vol.I, pp.652–3.
114. RGBl., Jg.1933, Teil I, Nr.81, p.479.
115. Jacobsen and Jochmann, *Ausgewählte Dokumente*, Bd.II.
116. Quoted in Peter Diehl-Thiele, *Partei und Staat im Dritten Reich* (Munich 1969), p.95.
117. Jacobsen and Jochmann, *Ausgewählte Dokumente*, Bd.II.
118. Timpke, *Dokumente zur Gleichschaltung des Landes Hamburg*, pp.217–18.
119. ND 951–D.
120. Heinrich Bennecke, *Hitler und die SA* (Munich 1962), p.82.
121. Jacobsen and Jochmann, *Ausgewählte Dokumente*, Bd.II.
122. Bennecke, *Hitler und die SA*, p.85.
123. *Ursachen und Folgen: Vom deutschen Zusammenbruch 1918 und 1945 bis zur staatlichen Neuordnung Deutschlands in der Gegenwart*, ed. H. Michaelis et al. (Berlin, undated), Bd. X, pp.168–72.
124. E. von Aretin, *Krone und Ketten: Erinnerungen eines bayerischen Edelmannes*, eds. Karl Buchheim and Karl Otmar von Aretin (Munich 1955), pp.365–6.
125. H.B. Gisevius, *Bis zum bittern Ende* (Zurich 1954), pp.142ff.
126. *Deutsche Allgemeine Zeitung*, Nr.302, 2.vii.34.
127. *Völkischer Beobachter* 3.vii.1934.
128. *Völkischer Beobachter* 5.vii.1934.
129. Baynes, *The Speeches of Adolf Hitler* vol.I, pp.311–13.
130. Staatsarchiv Bremen, N7 P ia, No.1149.
131. *Völkischer Beobachter*, 26.vii.1934.
132. RGBl., Jg.1934, Teil I Nr.89, p.747.
133. RGBl., Jg.1934, Teil I Nr.98.
134. *Völkischer Beobachter*, 21.viii.1934.
135. Niederśachsisches Hauptstaatsarchiv, Hanover, Hann.Des., Lüneburg III XXV, Nr.5.
136. *Terror und Hoffnung in Deutschland 1933–1945. Leben im Faschismus*, Herausgegeben von Johannes Beck et.al. (Hamburg 1980), pp.63–65.

A Selective Bibliography for Part I

D. Abraham, *The Collapse of the Weimar Republic. Political Economy and Crisis* (Princeton 1980)

W.S. Allen, *The Nazi Seizure of Power: the Experience of a Single German Town* (London 1966).

P. Aycoberry, *The Nazi Question. An Essay on the Interpretation of National Socialism* (New York 1981).

R. Bessel, *Political Violence and the Rise of Nazism. The Stormtroopers in Eastern Germany 1925–1934* (London 1984).

R. Bessel & E.J. Feuchtwanger, *Social Change and Political Development in Weimar Germany* (London 1981).

K.D. Bracher, *The German Dictatorship: the Origins, Structure and Effects of National Socialism* (London 1971).

M. Broszat, *The Hitler State* (London 1981).

A. Bullock, *Hitler. A Study in Tyranny* (London 1962).

J. Caplan, *Government Without Administration. State and Civil Service in Weimar Germany* (Oxford 1989).

W. Carr, *Hitler. A Study in Personality and Politics* (London 1978).

F.L. Carsten, *The Reichswehr and German Politics* (Oxford 1966).

T. Childers, '*The Nazi Voter. The Social Foundations of Fascism in Germany* (Chapel Hill, 1983).

T. Childers, ed., *The Formation of the Nazi Constituency 1919–1933* (London 1986).

J.M. Diehl, *Paramilitary Politics in Weimar Germany* (Bloomington, Ind. 1977).

G. Eley, 'What Produces Fascism: Pre-industrial Conditions or a Crisis of the Capitalist State?' *Politics and Society* 12 (1983).

T. Eschenburg, ed. *The Road to Dictatorship 1918–1933* (London 1974).

R.J. Evans and R. Geary, eds., *German Unemployed 1918–36* (Beckenham 1986).

J. Fest, *Hitler* (London 1974).

C. Fischer, *Stormtroopers: A Social Economic and Ideological Analysis 1929–35* (London 1983).

D. Gessner, 'Agrarian Protectionism in the Weimar Republic', *Journal of Contemporary History* 1977 12..4.

G. Eley, *The Reshaping of the German Right* (New Haven 1980).

J. Goebbels, *The Early Goebbels Diaries* ed. H. Heiber (London 1962).

R.H. Hamilton, *Who voted Nazi?* (Princeton 1982).

R. Heberle, *From Democracy to Nazism. A Regional Case Study on Political Parties in Germany* (New York 1970).

A. Hitler, *Mein Kampf* (London 1969).
H. Holborn, ed., *From Republic to Reich*. (New York 1972).
E. Jaeckel, *Hitler's Weltanschauung* (Middletown, Conn. 1972).
E. Jaeckel, *Hitler in History* (London 1984).
H. James, *The German Slump. Politics and Economics 1924–1936* (Oxford 1986).
L.E. Jones, 'The Dying Middle. Weimar Germany and the Fragmentation of Bourgeois Politics', *Central European History* 5 1972.
M. Kater, *The Nazi Party. A Social Profile of Members and Leaders 1919–1945* (Oxford 1983).
A. Krebs, *The Infancy of Nazism: The Memoirs of ex-Gauleiter Albert Krebs 1923–1933* ed. W.S. Allen (London 1978).
H. Lebovics, *Social Conservatism and the Middle Classes in Germany 1914–1933* (Princeton 1969).
M.R. Lepsius, 'From Fragmented Party Democracy to Government by Emergency Decree and National Socialist Takeover' in J.J. Linz and A. Stephan eds. *The Breakdown of Democratic Regimes. Europe* (Baltimore 1980).
P.H. Merkl, *Political Violence Under the Swastika* (Princeton 1975).
H. Mommsen, 'National Socialism: Continuity and Change' in *Fascism. A Reader's Guide* ed. W. Laqueur (London 1976).
A.J. Nicholls, *Weimar and the Rise of Hitler* (London 1980).
A.J. Nicholls & E. Matthias eds. *German Democracy and the Triumph of Hitler* (London 1971).
J. Noakes, *The Nazi Party in Lower Saxony 1921–1933* (Oxford 1971).
E. Nolte, *Three Faces of Fascism* (New York 1965).
J. Nyomarkay, *Charisma and Factionalism in the Nazi Party* (Minneapolis 1967).
D. Orlow, *A History of the Nazi Party Vol.1 1918–1933* (Newton Abbot 1969).
D. Petzina, 'Germany and the Great Depression', *Journal of Contemporary History* 1969.
G. Pridham, *Hitler's Rise to Power. The Nazi Party in Bavaria 1925–1933* (London 1973).
B. Smith, *Adolf Hitler. His Family, Childhood and Youth* (Stanford 1967).
P. Stachura, ed., *The Nazi Machtergreifung* (London 1983).
P. Stachura, ed., *Unemployment and the Great Depression in Weimar Germany* (London 1986).
W. Struve, *Elites against Democracy* (Princeton 1973).
T.A. Tilton, *Nazism, Neo-Nazism and the Peasantry* (Bloomington Ind. 1975).
H. A. Turner, *Germany Big Business and the Rise of Hitler* (Oxford 1985).
R. Waite, *Vanguard of Nazism. The Free Corps Movement in Post-War Germany 1919–1923* (Cambridge, Mass. 1952).
B. Weisbrod, 'Economic Power and Political Stability Reconsidered' *Social History* 1979.
J. Wheeler-Bennett, *Nemesis of Power. The German Army in Politics 1918–1945* (London 1967).
H.A. Winkler, 'The Social Conditions of Hitler's Rise to Power', *Journal of Contemporary History* 1976.
The despatches of the British Ambassador in Berlin, Sir Horace Rumbold, provide an illuminating account of developments in Germany in 1930–34. Cf. *Documents on British Foreign Policy 1919–1939* Second Series Vols.II–IV.

PART II
STATE, ECONOMY AND SOCIETY
1933-1939

CHAPTER 6

The Nazi Political System

The political system of the Third Reich was determined above all by two main features. Firstly, it was a personal dictatorship under a charismatic leader—that is a leader whose authority derived not from tradition or from office but from his possession of exceptional gifts in the eyes of his followers, first the Nazi Party and then the German people. This does not of course mean that Hitler was free to act as he wished, nor even that he initiated every major development in the Third Reich. Nevertheless, it would be foolish to deny that Hitler's role as dictator had major implications for what happened and for how it happened. Secondly, the Nazi regime was a one-party state in which the Nazi Party claimed supreme political authority in virtually every sphere. Here the emphasis must be on *claimed*. The extent to which the Party achieved political power and influence varied very much according both to period and to circumstances. Nevertheless, the fact that the Third Reich was a one-party state and that that party had totalitarian ambitions produced a major impact on developments in most areas.

(i) The Führer

Although in theory unlimited, in practice Hitler's power was restricted in a number of different ways. Above all, there was the sheer impossibility of one man keeping abreast of, let alone controlling, everything that was going on. Every day an enormous number of decisions had to be taken on a vast range of issues. Hitler could not know about, even less decide upon, more than a tiny fraction of these questions. There is of course nothing unusual about this; it is true of all heads of modern governments. But it does mean that excellent channels for and filters of information are necessary to select, process, and feed in those pieces of information which the head of government needs to know and convey those decisions which he needs to take. And the less work the head of government is prepared to put in himself, the more he is dependent on those channels and filters. Finally, even after a decision has been taken, it has to be implemented and this requires an administration which is efficient and whose performance can be monitored.

It is, in fact, notoriously difficult to chart the channels through which information and power flowed to and from the Führer. Hitler was averse to paperwork; most of his involvement in government took the form of face to face encounters between himself and his subordinates of which little or no record survives save brief comments about his wishes or simply that 'the Führer has been informed'. Furthermore, the official hierarchies of authority in the various spheres of government are even more misleading than usual as a guide to the real distribution of power. In a personal dictatorship such as Hitler's the key to the acquisition and maintenance of power was the ability to persuade people that one was acting with the support of the dictator. The key to power, therefore, became access to Hitler, not simply as a means of securing influence over him, but as a confirmation in the eyes of colleagues and rivals of one's own position within the regime. Access to Hitler, therefore, became the key factor in the political process overriding formal status of office in importance. As Hugh Trevor-Roper pointed out long ago, in many ways Hitler's government had more in common with a court than with twentieth-century cabinet or even presidential government.

Some of the implications of Hitler's role as a dictator are described in the following post-war reflections of Carl Schmitt, a leading constitutional lawyer, and Ernst von Weizsäcker, State Secretary in the Foreign Ministry:

137

(a) Such a concentration of total power in the hands of a single human individual, who claimed to rule a modern industrial state of 70 million people right down to every detail and to conduct a modern total war personally right down to orders to the individual surpasses all known examples of a 'personal regime'.... Correspondingly, the importance of those around Hitler surpasses the analogous phenomena of the other cases mentioned (e.g. William II).

Hitler's chauffeurs became high dignitaries of the regime. They received the rank of *Gruppenführer*, i.e. a general's rank.... A *Gau* leader who had access to Hitler was politically more important than a Reich Minister who did not see his Head of State for years. Thus, all concepts of a regulated and calculable distribution of responsibilities cease to be applicable.

Hitler's personal position of power involved an immense claim to omnipotence but also the claim to omniscience. His omnipotence existed to a large extent in fact and was highly effective. His omniscience, however, was purely fictitious. The first practical question therefore was who conveyed to the omnipotent Führer the material on which his decisions were based and who selected from the mass of mail which arrived and decided what was or was not to be shown him. The second question concerned the other aspect of dealing with things, the passing on of orders and decisions to the executive, a question of special importance because there were no clearly defined forms for the so-called Führer orders and the orders were often brief and abrupt. . . .

The higher Hitler climbed, and with him everyone who had access to him and who was in personal contact with him, the lower the Reich ministers who did not belong to these privileged people (e.g. Reich Minister of the Interior Frick) sank to the level of mere civil servants. The Reich Cabinet did not meet after 1937. Between the top level of political power and the previous highest posts which were sinking, a vacuum developed that had to be filled by new 'superministerial' structures corresponding to the extremely personal character of this kind of power and use of power. They could not be authorities in the sense of a rationally and functionally developed hierarchy, but could only be a highly personal staff regardless of any name under which they were registered. The usual, and in a certain sense typical, term which emerged to describe them was 'Chancellery' [*Kanzlei*]. . . .

(*b*) Hitler did not love Berlin. Mostly he was in Berchtesgaden in the Berghof. There was no such thing as a Government with Cabinet meetings. Ministers in charge of departments might for months on end, and even for years, have no opportunity of speaking to Hitler. As early as 1938 there was, as it were, a Supreme Headquarters. Anything that could not be settled between departments on their own account was referred there, in order that it might be brought to Hitler's attention by the Head of the Chancellery; or else the matter was simply put on one side as 'pending'. Ministerial skill consisted in making the most of a favourable hour or minute when Hitler made a decision, this often taking the form of a remark thrown out casually, which then went its way as an 'Order of the Führer'. . . .

In order to keep oneself informed of Hitler's opinion at any time, it was desirable to have one's own representative on his staff. The Army and Navy had their permanent adjutants there. Göring had a General Bodenschatz stationed there. Goebbels often visited Hitler's quarters personally. Ribbentrop, who had made the handling of Hitler a special study, posted his own *homme de confiance*, Hewel, later an ambassador, in Hitler's innermost circle. But apart from this, Ribbentrop, whenever he could do so, followed Supreme Headquarters from place to place. He then used to settle down somewhere half an hour or an hour away from where Hitler was, since the latter did not always want to have him around, and there he used to stay, on his toes, so to speak, and ready to appear on the scene at any moment. And so it came about that I was often alone in Berlin with the foreign ambassadors and envoys, reduced to guessing what had been planned in our foreign policy, or constrained to intercept rude aphorisms from Supreme Headquarters. Up to autumn 1938 I had not abandoned the attempt to influence political developments through the normal channel, by way of the Foreign Minister. From winter 1938/39 onwards, my notes of such efforts became ever rarer. . . .

The nature of Nazi rule was profoundly influenced by the style of leadership developed within the Nazi Party before 1933 and characterized by a peculiar combination of charisma and bureaucracy. The bureaucratic element had grown rapidly in importance after the electoral breakthrough of 1930 as the Party fought, with considerable success, to cope with the large number of new members and organize effective propaganda campaigns. In fact, however, its basis of authority remained not bureaucratic but charismatic, that is to say Hitler's absolute authority was derived not from his *office* as leader but from his exceptional qualities as an individual and leader in the eyes of his followers. All authority within the Party was ultimately concentrated in the hands of the leader, Hitler. It is true that some form of hierarchy was necessary for the functioning of such an elaborate organization. In theory, the Party organization was based on the so-called *Führerprinzip* or 'principle of leadership'. This principle laid down that at all levels of the organization authority was concentrated in a single individual or leader rather than in a committee or in the membership as a whole. Furthermore, it laid down that the authority of this leader over his subordinates was absolute. Again, in theory this made for a very simple and clear-cut hierarchical structure of authority deriving from military models. In practice, however, even before 1933, the situation was much more complex and confused. Those who held authority at subordinate levels did so in the final analysis as Hitler's direct representatives rather than as officials within a hierarchy. Hitler, as the charismatic leader, was never bound by the hierarchy and could go outside it whenever he chose. This is illustrated by the fact that, even before 1933, the hierarchy of the political organization of the Nazi Party was undermined by the tenuous control of the headquarters over the regional leaders or Gauleiters, who regarded themselves as Hitler's personal agents in their area, answerable only to him.

After 1933, this charismatic form of leadership was transferred from the Party to the German State and nation to form the basis of the Nazi regime. The constitutional turning point came with the Law concerning the Head of State of the German Reich of 1 August 1934, in which the offices of Reich President and Reich Chancellor were merged to form the new office of 'Führer and Reich Chancellor', later significantly shortened to 'Führer'.[1] The key concept of 'Führer power' [*Führergewalt*] was defined by the leading constitutional theorist of the Third Reich, Ernst Rudolf Huber, as follows:

138

The office of Führer has developed out of the National Socialist movement. In its origins it is not a State office. This fact must never be forgotten if one wishes to understand the current political and legal position of the Führer. The office of Führer

---

[1] See p. 185 above.

has grown out of the movement into the Reich, firstly through the Führer taking over the authority of the Reich Chancellor and then through his taking over the position of Head of State. Primary importance must be accorded to the position of 'Führer of the movement'; it has absorbed the two highest functions of the political leadership of the Reich and thereby created the new office of 'Führer of the Nation and of the Reich'. . .

The position of Führer combines in itself all sovereign power of the Reich; all public power in the State as in the movement is derived from the Führer power. If we wish to define political power in the *völkisch* Reich correctly, we must not speak of 'State power' but of 'Führer power'. For it is not the State as an impersonal entity which is the source of political power but rather political power is given to the Führer as the executor of the nation's common will. Führer power is comprehensive and total; it unites within itself all means of creative political activity; it embraces all spheres of national life; it includes all national comrades who are bound to the Führer in loyalty and obedience. Führer power is not restricted by safeguards and controls, by autonomous protected spheres, and by vested individual rights, but rather it is free and independent, exclusive and unlimited.

Thus Hitler's position of absolute power was justified not in rational-legal terms through his constitutional position as Reich Chancellor and Head of State, which would have imposed constitutional limitations on his authority, but in charismatic terms through his role as Leader of the German people, as the sole and exclusive representative of the nation's will and of its historical mission. This is made clear in a speech by Hans Frank, the head of the Nazi Association of Lawyers and of the Academy of German Law, in 1938:

139

. . . Even if no further decisions or legal formulations were added to the present laws of the Third Reich governing its legal structure, as a result of five years' government by the Führer there can be no juridical doubts about the following absolutely clear principles of the Reich:

1. At the head of the Reich stands the leader of the NSDAP as leader of the German Reich for life.
2. He is, on the strength of his being leader of the NSDAP, leader and Chancellor of the Reich. As such he embodies simultaneously, as Head of State, supreme State power and, as chief of the Government, the central functions of the whole Reich administration. He is Head of State and chief of the Government in one person. He is Commander-in-Chief of all the armed forces of the Reich.
3. The Führer and Reich Chancellor is the constituent delegate [*verfassunggebende Abgeordnete*] of the German people, who without regard for formal pre-conditions decides the outward form of the Reich, its structure and general policy.

4. The Führer is supreme judge of the nation.... There is no position in the area of constitutional law in the Third Reich independent of this elemental will of the Führer.

The real characteristic of constitutional law in the Third Reich is that it does not represent a system of competencies but the relation of the whole German people to a personality who is engaged in shaping history. We are in a juridical period founded on the Führer's name, and shaped by him. The Führer is not backed by constitutional clauses, but by outstanding achievements which are based on the combination of a calling and of his devotion to the people. The Führer does not put into effect a constitution according to legal guidelines laid before him but by historic achievements which serve the future of his people. Through this, German Constitutional Law has produced the highest organic viewpoint which legal history has to offer. Constitutional Law in the Third Reich is the legal formulation of the historic will of the Führer, but the historic will of the Führer is not the fulfilment of legal preconditions for his activity. Whether the Führer governs according to a formal written Constitution is not a legal question of the first importance. The legal question is only whether through his activity the Führer guarantees the existence of his people.

(ii) The Party

Nazi Germany, however, was not only a personal dictatorship, it was also a one-party state. Many of the problems which developed for the regime sprang from the tensions created by the inadequate integration of the new Party and old civil service elites with their very different styles and mentalities. For the 'seizure of power' in 1933 brought two very different organizations, the Party and the Civil Service, face to face with one another.

In addition to the charismatic basis of authority within the organization, the Nazi Party was characterized by a conception of its own role as a political crusade. It saw itself engaged on the vital task of saving the German people from what it regarded as the fatally debilitating democratic political structures and corrupting intellectual, social, and moral values associated with the liberal, democratic, and Socialist forces of the Weimar Republic. The Party aimed to overcome the various divisions hitherto setting German against German—through class, status, religion, regional loyalties by creating a 'national (or people's) community' (*Volksgemeinschaft*) based on ties of blood or race, a shared destiny, and a common set of values founded on the Nazi *Weltanschauung* and on, 'healthy popular sentiment' (*gesundes Volksempfinden*). This united 'national community' would in turn enable the German people to generate the strength and energy necessary not only for their revival but for a renewal of their bid to become a dominant world power.

This crusading vision of its own role contributed to the Party's ruthless and intolerant attitude towards any obstacles in its path, including those provided by legal rules and State regulations. Moreover, the leaders of the Party cadres—the hard core Nazis—were for the most part men who had been formed in the tough and often brutal world of the Free Corps and the Party's 'time of struggle' before 1933. Most were ruthless political entrepreneurs, determined to gain power and then to keep it, openly contemptuous of bureaucratic and legal 'clauses'. Apart from their own personal interests and those of their cliques, they were loyal only to the Führer and to what they (rightly) saw as his main aims—the racist and imperialist goals at the core of Nazi ideology. Party contempt for the bureaucracy and its regulations was encouraged by Hitler himself both in statements in *Mein Kampf* and in frequent comments to his entourage.

Hitler identified the vital political entity as the German *Volk*—the German nation as a racially-determined entity—not the State, which for Hitler was merely a 'vessel' for the race. As he put it in *Mein Kampf*: 'We must distinguish in the sharpest way between the State as a vessel and the race as its content. This vessel has meaning only if it can preserve and protect the content; otherwise it is useless'. The true interests of the *Volk* were articulated not by 'the State' but by Hitler as the leader of the *Volk*, who used his Party as his main instrument for guiding the State in the right direction. The Party was envisaged as both a check and a goad for the State machine and as a substitute for it where State officials proved unsuitable for carrying out particular policies deriving from the Party's ideological goals. An example was extreme measures against the Jews. Hans Frank commented in his Memoirs on Hitler's attitude:

140

Hitler had been a Party man. As such he had come to power and he remained one as a statesman: he always kept the position of supreme leader of the NSDAP as well as his Reich positions. On 30 January 1933 the investiture of this function in his person was clarified and consolidated. It was also formally secured. His will was Party law. He was the absolute autocrat of the NSDAP. The Reich, however, especially the State apparatus bound by formal lines of jurisdiction and a hierarchy of command, was unfamiliar and strange to him. On 30 January 1933 his will alone was not yet 'law' in this area. Therefore he felt insecure and inhibited towards it. But since he believed he had been victorious in pushing through his concept of the Party, he saw the organizational form of the NSDAP as suiting him best: instead of transferring to the Party the traditional form of a legally ordered, expertly supervised, formally interdependent, juridically controlled State executive, his whole aim was to transfer the independent position he had in the NSDAP and its inner structure to the State. On 30 January 1933 he brought this aim with him.

It was in this context that Party/State relations developed. The problem of dealing with a Civil Service committed to legality and bureaucratic rules was met, first, by using the Party and SS as two distinct executive agencies independent of, though partially linked to, the State machine, to keep a check on the Civil Service and carry out measures beyond the law; secondly, through the tendency for leading Nazis, bent on expanding their empires, steadily to encroach on the responsibilities previously exercised by departments within the official hierarchy of the State; and, thirdly, through Hitler's practice of creating new departments, often headed by Party heavyweights, who were determined to capture power and responsibility from the rival state bodies.

The tendency for Party agencies to encroach on those of the state was encouraged by Hitler's invariable failure to allocate to them specific areas of competence, with the result that there was no means of calling them to order. In any case, only Hitler would have had the power to do so and he was always loath to get involved in such struggles over competence. Indeed, he tended, either explicitly or often merely implicitly, to sanction this development, in effect encouraging these Nazi leaders to build up their own machines in rivalry with the government departments traditionally responsible for those particular spheres. These men were effectively agents of Hitler as the Führer and hence free to act outside the official state hierarchy. Notorious examples were Heinrich Himmler, who, as Reichsführer SS, usurped the vital police powers of the Ministries of the Interior, and Robert Ley, who, as leader of the German Labour Front, absorbed responsibilities from the Reich Ministry of Labour and endeavoured to encroach on the Reich Ministries of Economics and Agriculture.

Increasingly, government in the Third Reich came to resemble a war of all against all, with Hitler standing above the fray, intervening only very occasionally and even then not necessarily decisively. Moreover, as the regime continued, decisions tended to be reached in an increasingly arbitrary and irrational fashion. Hitler increasingly listened and responded to those Nazi Party heavyweights with access to him instead of acting on the basis of evidence put forward by the officials best qualified to prepare the data for a sound decision. Given Hitler's revolutionary goals, his unwillingness to rely on conventional civil service advice was understandable but the costs could be high. Moreover, he was often not prepared to listen to anyone, believing that he had a unique grasp of problems. The following, letter, dated 5 June 1935 is from Hitler's adjutant, Fritz Wiedemann, to Martin Bormann; it concerns the question of youth, on which the latter had submitted a long memorandum, and is suggestive of this very attitude.

141

I am returning to you the enclosed memorandum. The Führer received it but then gave it back to me at once unread. He himself wishes to deal with this question in his major speech at the next Party Rally and thus does not want his thinking to be influenced in any way from any quarter.

There was in fact a growing tendency for Hitler to opt out of active participation in the day-to-day running of the government and to concentrate on those aspects which particularly interested him—foreign policy, military questions, and pet architectural projects. Except where his major goals were directly concerned as, for example, with the launching in 1936 of the Four Year economic plan[2], which was intended to prepare the German economy for war, his interventions in domestic affairs became increasingly sporadic and haphazard. Even with the launching of the Four Year Plan Hitler's options had already been largely preempted by his failure to intervene decisively during the previous twelve months, with the result that the initiative had been taken by Göring and the lobby formed by the powerful IG Farben chemicals combine. Finally, during the war years, he was so preoccupied with the day-to-day running of the war that his interventions were reduced still further.

(iii) A Polycratic Regime

There increasingly emerged two coexistent but alternative spheres of authority—that of the normal State and legal system and the exceptional sphere of 'Führer power'. The State machine and the legal system were of course ultimately subordinate to the Führer. But in many areas and for much of the time they were permitted to operate as before. Laws were passed and administered, bureaucratic regulations were issued and implemented in accordance with constitutional and official procedures. This provided the essential element of rationality and predictability without which no modern, highly organized society can function. Civil servants, businessmen, and ordinary citizens knew to some extent where they were, and what rules they should follow in pursuing their various occupations and going about their private affairs. At the same time, however, this relative normality in State and society was increasingly liable to be breached at any moment by an intervention from the sphere of 'Führer power'. This would characteristically take the form of an assertion of the overriding importance of 'political priorities', enabling, for example, the Gestapo to consign anyone to a concentration camp without right of appeal even if he had just been found not guilty by the courts. At the same time, there was a progressive seepage of Nazi ideology into more and more spheres of life, including the interpretation of the law, and an insistent claim by Nazi party organizations to take over more and more of the activities hitherto covered by the state

---

[2]See below, pp. 289ff.

and local government. This was grounded in their role as the agencies of 'Führer power' and as the qualified exponents of Nazi ideology. The whole basis of the State and of the legal order in Germany as developed over the previous hundred and fifty years was being progressively eroded by the corrosive effects of 'Führer power'.

In place of the old image fostered by Nazi propaganda of the regime as a coldly calculating, ruthlessly efficient machine, research over the past twenty years has revealed the Third Reich to have been a labyrinthine structure of overlapping competencies, institutional confusion and a chaos of personal rivalries. The fields of propaganda and cultural policy, for example, saw permanent internecine warfare between Goebbels as Reich Minister of Propaganda, Rosenberg as the agent for the supervision of the Nazi *Weltanschauung*, Otto Dietrich as the Nazi Press Chief, Bernhard Rust as Reich Minister of Education, and Philipp Bouhler as head of a censorship office—among others! In addition to these rivalries among the various Party bosses, the regime as a whole was also riven by tension between the major power centres within it, each of which had varying degrees of autonomy and endeavoured to assert its interests vis-à-vis the others; the Wehrmacht leadership, Big Business, the SS, the senior ranks of the State bureaucracy, the Office of the Führer's Deputy/Party Chancellery and the Party's cadre organization. These blocks were themselves divided and internally at odds. Although institutional conflict is endemic in virtually all governmental systems and the chaos of Nazi rule appears striking only in contrast with the false monolithic image which had concealed it, the student of Nazi government cannot avoid the impression that the Third Reich was characterized by a degree of institutional anarchy that was unique—certainly in modern German history.

However, the new picture of a regime riven by internal conflict and characterized by a polycratic rather than a monolithic structure raises questions still not satisfactorily resolved. The first is the reason for this state of affairs, the second its implications for the regime's actions. On the first issue two main views have emerged. One insists that this institutional conflict represented the intentions of the Führer, who was consciously following a policy of 'divide and rule'. His power was based on the plethora of competing individuals and organizations so that nowhere could concentrations of power develop which might threaten the leader's position. The absence of clear lines of competence between the various sub-leaders and their organizations obliged them continually to refer to Hitler to confirm their authority, and also to compete with one another for his approval. One of the first statements of this view was made by Otto Dietrich, Hitler's Press Chief, in his Memoirs:

142

In the twelve years of his rule in Germany Hitler produced the biggest confusion in government that has ever existed in a civilized state. During his period of government, he removed from the organization of the state all clarity of leadership and produced a completely opaque network of competencies. It was not laziness or an excessive degree of tolerance which led the otherwise so energetic and forceful Hitler to tolerate this real witch's cauldron of struggles for position and conflicts over competence. It was intentional. With this technique he systematically disorganized the upper echelons of the Reich leadership in order to develop and further the authority of his own will until it became a despotic tyranny.

It has also been suggested that Hitler's encouragement of conflict through his continual creation of new agencies and his refusal to define competencies reflected his social darwinist belief that through conflict the best and most effective individuals would emerge on top and the weakest would be weeded out. Hitler, that is, encouraged a kind of institutional struggle for the survival of the fittest.

What implications had this chaotic administrative system for the policies and actions of the regime? Those historians who attribute it largely to Hitler's conscious intentions also tend to claim that it did not in fact affect decisively the implementation of major objectives. These are seen as being the acquisition of *Lebensraum* in the East and the campaign against the Jews. It is argued that the most serious effects of the institutional chaos were felt in the field of domestic policy, an area in which Hitler himself was little interested and, therefore, was loath to intervene. As far as foreign policy and antisemitism are concerned—the two key areas for Hitler—the lack of administrative coherence in other spheres merely affected the *timing* of diplomatic and antisemitic measures rather than the nature of the measures themselves. Here, allegedly, Hitler retained the reins in his own hands and was able to secure the effective implementation of his major ideological goals.

A number of historians, however, have cast doubt on this 'intentionalist' view of the regime in general and on Hitler's role in it in particular. They adopt a 'structuralist' or 'functionalist' approach and cast doubt on the extent to which the Nazi system was a product of conscious intention on Hitler's part. Indeed, Hans Mommsen has gone so far as to suggest that it derived, in part at any rate, from a lack of decisiveness by Hitler and to claim that he was, in a sense, a weak dictator.

There is certainly evidence that Hitler often avoided decisions or delayed them as long as possible. In particular, he frequently declined to get involved in disputes between subordinates, preferring to leave them to sort the matter out among themselves. How far this was a calculated tactic on Hitler's part to preserve his nimbus of authority or how far it reflected a basic indeciseveness is a moot point. The following reported comment by Hans-Heinrich Lammers, the head of the Reich Chancellery, and therefore one of those best qualified to observe Hitler's style as a ruler, is illuminating. It was made during a discussion about the Reich Ministry of Economics to the Lord Mayor of Hamburg in the Autumn of 1937, who noted it in his diary:

143

...I had a long talk with State Secretary Lammers about Schacht. He said the Führer found it so difficult to make decisions about personnel. He always hoped that things would sort themselves out on their own. A decision had not yet been made because the Führer was not satisfied with the nomination of only one state secretary and would prefer to appoint a minister. He kept hoping that the question of personnel would solve itself. He, Lammers, had proposed the appointment of super ministers to whom some of the ministers would be subordinated as far as particular issues were concerned. The reason was that he found it extremely difficult to work with this large cabinet...

Secondly, these historians suggest that many of the regime's measures, even in such crucial spheres as the anti-Jewish campaign, were not, in fact, the result of long-term planning or even in some cases intention. They were rather ad hoc responses to the pressure of circumstances not only by Hitler himself but also on the part of particular agencies acting more or less autonomously. In other words, the state was not only an inefficient machine for the implementation of an irrational programme, but, if anything, its uncoordinated workings influenced—in some cases profoundly—the way in which ideology was actually translated into practice. In particular, there tended to be what Hans Mommsen has termed a process of 'cumulative radicalization', as subordinate organizations vied with one another to maintain or acquire responsibilities and in the process tended to adopt the more radical of the available alternatives on the assumption that this reflected the Führer's will.

It could, of course, be argued that this process ensured that in practice things moved in the general direction Hitler wanted to go without requiring his direct involvement. The following statement by Werner Willikens, State Secretary in the Reich Ministry of Agriculture and an old guard Nazi, made to a meeting of state agricultural representatives on 21 February 1934 is suggestive here:

144

Everyone who has the opportunity to observe it knows that the Führer can hardly dictate from above everything which he intends to realize sooner or later. On the contrary, up till now everyone with a post in the new Germany has worked best when he has, so to speak, worked towards the Führer. Very often and in many spheres it has been the case—in previous years as well—that individuals have simply waited for orders and instructions. Unfortunately, the same will be true in the future; but in fact it is the duty of everybody to try to work towards the Führer along the lines he would wish. Anyone who makes mistakes will notice it soon enough. But anyone who really works towards the Führer along his lines and towards his goal will certainly both now and in the future one day have the finest reward in the form of the sudden legal confirmation of his work.

(iv) The Hitler Style of Leadership

One of the keys to understanding the Nazi regime lies in Hitler's characteristics as a leader and in the nature of the Nazi movement as it had developed before 1933. While the Nazis were still trying to gain power, the main requirements were to mobilize energy and support and also to appeal to as wide a section of the community as possible. What was needed was a dynamic and inspirational kind of leadership; something was offered to everybody and the contradictions seemed not to matter. But after 1933 the task was no longer to win power but to retain it and to achieve goals. It was necessary to make decisions between competing choices on the basis of a rational assessment of priorities and to do so in the light of the maximum amount and optimum quality of available information. It was here that the limitations of Hitler's own personality and political background and those of his movement became apparent. Hitler was essentially a propagandist— he was an inspirational kind of politician. What he had always lacked was an awareness of the problems involved in translating policy into action, problems of organization and administration. Hitler hated bureaucratic structures and procedures and the mentality which went with them. He saw politics essentially as the actions of great individuals such as himself. He saw the solving of problems as a matter of determination and will-power—the ability to galvanize people by a combination of personal inspiration and intimidation. After the war, Fritz Wiedemann, one of Hitler's adjutants commented in his memoirs on Hitler's style of work:

145

In 1935 Hitler kept to a reasonably ordered daily routine.... Gradually, this fairly orderly work routine broke down. Later Hitler normally appeared shortly before lunch, quickly read through Reich Press Chief, Dietrich's press cuttings, and then went into lunch. So it became more and more difficult for Lammers and Meissner to get him to make decisions which he alone could make as Head of State.... When Hitler stayed at Obersalzberg it was even worse. There, he never left his room before 2.00 pm. Then, he went to lunch. He spent most afternoons taking a walk, in the evening straight after dinner, there were films. There can be no question of Hitler's work habits being similar to those attributed to Frederick the Great or Napoleon. He disliked the study of documents. I have sometimes secured decisions from him, even ones about important matters, without his ever asking to see the relevant files. He took the view that many things sorted themselves out on their own if one did not interfere. And, he was by no means wrong about that. But the question was *how* did they sort themselves out? The Party leaders found it easiest to get something out of him. If they belonged to the top ranks they could always come to lunch. During coffee in the Winter Garden they quickly explained their problem to him and normally got the decision they wanted. It was not surprising that the State offices were outmanoeuvred.... He let people tell him the things he wanted to hear, everything else he rejected. One still sometimes hears the view that Hitler would have done the right thing if the people surrounding him had not kept him wrongly informed. Hitler refused to let himself be informed. Unfortunately, that was not only the case in domestic affairs but in foreign affairs as well.... How can one tell someone the truth who immediately gets angry when the facts do not suit him. Perhaps that may have been part of his strength. I once discussed with Hess Hitler's characteristic of simply refusing to accept certain things. Hess told me that this was already the case during the time of struggle and gave me an example. Hitler repeatedly gave the Reich Party Treasurer instructions to let him have say 200,000 RM on the following day. If Schwarz replied: 'You can't have it, there's no money in the coffers!', Hitler invariably replied: 'I don't care, the money must be there by tomorrow! 'And it always was there! Schwarz had somehow got it together. 'Do you see', Hess continued, 'in this way Hitler gradually got used to being able to overcome all objections. And he is still doing it now'.

Hitler's style of leadership sprang partly from his own personality and from his experience during the 'time of struggle', but it also derived from the nature of his position as a charismatic leader. Clearly, it would be impossible for him to retain his nimbus as the great *Führer* if he became too involved in day-to-day politics. Hitler was a master of the theatrical aspect of politics and was aware that this was one of his greatest strengths. He thus preferred to stand aloof as far as possible.

In any government, however, people tend to look to the head of government for instructions and decisions. This is even more true of a dictatorship in which authority is concentrated in the hands of the dictator. Should the dictator avoid decisions or decline to get involved, something like a vacuum develops at the heart of government. This increasingly happened in the Third Reich. The vacuum was filled by confusion and dissension which could not be resolved by the sporadic and arbitrary interventions of the

Führer. Moreover, although he was not prepared to take on the burden of coordinating and giving an active lead to the government, he was not prepared to risk letting anybody else do it and certainly not the bureaucracy itself. Hitler failed to understand that for any system to function effectively individuals and their actions must be integrated into an ordered structure. He emasculated the existing bureaucratic structures without putting effective alternatives in their place. He retained, for example, the Reich Chancellery and used it to supervise the routine legislative and administrative functions of government, while increasingly undermining it by his growing tendency to bypass it in important areas of policy and deal directly with the particular individuals concerned.

Indeed, the situation was further complicated by Hitler's refusal to define a system of spheres of competence. As a result, in place of the requisite team spirit within the government there was a destructive struggle over competences which consumed vast amounts of time and energy and encouraged the dominance of arbitrary and uncontrolled forces, making coherent planning impossible. Moreover, in such a state of internecine warfare it was in the interests of each organization to hoard its information and conceal its plans. This tendency was increased by the paranoia induced by a dictatorship in which the expression of opinion and the release of information was strictly controlled through censorship and the operations of a police state. Hitler himself contributed to this situation by his insistence that information should be confined to those directly involved: a fetish was made of secrecy. The result of all this was that the regime tended to disintegrate into separate components, each of which pursued its own particular interests without reference to the others or to overall objectives, which, except in a few instances, were never really clearly defined. This tendency towards disintegration was further encouraged by Hitler's practice of creating or tolerating the creation of new agencies to take over responsibilities from existing government departments. Thus, by 1942, there were eleven new agencies at Reich level established in specialist areas covered by existing ministries but not subject to ministerial supervision; one of these, the Office of the Director of the Four Year Plan, had seventeen subordinate agencies of its own, all equally un-coordinated with relevant agencies in the sub-ministerial system. Thus, to return to the analogy used at the beginning, the conventional channels and filters silted up or found their sources of information and power reduced or cut off. New bypass channels were created, but the old ones were not removed, until the whole system came to resemble the delta system of a very large river.

It could be argued, however, that this picture of 'authoritarian anarchy[3] does not fit the remarkable successes of the regime in various fields and, in

[3] A term used as the title of the first analysis of the Nazi system by an insider after 1945. Cf. W. Petwaidic, *Die autoritäre Anarchie* (Hamburg 1946).

particular, the conquest of virtually the whole of Europe. These ' achievements', however, can be attributed first to Hitler's exceptional political skill in gauging and exploiting the weaknesses of his opponents, and secondly to the work of such traditional German elites and institutions as the Army, industry, the Civil Service, and the universities. For, up until 1939, indeed arguably well into the war, the regime was based on an alliance between the Nazi movement and the traditional German elites, an alliance founded on 'a partial identity of views'. The Nazis succeeded in mobilizing these elites by harnessing their patriotism, exploiting the profit motive and their fears of Bolshevism, and focusing their energies on the goal of mobilization for war. But the regime's achievements were, to some extent, secured in spite of rather than because of Nazi leadership, as, for example, in the case of German science and technology, where the effects of an irrational ideology and weaknesses of organization combined to undermine one of Germany's main strengths.

What the Nazis were good at was mobilization, the unleashing of energy. The nature of Nazism was such that that very dynamic was bound to be destructive not only of others but also of themselves. A potentially fatal weakness of the regime was its inability to create an effective political and administrative apparatus which could, first of all, define realistic objectives related to the resources available and then deploy the resources of the community with maximum efficiency in order to achieve those objectives. For example, Hitler's failure to plan and coordinate a comprehensive and balanced armaments programme produced a damaging arms race between the three armed services, each of which went its own way. Attempts by agencies such as the Wehrmacht Armaments' Office to define priorities, build up reserves and, above all, match rearmament goals to available resources were stymied by Hitler's practice of dealing with the leaders of the Armed Services individually, egging each of them on to achieve totally unrealistic targets. These developments produced an overstrained economy and contributed to a dynamic which helped to push Germany into a war for which she was not adequately prepared.

Hitler no doubt sensed that the introduction of rational administrative procedures would not only have strengthened the role of the despised civilian and military bureaucracies, but would have sapped the dynamic of Nazism, its essential feature. Rational methods were inappropriate to an essentially irrational movement. Indeed, Hitler's growing unwillingness to get involved in decision-making, in the domestic field at any rate, was almost certainly due in part to the intractability of the problems confronting him. In this situation it was far easier just to press ahead on all fronts without thinking too hard about priorities. Thus, the final bankruptcy of Nazism was not just the product of the clash of the irrational goals of Nazism with the realities of the international situation. It was also encouraged by the defects of the apparatus of government itself, defects deriving both from Hitler's own limitations as a dictator and from the kind of movement and regime which he had created.

CHAPTER 7

Central Government and the Role of the Reich Chancellery

During the first few months after Hitler's appointment as Reich Chancellor, the Reich government continued to operate much as before. While President Hindenburg remained next door to him in Berlin and total power was not yet concentrated in his hands, Hitler followed a more or less orderly office routine and there were fairly frequent and regular cabinet meetings. With the passage of the Enabling Act of 24 March 1933, however, Hitler no longer needed to pay much attention to his Nationalist allies in the government and no longer needed the President's signature for legislation. Exploiting his growing freedom of manoeuvre, Hitler increasingly opted out of what he found to be the tedious routine of day-to-day government. On the grounds that he had to free his mind from detail in order to be able to concentrate on the big decisions—although he was quite happy to immerse himself in the detail of any architectural project—Hitler gradually reverted to his pre-1933 style of life, which involved turning night into day and marked the end of a conventional office routine. In particular, cabinet meetings became less and less frequent: there were 72 in 1933, 19 in 1934, 12 in 1935, 4 in 1936, 7 in 1937, and the last one was held on 5 February 1938. They also changed their nature. They ceased to be a forum for discussion, for the reconciliation of conflicting views, and for the coordination of policy. Hitler disliked this kind of discussion and hated being disagreed with—at any rate publicly. In any case, when the meetings became infrequent too much business had accumulated for them to be anything more than largely formal affairs. The cabinet became simply a sounding board for Hitler. Increasingly, legislation was not settled at cabinet meetings but instead was issued after a so-called *Umlaufverfahren* or circulation process. Under a change in the Government Rules of Procedure of 20 July 1933, legislation no longer required oral discussion between ministers but could be settled by circulating drafts among the responsible ministers provided they could agree on a final draft. This development and some of its implications were described after the war by Dr Leo Killy, the desk officer in the Reich Chancellery responsible for Civil Service matters:

146

I see the main complication caused by the demise of the cabinet in the fact that for the passing of important and complicated laws the process of oral discussion in cabinet, which simplified matters a great deal and was really the natural way of doing things, no longer took place. Oral discussion, which had hitherto occurred under the chairmanship of the Reich Chancellor, had also served to keep him thoroughly informed through the departmental minister responsible about the contents of and the issues involved in the particular law concerned. This had previously simplified the head of the Reich Chancellery's task of supplying information. Also, whereas previously differences of opinion between individual government departments could be discussed in the cabinet meetings and, in the event of an irreconcilable division, could be decided directly by the Reich Chancellor, this was now no longer possible. This situation was made even more difficult by the fact that, soon after the ending of cabinet meetings, Hitler no longer received the departmental ministers. This not only produced an increase in work but also added complications for Dr. Lammers. They manifested themselves in the unavoidable increase in correspondence with the departments after oral discussion of these matters had ceased. It also showed itself, however, in an increase in meetings and in the material which had to be reported orally to Hitler. Hitler had instructed that he would receive such reports only after all the participants had been heard and when there were no more objections or differences of opinion or they were demonstrably irreconcilable.

After the ending of cabinet meetings the method of dealing with draft laws through written agreement became the general rule whereas previously it had been the exception. The Reich Chancellery was responsible for the formal and technical preparation of this legislative process and for the supervision of its formal procedures. The process worked as follows: If a department wished to secure agreement to a draft law, it sent the draft with a sufficient number of copies to the Reich Chancellery. There it would be stamped in the office for distribution with a date within which objections had to be lodged. If no objections were made within this period, the Reich Chancellery merely had to note the fact. Then it was up to the head of the Reich Chancellery to inform the Reich Chancellor. If he also agreed the law was passed. The departmental minister was then informed of this and it was his responsibility to prepare the law itself, secure the signatures of the relevant ministers involved, and then send on the completed law for signature by the Reich Chancellor.

Even in the case where objection was made, it was not the task of the Reich Chancellery to exercise influence. It was up to the departmental minister involved to discuss the matter with whoever had raised objections and to reach agreement. In this process the Reich Chancellery only had the role of a mediator. In general, objections were made in written form. This objection was then, as with the draft itself, circulated to the departments. If the discussion led to the withdrawal of the objection, this would be noted in the Reich Chancellery and the process then operated as normal. If the disagreement could not be resolved, the head of the Reich Chancellery then had to seek the decision of the Reich Chancellor, who made the final binding decision.

As far as Hitler was concerned, this process had the advantage of reducing his role in the proceedings to a minimum. He could simply approve or disapprove the final draft or suggest amendments. On the other hand, he could, if he wished, influence the actual drafting of the legislation by making his views known either to the particular minister primarily responsible or to the head of the Reich Chancellery, Hans-Heinrich Lammers, or to the Party Minister, Rudolf Hess, or his deputy, Martin Bormann. This not only avoided the tedious and unpleasant task of trying to mediate between his ministers and reach an agreement, above all it preserved his unique status as the Führer standing above the arena of internal conflict. Finally, it accorded with his tendency to avoid decisions and hope that matters would sort themselves out.

The replacement of cabinet meetings by the circulation process had a number of important results. Above all, it reduced the corporate character of the Government. The Government tended to disintegrate into its component ministries whose contacts with one another were reduced to written comments on each other's draft legislation and the occasional inter-departmental meeting to discuss a draft bill or, more rarely, some particular sphere of policy. When Hitler learnt of the attempt by Lammers to revive a kind of informal cabinet by arranging beer evenings for the Reich Ministers, he immediately vetoed it. Under this system there was no more opportunity for the discussion of the general lines of Government policy. One can, of course, easily exaggerate the peculiarity of this development. The *Crossman Diaries* demonstrated how, even under the British system of cabinet government, departmental ministers tend to be so preoccupied with their own particular field that they have little time or energy left to devote to more general questions of policy. Nevertheless, the fact that in Nazi Germany the Government no longer met regularly as a group, apart from the so-called 'little cabinet' of state secretaries after 1937–38, undoubtedly reduced its cohesion and the coordination of its policies in the various fields. Above all, the failure of Hitler himself to perform a coordinating role meant that something like a vacuum developed at the top of government.

From 1934–35 onwards, the Reich Chancellery in effect replaced the cabinet as the main centre of coordination of the Government. It had no *formal* role in the policy-making process. Officially, its function was to make sure that the rules of legislative procedure had been adhered to; that the ministries had had an opportunity to comment on draft legislation; that any objections had been met; and then, finally, to act as the link between the Government and the Chancellor. In fact, however, the position of the Reich Chancellery as an office and of its head, State Secretary (after 1937 Reich Minister) Lammers, as an individual increased in importance parallel to the increase in importance of the Reich Chancellor vis-à-vis the rest of the government.

In a newspaper interview in November 1938 Lammers defined his role as follows:

147

If I as head of the Reich Chancellery . . . must above all keep the Führer up to date on all important legislative and administrative matters, then it is particularly important for me to keep peripheral matters away from him. Through correct timing and orderly presentation I must ensure that the mass of pressing problems do not become overwhelming and are presented to the Führer in a form in which they are ready for a decision . . . . It is one of my most important tasks as head of the Reich Chancellery to ensure that the overall view is not lost in the particular activities of the government departments. The Reich Chancellery, therefore, must act as a kind of magnifying glass for the various administrative and legislative branches, concentrating the mass of individual rays into a total picture . . .

After the war, State Secretary in the Reich Chancellery from 1938–1945, Kritzinger, explained Lammers's influence as follows:

148

. . . His influence lay essentially in the fact that he reported to Hitler on every conceivable sphere of government activity and in the process could naturally express his viewpoint. We reported to the head of the Reich Chancellery either verbally or in writing on how we thought particular issues should be handled. In addition, we drafted the papers necessary for the preparation or the transmission of a decision by the Reich Chancellor. We did not have a direct concrete influence on developments; we could only achieve anything through the way we handled particular issues . . .

There were, however, a number of cases in which Hitler adopted our point of view. I have already mentioned that these were mostly matters of little political importance, often matters of purely organizational significance. The most important method at our disposal for influencing Hitler's decisions was for us to involve other ministers from whom we could expect a sensible point of view . . .

There was little we could do about complaints concerning Gestapo measures. Lammers told me that before I joined the Reich Chancellery [1938], he had secured Hitler's authority to visit a concentration camp to investigate a complaint about abuses in it. But some time later—presumably as a result of pressure from Himmler—he was ordered to leave such complaints exclusively to Himmler to investigate. In politically important cases we advised Lammers to speak to Himmler in person which he usually did. Apart from Best,[4] we had no contacts among senior officials in the Gestapo such as we had with other government departments and which we could have used to deal successfully with requests and complaints . . .

In practice, the influence of the Reich Chancellery took various forms. Firstly, in the process of drawing up legislation the Reich Chancellery often suggested alternative or compromise formulations to drafts put forward by departmental ministers. Indeed, often the Reich Chancellery played a key role here because it alone had an overall view and knew what other ministries would accept. Secondly, although debarred from making formal objections itself, if it opposed a particularly piece of legislation, it could alert other ministries which it believed might also object and leave them to take the initiative. Above all, however, it could exploit the fact that Hitler, wishing to avoid becoming embroiled in interdepartmental disputes, insisted that all legislative matters must be put to him through Lammers. Most ministers most of the time were obliged to rely on Lammers to put their case to Hitler and were forced to accept *his* account of Hitler's views. Although officially Lammers was expected simply to act as a mouthpiece for both parties, in fact of course it was possible for him within certain limits to put the particular case across in either a more or less favourable light. It was equally possible for him within limits to suggest that Hitler was unlikely to approve of a particular proposal and therefore suggest modification.

Finally, a Führer decree of 20 March 1935 laid down that appointments and promotions of administrative grade civil servants should be referred to the head of the Reich Chancellery for approval. Under the authority of this decree the responsible desk officer within the Reich Chancellery, Dr Killy, was able to cooperate with his opposite number in the Reich Finance Ministry, which was also involved in all appointments, in blocking some of the more obviously unsuitable appointments of Party hacks or militants. There were, however, strict limits to the influence of the Reich Chancellery in this sphere, as Dr Killy recalled under interrogation after the war:

---

[4] Dr Werner Best, a lawyer, 1934–36 deputy chief of the Gestapo and from 1936–40 of the Security Police and SD.

150

There have recently been repeated instances in which projects, which are being dealt with by my department but which are not yet ripe for decision, have been referred to the Führer by other agencies without the participation of my department. What is more, decisions are being secured from the Führer concerning these plans. There have also been repeated instances of draft legislation being put forward by other departments or Party agencies (among others the Labour Front) which directly concern my department and which have been taken to the Führer for a decision without either me or my administration having been consulted at all about the preparation of these drafts.

If decisions by the Führer are secured in this way it causes great difficulties for me because then the installations and arrangements required for transport purposes have to be subsequently included in such plans when they have already been fixed.

This method of initiating legislation directly with Hitler was particularly associated with a growing tendency for laws (*Gesetze*), which had to go through the time-consuming 'circulation process', to be replaced by Führer edicts (*Erlasse*) to which Hitler's signature could be secured immediately or after a much shorter circulation process involving only one or two ministers. These developments sometimes cut through red tape, but they also inevitably increased the disintegration of the government and the problems of coordination, with ministries finding that decrees had been issued which adversely affected their own spheres of competence without their having been consulted at all. Sometimes, indeed, such decrees had to be revised by subsequent administrative regulations. Lammers repeatedly brought these problems to Hitler's attention and was repeatedly authorized by him to issue instructions that ministries should abide by official administrative procedures. But no sooner had they been issued than Hitler would once more undermine them by granting decrees to particular ministers which short-circuited the process and increased the confusion.

The key problem was that, although Lammers had joined the Party in 1932, he was not really a Party man. He had been a senior civil servant in the Reich Ministry of the Interior. Hitler respected him as 'the only jurist among my collaborators who is worth a damn';[5] he was, however, still a 'jurist'. According to one of his subordinates, Hans Ficker, Lammers was described in 1935 as 'lying on the threshold like a St Bernhard'. 'That was meant to imply on the one hand how faithful he was, on the other hand, how lacking in initiative.'[6] Unfortunately, Lammers and the Reich Chancellery found their claim to act as the hub of government increasingly challenged by a formidable rival in the shape of a Party office, effectively

---

[5] Cf. *Hitler's Secret Conversations* (New York 1953) p. 436.
[6] Hans Ficker Zeugenschrifttum Institut für Zeitgeschichte ZS 893.

149

...Particularly in connexion with the Reich Regulations [for civil service appointments and promotions] it was, I must say, a real game for the Reich Chancellery to queer the pitch of appointments and promotions which were being made for political reasons. In these cases, in particular, I made repeated use of the friendly assistance of the civil service department of the Reich Ministry of Finance ... Dr Lammers did not hinder this game. On the contrary, he supported us—me and my colleagues—when we, as the saying goes, wanted to be bloody minded. But if a proposal for a promotion or an appointment was blocked by us and the minister making it—Goebbels, for example—learnt of our objections, which we made with the help of the departments involved [i.e. Interior and Finance], he simply went round to the back door to Hitler and got him to sign the appointment...

The role of the Reich Chancellery in general and of Dr Killy in particular in trying to reduce the arbitrary nature of the regime was significant. Dr Killy had joined the Nazi Party in 1932 from the same motives of nationalism, conservatism and self-interest as other high-ranking civil servants such as Lammers himself. He was, however, a half Jew married to another half Jew and was protected by Lammers from the Party represented by Bormann until in the last few months of the war he was finally forced out of the Reich Chancellery.

In the meantime, however, the position of the Reich Chancellery was being undermined by other developments. As was mentioned earlier, Hitler established new ministries and agencies of various kinds which removed more and more authority from the traditional government departments. Many of these covered important areas of policy. The first example was Goebbels's Reich Propaganda Ministry set up in March 1933. It was followed by Himmler's take-over of the police powers of the Reich and state ministries of the Interior between 1934 and 1936, and then by Göring's absorption of many of the powers of the Economics Ministry into his Four Year Plan Office after 1936—to name only three of the most important examples. For the Reich Chancellery this was significant, for, whereas with such ministries as Justice, Education, and Posts Lammers was virtually the sole avenue to Hitler, men like Goebbels, Himmler, and Göring had direct access to the Führer. Lammers was, therefore, faced with a proliferation of new government departments or quasi-governmental agencies which made the problem of coordination much more difficult and with the problem of those ministers or 'Reich Commissioners' who could go their own way, sometimes abiding by the official procedures and using the Reich Chancellery as their channel to Hitler, but often exploiting their direct line in order to bypass Lammers. The following letter from the Reich and Prussian Minister of Transport to Lammers dated 31 January 1938 illustrates this problem:

dominated by a man of great initiative and very sharp elbows, a man who was no mere apparatchik but a Nazi fanatic. The office was the Staff of the Führer's Deputy, renamed in 1941 the Party Chancellery; the man was Martin Bormann. The rivalry between these two bodies reflected the tension, built into the regime between Party and State.

CHAPTER 8

The 'Coordination' of the Civil Service

One of the main issues facing the Nazis on coming to power was the need to regulate relations between the Party and the State. Here they were faced with conflicting priorities, for while the Nazi leadership was anxious to establish Nazi control over the State, at the same time it could not afford to allow the bureaucratic machine to be damaged through disruption by unqualified Party elements. This problem arose first in relation to the question of the reliability of the civil service to the new regime.

In 1933, the Party found itself faced with a very different form of organization—the German Civil Service. It was composed of the Reich or national civil service, which—apart from such bodies as the railways and the Post Office—was small in numbers, and the much larger *Länder* or state civil services, notably that of Prussia. These were all bureaucracies of high competence and long traditions. In 1933, many civil servants were sympathetic to Nazism. During the years 1930–33, the Party had made vigorous efforts to cultivate civil service support and these efforts had met with a positive response among a group demoralized by salary cuts under the Brüning government. Civil Servants, however, had more fundamental reasons for disliking the Weimar Republic. Before 1918, they had formed part of the Establishment of Wilhelmine Germany. Loyal to the Kaiser and his government, for which they, rather than the political parties, provided the personnel, they saw themselves as the true interpreters and guardians of the best interests of the State, which in turn represented the highest expression of the nation. They regarded party politics as the manifestation of selfish and divisive interests and parliament as a cockpit in which the welfare of the state was at the mercy of the struggle between these selfish interests. With the introduction of full parliamentary democracy in 1918–19 not only did they forfeit to party politicians some of the power they had formerly exercised, but party politics itself intruded directly into the civil service since, albeit only to a limited extent, membership of a political party could become a factor in career prospects. Many civil servants believed an authoritarian dictatorship, such as they envisaged would follow Hitler's appointment, would free the civil service from 'political interference', that is to say from party political interference. They assumed the conservative members of the Government would control the Nazis and restore a regime similar to that of Wilhelmine Germany. In any event, the civil service had survived the revolution of 1918, and assumed that the same would be true again.

As it became clear that the Nazis were in control, some civil servants justified to themselves their continuation in office with the argument that they were remaining 'to prevent worse things happening' under a Nazi replacement. However, by participating in the regime they were forced more and more to compromise their principles, losing their moral integrity until they were debased into mere functionaries. This dilemma is starkly revealed in the attitudes of two leading diplomats to the Nazi takeover, Bernhard von Bülow, State Secretary in the German Foreign Ministry until his death in 1936 and a highly civilized diplomat, chose to stay in office in the hope of keeping German diplomacy out of the hands of the Nazis and of preventing extreme policies which might jeopardize Germany's security. Yet he merely made the Nazis' task of persuading other countries to come to terms with the new regime that much easier by giving it an aura of respectability and the appearance of continuity. Shortly before his death he justified his attitude: 'One can't leave one's country in the lurch because it has a bad government.' The German ambassador in the United States, Friedrich von Prittwitz, on the other hand, resigned his post as early as 6 March 1933. He explained to a friend: 'One must only put onself at the disposal of a government for which certain basic values of humanity and justice are sacred. Coming to terms with inhuman principles in order to avoid something allegedly worse leads to disaster.'[7]

Apart from the particular notion of patriotism current among the German middle class which tended to believe in 'My country, right or wrong', there was another factor. Crucial to an understanding of the outlook of the German Civil Service and in particular of their attitude towards the new regime was the extremely legalistic Civil Service training. Apart from those in technical fields, Civil Service recruits had invariably studied law at the university and their initial in-service training continued to have a strong legal bias. Unlike the Anglo-Saxon legal system, based on a combination of

[7] Peter Krüger & Erich J. C. Hahn, 'Der Loyalitätskonflikt des Staatssekretärs Bernhard Wilhelm von Bülow im Frühjahr 1933', *Vierteljahrshefte für Zeitgeschichte*, vol. 20 (1972), p. 410.

precedent as embodied in the Common Law and statutes passed by the legislature, German law followed the Roman system and was derived almost entirely from legislation initiated by the Government. Whereas the Anglo-Saxon Common Law reflected a tradition of the defence of individual rights against the State, German law reflected the tradition of a strong state as the embodiment of the community by which individuals would be granted such rights as were considered compatible with its interests. During the nineteenth century German jurisprudence had come to be dominated by the theory of legal positivism which rationalized this tradition. The legal positivists conceived law as a manifestation of the authority of the State. It was law because the State had decreed it to be so. The sovereign State could not be bound by any prior moral order against which the justice or otherwise of the laws could be measured. In holding this view they were reacting against the theory of natural law which had maintained that certain moral precepts of natural justice must form the basis of all law. The legal positivists considered the natural law theory irrational and unscientific since there would always be different views about what exactly constituted natural law. They preferred the clarity of a legal system based on legislative enactment by the State. It is important to note that, so far as the legal positivists were concerned, the nature of the regime which controlled the State or the methods by which that regime had been established were immaterial. The important fact was that it was the sovereign State. It was this fact which conferred authority on its laws.

The dominance of legal positivism in German jurisprudence during this period and the fact that the Civil Service received a predominantly legal training greatly facilitated the Nazi take-over of power. It reinforced the emphasis on conformity inherent in any bureaucracy by enabling the Civil Service to rationalize almost any action, however immoral, provided it took the form of a law or a decree. It is clear that without the assistance of the Civil Service the Nazis could never have consolidated their power.

Yet, ironically, it was precisely this legalistic bias of the German Civil Service which made the Nazis, and Hitler in particular, so suspicious of it. Its adherence to rational procedures and legal norms and its bureaucratic concept of authority was in complete contrast to the irrational and arbitrary temper of the Nazi Party as it had developed in 'the years of struggle' before 1933, and above all to its charismatic basis. In the view of the Nazis, therefore, the Civil Service represented a serious obstacle to the arbitrary exercise of power which was their characteristic way of operating and to a limited extent this view was justified. With its insistence on 'going by the book', its contempt for professional incompetence, and its disapproval of corruption, endemic within the Party, the Civil Service did on occasion complicate the achievement of Nazi objectives. Yet Hitler clearly needed the Civil Service to ensure the stability of his regime.

During the first weeks of the 'revolution from below' in March–April, 1933, many officials in local and regional government were forced to resign and were replaced by Party men. In this the initiative was often taken by the local Party organizations with little or no direction from the top, except in the case of the most senior regional officials. At the same time, during 1933, a large number of SA 'commissars' moved into Government offices at various levels, with the excuse that they were making sure that the civil servants were acting in accordance with the principles of the new regime.

In the first few months, the Government did little to prevent this upheaval, partly because it favoured the purging of its political opponents from their offices, but partly because it sometimes found it difficult to control the SA and the local Party organizations. The Government was often confronted with local *faits accomplis*. The various Party organizations all tended to go their own way. Yet this arbitrary behaviour by the local Party organizations and the continual interference by the various 'commissars' threatened to alienate the Civil Service and to undermine the administrative effectiveness essential for the stabilizing of the new order. Both Frick, Reich Minister of the Interior, and Göring, Prussian Minister of the Interior, were anxious to purge the Civil Service of politically and ideologically objectionable elements, but at the same time to cause minimum disruption in doing so. In this they were able to rely on the cooperation of a bureaucracy very anxious to see a return to order.

This was the background to the Law for the Restoration of the Professional Civil Service of 7 April 1933. The law owed its title to an attempt by the Government to exploit an allegation made by the Right in the Weimar period that the Left had filled the bureaucracy with unqualified people who carried the right party card. During the implementation of the law the assertion was shown to be untrue. The law provided for the purging of Jews (Art. 3) and known opponents of the regime (Art. 4) and for the retirement or transfer of officials for technical reasons (Arts. 5 and 6), which had previously been prevented by the Civil Service regulations. These last two clauses were sometimes used as a means of evading political pressure on an individual from the Party which would otherwise have required the use of Article 4. They did, however, give very wide scope for interfering with civil servants' careers, previously impossible under the Civil Service regulations. Thus among other things the Law facilitated the removal of dead wood.

151

I 1. In order to restore a national professional Civil Service and to simplify the administration, officials may be dismissed under the following regulations, even when the necessary conditions under the relevant law do not exist.

2. The term 'officials', as used in this law, means direct [*unmittelbare*] and indirect [*mittelbare*] officials of the Reich, direct and indirect officials of the federal states, officials of local government and local government associations, officials of public corporations as well as institutions and undertakings of the same status as these public corporations. The regulations apply also to employees of agencies supplying social insurance, who have the rights and duties of officials.

3. 'Officials', as used in this law, also includes officials in temporary retirement.

4. The Reich Bank and the German State Railway are empowered to make corresponding regulations.

II 1. Officials who attained the status of officials after 9 November 1918 without possessing the requisite or usual training or other qualifications are to be dismissed from the service. Their previous salaries will be accorded to them for a period of three months after their dismissal.

2. They have no right to allowances, pensions, or dependants' pensions nor to the continued use of the official designation, the title, the official uniform and the official insignia.

3. In cases of need, a pension, revocable at any time, equivalent to a third of the normal basic salary of the last position held by them, may be granted them, especially when they are caring for dependent relatives; reinsurance according to the provisions of the Reich social insurance law will not occur.

4. The provisions in Sections 2 and 3 will be applied in the case of persons who come under the provisions of Section 1 and who had already been retired before this law came into effect.

III 1. Officials who are of non-Aryan descent are to be retired;[8] honorary officials are to be dismissed from office.

2. Section 1 does not apply to officials who were already in service on 1 August 1914, or who fought in the world war at the front for the German Reich, or who fought for its allies, or whose fathers or sons were killed in the world war. The Reich Minister of the Interior, with the agreement of the competent departmental minister, or of the highest authorities of the federal states, may permit further exceptions in the case of officials who are abroad.

IV Officials who because of their previous political activity do not offer security that they will act at all times and without reservation in the interests of the national state can be dismissed from the service.[9] They are to be accorded their previous salary for a period of three months after dismissal. From then on, they will receive three-quarters of their pension and corresponding dependants' benefits.

V 1. Every official must allow himself to be transferred to another office in the same or equivalent career, even to one carrying a lower rank or regular salary—reimbursement for the prescribed costs of transfer will be given if the needs of the service require it. If the official is transferred to an office of lower rank and regular salary he retains his previous official title and the official income of his former position.

---

[8] On 11 April 1933 'non-Aryan' was defined to include persons with only one non-Aryan grandparent; and on 30 June this provision was extended to those married to non-Aryans.

[9] A supplementary law of 20 July 1933 ruled that civil servants who belonged to any party or organization which furthered the aims of Communism, Marxism or Social Democracy were to be dismissed.

2. In place of transfer to an office of lower rank and regular income, the official can request to be retired.

VI Officials can be retired for the purpose of rationalizing the administration even if they are not yet unfit for service. If officials are retired for this reason, their places may not be filled again.

VII 1. Dismissal from office, transfer to another office and retirement will be ordered by the highest Reich or federal state agency which will make the final decision without right of appeal against it.

2. The dispositions according to Articles II–VI must be made known to those affected by 30 September 1933 at the latest. The time may be shortened by agreement with the Reich Minister of the Interior, if the relevant Reich or federal state agency declares that the measures authorized in this law have been carried out.

VIII A pension will not be granted to the officials dismissed or retired in accordance with Articles 3 and 4, if they have not completed a term of service of at least ten years: this applies also to the cases in which, according to the existing regulation, a pension is accorded after a shorter term of service . . .

The desire to cause minimum disruption in the administration informed the official instructions for implementing the law. In fact, its effects were comparatively small, though greater in Prussia than elsewhere. 12.5 per cent of the 1,663 administrative grade civil servants in Prussia were affected by Sections 2–4 and 15.5 per cent by Sections 5–6. This does not, however, give a complete picture of the situation, for many Socialist and Democrat officials in Prussia had already been dismissed before the Nazis came to power under the regime of Dr Bracht, appointed State Commissioner in Prussia on 20 July 1932 by the then Reich Chancellor, Papen. In the other states 4.5 per cent of administrative grade civil servants were affected by Sections 2–4 and 5 per cent by Sections 5–6. An even smaller percentage of middle and lower-ranking civil servants were affected. The administration of the law was placed in the hands of the State authorities, enabling them—for the time being at any rate—to regain full control of personnel policy from the Party.

The following record of the ministerial discussion of the Law on 25 April 1933 indicates the Government's guidelines for its implementation:

152

. . . The Prussian Minister-President[10] Göring in very forceful and impressive words said roughly the following: The Reich Chancellor had asked him to draw up certain guidelines. It was an unusual and extremely important law, therefore only the Minister could make the final decisions. Half a year was hardly enough time to carry out a purge of the administration in Prussia. The Fascist purge law had had a duration of two years.

---

[10] On 11 April Hitler had appointed Göring Minister-President (Prime Minister) in Prussia.

There was no question of justice being in acute danger. It did not say much for the judges if they felt concerned about such a law. Civil servants who somewhere some time had made some human error were not to be touched by the law.

He particularly wished to point out the dangers to which the law could lead under confined local circumstances where everyone more or less knew everyone else. A strong personality must be able to overcome any personal hostility he may have or possible feelings of revenge. 'Someone who has grumbled at us some time somewhere' may be a very capable civil servant and need not be damned just like that.

The carrying out of the law in the states was the responsibility of the governments there. The question of how far the parties could be involved depended on the circumstances. But it was very important that only such people should take part in the preparations for the decisions who were absolutely decent characters and not themselves aspirants for the new vacancies. National Socialists were not immune from human weakness. A law was being passed for Prussia that every informer who could not absolutely prove the truth of his statements should be punished with the full force of the law.

Civil servants carrying a Party card should be dismissed. So one should not simultaneously create new Party-card-carrying civil servants. That did not of course exclude isolated cases of people being made civil servants who did not have full training, if this lack of a general Civil Service training was made up for by a clear eye for the political situation and a decent character. In this context, the Minister-President sharply attacked time-servers who often seemed to be more papal than the Pope. It had riled him to see how in his ministry, in which it was notorious that 60 per cent of the civil servants had been followers of Severing, within a few days the swastika badges had popped up out of the ground like mushrooms and after only four days the clicking of heels and raising of hands had become a common sight in the corridors. The Minister-President gave his full approval to those civil servants who because of their character and sense of decency had certain inhibitions about joining the Party at this particular moment and who, because of this, were especially exposed to the pressure and enmity of those who had already climbed on the bandwagon. Such civil sevants were 'the most valuable workers' for the new government as well.

'The army of commissars' threatened gradually to undermine and shatter the authority of the State. Yesterday he had abolished these commissars in Prussia. They produced great confusion. They created considerable disruption in private firms. In practice, they had often turned out to be aspirants for directorships, insisting on creating vacancies for themselves: . . .

The Reich Chancellor had pointed out emphatically that there were two things which must not be overlooked in carrying out the law: 1. The Reich President; 2. Foreign countries.

1. The Reich President and Reich Chancellor both wished that, in particular, the withdrawal of pensions should be handled carefully and with a certain generosity. A petty attitude only created hotbeds of hatred and embitterment. Such imponderables should not be weighed lightly . . . Political activity from personal initiative must be distinguished from political activity under official instructions. Swamping the Reich President with complaints about the effects of the law must be avoided at all costs.

2. Germany could not simply say we shall do what we like. The isolation of Germany was unique. The Jews were working extremely hard to aggravate it. Therefore we must hit the Jews hard, but we must not give them a chance to malign us as barbarians in places where it could be interpreted in the wrong way. A Jew who had contributed something scientifically important for humanity must not be removed; the world would not understand that. The Reich President would examine again the question whether such scientific experts were not in the same category as soldiers.

In conclusion, the Minister-President made the following point with great gravity: 'I remind you of the seriousness of the law, you must bear in mind that your signature is often equivalent to a death sentence. This you must settle with your conscience. The Führer is responsible to history for your decisions. The dismissal, the assessment and the weeding out of individuals must therefore lie only in the hands of men of character.'

The limited nature of the purge within the Civil Service provoked resentment among Party militants as is clear from the following memorandum, dated 26 May 1934, by Hans von Helms, a Nazi activist and senior civil servant in the Reich and Prussian Ministry of the Interior.

153

Among the most difficult tasks which the National Socialist State still has to solve during the next few years is the question of 'Party and State'. Although the identity of Party and State must be our ultimate aim, the realization of this aim is at the moment a long way off. Anyone who has had the opportunity, on the one hand, of closely following the organization of the Party through all the phases of its development from its beginnings to the seizure of power by the Führer and of playing an active part in its success, and on the other hand of working in the State apparatus of the new Reich, must unfortunately admit that the influence of the Party on the State and the permeation of the State with National Socialist ideas does not correspond with the sacrifices made by the movement. The last few months in particular show a considerable decrease in the rate of growth of National Socialist influence upon the State.

The State apparatus, whose character, and particularly whose methods of administration and bureaucracy, represents in itself a certain element of danger for a National Socialist Government with different methods, is still far from making National Socialist ideas its most important tools. This is most strongly pronounced in the behaviour of a large section of the representatives of our State, the civil servants. The best gauge for the permeation of a State by an idea is still the appointments policy pursued by that State. Since everyone knows that 'men make history' one will be able to tell by the faces of people employed in decisive positions whether they are willing to pull their weight for the new State or whether they have no comprehension of, or sympathy for, National Socialism .... Once again people are beginning to value a person's knowledge more highly than his character. Once again people are daring to defame old experienced fighters in our movement who have been taken into the administration for political reasons in order to form a counterweight to old, burnt-out, unreliable hangers-on. They are reproached with lack of knowledge and recommended to learn administrative techniques, whereas in fact these officials are the best guarantee of the thorough permeation of the State by National Socialism.... Very often it would be better if the administrative bosses used the old Party warriors instead of falling for those who joined the Party after the March 1933 election [*Märzgefallene*]. In part, this is the result of fundamental errors made during the first months in the form of compromises which were probably unavoidable because National Socialism had not yet acquired total control over the State. So now also unfortunate compromises have to be put up with in the filling of posts. But even now there would be time to improve things if a consistent appointments policy were pursued, a policy which would prove particularly productive in the central administration. It must be self-evident for the National Socialist State that the head of a personnel department and the official in charge of personnel in the central administration, who in their turn have to be entrusted with the personnel files of their subordinate offices, should be trusted agents of the Party, men who have proved themselves as old Party fighters before the seizure of power....

Circumstances have brought it about that people often fill decisive positions in the State apparatus who are either not National Socialists or who, even as National Socialists, have been infected by other ideologies in such a way that they no longer detect a policy that is disloyal to National Socialism. It is therefore particularly important that measures taken by the central authorities, among them their appointments policy, are examined to see whether they are correct from a National Socialist point of view.

Is it possible for a Party member or the representative of the Party within the administration (the Federation[11]) to report any abuses to the Party leadership and thus act as the eyes and ears of the Party? Unfortunately the answer is No!

As can be seen from the enclosed decree of the Prussian Minister-President of 4 October 1933 and the Prussian Minister of the Interior of 4 August 1933, the Federation is even forbidden to report un-National Socialist behaviour to the Party or to disclose abuses unless the person reporting wishes to expose himself to the risk of disciplinary action....

There is a great danger that in the near future even National Socialist ministerial chiefs will have only a bureaucratic apparatus behind them whose representatives lack true National Socialist principles. The pillars of the Party in times of need were always the old Party fighters. This must not be underestimated!!

Over the next few years, the Civil Service became increasingly disillusioned with the regime. Continual denigration by the Party with Hitler's barely concealed connivance undermined its morale, already affected by relatively low pay, and thereby made it all the more vulnerable to Party interference. The following documents illuminate this change in the attitude of the Civil Service. They are two memoranda by Fritz-Dietlof Count von der Schulenburg, a young Prussian aristocrat who was a junior official in the field

---

[11] The *NS Beamtenbund*, the Nazi Civil Service organization.

administration of the Prussian Ministry of the Interior. Initially, he was sympathetic to Nazism and joined the Party in February 1932. But over the years his disillusionment with the regime in general and its negative effects on the Civil Service in particular led him into increasing opposition until finally he was executed for his participation in the plot against Hitler of 20 July 1944. The first memorandum by von der Schulenburg was dated April 1933 and was probably submitted to the Prussian Ministry of the Interior:

154

Reconstruction of the Higher Civil Service
In the period after the Revolution [of November 1918] there was no political concept of the State behind the State itself. The parties ruled and through them the powers which stood behind them—the Jews, Capital, and the Roman Catholic Church. The civil servant became a tool of the parties. In fourteen years of party rule, he was continually forced to bend to them and became—apart from a few exceptions—inwardly a slave. The distinctive character of the civil service disintegrated. The parties had no experience of the value of character. The cream of the parties judged according to the party card or, at the most, on the basis of rootless intellect. There was no longer any specific training for the civil service. The democratically individualistic age saw in the training of civil servants interference in their sacrosanct individual rights. The civil service as an estate died, since it could not survive without the cohesive force of an ideology. The honour of the civil service faded away under the dirt of party rule. There was no more responsibility in the new state since the discipline of responsibility can only be demanded from the upholders of an ideology. The technical ability and knowledge of the civil service declined more and more; the party card and a metropolitan intellect dominated the administration, particularly in the ministries. In the age of democracy training was restricted to the study of private law; for, it was characteristic of the thinking of this phase in the life of the State that protection of the rights of the individual took precedence over the rights of the State. During this period, training reached the pinnacle of absurdity. The trainee civil servant (*Assessor*) spent seven years on the theory and practice of private law before he even approached administration and the great problems of nation and State.

The result of this development is: the old Prussian civil service with its magnificent qualities of intellect, character, and ability is shattered. It must be reconstructed on the basis of a completely new spirit.

The significance of this reconstruction cannot be overemphasized. The most important thing is the question of selection and recruitment. The National Socialist leaders are confronted with the task of forming the State along National Socialist lines. The leaders are political fighters who in many respects lack expertise and knowledge of administrative techniques. The cooperation of the bureaucracy which has expertise and administrative skills is indispensable. The bureaucracy, which for the most part confronts National Socialism without any real understanding, works without enthusiasm, hinders the work and in some commits sabotage. The political will of National Socialism must, however, be implemented under all circumstances. The principle of a professional civil service must be recognized; nevertheless, during this transitional phase, *one cannot avoid using non-professional civil servants in the posts of Oberpräsident, Regierungspräsident, and Landrat* in order to implement the political will of National Socialism; *for true political leader-types with a real sense of responsibility and a sure instinct will be able to implement the political will of National Socialism more effectively even on a practical (fachlich) basis* than uncomprehending bureaucrats, who sabotage the Government's work. The partial use of non-professional civil servants is, however, conceivable only during a transitional phase. *In a National Socialist state it is obvious that the State will recruit its new leaders from within the administration itself* . . .

The permeation of the young civil service recruits with the National Socialist concept of the State is the task of the political leadership. This permeation cannot originate in the universities. It is the task of fanatical political leaders and fighters. Character must again be considered the highest value. Faith, character, judgement and drive are decisive for the quality of a civil servant. The selection must include the biologically best from all classes; it must not remain a privilege of the so-called educated classes. Fighters from the SA, SS, and the paramilitary leagues are to be given priority. The training of civil service recruits must be entirely concentrated on steeling character and will and testing courage. The young civil servant must engage in sports which place a high premium on daring, will, and endurance (flying, mountaineering, skiing, riding, fencing). An essential part of training must lie with the civil service itself which must once again arise as an estate. In this community the whole of life must revolve round the poles of honour, comradeship, and loyalty. By a process of constant coexistence, and constant shaping, a new type of civil servant must emerge who possesses true fighting spirit and exemplary attitudes. The civil servant of the future must differ from the civil servant of today as much as the Commando leader of the World War differed from the sentry of the Ancien Regime. True responsibility must live again . . . .

The proposed reconstruction of the civil service represents a complete rejection of previous principles. It requires radical, *bold decisions.* Without such decisions, however, it will be just as impossible to carry through the revolution in the civil service as it will be in the sphere of general State policy. The Liberation of 1813 was only conceivable with an army which had been reconstructed out of a revolutionary spirit. In the same way the Civil Service and the State can liberate Germany and secure it the necessary space for its development only if the Civil Service is reconstructed out of the spirit of the national revolution.

The following memorandum on the crisis in the Civil Service, dated September 1937, was presented to the Reich Ministries of the Interior, Economics, Finance, and to the OKW:

155

The Civil Service: Crisis and Remedies
1. *The Civil Service—the main pillar of the State.* In the Reich Civil Service Law [of 1937] the Civil Service is termed the main pillar of the State. And this is really what it is. However the bureaucracy may be abused, every responsible statesman in his political calculations counts on the work of the Civil Service.

Without a stable Civil Service no work can be achieved, no economy, especially in its financial aspects, can be run, but *above all no Four—Year Plan can be carried out, no war can be won. It is an appalling error for other institutions to think that there is no need of a creative Civil Service,* that it will be sufficient to replace its work or steer it from outside. For, in the first case, they would themselves ossify into complete bureaucracies. In the second case, the heavy weight of a stagnating bureaucracy would drag down anyone, even the highest flier. *Therefore, the only way left is to put the Civil Service itself into shape.*
2. *Situation.* The Civil Service, however, especially at the top levels, finds itself in a *situation which is beginning to destroy the prerequisites of creative work.*

(a) *The clear objective task* of the Civil Service and of the individual official *is more and more lost to sight* since the formerly unified State power has been split into a number of separate authorities; Party and professional organizations work in the same areas and overlap with no clear divisions of responsibility, while the whole is not always given priority over the particular aim, nor the cause over the individual. The Civil Service, as well as the individual official, lacks both clear directives from the State as well as objective backing when acting according to its laws. The civil servant too often stands alone and unprotected.

(b) *Politically* the Civil Service has already been purged for four years since 1933. Of 1600 administrative grade civil servants of the Prussian interior administration about 400 have left. Moreover, about 750 young referendars[12] and assessors were taken on, of whom up to 75 per cent were old Party members, to a great extent pre-1930. *Despite all this* the Civil Service is still *exposed to political discrimination.* Although it has considerable achievements to its credit since the take-over of power, it is publicly *ridiculed* as a 'bureaucracy', devalued as a mere piece of machinery, given no part to play or authority either by the Führer or by the community and decried as alien to the people, even as disloyal, without anyone being prepared to reject officially this disparagement of a class on which the State depends. Civil servants, especially leading ones, are *exposed to attacks* on their work, *which in fact are directed against the State as such*; if the matter comes to an argument they are never protected politically, but are let down even if they are doing no more than their duty. Despite the purge and the new recruitment of staff, they are under *special political control.* Through the *declaration of political reliability* they are judged by outsiders who, without a feeling for the State and authority, often cannot appreciate the nature and value of their work.

But, short of respect and appreciation, the historic achievements of the Civil Service, which the Führer himself has expressly acknowledged, are unthinkable. If

---

[12] Junior civil servants or lawyers who have not yet passed the final examination.

the *honour of the Civil Service is no longer protected, results cannot be expected.* Furthermore, achievement must be recognized by a post corresponding to it: the highest post for the highest achievement. *What is given to all other great institutions is denied to the State: no young civil servant today carries 'the field-marshal's baton in his knapsack'*, since the highest posts are filled from outside.

The consequences of this treatment of the Civil Service are that the Civil Service feels increasingly *defamed, without honour, and in some degree of despair. New recruitment is beginning to dry up.* Whereas in 1933 applications exceeded vacancies by 4–5 times, now vacant Civil Service posts can no longer be filled. Young law students who, for all the interest they showed in the State and administration, did not become civil servants openly give as their reason that there is no protection of professional honour nor any promotion on the basis of merit. For the same reasons able people are now already resigning and a growing number are about to do so. The Army, business, and the Party administration increasingly attract the best material. The only people who remain in the State and independent sector are those who become civil servants for the sake of the pension or the rank. This will mean the end of a true Civil Service and the emergence of a subservient bureaucracy.

(c) The Civil Service is largely reduced to the economic status of the proletariat. Its loss of capital is a consequence of war and inflation which it willingly bears together with large sections of the population. Financial stringency and reductions in salary, however, exceed what is bearable, and bring constant financial worries, distress and debts, especially to those who have many children or are sick; they close educational opportunities and do not allow the necessary freedom and sense of independence. By comparison, business offers many times the salary and attracts able civil servants whom the State needs (namely, in the Ministry of Economics) in order to control business.

The position is clear: because of all these stringent conditions the Civil Service is in a crisis which is dangerously sapping its substance, something which even the 'period of the system' [Weimar] was unable to destroy. Another few years and the substance will disintegrate; and that which it took generations to build up, it will take generations to rebuild . . . .

CHAPTER 9

Party/State Relations— at the Centre

Initially, Hitler does not seem to have had a clear idea about the future relationship between the Party and the State. In the first months the main danger was felt to be that the Party might get out of hand. One suggestion for regulating the relationship was for the Party to be integrated with the State in some form. This idea found expression in the Law to ensure the Unity of Party and State of 1 December 1933:

156

1. After the victory of the National Socialist revolution, the National Socialist German Workers' Party is the bearer of the concept of the German State and is inseparably linked with the State.

It is a corporation under public law.

2. The deputy of the Führer and the Chief of Staff of the SA will become members of the Reich Government in order to ensure close cooperation of the offices of the Party and the SA with the public authorities.

3. The members of the National Socialist German Workers' Party and the SA (including their subordinate organizations) as the leading and driving force of the National Socialist State will carry greater responsibilities towards Führer, people and State.

In the case of violation of these duties, they will be subject to special jurisdiction by Party and State.

The Führer may extend these regulations to include members of other organizations.

4. Every action, or failure to carry out an action, on the part of members of the SA (including their subordinate organizations), which threatens the existence, organization, activity or reputation of the National Socialist German Workers' Party, in particular any infringement of discipline and order, will be regarded as a dereliction of duty.

5. Custody and detention may be imposed in addition to the usual penalties.

6. The public authorities are bound to grant legal and administrative assistance to the offices of the Party and the SA, which are entrusted with the exercise of jurisdiction over the Party and the SA.

7. The law of 28 April 1933 regarding the authority to inflict penalties on members of the SA and SS is revoked.

8. The Reich Chancellor, as Führer of the National Socialist German Workers' Party and as supreme commander of the SA, will issue the regulations required for the execution and augmentation of this law, particularly with regard to the juridical organization and procedure of the Party and the SA. He will determine the date on which the regulations concerning this jurisdiction will become effective.

This law proved to be highly ambiguous and completely failed to define and regulate Party/State relations satisfactorily. It is significant, for example, that neither the Party nor the State could claim superiority to the other. For, while the Party is considered 'the bearer of the concept of the German State', this is never defined in legal or institutional terms. In addition, by being made a corporation under public law, and through the appointment of the deputy Führer (Hess) and the Chief of Staff of the SA as Ministers, the integration of the Party into the State appeared to mean its subordination to the State, though this was by no means so, as will become clear. The only unqualified gain for the Party was its right as a public corporation to claim money from the State, though even here its demands had to be granted by the Reich Finance Minister. In practice, however, the non-Nazi Reich Minister of Finance, Schwerin von Krosigk, dared not exercise more than a very limited supervision.

At a conference of Gauleiters on 2 February 1934, Hitler defined the tasks of the Party in limited terms. It was to be used primarily for propaganda and indoctrination as well as to perform auxiliary functions for the State Hitler was clearly also anxious about faction within the Party:

157

The Führer stressed:
The most essential tasks of the Party were:
1. to make the people receptive for the measures intended by the Government;
2. to help to carry out the measures which have been ordered by the Government in the nation at large;
3. to support the Government in every way.

Furthermore, the Führer stressed that those people who maintained that the revolution was not finished were fools; they did this only with the intention of getting particular jobs for themselves. The Führer described what difficulty he had had in filling all the posts with the right people and went on to say that we had people in the movement whose conception of revolution was nothing but a permanent state of chaos. But we needed an administrative apparatus in every sphere which would enable us to realize National Socialist ideas at once. And to achieve this, the principle must remain valid that more orders must not be given, and more plans must not be discussed, than the apparatus could digest; there must be no orders and plans beyond what could be put across to the people and actually carried into effect. The question of the amalgamation of Party and State was of fundamental importance; upon it Germany's future essentially depended.

The Führer described our main immediate task as the selection of people who were on the one hand able, and on the other hand willing, to carry out the Government's measures with blind obedience. The Party must bring about the stability on which Germany's whole future depended. It must secure this stability; this could not be done by some monarchy or other. The first Führer has been chosen by fate; the second must have right from the start a faithful, sworn community behind him. Nobody with his own power base must be chosen! What is vital is that he should have everyone completely behind him from the outset. This fact must be well known, and it will then be clear that there is no point in trying to assassinate him.

Apart from this: Only one person at a time can be Führer; who it is, is not so important; the important thing is that everybody should back up the second and all subsequent leaders. An organization with such inner solidity and strength will last for ever; nothing can overthrow it. The sense of community within the movement must be inconceivably intense. We must have no fighting among ourselves; no differences must be visible to outsiders! The people cannot trust us blindly if we ourselves destroy this trust. If we destroy other people's trust in us, we destroy our own trust in ourselves.

Even the consequences of wrong decisions must be mitigated by absolute unity. One authority must never be played off against another. There must be only *one* view, that of the movement.

To work against someone in an official position, who embodies part of this authority, is to destroy all authority and trust completely.

There must therefore be no superfluous discussions! Problems not yet decided by individual officials must under no circumstances be discussed in public. Otherwise, this will mean passing the decision on to the mass of the people. That was the crazy idea behind democracy. By doing that, the value of any leadership is squandered. The man who has to make the decisions must make them himself and everyone else must back him up. The authority of even the most junior leader is the sum of the authority of all leaders and vice versa.

Apart from this we must carry on only one fight at a time. The saying, 'Many enemies, much honour' should really run: 'Many enemies, much stupidity'. In any case, the whole nation cannot engage in twelve campaigns at the same time and understand what is involved. For this reason, we must always instil the whole nation with only one idea, concentrate its attention on *one* idea. In questions of foreign policy it is particularly necessary to have the whole nation behind one as if hypnotized. The whole nation must be involved in the struggle as if they were passionate participants in a sports contest. This is necessary because, if the whole nation takes part in the struggle, they also will be losers. If they are not involved, only the leadership loses. In the one case the wrath of the nation will rise against the opponent, in the other against their leaders.

During this period, Hitler was endeavouring to limit the disruptive interference of the Party in the State and economy while at the same time retaining its morale and future political potential. Thus, at the Party Congress in September 1934, he felt obliged to reassure the Party that, despite the ending of the revolution, the position of the Party was secure. He told the serried ranks of Party officials:

It is not the State which commands us but rather we who command the State. It was not the State which created us but rather we who created our own State.

This statement was, however, immediately used by Party officials to justify further interference in State affairs. The Reich Minister of the Interior, therefore, published the following defensive interpretation of Hitler's remarks:

158

Party offices have no authority whatever to issue instructions to agencies of the State. These agencies receive their instructions solely from their superiors within the State apparatus. They can never, therefore, escape the responsibility for their actions by referring to an instruction from a Party office. People who interpreted the Führer's well-known statement 'It is not the State which commands but rather we who command the State' to mean that the Party was thereby made superior to the State have completely misunderstood him. This statement merely implies that the leaders of the Party fill the top posts in the State and govern it. The Party organization and the State apparatus are the two pillars of the State. The State is, therefore, the more all-embracing concept. The relationship between the two is defined even more clearly by the fact that the Party offices have no direct executive power because otherwise a disastrous duplication and parallel government would develop...

In fact, however, it soon became clear that Hitler was not prepared to allow the Party to be reduced to a mere propaganda organization of the State. Indeed, in his speech to the Nuremberg Party rally on 15 September 1935 he warned the Civil Service that he would allow the Party to take over their functions in any sphere where they proved insufficiently zealous in carrying out Nazi policies and, in particular, in dealing with the political (and ideological) opponents of the regime:

159

... I should like to make it quite clear that the fight against foes within the nation will never be defeated by the inadequacy of a formal bureaucracy; wherever the formal bureaucracy of the State proves itself unfitted to solve a problem, there the German nation will bring into play its own more living organization in order to clear the way for the realization of its vital necessities. It is a great mistake to suppose that the nation exists to defend any formal institution [*Erscheinung*], or that, if an institution is incapable of solving the problems set it, the nation must therefore capitulate before these problems. On the contrary, whatever can be solved by the State will be solved through the State, but any problem which the State through its essential character is unable to solve will be solved by means of the Movement. For the State itself is but one of the forms of the organization of the *völkisch* life; it is set in motion and dominated by the immediate expression of the *völkisch* vital will [*Lebenswillens*], the Party, the National Socialist Movement... Party, State, Army, Economics, Administration are all but means to the end, and that end is the safeguarding of the nation. That is a fundamental principle of National Socialist theory. What is obviously damaging to the safeguarding of the nation must be removed. If an institution proves unfitted to undertake this task, then another institution must undertake the task and carry it out. All of us, my comrades, and especially you who hold positions of leadership in the State and the Movement, will not be judged by your observance of forms [*nach Ihrem formalen Verhalten*] but by your successful realization of our programme, i.e. by the measure in which you defend our *völkisch* life. And especially one principle must be maintained with fanatical obstinacy: an enemy of the National Socialist State—it matters not whether he be a domestic or a foreign foe—must never know of, must never find, any authority [*Stelle*] which will meet him with understanding or with assistance. We live in the midst of a world which is in ferment. Only iron principles and their ruthless application will make us strong so that Germany may not sink into Bolshevist chaos....

This resolute determination under any conditions to nip certain dangers in the bud will never hesitate, should the need arise, to hand over, through legislation, functions for which the State is obviously unfitted (since they are alien to its essential character) to institutions which appear better fitted to solve such problems. But on that point the will of the leadership alone decides, not the will of the individual. Our strength lies in our discipline.

The problem remained, however, of how to ensure that the Party exercised control over the State without jeopardizing its effectiveness through constant arbitrary interference. Part of the problem lay in the nature of the Party. In the 'time of struggle', in addition to its cadre organization (the Political Organization or PO), the Party had acquired a multiplicity of auxiliary organizations—paramilitary such as the SA and SS, occupational such as the NS Teachers' League, and social such as the Hitler Youth. Even before 1933, they had tended to emancipate themselves from the PO. With the take-over of power this process accelerated dramatically as each organization sought to establish its own autonomous niche within the new regime. The Party had effectively disintegrated into its component parts. Moreover, with the take-over of power the PO appeared to have lost its *raison d'etre*. This situation was described in a report by an SPD contact man to the SPD headquarters in exile (SOPADE) in June 1935:

160

The NSDAP is no longer a unified whole. Nobody really talks of the Party any more but rather of the Labour Front, the Air Defence League etc. The Party is the basis for job advancement and in many jobs one has only got prospects if one is in the Party. Otherwise the Party plays no role. It is torn apart internally by a plethora of intrigues and is pushed out of the spotlight by other organizations which arouse more interest among the public. At the Gau rally in Hessen the Party itself [i.e. the PO] remained almost completely in the background behind the parades of the SA, Hitler Youth, Labour Front, NSV etc. The conference itself was composed of sessions for the specialist organizations such as the NS Doctors' League, the NS Teachers' League etc. There can be no question of the Party's having a unified political line. Everywhere the 'old fighters' complain that the new members are given precedence over them. People do not bother to try and join the Party any more. In order to belong to an organization and so 'escape the whole swindle', people join the Air Sport League or some other organization but not the Party . . .

This was a situation which could be remedied only by action from above. The problem was that Hitler's destruction of Gregor Strasser's bureaucratic apparatus after his resignation in December 1932 had removed any effective central authority within the Party. The vacuum was filled by a struggle between Strasser's replacements: the so-called Chief of Staff of the PO, Robert Ley, and the head of the newly created Political Central Commission, Rudolf Hess, both of whom were ignored with impunity by powerful Party figures such as the various Gauleiters. The dangers of this situation were apparent. It caused disruptive confusion within the State administration, which was bombarded with contradictory instructions and requests from various sectors of the Party. On the other hand, it enabled the Civil Service to play the various Party agencies off one against the other. Hitler needed to create some sort of order within the Party and particularly in its relations with the State, while at the same time avoiding the kind of strong central apparatus which Strasser had been in the process of creating before his resignation and which might once again threaten Hitler's position. His solution was to delegate overall authority in the political sphere to the man whom he knew he could trust more than anybody, his faithful secretary, Rudolf Hess. In order to underline the significance of the move, on 21 April

1933 he gave him the title 'the Führer's deputy for Party affairs', authorizing him 'to take the decisions in my name in all matters concerning the leadership of the Party'. At the same time, however, he did not transfer to Hess control over the Party *machine*. This remained in the hands of the leaders of the various Party organisations, while the routine administration of the PO remained with Ley. Inevitably, this demarcation of responsibilities caused endless disputes in which Ley attempted to assert overall authority and was resisted both by Hess at Reich level and by the Gauleiters in the regions. But now, with Hitler's active support, Hess was able to assert his authority to represent the Party vis-à-vis the State. This was underlined when, on 27 June 1933, Hess was given permission to attend all cabinet meetings and, on 1 December, made a Reich Minister.

However, with the rapid decline in significance of the cabinet and without a portfolio, Hess found it impossible to exert any influence on government policy. On 27 July 1934, Hitler largely rectified this situation by issuing the following decree:

161

I decree that the Deputy of the Führer, Reich Minister Hess, will have the status of participating Reich Minister in connection with the preparation of drafts for laws in all Reich Government departments. All legislative work is to be sent to him when it is received by the other Reich Ministers concerned. This also applies in cases where no one else participates except the Reich Minister making the draft. Reich Minister Hess will be given the opportunity of commenting on drafts suggested by the civil servants concerned.

This order will apply in the same sense to legislative ordinances. The Deputy of the Führer in his capacity as Reich Minister can send an expert on his staff as his representative. These experts are entitled to make statements to the Reich Ministers on his behalf.

This decree, which was extended on 6 April 1935 to cover executive regulations also, provided the Party with a means of blocking or modifying legislation of which it disapproved. The following year Hess's office increased its influence over the State with the following decree from Hitler of 24 September 1935:

162

I. The Deputy of the Führer must participate in the appointment of officials who are appointed personally by the Führer and Reich Chancellor . . .

II. The participation of the Deputy of the Führer will take the form of his receiving a copy of the recommendation for promotion which must contain more detailed information about the official to be promoted. The Deputy of the Führer must be given reasonable time to express his opinion.

This decree gave the Party, through Hess's office, the right to vet the appointment and promotion of all civil servants of any importance. Generally, on receiving details of a proposed appointment, Hess's office would make enquiries of the Gauleiter of the area in which the civil servant lived, to make sure he was politically reliable. This, of course, gave considerable influence to the Gauleiter.

Clearly, these important new responsibilities of vetting both legislation and civil service appointments required considerable expertise. Hess had begun his task as the Führer's deputy with very inadequate resources in terms of trained personnel. The turning-point came with his appointment of Martin Bormann as his Chief of Staff on 1 July 1933. Bormann had hitherto run the SA Insurance Office. With the Nazi takeover of power, however, there was little need for the SA to be insured against injury or causing damage to property and, furthermore, his chief, the Party treasurer, Franz Schwarz, had shown no inclination to promote Bormann. With his well-attuned sense of power Bormann had realized that, in the Third Reich as in the pre-1933 Nazi Party, power would flow from Hitler. He therefore applied for a job with the man who had hitherto been closest to the Führer, Rudolf Hess.

Hess was evidently already aware of Bormann's formidable administrative skills which were allied to a tremendous capacity for hard work. Above all, however, Bormann combined his very well-developed sense of power, with a personal ambition and a ruthlessness unmatched by any other leading figure in a regime in which those qualities were at a premium, since no one could retain power without them. Following his appointment, and using Hess's prestige as a shield, Bormann worked behind the scenes to achieve his major goal of turning the Nazi Party into an elite corps which would provide Germany's political leadership at all levels. To secure this he needed both to turn the Party organization into a disciplined instrument obedient to the instructions of his office and to establish the Party's dominance over the State. He envisaged the party formulating policy while the State implemented it under continuing Party supervision.

By the end of 1934, Bormann had established an administrative apparatus—the Staff of the Führer's deputy—with its headquarters in Munich and based on two main departments: II and III. Department (*Amt*) II under Hellmuth Friedrichs had the title 'Department for Internal Party Affairs' and henceforward concentrated on trying to impose its authority on Ley and his Party apparatus and on the Gau organizations. On 25 October

1934, Hess issued the following directive to the Party, asserting both the political supremacy of the cadres at the various levels and the Führer's Deputy's monopoly of the representation of the Party vis-à-vis the Reich government:

163

The definition of the political line to be followed by the NSDAP, its subdivisions, as well as its subordinate organizations is solely a matter for the Führer. He has given me the responsibility for ensuring that political guidelines laid down by him are punctiliously observed by all branches of the Party and for ensuring uniformity in the implementation of policy. To guarantee this I decree the following:

1. The political leadership within the Party and its political representation vis-à-vis all state and other offices outside the Party is solely a matter for the cadres (*Hoheitsträger*) i.e. myself, the Gauleiters, district and branch leaders.
2. The cadres alone have the right to make agreements with the State and other agencies which are based within their particular area in accordance with the guidelines laid down by the Führer or by me on his authority. In the case of the Gauleiters these agencies include provincial authorities [*Provinzialbehörden*], state [*Land*] employment offices etc., even if their headquarters lie outside the particular Gau concerned.
3. The responsible Gauleiter represents the Party vis-à-vis the states whose boundaries fall within a Gau or embrace a Gau.
4. I reserve for myself the representation of the Party vis-à-vis the Reich Government in all matters. This also includes the representation of the Party vis-à-vis the governments of those states which contain several Gaus i.e. Prussia and Bavaria. The Party cadres are, therefore, in future obliged to pass on to me all matters for which these governments are responsible.
5. The specialists within the PO such as the *Reichsleiter*, the departmental officials, etc. as well as the leaders of the SA, SS, Hitler Youth, and the subordinate organizations are permitted to make binding agreements of a political nature with state or other agencies only with the approval of the responsible cadres . . .

By 1945 Department II's success had been incomplete, but it had made remarkable progress, particularly in the years 1941–45. The main barrier to its attempt to achieve absolute control over the Party was the independence of the Gauleiters. This could be bypassed to some extent by establishing close links with the Deputy Gauleiters and the district leaders, many of whom were seconded to the Staff of the Führer's Deputy in Munich for short periods and came under its influence. Moreover, as Hitler's old companions died, they tended to be replaced as Gauleiters by apparatchiks who had been trained by and owed their appointment to Department II, so that the future of this office as the acknowledged headquarters of the Party cadres looked quite promising in the long run.

The following notes for speeches made by Friedrichs, first at the Party's indoctrination centre for civil servants at Bad Tölz on 26 June 1939, and secondly, to Gauleiters and district leaders in Austria on 12 July 1938 give some idea of the outlook of him and his office:

164

(a) The struggle for existence and the racial (*völkisch*) self-assertion of a nation is a process which eternally repeats itself. There is no end to it, for there are always new tasks since each new generation must once again be trained for this responsibility. In this struggle for its existence the nation must be turned into a body capable of resistance through education, work, and the supervision of its morale. This body must be immune to all kinds of bacteria and external influences.

The Party is the barometer. It must know the state of the health of this body. It must examine what benefits or what damages the nation. It must analyze and get to know its innermost being and then draw practical conclusions. The Party represents the link between the leadership and the retinue. It prepares the ground among the people for the leadership to introduce those measures which are beneficial for the nation . . .

The Party must set great goals; it is the eternal engine in the nation's power house. It must warn and correct if something goes wrong but only through State methods and State institutions.

The *apparatus* of the State; the *leadership* of the people.

Why have an NSDAP?

November revolution of 1918 is a lesson to us. National divisions of that time a faithful mirror of the spiritual, cultural, and economic confusion. Party—the fervent will: State—the implementer of this will.

All the branches and organizations of the Party have the same task: leadership and character training.

Instruments for the leadership of the people—above all National Socialist propaganda and press. Influence on opinion [*Willensmeinung*] and on opinion formation of every single compatriot.

Importance of indoctrination.

Power and strength of a nation not simply based on weapons and the economy, above all through cementing the foundations of morale and ideology.

Previous occupational organizations liquidated and transformed into National Socialist organizations not for any occupational reason but as a means of influencing people from the occupational angle . . .

(b) 7. Relationship of the Party to the State.

(a) The Party is the creator [*Gestalter*], the State the administrator.

(b) The Party claims total control over the leadership of the people [*Menschenführung*], the state is responsible for carrying it out (Executive).

Department III of the Staff of the Führer's Deputy, with the title 'Department for Affairs of State' handled relations between the Party and the State and, with the significant exceptions of the SS and the German Labour Front, was increasingly successful in asserting its monopoly in representing the Party in its relations with the State. In September 1934, Bormann had succeeded in recruiting two administrative grade civil servants from the Thuringian state civil service. From then onwards, under the leadership first of one of these, Walter Sommer, and then, from 1941 onwards, of Dr. Gerhard Klopfer, Department III recruited a growing number of civil servants. By 1936 it has already overtaken the Reich Chancellery in size. These trained officials had the necessary skills to cope with the drafting of legislation and could face their ministerial opposite numbers on equal terms.

The following excerpt from an article entitled 'Party and State' by Walter Sommer, which appeared in a legal journal on 19 May 1936, gives some idea of the outlook of the office under his leadership:

165

A...Party and State form, it is true, a unity, but they are not a single entity, not one and the same thing. Party and State have different tasks and to fulfil these different tasks have separate administrations, separate laws, and separate judicial systems.

B. The Führer defined the respective tasks of Party and State in bold and clear strokes in the final speech of the Party Congress in 1935.[13] This declaration will be the basis of the future State law.

(a) The Party has the task of leading people and educating them in the way needed by the National Socialist State for the realization of its goals.

(b) The State has the task of administration. The State administration is specifically excluded from interference by the Party.

(c) A degree of influence by the Party on the State administration has, however, been secured for a transitional period. The Führer considers this transitional period as necessary so long as the State apparatus has not yet been transformed along Party lines...The transformation of the State must continue slowly step by step depending on the prevailing administrative burdens. The new people coming up from below into the State apparatus from the younger generation will bring this about by themselves. Thus, during the transitional period, we shall have to put up with some things which do not accord with the Party's programme and with some people who do not accord with its conception of the future German man [Mensch].

(d) It is the Führer's wish that the Party should exert influence on the State only in ways which are legally sanctioned. Party offices must not interfere directly in the work of government bodies. All complaints about the State administration must be forwarded to the responsible Reich Minister via the mediator between Party and State appointed by the Führer—his deputy, Reich Minister Hess.

---

[13]See doc. 159, p. 237 above.

(e) The strongest pressure on the State administration to gear itself to the Party lies in the Führer's statement: tasks which the State cannot fulfil will, if necessary, be transferred to the Party.[14] Up to now it has not been necessary to put this statement into effect.

C. The Party is independent of the State even in its administration, its jurisdiction, and in its legal system. Although it has become a body under the public law through the Law of 1 December 1933, this signifies only that this is the form in which it participates in legal processes. The Party is not under any kind of State supervision, it also does not owe its existence to any kind of State decree...

Sommer's successor, Dr Klopfer, appears to have been somewhat less of a Party militant, although of course his freedom of action was narrowly circumscribed by Bormann. At any rate, it was by no means true that there was a permanent state of confrontation between Bormann's office and the State Civil Service. The fact that the members of Department III and the ministerial civil servants shared a common background and training tended to give them a similar outlook on many matters, which could differ substantially from that of party militants. As late as 1944, for example, relations between Dr Klopfer and Lammers's deputy in the Reich Chancellery, State Secretary Dr Kritzinger, were quite cordial and they sometimes found themselves working together to defeat some abitrary or half-baked proposal from a Party figure—although this cooperation was largely limited to preserving administrative rationality.

Nevertheless, with the emergence of the Staff of the Führer's Deputy, and particularly the functions performed by Department III, the Reich Chancellery found itself faced with a new and potentially dangerous competitor. After all, unlike the various government departments and Party organizations, both agencies had the role of surveying the whole range of legislation and policy, at any rate in the domestic sphere. The crucial factor was access to Hitler. Who would succeed in acquiring Hitler's confidence to the degree which would enable him to assert the authority of his agency?

As we have seen, Hitler began by following a more or less orderly office routine in the Reich Chancellery. Until about 1935, Lammers saw Hitler regularly, but increasingly the Führer began to spend more and more time at Obersalzberg. The Reich Chancellery opened a special office in Berchtesgaden so that Lammers could be near Hitler. It was not, however, in the Berghof itself, and Lammers had no right of access to Hitler on a regular basis. Like everybody else, if he wanted an appointment he had to apply to the Führer's adjutants who would then pass on the request to Hitler. Such requests were frequently ignored as is clear from the following desperate appeal from Lammers (in Berchtesgaden) to Brückner, Hitler's adjutant (in the Berghof) only a few miles away, dated 21 October 1938:

[14]*Ibid.*

166

Because of his preoccupation with foreign policy I have been unable to make a detailed report to the Führer since 4 September. During my interview at the end of September in Berlin, shortly before his departure for the Sudetengau, I could report to him only on the most important questions and largely restricted myself to giving him a number of urgent laws to sign. In the meantime, matters on which I need to report to the Führer have piled up to such an extent that an interview during the next few days is extremely urgent. Since the Führer's decision must be secured by 1 November in a number of cases, I am being pressed daily by the responsible Reich Ministers to get an immediate decision from the Führer. I would, therefore, be grateful if you would inform the Führer of this and give me an appointment as soon as possible.

Martin Bormann saw the opportunities offered by proximity to Hitler more clearly and pursued them with more determination than anybody else. After 1933, his superior, Rudolf Hess, was for various reasons no longer on such intimate terms with Hitler and Bormann seized the opportunity. He increasingly took over from Hess the role of Hitler's unofficial private secretary. In 1935, for example, he acquired control over the administration of the Obersalzberg complex, Hitler's Bavarian estate. Unlike Lammers, therefore, Bormann secured permanent access to Hitler, and moreover, increasingly exploited his position to claim the right to pass on Hitler's instructions to Ministers and leading Party figures as the following letters indicate:

167

Bormann to the Reich Minister of Justice 24.8.1936
With reference to the discussion in your Ministry on 5 August 1936 concerning the admission of women to the legal profession. Since as the course of the discussion indicated, the Party has a particular interest in these things, I put the matter to the Führer. He has decided that women should become neither judges nor lawyers. Female law graduates, therefore, can be employed only in the Civil Service...

168

Bormann to Ley 8.2.1939
For your information the Führer wishes to see an end to the use of waiters in all restaurants. The job of a waiter is, in the Führer's view, not the right sort of work for a man but rather appropriate work for women and girls.

It was, however, only during the war years that Bormann succeeded in establishing a dominant position for himself and his office in the domestic sphere.

CHAPTER 10

Party/State Relations at Regional and Local Level

It was at regional and local level that tension between Party and State was most acute because it was there that the main power of the Party organization (PO) lay. The Gauleiters and district and local Party leaders were determined to hang on to the authority which they had won for themselves in the first months of 1933, and which they believed was theirs by right of conquest and by virtue of their Führer's role as Head of State.

On coming to power, the new regime was faced with the problem of Germany's unsatisfactory federal structure, bequeathed by Bismarck, which contained states which were grossly disproportionate in size and importance. Thus, at one extreme was the state of Prussia with three fifths of the area of the Reich and half of its population. The Prussian Civil Service was many times the size of that of the Reich and the Prussian state government in Berlin had always been more or less a rival to that of the Reich. At the other extreme was the state of Schaumburg-Lippe, which was about the size of an English rural district council. Proposals for federal reform had been discussed during the Weimar period but had been overtaken by the crisis of 1930–1933. The deposition of the Prussian government on 20 July 1932 and the installation of a Reich Commissioner in its place had prepared the way for major changes and the first two years of the new regime saw a great preoccupation with the issue of *Reichsreform*.

The Nazi seizure of power in the states in March 1933 involved both the takeover of the state governments and also the 'coordination' of the state parliaments (First Law for the Coordination of the Federal States of 31 March 1933). The takeover was engineered by the local Nazi party organizations in association with the Reich Ministry of the Interior in Berlin and the Ministry was determined to assert central control over the states. This appears to have been the main motive behind the Second Law for the Coordination of the Federal States under the Reich of 7 April 1933, which created the new post of Reich Governor (*Reichsstatthalter*) of which there were ten in all. With the exception of Bavaria (General von Epp) and Prussia (Hitler) the senior Gauleiter of each state was appointed. In some cases, one Reich Governor covered more than one state (e.g. Bremen-Oldenburg). The Reich Governors had the function of supervising 'the observance of the general policy laid down by the Reich Chancellor' by the state governments. It appears to have been Hitler's intention to use them to counteract the centrifugal tendencies which had resulted from the seizure of power by the Party in the states. The Reich Governors were to act as representatives of the Reich in the states, presumably on the principle of using the Gauleiter-poachers as gamekeepers.

The large state of Prussia was divided into provinces (e.g. East Prussia), in which the senior administrative official was the *Oberpräsident*. Many of these Oberpräsident posts had been taken over by Gauleiters. Although, as with the post of Reich Governor, this concentration of Party and State power was considerable, it did not ensure supreme authority within the province because the post of *Oberpräsident* had only a supervisory function over the real centres of Prussian state authority, which were the *Regierungspräsidenten* in charge of the *Regierungsbezirke* into which the Prussian provinces were sub-divided. The *Regierungspräsidenten* tended to resist the supervisory authority of the Oberpräsident so that the Ministry of the Interior in Berlin could use the *Regierungspräsidenten* as a check on the *Gauleiter-Oberpräsidenten*.

Thus, at regional level Party/State relations tended to take the form of an endemic conflict between the Reich Governors and the heads of the state governments, the Minister-Presidents, and in Prussia between the Gauleiter-Oberpräsidenten and the Regierungspräsidenten. A typical instance of this conflict was the following clash in August 1933 between Professor Werner, the Minister-President of Hesse and himself a leading local Nazi, and Jakob Sprenger, the Reich Governor-Gauleiter of Hesse over their respective claims to authority:

169

Werner: These things have unfortunately not been settled in detail. Because of this it was possible for the State Secretary, when going away on holiday, to tell me that he had appointed Herr Ringshausen as his deputy. That is preposterous. I am the only person who can be deputy and when I go on holiday the State Secretary deputizes for me. Thus the whole thing is fluid and gives rise to misunderstandings which must be removed. Clear lines of demarcation are best: clear lines of demarcation as to the position of the state government in relation to the representative of the Führer, the Reich Governor, and clear lines of demarcation between the Minister-President and the State Secretary, and between him and the Government. I once told the Führer in a conference: Transfer all authority to the Reich Governor. Since he rejected this and declared that it did not correspond to the intentions of the Reich Governors' Law, a separate head became necessary for the Government. This entailed a demarcation of areas of authority. How far does the power of the Reich Governor reach into the state government? A commentary is needed for the Reich Governors' Law and for the state governments. The governments are not simply organs of administration. That is clear from the fact that they have the right of nominating civil servants. In fact, generally speaking, I complied with all requests regarding personnel. In one or two cases I was unable to do so and have freely expressed my opinion on this, as you have repeatedly asked me to do.

Sprenger: Everything that you regard as unsettled, I now regard as settled. From a formal point of view the letter of the law prevails; beyond this the unwritten law of evolution. The Chancellor has declared: 'Revolution is dead, evolution has begun.' I remind you of the speech of the Führer in Berchtesgaden and at the Nuremberg Party Rally. In both speeches the theory of evolution is expressed entirely unambiguously. The Chancellor made a quite definite decision during the Berlin discussion. He refused to be regarded as a court for dealing with complaints and, as you, Herr Minister-President, will remember, he named me, the Reich Governor, as your superior. All the things you mention here, based on past legislation, must evolve in this direction. The Party takes precedence and is responsible for political questions. The Government is there to administer. The Gauleiter has determined political questions since the Party began. This principle was explicitly mentioned by the Führer at the time we took over power. The Gauleiters were the holders of power

---

Note and footnotes to diagram on facing page:

Perhaps the most outstanding characteristic of the political system of the Third Reich was its lack of formal structure. This diagram, therefore, should be regarded as no more than a rough indication of the position of the various State and Party offices and their relationship to one another. It was difficult to get agreement on policy at ministerial level except in the comparatively rare event of Hitler issuing a clear-cut Führer order. But because of the lack of an effective hierarchy it was equally difficult to ensure a uniform and comprehensive implementation of policy at the lower levels.

[1]On 11 April 1933, Hitler appointed Göring Prussian Minister-President in addition to his post as Minister of the Interior. On 1 May 1934, however, Hitler, at Göring's request, transferred the Prussian Ministry of the Interior to Frick, who then became Reich and Prussian Minister of the Interior, though the Prussian administrative apparatus as such remained intact.

[2]After 1928 the *Gaue* came to correspond, broadly speaking, with the electoral districts. Over the years, however, there were a number of amalgamations and subdivisions as well as the addition of the annexed territories after 1938, so that during the years 1928–45 the *Gaue* varied in number between thirty and forty. The area of the individual *Gaue* varied considerably. Some, such as East Prussia or Baden, corresponded to a Prussian province or a large federal state; others were smaller—Hanover-East, for example, embraced two *Regierungsbezirke* and was less than half the size of the Province of Hanover. The importance of the individual Gauleiter was, however, related more to his length in office and his relations with Hitler than to the size of his *Gau*.

[3]In large cities such as Leipzig or Cologne the Oberbürgermeister had traditionally been sufficiently important to have a direct line to the Ministry of the Interior.

Party/State Relationships in the Third Reich

For footnotes see facing page.

and as things have developed the Government has also been determined by the Gauleiters. Let me repeat, not for the first time, everybody can express his view like a man. I have never been biased. But if differences of opinion occur, only one person can decide: namely, myself as Gauleiter. And when I have made my decision, there must be no further speculation. Contact with Reich Government offices or the Chancellor is allowed only after consultation with and with the permission of the Gauleiter and Reich Governor, not otherwise. For those bodies have no authority over this. . . .

From this particular confrontation Sprenger emerged victorious. He succeeded in removing the Minister-President and eventually in combining the Minister-Presidency with the position of Reich Governor. But other Reich Governors were less successful and the situation remained ambiguous.

The civil servants in the Reich Ministry of the Interior had long wished to curb the powers of the states and saw the new regime as a golden opportunity. Their centralising ambitions met with the full approval of the new Nazi Minister, Wilhelm Frick, who wished to turn his department into the hub of government with the federal states reduced to the role of a field administration of his ministry. This goal found expression in the Law for the Reconstruction of the Reich of 30 January 1934 which effectively abolished the federal system. The state governments remained in existence but were subordinated to the Reich authorities:

170

The referendum and the Reichstag election of 12 November 1933 have demonstrated that the German people have attained an indestructible internal unity superior to all internal subdivisions and conflicts of a political character.

Consequently, the Reichstag has enacted the following law which is hereby promulgated with the unanimous vote of the Reichstag after ascertaining that the requirements of the Reich Constitution have been met:

Article 1.   Popular assemblies of the federal states shall be abolished.

Article 2.   (a) The sovereign powers of the federal states are transferred to the Reich.
(b) The federal state governments are subordinated to the Reich Government.

Article 3.   The Reich Governors are placed under the administrative supervision of the Reich Minister of the Interior.

Article 4.   The Reich Government may issue new constitutional laws.

Article 5.   The Reich Minister of the Interior issues the necessary legal and administrative regulations for the execution of the law.

Article 6.   This law becomes effective on the day of its promulgation.

Although the Law for the Reconstruction of the Reich removed from the states the remnants of their independent authority, reform of the federal structure soon came to a halt. This was partly because Hitler decided that the resultant administrative upheaval would interfere with the achievement of his major goals of economic recovery and rearmament and partly because of opposition from the vested interests involved, notably the local Gauleiters in the states scheduled for merger or dissolution. Reform was largely restricted to a merger of most of the Reich and Prussian ministries, including Interior, in April 1934. Göring was pacified by promotion to Minister-President of Prussia and plans for the abolition or full-scale restructuring of Prussia were shelved.

Among the anomalies left by this situation was the position of Reich Governor, which was now superfluous. Since the Minister-Presidents of the states were now directly subordinate to the Reich/Prussian Ministry of the Interior, there was no longer any need to have a representative of the Reich Chancellor supervising the implementation of Reich policy in the states. It was, however, characteristic of Hitler's style that the post of Reich Governor was not abolished, as the principles of good administrative order required, but left in continuing rivalry with that of the Minister-President. But the Law did subordinate the Reich Governors to the Reich Minister of the Interior (Art. 3), and this was something which senior Gauleiters were not prepared to tolerate, as is shown by the following letter of 9 April 1934 from the Reich Governor of Brunswick and Anhalt, Wilhelm Loeper, to State Secretary Lammers at the Reich Chancellery:

171

I am taking the liberty below of asking you for your opinion on the following matter:

The position of Reich Governors seems to me unclear at the moment. Whereas, on the one hand, the Reich Governor has been appointed by the Reich President and sworn in by him personally, and whereas, as regards salary, he is also on the same level as the Reich Ministers, on the other hand he is subject to instructions from the Reich Ministry of the Interior. With this new law[15] it is now not quite clear whether the Reich Governor has retained his old position or whether he has become an authority subordinate to the Reich Ministry of the Interior. Owing to this lack of clarity, there is uncertainty about the actions of the Reich Governor. One is often in the position of not knowing whether one is allowed to act independently in accordance with the policy of the Führer, or whether one is merely an executive organ of the Reich Ministry of the Interior. If the old position of the Reich Governor is to be retained, the subordination to the instructions of the Reich Ministry of the Interior must be of a purely general character and this fact should be manifest in

---

[15]Law for the Reconstruction of the Reich, of 30 January 1934; see p. 250 above.

externals as well. Just as one Reich Ministry cannot give orders to and make requests of another but must *invite* it to do something, the same practice should be observed towards the Reich Governor. But in fact the practice has developed of the Reich Governor himself (not only his office) receiving requests signed by some *Minis-terialrat* and certified by some Chancellery secretary. . . .

I do like clarity in all things. It is in such external matters that one's position is defined for officialdom and for the public. I can very well imagine that the professional bureaucracy is happy to make use of the opportunity of reducing the position of the Reich Governor below that intended by the Führer. But I also recall the words of the Führer during a conference of Reich Governors when he declared: 'You are the first Reich Governors and what you make of this position will determine what it will be in the future.' This comment by the Führer gives me the right to make this inquiry.

The Reich Governors insisted on their right to appeal to Hitler direct. But Frick, the Minister of the Interior, resented this attempt to go over his head and appealed to Hitler, Hitler's reply made it clear that he wished to keep important decisions in his own hands:

172

Reich Minister of the Interior Frick to the Reich Chancellery, 4 June 1934:

If we are to stick to the idea of a central and unified leadership of the Reich through the Reich Chancellor and the departmental ministers assisting him, who corporately together with the Reich Chancellor form the Reich Government, then it is impossible to leave differences of opinion between a departmental minister on the one hand and a governor on the other . . . to be decided by the Reich Chancellor. On the contrary, the decision of the Reich Minister who represents the Reich Government in his area of responsibility must be accepted by the Reich Governor without allowing him a form of legal redress against the decision of the Reich Minister in the field of legislation.

State Secretary Lammers to Frick, 27 February 1934:

The Reich Chancellor agrees that, generally speaking, differences of opinion between a departmental minister and a Reich Governor on the legality or expediency of a State law cannot be left to his decision. In the Chancellor's view an exception must be made for those cases which are concerned with questions of special political importance. In the view of the Reich Chancellor such a regulation is consistent with his position of leadership.

The regional state authorities could not afford to ignore the wishes of the Gauleiter-Reich Governors and Gauleiter-Oberpräsidenten, but during the period 1935–39 they could usually bring the authority of the Reich/Prussian Ministry of the Interior into play to maintain much independence of action. They also possessed greater skill as professional civil servants. The Reich

Governor and Gauleiter of Thuringia, Fritz Sauckel, for example, complained about the growing centralization of the Reich authorities which was reducing the position of Reich Governor to that of a figurehead. After an interview in January with Hitler, attended also by Hess and Frick, Sauckel wrote a thirty-six page memorandum, dated 27 January 1936, with the title. 'On the transfer of Spheres of Authority and Responsibility from the States and Regional Offices to the Government Departments in Berlin and the Political and Administrative Consequences', which he then passed to Hitler at lunch in the Reich Chancellery. This memorandum, from which the following extracts are taken, provides a very good insight into administrative developments during the years 1934–39 in general, and the relative weakness of the Party authorities vis-à-vis those of the state in particular. According to Sauckel, Hitler had 'expressed strong agreement with my views' at the January interview, but then, typically, had not acted on the memorandum. Sauckel was, therefore, obliged to write to the head of the Reich Chancellery, Dr Lammers, to ask him to place the memorandum before Hitler again. Once again there was apparently no result:

173

I. *The influence of the leading men in the Party in the regions* [Aussenbezirken] *is in danger of being absorbed back into the Reich administration.*
. . . 2. Often the members of the state governments are not even notified of the plans of the Reich Government departments and of the drafts of laws and decrees which affect their sphere of operations and indeed the very existence of their offices and subordinate offices. . . . Thus a directive from the Reich and Prussian Minister of Education of 23 February 1935 to the Education Departments of the states, following on the Law on University Teachers of 21 January 1935 and the 2nd Reich Governors' Law of 1 February 1935, subordinated the appointment of university teachers to 'Office W' in the Reich and Prussian Ministry of Education. . . . In this way, bit by bit the powers of those people in the regions who have the confidence of the movement are being absorbed into the central authorities in Berlin. There the ministers of the states often have to see a bunch of desk officials to get permission for the most trifling matters which were previously within their own discretion.

In many cases which could be dealt with by the state ministries without any difficulty, the red tape and waste of time involved in the relations between the state and Reich authorities reaches grotesque proportions. The initiative of the Reich field administration is often restricted because the individual Reich Government departments in the various spheres declare that a Reich regulation is to be issued. It then often appears that they have only just begun formulating these Reich regulations or that their formulation has been shelved. And yet, all this while, measures urgently necessary for local reasons are not introduced in the states and so damage is done both to the movement and to the State.

The progressive restriction of the sphere of activity at the level of both state and *Gau* has occasionally led to irritability even between leading Party members, indeed to friction and tensions. This is particularly apt to happen since these personalities are forceful and independent, refractory and self-willed, shaped by struggle rather than smooth administration. . . .

3. *The position of the Reich Governors has in reality even less substance than that of the state ministers.* The Reich Governors have hardly any direct legal responsibilities in the day-to-day affairs of state. . . . [After describing their legal responsibilities Sauckel continued:] It is not true that the activities of a Reich Governor need be restricted to these paltry legal responsibilities. He can act as the official representative of the Reich Government which he is officially declared to be. He can hurry from rallies to receptions, from public addresses to serious accidents, from dedication ceremonies to meetings—but he can give no orders. He is by no means without influence; he can get somewhere by diplomacy, by persuasion, by threats, or through the Party—but he can give no orders. He can make suggestions, he can request information, he can make inquiries and complaints—but he can give no orders. To make a comparison, he has a similar position in his district to that of the English king in England. He can make quite a lot of his position through his energy and skill but largely outside the legal limits. There can be differing opinions about the expediency of having such representative figures in the regions; but whether the most combative and active personalities in the movement are the most suitable people for such a purely representative role is questionable, except perhaps when they are near retirement.

The Reich Governors, who have after all been officially declared to be the representative of the Reich Government and the men responsible for seeing to the carrying out of its policies and are intended to be particularly well-informed agents and interpreters of its plans and intentions, are usually even less well informed than the state ministers about its legislative and administrative plans. . . .

4. The constitutional position of the Prussian *Oberpräsidenten* is equally weak. The administrative responsibilities attached to them are limited and fairly remote from politics. Their real function is almost entirely informatory and representative in character. As is well known, the *Regierungspräsidenten* are not subordinate to the *Oberpräsidenten*. Under Prussian law the *Regierungspräsidenten* and the Ministry can work together with one another, by-passing the *Oberpräsidenten*, and to my knowledge they make full use of this. The *Oberpräsidenten* hang, as it were, in the air.

5. As a result the leading personalities in the movement in the provinces who occupy such positions appear in the eyes of the people as the most senior exponents of a political development over which they basically have hardly any influence. . . .

II. *The shift in the seat of power as a result of the centralization in the hands of the Reich does not benefit the Führer and Reich Chancellor or the Reich Ministers as individuals so much as mainly the anonymous central bureaucracy.* . . .

III. *Overcentralization does not bring unity but rather inflates the administration, makes it cumbersome and difficult to supervise: it breeds departmental particularism and splits up the authority of the State.* . . .

The Reich Government departments clearly desire—and all of them are more or less forced by one another's actions to follow suit—to establish for themselves their own self-contained field organizations with a separate identity, imposing sharper and sharper lines of demarcation from the other administrative bodies and seeking to achieve independence of them. These huge administrative bodies are therefore bound in the long run to diverge more and more from one another; each one creates a state within the State. Instead of seventeen federal states there will be in the end fourteen departmental bodies which at their middle and lower levels are cutting themselves off more and more from one another. It only requires the shock of a crisis to bring about open chaos.

Instead of state particularism we are getting departmental particularism....

The centralism and the departmental point of view are leading to the complete disintegration of the field administration. And the main point is that the Party men, whether Reich Governors, Minister-Presidents or state ministers, are being more and more excluded from the administration. The whole process shows the infinitely subtle, secret and persistent endeavours of particular Civil Service cliques to acquire sole authority and to neutralize the influence of the Party representatives....

Party interference in the administration tended to be most prevalent at district and local level and the Gauleiters exercised greatest influence here. They had in most cases been responsible for building up the Party *apparat* in their region from the earliest times after the refounding of the Party in 1925. They were usually local men who had over the years built up a clique of loyal supporters, particularly at district level the district leaders or *Kreisleiter*. This gave the Gauleiters considerable independence of the central Party organization.

The control of the Gauleiters over the district and local Party *apparats* also gave them a large measure of influence over local government, since the district and local branch leaders were determined to dominate the state and local government officials in their district. The Party had won considerable influence over local government at the time of the seizure of power by packing the local councils and in some cases by taking over the office of mayor. But, as in most other spheres, this influence was then given legal expression although it was also delimited by legislation, in the form of the Prussian Local Government Law of 15 December 1933 and the Reich Local Government Law of 30 January 1935. The Prussian Law laid down, first, that the mayors were in future to be nominated (to serve for twelve years) rather than elected: in large cities by the Minister of the Interior (Göring); in towns by the *Regierungspräsident* 'in consultation' with the Gauleiter. Secondly, it laid down that, subject to the general supervision of the Ministry of the Interior, the mayor was to have absolute authority in his town. In some cases, the mayor was at the same time local branch leader of the Party. But in many cases this law actually had the effect of strengthening a non-Nazi or nominal Nazi mayor against the Nazi-dominated town council which had been reduced to a mere advisory body. As a result, the law met with considerable opposition from the Party.

This opposition was taken account of to some extent in the Reich Local Government Law of 30 January 1935. This law also gave the mayor dictatorial powers but introduced a so-called 'Delegate of the NSDAP in the Municipality'. This Nazi delegate had the right of participation in the appointment and dismissal of the mayor and his deputies, in the appointment and dismissal of the local councillors, and in the drawing up of the bye-laws. The district Party leaders (*Kreisleiter*) were appointed to this post, which meant that any local branch leader was officially excluded from effective influence on local government unless he happened to be mayor. Furthermore, the powers of supervision over local government remained with the Ministry of the Interior acting through the district and regional state authorities—the *Landräte* and the *Regierungspräsident* or Minister-President. These laws operating against the background of ambitious local Party leaders created patterns of conflict within local government. Thus the mayor, unless he was simultaneously local branch leader, would have to face interference both from the district leader in his capacity as 'Delegate of the NSDAP' and from the local branch leader who resented the mayor's role. The mayor could to some extent call on the support of the supervisory state authorities to help him to resist interference by the Party, but the *Landräte* and the *Regierungspräsidenten* were also having to fight off interference from the district Party leaders and the Gauleiters. The result was a constantly fluctuating power relationship within the localities. The following account of the *Landrat* of Kreuznach in the Rhineland for December 1935 indicates the extent of Party interference at district and local level:

174

I have often reported that the subordinate Party posts are still frequently filled with unsuitable persons and this is still so today. It is true that I was told by the mayors and police officers at the last official meetings that cooperation had improved between the offices of the Party and those of the administration. But against that is the statement from a reliable source that the Party itself does not find cooperation with the administration satisfactory because the offices of the administration are not sufficiently 'obedient'. In my opinion, the relationship between Party and administration can be described as follows: the heads of the administration, especially of the public administration, have gradually got so used to constant interference by political leaders in purely administrative matters that they have come to regard this state of affairs as tolerable only so long as these conflicts do not become too violent. But it is an unhealthy state of affairs if, in the interests of cooperation and their public image, the authorities are invariably lenient, often to the detriment of the cause. After nearly three years' service in the district, I feel obliged to say again clearly that the duplication in the work of the Party and of the authorities in administrative matters is intolerable in the long run and tends to jeopardize constructive work. This is not only my view but that of old Party comrades who have for many years occupied leading posts as administrative officials. It is they particularly who complain to me that the subordinate Party officers, obviously because of their training by their superiors, are convinced that the authorities are nothing more than their executive organs. In fact, the local district leader [of the Party] is of the opinion that in the district of Kreuznach there can be no other will but his. This principle is of course employed even more rigidly by the subordinate local Party leaders. They are often on the look-out for cases of complaint and possibilities of interference, in order to keep the authorities aware of Party supervision. Having no competently trained apparatus at their command, Party offices deal with administrative matters and prejudge questions which either have already been officially dealt with by the authorities or are undecided and in the end have to be left to the authorities for examination and final decision on their own responsibility. But by then much work has been duplicated and time and energy wasted. I get the impression that the main cause of all this is the personal ambition of the political leaders. They seek to claim success for administrative work and exploit it with the public and in the press, while their failures are blamed on the authorities which in any case have to bear the responsibility. . . .

The endeavour of the political leaders to fill civil servants' and employees' posts in Government offices solely on the ground of length of Party membership often reaches the point of excluding non-Party members and those Party members who joined the Party after 30 January 1933, even if they have far more skill and higher moral qualities. A particularly striking case was one in which other suitable applicants were turned down for the post of district welfare leader here, and the district committee proceeded to elect a civil servant who was an old Party member but who was not suited either by character or technical qualifications and whom meanwhile the police had to arrest for embezzlement in his previous post. No wonder, then, that people often express the view that the Party is pursuing the policy of getting Party members into public appointments regardless of their suitability, and is thereby doing exactly what it fought against in the old system.

Old Party members also confirm this view. But they are usually those who refrain on principle from turning their Party membership to any personal advantage.

It appears urgently necessary, in the interests both of the authority of the State and of constructive progress, to clear up the unsatisfactory situation I have described. Responsibilities for actual Party tasks must be clearly defined. I can see no solution in the linking up of Party offices with the State offices, whether with the district administration or with the local authorities. Moreover, the responsibility of the political leaders must, in my opinion, not only be a moral responsibility, but it must be emphasized by legal regulations.

At each level of the administration, therefore, the State authorities, frequently headed by nominal Nazis, had to fight off interference by the Party organization at their level. How successful they were in doing so was partly a matter of personality, depending on how good the connexions of the respective combatants were with those at the top and particularly with the Führer, and also on how good they were at this kind of political in-fighting. The State authorities tried to insist that since the State was now a Nazi State with a Nazi Head of State and Nazi ministers, they must be allowed to carry out the decisions and policies of the Government in accordance with official procedures and without interference by the Party, which would introduce an entirely arbitrary element. This attitude on the part of the Civil Service received the support of the Government ministers, even of Frick and Göring, Nazi leaders of long standing. It also had support from the Party chief, Rudolf Hess. While keen to ensure Party influence, Hess wished it to be secured in an orderly fashion through his office. Thus he regularly lectured the Party cadres on their responsibilities, as in his speech to the Party Congress of September 1935 from which the following extract is taken:

175

... Party and State are still by no means everywhere attuned to one another. As they take on new tasks the particular formations within the movement itself come up against new points of friction between each other.

State offices have not yet come to terms with the fact that the Party is a part of the State, that Party cadres [Hoheitsträger] are officials of the State. It has still not penetrated into the sub-consciousness of the Party offices that the State is our State that the laws are our laws, that the executive force is our force. . . . It causes damage if, for example, officials of the NSDAP attack civil servants or put down local policemen in front of the public—men who are only acting in accordance with the commands of our own State.

Lack of agreement, the occurrence of difficulties must never become public knowledge. Both sides must always be clear that both—State and Party—will suffer because the prestige of both will be damaged. . . . The Führer uses two arms with which to lead the nation: the Party apparatus and the governmental apparatus. The Party apparatus maintains the contact between government and people. The Party has the job of ensuring national discipline. . . . Let us prevent a vacuum from emerging between the people and the leadership. Top leaders must be available from time to time for the ordinary national comrade to speak to. They must retain the common touch and national comrades must retain the impression that the leaders of the movement have an open heart for them . . .

Nazi Party officials were, however, determined not to allow themselves to be ordered about by the State authorities. They claimed, as the true representatives of the will of the Führer, to be fighting a reactionary and formalistic bureaucracy which was always blocking the implementation of Nazi policy on the grounds that it was 'against regulations'. They believed, and basically with good reason, that they were 'working towards the Führer'. This tension between Party and State was built into the system and remained unresolved.

CHAPTER 11

The Nazi Economic Programme

The Nazis were very late in developing a coherent economic programme. The economic points contained in the Twenty-Five Point Programme of 1920 reflected the outlook of the urban lower-middle-class.[16] They were hostile to those living on investments, to big business, and above all high finance and the stock market (§§11,13,14). They also expressed the hostility of the small shopkeepers and artisans to the big department stores and consumer cooperatives and demanded special consideration for the small man (§16). During 1932, however, as the Party's prospects of achieving power grew brighter, so the need to produce an economic programme that would be acceptable to the main power groups became more acute. At the same time, the Party's new potential attracted the interest of various industrialists and economists who sought to influence a movement which was rising so rapidly. By 1933, the Nazis had established the broad outlines of an economic programme which derived from two main sources.

The first main source of Nazi economic policy was a group of unorthodox economists—the so-called 'Reformers' who, in the early 1930s, put forward a programme with two main components. The first consisted of a campaign for autarky (i.e. economic self-sufficiency) and, since Germany within its existing boundaries was incapable of achieving self-sufficiency, the creation of a 'large economic area' (*Grosswirtschaftsraum*) protected behind tariff barriers and dominated by Germany. This campaign was prompted by the collapse of the international trading system in the wake of the slump, the revival of world-wide protectionism and, specifically, the creation of imperial

---

[16]See above, pp. 14–16.

or regional preference areas such as the Ottawa Agreement. The impression became widespread that the old international economic order had broken down and that a new order was in the process of emerging. If Germany's economy was to compete with those of the United States, the British Empire, and Japan, it would need to create a rival economic block. The campaign also reflected the extreme nationalism prevalent in Germany. The idea of autarky and of Germany dominating a large economic area had a long history as a component of the German nationalist tradition, dating back to the writings of Adam Müller and Friedlich List at the beginning of the nineteenth century. It had resurfaced at the end of the century in the form of the concept of *Mitteleuropa*, an economic block in Central and South-Eastern Europe dominated by Germany, which gained an influential following among academic economists such as Gustav Schmoller who taught these ideas to the generation of economists, politicians, civil servants, and businessmen who were in power between the wars. *Mitteleuropa* had, in fact, been a key war aim during World War I and was then revived by the Brüning and Papen governments after 1930.

The second component of the 'Reformers'' programme was in the domestic sphere. Once again, in their view, the apparent bankruptcy of Liberalism, both in its political form (the democratic system of Weimar) and in terms of its economic policies, seemed to require a fundamental re-orientation of policy. They advocated much greater intervention by the State in the economy and, specifically, a policy of deficit-spending through a major programme of public works. Following the new ideas of Keynes, they argued that this would provide a solution to the unemployment problem both directly and also indirectly by reviving the economy through an increase in domestic demand. Again, it was a central part of the German nationalist economic tradition to favour such State intervention in the economy for the sake of furthering national political goals.

These 'Reformers' and Autarkists sought to gain political influence through the Nazi Party. The Party was on the look-out for new ideas and solutions to the economic crisis. It was already opposed to Liberal ortho-doxies and had no objection in principle to a policy of deficit-spending. Similarly, the Party's extreme nationalism was part of that same Pan-German tradition which had spawned the concept of *Mitteleuropa*. Indeed, during the early 1920s, Hitler had been converted to a version of this theory by Karl Haushofer, an ardent advocate of the new 'science' of Geopolitics. However, partly under Haushofer's influence, Hitler shifted the emphasis from economic to political and racial priorities and used the concept of *Lebensraum* or 'living space', seeing this living space not so much in south-eastern Europe as in Western Russia. In Hitler's view, economics was subordinate to politics and he regarded it as the function of economic policy to provide the material resources necessary for the political and military leadership to acquire by conquest or otherwise the land and natural resources (*Lebensraum*), which in turn would provide the wherewithal for further territorial acquisitions and the basis for the growth of a strong and healthy race.

In 1932, a leading Reformer, Heinrich Dräger, published a pamphlet with the title 'Work Creation and the Productive Creation of Credit' in a Nazi series, the 'National Socialist Library'. On 10 May 1932, Gregor Strasser, the Party's organization chief, made a major speech in the Reichstag which was later published with the title 'Work and Bread'. It expounded many of the Reformers' views:

176

This great anti-capitalist longing—as I call it—which is going through our nation and which has gripped perhaps as many as 95 per cent of our people is interesting and valuable. It by no means represents a rejection of property which is morally justified because it has been produced through work and saving. Above all, it has nothing to do with the senseless, unsuccessful, and destructive tendencies of the International. It is rather the protest of the productive sections of the nation against a degenerate theory of economics and it demands from the State that, in order to secure its own right to live, it must break with the demons of gold, the world economy, materialism, with the exclusive preoccupation with export statistics and the Reichsbank rate and reestablish a situation in which honest labour receives an honest reward.

This great anti-capitalist longing is proof of the fact that we are on the threshold of a great, a tremendous new epoch: the overcoming of Liberalism and the emergence of a new kind of economic thinking and a new attitude to the State ...

Article 163 [of the Weimar Constitution] will one day have to be altered to the effect that every German must have the right to work and people will have to be aware of the full significance of this alteration ...[17]

The necessities of life come from work: food, accommodation, clothing, light, and heat. The wealth of a nation lies in labour not capital and that is the point. And so when it is dealing with the question of work creation the State must never ask: Have I got the money for it? But rather, there is only one question: What should I use the money for? There is always money for work creation and in the last resort one should use productive credit creation [i.e. deficit-spending], which is economically entirely justified ...

In the case of work creation, therefore, the only question can be: where should one begin? The starting-point must be found. Here I must make the following point: Germany is still dependent on foreign countries for the most important human need: namely foodstuffs. A nation which is dependent on foreign countries is in the final analysis never in a position to solve its foreign policy problems, the problems of its freedom as it would wish. In other words, we must enable sufficient essential

---

[17]Article 163 laid down that 'Every German should be given the possibility of earning his living through work ...'.

foodstuffs to be produced on German soil to feed the whole population. One should have done that before the present level of unemployment was reached, as a response to the Treaty of Versailles which reduced our living space and which should have automatically produced a response in the form of a reorganization of agricultural production. In addition, we need in Germany an ambitious housing and population policy, i.e. the resettlement of people away from the big cities ...

Strasser incorporated these views in the 'Emergency Economic Programme of the NSDAP', published for the election of July 1932, and although this was later replaced by a more moderate programme which dropped Strasser's demand for the right to work in order to conciliate business, the basic policies remained the same.

This set of policies advocating, on the one hand, a shift of emphasis from world trade to autarky, particularly in foodstuffs, and the creation of a German economic sphere of influence in central and south-eastern Europe and, on the other hand, a programme of deficit spending was unorthodox and had a mixed reception within the business community. It did, however, broadly coincide with the views of those who provided the second main source of the Nazi economic programme—the advocates of a *Wehrwirtschaft*.

The concept of a *Wehrwirtschaft* (defence economy) may be defined as the gearing of the whole economy in peacetime to the needs of future war. It had been coined in the 1920s as military men and economists had reflected on the lessons of World War I. They concluded that a major reason for Germany's defeat had been the failure to organize the economy effectively in order to cope with the massive economic and technological demands of the war machine and the problems posed by the Allied blockade. In future Germany must be prepared to fight a 'total war' (Ludendorff) requiring the mobilization of the whole of the nation's resources and this must begin in peacetime.

Hitler had been impressed by these ideas and above all by Germany's experience during World War I, and the concept of a 'defence economy' provided the main goal of Nazi economic policy prior to the outbreak of war. He made this clear at a Cabinet meeting on 8 February 1933, just over a week after coming to power. He replied to a proposal by the Reich Ministry of Transport to build a reservoir as follows:

177

The Reich Chancellor stated that in judging the request by the Minister of Transport, another decisive consideration had to be taken into account. Germany was now negotiating with foreign countries about her military equality of rights. The recognition of a theoretical equality of rights was bound to follow in the very near future. But Germany could not content herself with that. This theoretical recognition must be followed by practical equality of rights, that is to say, by German rearmament. The world, especially France, was entirely prepared for German rearmament and regarded it as a matter of course. The next five years in Germany had to be devoted to rendering the German people again capable of bearing arms [*Wiederwehrhaftmachung*]. Every publicly sponsored measure to create employment had to be considered from the point of view of whether it was necessary with respect to rendering the German people again capable of bearing arms for military service. This had to be the dominant thought, always and everywhere.

The Reich Minister of Labour supported these statements of the Reich Chancellor, but added that besides the purely military tasks there was also other economically valuable work which ought not to be neglected.

The Reich Minister of Transport pointed out that the development of German waterways was also a military necessity. In the event of an emergency the entire German traffic system must be in order, and this included the operation of the waterways.

The Reich Commissioner for Air felt he must emphasize on the other hand that the improvement of the German highway system was even more important.

The Reichswehr Minister expressed the point of view that in the first place the immediate needs of the Army had to be considered. The German Army was disarmed to such an extent that the prime necessity was to provide the material foundation for armaments. Only after the emergency armament had been completed would it be possible to tackle larger tasks.

The Reich Chancellor again stressed that for the next 4–5 years the main principle must be: everything for the armed forces. Germany's position in the world depended decisively upon the position of the German armed forces. The position of the German economy in the world was also dependent on that.

The Reich Cabinet decided to have the total budget for 1933 submitted first, then to examine what could be done especially for the armed forces, and finally to see what funds were left for the development of the waterways, especially for the building of a reservoir in Upper Silesia, now under discussion.

There were, however, limits to the extent to which any government could impose a war economy in peacetime. First, for the sake of morale it was vital to retain the support of the mass of the population who expected a reasonable standard of living: an acceptable level of wages and an adequate supply of foodstuffs and consumer goods. Secondly, there was the problem of how to persuade private firms to gear their business activities to the requirements of a defence economy without thereby alienating a powerful elite whose cooperation was essential—the problem, that is, of reconciling the need for state direction with traditional business hostility to bureaucratic controls, an attitude shared by Hitler himself. Finally, there was the problem of Germany's dependence on international sources of supply for a substantial number of industrial raw materials and foodstuffs.

German economic policy between 1933 and 1939 was governed by the regime's attempts to overcome these difficulties and reconcile often conflicting priorities in the pursuit of its goal of a defence economy. An increasingly dominant element in that policy was the growing emphasis on performance (*Leistung*) as a key value. Both in the economic and in the social fields the regime's policies were increasingly geared towards rewarding the strong and efficient and penalising the weak and inefficient. Hitler himself made it clear that in the economic sphere his main priority was to maximize production, as he told the building workers constructing his estate in Berchtesgaden on 20 May 1937:

178

...A lot is talked about the question of a private enterprise economy or a cooperative economy, a socialised economy or a private property economy. Believe me here too the decisive factor is not the theory but the performance of the economy... Business is quite brutal. You know, one notices a businessman who has made it, but one doesn't notice the tens of thousands of others who have gone bust. But it is in the nation's best interests for its economy to be run only by able people and not by civil servants. You can be sure that it would be a catastrophe if the Civil Service were to run the German economy. We would not have one tenth of the production that we have... I am not there to subsidize incompetent business leaders for the sake of the State. I wouldn't dream of it. I place orders. Who completes them I regard as irrelevant. If you tell me that a thousand will go bust if I don't subsidize them, then they'll go bust. That's fine by me. They're merely good-for-nothings, incompetents—they can go bust.

Although this speech was clearly geared to its audience, it shows how Hitler regarded economic life as a model of the operation of the law of the struggle for the survival of the fittest, which in his view governed all of nature. He believed maximum productivity would be achieved where that law could operate most ruthlessly with minimal interference from the State bureaucracy. At the same time, however, business must gear its activities to the needs of the State which placed the orders. Thus, although the criterion of performance appeared on the surface ideologically neutral, in fact it reflected the Social Darwinist mentality at the core of Nazism. It also coincided with a central tenet of capitalist economics and thereby won the support of the most influential groups within the various sectors of the economy. In effect, the regime encouraged a process of differentiation in business, agriculture, and even within the labour force. It was a process based partly on performance, which in turn depended largely on size—the larger firms tended to be better equipped and to use more modern techniques. However, since the economy was geared primarily to rearmament, it also depended above all on the extent to which the particular business or individual worker was engaged on rearmament projects. Those on the capital goods side of the economy tended to benefit, those on the consumer goods side to lose out. The fact that there were both winners and losers undermined solidarity within the various economic sectors, putting their members at odds with one another. Through its favours the regime in effect recruited the more powerful members of each group as its clients, thereby neutralizing potential centres of opposition. This was of course in addition to its general concern of improving productivity as a whole. Here again the regime was able to work with the grain of existing trends and values within German society.

CHAPTER 12

The Policies of Schacht

Hitler's main objective as he took office at the end of January, was the winning of the election in March. As for economic policy, he contented himself with a general commitment in his Appeal to the Nation to solve what he described as the two major economic problems—unemployment and the agrarian crisis.[18] He made no detailed proposals. Indeed, on 8 February he informed his Cabinet that they 'should avoid all detailed statements concerning an economic programme of the Government'. Hitler, anxious to secure the widest possible support before the election, did not wish to risk alienating any social or economic group by putting forward specific proposals at this stage.

One of Hitler's most important decisions during his first weeks in office was to appoint Dr Hjalmar Schacht on 16 March 1933 to the Presidency of the Reichsbank. Schacht's predecessor, Hans Luther, was a very conservative financier who had insisted on restricting the previous government's attempts to provide State finance for the work-creation programme for fear of encouraging inflation. When Luther endeavoured to impose the same restrictions on Hitler he was forced to resign. In Schacht, Hitler found an ideal replacement. President of the Reichsbank in the 1920s, Schacht had resigned over the Young Plan and had joined the 'nationalist opposition' to the Republic. During 1931, he had established links with Hitler and had continued to support him even when his prospects had not looked bright. Hitler was fortunate in finding in Schacht someone who was both a sympathizer and an acknowledged expert with whom the business community could feel secure. But Schacht was above all a brilliant financier and he now devoted his considerable gifts to the economic consolidation of the Nazi regime and, in particular, to facilitating the rearmament programme.

---

[18]Cf. above, pp. 131–4.

(i) Financial Measures 1933–34

Schacht at once began to develop the methods of deficit financing practised only tentatively by his predecessors and to use them to finance rearmament. One of his most important innovations was the so-called 'mefo' bills. After the war Emil Puhl, a director of the Reichsbank, described to the Nuremberg tribunal how this method worked:

179

Dr Schacht, President of the Reichsbank, after considering various techniques of financing, proposed the the use of 'mefo' bills to provide a substantial portion of the funds needed for the rearmament programme. This method had as one of its primary advantages the fact that secrecy would be possible during the first years of the rearmament programme and figures indicating the extent of rearmament which would have become public through the use of other methods could be kept secret through the use of 'mefo' bills.

'Mefo' bills, abbreviation for 'mefo-wechsel', were drawn by the armament contractor and accepted by the *Metallurgische Forschungsgesellschaft G.m.b.H.*[19] These bills ran for six months with extensions running for three months each consecutively. The total life of these bills varied and in some instances exceeded four years. The Reichsbank could discount the original bill any time within its last three months. The co-endorser and drawer did not have to accept any liability. (This provision results from a guarantee of the bill by the Reich.)

The 'mefo' bills were used exclusively for financing rearmament, and when in March 1938 a new finance programme dicontinuing the use of 'mefo' bills was announced by Dr Schacht, there was a total volume outstanding of twelve billion marks of 'mefo' bills which had been issued to finance rearmament. One of the primary reasons for discontinuing financing rearmament with 'mefo' bills was that by the spring of 1938 it was no longer considered necessary to keep the progress of German rearmament secret. The rearmament boom had by then reached such proportions that it became possible by taxation and by the sale of Government securities to raise sums which could never have been raised when the rearmament programme acceleration began in 1935.[20] . . .

During 1934–36, the mefo bills accounted for 50 per cent of arms expenditure. Thereafter, as the economy recovered, it became possible to finance rearmament from Government loans and taxation and as the need for secrecy decreased, they declined in importance. During 1933–34, however, Germany's rearmament programme was threatened by two major problems: Germany's foreign debts, and the balance of payments. As for the

---

[19] This company was formed in May 1933 by four armament firms but existed on paper only and served as a front for the Reichsbank, which was legally prohibited from discounting Government bills.
[20] In fact the 'Mefo' bills were introduced in 1933.

former, Hitler's Government was in a better position than any of its predecessors in one sphere—reparations. Hitler reaped the fruits of Brüning's long negotiations with the Allies which had resulted in the cancellation of reparations at the Lausanne Conference in June 1932. Yet Germany still owed substantial debts on loans which had been raised to pay the reparations under the Dawes and Young Plans. In addition, a large number of commercial debts were outstanding. Puhl described Schacht's policy on German foreign debts:

180

After Hitler came to power and after Schacht returned to the presidency of the Reichsbank, the problem of Germany's long- and medium-term indebtedness was met by the declaration of a transfer moratorium. By law, starting 1 July 1933, German debtors were compelled to make payments in Reichsmarks (instead of the foreign currency in which the debt might have been incurred) on all interest and amortization payments of foreign debts incurred before the July 1931 crisis to the *Konversionskasse für Auslandsschulden* [Conversion fund for foreign debts] which was under the supervision of the Reichsbank. The law was not applicable to debts for which standstill agreements had been concluded, the Dawes loans, the Young loans, or other foreign loans for which special arrangements were made. It was left to the discretion of the Reichsbank to determine when, if ever, transfer into foreign currency should be made from the funds of the *Konversionskasse*. Immediate threats of retaliatory measures by foreign countries brought a partial payment of interest charges in foreign exchange and in 'scrip' which were sold at a substantial discount. However, after 1 July 1934, a complete transfer moratorium was put into effect and no more foreign exchange transfers for payment of interest and amortization took place, as funding bonds were offered the foreign creditor as payment.

This policy met with considerable opposition from the creditor countries. If they had taken a united stand on the issue, Germany would have been forced to divert foreign exchange from paying for raw material imports for the rearmament programme towards paying off her debts. Yet the decline in international economic cooperation resulting from the depression meant that Germany could exploit the self-interest of the various powers and make bilateral agreements with each one individually.

The second major problem facing the Government during 1933–34 was the balance of payments. During 1933, there was a favourable trade balance of 667 million RM, partly because of a decline in food imports as a result of Hugenberg's protectionist measures. But in 1934 the German balance of payments showed a deficit of 284 million RM.

This adverse balance of payments situation was essentially a result of two separate developments. The programmes of rearmament and work creation required large amounts of raw materials much of which had to be imported, and they also increased consumer demand with the same result. Secondly, whereas most countries had devalued their currency since 1931, Germany had insisted on retaining the old parity of the mark for fear of public reaction and in order not to increase the value of her foreign debts. German exports therefore tended to be too expensive compared with those of other countries. In any case, as a result of the economic crisis many countries introduced various protectionist measures.

By mid-June 1934, the gold and foreign exchange reserves in the Reichsbank had sunk to only 100 million RM and the Government was forced to take emergency action. Foreign exchange controls had in fact been introduced as early as August 1931, but only in the form of the allocation of a fixed quota of foreign exchange to importers, without any attempt by the Government or the Reichsbank to specify how it should be used. This measure, however, had clearly proved inadequate during the foreign exchange crisis of 1934. From 25 June onwards, therefore, the Reichsbank was forced to allocate foreign exchange on a day-to-day basis, giving out no more foreign exchange than it received. Although a list of priority categories was drawn up, only a few of these could in fact be satisfied. A number of vital raw materials could no longer be imported, and the work-creation programme and therefore also the rearmament programme were threatened.

This latter threat prompted the intervention of the armed forces. The Wehrmacht was discontented with the Minister of Economics, Dr Kurt Schmitt. They considered he was not firm enough and they disliked his economic policy. Schmitt wished to solve the unemployment problem by increasing the purchasing power of the masses through reducing the unemployment insurance contributions of the workers. This policy of increasing consumption would, however, lead to an increase in the demand for consumer goods and thus in imports, worsening the foreign exchange situation. Furthermore, an increase in consumption would mean a competition for scarce raw materials between the consumer goods industries and the armament programme. The armed forces received support in their opposition to Schmitt from industry, which resented his dislike of cartels.

The initiative was now taken by Colonel Georg Thomas, the head of the Defence Economy and Weapons (*Wehrwirtschaft und Waffenwesen*) Bureau in the Wehrmacht office. In a memorandum dated 20 June 1934 which reached Hitler's desk Thomas pressed the view of the armed forces that decisive action must be taken to solve the foreign exchange crisis:

181

The Reich Defence Ministry has for years been pointing out the necessity of preparing the economy for the event of war. It has demanded stockpiling, revealed the dangers of the loss of foreign exchange and the collapse of exports for the defence of the country and has especially requested the regulation of the peacetime economy in accordance with the needs of war. Only the present Reich Government has decided to fulfil these demands, but unfortunately economic developments threaten to nullify these efforts which have hardly begun.

The information from industry and the reports from the supervisory offices for raw materials show clearly that the raw materials situation is becoming daily more acute. Not only does this endanger the Government's work programme, but also the basis for an operational commitment of the Wehrmacht is becoming more and more remote and everywhere the question is being asked, What is the point of a larger army if it lacks supplies, its lifeblood? The raw materials situation is taken far more seriously by the business community than by the Reich Economics Ministry, and since everybody is clear about the fact that we are in the middle of an economic war, it is incomprehensible that decisions are not taken to overcome the danger which threatens. For months we have noticed the drain of foreign exchange followed by the melting away of stocks of raw materials, but so far there has been no firm intervention to remove the danger, with a few exceptions which have proved insufficient. What has happened to all the lessons we have learned from the Great War in the economic field? Because of struggles between capitalist interest groups, the wishes of Party offices, and the misguided interventions and opinions of individuals, no decisions are taken. . . .

The economic crisis, which is imminent because of the raw materials and foreign exchange situation, is recognised in all informed quarters; the will of the Führer to overcome it is irreversible. Why is the nation not urged to undergo self-denial and restrictions in order to overcome this economic crisis? The measures of individual leaders of the Labour Front run directly counter to these requirements. In this situation employees should not be lectured about the necessity for a higher standard of living, which leads everywhere to the desire for wage increases. The Labour Front imposes financial demands on employers, which small and medium-sized industry cannot endure in the long run and which are not intelligible so long as the Labour Front spends large amounts on buying luxurious houses and similar extravangances. Actions of this kind weaken the financial power of industry and what must be particularly avoided, weaken confidence in the leadership.

These impressions of economic life today keep reappearing and can now no longer be wished away with hopeful optimism. They are supported by the news about the harvest situation which may well give cause for further disquiet about the economy. It must be clear that in overcoming the crisis we have to fight for time, that the economy will not survive the coming struggle if this conflict between the various authorities and the present indecisiveness of the economic leadership continues.

The whole situation calls for a resolute and unified economic leadership which can direct the work of the Ministries of Economics, Agriculture, Labour, and Finance, the Reichsbank and all offices of the Labour Front by dictatorial methods. If one returns to question (b)[21] posed at the beginning, one must come to the unequivocal conclusion that, with regard to the situation of the German economy described

---

[21] This question, which appeared earlier in the memorandum, ran as follows: 'What effect does the current economic situation have on the maintenance of the Army in the event of war and how will this influence the expected increase in German defensive strength through the accelerated reconstruction of the Army?'

above, the economic crisis represents a serious threat to the defence of the country and that in these circumstances the economy is not in a position to meet the supply requirements of the Wehrmacht in its enlarged form.

As the Ministry responsible for the security of the Reich, the Reich Defence Ministry must now demand sweeping measures. . . .

I wish to make the following proposals to deal with this situation:

1. The Führer should assume economic leadership. A permanent official should be appointed as his subordinate with the title of Economics Deputy of the Führer, together with an adviser on industry, agriculture, commerce and banking respectively, and also one liaison officer from the Reich Defence Ministry.

The Economics Deputy must be an exceptionally able man, enjoying the confidence of the widest and most authoritative circle and possessing the utmost resources of energy and authority. He must have the power to issue decrees of decisive importance and have the means to carry them through ruthlessly in the face of all authorities and Party offices.

The Reich Ministries of Economics, Agriculture, Labour and Finance, the Reichsbank, the leaders of industry and the Labour Front shall be subordinate to him.

2. All Party and other offices should be prohibited from carrying out any economic measures which do not come from the Economics Deputy and have not been approved by him.

3. The branches of the economy which are important for war and are still unattached should be integrated in a planned economy.

For this purpose the following are necessary:

The creation of trade monopoly offices for all raw materials which are important for war.

The detailed regulation of the import, export and supplies of all materials pertaining to war.

An immediate start with this process of mobilization [*Erschliessung*] and a clear lead from the Government in building up the country's sources of raw materials.

The establishment of a central office for all foreign trade.

4. The nation should be thoroughly informed about the serious state of the economy, and determined measures should be taken to train the people in thrift and moderation.

5. Measures should be taken to overcome this year's bad harvest.

Thomas almost certainly envisaged Schacht for this position of 'economic dictator'. On 28 June, Schmitt fell ill and went on leave and, on 2 August, Schacht was designated acting Minister of Economics. In the meantime, on 3 July, a law was passed giving the Minister of Economics dictatorial powers.

At first sight, it seems surprising that Hitler should have agreed to such a concentration of economic power (Reichsbank and Ministry of Economics) in the hands of a non-Party man. It is probable that the economic crisis, which coincided with the SA crisis,[22] gave him very little choice. The

---

[22] See above, pp. 167ff.

purge of the SA represented a necessary concession to the Army and the business community and the same is almost certainly true of the appointment of Schacht. Schacht was the one man who commanded sufficient respect both at home and abroad and sufficient financial ability to master an economic crisis which threatened the major objectives of the regime. Certainly the concession was a real one. For the next two years Schacht's position was extremely strong and he was largely successful in resisting attempts by the Party organizations to interfere with the business community. And yet, although from one point of view the appointment of Schacht was a concession by Hitler, Schacht in fact, by solving the economic crisis and by evolving economic techniques to ensure the progress of the rearmament programme, made a considerable contribution to the regime.

(ii) The 'New Plan'

In September 1934, in order to deal with the foreign exchange crisis, Schacht introduced a number of new policies. Apart from imposing an absolute moratorium on Germany's foreign debts in order to check the outflow of foreign exchange in the form of interest payments, he also introduced a so-called 'New Plan,' which represented a radical extension of a trade policy already begun before 1933. An explanation of the substance of the plan was sent to all German embassies by Dr Karl Ritter, the extremely influential Director of the Economics Department in the Foreign Office:

182

2. . . . In future, all German imports will be regulated and they will be controlled by Supervisory Offices. Within the framework of a general allocation system the Supervisory Offices will issue foreign currency permits to importers before transactions are concluded if, judging by the amount of foreign exchange received, it could be assumed that the foreign currency would be available on the due date. These foreign currency permits ensure priority for foreign exchange allotments. Thus, provided that the foreign exchange received comes up to our expectations, foreign exporters will be given a substantial assurance that their claims will be met on the date. Where transactions are concluded without a prior foreign currency permit, however, the importer cannot count on being considered for an allocation of foreign exchange in the near future.

3. It is assumed under the New Plan that, in view of the decline in German exports and the consequent decline in foreign exchange receipts, the issue of foreign currency permits will be to a large degree restricted to vital foodstuffs as well as to raw materials and semi-manufactured goods. Even here considerable restrictions will have to be imposed. Outside the foreign exchange plan the system of barter transactions will be expanded. As regards essential commodities, barter transactions

will be sanctioned provided that they do not require foreign exchange. In the case of non-essential commodities, an effort must be made to obtain foreign exchange through barter transactions too, for example by exporting more goods from Germany than are imported.

4. Treaty arrangements will not be infringed. The import of goods in itself can continue in the same way as hitherto, but the German importer who concludes transactions and imports goods without previously receiving a foreign currency permit will be aware from the outset that he cannot count on an allocation of foreign exchange. Consequently, in future the foreign exporter will also be able to satisfy himself as to whether the German buyer and importer will be supplied with foreign exchange and whether, therefore, he himself can expect payment. Thus any complaints about allotment of foreign exchange and non-payment will in future be deprived of justification.

Where exchange agreements or clearing arrangements are in force, they will not be affected by the New Plan for the time being, but they must, if necessary, be adjusted to the new situation by negotiation in the sense that the clearing will remain limited to certain goods and quantities. Payments agreements containing the so-called Swedish clause[23] will be applicable only to such goods as are not subject to special management. As, however, all German importers will be subject to management, the payments agreements will, although without any formal infringement of the law, become unworkable in practice. What the effects will be of this undermining process [Aushöhlung] in respect of the various countries concerned remains to be examined. . . .

The principle of this New Plan—the regulation of imports through Government supervision of the allocation of foreign exchange—was not new. The New Plan, however, represented a far more comprehensive and detailed application of these principles of exchange control and import regulation than had previously existed. Whereas previously foreign exchange was allocated *after* the imports had arrived, the New Plan required importers to obtain foreign exchange clearance *before* importing goods. Special supervisory offices, established for each group of commodities, issued permits, which importers were obliged to secure for each individual transaction. This enabled the Government to plan ahead for imports and to allocate foreign exchange according to its own priorities rather than those of the individual importers. The Government could determine not only *what* goods and raw materials should be imported, but also *where* they should come from. This in turn facilitated the trend towards bilateralism already apparent in German trade.

The introduction of exchange controls in 1931 by several major countries, including Germany, dealt a severe blow to multilateral trade and to the 'most favoured nation' principle. As the various note-issuing banks became

---

[23] This referred to Clause 10 of the standstill agreement of 1931 which had been renewed in February 1933. It dealt with the payment of certain German debts in marks which were paid into special accounts in Germany and could only be used for authorized purposes such as tourism.

unwilling to provide foreign exchange for the payment of imports, there was an inevitable trend towards quotas and barter and clearing agreements by which in effect two countries exchanged goods with one another without recourse to the reserve currencies or even in many cases to their own. This bilateral trade, regulated by agreements between the two Governments gave them the power to regulate trade in accordance with political objectives, discriminating between one country and another on diplomatic or strategic grounds.

This tendency had already begun to dominate German trade policy during 1933–34. Germany's main foreign trade problem was that while her imports of raw materials tended to come from overseas, her exports went mainly to Europe. This worsened during the economic crisis because the countries exporting raw materials tended to be colonies or dominions which now entered preference systems with their mother countries (e.g. the Ottawa Agreement). Germany's exports were still at a disadvantage because of her unwillingness to devalue the mark. It became the main aim of German foreign trade policy to reorientate German trade to Europe and to those parts of the world not subject to colonial preference agreements, in particular South America. Apart from the economic aspect, however, political considerations played a part in this. The economic policy of the German Right in general and the Nazis in particular, had always aimed to make Germany as self-sufficient as possible—for strategic reasons. The lesson of the Allied blockade during the First World War had been learnt. By acquiring sources of raw materials in south-east Europe rather than overseas, Germany would be economically far more independent in the event of war, for it was assumed that German economic penetration would have turned south-east Europe from a French into a German sphere of influence.

This trend in German foreign trade policy was described by the German Foreign Office in an explanatory circular to its embassies in June 1934:

183

... V. The concept of barter in German commercial policy
German import requirements, particularly in respect of raw materials and consumer goods, are, in spite of the decline in purchasing power, still an important factor in a highly industrialized country with a population of about 65 million. This factor will in future be made use of even more than was possible under the unrestricted application of the 'most favoured nation' treatment, for the purpose of making producers and suppliers of these raw materials and consumer goods aware of the necessity of accepting increased imports of German industrial products in return.

VI. Possibilities of reorientating German imports
Closely bound up with the objectives of the barter system is the question of how far it is possible to transfer German imports of raw materials and consumer goods to

the countries which take German manufactures in larger quantities than do those countries which have previously been supplying us.

It is a general aim of German commercial policy to transfer the purchase of raw materials and consumer goods from Africa and from the British overseas territories (Ottawa policy) to countries which offer greater future possibilities to German exports, as for instance South America and the Dutch Indies.

VII. New trade treaties concluded by Germany in the course of the past year
The principles of German commercial policy as expounded above have been set down in various forms in fresh treaties concluded by the Reich Government during the course of the last eighteen months.

Particularly noteworthy in this connexion are two further treaties of a special kind which have been concluded in the course of this year and which have political significance above their actual commercial content, namely the treaties with Hungary and Yugoslavia. These treaties are designed to create in Hungary and in Yugoslavia two points of support for German policy in the Danubian region, in order above all to counteract French and Italian policy directed against German policy in the Danubian region. In view of the special purposes which these two treaties serve, a system of secret financial privileges has been embodied therein whereby both countries, without being granted open preferences, are in fact by means of subventions obtaining preferential treatment of their exports to Germany in comparison with their competitors. The Reich Government have in this case consciously made certain financial sacrifices in the interests of German foreign policy in south-east Europe. Nevertheless it was clearly established, when these decisions were taken, that such procedure was only justified by the special reasons in favour of the conclusion of both treaties, and that to apply these methods to commercial policy in general could not be considered, if only on account of the heavy calls on Reich finance which would result therefrom.

In fact, for a time after 1933, Germany carried out a policy of economic exploitation in the Balkans by using her position as a massive buyer of foodstuffs and raw materials. The Balkan countries, unable to find export markets for their produce, particularly since their price level was high by world standards, found only Germany prepared to buy these expensive commodities. Schacht developed a technique whereby Germany built up a large trade deficit with these countries. The imports were paid for by special mark accounts which remained frozen in Germany until they were periodically released by special agreement. These countries were then obliged to use the mark accounts either to buy German goods or to invest in their countries in plant which would produce goods which Germany required. The German Government fixed the exchange rate at a relatively high level so that these German exports were expensive and thereby balanced out the expensive imports. By this method Germany was able to acquire imports of raw materials on credit, to subsidize her exports, and to acquire economic influence over the Balkan countries. After a time, however, these countries began to resist this type of pressure and to demand payment for their goods in foreign exchange and in cash. It was only after the German take-over of Austria and Czechoslovakia in 1938–39 that Germany acquired a dominant economic position in south-east Europe.

To sum up, the regime exploited the general trend towards Government regulation of the economy, which was accelerated by the world economic crisis, for its political and military objectives. By subjecting her foreign trade to strict Government control through highly specific foreign exchange regulations and bilateral trade agreements, Germany was able to subordinate foreign trade to her political goals of rearmament and of the economic penetration of south-east Europe for strategic and diplomatic purposes. Germany's rearmament programme and her aim of maximum economic self-sufficiency benefited enormously from the breakdown of the world monetary system and multilateral trade, just as her foreign policy was facilitated by the collapse of international cooperation. On the other hand, Schacht's New Plan was not the only possible response to the economic situation. In July 1934, the Mayor of Hamburg, Karl Krogmann, put forward an alternative scheme which envisaged a liberalizing of foreign trade, emphasized the need to encourage exports, and advocated the replacement of strict import controls by a more flexible system. This plan had the backing of influential figures in the worlds of finance and commerce. Nevertheless it was rejected because, unlike Schacht's New Plan, it did not ensure priority for raw materials essential for the rearmament programme. Although Schacht later came to deplore the trend towards autarky, in effect the trade policies he initiated in 1934 prepared the ground for the implementation of the programme of *Grossraumwirtschaft* adopted by the Nazi movement before 1933 as a crucial element in the establishment of a 'defence economy'.

CHAPTER 13

The Four-Year Plan, 1936–39

(i) The Crisis of 1935–36

Schacht's New Plan solved the balance of payments crisis of 1934 and in the following year there was a trade surplus. But during the second half of 1935 an adverse trend developed, and early in 1936 fears grew of an even worse balance of payments crisis than that of 1934. The New Plan had been unable to alter fundamentally the basic factors governing Germany's balance of payments position. Since 1933 the 'terms of trade' had moved against Germany. Between 1933 and 1936 export prices declined by 9 per cent on average while import prices rose by 9 per cent. In 1936 Germany had to export 18 per cent more to be able to import the same amount as in 1933. Schacht had in fact introduced measures to try to encourage exports. He forced creditor countries to take as payment of German debts special marks which could be used only for buying German goods or for travel in Germany. He also introduced a levy on firms which was used to subsidize exports. Yet these measures could only mitigate the second basic problem, which was the enormous increase in Germany's demand for imports owing to the work-creation and rearmament programmes. Moreover, the revival of the economy at home meant that firms found it far more attractive to sell on the home market than to try to export in the face of protectionist measures abroad which had contributed to a sharp decline in world trade.

The third basic problem was the conflict between 'guns and butter'. There was a direct relationship between rearmament and the standard of living of ordinary people, as Schacht pointed out in a speech on 29 November 1938:

184

... Reduced to a simple formula, the problem is as follows: The credit money made available for armament purposes produces a demand for consumers' goods through the payment of wages and salaries. The armament manufacturers, however, deliver military goods which are produced but not put on the market. From this follow two consequences: first, care must be taken that aside from armament manufacture sufficient consumer goods are produced to sustain the population including all those working for the armament industry; second, the less there is consumed, the more labour can be used for armaments; but the higher consumption rises, the more manpower must be left for the production of consumer goods. Therefore, the standard of living and the extent of armament production are in an inverse ratio....

This relationship became critical in 1935, when a conflict of priorities developed between raw material imports required for rearmament and the import of foodstuffs. Germany's foreign exchange reserves could not cover unlimited quantities of both. Since 1933, German agricultural production had failed to keep pace with the rising demand which followed increasing employment. This was partly because the Reich Food Estate had discouraged expansion in order to maintain high prices. The most serious shortage was of fats and meat. The regime—and here the Party authorities were particularly adamant—felt that it could not afford to damage its prestige by introducing rationing. During 1935, Darré, the head of the Reich Food Estate, demanded from Schacht large allocations of foreign exchange for the purpose of importing butter, vegetable oil and fodder. Schacht was opposed to this because, with the shortage of foreign exchange, such a grant would compel a reduction in the import of industrial raw materials and therefore would damage the rearmament programme. Hitler, characteristically, was loath to make a decision between the two and appointed Göring to arbitrate in the dispute. Göring, fearful of discontent over high food prices and of the reaction to the introduction of rationing, which seemed the only alternative, came down in favour of Darré. Clearly, however, the import of agricultural products could not permanently take precedence over industrial raw materials without undermining the rearmament programme. Indeed, in December 1935 Schacht informed the Defence Minister, Blomberg, that he was unable to provide the necessary foreign exchange to pay for the doubling of copper and lead imports requested by the armed forces, and that raw material supplies for rearmament could not be guaranteed even at the existing level. The problem was pressing.

One solution would have been to increase exports to provide the foreign exchange to pay for raw materials. This was urged by Schacht, although he appreciated that, considering the international trade situation, it could only be a medium- to long-term solution. Moreover, this solution contradicted the principles of his New Plan. Germany could hardly carry out a policy of ruthless import controls and bilateralism and at the same time expect other countries to welcome her exports. Above all, an expansion of exports would mean a reduction in the rearmament programme which the regime was not prepared to tolerate.

The alternative was to try to cut down on imports and meet the demand for raw materials as far as possible by expanding home production. Such a policy of maximum economic self-sufficiency fitted well with the ideas of autarky in the Nazi agricultural programme of 1930 and which were current among influential circles outside as well as inside the Party. An attempt to expand agricultural production was, indeed, already in progress. The so-called 'Production Battle' began in the autumn of 1934. But agriculture was increasingly compelled to compete with industry for manpower, and industry could afford to pay higher wages.[24] One remedy would have been the growing mechanization of agriculture, but this required extensive capital investment by individual farmers, and severe restrictions had been placed on loans and mortgages by the Reich Entailed Farm Law. In any case, it was difficult to expand production of agricultural machinery in view of the priority given to rearmament. As a result, the achievements of the 'Production Battle' were comparatively small. By 1938–39 Germany was still importing 17 per cent of her agricultural needs (compared with 20 per cent in 1934) and in particular was dependent on imports for 45 per cent of her fats and 30 per cent of her fodder.

As crucial as the need to expand agricultural production was the need to provide industrial raw materials, above all, oil, rubber, and metals The economic revival under the New Plan had depended largely on the consumption of Germany's raw material reserves and they had now been used up. By 1936 Germany was having to buy the bulk of her requirements on the world market and in cash. The Romanians, for example, were insisting on payment in cash for their oil. A solution to this problem was now offered by the giant chemicals firm of IG-Farben. During the 1920s they had developed techniques for the synthetic manufacture of oil and rubber. Because these processes were expensive, the firm had been unsuccessful in its attempts to persuade previous German Governments to underwrite their development. In the winter of 1933, however, a director of IG-Farben, Carl Krauch, persuaded the new regime to sign the so-called Feder-Bosch Agreement, which guaranteed, for a period of ten years, a price and a market for oil produced by the hydrogenation process. From then onwards IG-Farben lobbied intensively for further Government support for the programme. Given the chronic crisis in foreign exchange and raw materials, it gained influential converts, of whom the most important was Göring, Chief of the Air Force. Fuel was of vital importance to the new Luftwaffe and

---

[24] For details on agriculture and labour see below pp. 316ff. and pp. 327ff.

Göring was determined to secure supplies at any cost. He evidently convinced Hitler of the need for more action in the sphere of raw material production and on 4 April 1936 was appointed by Hitler Commissioner of Raw Materials with authority to give orders to the departmental ministers on matters of foreign exchange and raw materials.
During the summer, however, the crisis intensified. Munition factories were only producing 70 per cent of their capacity because of the shortage of raw materials stemming from the lack of foreign exchange. Hitler became convinced that if the momentum of the rearmament programme was to be sustained a reorientation of the economy in the interests of maximum self-sufficiency in raw materials was necessary. This would subordinate it even more directly to the needs of rearmament than had Schacht's New Plan.
The trend towards autarky, however, did not go unchallenged. Schacht had resented Hitler's appointment in 1934 of Keppler to head a special office for raw materials with the aim of replacing foreign with German ones as far as possible. Although Hitler had not given Keppler much support, Schacht was aware that the recent appointment of Göring represented a far greater danger to his position. It was not simply a question of power but of policy. Although Schacht had accepted the Feder-Bosch Agreement, he was suspicious of the production of synthetic raw materials. He believed they were uneconomic and that is was far cheaper to import the raw material itself. In an attempt to win the support of the Defence Minister, he argued. 'If we now proclaim to the world yet again our determination to achieve economic independence, we will be cutting our own throats because we can no longer last out the necessary transition period. In addition, it must be continually emphasized that German raw materials are at the moment much too expensive to be used in goods intended for export, and only exports can make possible further rearmament.' To this appeal Blomberg replied, characteristically: 'Herr Schacht, I realize you are absolutely right but I am convinced that the Führer will find a way out of all these difficulties.' Schacht's doubts were shared by the influential Reich Price Commissioner, Carl Goerdeler, later a leader of the opposition to Hitler, who urged a large cut in raw material imports and a return to freer trade. In 1936, however, this was tantamount to advocating a return to mass unemployment and was therefore ruled completely out of court.

(ii) The Launching of the Four-Year Plan

In their opposition to a policy of autarky, Schacht and Goerdeler had the support of commerce and the more export-minded sections of industry, particularly coal, iron and steel. It was in the light of this opposition that, some time during August, Hitler composed the following memorandum, one of the basic documents of the Third Reich:

185

This memorandum was given to me personally by A.H. in 1944 with the following statement:
  The lack of understanding of the Reich Ministry for Economics and the opposition of German business to all large-scale plans induced him to compose this memorandum at Obersalzberg.
  He decided at that time to carry out a Four-Year Plan and to put Göring in charge of it. On the occasion of Göring's appointment as the official in charge of the Four-Year Plan he gave him this memorandum. There are only three copies, one of which he gave to me....

[signed] ALBERT SPEER

The political situation

Politics are the conduct and the course of the historical struggle of nations for life. The aim of these struggles is survival. Even ideological struggles have their ultimate cause and are most deeply motivated by nationally determined purposes and aims of life. But religions and ideologies are always able to impart particular bitterness to such struggles, and therefore also to give them great historical impressiveness. They leave their imprint on centuries of history. Nations and States living within the sphere of such ideological or religious conflicts cannot opt out of or dissociate themselves from these events. Christianity and the barbarian invasions determined the course of history for centuries. Mohammedanism convulsed the Orient as well as the Western world for half a millennium. The consequences of the Reformation have affected the whole of central Europe. Nor were individual countries—either by skill or by deliberate non-participation—able to steer clear of events. Since the outbreak of the French Revolution the world has been moving with ever-increasing speed towards a new conflict, the most extreme solution of which is Bolshevism; and the essence and goal of Bolshevism is the elimination of those strata of mankind which have hitherto provided the leadership and their replacement by world-wide Jewry.
  No nation will be able to avoid or abstain from this historical conflict. *Since Marxism, through its victory in Russia, has established one of the greatest empires as a forward base for its future operations, this question has become a menacing one. Against a democratic world which is ideologically split stands a unified aggressive will, based on an authoritarian ideology.*
  The military resources of this aggressive will are in the meantime rapidly increasing from year to year. One has only to compare the Red Army as it actually exists today with the assumptions of military men of ten or fifteen years ago to realize the menacing extent of this development. Only consider the results of a further development over ten, fifteen or twenty years and think what conditions will be like then.

Germany

Germany will as always have to be regarded as the focus of the Western world against the attacks of Bolshevism. I do not regard this as an agreeable mission but as a serious handicap and burden for our national life, regrettably resulting from our disadvantageous position in Europe. We cannot, however, escape this destiny. Our political position results from the following:

At the moment there are only two countries in Europe which can be regarded as standing firm against Bolshevism—Germany and Italy. The other nations are either corrupted by their democratic way of life, infected by Marxism and therefore likely to collapse in the foreseeable future, or ruled by authoritarian Governments, whose sole strength lies in their military resources; this means, however, that being obliged to protect their leadership against their own peoples by the armed hand of the Executive, they are unable to use this armed hand for the protection of their countries against external enemies. None of these countries would ever be capable of waging war against Soviet Russia with any prospects of success. In fact, apart from Germany and Italy, only Japan can be considered as a Power standing firm in the face of the world peril.

It is not the aim of this memorandum to prophesy the moment when the untenable situation in Europe will reach the stage of an open crisis. I only want, in these lines, to express my conviction that this crisis cannot and will not fail to occur, and that Germany has the duty of securing her existence by every means in the face of this catastrophe, and to protect herself against it, and that this obligation has a number of implications involving the most important tasks that our people have ever been set. *For a victory of Bolshevism over Germany would lead not to a Versailles Treaty but to the final destruction, indeed to the annihilation, of the German people.*

The extent of such a catastrophe cannot be estimated. How, indeed, would the whole of densely populated Western Europe (including Germany) after a collapse into Bolshevism, live through probably the most gruesome catastrophe which has been visited on mankind since the downfall of the states of antiquity. *In face of the necessity of warding off this danger, all other considerations must recede into the background as completely irrelevant.*

Germany's defensive capacity

Germany's defensive capacity is based upon several factors. I would give pride of place to the intrinsic value of the German people *per se*. The German nation with an impeccable political leadership, a firm ideology, a thorough military organization, certainly constitutes the most valuable factor of resistance in the world today. Political leadership is ensured by the National Socialist Party; ideological solidarity has, since the victory of National Socialism, been introduced to a degree that has never previously been attained. It must be constantly deepened and strengthened on the basis of this concept. This is the aim of the National Socialist education of our people.

The development of our military capacity is to be effected through the new Army. *The extent of the military development of our resources cannot be too large, nor its pace too swift.* It is a major error to believe that there can be any argument on these points or any comparison with other vital necessities. However well-balanced the general pattern of a nation's life ought to be there must at particular times be certain disturbances of the balance at the expense of other less vital tasks. *If we do not succeed in bringing the German Army as rapidly as possible to the rank of premier army in the world so far as its training, raising of units, armaments, and, above all, its spiritual education also is concerned, then Germany will be lost!* In this the basic principle applies that omissions during the months of peace cannot be made good in centuries. Hence all other desires without exception must come second to this task. For this task involves life and the preservation of life, and all other desires—however understandable at other junctures—are unimportant or even mortally dangerous and are therefore to be rejected. Posterity will ask us one day, not what were the means, the reasons or the convictions by which we thought fit today to achieve the salvation of the nation, but *whether* in fact we achieved it. And on that day it will be no excuse for our downfall for us to describe the means which were infallible, but, alas, brought about our ruin.

Germany's economic situation

Just as the political movement among our people knows only one goal, the preservation of our existence, that is to say, the securing of all the spiritual and other prerequisites for the self-assertion of our nation, so neither has the economy any other goal than this. The nation does not live for the economy, for economic leaders, or for economic or financial theories; on the contrary, it is finance and the economy, economic leaders and theories, which all owe unqualified service in this struggle for the self-assertion of our nation. Germany's economic situation is, however, in the briefest outline as follows:
1. We are overpopulated and cannot feed ourselves from our own resources.
2. When our nation has six or seven million unemployed, the food situation improves because these people lack purchasing power. It naturally makes a difference whether six million people have 40 marks a month to spend, or 100 marks. It should not be overlooked that a third of all who earn their living is involved, that is to say that, taken as a proportion of the total population, through the National Socialist economic policy about 28 million people have been afforded an increase in their standard of living of, an average, from at least 50 marks a month to at most 100–120 marks. This means an increased and understandable run on the foodstuffs market.
3. But if this rise in employment fails to take place, the effect of undernourishment will be that a higher percentage of the population must gradually be deducted from the body of our nation, so far as its effective contribution is concerned. Thus, despite the difficult food situation, the most important task of our economic policy is to see to it that all Germans are incorporated into the economic process, and so the prerequisites for normal consumption are created.
4. In so far as this consumption concerns articles of general use, it can be satisfied to a *large* extent by an increase in production. In so far as this consumption falls upon the foodstuffs market, it cannot be satisfied from the domestic German economy. For, although the output of numerous products can be increased without difficulty, the yield of our agricultural production can undergo no further substantial increase. It is equally impossible for us at present to manufacture artificially certain raw materials which we lack in Germany or to find other substitutes for them.
5. There is, however, no point in endless repetition of the fact that we lack foodstuffs and raw materials; what matters is the taking of those measures which can bring about a *final* solution for the *future* and a *temporary* easing of conditions during the *transition* period.

6. The final solution lies in extending our living space, that is to say, extending the sources of raw materials and foodstuffs of our people. It is the task of the political leadership one day to solve this problem.

7. The temporary easing of conditions can be achieved only within the framework of our present economy. In this connexion, the following must be noted:

(a) Since the German people will be increasingly dependent on imports for their food and must similarly, whatever happens, import a proportion at least of certain raw materials from abroad, every effort must be made to facilitate these imports.

(b) An increase in our own exports is possible in theory but in practice hardly likely. Germany does not export to a political or economic vacuum, but to areas where competition is very intense. Compared with the general international economic depression, our exports have fallen, not only *not more*, but in fact *less* than those of other nations and states. But since imports of food on the whole cannot be substantially reduced and are more likely to increase, an adjustment must be found in some other way.

(c) It is, however, impossible to use foreign exchange allocated for the purchase of raw materials to import foodstuffs without inflicting a heavy and perhaps even fatal blow on the rest. *But above all it is absolutely impossible to do this at the expense of national rearmament.* I must at this point sharply reject the view that by restricting national rearmament, that is to day, the manufacture of arms and ammunition, we could bring about an 'enrichment' in raw materials which might then benefit Germany in the event of war. Such a view is based on a complete misconception, to put it mildly, of the tasks and military requirements that lie before us. For even a successful saving of raw materials by reducing, for instance, the production of munitions would merely mean that we should stockpile these raw materials in time of peace so as to manufacture them only in the event of war, that is to say, we should be depriving ourselves during the most critical months of munitions in exchange for raw copper, lead, or possibly iron. But in that case it would none the less be better for the nation to enter the war without a single kilogram of copper in stock but with full munition depots rather than with empty munition depots but so-called 'enriched' stock of raw material.

War makes possible the mobilization of even the last remaining supplies of metal. For it then becomes not an *economic problem*, but solely a *question of will*. And the National Socialist leadership of the country will have not only the will but also the resolution and the toughness necessary to solve these problems in the event of war. But it is much more important to prepare for war in time of peace. Moreover, in this respect the following must be stated:

There can be no building up of a reserve of *raw materials* for the event of war, just as there can be no building up of foreign exchange reserves. The attempt is sometimes made today so to represent matters as if Germany went to war in 1914 with well-prepared stocks of raw material. That is a lie. No country can assemble in advance the quantities of raw materials necessary for war lasting longer than, say, one year. But if any nation were really in a position to assemble those quantities of raw material needed for a year, then its political, military and economic leaders would deserve to be hanged. For they would in fact be setting aside the available copper and iron in preparation for the conduct of a war instead of manufacturing shells. But Germany went into the world war without any reserves whatsoever. What was available at that time in Germany in the way of apparent peacetime reserves was counterbalanced and rendered valueless by the miserable war stocks of ammunition. *Moreover, the quantities of war materials that are needed for a war are so large that there has* NEVER *in the history of the world been a real stockpiling for a period of any length!* and as regards preparations in the form of piling up foreign exchange it is quite clear that:

1. War is capable of devaluing foreign exchange at any time, unless it is held in gold.
2. There is not the least guarantee that gold itself can be converted in time of war into raw materials. During the world war Germany still possessed very large assets in foreign exchange in a great many countries. It was not, however, possible for our cunning economic policy-makers to bring to Germany, in exchange for them fuel rubber, copper or tin in any sufficient quantity. To assert the contrary is ridiculous nonsense. For this reason, and in order to secure the food supplies of our people, the following task presents itself as imperative:

It is not sufficient merely to establish from time to time raw material or foreign exchange balances, or to talk about the preparation of a war economy in time of peace; on the contrary, it is essential to ensure all the food supplies required in peacetime and, above all, those means for the conduct of a war which can be secured by human energy and activity. I therefore draw up the following programme for a final provision of our vital needs:

I. Parallel with the military and political rearmament and mobilization of our nation must go its economic rearmament and mobilization, and this must be effected in the same tempo, with the same determination, and if need be with the same ruthlessness as well. In future the interests of individual gentlemen can no longer play any part in these matters. There is only one interest, the interest of the nation; only one view, the bringing of Germany to the point of political and economic self-sufficiency.

II. For this purpose, foreign exchange must be saved in all those areas where our needs can be satisfied by German production, in order that it may be used for those requirements which can under no circumstances be fulfilled except by import:

III. Accordingly, German fuel production must now be stepped up with the utmost speed and brought to final completion within eighteen months. This task must be attacked and carried out with the same determination as the waging of a war, since it is on the discharge of this task, not upon the laying in of stocks of petroleum, that the conduct of the future war depends.

IV. The mass production of synthetic rubber must also be organized and achieved with the same urgency. From now on there must be no talk of processes not being fully determined and other such excuses. It is not a matter of discussing whether we are to wait any longer; otherwise time will be lost, and the hour of peril will take us all by surprise. Above all, it is not the job of the economic institutions of Government to rack their brains over methods of production. This has nothing whatever to do with the Ministry of Economics. Either we possess today a private industry, in which case its job is to rack its brains about methods of production; or we believe that it is the Government's job to determine methods of production, and in that case we have no further need of private industry.

V. The question of the cost of producing these raw materials is also quite irrelevant, since it is in any case better for us to produce expensive tyres in Germany which we can use, than to sell theoretically cheap tyres, but tyres for which the Minister of Economics cannot allocate any foreign exchange, and which therefore cannot be produced for lack of raw materials and consequently cannot be used at all. If we really are obliged to build up our domestic economy on autarkic lines, which we are—for lamenting and harping on our foreign exchange plight will certainly not solve the problem—then the price of raw materials individually considered no longer plays a decisive part.

It is further necessary to increase German iron production to the utmost limits. The objection that with German ore, which has a 26 per cent ferrous content, we cannot produce pig iron as cheaply as with the 45 per cent Swedish ores, etc., is irrelevant; we are not faced with the question of what would *rather* do, but what we *can* do. The objection, moreover, that in that event all the German blast-furnaces would have to be converted is equally irrelevant, and, what is more, this is no concern of the Ministry of Economics. The job of the Ministry of Economics is simply to set the national economic tasks; private industry has to fulfil them. But if private industry thinks itself incapable of doing this, then the National Socialist State will know how to resolve the problem on its own. In any case, for a thousand years Germany had no foreign iron ores. Even before the war, more German iron ores were being processed than during the period of our worst decline. *Nevertheless, if there is still the possibility of our importing cheaper ores, well and good. But the future of the national economy and, above all, of the conduct of war, must not depend on this.*

Moreover, the distillation of potatoes into alcohol must be prohibited forthwith. Fuel must be obtained from the ground, not from potatoes. Instead it is our duty to use any arable land that may become available either for human or animal foodstuffs or for the cultivation of fibrous materials.

It is further necessary for us to make our supplies of *industrial* fats independent of imports as quickly as possible. This can be done by using our coal. This problem has been solved by chemical means and the technique is actually crying out to be put into practice. Either German industry will grasp the new economic tasks or else it will show itself incapable of surviving any longer in this modern age in which a Soviet State is setting up a gigantic plan. *But in that case it will not be Germany that will go under, but at most a few industrialists.* Moreover, the extraction of other ores must be increased, *regardless of cost,* and, in particular, the production of light metals must be increased to the utmost limits, in order to produce a substitute for certain other metals.

Finally, it is also necessary for the rearmament programme to make use even now whenever possible of those materials which must and will replace high-grade metals in time of war. *It is better to consider and resolve these problems in time of peace than to wait for the next war and only then, in the midst of a multitude of tasks, to try to undertake these economic researches and experiments with methods.*

In short, I consider it necessary that now, with iron determination, a 100 per cent self-sufficiency should be attained in every sphere where it is feasible, and that not only should the national requirements in these most essential raw materials be made independent of other countries, but we should also thus save the foreign exchange which in peacetime we need for our imports of foodstuffs. *In this connexion, I want to emphasize that in these tasks I see the only true economic mobilization and not in the throttling of armament industries in peacetime in order to save and stockpile raw materials for war.*

But I further consider it necessary to make an immediate investigation of the outstanding debts in foreign exchange owed to German business abroad. There is no doubt that the outstanding claims of German business abroad are quite enormous. Nor is there any doubt that behind this in some cases there lies concealed the contemptible desire to possess, whatever happens, certain reserves abroad which are thus withheld from the grasp of the domestic economy. I regard this as deliberate sabotage of our national self-assertion, that is to say, of the defence of the Reich, and I therefore consider it necessary for the Reichstag to pass the following two laws:

1. A law providing the death penalty for economic sabotage, and
2. A law making the whole of Jewry liable for all damage inflicted by individual specimens of this community of criminals upon the German economy, and thus upon the German people.

Only the fulfilment of these tasks, in the form of a Several Years Plan for rendering our national economy independent of foreign countries, will make it possible for the first time to demand sacrifices from the German people in the economic sphere and in that of foodstuffs. For then the nation will have a right to demand of their leaders whom they blindly acknowledge, that they should not only talk about the problems in this field but tackle them with unparalleled and determined energy, not only point them out but solve them.

Nearly four precious years have now gone by. There is no doubt that by now we could have been completely independent of foreign countries in the spheres of fuel supplies, rubber supplies, and partly also iron ore supplies. Just as we are now producing 700,000 or 800,000 tons of petroleum, we could be producing 3 million tons. Just as we are today manufacturing a few thousand tons of rubber, we could already be producing 70,000 or 80,000 tons per annum. Just as we have stepped up the production of iron ore from $2\frac{1}{2}$ million tons to 7 million tons, we could process 20 or 25 million tons of German iron ore and even 30 millions if necessary. There has been time enough in four years to find out what we cannot do. Now we have to carry out what we can do.

I thus set the following tasks;

I. The German armed forces must be operational within four years.
II. The German economy must be fit for war within four years.

On 4 September, Göring read out Hitler's memorandum to the Cabinet and emphasized its implications for the economy;

186

Min.-Pres. Göring: Today's meeting is of greater importance than all previous meetings.

At the last Cabinet meeting of 11 August 1936 it was agreed that supplementary material was needed in order to make it possible to reach a decision.

Meanwhile new trouble has arisen, especially in connexion with non-precious metals and rubber; even the Führer has been drawn into this affair....

... Certain persons have been asked for memoranda on the basic conduct of the economy. So far only one has been presented, by Dr Goerdeler, and it is absolutely useless. In addition to many other erroneous ideas it contains the proposal for a considerable limitation of armaments.

In this connexion it should be staed that the mandate of the Colonel-General [Göring as Commissioner for raw materials] refers to the 'ensuring of armaments' which must rather be speeded up than slowed down.

The Führer and Reich Chancellor has given a memorandum to the Colonel-General and the Reich Defence Minister which provides general instructions for putting it into effect.

It starts from the basic premise that the showdown with Russia is inevitable. What Russia has done in the field of reconstruction, we also can do.

Just what sort of risk is it that our industry is afraid of, compared to the risk in the sphere of foreign affairs which the Führer runs so continually?

The Führer is about to have a memorandum issued concerning the financial angle of this problem.

Research on the problem of increasing exports, for instance, has shown that there are hardly any fundamentally new ways to be found. It will not be possible to create a balance of foreign exchange merely by means of exports. The 'New Plan' of the Reich Minister of Economics is acceptable in its basic features, but it can be improved in detail.

The Colonel-General reads the memorandum of the Führer.

The Colonel-General is responsible for the execution of the tasks outlined in the memorandum.

If war should break out tomorrow we would be forced to take measures from which we might possibly still shy away at the present moment. They are, therefore, feasible. Two basic principles:

1. We must strive with the greatest energy for autarky in all those spheres in which it is technically possible; the yearly amount of foreign exchange savings must still surpass that of the first proposal made by the raw materials and foreign exchange staff anticipating savings of 600 million Reichsmarks.

2. We have to tide over with foreign exchange all cases where it seems necessary for armaments and food.

In order to provide for foreign exchange, its flow abroad must be prevented by every means; on the other hand, whatever is abroad must be collected.

The Führer is going to speak very soon to the industrial leaders and disclose to them his basic ideas.

In view of the authority of the State the necessary measures are definitely feasible. Frederick the Great, to whom reference is being made from the most diverse quarters, was in his financial policy a strong inflationist.

Through the genius of the Führer things which were apparently impossible have very quickly become reality; most recent example: introduction of the two-year military service and recognition on the part of France that we need a stronger Wehrmacht than France herself. The tasks now ahead of us are considerably smaller than those we have already accomplished.

All those measures which can be carried through with domestic German money are possible and should be carried out. By their means the requirements of industry and food supply needing foreign exchange must be given a lower priority. All measures must be taken as if we were actually at the stage of imminent mobilization.

The execution of the order of the Führer is an absolute command.

End of meeting: 1300 hrs.

187

Decree on the Execution of the Four-Year Plan, 18 October 1936

The realization of the new Four-Year Plan as proclaimed by me at the Party Congress of honour [*Parteitag der Ehre*] requires the uniform direction of all the powers of the German nation and the rigid consolidation of all pertinent authorities within Party and State.

I assign the execution of the Four-Year Plan to Minister-President General Göring.

Minister-President General Göring will take the necessary measures for the fulfilment of the task given him, and in this respect he has authority to issue legal decrees and general administrative regulations. He is authorized to hear and to issue instructions to all authorities, including the Supreme Authorities of the Reich, and all agencies of the Party, its formations and affiliated organizations.

ADOLF HITLER

(iii) The Organization and Impact of the Four-Year Plan

Armed with these far-reaching powers, Göring set about establishing an organization for the putting of the Four-Year Plan into operation. In this he followed two different lines of approach. On the one hand, he established a separate. Four-Year Plan organization. This consisted of six departments responsible for (1) the production of German raw materials, (2) the distribution of raw materials, (3) the labour force, (4) agricultural production, (5) price supervision, and (6) foreign exchange matters. The responsibility for the production of raw materials was then distributed between an Office for German Raw Materials and an Office for the Planning and Production of Industrial Fats. The coordination of these six departments was carried out by *Ministerialdirektor* Neumann of the Prussian State Ministry, who was simultaneously head of the Four-year Plan department for foreign exchange.

The most important of these departments was the Office for German Raw Materials, which was responsible for the main objective of the Four-Year Plan—the production of raw materials. Headed by a Colonel Löb, who came from Göring's Air Ministry, it was staffed by a combination of Air Force officers and representatives of private industry, of whom the most important was Carl Krauch of IG-Farben who was responsible for research and development in the vital chemicals sector. At the beginning of 1938, Krauch replaced Löb, and the Office for German Raw Materials was transformed into the Reich Agency for Economic Consolidation (*Reichsstelle für Wirtschaftsausbau*), a separate Reich authority. Under Krauch emphasis within the plan switched from general expansion of the raw materials sector to concentration on specific items most urgently needed for rearmament purposes: oil, rubber, light metals and, in particular, gunpowder and explosives for which a special 'express plan' was introduced. This new 'Krauch plan', introduced on 30 June 1938 and intended to cover a period of four years, reflected the new tempo in German foreign policy during 1938 and significantly the 'express plan' was intended to increase Germany's capacity in the areas it covered so that by the end of 1939 it would have reached 'the maximum level of productive capacity achieved in the World War'.

The emergence of Krauch as the most influential figure within the Four-Year Plan organization under Göring set a pattern for the employment of representatives from private industry in semi-official capacities which subsequently became a characteristic feature of German economic organization. It provided both expertise and administrative flexibility, but at the cost of undermining the structure of the Civil Service, since these men from industry were outside the Civil Service hierarchy and subordinate only to Göring. There has been some controversy among historians, particularly between Western historians and those from East Germany, about the significance of that close relationship between private industry and the Nazi State of which this is by no means the only instance. Historians in East Germany seek to show that the regime was being used by 'monopoly capital' for its own ends and was, indeed, to a large extent its creation. They have, however, been unable to provide any convincing evidence that the regime's policies and goals were determined by big business. Western historians, on the other hand, tend to argue that it was the State that used industry rather than the other way round, and that politics rather than economics provides the key to understanding the regime, although they admit that big business profited from it.

Although a separate organization was created for the Four-Year Plan, Göring simultaneously followed another line of approach by appointing the State Secretaries in the Ministries of Labour and Agriculture to head the Labour and Agricultural departments in his Four-Year Plan organization. In this way, he effectively coordinated the two Ministries in the interest of the Four-Year Plan. The Ministers of Labour and Agriculture (Seldte and Darré) increasingly found their power being drained off by way of their State Secretaries to the Four-Year Plan organization which had the mighty

Göring behind it, and behind him Hitler. Their own lines of communication with the Führer were not nearly so good. During the following months Schacht also shared this experience. Increasingly he found his previous power over the economy being undermined by decisions of the Four-Year Plan taken independently of the Economics Ministry in spheres which had hitherto been within its sole competence. Thus, in 1937, a mining ordinance taking over a mining company was issued by the Four-Year Plan, despite the fact that this sphere came under Schacht's responsibility as Minister of Economics. This brought to a head Schacht's growing discontent with what he regarded as the excessive speed of rearmament and the priority given to the uneconomic production of raw materials instead of resources being devoted to exports. After a rather acrimonious correspondence with Göring, he offered his resignation as Minister of Economics, which was eventually accepted on 26 November 1937. He was replaced by the pliable Walther Funk, so that in effect the Ministry of Economics had now also been absorbed within the power orbit of the Four-Year Plan.

The Four-Year Plan, then, was initiated because Schacht's New Plan had failed to solve the problem of providing sufficient raw materials to sustain the rearmament drive as well as tolerable levels of consumption. Although it marked a watershed in German economic policy in a number of ways, it was not in fact a comprehensive and well co-ordinated plan but rather a collection of individual measures in particular areas. It inaugurated a period of tighter controls on prices—a new Reich Price Commissioner was appointed on 29 October 1936 with extensive powers—on wages, and on the labour and financial markets. Above all, however, it represented a reorientation of the economy in the interests of the manufacture of synthetic raw materials and of an increase in the production of Germany's own sources of raw materials, such as coal and iron ore, even where these were uneconomic compared to the price levels of the world market. Between 1936 and 1942, the Four-Year Plan projects absorbed 3.25 billion RM or 50 per cent of the total industrial investment. The figures on page 292 show the degree of success achieved in reaching the targets in the most important spheres.

The most striking failure to match the target was in synthetic oil, despite the fact that, in the years 1937–42, 40–50 per cent of total investment under the plan went into the production of synthetic fuel. In fact, although the production of synthetic fuel increased by 130 per cent in the years 1936–39, it still only covered 18 per cent of the demand. A major problem was the long time taken by the construction of the factories, which only really began to make themselves felt during the war. In general, by the outbreak of war, Germany was still dependent on foreign sources of supply for one-third of her raw material requirements. Moreover, despite the Four-Year Plan, the

188

(in thousands of tons)

Commodity	1936 output	1938 output	1942 output	Plan target
Mineral oil*	1,790	2,340	6,260	13,830
Aluminium	98	166	260	273
Buna rubber	0.7	5	96	120
Nitrogen	770	914	930	1,040
Explosives	18	45	300	223
Powder	20	26	150	217
Steel	19,216	22,656	20,480	24,000
Iron ore	2,255	3,360	4,137	5,549
Brown coal	161,382	194,985	245,918	240,500
Hard coal	158,400	186,186	166,059	213,000

* Including synthetic petrol

German economy had been subjected to no more than partial mobilization for the purposes of rearmament and large areas of it remained relatively unaffected.

The problem was, as Tim Mason has put it, that the regime 'was trying to have its cake and eat it'. It wanted to rearm as fast as possible and at the same time protect the consumer; it wanted to have both guns and butter. At the same time, it wanted to construct massive prestige buildings such as the Nuremberg complex, with which to overawe its own subjects and the rest of the world and impress future generations. The problem was that the German economy lacked the resources to sustain the simultaneous pursuit of all these goals. In July 1938, an SPD analyst produced a very shrewd assessment of the constraints on the German economy and of the dilemma which faced it during 1938–39:

189

The Nazis try to persuade the nation that the problem of economic constraints is nothing but a foreign exchange problem, whereas in reality it is a problem of the capacity of the economy and of the nation's willingness to make sacrifices. This problem has two aspects: on the one hand, the problem of economic resources, of the maximum level of production and the minimum level of consumption; and, on the other hand, the problem of money, of the financial constraints. What the superficial observer normally notices, however, is the constricting effect of the foreign exchange shortage with which Germany continually has to cope. If the German people do not get enough butter and fats, if they have to stuff their stomachs with inferior war-type bread, if, one after the other, the objects of daily use have to be made of dubious *ersatz* materials, then it seems at first sight—and that is what the Nazis try and persuade the people—as if the blame for that lies in Germany's one-sided dependence on foreign countries, which finds technical expression in the shortage of foreign exchange.

This superficial view makes the false theory of autarky popular in Germany: if only one could succeed in reducing or removing the dependence of the German economy on foreign countries by ensuring that a large part of the goods which hitherto had to be imported could be made at home, then the crisis would disappear and then the constraints on rearmament could be removed altogether. This theory completely conceals and falsifies the true situation . . .

If, in contrast to the foreign trade of America and Britain and that of other industrial countries, German foreign trade cannot recover, the cause lies primarily in the enormous demands placed on the German economy by rearmament. In a full-employment economy new scope for one sector of production can only be created at the expense of other sectors of production. If production geared to rearmament and the autarky programme is set against the production for export and consumption (including production geared to the expansion of the consumer goods industries), it is clear that the one can grow only at the expense of the other. To the extent that the hunger belt cannot be tightened further—for physiological and political reasons—exports must be the sector that suffers at the expense of re-armament and autarky and that is in fact the case. . . .

The shortage of foreign exchange is, therefore, in reality only a reflection of the overloading of Germany's economic strength through rearmament and the autarky programme. It is here, in the strength of the German economy, and not in technical aids for foreign exchange services that the real constraints on rearmament lie. The constraints operate on two sides: on the one hand, through the maximum level of activity of the economic factors, on the other hand, through the maximum extent to which consumption can be choked off.

Under the lash of the dictatorship the level of economic activity has been greatly increased. The exploitation of labour has been greatly increased by the *de facto* abolition of the 8 Hour Day, which had been gained over generations, and by the extraordinary increase in the work rate; female employment has been increased despite the totally contradictory National Socialist ideal of womanhood; and a large number of self-employed people [*Mittelständlern*] have been transformed into wage labourers despite the totally contradictory National Socialist ideal of their occupational status. But there are psychological and political barriers to the extension of wage labour to new status groups which have apparently not only been reached but already represent a potential source of danger for the system.

The same is true of the reduction in consumption which has been practised since the beginning of the Nazi regime. Can one keep down consumption permanently at its present level without building up an explosive charge? One must not only consider the consumption of foodstuffs but also the consumption of consumer durables and the expansion of the consumer goods industries in proportion to the growth of the population.

The most important consumer durable is the dwelling. One can neglect housing construction for a few years, as occurred during the war. But, in the process, such a demand for housing develops that afterwards extraordinary efforts are necessary to get on top of the worst housing shortage. Similarly, the expansion of the consumer goods industries can cease for a time, but, in the process, one creates for the future a dangerous 'contraction in the capacity for foodstuffs', particularly if one encourages the procreation of children as much as the Nazis do.

Since the same steel and the same cement, the same copper and the same wood are used for rearmament and for the installations of the autarky programme as for the construction of dwellings and for the expansion of the consumer goods industries, and since human labour power, which is required for the production of all these goods, is only available in a limited amount, the resource limitations to the expansion of rearmament have finally been reached. (through the annexation of Austria these limits have once more been somewhat extended because in Austria there are reserves of labour and industrial capacity which have not yet been used. But these reserves will soon have been used up as well.)

In a money economy all resource constraints express themselves as financial constraints . . . As far as the individual is concerned, the most important constraint on consumption continues to be the size of his purse. The quality and amount of the foodstuffs, clothing, shoes, radios which someone can buy is still determined in the first instance by the size of his net income—after the deduction of all taxes, social security contributions, contributions to the Labour Front, 'donations' etc. . . . It follows from this that the most important method of 'diverting' production from the consumer goods sector to the rearmament industries consists in pinching the consumer's purse as hard as possible. That can be achieved by keeping down wages or by raising taxes and contributions. And both of those are indeed happening. But the limits on the wage and of the tax policies of the regime are identical to the resource constraints on the reduction in consumption which have been referred to above.

Just as the financing of rearmament via taxation represents the mechanism whereby production is transferred from the consumer sector to the rearmament sector, so the financing of rearmament via floating loans raised from banks and businesses and via government bonds represents the mechanism whereby production is diverted from housing and from the expansion of the consumer goods industries to the rearmament industries.

It has been demonstrated above how the financing of housing and the financing of private industry through the banks and the capital market has been blocked through the ruthless exercise by the Reich of its monopoly of credit. The same is true to some extent even of the reinvestment by firms of their own profits. For, if firms are compelled to purchase work creation bonds or Reich bonds for their portfolios, or if they are compelled to finance installations for the autarky programme, then the freedom of action which remains to them for investing in the expansion of their production facilities is correspondingly reduced.

But there are constraints here as well. A fascist system, which makes marriage and the procreation of as many children as possible the highest duty of a subject, cannot afford in the long run continually to reduce housing capacity for the expanding and increasing number of households. The closing of the capital market for mortgage bonds and the ban on the issuing of mortgages by the Savings Banks will have to be relaxed sooner or later in order to free more capital for housing construction. And the same thing will have to happen to provide finance for the expansion of the productive capacity of the consumer goods industries because otherwise, in view of the growth in population, the provision of consumer goods will shrink permanently. None of the constraints described here is absolute. But, taken together, they ensure that even Nazi trees cannot grow up to the sky. It is true that as long as the German people are prepared to put up with their living standards being held at the lowest of crisis levels, the mechanism by which each year 12–13 billion RM are squeezed from the national income for rearmament will keep on functioning. But even then one cannot do everything at once with the extorted billions. One cannot simultaneously use them to increase armaments for the land and air forces *ad infinitum*, to build up a massive battle fleet, to fortify new extended borders, to build gigantic installations for the production of *ersatz* materials, to construct megalomaniacal grandiose buildings, and to tear down large parts of cities in order to build them somewhere else. On the basis of the living standards of the German people hitherto, one can either do one or the other or a bit of everything, but not everything at the same time and in unlimited dimensions. . . .

The regime had succeeded in gearing much of Germany's economic activity to rearmament and the country was better prepared for war in 1939 than it had been in 1914. At the same time it had also managed to sustain tolerable levels of consumption. This was largely because it had been able to mobilize the vast amount of resources in terms of plant, labour and technology which had been idle during the slump. Nevertheless, the goal of achieving a 'defence economy' had not been realised. First, the priority of sustaining politically acceptable levels of consumption had prevented the full-scale mobilization of Germany's resources for war. Secondly, the inadequacies of the German planning apparatus, which in turn reflected the flaws within the political system itself, prevented the adoption of a coherent strategy for rearmament. Moreover, the cracks in an economy which was operating beyond its capacity were beginning to show. Although use of the term 'crisis' to describe the German economy in 1939 may be an over-statement, it was already clear to the regime's leaders that a serious economic crisis was indeed just round the corner. However, the remarkable fact was that the regime had succeeded in imposing a massive rearmament burden on the population without either a wages explosion or serious price inflation and above all without mass opposition. As we have seen, one reason for this was the fact that there had been a distinct improvement in most people's material circumstances since 1933. Two further reasons were the regime's monopoly of the media of information and the system of terror which it imposed on its subjects.

(iv) Economic Statistics

190

The Balance between Production Goods and Consumer Goods in the Development of Industrial Production from 1933–1938

	Total industrial production	Production goods	Consumer goods
1933	100	100	100
1934	130.8	144.9	114.2
1935	149.5	177.3	116.5
1936	168.9	206.7	124
1937	187.2	231.1	135.1
1938	205.1	255.6	145.1

191

The Percentage Increase in Production 1934–1939

	Production goods %	Consumer goods %
1934	44.9	14.2
1935	22.3	2.0
1936	16.6	6.4
1937	11.8	9.0
1938	10.6	7.3
January–April 1938	9.1	8.9
January–April 1939	9.5	9.9

192

Estimated investment in the German economy, 1928–38, classified in relation to military potential

(in billions RM)

Year	Total investment	Military investment (a)	Basic (incl. Four-Yr. Pl.) (b)	Industry (Four-Year Plan only)	Major transport and roads	Civilian economy (c)
1928	13.8	0.5	2.7	—	1.3	9.3
1933	6.8	1.0	0.5	—	0.8	4.5
1934	10.6	3.4	1.0	—	1.2	5.0
1935	14.4	5.0	1.6	—	1.4	6.4
1936	21.1	9.3	3.0	(0.8)	1.6	7.2
1937	23.2	9.5	4.3	(1.5)	1.8	7.6
1938	29.8	13.6	5.6	(2.0)	2.6	8.0
Totals						
1933–8	105.9	41.8	160.0	(4.3)	9.4	38.7

(a) Military expenditure for buildings, armaments, ships, vehicles, industrial sub-sidies, etc. Excludes administrative and personnel expenditure.

(b) Includes: Mining and metallurgy; chemical and fuel industries; other producer goods; machinery, automotive and electrical industries; locomotives and cars; ship-building; power and water; iron, steel and metal-working; optical and precision instruments.

(c) Agriculture, light industries, post office and communications, civilian construction (private, state, municipal, and NSDAP).

193

Gross national product and military expenditure in Germany, the United States and Britain, 1929–45

Year	Germany RM billions			United States $ billions			Britain £ billions		
	GNP (a)	Mil. exp.	Per cent	GNP (b)	Mil. exp.	Per cent	Natl. inc. (c)	Mil. exp.	Per cent
1929	89	0.8	1	104	0.7	1	4.2	0.1	2
1932	58	0.8	1	59	0.6	1	—	0.1	—
1933	59	1.9	3	56	0.5	1	3.7	0.1	3
1934	67	4.1	6	65	0.7	1	3.9	0.1	3

Year	Germany			United States			Britain		
	RM billions			$ billions			£ billions		
	GNP (a)	Mil. exp.	Per cent	GNP (b)	Mil. exp.	Per cent	Natl. inc. (c)	Mil. exp.	Per cent
1935	74	6.0	8	73	0.9	1	4.1	0.1	2
1936	83	10.8	13	83	0.9	1	4.4	0.2	5
1937	93	11.7	13	91	1.0	1	4.6	0.3	7
1938	105	17.2	17	85	1.0	1	4.8	0.4	8
1939	130	30.0	23	91	1.3	1	5.0	1.1	22
1940	141	53.0	38	101	2.2	2	6.0	3.2	53
1941	152	71.0	47	126	13.8	11	6.8	4.1	60
1942	165	91.0	55	159	49.6	31	7.5	4.8	64
1943	184	112.0	61	193	80.4	42	8.0	5.0	63
1944	—	—	—	211	88.6	42	8.2	5.1	62
1945	—	—	—	214	75.9	36	8.3	4.4	53

(a) For the years 1939–43, includes Austria and Sudetenland. Figures are rounded to the nearest billion.
(b) Figures are rounded to the nearest billion.
(c) Britain's gross national product may be estimated at about one billion above national income, resulting in a slightly downward revision of the percentages calculated here. For example, military expenditures calculated against gross national product would give 7 per cent in 1938, 18 per cent in 1939, and a peak of 57 per cent in 1942.

194

German Visible Foreign Trade: Exports and Imports 1928–1938
(in millions RM)

	Imports	Exports[1]		Imports	Exports[1]		Imports	Exports	Imports	Exports
Year	(a) At current prices		Balance	(b) At 1928 prices		Balance	Movement of prices 1936 = 100		Movement of volume 1928 = 100	
1928	14,001[2]	12,276[2]	−1,725	14,001	12,276	−1,725	204.1	169.8	100	100
1929	13,447	13,483	+36	13,512	13,669	+157	203.1	167.6	96.5	111.3
1930	10,393	12,036	+1,643	12,039	12,958	+919	176.1	157.7	86.0	105.6
1931	6,727	9,599	+2,872	10,156	11,771	+1,615	135.1	138.4	72.5	95.9
1932	4,667	5,739	+1,072	9,466	8,123	−1,342	100.6	120.0	67.6	66.2
1933	4,204	4,871	+667	9,312	7,627	−1,685	92.2	108.5	66.5	62.1
1934	4,451	4,167	−284	9.809	6,810	−2,999	92.4	103.9	70.0	55.5
1935	4,159	4,270	+111	8,956	7,334	−1,622	94.7	98.8	64.0	69.7
1936	4,218	4,768	+550	8,610	8,092	−518	100.0	100.0	61.5	65.8
1937[3]	5,468	5,911	+443	10,089	9,360	−729	110.6	107.1	72.0	76.2
1938[4]	5,449	5,257	−192	10,792	7,937	−3,455	103.1	112.4	85.5	69.2

[1] From 1928 to 1932 including reparations deliveries.
[2] Corrected totals.
[3] From 1937 onwards including silver.
[4] Excluding trade with Austria.

Imports 1928–1938: subdivided into agricultural and industrial goods
(a) At current prices

Year	Total (5,6)	AGRICULTURE					INDUSTRY				
		Total	Live animals	Foodstuffs — Animal	Foodstuffs — Plant	Luxuries (e.g. tea and coffee)	Total	Raw materials	Semi-finished goods	Finished goods	Returned goods (7)
1913	10,769.7	4,111.4	299.7	906.5	2,452.7	462.5	6,658.3	3,762.0	1,850.4	1,045.9	—
1928	14,001.3	5,721.9	144.8	1,493.9	3,380.3	702.9	8,279.4	3,968.8	2,503.2	1,807.4	—
1929	13,446.8	5,380.6	149.7	1,544.5	2,943.1	743.3	8,066.2	3,927.4	2,374.0	1,764.8	—
1930	10,393.1	4,229.7	118.3	1,310.3	2,166.1	635.0	6,163.4	2,904.4	1,848.1	1,410.9	—
1931	6,727.1	2,783.2	54.9	857.1	1,432.7	438.5	3,943.9	1,832.2	1,145.3	966.4	—
1932	4,666.5	2,132.7	34.3	593.8	1,182.1	322.5	2,533.8	1,271.7	704.3	557.8	—
1933	4,203.6	1,629.7	30.9	432.5	869.9	296.4	2,573.9	1,367.6	701.4	504.9	—
1934	4,451.0	1,543.2	33.3	385.7	827.5	296.7	2,907.8	1,540.7	791.5	575.6	—
1935	4,158.7	1,435.2	45.1	405.5	704.9	279.7	2,723.5	1,567.9	747.5	408.1	—
1936	4,217.9	1,499.4	96.3	443.7	670.2	289.2	2,718.5	1,571.1	750.0	397.4	—
1937	5,468.4	2,045.1	107.5	479.7	1,135.2	322.7	3,373.1	1,996.2	980.3	396.6	50.2
1938	6,051.7	2,393.8	185.8	508.7	1,332.7	365.1	3,607.4	1,991.4	1,139.8	476.2	51.3

Imports 1928–1938: subdivided into agricultural and industrial goods
(b) At 1928 prices

Year	Total (5,6)	AGRICULTURE					INDUSTRY				
		Total	Live animals	Foodstuffs — Animal	Foodstuffs — Plant	Luxuries (e.g. tea and coffee)	Total	Raw materials	Semi-finished goods	Finished goods	Returned goods (7)
1913	14,599.9	5,870.1	307.8	1,232.0	3,599.5	730.8	8,729.8	4,967.4	2,206.9	1,555.5	—
1928	14,001.3	5,721.9	144.8	1,493.9	3,380.3	702.9	8,279.4	3,968.8	2,503.2	1,807.4	—
1929	13,511.9	5,522.9	150.2	1,555.7	3,114.2	702.8	7,989.0	3,980.5	2,308.3	1,700.2	—
1930	12,039.0	5,013.8	122.0	1,489.0	2,701.4	701.4	7,025.2	3,617.2	1,995.9	1,412.1	—
1931	10,156.4	4,245.9	71.1	1,233.1	2,339.1	602.6	5,910.5	3,140.7	1,700.4	1,069.4	—
1932	9,464.6	4,212.1	71.2	1,179.9	2,420.1	540.9	5,252.5	3,045.9	1,417.8	788.8	—
1933	9,311.9	3,601.9	69.0	921.6	2,045.8	565.5	5,710.0	3,425.4	1,508.9	775.7	—
1934	9,809.4	3,676.8	71.2	855.1	2,107.2	642.3	6,132.6	3,447.8	1,768.8	916.0	—
1935	8,956.2	3,180.6	85.1	892.0	1,575.4	628.1	5,775.6	3,423.9	1,695.8	655.9	—
1936	8,610.0	3,194.0	166.9	887.5	1,494.2	645.4	5,416.0	3,155.9	1,640.3	619.8	—
1937	10,089.3	4,133.6	168.2	993.9	2,262.1	712.4	5,876.5	3,486.5	1,786.7	603.3	79.2
1938	11,973.3	5,018.5	276.6	1,077.6	2,854.5	809.8	6,878.8	3,812.3	2,303.6	762.9	76.0

5 Up until 1936 the returned goods are included in the totals of the individual goods.
6 Until 1936 excluding silver.

Exports 1928–1938: subdivided into agricultural and industrial goods
(a) At current prices

Year	Total (5,6)	AGRICULTURE					INDUSTRY				
		Total	Live animals	Foodstuffs Animal	Foodstuffs Plant	Luxuries (e.g. chocolate)	Total	Raw materials	Semi-finished goods	Finished goods	Returned goods (7)
1913	10,097.2	1,213.8	7.4	57.0	1,050.7	98.7	8,883.4	1,346.9	1,082.7	6,453.8	—
1928	12,275.6	787.8	18.8	51.1	651.3	66.8	11,487.8	1,498.0	1,491.5	8,498.3	—
1929	13,482.7	869.9	22.0	56.7	721.5	69.7	12,612.8	1,582.0	1,596.3	9,434.5	—
1930	12,035.6	660.7	68.7	77.9	450.0	64.1	11,374.9	1,332.5	1,333.2	8,709.2	—
1931	9,598.6	483.8	46.9	64.1	318.7	54.1	9,114.8	989.6	985.1	7,140.1	—
1932	5,739.2	260.0	14.5	35.8	177.8	31.9	5,479.2	577.6	556.3	4,345.3	—
1933	4,871.4	222.3	9.0	29.3	146.4	37.6	4,649.1	515.9	473.7	3,659.5	—
1934	4,166.9	150.3	3.8	21.3	89.0	36.2	4,016.6	463.5	404.7	3,148.4	—
1935	4,269.7	95.7	2.9	13.4	49.6	29.8	4,174.0	446.7	415.7	3,311.6	—
1936	4,768.2	87.6	2.6	9.7	45.4	29.9	4,680.6	419.2	459.1	3,802.3	—
1937	5,911.0	88.8	9.6	9.6	45.7	30.7	5,820.8	577.6	543.2	4,700.0	1.4
1938	5,619.1	66.7	2.0	9.7	30.0	25.0	5,549.0	534.3	473.0	4,541.7	3.4

Exports 1928–1938: subdivided into agricultural and industrial goods
(b) At 1928 prices

Year	Total (5,6)	AGRICULTURE					INDUSTRY				
		Total	Live animals	Foodstuffs Animal	Foodstuffs Plant	Luxuries (e.g. chocolate)	Total	Raw materials	Semi-finished goods	Finished goods	Returned goods (7)
1913	14,885.6	1,612.4	12.8	85.7	1,360.2	153.7	13,273.2	1,947.8	1,324.1	10,001.3	—
1928	12,275.6	787.8	18.8	51.1	651.3	66.6	11,487.8	1,498.0	1,491.5	8,498.3	—
1929	13,669.2	950.2	19.5	56.0	803.7	71.0	12,719.0	1,632.5	1,636.9	9,449.6	—
1930	12,957.5	877.6	78.1	87.1	641.0	71.4	12,079.9	1,549.7	1,460.9	9,069.3	—
1931	11,770.6	778.4	68.7	84.0	555.7	70.0	10,992.2	1,421.5	1,330.9	8,239.8	—
1932	8,122.8	490.4	27.2	56.4	362.6	44.2	7,632.4	1,062.5	981.9	5,588.0	—
1933	7,627.1	520.7	17.1	47.5	409.8	46.3	7,106.4	1,016.8	943.0	5,146.6	—
1934	6,810.3	349.2	5.6	35.0	262.1	46.5	6,461.1	936.4	858.9	4,665.8	—
1935	7,333.6	169.6	3.9	22.4	101.6	41.7	7,164.0	932.1	938.3	5,293.6	—
1936	8,091.6	159.4	3.9	14.3	93.8	47.4	7,932.2	833.5	989.1	6,109.6	—
1937	9,360.0	154.9	2.8	15.3	85.2	51.6	9,202.6	1,014.3	1,059.5	7,128.8	2.5
1938	8,491.9	121.2	2.0	19.4	57.3	42.5	8,364.0	866.7	885.3	6,612.0	6.7

5 Up until 1936 the returned goods are included in the totals of the individual goods.
6 Until 1936 excluding silver.

CHAPTER 14

Business

The take-over of power required the new regime to respond to the often conflicting demands of the various sections of the German business community and to gear business to the requirements of a defence economy. The regime was bound in general to favour the interests of big over small business. Big business was on the whole more productive and efficient; above all, its role in the economy was far larger and its cooperation was essential for economic revival and the rearmament programme. On the other hand, however, small business could hardly be ignored. First, it represented a significant slice of the economy. In 1936, for example, handicrafts supplied 10 per cent of total turnover in the economy and 25 per cent of business turnover. Moreover, some of these small artisan businesses were important suppliers of big business, including armament firms. Secondly, small retailers played a crucial role in the distribution network of consumer goods in general and foodstuffs in particular. There were 540,000 retailers in the Special Group Retail Trade, forming by far the largest group in the Reich Group Commerce. Finally, this section of the community—the 'old middle class'—was an important potential basis of support, particularly in view of the unreliability of the working class. Indeed, it supplied a hard core element of the Party's rank and file, and this was to complicate the situation during 1933.

(i) Small Business

After the March election, the local Party and SA organizations tried to take the initiative in putting into effect the economic principles embodied in the 1920 Programme. The tradesmen, artisans, and unemployed who filled the ranks of the SA believed that with Hitler's appointment the opportunity to eliminate their business competitors for which they had been waiting so long had at last arrived. As a result SA and Party 'commissars' moved into businesses and in some cases started to order the sacking of Social Democrat workers and the employment of Nazis in their place. Pressure was particularly strong from the so-called 'Combat League of Middle Class Tradespeople' which embraced the artisans and small shopkeepers in the Party. These small traders had long resented the dominant influence of the big department stores and consumer cooperatives which had flourished since the end of the nineteenth century. Indeed, in the period before 1933, the Nazis had exploited this resentment as one of their major propaganda themes, promising to destroy them. This Combat League now organized boycotts of department stores and cooperatives and interfered in business in various other ways. Soon the disruption of business activity became such a problem that the Government and Party authorities were obliged to intervene. On 13 May 1933 Dr Wagener, Reich Commissioner for the Economy and Head of the Economic Department of the NSDAP and Dr von Renteln, Leader of the Reich Combat League, issued the following directive:

195

The organization of the Combat League of Middle Class Tradespeople is an instrument for carrying out specific economic duties and the setting of these tasks is the sole responsibility of the leadership of the Reich Combat League.

Under no circumstances do the following form part of these duties: the appointment of commissars, the coordination of associations and plants, the dismissal and replacement of undesirable people, the exercise of direct influence on prices or of direct influence on business activity.

These tasks have been delegated to the State and local authorities as well as to the Reich Commissioners for the Economy and their representatives and delegates. All offices of the Combat League, therefore, are strictly forbidden to take unauthorized action of the kind described above. Contravention will from now onwards be punished by the law.

Nevertheless, the Combat League and the small business interests it represented continued their efforts to seize positions of influence, and so, on 2 June, Göring and Hugenberg wrote to von Renteln as follows:

196

Even recently the complaints about interference by the Combat League have not ceased, despite the fact that 'coordination' can no longer be used as an excuse for this interference. In particular, public bodies and business institutions are suffering from these interventions by the Combat League. For example, frequently during elections to the Chambers of Industry and Commerce, owing to the intervention of the Combat League, which is naturally more representative of the interests of the small business, medium-sized and large businesses have been excluded from participation in the leadership of the Chambers. . . . We therefore request that in future all interference in public bodies and business institutions and in their associations should cease.

The local Party and SA organizations nevertheless continued their harassment of department stores. They justified their behaviour by claiming to act on Point 16 of the 1920 Programme. But the Nazi leadership was forced to take a wider view. Destruction of the department stores, which were organised in five leading concerns with 176 branches, would mean putting thousands of employees out of work and would jeopardize their suppliers. Finally, the banks had loaned millions of marks to these stores, and their elimination would cause widespread economic disruption at a time when it was essential for the Government to improve the economic situation. The department stores were, in fact, in such a critical position that the Government was forced with a large loan to bail out one of the biggest, the firm of Tietz, despite the fact that it was Jewish. To prevent local Party organizations from destroying the department stores, Rudolf Hess was forced to issue the following directive to the Party on 7 July 1933:

197

The attitude of the NSDAP toward the 'department store question' is in principle unchanged. Its solution will follow at the appropriate time in accordance with the National Socialist programme. In view of the general economic situation, the Party leadership considers action intended to paralyse department stores and similar institutions to be inadvisable for the time being. At a time when the National Socialist Government sees its main task as helping as many unemployed citizens as possible to find work and bread, the National Socialist movement must not counteract this by taking away their jobs from hundreds of thousands of workers and employees in department stores and in the firms dependent on them. The sections of the NSDAP are therefore forbidden to undertake further action against department stores and similar firms until further notice. On the other hand, it is forbidden for members of the NSDAP to make propaganda for department stores.

Although this averted the collapse of the department stores, it did not completely end harassment. During the following years local Party organizations continued to subject the department stores to various kinds of sanction, such as this boycott organized by the Dortmund local branch at Christmas 1933:

198

We expect all our members and their relations to pay close attention to the following brief instruction:

Racially conscious Germans make all their purchases for the Christian festival of Christmas only in Christian German shops, whose owners share our ideology. They support German retail trade and German craft. They despise those weak characters who have the nerve to buy presents for the most German of festivals from people who cannot have any feeling for the values of our blood or the sacredness of our creed.

Keep away from Jews and the friends of Jews!

Set an example as National Socialists and avoid firms, stores and department store palaces which, contrary to National Socialist principles, still exist.

Show by your own attitude and by enlightening those around you that you are National Socialist fighters.

Then you will be able to celebrate a German Christmas with a contented heart.

The regime therefore blocked the bid by small business for radical changes in its favour. In the summer of 1933 the Nazi Combat League of Middle Class Tradespeople was dissolved and replaced by a new body for Nazi small businessmen, the NS Hago, which could be more strictly controlled and was designed primarily for political indoctrination. Nevertheless, the Government made significant concessions to small business where these coincided with its main goals of improving efficiency and facilitating control, or where they did not seriously interfere with big business and so jeopardize rearmament. The years 1934–35, in particular, saw a number of measures designed to satisfy small business demands.[25]

Although the regime had prevented Nazi small retailers from destroying the department stores, it did go some way towards meeting their wishes. The Reich Minister of Economics summed up the policy as 'putting a curb on the development of department stores but not allowing them to collapse'. Thus the Law concerning the Protection of Retail Trade of 12 May 1933 imposed a general ban on new department stores and on the expansion of existing ones which lasted till 1945. Also, Party and government agencies discriminated against department stores in their purchasing policies and in other ways such as through special taxes. The result was that in 1938, while the turnover of retail trade as a whole had reached 93.7 per cent of the record result of 1928, that of department stores had only reached 70.1 per cent. Also, the percentage taken by consumer cooperatives of the total retail trade turnover fell from 4.1 per cent to 1.8 per cent. Seventy-two consumer cooperatives—half of the total—were closed by the Law concerning Con-

---

[25] This section is particularly indebted to A. von Saldern, *Mittelstand in Dritten Reich* (Frankfurt 1979).

sumer Cooperatives of 21 May 1935 'in order thereby to create new middle class livelihoods'.

The slump had seen a marked expansion in the number of retail businesses, as unemployed workers sought an alternative source of income. The Law for the protection of Retail Business of 12 May 1933 introduced a ban on the establishment of new retail business, which was then loosened into a requirement for an official permit. This enabled the trade itself to control the influx of new members and on average approximately half of the requests were approved. This ensured that competition was kept in check and, from the point of view of the regime, prevented the inefficient use of labour and resources by marginal businesses. The regime also benefited small retailers by imposing strict controls on door-to-door salesmen and mail order firms.

Finally, the so-called 'aryanization' programme i.e. the expropriation of Jewish businesses, provided a windfall for small retailers both by excluding Jewish competitors and by enabling some businesses to take over their Jewish rivals. In Berlin, for example, there were 3,700 Jewish retail businesses. During Aryanization, there were 3–4 applicants for each business; the selection process was overseen by the Party district leader who favoured reliable Party members. In fact, however, only one third of the Jewish shops were aryanized; the remainder were closed 'to relieve the traditional German retail businesses'. Nevertheless, the department stores were not destroyed in the aryanization programme because their role as efficient retailers was too important—the criterion of 'performance' proved decisive.

The artisans also benefited in various ways from the regime. Ever since the late nineteenth century independent artisans had sought to develop their own organizations in order to increase their influence within the economy, thereby protecting themselves against competition from industry and winning greater recognition of their interests from the state. Their dream was to create a new version of the old medieval corporate system with compulsory guilds forming a craft estate (*Stand*). Their organization had made some progress. In 1919 a Reich Association of German Craft Trades had been established and, by 1932, 64.5 per cent of all trade guilds were compulsory with 772,981 members representing 79.5 per cent of all guild members. But with only 56 per cent of German artisans in these compulsory guilds they were still some way off their goal. Moreover, this organization had proved an inadequate defence against the deterioration of their economic position and social status, through the pressure of big business and organized labour in the less sympathetic climate of the Weimar Republic.

The Law for the Provisional Construction of German Craft Trades of 29 November 1933 was drawn up in close consultation with representatives of the industry and went a long way towards satisfying their demands. In the first place, it insisted that only those artisan businesses could operate whose owners were members of the relevant guild, which was in effect made compulsory. Each guild had a leader appointed from above and empowered to impose fines for breaches of guild regulations, including failure to attend meetings. Although the operation of these guilds and, in particular, the high membership contributions and discipline were sometimes resented by the membership, the principle of compulsory guilds had been a major goal of the artisan community for over fifty years.

Secondly, the Law fulfilled another long-standing artisan demand by introducing the so-called 'Major Certificate of Qualification' (*Großer Befähigungsnachweis*). This meant that in future only those artisans who had taken a 'master's examination', which also included criteria of personal and political reliability, could open an artisan workshop or business. At that time, only about 40 per cent of the owners of artisan businesses had taken a Master's Examination. The intention behind the measure, which had been opposed by big business as the thin end of the wedge of controls, was to improve standards, to raise the prestige of the craft trades and reduce the surplus of artisan businesses. Once again, it was clearly in the interest of the more established artisans, while fitting in with the regime's aim to improve efficiency. The state also satisfied the demands of artisans by mounting a campaign against moonlighting by unqualified people and by discouraging state and municipal workshops.

The guilds provided the base for the reorganization of the craft trades. They were organized both vertically into Reich Guilds for each trade, and horizontally at district level in Chambers of Trade (*Handwerkskammer*), which brought the various trades together and supervised the operation of the guilds. Although superficially the new organization appeared corporatist in style, like an estate of the craft trades, in practice tight political control was ensured by the operation of the leadership principle at all levels and the appointment of reliable Party members as leaders. The system provided the regime with a means of controlling the artisan community indirectly through its own members. Normally, these leaders were appointed from the more established artisans and they in turn could use the organization to weed out marginal members. The controls were enforced by a system of Courts of Honour which also had limited powers of intervention against sharp practice or price cutting. The guilds also had substantial control over craft training, successfully fighting off a challenge from the Labour Front thanks to the support of the Ministry of Economics.

Clearly, concessions to small business found their limits where they conflicted significantly with the interests of big business. The main difficulties for small business occured first as a result of a growing competition with big business for increasingly scarce supplies of labour and raw materials, and secondly through their inability to pass on to their customers increases in raw material and labour costs as a result of price controls. In general, it appears to have been the smaller and more marginal businesses which suffered most. The small business organizations needed little encouragement from the state to close down their weaker members. Between 1936 and 1939, under the harsher climate of the Four Year Plan, the number of self-employed artisans declined from 1.65 million to 1.5 million. The following SPD report describes the difficulties of the more marginal small businesses:

199

Central Germany, July 1939
The small businessmen are in a condition of gloom and despondency. These people, to whom the present system to a large extent owes its rise, are the most disappointed of all. The shortages of goods restrict their turnover, but they cannot respond by putting up their prices because the price decrees prevent them from doing so. The artisans complain about raw material shortages—shoemakers, for example, have not enough leather and so on, and the burden of taxes and other contributions grows. The compulsory maintenance of very detailed accounts, which are frequently checked, has a very demoralising effect. In addition, the indignation of the consumers about goods being unobtainable and contracts not being fulfilled on time often finds expression in a very unpleasant fashion. Thus the mood is often strained.

But if a small artisan has reached the point where his business can no longer provide him with a living, the authorities are quick to close it and pass him on to the employment exchange. The loss of their imaginary independence and the fact that they are compelled to take up a new job to which they are not used, possibly in a strange place, hangs like a threat over the small men and takes away their courage to face life. One can say of many of them that inwardly they have long since turned away from the system and would welcome its fall . . .

Figures for both craft trades and retail trades suggest, however, that there was in fact a steady increase in turnover in the pre-war years:

200

The Development of Turnover in the Craft Trades in Billion RM

1929	19–20	1937	17–18
1932	10–11	1938	19
1933	10–11	1939	20
1936	15–16		

201

The Development of Turnover in the Retail Trades 1929–39 (1933 = 100)

Year	Total	Dept. Stores	Consumer Co-operatives
1929	168	183	191
1932	104	120	152
1933	100	100	100
1934	111	105	91
1935	116	100	70
1936	128	109	71
1937	142	118	74
1938	155	129	77
1939	173	—	79

The more economically viable small businesses reaped some benefit from the rearmament boom and were no doubt content to see their less successful colleagues closed down. For this group, the improvement in their economic position, the—at least partial—satisfaction of some of their long-standing demands, e.g. for a corporate-style organization and for restrictions on department stores, and the flattery bestowed on them as the 'healthy core of the nation' by the regime's propaganda—in sharp contrast to their experience under Weimar—may have made them relatively content with their situation.

(ii) Big Business

The attitude of big business to the Nazis take-over was mixed. A section of heavy industry—coal mining and steel manufacture—led by Fritz Thyssen welcomed it unreservedly. Much of industry, however, and particularly those firms oriented towards exports were opposed to Nazi plans for greater state intervention, deficit-spending and autarky. This attitude found expression in attempts by the main industrial pressure group, the Reich Association of German Industry (RDI) to frustrate these plans, attempts which were sharply criticized by Thyssen at a committee meeting on 23 March 1933:

202

... The General Secretary of the Reich Association actually managed to intervene with the Reich President on the day before Hitler's appointment as Reich Chancellor [i.e. against it]. Even after Hitler's appointment, the Reich Association attempted to form a *Fronde* with the Trade Unions against the Government. On the day before

Schacht's appointment as President of the *Reichsbank*, a meeting summoned by the Reich Association took place, or a meeting of the members of the General Council of the Reichsbank at which the Reich Association participated. At this meeting ways and means were discussed where by the previous President, Luther, could be kept in office and the choice of President Schacht be prevented.

On 13 March, the nationally-inclined members of the Executive Committee had to remind the officers of the Association that it was necessary to hang out the swastika flag, the flag of the National Uprising, alongside the Black-White-Red flag. Under pressure from the national[ist] section of the Committee the officers were compelled to purchase a swastika flag and this flag was then hung out by the national members of the Committee on the third day of the celebration of the National Uprising. Nevertheless, on 21 March, the Reich Association still only hung out a Black-White-Red flag. But this refusal had unpleasant consequence for the Committee. For, a detachment of SA then visited the General Secretary and compelled him to hang out the swastika flag. He [Thyssen] welcomed this deed which taught the Reich Association respect for the new flag. . . .

The Nazis managed to overcome the opposition within the RDI by a combination of pressure from without and collaboration from within. On 1 April 1933, Otto Wagener, the Nazi Reich Commissioner for the Economy, arrived at the RDI offices and demanded the resignation of the General Secretary since the Association had so far avoided 'taking any notice of the revolution' and acted 'as if everything was as before'. He also demanded the replacement of three Jewish members of the Committee by two Nazis. Appeals for help against this 'coordination' fell on deaf ears. Hugenberg declared himself 'extremely shocked' but declined to intervene on the grounds that Hitler 'was always extremely loath to disavow his own people'. Hindenburg was reported to be 'indignant' but also failed to act. The opposition within the RDI was undermined by the willingness of its President, Krupp, and of the new General Secretary, Herle, to cooperate with the new order. On 3 May, Krupp declared that he was introducing the leadership principle into the organization and would use it 'to bring the new organization into line with the political goals of the Reich Government'.

The regime was not, however, content with a mere replacement of personnel in existing associations. To secure the influence of the state over the business community without imposing too many bureaucratic controls it needed a more highly structured organization. At the same time, however, business was seeking maximum independence within the regime and tried to achieve this by utilizing the fashionable concept of Corporatism. A corporatist structure for business such as existed in Fascist Italy would, it was hoped, secure it a large measure of autonomy. After flirting with the idea for some months, however, the Nazi leadership dropped it for fear of establishing a power block resistant to political control. Instead, they decided to establish a less independent system which might act as a transmission belt between the State and business and through which business would in effect control itself in the service of the State. The structure of this new organization was laid down in the Law for the Preparation of the Organic Construction of the German Economy of 27 November 1934:

203

§1 In order to prepare for the organic construction of the economy, the Reich Minister of Economics is empowered
1. to grant recognition to economic associations as the sole representatives of their branches of economic activity.
2. to establish, dissolve, or amalgamate economic associations.
3. to alter and amend the statutes and articles of association of economic associations and, in particular, to introduce the leadership principle.
4. to appoint and dismiss the leaders of economic associations.
5. to oblige employers and business undertakings to join economic associations.
Economic associations are those associations and combinations of associations which are responsible for looking after the economic interests of entrepreneurs and business undertakings.

The first decree implementing this law was issued on the same day;

204

I *The structure of Business*

§1 Business will be unified and structured both by sector and regionally. The organization and the official representative bodies of business will be organically linked.
§2 Business will be unified in sectors viz: in a Reich Group Industry, subdivided into Main Groups, and in the Reich Groups Handicrafts, Commerce, Banking, Insurance and Energy.
Economic Groups will be formed within the Main Groups of Industry and in the Reich Groups of the rest of Business and where appropriate will be subdivided into specialist groups or sub-groups.
§3 Industry will be unified regionally in Economic Districts. . .
§6 The existing economic associations are to be transferred into the sectoral or regional structures where appropriate and thereby receive the new legal form . . . The transfer will be ordered by the Reich Minister of Economics insofar as it is not carried out by the associations themselves. . . .

IV *Tasks and Duties*

§16 The Business Groups will advise and supervise their members in their particular field.

THE STRUCTURE OF BUSINESS ORGANISATION

Reich Ministry of Economics

Reich Chamber of Economics

REICH GROUP

Industry | Handicrafts | Commerce | Banks | Insurance | Energy | Tourism

7 Main Groups

Economic Groups

Sector Groups

Sector Sub-Groups

1 East Prussia
2 Silesia
3 Brandenburg
4 Pomerania
5 North Mark
6 Lower Saxony
7 Westphalia
8 Rhineland
9 Hesse
10 Central Germany
11 Saxony
12 Bavaria
13 South-west Germany

REGIONAL STRUCTURE

District Chamber of Economics

Chambers of Industry and Commerce

Chambers of Trade

The director of the Group will lead the Group according to the principles of the National Socialist State and will further the affairs of the Group and its members taking into consideration the overall interests of industry and safeguarding the interests of the State. The director is responsible to the Group and to the directors of the Groups in authority over him for the proper leadership of the Group. Instructions from the director which are determined by the function of the Group or by the restructuring of Business must be followed by the membership.

This practice of indirect control by the State through a system of 'self-regulation' by Business, exercised via a network of business organizations, created a complex and shifting pattern of interdependence between State and Business. For, although the Reich Groups etc. were obliged to implement regulations issued by the Government, at the same time, the State was dependent on the business organizations for their expertise and for the smooth operation of its economic controls. This situation ensured Business a measure of autonomy vis-à-vis both State and Party. This was particularly true under Schacht as Reich Minister of Economics (till November 1937). Even after his resignation, the inauguration of the Four-Year Plan and the widespread recruitment from Business to staff its various agencies, intensified this interlocking relationship between Government bureaucracy and Business.

In general, the cooperation of big business with the new order was brought about by a combination of the carrot and the stick. The carrot was provided, firstly, by the new business opportunities and profits offered by the rearmament programme and, secondly, by the destruction of the Trade Unions and the restoration of the employer's role as 'master in his own house' through the concept of the 'plant community'.[26] The stick was provided by the atmosphere of barely concealed terror and the threat that the regime would favour the small business interest, so heavily represented among its supporters, or encourage the ambitions of the German Labour Front. This was arguably an empty threat in view of the regime's dependence on big business for rearmament, but it may not have appeared so at the time. Indeed, a number of small-scale manufacturers who were Nazis were appointed to important posts in the Four Year Plan apparatus (e.g. Hans Kehrl—textiles) with the function of bringing the firms in their sector into line.

Where Business was not prepared to cooperate with the regime on the grounds that its proposals were uneconomic, the Government was ruthless in stepping in and setting up its own plant. This point was put very firmly by Göring at a meeting of the Economic Group of the Iron Making Industry on 17 March 1937:

---

[26]See below p. 342.

205

... It is a project such as when one prompts an armaments firm, the capacity of whose plant is only partially utilized by the normal level of orders, nevertheless to expand their plant even though it will be uneconomic to do so. And yet this will have to be done. I am intentionally leaving on one side the question of how far the iron industrialists can manage to do it on their own and how far they will have to be assisted. In the case of vital plants, where the State cannot put so many demands that the firms might go bust, then the State will have to step in and help since these measures must under all circumstances be prepared. The same is true of the production of explosives or field guns, where one also cannot require these projects to be economic. The same is valid for low grade iron ores. For provision must be made so that in the event of Germany being cut off from foreign supplies of iron ore the defence programme can still be carried through in toto. This does not, of course, imply that the import of rich ores from abroad can be ended but rather that large reserves must be built up so that Germany can stand on its own feet. In the name of the Führer, who has expressly instructed me to declare to you that he does not intend to depart from this path, I state as my view that it must be possible to secure from German soil sufficient ores for military requirements. And, if three times the number of blast furnaces have to be built then three times that number must be built. The programme of munitions production and armaments must not be jeopardized, in the event of war, by a shortage of ore. Everything possible must be done by the firms, and the State must step in where the firms are clearly no longer in a position to do so. It is the same for the State as when it has to build battleships, field guns etc.

In this connexion, it is important that, in the event of war, Austria's soil will belong to Germany. We must get hold of all the Austrian deposits we can, in order to increase our reserve capacity. Austria is rich in ores.

The unwillingness of the Ruhr iron industrialists to go ahead with the construction of extra capacity to process uneconomic German ores prompted Göring to establish a massive State plant in Salzgitter in North Central Germany, the Reich-Works-Hermann-Göring, in direct competition with them, which was also given priority in the allocation of raw materials and labour.

By 1939, businessmen were subject to a whole range of controls—on imports, the distribution of raw materials, prices, wages, employment, capital markets and so on. The Government dictated to a large extent what and how much they should produce, the amount of new investment, where new plants should be built, the type and amount of raw materials to be used, what prices to charge their customers and what wages to pay their employees, the amount of profit they could take and how it should be used—largely in reinvestment or for the purchase of Government bonds. Government spending as a percentage of national income had risen from 23 per cent in 1929 to 35 per cent in 1938. On the other hand, business remained in private hands and the impact of these controls varied from industry to industry with those involved in the rearmament drive faring best. This differentiation between industries undermined any united front of business since for those firms which were both cooperative and efficient and also in the right sector the pickings could be rich.

The firm which benefited most was the massive chemicals combine IG Farben. Not only did it play the major role in the crash synthetics programme of the Four-Year Plan but it also—along with other firms—benefited from the regime's expansion of territory, as is clear from the minutes of its 'Austria Meeting' held on 19 April 1938.

206

Reports from Haefliger, Haager, and Schiller, some already in writing and some repeated orally at the meeting, show that both the Party and the State authorities in the Old Reich and in Austria have no basic objections to our long-standing plan for a coordination of the Austrian chemical industry, i.e. the DAG, the Deutsch-Matrei and SWW, and regard our presence on the boards of the two firms, which occurred in response to the wishes of the gentlemen in authority there, as a logical development.

In addition, a detailed discussion will take place concerning the possibility for a union of the various firms in Austria and concerning a general reorganization of our industrial interests in South-East Europe in so far as it is required by the new situation, i.e. the incorporation of Austria into the Reich.

Plans, previously discussed, to dispense with one or other of the spheres of influence linked to the DAG in return for greater participation in the Austrian firm will be dropped.

On the occasion of his visit to Budapest next week, Krüger will be instructed to explore the possibility of acquiring the Pest Hungarian Bank's minority holding in the DAG Bratislava. If this attempt fails, then the possibility must be examined of a pooling agreement with the Hungarians concerning the common ownership of shares in the DAG Bratislava and a leasing of the Austrian plants of the DAG Bratislava. In view of the fact that it is still an open question whether a fusion or a leasing arrangement will occur, and whether the individual companies and their management will remain, the drawing up of a shortlist for the appointment of the board of the new company (Ostmark Chemicals) will be postponed for the time being. On the other hand, we must examine right away the question of how far changes are necessary in the personnel and organization of the South East European subsidiaries of DAG Bratislava and of the firm itself.

The following figures indicate both the importance to IG Farben of the Four-Year Plan and the fact that they were conscious of the need to demonstrate their gratitude to the regime in tangible form:

207

Contributions and Net Profits of the IG-Farben Concern
(in RM)

Year	Contributions to the NSDAP	Net Profits
1933	3,584,070	74,000,000
1934	4,020,207	68,000,000
1935	4,515,039	71,000,000
1936	4,960,636	140,000,000
1937	5,467,626	188,000,000
1938	8,156,315	191,000,000
1939	7,538,857	240,000,000

IG Farben was only the most extreme example. Between 1928 and 1939 there was an increase in the undistributed profits of Big Business from 1.3 billion RM to 5.0 billion RM.

CHAPTER 15

Agriculture

By January 1933, German agriculture had been suffering from five years of crisis. Twenty-nine per cent of the population were engaged in agriculture and the rural population had provided the backbone of the Party's electoral support between 1930 and 1933. In the first Four-Year Plan which the government had announced in its Appeal to the Nation on 31 January 1933[27] a new deal for agriculture was given top priority along with the solving of the unemployment problem, and on 8 February Hitler informed his Cabinet of 'the need to satisfy the wishes of at least one section of the nation, namely the German peasantry'.

Nazi agricultural policy was determined by a number of different and sometimes conflicting priorities. First, it aimed to secure 'nutritional freedom' (*Nahrungsfreiheit*) i.e. maximum independence from foreign sources of supply. This would both secure Germany against the effects of any future enemy blockade and also minimise the foreign exchange expenditure on food imports, thereby freeing foreign exchange for the purchase of industrial raw materials for the rearmament programme. Secondly, it aimed to secure a healthy and prosperous peasantry as the 'blood spring' of the nation. For, in the view of the Nazi agricultural leader, Richard Darré, the peasantry was the key to Germany's racial health, both in terms of the quantity and quality of its offspring and in terms of its values, a view shared by Hitler himself. Finally, Nazi policy needed to keep food prices stable so that wages could also be kept stable and not disrupt rearmament through a wage-price spiral.

Initially, however, agrarian policy was formed by Alfred Hugenberg, the leader of the German Nationalists. Hugenberg combined the posts of Reich Economics Minister and Reich Minister of Agriculture, but concentrated his

---

[27] See above, pp. 131–4.

attention on agriculture, which was the main concern of his party's supporters, the Prussian Junkers and other landowners. In his first weeks in office Hugenberg introduced a ban on the foreclosure of farms for debt, valid until 31 October 1933. He also increased tariffs for the most important agrarian products. In March, he introduced a plan for the compulsory addition of butter to margarine and for reducing the production of margarine to 60 per cent of current production. The result of this measure was to increase the price of fats by between 40 and 50 per cent. Finally with the Debt Regulation Law of 1 June 1933, the Government initiated a programme designed to alleviate the problem of agricultural debt by providing finance for the reduction of interest rates and the part cancellation of debts.

These one-sided measures in the interests of agriculture, and particularly the marked increase in the price of fats, were unpopular with the general public and therefore provoked the hostility of the Party. Despite his desire to conciliate the agriculture population, even Hitler began to have second thoughts. At this stage, however, Hitler was still dependent on the Nationalists, particularly since in this case they had the support of Reich President von Hindenburg. He was therefore obliged to accept Hugenberg's policy.

Soon, however, Hugenberg's position was undermined both within the agricultural sector and within the Government. Even before 1933, the Nazis had managed to acquire considerable influence within the agricultural organizations, notably the Reichslandbund and so they had no difficulty in 'coordinating' these organizations when it was no longer necessary to conciliate the nationalists. During April and May 1933, Darré took over the agricultural organizations and, when Hugenberg resigned as Minister of Agriculture at the end of June, Darré replaced him.

During September 1933, Darré launched an ambitious reorganization of German agriculture, which had two aspects. The first exploited the corporatist ideas current during 1933 and involved the formation of a huge new corporate-style organization known as the Reich Food Estate (*Reichsnährstand*), thereby fulfilling a long-standing demand of agricultural associations. The initial measures were contained in the Law concerning the Provisional Establishment of the Reich Food Estate of 13 September:

208

---

§1. (i) The Reich Minister of Food and Agriculture is empowered to make provisional arrangements for the establishment of the Estate of German Agriculture (Reich Food Estate). (2) German agriculture within the meaning of this law also embraces forestry, horticulture, fisheries, and hunting. The Reich

Food Estate also includes the agricultural cooperatives, rural commerce (large-and small-scale), and those who process agricultural produce.

§2. The Reich Minister of Food and Agriculture can empower the Reich Food Estate or one of its groups to regulate the production, distribution, as well as the prices and price margins of agricultural produce when it appears desirable, having taken into consideration the interests of the economy as a whole and of the common good.

§3. For the purposes of regulating the production, distribution as well as the prices and price margins of agricultural produce the Reich Minister of Food and Agriculture can amalgamate or include in existing amalgamations, groups, and members of the Reich Food Estate and other undertakings and institutions which produce or sell agricultural products, if the amalgamation appears desirable, having taken into consideration the interests of the economy as a whole and of the common good . . .

§6. The Reich will not provide any compensation for damage caused by any measure arising from this law. . . .

§9 (1) The Reich Minister of Food and Agriculture can determine that anyone who contravenes regulations issued on the basis of this law will be punished with imprisonment and with fines of up to RM 100,000 or with one or other of these penalties. (2) He can further determine that the continued operation of businesses can be forbidden if a penalty had been legally imposed because of a contravention of one of the regulations issued on the basis of this law. . .

The Reich Food Estate was headed by Darré as Reich Peasant Leader and subordinate to him was a cadre organization of state, district, and local peasant leaders. It acquired the function of strictly controlling the movement of German agricultural produce from the producer to the consumer. These controls required an elaborate organization to enforce them. This consisted of two main sections. Firstly, the producers, processors, and distributors of a particular product such as grain, milk, fish, fruit etc. were combined together into district organizations (*Wirtschaftsverbände*), which were in turn subordinate to a central marketing board (*Hauptvereinigung*) with its headquarters in Berlin. Secondly, so-called Reich Agencies (*Reichsstellen*) were established to control the import of various agricultural products. The first of these—that for wheat—had in fact been established by the Brüning government in 1931. From 1936, farmers were given annual delivery quotas for certain products notably for milk (17.4.1936) and grain (22.7.1937), taking into account such factors as size of farm and quality of soil. Thus, through the Reich Agencies and the Central Marketing Boards the Reich Food Estate could control the production and distribution of all foodstuffs and fix their prices.

The second aspect of Darré's reorganization of agriculture in September 1933 was embodied in his Reich Entailed Farm Law (*Reichserbhofgesetz*) of 29 September 1933. This represented an attempt to guarantee the future of medium-sized peasant farmers who were expected to be the 'blood spring' of the German nation:

209

By upholding the old German custom of entailment, the Reich Government wishes to retain the peasantry as the blood spring of the German nation.

The peasant farms are to be protected from heavy indebtedness and from being split up in the course of inheritance, so that they may remain in the hands of free peasants as the inheritance of their kin.

It is intended to work towards a healthy distribution of agricultural units, since a large number of viable small and medium-sized farms, distributed as evenly as possible over the whole country, forms the best guarantee for the maintenance of the health of the nation and of the State.

The Reich Government therefore promulgates the following law.

The basic principles of the law are:

An agricultural or forestry property consisting of at least 7.5 hectares and at most 125 hectares is an entailed-farm provided it belongs to a person qualified to be a peasant

The owner of the entailed-farm is called a peasant.

Only German citizens of German blood or of that of a similar race and who are respectable are eligible to be peasants.

The entailed-farm is passed on undivided to the heir.

The rights of the co-heirs are limited to the remaining property of the peasant. Those descendants not qualified to be heirs receive a dowry and occupational training corresponding to the resources of the farm; if through no fault of their own they get into difficulties, they will be permitted to seek refuge at home.

The right of inheritance cannot be excluded or limited by instructions because of death.

The entailed-farm is absolutely barred from encumberment and is inalienable. . . .

5. The creation of an entailed-farm through special dispensation.

(1) The Reich Ministry of Food and Agricultural may, after consultation with the District [*Kreis*] Peasant Leader and the *Gau* Peasant Leader, permit exceptions to the requirements of section 3.

[These requirements referred to the maximum size of the farm—125 hectares—and to the need for the farm to be operated without farm steading.]

(2) But a size in excess of 125 hectares should normally only be permitted:

1. When it appears imperative owing to the type of soil or the climate.

2. When it concerns a farm which is economically self-contained and whose estates have been rounded off and when it can be proved to have been in the possession of the family of the peasant for more than 150 years.

3. When a German who has made a particular contribution to the welfare of the German people is to be honoured either personally or through his descendants.

4. When the family which resides on the farm has created works of value there (for example, buildings of artistic interest or of importance in the history of art) for which a size of no more than 125 hectares would provide an inadequate economic foundation.

(3) The precondition that the farm should be capable of being farmed without farm steading can be lifted only if special operating conditions require the farm steading....

38. Foreclosures for debt cannot take place on an entailed-farm.

Statistics show that the law failed in its main objectives. It applied to some 700,000 farms, only 22 per cent of the total, 85 per cent of which were between 20 and 50 hectares in size. Only about 6 per cent were over 50ha. They made up some 37 per cent of the total agricultural and forest area and were unevenly distributed, with the weakest concentration in Mecklenburg and the South West and the strongest in southern Bavaria. Under the provisions of the law the peasantry acquired security against foreclosure—a long-standing demand—but at the price of a loss of freedom to sell or mortgage the property. The law had similarities with the law of primogeniture which governed inheritance in four-fifths of Germany. The other one-fifth, mainly in South-West Germany, was governed by the practice of dividing up the farm among the various heirs. However, it differed from existing practice in a number of important ways: first, in not permitting other heirs to receive cash payments through mortgages and loans using the farm as collateral, and secondly, by discriminating against the female heirs of the family. A report by a district government office in Eastern Bavaria of 4 January 1934 summed up the mixed but generally hostile reaction to this law:

210

Although the Entailed Farm Law was passed for the protection of the peasantry, it does not receive wholehearted approval even among the farmers. It is naturally welcomed by those peasants whom it saved from foreclosure. On the other hand, the efficient farmers, who have always endeavoured to fulfil their responsibilities and to keep their farms free from debt, are unpleasantly surprised when banks etc, no longer grant them credit precisely because they are owners of entailed farms and thus treat them more or less as no longer creditworthy. Since the entailed farm can no longer be used as collateral and, together with all its equipment, is out of the reach of creditors, all cautious businessmen understandably decline to grant credit to owners of entailed farms.... A further consequence of the ineligibility of the entailed farms for mortgages is the fact that the existing owners, who do not feel that their futures are sufficiently secure under the agreements for a compulsory transfer of ownership, increasingly endeavour to provide for their old age through life assurance. The high premiums involved must naturally be paid from the profits of the farm. As a result of this and of the shortage of credit (for example for the purchase of machinery), a decline in the quality of farm management must be anticipated. A further and even more serious reservation about the Entailed Farm Law is expressed about the fact that most of the entailed farms will not be in a position to provide an adequate inheritance for their children—apart from the heir himself. The positions of the heir and of the other children will in many cases be so unequal that a father who loves all his children equally will find this regulation inequitable. The contrast between the provision for the heir and for the other children will be even sharper the more children there are. As a result, as long as he is the owner of the farm, the father will remove capital from it for the sake of the other children (e.g. through life assurance etc.) or, which seems more likely, reduce the number of children, as is already apparently the case in Westphalia, the homeland of the law of primogeniture.

The farmers who owned entailed farms tended to feel that they were in fact no longer the owners but merely administrators. Moreover, concern about the children who were not heirs was all the greater because many of these children had spent years workings on the farms for little or no wages on the assumption that even though they would not inherit the farm, they would at least receive a substantial cash payment or dowry. Now, overnight, those hopes were to be disappointed. Finally, by preventing the sale of entailed farms, the law automatically increased the demand for, and therefore the price of, non-entailed farmland, thereby discouraging upward social mobility by efficient labourers and small farmers and encouraging the 'flight from the land'.

It was not only the Entailed Farm Law which proved controversial among the peasantry. The controls on the sale of produce introduced by the new marketing boards established by the Reich Food Estate—initially for eggs, milk, and butter in December 1933—were highly unpopular. The mood of the dairy and livestock farmers in an area which since 1928 had been a major centre of Nazi support[28] was reported by an SPD agent in the Summer of 1934;

211

North-West Germany, June/July 1934
The medium sized and big peasants of Oldenburg and East Friesland, who were once enthusiastic Nazis, are now virtually unanimous in rejecting the Nazis and in reaffirming their old Conservative traditions. Among the East Frisian animal breeders and rich polder peasants the Entailed Farm Law bears the main responsibility for this. Among the medium-sized farmers it is mainly the controls on the sale of milk and eggs which are responsible. The farms near towns previously delivered their milk direct to the consumer and recieved 16 pf. per liter. Now the consumer pays 20 pf. per liter for delivery via the central cooperative, while the peasant only receives 10–12 Pf. There is a similar situation with the sale of eggs. The ensuing losses for the peasant farms are in proportion to their size, very large. the

---

[28]See above, pp. 59ff.

hostility to the Nazis goes so far that East Frisian farmers kicked out representatives of the NSBO who were demanding the reemployment of dismissed workers. When the Nazis threatened to come back and bring the SA with them, the peasants replied that then there would be deaths. A peasant who was arrested after an incident with Nazis received support from his colleagues in the form of them doing his work for him, thereby demonstrating to the system their solidarity with the arrested man.

At the same time, however, the following SPD reports suggest that in assessing peasant morale one must differentiate between peasants and also not exaggerate the extent of their opposition:

212

Southern Bavaria, November/December 1934
As far as we can observe the mood of the countryside, one must make a distinction between the older and the younger generation of peasants. The older peasants are very critical, find it very difficult to get used to the new situation and can hardly get over the fact that their influence in the parish councils etc. has been excluded by the opposition forces. The younger generation, on the other hand, which now often sits on the parish councils, appears National Socialist to a high degree...

213

Bavaria, August 1937
I spoke with a peasant with a medium-sized farm, a former supporter of the Bavarian People's Party. He reckoned the regime had brought the peasants some advantages as well, particularly for those whose farms were heavily in debt and had faced foreclosure. The Entailed Farm Law has advantages as well as disadvantages just like the controlled market. Many peasants find it difficult to distinguish between advantages and disadvantages. They grumble non-stop and many are under heavier financial pressure than before, but others are better off. The peasants are more upset by the regime's fight against Christianity than by economic difficulties because religious questions preoccupy them a great deal. They wanted nothing to do with Communism—at least the peasants with medium-sized farms didn't. They were afraid that Bolshevism would take away their land and they would prefer to come to terms with the Nazis who only dispossess them of half their property.

Most farmers must indeed have had mixed feelings about Nazi policies. While they may have been flattered to some extent by propaganda rhetoric of the 'blood and soil' variety, almost certainly more important were the concrete material results and these were mixed. First, the regime had had some success in alleviating the financial problems of German farmers. Thus, whereas between 1926 and 1933 Weimar governments had paid out 453.6 million RM to clear farm debts, between 1933 and 1936 the Nazi government paid out 650 million RM. The bulk of this money, however, went to the large and medium-sized farms. It was only after 1935 that smaller farms benefited and, even then, much of the money was channelled towards the entailed farms.

Secondly, while the Reich Food Estate may have partially succeeded in increasing production and rationalising the distribution of foodstuffs, in evening out shortages, in controlling prices, and in preparing the ground for war-time controls and rationing, the cost in terms of bureaucratic waste and peasant resentment was quite high. Above all, however, Darré failed in his main intention of taking agriculture out of the market economy. For, although the central objective of making Germany as far as possible independent of foreign sources of supply—enshrined in the so-called 'Battle of Production' launched in 1934—met with considerable success, it failed totally in the crucial sphere of fats. Moreover, while the arable landowners benefited from subsidies, livestock farmers dependent on expensive fodder, much of it imported, were hard hit. Germany was in fact subject to world market conditions which meant a rise in the price of imports during the 1930s. As a substitute for animal fats, attempts were made to increase the area devoted to the cultivation of oil seed plants. But this was both uneconomic and of marginal significance. A propaganda campaign was also launched by the Party organizations to try and change people's habits. They were encouraged to switch from meat to fish and to use jam as a substitute for sausage on bread. There was some success; the consumption of jam went up three times by 1938; fish consumption increased and that of fats went down by 15 per cent. The consumption of meat per head (48.6 kilos) in 1938 was still under the 1929 level of 51.7 kilos. Nevertheless, these measures could not have a decisive effect.

214

Self-sufficiency in Important Foodstuffs (in %)

Foodstuff	1927/28	1933/34	1938/39
Bread grains	79	99	115
Pulses (without lentils)	62	50	71
Potatoes	96	100	100
Vegetables	84	90	91
Sugar	100	99	101
Meat	91	98	97
Eggs	64	80	82
Fats	44	53	57
Total Foodstuffs	68	80	83

By 1938 levels of food consumption had only increased marginally from those in the crisis year 1932:

215

Food Consumption per head of the Population

	Calories	Protein	Fats	Carbohydrates
1932	100	100	100	100
1933	99.1	100.5	96.3	100.4
1934	100.5	102.1	96.3	102.2
1935	100.6	103.4	95.7	102.2
1936	103.0	104.9	98.8	104.3
1937	104.7	107.4	97.7	107.4
1938	105.0	107.7	100.7	105.6

The above figures are probably an overestimate.

The price of foodstuffs was strictly controlled after 1935 but was allowed to rise more than farm costs, with one crucial exception—labour. Since production also increased after 1935 farmers' incomes went up by 41 per cent between 1933 and 1938. This increase was, however, modest compared with that of trade and industry (116 per cent), though substantial compared with that of industrial workers (25 per cent).

216

The Proceeds and Costs of Agriculture 1928/29–1938/39
1932/33 = 100

Year	Proceeds	Costs
1928/29	163	145
1932/33	100	100
1933/34	117	102
1934/35	132	103
1935/36	141	111
1936/37	145	116
1937/38	157	124
1938/39	172	133

217

The Development of Agricultural Prices 1928/29–1943/44
1909/10–1913/14 = 100

1928/29	132	1938/39	104
1931/32	89	1939/40	106
1932/33	77	1940/41	109
1933/34	84	1941/42	113
1935/36	102	1942/43	118
1936/37	101	1942/42	118
1937/38	102	1943/44	121

Price increases varied of course from foodstuff to foodstuff. Prices all, however, remained below those for 1928/29—wheat by 7%, rye by 13%, pigs by 30%, beef cattle by 9%, butter by 28%, eggs by 20%, potatoes by 14%, and vegetables by 30%.

By the late 1930s, the main barrier to an increase in agricultural production and the main reason for a sharp deterioration in peasant morale was the shortage of labour, which had reached crisis proportions. The restrictions on food prices from 1935 onwards meant that farmers could neither afford to pay competitive wages nor invest in labour-saving machinery, the production of which was in any case restricted by the priority given to rearmament. By 1938–39, the situation was so serious that the Army's Economic Inspectorate warned that 'if the labour shortage persists or gets even worse there will be nothing left for it but to go over to more extensive forms of cultivation.' The crisis was summed up in a letter from the Reich Minister of Labour to the Head of the Reich Chancellery on 4 February 1939:

218

... Following on from these general comments, I now wish to refer to the particularly difficult labour situation in agriculture.

In 1933, 2,230,000 non-family workers were employed in agriculture, horticulture and animal-breeding. As is shown in the Work Book census of the middle of last year, this number has now fallen to 2,030,000, i.e. by 200,000 or nearly 10 per cent. But it is probable that the number of independent and family employees in agriculture has also dropped sharply. In 1933 there were engaged in agriculture, apart from the $2\frac{1}{4}$ million non-family workers, another 2.2 million independents and $4\frac{1}{2}$ million family workers. Unfortunately there are no statistics on the last two groups. But even on the most optimistic estimate it must be assumed that, in view of the increased flight from the land, agriculture has perhaps $\frac{1}{2}$ million fewer workers at its disposal in 1938 than in 1933. The reasons for this development are well known: the difference between working conditions and living conditions in the towns compared with the countryside, the excessive opportunities for employment in industry, particularly in the building industry which is closely related to agriculture, and the call-up to labour service and military service.

Considering the increased demands made upon agriculture by the battle for self-sufficiency, this drop of approximately $\frac{1}{2}$ million workers is particularly serious.

Over the last few years, therefore, I have tried within my own sphere to alleviate the shortage of labour in agriculture by taking appropriate action in the labour field, and will endeavour to expand these measures in the coming year. I would like to mention in this connexion the recent extension of the year of compulsory domestic service to all female youth who wish to take up a career and the increased importing of foreign agricultural workers within the limits permitted by the foreign exchange situation. Negotiations for the year 1939 have already been concluded with a few states particularly with Italy. With others, and particularly with Poland, they are at the moment still in progress.

Not only agriculture suffered from a severe labour shortage. Labour represented the most serious bottleneck for industry too and in particular for the Four-Year Plan. The exploitation of labour raised major political issues for the regime.

CHAPTER 16

Nazism and the Working Class

From the beginning one of the basic aims of the Nazi Party, expressed even in the name of the Party—the National Socialist German Workers' Party, had been to win over the workers. Hitler had seen the *raison d'être* of the Party in the attempt to win the workers away from 'Jewish' Marxism and Internationalism and for nationalism and antisemitism. This he regarded as the prerequisite for the national unity so vital for German expansion. Yet, in the period before 1933, workers had on the whole remained loyal to the Social Democratic Party. The more radical of them tended to support the Communists rather than the Nazis. The National Socialist Factory Cell Organization (NSBO), which had attempted to provide a Nazi alternative to the trade unions, had had comparatively little success among blue-collar workers. On coming to power, therefore, the Nazis were determined to eliminate hostile working class organizations and to win the support of the workers for the new state. Indeed, if the new regime were to be successful in its goal of concentrating Germany's economic resources on rearmament, it would be essential to eliminate the independent power of organized labour. Moreover, such a policy was part of the implicit bargain with the German elites on the basis of which the Nazis had come to power. However, labour could not be simply ignored or repressed without adverse effects on economic performance and social stability. The trauma of November 1918 was still a powerful influence on the thinking of Nazi leaders, notably Hitler himself. Thus, having destroyed existing labour organizations, the Nazis would be faced with the task of establishing a new one as well as a new system of labour relations.

(i) Labour Organization and Labour Relations in January 1933

Modern German labour organizations had developed during the last third of the nineteenth century, while the basis of the system of labour relations in force in January 1933 had been laid during the first year of the Weimar Republic. Three separate trade-union organizations had established themselves: the so-called Free Trade Unions which were close to the Social Democratic Party and were by far the largest; the Catholic Christian Trade Unions which were quite influential in the predominantly Catholic industrial areas such as the Rhineland and were close to the Centre Party; and finally, the small Hirsch-Düncker unions traditionally linked with the Liberals. These divisions within the trade-union movement were to weaken it in the face of Nazism.

Before 1914, both employers and the State refused to recognize independent trade unions as proper representative bodies of the working class. They encouraged so-called 'yellow' or company unions. However, by 1916, the need to win the cooperation of workers for the war effort had set in motion a trend by which, under pressure from the military authorities, employers were obliged to come to terms with the trade unions and grant them a measure of participation in the running of their plants.

At the end of 1918, under the pressure of the revolution, this trend culminated in official recognition, first by the employers and then by the State, of the trade unions as the competent representatives of the workers and of their right to participate in the regulation of wages and working conditions through the conclusion of collective agreements with employers. At the same time, the employees' right to strike and the employers' right to lock workers out were both recognized. The workers' right to join trade unions was incorporated in the Weimar Constitution of 1919 and in the same year workers were guaranteed a measure of participation in the running of their plants through the establishment by law of works councils, on which both workers and employers were represented. The workers' representatives were freely elected by the employees of the plant. Finally, a system of labour courts was subsequently established to deal with disputes. This, then, was the system which confronted the Nazis on their take-over of power and which they were determined to destroy. They struck first at the Trade Unions.

(ii) The Destruction of the Trade Unions

During March 1933, as part of the Nazi campaign against the Left, a number of Free Trade Union offices were ransacked by the SA and many of their officials were arrested and beaten up.[29] Furthermore, during March many

---

[29]See above, pp. 146–50.

leading Socialists and Communists were purged from works councils in factories by the SA and the NSBO. Despite their pressure, in the works council elections in March NSBO candidates still only won 25 per cent of the vote. The regime was therefore obliged to take official action to coordinate works councils. On 4 April, Nazi control over works councils was ensured by the Law on Plant Representative Councils and Business Organizations which enabled the authorities to postpone elections until 30 September and meanwhile to purge the councils of 'members who are opposed to the spirit of the State and the economy'.

Yet even in April 1933 some trade-union leaders still hoped that the purge would be restricted to political organizations and that they would be able to come to an arrangement with the new regime by adopting a non-political stance. This attitude reflected an influential strand in trade-union thinking which had first manifested itself in the cooperation which the Free Trade Unions had given to the military authorities during the First World War. The Executive Committee of the umbrella organization of the Free Trade Unions offered its cooperation in reorganizing the trade unions, issuing the following statement on 9 April 1933:

219

Loyal to its duty to cooperate in the construction of a social order for the German people, in which the basic rights of the workers are secured in accordance with their national importance in the State and the economy, the General German Trade Union Federation[30] declares itself willing to place at the service of the new state the labour force's own organization which the trade unions have devoted years of activity to creating.

The trade unions recognize now as before that their own freedom of action must be limited by the higher law of the State acting in its role as the representative of the whole national community. The State must have the right to intervene to regulate and establish order within the economy; its duty is to create an economic constitution which binds the economic leadership to the fulfilment of overall economic obligations, because only in this way is it possible to achieve unity between the leadership of the State and of the economy.

The trade unions are therefore prepared to cooperate in the corporative structure of the German economy as planned by the Government in the conviction that, just as the Government decisively maintains the primacy of the Reich over the states, it will also ensure that the higher law of the needs of the economy as a whole will prevail over all tendencies towards disunity.

The ADGB welcomes the efforts to unify the trade unions. It will therefore gladly assist the new State in its attempt to carry out this unification and will put its experience at its disposal.

---

[30] The Allgemeiner Deutscher Gewerkschaftsbund (ADGB).

This reorganization of trade-union law will inevitably require new regulations for State supervision of the self-administration of the labour force.

In order to ensure both that the measures planned by the Government are uniformly carried out and that the trade unions can cooperate effectively, and in order to restore to the German workers and the German economy a sense of security which is necessary in the interests of the community as a whole, the Executive Committee of the ADGB recommends the appointment of a Reich Commissioner for the Trade Unions.

But the Nazis had no intention of compromising. It was essential that they should control the organization of labour. On 21 April 1933, plans were therefore drawn up to take over the trade unions which had already been weakened by the excesses of the 'revolution from below' in the previous month. Both planning and execution were to be carried out by the Party under the supervision of Dr Robert Ley, the head of the so-called Political Organization of the Party, who issued the following instructions:

220

On Tuesday, 2 May 1933, the coordination [*Gleichschaltungsaktion*] of the Free Trade Unions will begin. . . .

The direction of the entire operation lies in the hands of the Action Committee. . . .

The essential part of the operation is to be directed against the General German Trade Union Federation (ADGB) and the General Independent Employees' Federation (AFA). Anything beyond that which concerns the Free Trade Unions is left to the discretion of the Gauleiters.

The Gauleiters are responsible for the establishment of coordination in the individual areas. Those concerned in the operation should be members of the National Socialist Factory Cell Organization.

SA as well as SS are to be employed for the occupation of trade-union properties and for taking into custody the people concerned.

The Gauleiters must proceed on the basis of the closest understanding with the appropriate *Gau* factory cell leaders.

The action in Berlin will be carried out by the Action Committee itself.

In the Reich the following will be occupied: the headquarters of the unions; the trade-union buildings and offices of the Free Trade Unions; the party buildings of the Social Democratic Party of Germany in so far as trade unions are lodged there; the branches and pay offices of the Bank for Workers, Employees and Officials, Ltd; the district and local committees of the General German Trade Union Federation and of the General Independent Employees' Federation.

The following are to be taken into protective custody: all trade-union chairmen; the district secretaries and the branch managers of the Bank for Workers, Employees and Officials, Ltd.

The chairmen of local committees as well as the employees of unions are not be taken into protective custody but are to be urged to continue their work.

Exceptions are to be made only with the permission of the Gauleiters.

The taking over of the independent trade unions must proceed in such a way that the workers and employees will not be given the impression that this action is aimed at them, but, on the contrary, at a superannuated system which does not conform with the interests of the German nation.

The provisional local leadership of the General German Trade Union and of the General Independent Employees' Federation is to be taken over by a commissioner of the National Socialist Factory Cells Organization.

Negotiations with the authorities and other organizations are to be immediately put into the hands of the newly installed commissioners.

All funds and accounts of the independent trade unions are to be blocked immediately and to remain so until Thursday afternoon 1800 hours. In so far as incumbent cashiers are permitted to remain in office they will be subject to the authority of a commissioner. All receipts for payments must be countersigned by the commissioner.

After lifting the blocking of the funds, the usual payments for the support of individuals must be unconditionally assured, to avoid creating a feeling of uneasiness among members of the trade unions.

Mass meetings are to be arranged as soon as possible, to be freely attended by all trade-union members. In these meetings the significance of the action must be explained and it must be pointed out that the rights of the workers and employees are being unconditionally guaranteed . . . .

It must be understood that this operation is to proceed in a highly disciplined fashion. The Gauleiters are responsible for this: they are to keep the direction of the operation firmly in hand.

The Nazis disguised their intentions with a propaganda campaign stressing their sympathy with the workers. On 1 May, this culminated in massive parades in which employers and workers marched together and a big speech by Hitler to celebrate May Day, traditionally a Socialist festival and now turned by the Nazis for the first time into an official day of national celebration. Next day, detachments from the various Nazi organizations occupied the Free Trade Union offices throughout the Reich, confiscated their funds and arrested their leaders. Ley then issued a proclamation in which he frankly recognized that support from the workers for the new regime was inadequate:

221

German workers and employees! Working people in town and country! The bells have rung in honour of work. The entire German nation has sung the praises of the working man with a strength and an enthusiasm without precedent and thus has done honour to itself and the creative spirit. The wheels stopped. The sound of the anvil was not heard. The miner came out of his mine. Everybody had a holiday.

What trade unions of all shades, red and black, Christian and 'free' have not even come near to achieving, what even at the height of Marxism was only a shadow, a feeble, miserable imitation compared to the gigantic thing of yesterday, National Socialism has achieved at its first attempt.

It puts the worker and the peasant, the artisan and the employee, in short all working people, at the centre of its thought and action and therewith at the centre of the State, and it renders the grabbers and the functionaries harmless. Well, who was that servant of capitalism, that reactionary who was out to oppress you and rob you of your rights? Was it those red criminals who for years have abused you, well-meaning, honest and decent German workers, in order to deprive you and with you the whole German people of your rights? or we, who amidst unspeakable suffering and sacrifices fought against these insane and crazy ideas of devilish Jews and their cronies? Three months of National Socialist Government have already proved to you: Adolf Hitler is your friend! Adolf Hitler struggles for your liberty! Adolf Hitler gives you bread!

Today we are opening the second chapter of the National Socialist revolution. You may say, You have absolute power; what more do you want? True, we have power, but we do not yet have the whole nation, we do not have you workers 100 per cent; and it is you whom we want. We will not let you alone until you give us your entire and genuine support. You too shall be freed from the last Marxist manacles, so that you may find your way to your people.

For we know that without the German worker there is no German nation. And above all we must prevent your enemy, Marxism and its satellites, from stabbing you again in the back. . . . It is not as if we wanted to disrupt and destroy the unions. On the contrary, we have never disturbed anything which has, in any way, value for our people and we shall never do so in the future; that is a rule of National Socialism. This certainly goes for the unions which serve with hard work and were built up by the pennies taken from the pockets of the workers. No, workers! Your institutions are sacred to us National Socialists. I am myself the son of a poor peasant and I know what poverty is. I myself spent seven years in one of the biggest industries in Germany[31] and I know the exploitation of anonymous capital; above all I know its stingy commercial methods of business, for in 1928 I was sacked for my opinions.

Workers, I swear to you we shall not only preserve everything which exists, we shall build up even further the protection of the worker's rights, so that he can enter the new National Socialist State as a completely worthwhile and respected member of the nation.

Workers and peasants on a broad front, together with the professions and skilled labour—in this way we shall build a new Reich of well-being, honour and freedom. Forward with Hitler for Germany!

For this action there was no legal foundation whatever. But, two days later, the following 'official statement' appeared in the Party paper, the *Völkischer Beobachter*. An action was also brought against the leaders of the trade unions which enabled a warrant to be issued for confiscation of trade-union property. It is one of the first examples of what was to become

---

[31] Ley had been an industrial chemist with IG-Farben.

a common practice in the Third Reich—the retroactive legitimizing of arbitrary actions.

222

According to official sources, the action taken against the Free Trade Unions corresponds completely with the struggle against Marxism which has been proclaimed by the Führer, Adolf Hitler. The Reich Government believes that Marxism must not be allowed to hide behind the trade unions and to continue the struggle in disguise. The measures were not directed against the workers as such, but were aimed at guaranteeing to the workers their money and their full rights.

A few days later, the Hirsch-Düncker unions 'voluntarily' subordinated themselves to Ley's Action Committee. The Christian Trade Unions were spared for a time because of the intention of reaching a Concordat with the Vatican. At the end of June, however, when the Concordat had been secured, under its terms they too were disbanded. In the meantime, on 6 May, Ley had announced the creation of a new organization, the German Labour Front (*Deutsche Arbeitsfront*).

(iii) The organization of German Labour: the Trustees of Labour and the German Labour Front

The Nazi Factory Cells Organization (NSBO) tended to contain the most socially radical elements in the Party and now its leaders attempted to exploit their new power to force wage concessions from employers, to compel them to dismiss Social Democrat workers and replace them with unemployed Nazis, and generally to interfere with management. This activity, however, provoked the hostility of business which had no desire to see pressure from the Trade Unions replaced by pressure from the NSBO. Fearing that such radicalism would jeopardize economic recovery and the armaments programme, the Nazi leadership was obliged to cooperate with the state bureaucracy and the employers in resisting populist pressure from the Nazi movement. On 19 May 1933, therefore, the Law on Trustees of Labour transferred the ultimate authority for the regulation of wages, previously settled between the trade unions and the employers in the form of binding collective agreements, to new *State* officials—the Reich Trustees of Labour. There were twelve of these, each covering a separate district and they were subordinate to the Reich Ministry of Labour. Those appointed to the new posts were largely a mixture of officials from the federal states and lawyers associated with employers' organizations:

223

I 1. The Reich Chancellor appoints Trustees of Labour for the large economic regions upon the proposal of the competent state governments and in agreement with them.

2. The Reich Labour Minister will assign the Trustees either to the participating state governments, if they agree, or to the Reich authorities.

II The Trustees are to regulate the conditions for the conclusion of labour contracts pending a new revision of the social constitution. This practice is to be legally binding on all persons and replaces the system founded on combinations of workers, on individual employers, or on combinations of employers...

2. Moreover, the Trustees are also to supervise the maintenance of peace between employers and labour.

3. Furthermore, they are to be convoked for their cooperation in the preparation of a new social constitution.

III The Trustees are empowered to request aid from the competent Reich and state authorities for the enforcement of their regulations. They should contact the state government or one of its designated authorities before carrying out their measures, even though there is a danger of delay.

IV The Trustees of Labour are bound by the directives and decrees of the Reich Government.

V The Reich Minister of Labour in agreement with the Reich Minister of Economics will issue the necessary regulations for the enforcement of this law.

This law represents another example of the reaction against the Party's 'revolution from below' and typically it took the form of strengthening the State authorities and of regulating their position by legislation. At this period one of the main tasks of the Trustees was to intervene to prevent interference by the NSBO officials in labour disputes, as in the following case:

224

Düsseldorf-Oberkassel, 23 March 1934 Theodor Hutmacher, Assistant to the Trustee of Labour for the Economic Area Westphalia and Branch Leader of the Western branch in Gau *Düsseldorf*

To the Reich Chancellor Adolf Hitler

My Führer!

On starting work this morning, I received the confidential information that the Trustee of Labour for the Westphalia district, Dr Klein, has been transferred to Bremen by the Reich Minister of Labour. I consider this extremely dangerous for the future of the state.

Before the take-over of power, I worked in various ironworks and foundries, and was simultaneously a political leader in a Communist stronghold in *Gau* Düsseldorf. From my observations during the prewar, war, and postwar periods and the present, I think I have gained enough experience to be a good judge of affairs. After the take-over of power, I was commissioner of the Chamber of Industry and Trade in Düsseldorf and was in charge of Jewish affairs and foreign-exchange questions. I carried out these tasks under the guidance of Dr Klein and in collaboration with the *Gau* leadership, in accordance with the new regime, and in the spirit of my Führer as well as that of my local National Socialist leaders. With the introduction of the Trustees of Labour, Party comrade Dr Klein summoned me and transferred to me all labour questions in so far as they still needed to be dealt with. For ten months, the Trustees of Labour and I have stood between the devil and the deep blue sea: workers on one side, employers on the other.

The law of 19 May concerning the Trustees of Labour was very vague [*dehnbar*] and, by summoning all his strength and working day and night, Dr Klein mastered the growing disorder which was often reminiscent of class war. Since I alone intervened in disputes throughout the whole economic district of Düsseldorf, I am the best judge of how dangerous it is for the National Socialist State and for peace and order to remove the authority which Dr Klein represents and his knowledge and ability which has served the workers and the economic leadership. This would involve the danger of the non-National Socialist workers and a section of the employers again getting the upper hand. Frequently I came out of negotiations in which strikes and demonstrations were threatened. I rarely met a workers' leader who did not demand the arrest of his employer right at the start of negotiations, the moment after he had greeted me. During night-long negotiations in the Ruhr area I often had to threaten the NSBO agents and works council chairman with the Gestapo in order to achieve peace and order in the labour sphere. My conception of my duty, which was drummed into me by Dr Klein, has made me the worker most hated by the NSBO and the DAF far beyond the boundaries of the Düsseldorf district.

In the NSBO, which usually took part in negotiations between leader and retinue,[32] I found still, to a frightening degree, the spirit of pure class war. But I always managed with Dr Klein's help to keep it in check so that we obtained the best results for the State, the economy, as well as for the retinue. I have often sat in shabby clothes among miners in the Ruhr area, accompanied them on their way to and from the pit (as if I was looking for work) in order to find out the mood of these people. They have faith in our Führer all right but they often do not know how to give it expression. I fear that if Dr Klein is moved, these people, under new leadership, will fall back into the old ideas just as Marxism would have it: living well and sacrificing nothing.

In March 1933, I was elected a city councillor in Düsseldorf and, as the representative of the workers, I signed the letter conferring honorary citizenship on my Führer. Shortly afterwards, I was forced willy-nilly away from the task allotted me by having largely to take the side of the employers because the class war spirit on the part of the retinue threatened to ruin the economy and therefore people's jobs. . . .

---

[32] *Gefolgschaft*, i.e. the employees in the factory; see below, p. 342.

The problem of how to organize labour was serious. The radicalism of the NSBO during 1933, springing partly from its need to demonstrate its effectiveness to the working class, was alienating business. The founding of the German Labour Front (DAF) on 6 May had been largely a response to the need to provide some kind of substitute for the Trade Unions and to neutralize the NSBO. The following account by Ley of its first few months, given in a speech to the Fifth Annual Congress on 11 September 1937, while clearly somewhat exaggerated for effect, gives a good insight into the *ad hoc* way in which the Nazi regime established itself. There was no coherent planning; ideas were taken up and dropped in response to the requirements of a developing situation; individuals were given jobs to do and had to see what they could make of them with little or no guidance from Hitler:

225

When, in April 1933, I received the order from the Führer to take over the trade unions, I did not receive it because I was an expert on the trade unions. I hardly knew how many trade unions there were and I did not know the differences between them. I knew least of all about the way in which they were financed, about their structure and about their economic enterprises. In a word, I went there as a layman and I think I was myself more surprised than anyone to have been given the job. It was not as if we had a complete programme that we could haul out and according to which we could set up the Labour Front. Instead I received the Führer's order to take over the trade unions and then I had to see what I could make of it.

As you know, we were not given a legal status, we were not integrated in the State in any way. On the contrary, after the take-over of the trade unions I went to the Führer a few days later to report that I had taken over all the trade unions. When I said it was now time for us to receive a legal status and be recognized by the State as the Labour Front, the Führer replied in his benevolent, fatherly way: 'Let us wait and see what becomes of this changeling.' He did not want to give legal status to a chaos that was not yet sorted out, he did not want to create a public corporation with a constitution and statutes. The Führer indicated that this had to develop first.

I can say to you frankly, party comrades, that I felt embittered and defeated then because I saw how everyone else was getting laws and then developing their organizations on the basis of these laws. I almost thought at the time that the Führer mistrusted me since he did not give me the same.

When we took over the trade unions, what did we find, what was there in existence?

Ideologically speaking, the class war was anchored in the trade unions and the trade unions lived off this. On the one side stood the employers' associations, on the other side the employees' associations. The whole thing was seen as ordained by God. Nobody would ever have doubted that the Lord himself wanted it this way and that this could not be changed, that this was a natural law: that there were classes, that one had to recognize these classes, that they fight one another and that they each had to represent their interests as parties confronting one another.

Ideologically speaking, that was the state of affairs which we found. Apart from that, there was ideological chaos and muddled ideas about a corporate system. This was true of all of us. It only needed two National Socialists to meet and talk about the corporate system and there were bound to be ten different opinions, because each of these two had so many opinions on the corporate system. In practice, I have never met two National Socialists who were of one opinion on the corporate system. It was a real catastrophe in June and July 1933. I can tell you I did not sleep for several nights on account of the corporate system because I could not make head or tail of it and I began to believe I was more stupid than the others. But I did not want to accept this. So I bought all sorts of coloured pencils and made drawings and plans for days and nights on end. There were conferences. The others kept quiet and pretended to be unwilling to reveal their knowledge. They pretended to be very clever.

This corporate system turned out to be an absolute chaos of ideas, a complete muddle. I then tried to study Othmar Spann.[33] But he is unclear and confused like Marx. It is the language of the Jew, the old Moses which no German can understand. It is the language of Bolshevism and the Jew, the language of the Jesuit, the language and learning of Jesuit Rome which he speaks, mixed up with bits of National Socialist thought, of completeness and unity, and then again with Marxist thought, in short, a philosophical muddle which nobody understands. In a word, I was very unhappy during those days of June, July and August 1933.

As a third source of ideas, there was the NSBO, a Party institution, the factory cell organization. I must confess that until then I had dealt with it only on business. It was subordinate to me in my function as inspector under Strasser and I had the task of supervising it, of authorizing or not authorizing circulars and of supervising the finances, etc. I did not do all these things with great enthusiasm. Something prevented me from taking it seriously. Now I know what stopped me then. I can tell you today: the NSBO was, ideologically speaking, just as badly constructed. It did not fit into our National Socialist ideology and it was intentionally constructed like that by Herr Strasser. It was intended to become his power base and serve his treason. So he vetoed employers joining it. If it is intended to be a factory cell the employer must of course be represented as well. That is quite clear.

Thus the NSBO was essentially founded on the lines of the class war just like the trade unions. There was no difference of thought and ideology. People said it should be set up in the factories as a rival undertaking to the trade unions. I do not want to detract from the tremendous value which the NSBO had for our struggle. On the contrary, I would like here to sing the praises of all the men and women in the factories who took upon themselves a martyrdom of suffering during the time of struggle, who as individual NSBO members sometimes stood up to a horde of Marxists and who fought tenaciously and fanatically. But that does not prevent one from recognizing that the NSBO did *not* represent the ideology we National Socialists represent and must represent.

So at that time I found: the class struggle in its purest form, represented by the trade unions and employers' associations; a corporate structure, that is to say,

---

[33] An Austrian professor who advocated the corporate system.

essentially the class struggle, only in a different disguise; and the attempt by Strasser to introduce this divisive trade union element into the Party via the NSBO...

Employers were, however, concerned that in the DAF, and above all in the NSBO, they might be facing a new form of trade union, which could use the forces of the new regime—the SA or even the Gestapo—to impose its will more effectively than the old trade unions. In their hostility to the NSBO they had the support of the ministerial bureaucracy. Both employers and civil servants wanted to neutralize the working class completely. The Nazi leadership, however, while anxious to secure the cooperation of the employers for its rearmament programme, could not afford totally to ignore the workers, nor could they rely simply on represssion.

The solution reached was to purge the NSBO of its radical elements and totally subordinate it to the DAF. Moreover, in future the DAF was to incorporate the employers as well as the workers, thereby turning it into a symbol of the 'national community' or, in Hitler's own words, an 'honest broker' between the classes promoting social harmony. On 27 November 1933, Ley was obliged to reach a compromise with the bureaucracy and industry in which the role of the DAF was very narrowly defined. It was enshrined in the following agreement signed by Ley, on the one hand, and the Reich Ministries of Labour (Seldte), Economics (Schmitt), and Hitler's representative for economic affairs (Keppler) on the other:

226

The German Labour Front is the organization for all working people without reference to their economic and social position. Within it workers will stand side by side with employers, no longer separated into groups and associations which serve to maintain special economic or social distinctions or interests. The value of personality, no matter whether of worker or employer, shall be the determining factor in the German Labour Front.

In accordance with the will of our Führer, Adolf Hitler, the German Labour Front is not the place for deciding the material questions of daily working life, or for harmonizing the natural differences of interest between individual workpeople.

Methods of procedure will soon be formulated to regulate work conditions which will assign both to the leader and to the retinue of a plant the position prescribed to each by the National Socialist ideology.

The high aim of the Labour Front is to educate all Germans who are at work to support the National Socialist State and to indoctrinate them in the National Socialist mentality. In particular, it undertakes the indoctrination of those people who are called upon to play an influential part in the plant in the organs of the social constitution, the labour courts, and social insurance....

On 7 December 1933, the principles contained in this agreement were embodied in a reorganization of the DAF. It was now structured both regionally and according to branches of industry, trade, and commerce. A regional cadre organization was developed alongside that of the Party cadre (PO) with the DAF leadership at the various levels (Gau, district, branch) integrated with that of the PO which was of course organizationally already subordinate to Ley as Chief of Staff of the PO/Reich Head of Organization. The 'coordinated' blue- and white-collar unions, which had hitherto formed the core of the DAF were abolished and replaced by so-called Reich Plant Communities for the various sections of industry, trade and commerce which contained both employers and employees.

The 'methods of procedure' to regulate work conditions, mentioned in the November agreement, found expression in the Law for the Ordering of National Labour of 20 January 1934, which became the basic law governing labour in the Third Reich. It was drawn up by the Ministry of Labour in consultation with the Ministry of Economics. Apart from strengthening the hand of the Ministry of Labour, it was also shaped by the interests of the employers. The civil servant in the Ministry of Labour responsible for drafting it, Dr Werner Mansfeld, had previously worked for an association representing the interests of mine-owners. Significantly, the Party, including the DAF, had no part in its formulation:

227

SECTION I: THE LEADER OF THE PLANT AND THE COUNCIL OF TRUST

1 The employer works in the factory as leader of the plant, together with the employees and workers who constitute his retinue, to further the aims of the plant and for the common benefit of nation and State.

2 1. The plant leader makes the decisions for the retinue in all matters concerning the plant in so far as they are regulated by this law.
2. He is responsible for the well-being of the retinue. The retinue owe him loyalty according to the principles of the plant community....

5 1. Councillors of Trust recruited from the retinue act in an advisory capacity to the leader of a plant with as a rule at least twenty employees. They constitute, with the leader and under his direction, the Council of Trust of the plant.
2. Those persons who do piecework at home, and who work primarily for the same plant either alone or with their families, also count as retinue in the meaning of the regulations concerning the Council of Trust.

6 1. It is the duty of the Council of Trust to increase the mutual confidence within the plant community.
2. It is the task of the Council of Trust to discuss all measures concerning the improvement of output, the form and enforcement of the general conditions of

labour especially the plant regulations, the enforcement and improvement of safety measures, the strengthening of the ties between the members of the plant themselves and their ties with the plant, as well as the welfare of all members of the community. Furthermore, it is their task to resolve all disputes within the plant community. Their views must also be heard before any decision on punishment for the violation of the plant rules.

3. The Council of Trust can charge certain Councillors of Trust with the carrying out of certain of its tasks. . . .

9 1. Every year in March the leader of the plant, in collaboration with the representative of the National Socialist Factory Cell Organization, shall make a list of the Councillors of Trust and their deputies. Thereupon the retinue shall vote on the list in secret ballot.

2. If there is no agreement between the leader of the plant and the representative of the National Socialist Factory Cell Organization as to who shall be proposed as Councillors of Trust and their deputies or if a Council of Trust is not formed for other reasons, in particular if the retinue does not agree to the list, the Trustee of Labour can appoint the requisite number of Councillors of Trust and deputies. . . .

14 The Trustee of Labour can recall a Councillor of Trust on the grounds of professional or personal unsuitabililty.

16 A majority of the Council of Trust of a plant can without delay appeal in writing to the Trustee of Labour against decisions of the plant leader concerning the formulation of the general conditions of employment and in particular regarding the establishment of rules (Article 6), provided the decisions appear to be incompatible with the economic or social situation of the plant. The effectiveness of the decision made by the plant leader will not be impaired by the appeal. . . .

SECTION II: TRUSTEES OF LABOUR

18 1. Trustees of Labour shall be appointed for large economic regions of which the boundaries shall be fixed by the Reich Minister of Labour in cooperation with the Reich Minister of Economics and the Reich Minister of the Interior. They shall be Reich officials and shall be under the supervision of the Reich Minister of Labour. The Reich Minister of Labour in conjunction with the Reich Minister of Economics shall decide on their headquarters.

2. The Trustees of Labour are bound by the directives instructions of the Reich Government.

19 The Trustees of Labour shall ensure industrial peace. In order to fulfil this task they shall carry out the following:

1. They shall supervise the setting up and operation of the Councils of Trust and give decisions where disputes occur.

2. They shall appoint Councillors of Trust for plants and remove them from office in accordance with subsection (2) of Article 9, subsection (2) of Article 14, and Article 15. [Article 15: The Labour Trustee appoints new Councillors of Trust when no more substitutes are available.]

3. They shall decide appeals from Councils of Trust in accordance with Article 16.

4. They shall decide proposed dismissals in accordance with Article 20 [requiring the employer to inform the Trustee of redundancies of more than 10 per cent of the labour force].

5. They shall supervise the observance of the provisions regarding the plant rules (Articles 26ff.).

6. They shall lay down principles and collective rules under the conditions specified in Article 32 [giving the Trustees the right to fix minimum conditions of employment].

7. They shall cooperate in the exercise of jurisdiction of the Courts of Social Honour (in accordance with Articles 35ff.).

8. They shall keep the Reich Government informed regarding the development of social policy in accordance with detailed instructions issued by the Reich Minister of Labour and the Reich Minister of Economics....

22 1. Anyone who repeatedly and wilfully contravenes the written instructions of the Trustee of Labour, which have been issued in the course of his duties, will be punished with a fine; in particularly serious cases a prison sentence may be imposed in place of the fine or in combination with it...

SECTION III: PLANT REGULATIONS AND WAGE REGULATIONS

26 In every plant in which there are as a rule at least twenty employees and workers the plant leader shall issue in writing plant regulations for the retinue of the plant (Article 1).

27 (1) The following conditions of employment are to be included in the plant regulations:

1. the beginning and ending of the normal daily hours of work and of the breaks;

2. the times for the payment of remuneration and the nature thereof;

3. the principles for the calculation of piece or contract work, if work is done on a piece or contract basis in the plant;

4. regulations on the nature, amount and collection of fines if provision is made for them;

5. the grounds on which employment can be terminated without notice, in cases where this does not rest on statutory grounds;

6. the utilization of remuneration forfeited by the unlawful termination of employment in cases where the said forfeiture is prescribed in the plant regulations or in the contract of employment or in statutory provisions.

(2) In so far as regulations on the compulsory content of the plant regulations going beyond the instructions of subsection (1) are contained in other legislation or decrees, they retain their validity.

(3) Apart from the rules required by law, rules on the amount of remuneration and on other aspects of employment can be included in the plant regulations, as well as rules on discipline in the plant, the behaviour of the employees in the plant, the improvement of safety etc.

28 (1) The imposition of penalties on employees is permitted only for offences against the discipline or security of the plant. Financial penalties must not exceed half the average daily earnings; but for serious and specified offences of up to the full amount of the daily earnings may be imposed. The Reich Minister of Labour determines how the fines are to be utilized.

(2) The penalties are imposed by the plant leader or a person designated by him after consultation with the Council of Trust (Article 6), if there is one.

SECTION IV: THE JURISDICTION OF THE COURTS OF SOCIAL HONOUR

36 (1) Serious breaches of the social duties based on the plant community will be dealt with in the Courts of Honour as offences against social honour. Such offences shall be deemed to have been committed in the following cases:
1. when an employer, a plant leader or any other person in a supervisory capacity abuses his authority in a plant by maliciously exploiting the labour of any member of his retinue or by wounding his sense of honour;
2. when a member of the retinue endangers industrial peace in the plant by maliciously provoking other members of the retinue, and in particular when a Councillor of Trust wilfully interferes unduly in the conduct of the plant or continually and maliciously disturbs the community spirit within the plant community;
3. when a member of the plant community repeatedly makes frivolous and unjustifiable complaints or applications to the Trustees of Labour or obstinately disobeys instructions given to him in writing;
4. when a member of the Council of Trust reveals without authority any confidential information or technical or business secrets which have become known to him in the performance of his duties and have been specified as confidential matters.
(2) Civil servants and soldiers are not subject to the jurisdiction of the Courts of Social Honour...

41 (1) Breaches of social honour are to be judged on the application of the Trustee of Labour by a Court of Social Honour which is to be set up for each district in which there is a Trustee of Labour.
(2) The Court of Social Honour is to be composed of a member of the judiciary, appointed by the Reich Minister of Justice in cooperation with the Reich Minister of Labour, as chairman, and a leader of a plant and a Councillor of Trust as assessors. Leaders of plants and Councillors of Trust are to be chosen from short lists drawn up by the German Labour Front in accordance with Article 23; they are to be chosen in the order in which they appear, though it is desirable that persons should be chosen who are in the same line of business as the accused....

Influenced by a contradictory mixture of paternalist traditions characteristic of such conservative bosses as the Krupps, modern management techniques, and Romantic notions of social organizations current among Conservative intellectuals, the main aim of the new law was to create a new system of labour relations based on the concept of the individual 'plant community' (*Betriebsgemeinschaft*), formed by the 'plant leader' (employer) and his 'retinue' (the employees). Hitherto, relations between employer and employee had been based on contracts of employment which were legally enforceable and which regarded both sides as equal before the law. The conditions of employment contained in these contracts were normally agreed between employers' organizations and trade unions and defined in collective agreements covering all the plants in a particular branch of industry. The new law replaced the relationship of legal equality between employer and employee by a quasi-feudal relationship of leader and retinue based on mutual obligations as members of the Plant Community. The theory was that in place of the conflict between employer and employee there would be mutual trust and cooperation based on the common ethic of the National Socialist *Weltanschauung*. In practice, of course, the law greatly strengthened the hands of the employer at the expense of the employee, reflecting the determination of the employers to restore the position of 'master in their own house' which they had held before the rise of trade union power after 1918.

The employer could now draw up his own plant regulations whilst the Councils of Trust were only a pale reflection of the works councils they replaced. Furthermore, when in 1935 the results of the elections to these Councils proved unsatisfactory even this feeble form of workers' representation was rendered completely sterile by the repeated postponement of elections to the councils, until in 1938 they were postponed indefinitely. Finally, breaches of the assumed mutual trust between plant leader and retinue were no longer dealt with by Labour Courts but by the new Courts of Honour. The worker no longer had a legal right of redress but only a 'claim of honour' which he could no longer enforce himself or through his trade union but only via his local Trustee of Labour. In so far as they were used to protect workers, these courts acted mainly against small businessmen and artisans, where conditions tended to be particularly bad, and even then only in glaring cases of injustice such as the physical ill-treatment of apprentices. Out of a labour force of over 20 million only 516 cases were brought to the Courts in the years 1934–36 and of these only just over 300 ended with a definite penalty.

The powers of the Reich Trustees of Labour were strengthened and they were given the final decision on most matters. The intention was, however, that they should only intervene as a last resort where it proved impossible to reconcile conflicts within individual plants, or where employers created serious unrest by the abuse of their new powers. They were to act as a kind of safety net of state arbitration in the event of the failure of the 'plant community' to overcome class conflict. In practice, however their main role was to be in the wages field.

The DAF was given no official responsibilities by this law apart from the participation of the DAF shop steward in the drawing up of the list of 'councillors of trust'. The law was, therefore, deeply resented by the DAF as a sell-out to industry and the bureaucracy i.e. to non-Party elements. Ley, therefore, decided to seek the backing of Hitler and, by-passing official channels, persuaded him to issue the following Decree on the Nature and Goals of the Labour Front dated 24 October 1934:

228

1. The German Labour Front is the organization of creative Germans of brain and fist.

In particular, the members of the former trade unions, the former white-collar workers' unions and the former employers' organizations are united in it as members with equal rights.

Membership in professional, social, economic or ideological organizations cannot be a substitute for membership in the German Labour Front.

The Chancellor of the Reich can decreee that professional [*ständisch*] organizations which have been recognized by law belong corporatively to the German Labour Front.

2. The goal of the German Labour Front is to create a true national and productive community of all Germans.

Its task is to see that every single individual can take his place in the economic life of the nation in an intellectual or physical condition which enables him to work as effectively as possible, thereby ensuring the maximum benefit for the national community.

3. The German Labour Front is a branch of the NSDAP in the meaning of the Law for Securing the Unity of Party and State, issued on 1 December 1933.

4. The leadership of the German labour Front is the responsibility of the NSDAP.

The Reich Organization Leader[34] is the leader of the German Labour Front. He is appointed by the Führer and Reich Chancellor.

He appoints and dismisses the other leaders of the German Labour Front.

These posts should be given in the first instance to members of the existing branches of the NSBO and of the NS. Hago[35] which are in the NSDAP, and further to members of the SA and SS.

5. The regional organization of the Labour Front corresponds to that of the NSDAP.

The goal of an organic order as laid down in the programme of the NSDAP determines the professional organization of the German Labour Front. . . .

7. The German Labour Front has to secure labour peace by evoking sympathy among the plant leaders for the justified claims of their retinue and appreciation among the retinue for the position of their plant and what is practicable for it.

The German Labour Front has the task of finding the balance between the just interests of all participants which is in accordance with the basic principles of National Socialism and which reduces the number of cases which are to be referred to the state agencies which are solely responsible according to the law of 20 January 1934.

The representation of all the participants which is necessary for the process of conciliation is the exclusive task of the German Labour Front. It is prohibited to create other organizations in this field or to permit their activities.

---

[34] Until 12 November 1934 'The Chief of Staff of the Political Organization'—merely a change of title.
[35] *Nationalsozialistische Handwerks-, Handels- und Gewerbe-organisation*: the National Socialist Craft and Trade Organization.

8. The German Labour Front is responsible for the National Socialist Organization, 'Strength through Joy'.[36]

This characteristically vague degree potentially gave the DAF a wide-ranging role in the sphere of labour relations and social policy, thereby contradicting the provisions of the Law of 24 January. However, since it had not been discussed, let alone approved, by the ministries affected (Labour and Economics) or by Hess's office, it immediately provoked strong protests from all of them. At this stage, Hitler was anxious not to antagonize Schacht or industry and was obliged to retreat. He did not withdraw the order, for this would have been too great a blow to his prestige. It was merely ignored from then onwards with the tacit approval of Hitler, although Ley referred to it from time to time to try and legitimize the expansion of the DAF's role in social policy.

The DAF did in fact develop a remarkable dynamic fuelled by a combination of Ley's strong personal ambition, organizational momentum, and the total claims of Nazi ideology. Ley was not prepared to play a subordinate role to industry and the State bureaucracy. In his view, its responsibilities vis-à-vis labour required the DAF not only to play the dominant part in the whole sphere of social policy but, in view of the inter-relationship of economic and social policy, to participate fully in the shaping of economic policy as well. Thus, he was determined to ensure for the DAF the all-embracing role envisaged by the October 1934 decree. In 1936, he issued a commentary to the decree which re-emphasised the Labour Front's claim to total authority in the economic sphere. In 1938, he went even further and tried to claim for the DAF a position which would have usurped that of the Party itself. On this occasion, however, he only succeeded in uniting against him all the other leading figures in Party and State and, as a result, this most ambitious attempt to expand his authority failed.

Nevertheless, despite setbacks, the vast organization of the DAF with its insatiable appetite for responsibilities in the socio-economic field, which were rationalised in ideological terms, created its own momentum. It had begun with a sound financial basis in the shape of the funds confiscated from the trade unions. Although membership was in theory voluntary, by the end of the 1930s pressure from the employers and the authorities made it virtually compulsory for the bulk of the labour force. By 1939, its annual income from membership dues was 539 million RM, more than three times the income of the Nazi Party itself. It had acquired a large business empire comprising banks, insurance companies, housing associations, and even a car plant—the *Volkswagenwerk*. It had 44,500 paid functionaries who regarded themselves as the Party's representatives in the socio-economic sphere. They did not

---

[36] See below, pp. 346ff.

hesitate to apply pressure on employers whom they regarded as un-
cooperative, even if this meant exceeding their authority under the Law of
January 1934. On the other hand, they frequently sided with the employers
against labour where they felt workers were trying to assert an independent
voice in a potentially subversive way.

(iv) 'Beauty of Labour' and 'Strength through Joy'

The proclamation of 27 November 1933, had in effect allocated the DAF
the functions of ensuring harmony within the factories, increasing productivity for the sake of the rearmament drive, and in general reconciling the
working class to the loss of its freedom to organize itself and winning its
loyalty to the regime. But, in view of the overall priority of concentrating
the nation's resources on rearmament, there were strict limits to the extent
to which the DAF could seek working class support by pressing for
improved wages. It was obliged, therefore, to develop alternative induce-
ments to loyalty or at least acquiescence.

On 27 November 1933, Ley established two organizations within the
DAF 'Beauty of Labour' (*Schönheit der Arbeit*) and 'Strength through Joy'
(*Kraft durch Freude*).[37] The function of 'Beauty of Labour' was to persuade
employers to improve working conditions within factories. To this end, the
organization initiated a series of propaganda campaigns with the titles:
'Clean people in a clean plant', 'Greenery in the factories', 'Fight against
noise', 'Good lighting—good work', 'Good ventilation in the work place',
'Hot meals in the plant'. According to official estimates of the Labour Front
which, it was admitted, were not very adequate, these campaigns produced
the following results by 1939:

229

Total number of factory inspections	67,000
Improvements to work rooms	26,000
Improvements to factory yards and the creation of lawns	17,000
The provision of washing facilities and changing rooms	24,000
The provision of canteens and rest rooms	18,000
The provision of sports facilities	3,000

Total cost: RM 900 million

---

[37]Called at first 'After Work', following the Italian fascist organization, *Dopolavoro*, which was its model.

Much of this expenditure on improved facilities for the workforce would no doubt have occurred without the prompting of the 'Beauty of Labour' campaign, particularly in view of the competition between firms for labour from 1936 onwards. 'Strength through Joy' was to organize the leisure time of the labour force in the interests of the regime. This was carried out with the aim of ensuring maximum relaxation in order that the worker could return refreshed and therefore at his most efficient. It was also used to encourage a sense of egalitarianism and community spirit. This was intended to compensate for, and divert attention from, the regimentation of life, and to render more tolerable the inadequacy of the rise in wages which workers might have hoped for from the increase in national production since 1933, but which was ruled out by the paramount need to restrict consumption to permit rearmament. Much was made of the fact that thanks to 'Strength through Joy' ordinary people could now participate in luxury pursuits hitherto reserved for the rich such as sea cruises and the prospect of ownership of motor-cars (Hitler laid the foundation stone of the Volkswagen factory on 26 May 1938). Much was also made of the importance of sport as a means of encouraging both physical health and a 'healthy mental attitude'. In 1936 sports and physical training were introduced into factories and every youth in employment was obliged to spend two hours of his working week doing physical exercises. In the view of the Labour Front it was 'of great political importance that the community spirit associated with physical exercise can make a considerable contribution to the highest principle of National Socialist working life—the unity of the plant in the spirit of the plant community'.

The Labour Front also successfully exploited the personal ambitions of workers for the purposes of the regime. Thus the National Trades Competition, inaugurated in 1933 for apprentices and later expanded to adult workers, offered advancement to the able and ambitious, while simultaneously raising the standard of work all round, and thereby helping to provide the skilled workers so necessary for the rearmament programme.

Apart from the continual emphasis on 'performance', running through all the activities were two themes: the determination to submerge the individual in the mass (in Nazi terminology 'the community'), and, as a crucial aspect of this, an attempt to persuade workers to regard work not purely in material terms to finance their private activities, but in idealistic terms as a service to the community and therefore their highest duty in life, indeed the main reason for their existence. The Labour Front's continual endeavour to substitute psychological motivations for work in place of material motivations was an attempt to overcome the alienation of the modern industrial worker by submerging him first in the 'factory community' and then in the 'national community'. He was given a form of status instead of higher wages.

This was the essence of the Nazi conception of Socialism. Yet these 'communities' were in fact nothing but a mass of individuals manipulated by the organizations of the regime. It was hoped this would generate enormous poductive energy and simultaneously make the labour force a totally pliable instrument in the hands of the regime. The following documents from its official publications illustrate these various aspects of the Labour Front's activities.

230

Leisure-time activities organized by 'Strength through Joy' in 1934 and 1938

| | 1934 | | 1938 | |
	number	*participants*	*number*	*participants*
Concerts	1,020	576,594	5,291	2,515,598
Popular entertainments	725	285,037	54,813	13,666,015
Operas, operettas	959	540,841	12,407	6,639,067
Theatre	2,839	1,581,573	19,523	7,478,633
Variety, cabaret	1,315	481,855	7,921	3,518,833
Evening variety shows	3,189	1,228,457	10,989	4,462,140
Films	3,372	316,968	3,586	857,402
Exhibitions	72	237,632	555	1,595,516
Guided tours	1,528	90,242	676	58,472
Others	9,653	3,772,464	15,084	11,118,636
Events for the Autobahn workers	—	—	13,589	2,658,155
Total	24,672	9,111,663	144,434	54,568,467

231

Sports organized by 'Strength through Joy'

Type of course	1937	1938	of whom were female
Basic course	4,988,103	4,088,469	2,417,531
Special gymnastics	151,687	136,601	131,229
Light athletics	448,902	304,278	107,995
Swimming	1,809,873	1,582,427	710,416
Boxing, wrestling, etc.	208,762	203,252	8,415
Games	223,426	202,853	82,549
Water sports	19,393	9,641	5,399
Winter sports	53,839	92,631	55,656
Special sports	235,242	211,078	99,474
Youth in employment	1,262,267	3,004,071	140,720
Factory sports	—	12,297,026	2,048,200
Others (sailing, seaside resorts)	—	247,304	128,488
Total	9,401,494	22,379,631	5,936,072

232

Holidays and trips organized by 'Strength through Joy'

	participants 1934	1938
Vacation journeys	—[38]	1,447,972
Short trips	2,120,751	6,811,266
Cruises	61,151	131,623
Hikes	99,408	1,937,850

233

Motives behind the activities of the General Labour Front

If any institution of the National Socialist State has convinced the rest of the world that in Germany the national community and Socialism do not simply exist on paper but have become a living reality, it is the National Socialist Community 'Strength through Joy' [KdF]. One can no longer conceive of Germany without KdF as the expression of the affirmation of life of our people. Here I wish only to highlight a

---

[38] In fact, though no overall figure is available, the official record states that 'the first KdF vacation trains started on 17 February 1934. Twelve trains went to twelve different *Gaue*.'

few aspects of the work of KdF in order to deduce its basis and intentions from its effects, its aspirations from its achievements. German male and female workers are getting to know their homeland and the world through their holidays. The prerogatives of property over the beautiful things and comforts of life have been removed. It is no exaggeration to say that for millions of Germans KdF has made the world beautiful again and life worth living again. For reasons of self-preservation and in order to gain for itself the place among the nations appropriate to its greatness and befitting its achievements the German nation is compelled to make the fullest use of its labour resources. It is all the more necessary to ensure not only sufficient leisure time but also that this leisure time really enables the individual to relax. For this reason KdF ensures that everybody can travel, and entirely according to his own tastes, no matter whether the mountains or the sea provide him with greater relaxation. There is probably no better proof of the Socialist significance of the NS Community 'Strength through Joy' than the fact that hundreds of thousands have travelled into the wide world in our KdF ships. Not only has the KdF organized a travel and hiking programme but the idea of 'Beauty of Labour' has ensured that the factories are once more worthy of a human being. This too has a deeper significance. People can produce more in clean, airy and bright workplaces. . . .

One of the most important tasks of the German Labour Front is vocational training. Vocational training is not only a priority in view of the Four-Year Plan in order to make every working citizen into as valuable a worker for the nation as possible; it is also important for the individual. It is after all a fact that with few exceptions the man who gets on in life is the man who achieves the most. The few geniuses who starved because nobody recognized their importance are exceptions that merely prove the rule. It is well known that the German worker in particular has always felt a deep need to continue his studies because he has felt that he could only improve his social position by new achievements. In addition there is the current shortage of skilled workers. The German Labour Front has done, and is still doing, almost everything possible to alleviate this shortage. The establishment of training centres, the construction of training shops, the additional training of engineers and technicians, a comprehensive specialist press, the encouragement of technical colleges—these are the methods which the German Labour Front has adopted in the sphere of vocational training. The Reich Trades Competition, the Competition for German Factories, the programme for encouraging gifted people, the encouragement of the idea of craft work, also help to increase the productivity of our people. . . .

234

An improvement in status and working conditions as a substitute for wage increases

The Deputy Führer [Hess] began[39] by making the point that he was aware that some employees still hold against us the fact that, whereas we are always talking about the increase in production and the growth in the national product, our wages have not been correspondingly increased, so that in reality the employees are not sharing the fruits of this increase in production: 'I can only reply to them that the swimming

---

[39] At a meeting of the Reich Chamber of Labour, 30 April 1938.

pool in his plant, the canteens, the improvements in working conditions, all the advances in the social field which were endlessly described earlier [at the meeting], all these things are in the final analysis the result of the increase in production from which the individual benefits as part of the community. And the individual could only properly assess the significance for him of the increase in production if its main result, namely, the weapons of our forces, did not exist.'

It is therefore of great importance that we should assess the social position of the German worker, not on the basis of 'an increase in wages or no increase in wages', but from a consideration of what position the workers, the employees or the small tradesmen now hold within the national community. And in this case one need only go through Germany with one's eyes open to discover that the ordinary citizen can do things which in other countries are open only to a privileged class but never to the workers. . . .

235

A claim that 'Strength through Joy' was transforming social life

Out of the experience of the worker must be created the world picture of a new culture which is rooted in the living nationality [*Volkstum*]. Then the working man will become capable of recognizing his worth and he will be assisted in achieving an idealistic appreciation of his existence in the material sphere of life. The significance of his life must lie once more in work as the highest precept and the highest duty. Such an attitude will enable the individual to see his destiny in art as well. The work of 'Strength through Joy' is essentially the struggle for the soul of the worker, for leisure time and holidays presuppose the toil of the working day.

The comradely experience of work and the equally comradely community experience of leisure time belong together; in them lies the idea of social life itself. The 'Strength through Joy' land and sea trips mean far more than social travel in the normal sense: their value lies neither in the type of transport nor in the destination of the journey, but solely in the community experience. It is the great experience of nature which provides the best prerequisite for comradeship, so that one can say that these trips undertaken together and truly experienced represent the beginnings of a transformation of social life: a new type of culture is in process of being born. And by making the industrial and rural population aware of one another's style of life and needs one expands their vision and at the same time awakens the seeds of a culturally creative energy. . . .

How then did the workers respond to these programmes of 'Beauty of Labour' and 'Strength through Joy'? According to the reports of the SPD contact men in Germany to their headquarters in exile, the response was mixed. They appear to have been generally unimpressed with the Nazi community propaganda associated with the programmes and yet quite happy to take advantage of the benefits on offer and prepared to give the regime some credit for them. 'Beauty of Labour', which merely continued paternalist German business traditions and developments of the 1920s deriving from modern personnel management techniques geared to improving productivity, appears to have had little impact. 'Strength through Joy', on the other hand, and particularly the tourist branch of it, appears to have been quite popular. It was given added impetus by pressure on employers to increase workers' entitlement to holidays in lieu of wage increases—the average holiday entitlement increased from three days per year in 1933 to between six and twelve by 1939. Although few workers could afford to go on the prestige cruises to Madeira and Scandinavia, by introducing the modern tourist practice of the package tour, and with the help of special cheap fares from the railways, KdF managed to tap a large new market and win a good measure of approval in the process. Similarly, plans to build a 'people's car' (*Volkswagen*) and the opening of a savings scheme to facilitate purchase of it received quite an enthusiastic response. The Nazis succeeded in this field in building upon and exploiting a consumer taste which was already latent and prevalent in other countries. The following reports by SPD contacts are fairly typical:

236

Berlin, February 1938
Under the rubric 'Beauty of Labour' some large firms have laid out sports fields and built swimming baths etc. in their grounds for the use of their employees. But the workers are compelled to build these facilities in their spare time without pay. There is great indignation about this and many are of the opinion: 'It is simply intended to look good. The bosses are certainly not thinking of the workers and of their well being'.

237

Central Germany, April 1939
While Beauty of Labour makes no impression whatsoever—the splendours are normally built near the entrance to the plant so that visitors can see them—Strength through Joy is not without impact. However, workers' wages are only barely sufficient for essentials and nobody can afford a trip to Madeira, 150 RM per person—300 RM with the wife. Even the shorter trips produce so many additional expenses that they often double the cost. But some people like them nonetheless. Anybody who has never made a trip in his life and sees the sea for the first time is much impressed. The effect is:
'The Nazis have done some good things after all'. The enthusiasm is, however, greater on the first trip. On the second, many are put off by the crowds. . . .

238

Berlin, February 1938

Strength through Joy is very popular. The events appeal to the yearning of the little man who wants an opportunity to get out and about himself and to take part in the pleasures of the 'top people'. It is a clever appeal to the petty bourgeois inclinations of the unpolitical workers. For such a man it really means something to have been on a trip to Scandinavia, or even if he only went to the Black Forest or the Harz Mountains, he imagines that he has thereby climbed up a rung on the social ladder. . . .

239

Bavaria, April 1939

On the group tours there is a sharp social differentiation. The 'top people' only go on big trips where there will be a more select clientele. The big mass trips are for the proletariat. People now look for places where there are no KdF visitors. 'Not visited by KdF' is now a particular asset for summer vacations. A landlord in a mountain village in Upper Bavaria wrote in his prospectus: 'Not visited by KdF tourists'. The Labour Front, which was sent the prospectus by someone, took the landlord to court. He had to withdraw the prospectus and was not allowed to receive summer guests. Nevertheless, information about summer Pensions which are not used by KdF is becoming more and more widespread. . . .

240

Rhineland–Westphalia: April 1939

. . . For a large number of Germans the announcement of the People's Car came as a pleasant surprise. There developed a real KdF-Car psychosis. For a long time the KdF Car was a big talking point among all classes of population. . . . With the KdF car the leadership of the Third Reich has killed several birds with one stone. In the first place, it removes for a period of several years money from the German consumer which he would otherwise spend on goods which cannot be supplied. Secondly, and that is the most important thing, they have achieved a clever diversionary tactic in the sphere of domestic politics. This car psychosis, which has been cleverly induced by the Propaganda Ministry, keeps the masses from becoming preoccupied with a depressing situation. Hitler has acquired domestic political credit with the car savers until the delivery of the car. For, it is well-known that, while they are saving up for a particular commodity, people are prepared to make quite a lot of sacrifices. Another aspect must not be overlooked. Despite all the export subsidies paid by other countries for their cars, the KdF car will be at least half the price of an equivalent car from the other exporting countries. In all the markets of northern and southern Europe, Asia, South and Central America, everywhere where the market is open, the KdF car will beat all the other mass produced cars. . . .

(v) The Reich Labour Service

Another institution which combined material and ideological functions was the Labour Service. Inaugurated at the end of the Weimar Republic by political and youth groups as a means of absorbing the unemployed by putting them to work on projects requiring a large amount of labour, such as the reclamation of land and the digging of canals, the Nazis had regarded it with some suspicion before coming to power because it tended to be run by rival political organizations. Soon after coming to power, however, they saw its practical and ideological advantages. From a practical point of view it absorbed young people from the labour market and therefore opened scarce jobs to family men. Later when unemployment ceased to be a problem and a labour shortage developed, it provided cheap labour for projects of land reclamation for the 'battle of agricultural production'. The ideological advantages were that it provided an opportunity for giving young men political indoctrination and pre-military training. It also symbolized the 'Socialist' principles of the regime. Thus early on it was made obligatory for students so that they should learn to respect manual labour. Hitler referred to this aspect in a speech on May Day 1934, an occasion he invariably used to emphasize this aspect of Nazis ideology:

241

We want to destroy the arrogance with which unfortunately so many intellectuals feel that they must look down upon labour, and on the other hand we wish to strengthen their self-confidence through their consciousness that they too can perform manual labour. But beyond this we wish to contribute to the mutual understanding of the different classes in order to reinforce the tie which binds together the community of the people.... We all know that it is not words or outward professions that lead to the establishment of this community; that needs an inner unlearning, a new education of the people.

The gigantic organizations of our movement, their political bodies as well as the organizations of the SA and the SS, the building up of the Labour Front just as much as the organization of the Army, these are all national and social smelting-furnaces in which gradually a new German man will be formed.

Sickle and hammer were once the symbols of the German peasant and the German workman. The arrogance and unreason of a *bourgeois* age have sacrificed and lost these symbols. Men have praised and admired artists, architects, and engineers; they have spoken of German science, German handicrafts, German business life, but the working man they have for the most part forgotten.... The National Socialist State will put an end to this unhappy development. The hammer will become once more the symbol of the German worker and the sickle the sign of the German peasant, and with them the intellect [*Geist*] must conclude an alliance that nothing shall dissolve.... Today, on May Day, we meet to celebrate the fame of the army of those millions who, as unknown and nameless Soldiers of Work, in the sweat of their faces, in town and country, in the fields, in the factory and the workshop, cooperate to produce those goods which rightly raise our people into the ranks of the civilized nations of the world and enable it to hold that place of honour.

The Reich Labour Service Law of 26 June 1935 made labour service compulsory. According to Article 3 of the law, the Reich Labour Service was 'intended to educate German youth in the spirit of National Socialism to membership of the national community and to acquire a true conception of work, above all appropriate respect for manual labour.' Article 4 defined its task as 'the carrying out of public works'. In a decree of 26 September 1935 Hitler laid down the period of compulsory service as six months for all men between the ages of 18 and 25. For women it remained voluntary until 1939.

The reality of the Labour Service, however, often appeared rather different from the ideal to those who were obliged to participate, as is clear from the following SPD reports:

242

South West Germany, April/May 1938: A discharged labour service man reported as follows: When I arrived at the labour service camp, those in our group sniffed round each other for a long time. There was great mistrust. But the longer we were together the more our inhibitions disappeared. Above all, when all the bull hit us and embittered us, it soon loosened our tongues and so one gradually found out what each person was thinking. Most came to the Labour Service as supporters of National Socialism. But, after only a few weeks, that had changed radically. When we were discharged, one could say that while the majority of the comrades had not become conscious anti-fascists, they had at least become embittered and rebellious non-Nazis. In my experience one can regard this development as virtually universal in the Labour Service. The tension between the supervisors and the Labour Service people, the exaggerated discipline, the drill which had nothing to do with 'labour service', the sometimes senseless work, all this contributed towards removing the young people's illusions and towards showing them National Socialist reality without disguise. What is more, the food was completely inadequate for the demands of the work. We often went off in the morning hungry, got up from lunch hungry and went to bed hungry. I often remembered how my father had said that in the old days Prussian drill had been the best recruiting school for the Social Democrats. Now it is almost like those days except that now everything is much worse because there is no opportunity actively to resist these conditions. One restricts oneself to learning from the experience and gritting one's teeth. . . .

243

Saxony, April/May 1983: The daily programme of the labour service camp at Beiersfeld/Erzgebirge 9/165 looks like this: 4.45 am. get up. 4.50 gymnastics. 5.15

wash, make beds. 5.30 coffee break. 5.50 parade. 6.00 march to building site. Work till 14.30 with 30 minutes break for breakfast. 15.00 lunch. 15.30–18.00 drill. 18.10–18.45 instruction. 18.45–19.15 cleaning and mending. 19.15 parade. 19.30 announcements. 19.45 supper. 20.00–21.30 Sing song or other leisure activities. 22.00 lights out. The day is thus filled with duties. The young people, who have been deadened by excessive physical exertion, have neither the strength nor the time for the slightest flicker of independent intellectual life. The wage is 25 Pf. per day. For that the Labour Service man cannot even afford a beer which costs at least 30 Pf. . . . In some camps like . . . the students and intellectually superior people are grouped together in separate troops. They get easier work and are not bullied so much as the ordinary working class lads. . . .

(vi) The Labour Market: (a) The Work Creation Programme

The economic crisis which began in 1929 had been primarily responsible for the electoral success of the Nazi Party and Hitler was well aware that the stability of his regime would depend on whether or not it could solve Germany's economic difficulties. Foremost was unemployment. The Nazis began by putting into effect plans worked out by their predecessors, the Schleicher Government. On becoming Chancellor in December 1932, Schleicher had appointed a Reich Commissioner for Employment to devise an emergency programme for the creation of work. The Reich Commissioner, Dr Gereke, produced a scheme which included for the first time a programme of public works to be financed by the Reich, state, and local governments. The President of the Reichsbank and the Economics and Finance Ministers, however, out of financial conservatism, restricted the Reich's guarantee to 500 million RM. This programme had just been authorized when Schleicher was dismissed.

Hitler now put this public works programme into effect, at the same time making clear his intention of using it where possible to carry out projects which would assist rearmament. This also had the advantage of disguise. The projects of the public works programme, which were financed by the Reichsbank, would not appear in the budget of the Reich Ministry of Defence and would, therefore, not come to the notice of the Allies. However during 1933, the Wehrmacht was not in a position to spend more than 50 million RM of the Schleicher fund in addition to the substantial sums which had already been budgeted for under the so-called 'Second Rearmament Programme' prepared before the Nazi takeover and scheduled to begin on 1 April 1933.

The Nazis were, in fact, slow to introduce a work creation programme of their own. Hitler told his Cabinet 'to divert the whole nation's attention towards purely political activity because they will have to wait for the economic decisions'. The regime's work creation programme was finally launched on 1 June 1933 with the Law to Reduce Unemployment—the first

'Reinhardt Programme' based on plans drawn up by Fritz Reinhardt, the Nazi State Secretary in the Reich Ministry of Finance. The second plan appeared on 21 September. The scheme involved the granting of government loans and grants for the promotion of building and renovation projects by both government bodies and private concerns, and also the granting of tax concessions for the purchase of replacement stocks. The Law of 1 June insisted (§II.3) that 'all projects must be carried out with manual labour except where mechanical aids are essential and when the restriction to manual labour would result in excessive expense'. It also included a scheme of marriage loans conditional on women leaving their jobs on marriage. The loans were in the form of vouchers which could be spent on the purchase of furniture and household goods, thereby also giving a boost to those industries.

Finally, the programme of work creation was completed by a law of 27 June 1933 which initiated the construction of a network of autobahns. This was not an original idea of the Nazis. Already during the 1920s a pressure group had been founded to urge the building of a motorway from the northern Hansa cities through Frankfurt to Basle, the Verein zur Vorbereitung der Autostrasse, Hansestädte-Frankfurt-Basel (HAFRABA). A small section of this projected route had been built by 1933. The onset of the depression, however, brought these plans to a halt. Nevertheless, the work-creation programmes launched by Brüning, Papen and Schleicher in 1932 had included extensive roadworks.

The Nazi regime now took over this programme and expanded it significantly. The function of the autobahns is a matter of controversy among historians. Nazi propaganda made much of their role in creating work. In practice, however, they did not get under way quickly enough during the crucial early phase of work creation to make a significant impact. Between December 1933 and January 1935, there were never more than 84,000 workers directly involved and usually considerably fewer and, even assuming another worker was employed producing the materials for every worker directly employed on site, the numbers involved were still comparatively small. According to the head of the railways, Dorpmüller, Hitler was convinced 'that a mobilization . . . would not be feasible on our existing road network' and made no bones about the fact that, in building the autobahns he was pursuing 'in the first instance . . . military objectives'. However, although the military were involved in all stages of their planning, the routes were by no means always governed by military criteria and sometimes scenic priorities were decisive. Moreover, the Wehrmacht was not impressed with the contribution of the autobahns to Germany's military preparedness. It would have preferred direct investment in armaments or even in the railways. Thus, it is probable that Hitler used military arguments to justify a programme that derived more from his own fascination with the motor car and his conviction about its future importance as a form of mass transport.

The extent to which the work creation programme was geared to rearmament is somewhat controversial, and assessment is made more difficult by the fact that much of the initial rearmament expenditure was not on weapons but on infrastructure projects such as barracks, airfields, port facilities etc.

244

Public Expenditure on Civilian Work Creation Projects (in millions of RM)

Purpose	Up to the end of 1933	Total up to the end of 1934
Public building projects (Canals, roads, public buildings public utilities, bridges)	855.6	1,002.4
Housing (Renovation, urban redevelopment private housing)	723.3	1280.0
Transport (Railways, Shipping, Autobahns, Post Office)	950.8	1,683.9
(Autobahn total)	(50.0)	(350.0)
Agriculture and Fisheries (Land improvement, agricultural settlement)	337.4	389.2
Measures to encourage consumption	70.0	70.0
Reich Labour Exchange and Unemployment Welfare Office (including Labour Service)	164.0	568.0
Total	3,101.1	4,993.5
For comparison: Armament Expenditure	1,900.0	5,900.0

The Reinhardt programme took time to get under way and during the first months the regime used propaganda to create an image of hectic activity on the employment front and statistics were massaged to suggest that unemployment was in rapid decline. It was not until rearmament began to get properly under way during 1934 with state contracts to private industry and particularly to the building industry in order to provide the infrastructure (docks, barracks, new industrial plant) that the unemployment problem began to be solved on a lasting basis. In April/May 1934, the SPD agents in Germany reported the following practices involved in the reduction of unemployment:

245

1. The assignment of armament contracts. 2. The extension of short-time work through pressure on the employers to avoid redundancies and to take on new workers even when they are not needed. 3. Wage cuts. 4. Work-creation projects, mainly of highly dubious economic value. 5. The extension of the Labour Service. 6. The deportation of young unemployed workers to the countryside as farm labour. 7. The ruthless weeding through of those who receive welfare benefits.

246

South Bavaria. The people are exhausted by the heavy road works. They are mostly long-term unemployed lacking in strength because of poor nutrition. They must now carry out the heavy gravel work, if possible without machinery. Many of them previously had other occupations. At the concrete construction site in Pfraundorf, out of a work force of 140, 17 have reported sick in one week.

247

Baden. At the Autobahn construction site near Mannheim there is a terrible system of slave-driving: fear produces an unheard-of work tempo. When one sees the overseers standing on mounds watching the work going on and shouting at the workers one is reminded of descriptions of Ancient Rome.

248

Level of unemployment at the end of every month in the years 1933–39

	1933	1934	1935	1936	1937	1938	1939
January	6,013,612	3,772,792	2,973,544	2,520,499	1,853,460	1,051,700	301,900
February	6,000,958	3,372,611	2,764,152	2,514,894	1,610,947	946,300	196,800
March	5,598,855	2,798,324	2,401,889	1,937,120	1,245,338	507,600	134,000
April	5,331,252	2,608,621	2,233,255	1,762,774	960,764	422,500	93,900*
May	5,038,640	2,528,960	2,019,293	1,491,235	776,321	338,400	69,600
June	4,856,942	2,480,826	1,876,579	1,314,731	648,421	292,200	48,800
July	4,463,841	2,426,014	1,754,117	1,169,860	562,892	218,300	38,400
August	4,124,288	2,397,562	*1,706,230*†	1,098,498	509,257	178,800	34,000†
September	3,849,222	2,281,800	1,713,912	*1,035,237*†	*469,053*†	156,000	77,500
October	3,744,860	2,267,657	1,828,721	1,076,469	501,847	163,900	79,400
November	*3,714,646*†	2,352,662	1,984,452	1,197,140	572,557	*152,400*†	72,600
December	4,059,055	2,604,700	2,507,955	1,478,862	994,590	455,700	104,400

*216,000, including Austria and the Sudetenland.
†The italicized figures are the lowest level in each year.

(vii) The Labour Market (b): Problems created by the Rearmament Boom—and Responses

Government intervention in the labour market began in the years 1933–36. Trustees of Labour cooperated with employers in ensuring that wage rates did not rise above the level of 1933. Since there was a large pool of unemployed, there was little pressure on wages which helped them. Secondly, a decree of 26 July 1934 enabled employers to make a considerable number of exceptions to the Eight Hour Day limit on hours of work. Finally, a number of measures enabled the Government to exercise more control over the employment of labour. The Labour Exchanges were subordinated to the Ministry of Labour and on 10 August 1934 a decree was issued giving the official Labour Exchanges a monopoly in the supply of labour, thereby facilitating State intervention in the labour market. On 26 February 1935, 'work books' issued for all employees contained details of their qualifications, which were filed by the Labour Exchanges. This provided the necessary information for any future direction of labour. In addition, a law of 15 May 1934 required agricultural workers to obtain permission from their Labour Exchange before accepting employment in industry. In December similar restrictions were imposed on the movement of metal workers to prevent them being lured to the more lucrative aircraft industries of central Germany.

The labour situation in 1936
During 1936, the effects of the rearmament boom began to make themselves felt. Shortages of skilled labour began to appear in important sectors of industry and it became increasingly difficult either to maintain wage rates at the 1933 level or to enforce the decrees restricting the freedom of movement of agricultural and metal workers. Employers, anxious to acquire labour, cooperated with their employees in evading the restrictions. These developments, however, had serious economic and social implications, as was pointed out in a memorandum to Hitler from the Ministries of Economics and Labour, dated 6 October 1936:

249

I. *The shortage of skilled workers and its effects*
1. As a result of the strong revival in the German economy, a severe shortage of skilled workers has developed in the building trade, in the building materials industry and in the metal industry; furthermore, the satisfaction of the labour requirements of agriculture is causing difficulties. The number of workers lacking in these branches of the economy cannot of course be estimated in statistical terms, but according to

the available reports it runs into tens of thousands. And the demand will increase still further. For the new aircraft factories alone, 50,000 more metal workers will shortly be needed. The introduction of the two-year military service will make the shortage of workers even worse. Cuts in production which must be expected in view of the present raw materials and foreign exchange position will not for the time being bring the economic sectors referred to here, particularly the building industry, any relief.

2. This shortage of workers has produced many undesirable repercussions both economic and social. Under the pressure of delivery schedules which are too short, particularly for public contracts, the contractors feel compelled to use any means to get hold of the workers needed to fulfil the contracts. Since the Labour Exchanges are no longer in a position to provide the necessary workers, many contractors under the pressure of circumstances take the law into their own hands and in so doing follow paths which conflict with business ethics. Thus they frequently make attempts to poach skilled workers from other firms in order to carry out the contracts to which they are committed without any consideration for other factory leaders who have trained these skilled workers. The method of 'poaching workers' by the offer of excessively high wages is always successful. The wage increases occur so precipitately and so much at random that they can no longer be regarded as desirable from the point of view of social policy. On the contrary, they have serious economic and political repercussions in that they provide, if not a reason, at least an excuse for price increases such as have already occurred with building materials. The size of the wage increases is considerable. Rates of even three times the tariff minimum are being paid; in addition there are the overtime earnings for a working day of up to fourteen hours. These abnormal wages are especially prevalent in industries which have public contracts to fulfil, so that in the end the increase in earnings in the boom jobs is at the expense of the nation as a whole since the contractors undoubtedly pass on their increased costs, if they can, to the Government. The firms with big export business, which depend on a very fine calculation of prices and therefore cannot carry out similar wage increases, are badly hit by the migration of skilled workers. As a result of this, exporting is made more difficult and the desire to export diminishes.

The conditions described above have an extremely adverse effect on the worker's loyalty to his factory and on work morale. The frequent and unregulated switching of jobs produces discontent in the factories. In many instances people leave their factory without giving notice or provoke dismissal by undisciplined behaviour of inadequate work performance. Even strike attempts on the part of the favoured categories of workers (to get further wage increases) are unfortunately no longer exceptional. The flight from the land (the drift from agricultural work to better paid jobs, particularly in the building trade) is encouraged by these developments. Finally, discontent is growing among the workers who are employed in those branches of the economy which have not been so strongly affected by the recovery or are being hit by the shortage of raw materials. Those fellow citizens whose earnings are often down to subsistence level and for the time being cannot be significantly improved are beginning to feel that their situation shows unfair discrimination when they cannot help noticing that the skilled workers in trades which are particularly favoured by State contracts are now earning several times their own wages, though they are already better off than they are.

3. This unsatisfactory situation has developed into a serious threat to the great political tasks of the State and must be remedied without fail in order to safeguard the carrying out of the defence programme and of the new Four-Year Plan, including the Battle for Agricultural Production. For it has already become apparent that numerous building projects and other contracts placed by the armed forces cannot be carried out to schedule because there are not enough workers or they cannot be found in time, and it was only with the greatest difficulty that the labour force for the harvest could be organized. Apart from this a successful solution to our defence and raw material projects requires that the present wage and price levels be kept stable; but the existing situation exposes them to a growing upward pressure. Thus the elimination of these evils is of decisive importance for the carrying out of the special commission which the Minister-President Göring has received . . .

1. Measures to increase the supply of suitable labour are no longer possible because all the appropriate methods in this connexion have already been used. All those people in the relevant trades—that is, the building trade, especially bricklayers and carpenters, and in the metal industry, fitters, lathe operators, milling operatives, smiths, sheet metal workers—who are known to be unemployed are not sufficient to meet the shortage even if they could all be employed. But apart from this the available unemployed are in some cases unemployable or only partly employable, and some appear in the statistics only because they were changing their jobs on the day of the survey and therefore were temporarily unemployed. It can therefore be assumed that among the ranks of the unemployed there are no more reserves to cover the shortage. Moreover, the Reich Institute for Labour Exchange and Unemployment Insurance has exhausted the possibilities of adjustment between different areas (the transfer of skilled workers from surplus areas to areas of shortage). In our experience only a small number can be re-trained and this takes too long to solve the present difficulties as does the training of apprentices.
2. Changes in wage policy are just as incapable of eliminating the difficulties outlined above as are the measures hitherto taken. The idea of fixing maximum wage rates, which has been suggested by various people and which is intended to prevent the unscrupulous poaching of skilled workers by the offer of higher wages, would be a breach of one of the basic principles of the Law for the Organization of National Labour. If it was put into practice it would have the effect at once of making the maximum wage the mimimum wage and would leave no scope for rewarding people according to individual performance. It is probable that the maximum wage rates would be circumvented by disguised benefits and, as a result, the same situation as we have now would develop at the new level of maximum wage rates; this has been proved by an attempt which was undertaken along these lines in Danzig. It would hardly be possible to prevent such attempts at circumvention since in these cases (unlike the cases in which less than the minimum wage is paid) neither party would complain. In the final analysis, then, the fixing of maximum wage rates could weaken the authority of the State without achieving the desired effect. In addition, changes in wage policy cannot eliminate the shortage of workers.
3. Even a sharper control of prices when awarding public contracts cannot be effective on its own. It is nevertheless urgently necessary, not only for general fiscal reasons, but also in order to counteract dubious methods of 'poaching workers'.

These methods can be employed only when the contractor is not obliged to calculate very carefully what price he should charge. Like tougher price controls, a more generous calculation of delivery dates, which are often much too short, could remove many faults. Only recently those responsible for awarding public contracts again had their attention drawn to this point in the circular issued by the Reich Ministries of Labour and Economics. . . .

With the increasing tempo of rearmament after 1936, tension developed between the Ministries and the Army on the one hand and the Party and the Labour Front on the other. The Ministries and the Army wished to concentrate all resources on the rearmament programme and in particular to keep wages down. The Party and the Labour Front, on the other hand, were primarily interested in maintaining public morale and in particular in winning the workers' confidence in the regime. They also wished to assert the authority of the Labour Front as compared to the Government agencies. To this end, they were quite prepared to apply pressure on the employers to bring about wage increases or improvements in working conditions. On 29 August 1936, Ley persuaded Hitler to institute a competition between factories to encourage them to improve their working conditions as part of the 'Beauty of Labour' programme:

250

Plants in which the leader and his retinue have realized most completely the idea of the National Socialist plant community as expressed in the Law for the Organization of National Labour in the spirit of the German Labour Front may be awarded the title of

'National Socialist Model Plant'

This award will be made by me or by an authority commissioned by me, on the advice of the German Labour Front.

The award is made for the duration of one year; it can be re-awarded. The award will be withdrawn if the prerequisites for the award are no longer present.

The award will be made on the national holiday of the German nation and will take place through the handing over of a document to the leader of the plant.

The document shall state the reasons for the award.

A plant which has been awarded the title 'National Socialist Model Plant' is entitled to fly the flag of the German Labour Front with a golden wheel and golden fringes.

This ordinance comes into effect immediately.

This, however, was strongly resented by the Ministry of Economics, particularly since the criteria laid down by the Labour Front for the award included not only matters of social policy but also a more general economic assessment of each firm. This is clear from a letter from Schacht to Göring, dated 24.ii.37:

251

I consider that it is impossible to hold the competition instituted by the Führer decree of 29.viii.36 at the present time. The putting into effect of the Four-Year Plan and the rearmament programme already requires the total commitment of the whole economy and therefore of every single plant. It is for this very reason that we must at all costs avoid subjecting the plants to new demands which the factory competition would inevitably involve and which would divert them from their primary tasks, particularly those which are essential to the State. . . .

Furthermore, I cannot support the draft regulations of the Labour Front for the following basic reasons:

In the first place, I must object to the fact that, contrary to the sense and the wording of the Führer's decree, economic aspects also are to be taken into consideration for the judgement. It is absolutely clear from the Führer's decree that the plants are to be judged only on the basis of their social policy. Moreover, the fact that the Labour Front has been given responsibility for selecting the plants which are to be considered for the award shows that the question of social policy was to be the decisive factor in the award.

The draft regulations, however, show on the contrary that in its evaluation of the plants the DAF wishes to go far beyond the bounds set for it, since to a large extent it uses purely economic factors as its criteria and brings under consideration the whole economic attitude of the plants. I need only refer here to some examples mentioned in the draft: rearmament, Four-Year Plan, the acquisition of foreign exchange, increase in exports, etc. Apart from the fact that this is not the function of the DAF, it does not possess the necessary economic experience for it. Such a comprehensive evaluation of the plants would also interfere with the exclusive responsibilities of State agencies, including the Delegate for the Four-Year Plan [Göring]. Finally, there is the danger that a faulty economic assessment could introduce confusion and disruption into the economy, thereby endangering the smooth execution of the tasks to which the State has given prime importance.

If therefore, in view of all this, the criteria for the judging of the factory competition for the award of the title of Model Plant are restricted to social conditions, the Trustees of Labour in particular ought to be officially involved, since they have been given the duty of supervising social conditions in the factories under the Law for the Organization of National Labour. . . .

The following documents illustrate further this tension between the requirements imposed by rearmament, the central economic objective of the regime, and the need to conciliate workers and consumers. The basic conflicts of interest between employers and employees, between rulers and ruled, had not been removed by Nazi propaganda about a 'national

community' or a 'plant community'. Since the various elements in the
pluralist system of Weimar had been absorbed into various official organizations, the conflicts were transferred from society to the State itself.
They became aspects of the struggles between the rival bureaucracies
competing for spheres of authority. The Party and the Labour Front based
their claim to authority on their alleged popular support and on their
function as intermediaries between the people the State. The Gauleiters and
the Labour Front, therefore, became to a limited extent and for tactical
reasons defenders of the interests of workers and consumers against the
ministerial bureaucracy, the Army and employers. As such, although they
complicated the rearmament programme, they acted in effect as a stabilizing
force for the regime by helping to soften its impact on the masses. The
following documents illustrate these processes:

252

*Memorandum of the Reich Ministry of Labour on Interference by the Labour Front
(undated, c. Jan. 1938)*

Summary
The cases combined under 'interference by the Labour Front' can be grouped in two
categories, apart from a few irrelevant exceptions. They are the cases which:
1. show evidence of efforts to exclude the Reich Trustees of Labour as far as
possible;
2. aim at direct control over labour conditions and their improvement, frequently
in opposition to the line of social policy laid down by the State. Several methods have
been chosen to carry out these aims:
(a) through the labour committess.
    Here the Labour Front tries to achieve results with far-reaching social implications
by psychological pressure on the employers in the negotiations of the labour
committees; these results are then passed on to the participants with the 'expectation
that these decisions will become part of the factory regulations'.
(b) by direct influence on the drawing up of factory regulations.
    The Labour Front tries to obtain direct control of the factory regulations in order
to gain influence over the shaping of factory conditions and in order to limit the
effects of the external regulations laid down by the Reich Trustees of Labour.
(c) by direct influence on the individual employer for the purpose of improving
labour conditions.
    The Labour Front urges the plant leaders in direct negotiations to make
substantial social improvements, pointing out that rejection of these requests would
be an expression of anti-social attitudes. . . .

Rudolf Hess, as the Führer's Deputy for Party Affairs, reflected the overall interests of the leadership of the regime in concentrating the nation's resources on rearmament, which meant avoiding wage increases. On 1 October 1937 he issued a directive to the Party to this effect:

253

The Führer has repeatedly stated that under the present circumstances wage increases must lead to price increases. This in turn will lead to the endless vicious circle familiar to the German people from the time of the inflation. Wage increases, therefore, can only be damaging rather than beneficial to the general public and to the individual, and so must be avoided at all costs.

A gradual general rise in the standard of living can only take place if that part of national production which has been tied up for years in the elimination of previous damage and in the measures which are necessary to secure German living space, and which to some extent must always be tied up, becomes smaller than it is at present. And even then this can occur only if that part of the production which can be exploited directly or indirectly for raising the general standard of living has been correspondingly enlarged.

If follows from this that there is a binding obligation on all Party offices, their subdivisions and affiliated organizations, to desist from trying to win popularity by propagating and publicly advocating wage demands and from any attempts to press such demands by more or less forceful means.

Attempts to bring about wage increases in a firm which is fully employed, and then to make similar demands for all similar firms, must be resisted in view of the Führer's orders and of the extensive economic planning which will presumably still be necessary for a long time and which we must pursue if only in the interests of the Four-Year Plan.

The fact that the economic position of large sections of our people is not what we would wish and are striving for is the fault of the political, economic, and trade-union leadership of the postwar years.

One must not overlook the importance of the fact that the virtual elimination of unemployment at the present time is due solely to the Führer, his movement and his colleagues.

The honest intentions of the Führer should be sufficient guarantee for every German citizen that everybody will get his share as quickly as possible and that unusually high profits which are being made here and there will on the other hand be used to a very considerable extent in meeting general charges. With this kind of tax legislation and economic planning they will be utilized in every instance to increase production which is the decisive factor for raising the general standard of living. If particular cases of hardship should occur anywhere owing to the level of wages, the advice of the authorities responsible for the investigation and removal of such hardship should of course be sought.

Apart from this all Party offices and their organizations must assist the Führer in the solution of his great tasks by faultless behaviour over the whole wage question and must encourage an awareness of those tasks and understanding for his attitude on the wages question among all classes of the population.

Despite this directive from Hess, however, Gauleiter Bürckel of the Rhineland Palatinate, a particularly impoverished *Gau*, initiated a campaign for the payment of wages on public holidays. Reluctantly, the ministerial bureaucracy agreed to this measure in a decree signed by Göring on 3 December 1937:

254

The carrying out of the Four-Year Plan makes additional demands on all members of the retinue. Wage increases cannot be granted as compensation. But in order that those collaborating in the Führer's great work should be able to enjoy their public holidays I decree the following:

1. For the working time lost because of New Year's Day, Easter and Whit Monday, as well as the two days at Christmas, the members of the retinue are to be paid regular wages. This does not apply if New Year's Day and the Christmas days fall on a Sunday. The official regulations or factory (service) regulations can be used to determine what counts as regular wages....

It was not really necessary, however, for the Party or the Labour Front to press for wage increases, since the shortage of labour, or at least of skilled labour, ensured that wage rates rose. Rising wages, combined with the shortage of consumer goods owing to the emphasis on rearmament, posed the threat of inflation. To meet this threat the Government introduced a decree on the fixing of wages signed by Göring, on 25 June 1938 giving the Trustees of Labour power to fix maximum wages:

255

... 1. The Reich Trustees and Special Trustees of Labour are to supervise wages and work conditions and to take all measures necesary to prevent any weakening of the rearmament drive or of the enforcement of the Four-Year Plan through the trend of wages or of other conditions of work. They are authorized in particular to fix maximum and minimum wages with binding effect in the economic branches selected by the Reich Minister of Labour, even to the point of altering factory (service) regulations and labour contracts.

2. Those who act contrary to or evade the measures taken by the Reich Trustees or Special Trustees of Labour on the basis of this decree will be punished by a prison sentence and a fine of unlimited amount, or with one of these penalties. Prosecution will only be initiated at the request of the Reich Trustee or the Special Trustee of Labour...

Considering the shortage of labour, the Government was on the whole surprisingly successful at limiting the increase in wages. The following figures show that wages as a percentage of Gross National Product sank during this period. This compares with an increase of 36.5 per cent in the undistributed profits of business from 1933 to 1939:

256

The Development of Wages 1929–1939:

	1929	1932	1933	1934	1935	1936	1937	1938	1939
Nominal hourly wages (official)	122	100	97	97	97	97	97	97	98
Nominal hourly wages (actual)	133	100	97	99	101	102	105	108	111
Actual hourly wages (real)		100	99	99	99	100	101	104	107
Actual weekly wages (nominal)	149	100	102	110	112	117	121	126	131
Actual weekly wages (real)	118	100	104	109	110	112	115	119	123
Wages as a % of National income	56.6	57.0	56.0	55.5	54.6	53.5	52.7	52.4	51.8
Official cost of living index	128	100	98	100	102	103	104	104	105
Undistributed profits of private business as a % of national income			0.5	1.4	2.6	3.6	3.9	4.9	
Gross wages in the machine building industry			100	113	118	120	122		
Gross wages in the food processing industry			100	101	101	101	102		
Gross wages in the clothing industry			100	96	91	96	95		
Average hours of work per week for each worker in the processing industries	46	41.5	42.9	44.6	44.4	45.6	46.1	46.5	47.0[1]

[1]First six months.

An important reason for this relative success in wage control is suggested in the following SPD report of January 1939 from *Silesia*:

257

The company D reduced the piece work rates in the lathe shop, the paint shop, and for the boiler makers without having previously informed the work force. This produced a storm of protest and work came to a halt as groups of workers met to discuss the issue. The works manager charged furiously through the plant ordering people to resume work. When this had no effect he shouted to the workers: 'Go and see the Trustee, he ordered the reduction'. He vanished and phoned the Gestapo which came at once. There were informers among those involved in the discussions who denounced to the Gestapo those stirring up opposition. Twenty-two workers were arrested and taken to the Brown House in Görlitz. The other workers were threatened with immediate dismissal and transfer to forced labour in the event of a repetition. In the meantime 8 out of the 22 have been released. They did not, however, return to the factory but had to go to the fortification works in the West.

This report also illustrates the way in which employers were sometimes caught between the demands of labour, which they were at times inclined to heed in order to retain workers, sustain productivity and deliver orders, and those of the State expressed by the Trustees of Labour, also, however, a convenient scapegoat for the refusal of demands.

Whilst, the market mechanism operated fairly successfully in supplying labour to firms engaged in the rearmament programme, as the diplomatic situation became more and more tense during 1938 Hitler decided to strengthen his position by building a line of fortifications along the frontier with France, the West Wall or so-called Siegfried Line. This required a crash programme, for which, owing to the labour shortage, there were simply not enough people available. The Government had anticipated the need for civil conscription in the event of war in an unpublished statute of May 1935. But this statute was now superseded by a decree which became known as the Decree on the Duty of Service issued by Göring on 22 June 1938:

258

In order to be able to make available the labour necessary for particularly important tasks which, for political reasons, cannot be postponed, the possibility must be created of relying temporarily on labour employed elsewhere, In accordance with the Decree of 18 October 1936 for the Implementing of the Four-Year Plan I therefore decree the following:
1. The President of the Reich Institute for Labour Exchange and Unemployment Insurance can require German citizens to do service for a limited period in a workplace assigned them or to undergo a special training course.
2. The general service and social insurance regulations are valid for this new position in service or training. The position in service or training can, however, be dissolved only with the consent of the President of the Reich Institute for Labour Exchange and Unemployment Insurance.
3. Those people signed up for service and training who are employed at the time of their call-up must be given leave for the duration of their service. During their leave of absence the previous position in employment must not be cancelled. The person signed up for service cannot claim compensation and other fees from his previous employment during his leave of absence. The time spent fulfilling the service obligation based on this decree is considered as employment time in his previous job.
4. The regulations necessary for the execution and enforcement of this decree are laid down by the President of the Reich Institute for Labour Exchange and Unemployment Insurance.
5. This decree comes into effect on 1 July 1938.

Workers could now be compulsorily directed to jobs considered of importance to the State, and in February 1939 new regulations extended the decree to foreigners living in Germany and laid down that workers could be conscripted for an indefinite period. Apart from the West Wall, workers were conscripted to build the Four-Year Plan plants and to man the munitions industries. Over a million workers were conscripted, but less than 300,000 on a regular basis, out of a total work force of some 23 million. Indeed, such was the discontent aroused by the measure and the resultant low productivity that the authorities soon had second thoughts. In November 1939, Hitler insisted that workers should be employed in their home towns—a characteristic concession to working-class discontent. Above all, however, this decree did not solve the crucial problem of the labour shortage which jeopardized the whole economy.

(viii) The Morale of the Working Class

What then were the effects of Nazi economic and social policies on the morale of the working class? The situation was extremely complex. Workers' attitudes were influenced by many different variables: age, geographical location (city/small town), nature of occupation, size of plant, conditions within the plant, attitude of employers, extent and nature of previous political or trade union activity, attitude of local Nazi authorities and so on, quite apart from the incalculable effects of personality. Some workers—those in industries involved in the rearmament boom—were materially better off than in 1929—while others such as those in the consumer goods industries or in agriculture were worse off. Increases in real wages, however, had to be earned through large amounts of overtime, This in turn had an impact on productivity and on morale through increased sickness and absenteeism, as is clear from the following social report of the Reich Trustees of Labour for the third quarter of 1938:

259

... The discrepancy between the available labour force and the number of orders has in general led to a considerable increase in hours worked which has been made possible by flexibility in the use of the regulations governing working hours. Fifty-eight to sixty-five hours a week are no longer exceptional. And some factories continue overtime, even when there is a reduction in orders owing to seasonal factors, because they are afraid of losing workers. The extraordinary demands made upon the German workers particularly during the period of tension[40] have on the whole been met without any difficulties. Thus the Reich Trustee of Labour for the Saar-Palatinate reports that it is not uncommon for railway workers, for example,

---

[40]The Czech crisis of summer 1938.

to work up to sixteen hours a day. On being questioned by a commission of inquiry, the railway workers declared that normally they worked for eight hours and rested for sixteen hours, but now they worked for sixteen hours, and rested for eight hours because the Führer needed it. . . .

Owing to the tense situation in the labour sphere and the increase in hours of work in nearly all branches associated with it, certain reactions were unavoidable. The number of cases of sickness has risen considerably. . . .

A further reaction against continuous overtime, according to several Reich Trustees, is the tendency on the part of the retinues not to work for more than forty-eight hours a week. If this objective cannot be met, the result is a decline in productivity. There is also occasional absenteeism. Thus on several building sites the workers went home straight after the payment of their wages and did not return to work until Monday or Tuesday. . . .

Higher real wages were to some extent offset by shortages of particular foodstuffs and by the deterioration in the quality of food and consumer goods through the increasing use of *ersatz* materials such as the replacement of wool and cotton in textiles by fibres processed from wood pulp. The regime was faced with the need to increase workers' productivity without increasing wage levels and thereby encouraging consumption. This situation formed the background for a number of developments. In line with the concept of the 'plant community', employers were encouraged gradually to move from industry-wide wage agreements to those for individual plants. They were also prompted to move from hourly wage rates to piece-work rates in accordance with the principle of 'achievement' or 'performance' (*Leistung*) of which the regime made a veritable cult. These measures—as the SPD analysts shrewdly noted—had a number of advantages for the regime.

First, the introduction of an individual 'wage geared to performance' (*Leistungslohn*) ensured that the general level of wages remained stable, since increases were restricted to particularly skilled and energetic individuals and such increases could be controlled by the employer, who himself set the piece-rates. At the same time, however, it gave individual workers a sense of freedom of manoeuvre, of possessing a degree of responsibility for their own lives which was psychologically important within the general atmosphere of repression. Secondly, these measures encouraged a breakdown of workers' solidarity both across plants and within plants as individual workers sought to improve their own position relative to that of their work-mates.

The workers' sense of solidarity was also undermined by the tendency for general wage increases to be replaced by various substitutes such as holiday bonuses, improved sickness pay usually geared to length of service, and increases in the period for giving notice for both employer and employee. Such measures increased the worker's sense of dependence on the firm and encouraged him to expect such improvements as gifts from his employer as a reward for loyalty instead of—as in the past—having to fight for them through collective action via his trade union.

Finally, the regime's monopoly of the public sources of information and the system of terror enforced through informers and the Gestapo further encouraged the atomization of the working class and the spread of political apathy, already being induced by sheer physical exhaustion. On the other hand, many of the negative features of the regime were to some extent offset by its continuing provision of full employment. The experience of the slump had shaped the minds of a generation of workers. The following excerpts from SPD reports indicate the variety and complexity of working class attitudes to the regime.

260

Bavaria, September 1938: The incredible increase in the work rate has not generally strengthened the will to resist among the workers. The development of solidarity in the plants is very weak. The low purchasing power of real wages, their continual reduction through all manner of contributions etc., which do not appear in any statistics, are for the present not favourable to a strengthening of resistance. It is only among skilled workers that some stirrings of self confidence can be observed. Thus, a group of electricians in a big plant threatened to strike over wages. The threatened strike confronted the management with the decision of whether to bring in the Gestapo and, as a result, jeopardize the completion of the contract, or to agree to their demands. A works engineer, who is sympathetic to the workers, influenced the decision so that the workers demands were accepted.

Civil servants and white collar employees are also increasingly affected by the exploitation of labour. There are no signs of resistance from them but slackness and criticism are increasingly evident.

Relations between the workers suffer from the increasingly tight controls and supervision within the plants. The system of informers is continually being expanded within the plants. The result is that workers only establish personal relations with those whom they know well. The workers avoid each other as far as possible. Even the Nazi workers keep themselves more or less to themselves, apart from anything else because they are avoided by the others. They are not even trusted when they grumble because people are afraid that their complaints are merely provocations. . . .

261

Berlin, April 1936: In a large Berlin armaments plant a worker made a negative remark about National Socalism. He was denounced by a Nazi and, as a result, was fined a week's wages. Since he has a family, his workmates found ways and means of supporting him so that he did not lose money. The man responsible for denouncing him was boycotted by the shop floor. The Nazi complained to the management but without success. This is a by no means isolated example of the solidarity of skilled workers. . . .

But one cannot generalize from such examples of solidarity and expressly anti-fascist attitudes. New plants, in particular, which do not have an old established permanent workforce lack any sense of solidarity. Thus, a metal plant has opened in Tegel. All the workers employed there are new and most of them had not previously been organized in Trade Unions. Among them are many 'old fighters'. As a result, there is no political solidarity among the workers in this plant. Previously, the workers received weekly wages, now they are paid piece rates which the employers are continually trying to cut. The workers complain about it, but cannot mount any kind of resistance. If anyone mentions the possibility of doing so the other workmates immediately put on the brakes. In this plant the less well paid tend to envy the skilled and better paid. But one can no more generalize from the conditions in this plant than one can from the good ones mentioned above. It represents in a sense the extreme case of a bad plant. . . .

262

Saxony, May 1936: Some workers in West Saxony and in the Vogtland have taken the path permitted by the Labour Front by which individual workers are allowed to ask for wage increases. In individual cases they were successful but mostly they were unsuccessful. Basically, the employers are quite content with this system and, according to our information from Saxony, they do not systematically refuse to allow wage increases for *individual* workers. For, firstly, they save themselves the costs which would arise from general wage agreements. And, secondly, the workers are atomised through this system, class solidarity is destroyed, each man becomes the enemy of the other and envies him and that is what the employers want. They gladly pay the small premium against the return of general wage agreements in the form of modest wage increases for individuals, quite apart from the fact that in this system lies the whip by which "ambitious" workers are encouraged to allow their strength to be ruthlessly exploited—again an advantage for the employers.

263

Central Germany, September 1938: Among industrial workers there are many who do not give a damn about the successes of the Hitler system and have only scorn and contempt for the whole show. Others, however, say: 'Well, there are a lot of things Adolf does not know about himself and which he does not want'. But one is never quite sure with them whether they mean it seriously or only want to protect their backs. Naturally, there are also many who have become unpolitical. In particular, a large number of the skilled workers who were unemployed for a long time are not enthusiastic Nazis. They often complain about the fact that they earn much less now than in say 1929 but, at the end of the day, they always say: 'It's all the same to us; at least we have work'. The further one goes down into the poorer sections the more opposition there is. But even now—although they know there is a labour shortage—they are all scared of losing their jobs. The years of unemployment have not been forgotten.

Those who are still Nazis in the plant are subdued. One has the feeling that many of them only stay in the Party to get an easier life. If discussions occur they usually give in or do not get involved. They make no use whatsoever of the jargon employed at their meetings. The facts speak clearly enough for themselves. The fact that one's wages continually buy less and less and that the slave driving gets worse and worse every day cannot be denied by even the 'oldest fighter'. The 'old fighters' in particular, have mostly had enough of the Third Reich. But it is still a different matter as far as white collar employees are concerned. Among them those who have come up in the world through the Party make much of their decorations and titles.

The mood in the plants is one of depression. It's true that even in the old days work was no fun and was regarded by many as a necessary evil. But in those days one had the feeling: if you don't like something you can get it off your chest frankly and in public. Perhaps something will be done about it, in any case it will be a relief. Now one goes into the plant with a heavy heart because one is always afraid of saying a word too many and landing oneself in a spot. There is a dark cloud over one's whole life. One even looks forward less to getting home than in the old days because there is no longer any relaxed comradeship with friends and neighbours. Before, one always used to meet like-minded people in the workers sport and education associations, for a game of chess, or in the People's House. Now one leaves the factory, runs a few errands, goes home, reads the headlines in the paper, and goes to bed, and next morning the same monotonous cycle begins again. Those who have their 'duty' to perform whether in the SS, SA, Party, or Welfare are even worse off. They have to slave away in the evenings as well and moan a lot, particularly if they have been doing heavy physical work during the day. Most of them would gladly give up their posts. But they lack the courage to do so.

CHAPTER 17

The Regime and the People

In the eyes of the Nazis their 'seizure of power' in 1933 was more than just a change of government: it represented merely the start of a revolution which would transform German society in accordance with their ideology. Speaking to the Party faithful in September 1933, at the first NSDAP Rally at Nuremberg after the 'seizure of power', Hitler distinguished between the political and ideological revolution:

264

... On 30 January 1933 the National Socialist Party was entrusted with the political leadership of the Reich. At the end of March, the National Socialist revolution was completed on the external plane, completed so far as regards the entire take-over of political power. But only those who have not fully comprehended the character of this tremendous struggle can believe that the struggle between ideologies [*Weltanschauungen*] has thereby come to an end. This would be so if the National Socialist movement wanted nothing other than the ordinary parties. These do indeed seem to reach the peak of their ambition and therefore of their existence on the day of the take-over of political power. Ideologies, however, see in the achievement of political power only the prerequisite for the beginning of the fulfilment of their real mission. The word 'ideology' already contains the solemn proclamation of the decision to base all actions upon a particular initial position and therefore a clear orientation. Such an attitude may be right or wrong: it is the basis for the attitude to be adopted towards all the phenomena and processes of life and therefore is a law which binds and determines all action....

The starting-point for Hitler's domestic political 'programme' was the lessons which he drew from Germany's collapse in 1918. Like the rest of the German Right, he believed that Germany had not been defeated in the field but rather by the collapse of morale brought about by a combination of internal subversion by 'Jewish Marxist agitators' and 'truly brilliant' Allied propaganda. The main lesson drawn by Hitler, and in this he merely echoed the views of leading military commentators such as General Ludendorff, was that wars had ceased to be simply the province of professional soldiers; they were now fought between whole nations. As a result, they required the total mobilization not only of a nation's military and economic resources, but also and above all its morale.

Hitler regarded the last point as decisive. In his view, the most serious defeat Germany had suffered was not the loss of its arms but the imposition on the German people of a new ethos associated with the Weimar Republic and its dominant political parties. For, in his distorting vision, Liberalism with its emphasis on the priority of the individual over the community, democracy with its subordination of the 'creative' and 'heroic' individual to the mass, and Marxism with its advocacy of class war—all undermined German unity and morale. For these doctrines stressed international ties which led to pacifism and, by denying the significance of race, they paved the way for the Jews to establish hegemony.

Owing to the weakness of pre-war governments, these 'unnatural' ideas had exercised a pervasive influence over the previous decades and had deeply entrenched themselves in German society and culture, sapping the national will. To restore German unity and morale, therefore, would now require 'internal reforms'. First, the democratic system of Weimar must be overthrown and replaced by a dictatorship. And secondly, the new regime must then create a new social order in which class conflict and ideological cleavages would disappear and be replaced by a sense of national solidarity and by a commitment on the part of every individual to put the interests of nation before self (*Gemeinnutz vor Eigennutz*). The concept used by the Nazis to describe their social model was the 'national' or 'people's community' (*Volksgemeinschaft*), which would be created by the Nazi movement and whose interest would be expressed through Hitler's leadership. Like almost all Nazi ideological concepts it was by no means original. Indeed, it was a cliché among the German Right during the Weimar Republic as a counter-model to the 'class society' diagnosed by the Left. The assumption behind it was that membership of the German nation—being a 'national comrade' (*Volksgenosse*)—should transcend the differences of class and status in German society. Its prototype was the 'spirit of 1914', the mood of national unity in which Germany had entered the war in August 1914. The myth of the 'spirit of August 1914', in which class differences had allegedly been submerged by a wave of nationalist fervour, had become a very potent one for the German Right, particularly after the experience of the spirit of November 1918. The major domestic goal of the Nazis was in effect to recreate this spirit of a united nation ready and eager for war, to establish a 'fighting community'. In this they were in the mainstream of the German Right between the wars.

Like his Pan-German mentors, Hitler saw these 'internal reforms' in terms not of an economic and social revolution but of an ideological one to be achieved, on the one hand, through the inculcation of a new mentality and a new social ethos and, on the other hand, through the ruthless suppression of ideologies which ran counter to this new ethos. For the Nazis believed that social reality was determined above all by people's mentality and will. At the core of this new ethos would be an affirmation of the 'laws of nature', the social Darwinist doctrine that human life just like animal life is a struggle for the survival of the fittest and that anything which interfered with that struggle, such as moral inhibitions about letting the weak go to the wall, should be ruthlessly discarded. Moreover, this endless struggle not only took place between individuals but also between nations and between races. The German nation was involved in a struggle with its European rivals, but also, as Aryans, the Germans were engaged in the crucial struggle between Aryans and Jews which would decide the fate of humanity. The main function of domestic policy, therefore, was to prepare the German nation for struggle, both materially and above all psychologically. For as Hitler put it at the beginning of 1932:

265

Army institutions, even those of optimum military value, will be worthless in the future if the nations which stand behind them do not think in soldierly terms and are, therefore, not ready for such action and such sacrifices. Thus, the task of the really responsible politician and statesman is no longer to create a more or less well-trained army, but rather to place the whole nation in the mental state of absolute military commitment and preparedness.

For Hitler politics and war were merely two sides of the same coin: permanent mobilization for struggle which was the essence of life. Nazism was above all else an ideology of struggle, force, and violence.

In practice, this 'programme' meant the creation of a society governed by the rules of race, eugenics, social efficiency, and ideological conformity. To be acceptable as a 'national comrade' one was required to be of the correct racial type (Aryan), to be hereditarily healthy, to be socially efficient (*leistungsfähig*), and to be ideologically reliable. If one was unsatisfactory in any of these respects then one was outside the 'national community' and subject to the various penalties enforced by the agencies responsible for protecting the national community against biological or ideological corruption. Like a cell within a biological organism, the individual only had significance in terms of his function within the national community and his contribution towards its survival.

The problem came, however, with defining what was 'ideologically reliable'. For, apart from the racial and eugenic principles, which were fairly systematically and comprehensively enforced, and the inculcation of militarist values, most other aspects of Nazi ideology were confused and sometimes contradictory. In particular, archaic and modern features coexisted side by side. Thus, on the one hand, there were elements in Nazi ideology which were anti-capitalist, anti-industrial, and hostile to big cities. The 'Blood and Soil' ideology, which glorified the peasantry and regarded urban civilization as a form of disease, articulated the dream, which had haunted the German Right for the past sixty years, of a return to the age before modern capitalism and industrialization had disrupted the traditional patterns of the old society. At the same time, however, Nazism was itself a product of this process of modernization in its contempt for the old social hierarchy and its determination to create a society in which the old exclusive elite criteria of birth, property, and education would be replaced by the much more open criterion of 'achievement' (*Leistung*), in addition of course to racial and biological fitness and political reliability. Moreover, in its—largely unsuccessful—attempt to replace traditional ethnic, religious, social, and family ties by the one tie of personal subordination to the regime, to subsume all social roles in the one role of 'national comrade', it worked in direct conflict with those archaic 'community' (*Gemeinschaft*) values which it claimed to uphold.

The other major problem confronting the Nazi ideological revolution was the fact that its anti-capitalist, anti-industrial, and anti-urban goals conflicted with the dynamic and aggressive nature of the movement and with the requirements imposed by the major objective of its leader—territorial expansion. Rearmament and war required maximum industrial output and therefore an expansion both of the industrial and urban sector at the expense of agriculture and rural society, and of the big firms at the expense of the small man whom Nazi ideology was committed to encourage. There was no way out of this conflict between ideological theory and economic reality, despite the efforts of propaganda to persuade people to accept an alternative reality to the one that actually faced them. The Nazis, who came to power as the champions of the socially and economically most backward elements in the community, ended by taking Germany further forward on the path towards modernization.

In the light of this confusion, Nazi propaganda and indoctrination increasingly focused on those aspects of the ideology that were clear-cut and appeared realizable—antisemitism and eugenics, the strengthening of the 'will for defence', and the national comrade's duty to 'achieve'—while at the same time allowing pragmatism increasingly to dictate the style and content of cultural activities. Here the aim became increasingly one of providing relaxation for the population in the form of innocuous and undemanding entertainment rather than political indoctrination. Indeed, the regime came to pursue contradictory policies towards its people. For while, on the one hand, it attempted to organize, control, and mobilize them by requiring repeated gestures of conformity—the Hitler Salute, listening to broadcasts of political speeches, the hanging out of flags for the regular official rituals of the regime such as the celebration of Hitler's birthday, and contributions to endless public collections for Nazi causes—on the other hand, it aimed to depoliticize them by turning them into passive consumers who listened to undemanding radio programmes, watched entertaining films, interspersed with the occasional patriotic but not usually overtly Nazi one, followed the fashions, and aspired to purchase the ultimate consumer durable, the new *Volkswagen*. In fact, the Nazis proved far more successful with their second tactic than with their first. For while relatively few Germans were turned into committed Nazis, the overwhelming majority were reconciled with a regime which satisfied many of their basic needs and in many of its policies reflected their basic values. For although terror, both latent and active, provided a crucial element in the stability of the regime, consent was an equally or even more important foundation for it.

An important element in this consent, indeed in the effectiveness of the regime such as it was, was the appeal of Nazism to the younger generation— at any rate during the early years. The Nazis benefited enormously from the fact that they offered the generation of young men up to 35 years of age or so the opportunity not only of employment, but of appointments and promotions to positions of considerable responsibility. Through the impact of the Party and its organizations the Third Reich saw a changing of the guard at many levels—on village parish councils as well as in the State bureaucracy, though this varied from department to department. The top ranks in the Propaganda Ministry and the SS-police organization, for example, were full of young Nazis, whereas the Reich Finance Ministry saw far less change. The Nazis provided a vehicle for the ambitions of a younger generation which, during the Weimar period, had felt frustrated by what they regarded as the ossified structures and hidebound establishment of the older generation which was no longer capable of providing Germany with the dynamic leadership that was required to solve a grave national crisis.

Propaganda and Indoctrination

(i) The Reich Ministry of Popular Enlightenment and Propaganda

Goebbels had long seen his own Nazi Party Reich Propaganda Directorate, formed in 1930, as the model for a future Reich Propaganda Ministry, and Hitler himself had already referred to the need for such a Ministry in negotiations over Nazi participation in the Government during 1932. After the election of 5 March 1933, the Cabinet was quickly pressured into approving a decree establishing a 'Reich Ministry of Popular Enlightenment and Propaganda', which came into law on 13 March and defined the task of the new Ministry as the spreading of 'enlightenment and propaganda within the population concerning the policy of the Reich Government and the national reconstruction of the German Fatherland.' Goebbels, the new minister, was not particularly happy for psychological reasons with the use of the word 'propaganda' in the title and, in May 1934, tried to have it replaced by the word 'culture'. However, the Reich Minister of Education and Science objected to this and, in any case, Hitler insisted on the retention of the word 'propaganda'.[41]

Soon after his appointment Goebbels outlined his view of the role of the new Ministry at his first press conference on 15 March 1933:

266

I see in the setting up of the new Ministry of Popular Enlightenment and Propaganda by the Government a revolutionary act in so far as the new Government no longer

[41] See Ansgar Diller, *Rundfunkpolitik im Dritten Reich* (Stuttgart 1980) p. 127.

intends to leave the people to their own devices. This government is in the truest sense of the word a people's government. It arose out of the people and will always execute the will of the people. I reject most passionately the idea that this government stands for reactionary aims, that we are reactionaries. We want to give the people their due, though admittedly in another form than occurred under parliamentary democracy.

In the newly-established Ministry of Popular Enlightenment and Propaganda I envisage the link between regime and people, the living contact between the national government, as the expression of the people's will, and the people themselves. In the past few weeks we have seen an increasing coordination between Reich policy and the policy of the states, and in the same way I view the first task of the new Ministry as being to establish coordination between the Government and the whole people. If this government is determined never and under no circumstances to give way, then it has no need of the lifeless power of the bayonet, and in the long run will not be content with 52 per cent behind it and with terrorizing the remaining 48 per cent, but will see its most immediate task as being to win over that remaining 48 per cent.

... It is not enough for people to be more or less reconciled to our regime, to be persuaded to adopt a neutral attitude towards us, rather we want to work on people until they have capitulated to us, until they grasp ideologically that what is happening in Germany today not only *must* be accepted but also *can* be accepted.

Propaganda is not an end in itself, but a means to an end. If the means achieves the end then the means is good. Whether it always satisfies stringent aesthetic criteria or not is immaterial. But if the end has not been achieved then this means has in fact been inadequate. The aim of our movement was to mobilize people, to organize people, to win them for the national revolutionary ideal. This aim—even the most hostile person cannot dispute this—has been achieved and that represents the verdict on our propaganda methods. The new Ministry has no other aim than to unite the nation behind the ideal of the national revolution. If the aim has been achieved then people can pronounce judgment on my methods if they wish; that would be a matter of complete indifference for the Ministry would then by its efforts have achieved its goal. If, however, the aim is not achieved then although I might be able to prove that my propaganda methods satisfied all the laws of aesthetics I would have done better to become a theatre producer or the director of an Academy of Art not the Minister of a Ministry of Popular Enlightenment and Propaganda...

The most important tasks of this Ministry must be the following: first, all propaganda ventures and all institutions of public information belonging to the Reich and the states must be centralized in one hand. Furthermore, it must be our task to instil into these propaganda facilities a modern feeling and bring them up to date. We must not allow technology to run ahead of the Reich but rather the Reich must keep pace with technology. Only the latest thing is good enough. We are living in an age when policies must have mass support... the leaders of today must be modern princes of the people, they must be able to understand the people but need not follow them slavishly. It is their duty to tell the masses what they want and put it across to the masses in such a way that they understand it too...

Ten days later, on 25 March, he told a meeting of radio officials:

267

The Ministry has the task of achieving a mobilization of mind and spirit in Germany. It is, therefore, in the sphere of the mind what the Defence Ministry is in the sphere of defence. Thus, this ministry will require money and will receive money because of a fact which everybody in the Government now recognizes, namely that the mobilization of the mind is as necessary as, perhaps even more necessary than, the material mobilization of the nation. The proof is: in 1914 we had been mobilized in material terms as no other nation had—what we lacked was the mobilization of the mind within the country and in other countries which provided the basis for the material mobilization. We did not lose the war because our artillery gave out but because the weapons of our minds did not fire. Because people who knew nothing about it were employed to explain Germany to the world. Because people believed that any old privy councillor could do it, without his having any contact with every day life. No, this is a task for men who have come from the people and understand the people . . .

As a new creation, the new ministry was from the beginning more fully staffed with Nazis than the older ministries. Most of the high positions in the Ministry were held by officials from the Propaganda Department of the NSDAP. Many were young and with higher educational qualifications than the average Nazi activist. Like Goebbels himself, they retained their positions in the Party's propaganda apparatus and, in its power struggles with other bodies, the Ministry benefited from the fact that many of its officials straddled Party and State. By 8 April the Ministry had acquired its basic structure which was divided into seven departments: I Budget and Administration; II Propaganda; III Radio, IV Press, V Film, VI Theatre; VII Popular Enlightenment. These departments indicate the breadth of scope envisaged for the new ministry by Goebbels. However, before he could assert his authority over these various spheres, he was obliged to fight a bureaucratic war with the various ministries and agencies hitherto responsible for them. It was vital that he could count on Hitler's support and, on 30 June 1933, he successfully prevailed upon Hitler to issue a supplementary regulation which declared that:

268

The Reich Minister of Popular Enlightenment and Propaganda is responsible for all influences on the intellectual life of the nation, public relations (*Werbung*) for State, culture, and the economy, for instructing the domestic and foreign public about them and for the administration of all the institutions serving these purposes.

The regulation also laid down in detail those responsibilities which were to be transferred to the Propaganda Ministry from other departments.

(ii) Radio

Even before the take-over of power both Hitler and Goebbels were well aware of the importance of radio as a propaganda medium. Hitler regarded the spoken word as more effective than the written one, and through radio the regime could reach the masses directly. Goebbels demonstrated his grasp of the significance of radio by acting at once to exploit the new situation created by Hitler's appointment as Reich Chancellor. He mobilized the new Nazi Reich Minister of the Interior to instruct the Reich Radio Commissioner and the state radio commissioners to broadcast the torchlight procession held on the evening of 30 January 1933 to celebrate the new 'national(ist) government'. During the evening, however, the Bavarian radio station interrupted the broadcast when it became apparent that the celebration was being used for party political purposes.

This incident highlighted the major problem facing Goebbels in his attempt to concentrate power over the radio in his hands, namely the fact that the German radio had a federal structure over which the Reich had only limited economic control through the Reich Radio Commissioner of the Ministry of Posts and limited political control through the Reich Radio Commissioner of the Minister of the Interior. However, agreement had been reached with the Nationalists to share the 45 political broadcasts allocated for the election period 1 February–4 March: no other party was permitted to broadcast. Although the main process of coordination was postponed until after the election, within the first few weeks the two Reich radio commissioners were replaced as well as the controller of Berlin radio.

With the establishment of the Reich Propaganda Ministry on 13 March Goebbels set about trying to concentrate power over radio into his hands. Here, however, he came up against the resistance of Göring who, as Prussian Minister of the Interior, was determined to assert the responsibility of the states for radio and with this course of action threatened to provide a lead for the other states. Although Goebbels responded by persuading Hitler to issue his decree of 30 June 1933, in which the responsibility for radio was clearly vested with the Propaganda Ministry, it required a letter from Hitler to the *Reichsstatthalter*, dated 15 July, finally to clinch the matter. Even then it took several months before the final details were cleared up. From 1 April 1934, however, German radio was unified in the 'Reich Radio Company', of which the previous state stations were now merely branches with the title of 'Reich Radio Stations'. The Reich Radio Company in turn was in theory subordinate to Department III of the Propaganda Minstry. In practice, however, the key figure in German radio was the Reich Director of

Broadcasting, Eugen Hadamovsky, appointed head of the Reich Radio Company on 8 July 1933. Hadamovsky had a direct and close link to Goebbels and was responsible for approving all important broadcasts. Finally, the 'Wireless Service' (DDD), which was responsible for news broadcasts was attached not to the radio but to the press department of the Ministry under its existing director, Hans Fritzsche, who joined the Party on 1 May. Fritzsche remained in control of all German news broadcasts until his appointment as head of the press department in 1938.

Parallel with the reorganization of German radio went a purge of its personnel. In the weeks following the election of 5 March the directors of the Reich Radio Company, all but one of the controllers of the state stations (Stuttgart), and large numbers of staff at all levels were dismissed. The first six months of 1933 saw approximately 270 dismissals or some 13 per cent of total broadcasting staff.[42] This was a higher percentage than that of the Civil Service purge, reflecting both the fact that the Propaganda Ministry was run by fanatical young Nazis and the fact that many broadcasting staff were not civil servants but on fixed term contracts. At the end of March, the head of the radio department in the Ministry, Horst Dressler-Andress, told the Nazi radio journal, *Die Funk*, that all 'alien elements' would have to be excluded 'from the organization and programming of the radio.' 'Not only the whole Jews but also the half Jews' would have to 'disappear'.[43]

A clear impression of the impact of the Nazi take-over of the German radio is provided by the diary entries of the writer and broadcaster, Jochen Klepper, a devout Protestant and patriotic Prussian who happened to be married to a Jewess and to have been a member of the SPD:

269

30 March. I had just finished 'Atlantis' on time. Now it was a case of rehearsing it quickly for Saturday. The rehearsal had to be cancelled. The manuscript had not been duplicated because the firm with which the radio station had up to now been working quite happily is Jewish. The records I ordered were removed from me because either the firm or the composer ... or the conductor is Jewish. I had to dismiss my most reliable announcer because he is Jewish. What is left of the station is almost like a Nazi barracks: uniforms, uniforms of the Party formations.
25 May. Three hours before the beginning of the broadcast the controller received the denunciation. I was a member of the SPD. I was supposed to have said myself that I ought to be one of the first to go. Jewish family—The denunciation as effective as it could have been: it came via the National Socialist Radio Listeners [Association].

---

[42] *Ibid.* p. 127. This section depends heavily on this book.
[43] *Ibid.* p. 109.

26 May. Now the Damocles sword of denunciation is no longer hanging over me. The controller Arenhövel[44] knows that I was a Social Democrat and that my wife is Jewish. His response: close friends of his were also religious Socialists, that didn't bother him at all. My marriage was my own affair. But because of these things the renewal of my contract has to be postponed and my name can only rarely appear in the programmes.

5 June. Braun and Arenhövel are hard put to keep me on. I have no prospects and an income which in the opinion of my superiors in no way reflects my work and my achievements. I have to work anonymously. Whole series which from A to Z are my intellectual property and bear the ever-clearer stamp of my work go out under the name of other lazier and less talented authors! Even as a producer I have to remain anonymous, have to put up with everything simply because I was a religious socialist and have a Jewish wife.

7 June. When I arrived at the radio station I was asked to see the controller who informed me briefly that 'until my case had been finally settled I must stop work immediately and leave'.

On 25 March 1933 Goebbels told the Controllers of German radio the role he envisaged for the medium under the new regime:

270

We make no bones about the fact that the radio belongs to us and to no one else. And we will place the radio in the service of our ideology [*Idee*] and [the speaker bangs on the lectern] no other ideology will find expression here ... The radio must subordinate itself to the goals which the Government of the national revolution has set itself. The Government will give the necessary instructions ...

I consider radio to be the most modern and the most crucial instrument that exists for influencing the masses. I also believe—one should not say that out loud—that radio will in the end replace the press ...

First principle: At all costs avoid being boring. I put that before *everything* ... So do not think that you have the task of creating the correct attitudes, of indulging in patriotism, of blasting out military music and declaiming patriotic verse—no, that is not what this new orientation is all about. Rather you must help to bring forth a nationalist art and culture which is truly appropriate to the pace of modern life and to the mood of the times. The correct attitudes must be conveyed but that does not mean they must be boring. And simply because you have the task of taking part in this national enterprise you do not have *carte blanche* to be boring. You must use your imagination, an imagination which is based on sure foundations and which employs all means and methods to bring to the ears of the masses the new attitude in a way which is modern, up to date, interesting, and appealing; interesting, instructive but not schoolmasterish. Radio must never go down with the proverbial disease—the intention is clear and it puts you off.

---

[44] Friedrich Arenhövel had worked for the *Völkischer Beobachter* and Goebbels's *Der Angriff* and was head of the literature section of the Nazi cultural organization, *Kampfbund für deutsche Kultur*.

I am placing a major responsibility in your hands for you have in your hands the most modern instrument in existence for influencing the masses. By means of this instrument you are the creators of public opinion. If you carry this out well we shall win over the people and if you do it badly in the end the people will once more desert us . . .

The regime made great efforts to encourage the spread of radio ownership and of listening to the radio. Within months it had arranged with a group of industrialists for the production of cheap radios in two versions, one for 75 RM and the so-called 'people's receiver' for 35 RM payable in instalments. One-and-a-half million sets were produced during 1933 alone.[45] By 1939 70 per cent of German homes had a radio, three times the number in 1932 and the highest percentage of radio ownership in the world. The cheap radios were designed with a limited range so that they would be unable to receive foreign broadcasts.

In addition, the regime placed great emphasis on the encouragement of community radio listening in factories, offices, cafés etc. This was not simply in order to reach those who did not possess a radio at home but also because it was believed that the impact of rallies and speeches broadcast on radio would be greater if they were listened to in public where people would be more suggestible than in their familiar home surroundings. Thus, the local paper in Neu-Isenburg near Frankfurt announced on 16 March 1934:

271

Attention! The Führer is speaking on the radio. On Wednesday 21 March, the Führer is speaking on all German stations from 11.00 to 11.50 am. According to a regulation of the Gau headquarters, the district Party headquarters has ordered that all factory owners, department stores, offices, shops, pubs, and blocks of flats put up loud-speakers an hour before the broadcast of the Führer's speech so that the whole work force and all national comrades can participate fully in the broadcast. The district headquarters expects this order to be obeyed without exception so that the Führer's wish to speak to his people can be implemented.

In the summer of 1938 the first loudspeaker column was put up in Breslau to be followed by thousands of others elsewhere. State Secretary Hanke of the Propaganda Ministry summed up their roles as 'to provide a direct and rapid means of issuing orders'.[46]

---

[45] See E. K. Bramsted, *Goebbels and National Socialist Propaganda 1925–1945* (London 1965).
[46] See J. Sywottek, *Mobilmachung für den totalen Krieg. Die propagandistische Vorbereitung der deutschen Bevölkerung auf den Zweiten Weltkrieg* (Cologne 1976), p. 31.

At the same time, although the radio broadcast many speeches by Nazi leaders, it also paid attention to Goebbels insistence that the most important principle was not to be boring and, therefore, increasing emphasis was placed on light entertainment, particularly during the war years.

An important role in the regime's radio propaganda was played by the thousands of local 'radio wardens' who were responsible for encouraging the spread of radio, ensuring that the population fulfilled 'its political responsibility of regular listening to the radio', for encouraging community listening, and for monitoring audience reactions.

(iii) The Press

Since the radio was already controlled by the Reich and the states before 1933, its coordination proved relatively easy. The press, which was in the hands of private companies, political parties, and religious bodies was another matter altogether.[47] To ensure the regime control over the press three main policies were pursued: first, those involved in the newspaper business—publishers and journalists—were subjected to strict controls; secondly, the Party's publishing house, the Eher Verlag, acquired the ownership—either direct or indirect—of the bulk of the German press; thirdly, the Propaganda Ministry maintained a continuous control over the content of the press through the state-controlled press agency and via a stream of directives issued at daily press conferences.

After the Nazi take-over, the German publishers association, the VDZV, endeavoured to preserve the position of publishers by seeking a *modus vivendi* with the regime. They were encouraged in their 'self-coordination' by sympathetic noises from Hitler and other Nazi leaders. On 28 June 1933, they replaced politically obnoxious members of their council with Nazi publishers and appointed Max Amann, the head of the Eher Verlag, as their chairman and his right-hand man, Rolf Rienhardt, to the staff. Rienhardt soon effectively controlled the organization.

On 30 April 1933, the journalists' organization, the Reich Association of the German Press, felt obliged to elect the Nazi Press Chief, Otto Dietrich, as chairman and at the same time announced that in future membership of the association would be compulsory for all journalists and that all members would be vetted for 'racial and political reliability'.

On 4 October 1933, the regime transformed the position of editor and in particular the relationship between editors and publishers in a major piece of legislation, the so-called 'Editors' Law'. It was based on a Journalists Bill of 1924 which had been rejected and on Italian fascist press legislation:

---

[47] This section owes much to O. J. Hale, *The Captive Press in the Third Reich* (Princeton 1964).

272

§1. Participation in the shaping of the intellectual content of the newspapers or political periodicals published within the area of the Reich, whether by written word or by dissemination of news and pictures, and whether carried out as a main employment or based on an appointment to the position of editor-in-chief, is a public task, of which the professional duties and rights are regulated by the State through this law.

§2. 1. Newspapers and periodicals are printed matter, appearing in regular sequence at intervals of at most three months, not limiting its circulation to a certain group of persons.

2. All reproductions of writings or illustrations, destined for dissemination, which are produced by means of a mass reproduction process, are to be considered as printed matter.

§3. 1. The provisions of this law relating to newspapers are also valid for political periodicals.

2. This law does not apply to newspapers and periodicals published by official order.

3. The Reich Minister for Popular Enlightenment and Propaganda will determine which periodicals are to be considered as political within the meaning of the law. In case the periodical affects a specific vocational field, he will make the decision in consultation with the highest Reich or state agency concerned.

§4. Participation in the shaping of the intellectual content of the German newspapers is also considered as such, even if it does not take place in the management of a newspaper, but in an establishment which is to supply newspapers with intellectual content (the written word, news, or pictures).

§5. Only those persons can be editors who:

1. possess German citizenship;
2. have not lost their civic rights and the qualification for the tenure of public office;
3. are of Aryan descent, and are not married to a person of non-Aryan descent;
4. have completed their 21st year;
5. are competent at business;
6. have been trained in the profession;
7. have the qualities which the task of exerting intellectual influence on the public requires....

§14. Editors are especially obliged to keep out of the newspapers everything...(2) which is calculated to weaken the strength of the German Reich abroad or at home, the community will of the German people, German defence, culture or the economy, or to injure the religious sensibilities of others...

§20. 1. Editors of a newspaper bear the professional responsibility and the responsibility before the criminal and civil law for its intellectual content in so far as they have composed it themselves or have accepted it for publication.

2. The chief editor is responsible for the general stance of the text...

§22. The editorial group as a whole will watch over their individual professional colleagues' fulfilment of their duty and will look after their rights and their welfare.

§23. Editors are legally combined in the Reich Association of the German Press. Every editor belongs to it by virtue of his registration on the professional roster. By virtue of this law the Reich Association becomes a public corporation. It has its headquarters in Berlin.

§24. 1. The Reich Minister for Popular Enlightenment and Propaganda will appoint the head of the Reich Association who will issue a charter for the Reich Association, which will require the approval of the Minister. The head of the Reich Association will appoint an advisory council. . . .

§30. A publisher may only dismiss an editor because of his intellectual stance if it contravenes the public professional duties of an editor or the agreed guidelines . . .

§35. Apart from the proceedings before the professional courts the Reich Minister for Popular Enlightenment and Propaganda can order the removal of an editor from the professional roster if he considers it for urgent reasons essential for the public good.

§36. Whoever works as an editor despite the fact that he is not registered in the professional rosters, or despite the fact that he has been temporarily prohibited from exercising his profession, will be punished with imprisonment of up to one year, or fined. . . .

By placing responsibility for editorial content entirely in the hands of the editor and protecting him from dismissal, the law reversed the roles of publisher and editor, reducing the publisher to the level of a business manager. On the other hand, the editor's freedom was removed to such an extent that he became what the official commentary to the law described as 'a State organ who is called upon to fulfil one of the most important tasks of the State.' Furthermore, under the Law the Reich Association established a list of officially accredited journalists and a system of professional courts to enforce a journalists' code which operated on the basis that journalism was a public function. The Reich Minister of Propaganda was appointed President of the Association and was given a veto over admission to the occupational list. By 1935 1,300 'Jewish and Marxist' journalists had been purged from the profession. The Law represented a victory for Goebbels and Dietrich, whose influence operated via the editors and journalists, over Max Amann, who aimed to exercise power via the publishers.

On 15 November 1933, Amann acquired the key to control over German publishing with his appointment as President of the Reich Press Chamber which had been established by the Law relating to the Chamber of Culture of 22 September 1933.[48] Clause 4 of the regulations of the Press Chamber made membership of the chamber compulsory for all those engaged in publishing. Under clause 10 anyone could be excluded from membership who was considered politically unreliable or who lacked suitable qualifications for the profession, while clause 25 empowered the Reich Chamber to lay down the conditions for opening and closing down businesses and to regulate all important matters concerning the publishing

---

[48] See below pp. 397–8.

business. These clauses gave Amann complete power over German publishing. His power was largely exercised by Rolf Rienhardt, who ran the publishers' association which was reorganized on 18 February 1934 as a compulsory membership organization directly subordinate to the Reich Press Chamber. Armed with their new powers Amann and Rienhardt now set about radically reshaping the German newspaper industry.

In 1933 Germany had more daily newspapers than the United States and more than the combined total for France, Britain, and Italy. The city of Stuttgart alone (pop. 400,000) had nine and Stettin (pop. 254,000) five. Most small rural towns had at least one. Many of these papers were uneconomic and had been badly hit by the depression. At the end of 1932, the 59 Nazi daily newspapers had a combined circulation of only 782,121 and accounted for only 2.5 per cent of the total. They were poor in quality and had suffered from continual financial difficulties.

With the take-over of power the Nazis exploited the new situation to strengthen their position at the expense of the Socialist and Communist press. Socialist and Communist publishing houses were either destroyed or taken over by the Nazi newspapers. Some middle class democratic papers were also forced to sell to the Nazis since Nazi-controlled government agencies switched advertising and printing contracts to the Nazi press. By the end of 1933, the Nazis had acquired 27 daily papers and increased the total circulation of their daily press by 2.4 million copies per day. This process continued during 1934 which saw the demise of the large Jewish publishing firm of Ullstein. However, Amann and Rienhardt were clearly unhappy about the lack of Party control over German newspaper publishers. By March 1936, when action under clause 10 of the Press Chamber regulations had been completed, only around 100 newspaper publishers had been declared ineligible and large numbers of other middle-class publishers, while outwardly conforming, were clearly by no means National Socialist in spirit. The Nazi leadership was particularly concerned about the prosperous *Generalanzeiger* press usually owned by big concerns who were motivated primarily by profit and geared to maximising circulation and advertising revenue with little interest in politics. These papers provided serious competition for the Nazi press. They also disapproved of papers which were confessional in character and those that were sensational—with the exception of Streicher's *Der Stürmer*.

Amann and Rienhardt decided to deal with this problem by issuing in April 1935 three ordinances under clause 25 of the Reich Press Chamber regulations. These ordinances asserted Amann's power to close publishing enterprises where competition created unsound publishing conditions. They required detailed disclosure of the ownership of private publishing firms, including proof of Aryan ancestry, and details of any subsidies received. They excluded from future ownership of newspapers all corporate forms of business enterprise and legally registered societies, organizations, public or private foundations or trustee representatives. And finally, they prohibited newspapers designed to appeal to 'confessional, vocational or special interest groups'.

Rienhardt prepared a 'Brief Explanation' of his ordinances from which the following extracts are taken:

$$273$$

The National Socialist *Weltanschauung* sees in the press a means of educating the people for National Socialism. In consequence, the press is an instrument of the National Socialist State. The National Socialist *Weltanschauung* demands total acceptance and does not tolerate the propagation of other basic political ideas. On this basis a state whose foundation is the National Socialist movement recognizes only a National Socialist press. To achieve and give legal expression to these principles the National Socialist State formulated and published the Editors' Law and the Reich Chamber of Culture Law. Both laws enroll, on the basis of character and attitudes, all German citizens creatively employed in the press. Anyone who on professional or personal grounds is unsuitable for the fulfilment of the high demands of the press, loses all opportunity for activity in these callings by exclusion from the Reich Press Chamber . . .

The National Socialist revolution renounced the use of political force to suppress the entire non-National Socialist press, limiting its action to the suppression of the Marxist-Communist press. In consequence thereof, after the seizure of power, fewer than 100 National Socialist papers confronted about 3,000 papers which before January 30 1933 took it to be their duty to represent other viewpoints, parties, and groups opposed to National Socialism, and to hinder the movement and prevent its coming to power.

The repeated pronouncements by the highest authorities of Party and State, in agreement with the NS-programme, that 'There is only a National Socialist Press', stand in sharp contrast to the facts, namely that today a large number of publishing firms still exist of which no-one could say they were National Socialist, for the men who own them and direct them are everything but National Socialists . . .

The publisher personalities, whose political reliability and qualifications for activity in the publishing industry . . . must be denied and against whom the struggle of the Party is directed, are mainly the proprietors of those newspapers possessing the largest circulations . . .

As a result of the Amann ordinances over the next eighteen months, between 500 and 600 newspapers vanished, merged, or were bought by the Eher Verlag or one of its affiliates, many of them economically prosperous. During the following years, Nazi ownership of the press increased inexorably until by 1939 the Eher Verlag controlled either directly or indirectly around two thirds of the German press. Many of these papers kept their titles and even the old publishing imprint so that their readers were unaware of the change of ownership which had taken place.

In addition to controls over journalists and publishers and the ownership of a large percentage of the press, the Nazis also ensured their influence by strict regulation of the content of newspapers. This was achieved first through the State-owned press agency, the DNB, which was formed in December 1933 out of an amalgamation of Hugenberg's agency Telegrafen Union and the rival Wolffs Telegraphen Büro and directly subordinated to the Propaganda Ministry. Newspapers were obliged to acquire their news through the DNB, and its commentaries provided guidance for the line to be taken by the papers. It therefore acted as a kind of pre-censorship filter.

Secondly, the content of newspapers was also controlled through the directives issued by the Propaganda Ministry at its daily press conferences. During the Weimar Republic, journalists had organized daily press conferences in the Government Press Office at which the Press Chief and ministerial representatives had informed journalists about Government policy and responded to questions. Now Goebbels transformed these press conferences into official sessions chaired by the Government representative to which only accredited journalists were admitted and at which official instructions were issued for the treatment of the news. These instructions were so detailed that they sometimes even covered the length of articles to be devoted to particular topics, where they should be placed and the size of headlines to be used. For important events actual articles were issued which smaller papers printed as written, while others used them as the basis for their own articles. These instructions were then also passed on to the various publishing firms via the Gau Propaganda Offices. The proceedings of these conferences were secret. Fritz Sänger, who represented the *Frankfurter Zeitung* at them for eight years, commented:

274

The press conference *with* the Reich Government founded in 1917 was changed by the National Socialists on their seizure of political power in Germany in 1933 into a 'press conference *of* the Reich Government'. So it was now an institution of the Government. There it gave directives, laid down language regulations, and there were daily opportunities to give directives to the press 'to bring it into line' (a phrase in fashion then) and to inform it so far as seemed advisable. Before 1933, these press conferences were run by journalists and the Government was their guest; after they were run by the Government.

Every German paper was anxious to have a representative at the Reich Press Conference. Some papers (the big ones like the *Frankfurter Zeitung* of whose Berlin editorial office I was a member) had several representatives there, and some who attended the press conference represented several papers. Every representative in the press conference became a 'member' there, that is, he was admitted or accredited. Previously, the board of the press conference was responsible for admissions; after 1933 it was in the hands of the Reich Ministry for Popular Enlightenment and Propaganda—its German Press Department.

Several of the Berlin editors of the *Frankfurter Zeitung* were members, including myself. The Reich press conference took place at 12 noon on weekdays; later on, in the war years, at a second time, usually at 5 p.m., but occasionally also late in the evening and even during the night or very early in the morning. The summons came by telephone or telegram if it was not the daily noon or evening conference.

In these conferences there was no discussion, we were simply spoken to somewhat one-sidedly (by the Government) and at most the press asked questions.

At his first official press conference on 15 March Goebbels made clear his views on the role of the press and its relations with the Government:

275

... As I have emphasized already, the press is not only there to inform but must also instruct. In saying this I am directing my remarks above all to the national press. You will also recognize that it is an ideal situation for the press to be a tremendously important instrument for influencing the masses, which in the hands of the Government can be used in the areas for which it is responsible. It is possible for the Government and the press to cooperate with one another on a basis of mutual trust. I regard it as one of my principle tasks to achieve that. I am aware of the significance of the press. I recognize what it means for a government to have a good press or a bad press. I regard myself, therefore, so to speak as the senior link man between Government and press. I will make sure that the contact is never interrupted. For this reason I see in the task of the press conference held here daily something other than what has been going on up to now. You will of course be receiving information here but also instructions. You are to know not only what is happening but also the Government's view of it and how you can convey that to the people most effectively. We want to have a press which cooperates with the Government just as the Government wants to cooperate with the press ... We do not want a state of daily warfare, a state of continual bans, rather we wish Government and press to work together with mutual trust. You need not be afraid of making statements with obvious bias. There is nothing unbiased in the world. Anything unbiased is sexless and thus worthless. Everything has a bias whether acknowledged or concealed. In my view it is better for us to acknowledge our bias rather than conceal it. There is no absolute objectivity. Everyone who as a contemporary contributes to the formation of this epoch carries an enormously heavy responsibility in so far as he is shaping not only his own opinion but an article he writes in the press may communicate that opinion to hundreds and thousands of others.

The following are examples of official instructions issued at the daily press conferences in the Propaganda Ministry:

276

6.vii.33: The Propaganda Ministry once again points out that announcements about future journeys and visits of the Reich Chancellor must not be published under any circumstances, not even if local National Socialist offices give out these announcements. The *Dortmunder Generalanzeiger* yesterday publicized the fact that the Reich Chancellor was to speak at a big SA rally in Dortmund. Following this, the paper (although it is an official Party organ of the NSDAP *Gau* Düsseldorf) got a message from the Propaganda Ministry in which the behaviour of the *Dortmunder Generalanzeiger* was sharply criticized and disapproved of. National Socialist Party sources comment that the paper would have been banned for an indefinite period if it had been a bourgeois paper and not a Party organ. This measure shows clearly the necessity of watching out for and checking announcements of future visits by the Chancellor.

12.xi.33: Reports on the protective custody of Duke Albrecht of Württemberg must not be published under any circumstances. Purely for your information, Duke Albrecht this morning refused to take part in the election. This came to the notice of the public, which assembled in a great crowd in front of his flat. Duke Albrecht then made derogatory remarks to the crowd about the Reich Government and the new State. He had to be taken into protective custody because of pressure from the crowd.

6.iv.35: The Propaganda Ministry asks us to put to editors-in-chief the following requests, which must be observed in future with particular care:
  Photos showing members of the Reich Government at dining tables in front of rows of bottles must not be published in future, particularly since it is known that a large number of the Cabinet are abstemious. Ministers take part in social events for reasons of international etiquette and for strictly official purposes, which they regard merely as a duty and not as a pleasure. Recently, because of a great number of photos, the utterly absurd impression has been created among the public that members of the Government are living it up. News pictures must therefore change in this respect.

10.xi.38: With regard to last night's events throughout the Reich[49], Bareckow declared that papers could publish their own reports on the events following the DNB[50] report issued that morning, that is, they could state that here and there windows had been broken and that synagogues had gone up in flames. He requested that the reports should not be exaggerated—above all, no front page headlines. He also asked that no photos should published yet. Nor should collective reports from the Reich appear. Of course the papers could mention in their reports that there had been understandable indignation and corresponding actions by the population in other parts of the country.

---

[49] The *Reichskristallnacht*; see pp. 553ff.
[50] The *Deutsche Nachrichten-Büro*—the German Press Agency.

16.vi.39: Tomorrow, on Saturday evening, there will be an important political event, namely a great rally with a speech by Dr Goebbels in which the minister will make a strong demand for the reintegration of Danzig into the Reich. The papers may be given an excerpt of the Goebbels speech by the Berlin bureau during Saturday. It is a kite to test the international atmosphere for the regulation of the Danzig question, etc.

The regime orchestrated press campaigns geared to its foreign policy, as is clear from the following press conference directives:

277

15.5.38 Herr Berndt[51] said: It will prove necessary for every editorial board to appoint a specialist for the Sudeten German question. Editors must be found who know the subject and who also have material to hand. We need facts not generalities.

23.5.38 Make a big thing of any incidents. The Line is: Germany is peaceful, but the others [i.e. the Czechs] go in for reckless terrorism... The mobilization and the military measures of the Czechs have proved superfluous. We must demand their revocation.

28.5.38. From now onwards incidents must be downplayed.

1.6.38. The German press is requested to phase out the reporting of political events until after Whitsun. The art critics are requested to give large scale coverage even in the political section to the festivals in Bayreuth, Vienna, Salzburg, Heidelberg and Munich.

14.9.38. The press must take the line: peaceful coexistence between different ethnic groups in the same state is inconceivable.

17.9.38. General line: This state i.e. Czechoslovakia is a disgrace to Europe. It must be erased from the map, only then will there be peace. Gentlemen, you are the heavy artillery of the Reich. You must bombard the position ready for the final assault. Use every means possible to hold out for a few more days. At this moment the Reich has no other weapons but you. No paper must appear without major coverage. Even the front page must be striking. Up to now everything has worked well.

30.9.38. The Munich Agreement helps to ensure peace in Europe but we must not behave as if that was a load off our minds.

The result of this regimentation was that the press became boring and predictable. The regime tried to counter this by permitting one or two prestigious newspapers to take a slightly independent line, notably the *Frankfurter Zeitung*, which had an international reputation, and later by founding a paper designed for a more intellectual readership, *Das Reich*. It

---

[51] Alfred Berndt, director of the radio department in the Propaganda Ministry 1938–41.

also tried to introduce some variety by ordering different papers to deal with the various aspects of an issue, in effect increasing the regimentation still further. But these measures could not disguise the fact of a controlled press and the result was a decline in newspapers circulation of ten per cent between 1933 and 1939.

The extent to which the newspaper industry was controlled by the regime is strikingly apparent from the fact that not only the ownership, authorship, and content of the newspapers was strictly regulated, but even their outlets were supervised. One of the professional organizations under the direction of the Reich Press Chamber was the Reich Association of German Station Booksellers. Its function was to vet those who worked in railway bookshops:

278

Re: Karl Friedrich Menzel, Berlin-Wilmersdorf, Hildegardstr. 4. Born 30.x.96.

It follows from Section 10 of the first executive regulation of the Reich Chamber of Culture Law of 1 November 1933, that the admission of a station booksellers to the Reich Press Chamber and to the Reich Association of German Station Booksellers can be refused if facts are available which show that the station bookseller in question does not show the political and moral reliability necessary for carrying out his activity.

We therefore ask you to send us a short statement on the political, ideological, and denominational attitude and activities of the above mentioned, via the appropriate Reich Propaganda Office.

When writing this report it is necessary to start from the basic question of whether in your opinion it is justifiable and advisable for Herr Menzel to continue with his occupation as a station bookseller in the context of the reconstruction of the German press in the National Socialist State.

Evasion of official regulations usually came to the attention of the authorities. Railway stations were often important as meeting-places in the larger German cities, and station booksellers were under particular supervision since there had been complaints about the sale of foreign newspapers:

279

The main administration of the Reich railways has been informed that station bookshops have been offering travellers foreign papers even though they had not been asked for. Such a promotion of foreign papers is not approved by the Reich railways as it is laid down in a decree that it must be the first duty of station booksellers to spread German ideas. The leaseholders of station bookshops must be instructed to desist from everything that could promote the distribution of foreign papers. In the case of serious offences, the lease will be cancelled without notice.

(iv) The Arts

Goebbels's ambitions went beyond controlling and influencing opinion through the obvious propaganda media of the radio and the press. 'What we are aiming for', he told book dealers on 16 May 1933 'is more than a revolt. Our historic mission is to transform the very spirit itself [*den Geist an sich*] to the extent that people and things are brought into a new relationship with one another'(!). This great mission required the mobilization of the entire range of cultural activities in its service. As the Propaganda Ministry declared in connexion with the Theatre Law of 15 May 1934: 'The arts are for the National Socialist State a public exercise: they are not only aesthetic but also moral in nature and the public interest demands not only police supervision but also guidance.'

However, just as in the sphere of the press Goebbels was obliged to compete for influence with the Press Chief, Otto Dietrich, and the Nazi publishing czar, Max Amann, so in the cultural field he was faced with a major rival in the shape of Alfred Rosenberg. Before 1933, Rosenberg had gone some way towards establishing a claim to responsibility for cultural matters within the Party through the establishment of his 'Combat League for German Culture'. He regarded himself as the Party's ideologist in chief, a position which appeared to have received official recognition with his appointment in 1934 as the 'Führer's Commissioner for the Control of the Entire Intellectual and Ideological Training and Education of the Party and of All its Affiliated Bodies'. The conflict between Goebbels and Rosenberg over the control of cultural policy remained bitter during the following years and it had some impact on policy. For while Goebbels had a modicum of artistic taste and also saw the advantage of compromising ideological principles for the sake of propaganda advantage—for example, retaining outstanding film stars even though they had Jewish connexions—Rosenberg was a hard line Nazi ideologist of the most primitive kind. Since Hitler also took a hard ideological line on cultural matters, Goebbels was continually obliged to make sure that he was not outflanked by Rosenberg.

Goebbels triumphed in this struggle because unlike Rosenberg he possessed both State and Party functions and authority. The key to his power in the cultural field was the Reich Chamber of Culture which he established in his capacity as Reich Propaganda Minister with a Law of 22 September 1933:

280

§1. The Reich Minister for Popular Enlightenment and Propaganda is ordered and authorized to organize the members of those branches of activity which affect his sphere of competence into public corporations.

§2. Pursuant to §1 the following chambers are established:
1. A Reich Chamber of Literature.
2. A Reich Press Chamber.
3. A Reich Radio Chamber.
4. A Reich Theatre Chamber.
5. A Reich Music Chamber.
6. A Reich Chamber of the Creative Arts.

§3. The regulations and supplementary regulations which have already been issued for the film industry by the Law concerning the Establishment of a Provisional Film Chamber of 14 July 1933 are to be applied for the establishment of the Chambers referred to in §2...[52]

§5. The corporate bodies in Section 2, together with the Provisional Film Chamber, referred to as the Reich Film Chamber, are combined in a Reich Chamber of Culture. The Reich Chamber of Culture is under the supervision of the Reich Minister for People's Enlightenment and Propaganda. It has its headquarters in Berlin....

§7. The Reich Minister for People's Enlightenment and Propaganda is authorized to decree laws and general administrative regulations as well as amendments for the purpose of enforcing this law. The laws and general administrative regulations affecting the financial or trade interests of the Reich require the consent of the Reich Minister of Finance, in agreement with the Reich Minister of Economics.

By imposing on all those professionally engaged in the cultural sphere the requirement to belong to the Chamber relevant to their particular field and by giving the Propaganda Minister the power to approve or disapprove such membership, the Law conferred on Goebbels the power of professional life and death over all such persons, a power of which he made full use to exclude those writers, musicians, actors, artists etc. who were racially or ideologically objectionable. This Law enabled the regime largely to dispense with formal powers of censorship. In effect people were obliged to censor their own work knowing that the consequences of stepping out of line would be the loss of their livelihood.

What then were the criteria used by the Nazis to define what was or what was not artistically desirable? As an artist manqué, Hitler had strong views about art and, although he rarely intervened directly, it was his views, to which he gave vent in a number of speeches, which provided the basis of Nazi cultural policy. In his speech of 19 July 1937, opening the House of German Art in Munich, which was intended to house the officially approved art, he contrasted his own view of the artistic ideal with that expressed by the modern artists whose works were being displayed simultaneously in

---

[52] §3 of this law laid down that: 'Anyone who professionally or on a charitable basis produces, sells, or shows films or anyone who as a film maker participates in the production of film must belong to the Film Chamber. Acceptance into the Film Chamber can be refused or a member can be excluded if there is evidence which demonstrates that the applicant does not have the requisite reliability for the film trade...

Film makers are producers, directors, composers, script writers, musical directors, musicians, continuity men, architects, cameramen, sound technicians, principal actors, bit part players, extras etc....'

another building in an exhibition of 'Degenerate Art' organized by Adolf Ziegler, President of the Reich Chamber of Art:

281

... But the House is not enough: it must house an exhibition, and if now I venture to speak of art I can claim a title to do so from the contribution which I myself have made to the restoration of German art. For our modern German State, which I with my associates have created, has alone brought into existence the conditions for a new and vigorous flowering of art. It is not Bolshevist art collectors or their henchmen who have laid the foundations, for we have provided vast sums for the encouragement of art and have set before art itself great, new tasks. As in politics, so in German art-life, we are determined to make a clean sweep of empty phrases. Ability is the necessary qualification if an artist wishes his work to be exhibited here. People have attempted to recommend modern art by saying that it is the expression of a new age; but art does not create a new age, it is the general life of peoples which fashions itself anew and often looks for a new expression. ... A new epoch is not created by *littérateurs* but by the fighters, those who really fashion and lead people, and thus make history. ... It is either impudent effrontery or an almost inconceivable stupidity to exhibit to people of today works which perhaps ten or twenty thousand years ago might have been made by a man of the Stone Age. They talk of primitive art, but they forget that is is not the function of art to retreat backwards from the development of a people: its sole function must be to symbolize that living development.

The new age of today is at work on a new human type. Men and women are to be healthier and stronger. There is a new feeling of life, a new joy in life. Never was humanity in its external appearance and in its frame of mind nearer to the ancient world than it is today. ... This, my good prehistoric art stutterers, is the type of the new age, but what do you manufacture? Misformed cripples and cretins, women who inspire only disgust, men who are more like wild beasts, children who, were they alive, must be regarded as under God's curse. And let no one tell me that that is how these artists see things. From the pictures sent in for exhibition it is clear that the eye of some men portrays things otherwise than as they are, that there really are men who on principle feel meadows to be blue, the heaven green, clouds sulphur-yellow, or, as perhaps they prefer to say, 'experience' them thus. I need not ask whether they really do see or feel things in this way, but in the name of the German people I have only to prevent these miserable unfortunates, who clearly suffer from defects of vision, attempting with violence to persuade contemporaries by their chatter that these faults of observation are indeed realities or from presenting them as 'art'. There are only two possibilities here. Either these 'artists' do really see things in this way and believe in what they represent. Then one has only to ask how the defect in vision arose, and if it is hereditary the Minister for the Interior will have to see to it that so ghastly a defect of vision shall not be allowed to perpetuate itself. Or if they do *not* believe in the reality of such impressions but seek on other grounds to burden the nation with this humbug, then it is a matter for a criminal court. There is no place for such works in this building. The industry of architects and workmen has not been employed to house canvases daubed over in five hours, the patients being assured that the boldness of the pricing could not fail to produce its effect, that the canvas would be hailed as the most brilliant lightning creation of a genius. No, they can be left to cackle over each other's eggs!

The artist does not create for the artist. He creates for the people, and we will see to it that the people in future will be called in to judge his art. No one must say that the people has no understanding for a really valuable enrichment of its cultural life. Before the critics did justice to the genius of a Richard Wagner, he had the people on his side, whereas the people has had nothing to do with so-called 'modern art'. The people has regarded this art as the outcome of an impudent and shameless arrogance or of a simply deplorable lack of skill. It has felt that this art stammer, these achievements which might have been produced by untalented children of eight to ten years old, could never be considered an expression of our own times or of the German future. When we know today that the development of millions of years, compressed into a few decades, repeats itself in every individual, then this art, we realize, is not 'modern'. It is on the contrary to the highest degree 'archaic', far older probably than the Stone Age. The people in passing through these galleries will recognize in me its own spokesman and counsellor. It will draw a sigh of relief and gladly express its agreement with this purification of art. And that is decisive: an art which cannot count on the readiest and most intimate agreement of the great mass of the people, an art which must rely upon the support of small cliques, is intolerable. Such an art only tries to confuse, instead of gladly reinforcing, the sure and healthy instinct of a people. The artist cannot stand aloof from his people. This exhibition is only a beginning, but the end of Germany's artistic stultification has begun. Now is the opportunity for youth to start its industrious apprenticeship, and when a sacred conscientiousness has at last come into its own, then I have no doubt that the Almighty from the mass of these decent creators of art will once more raise up individuals to the eternal starry heaven of the imperishable God-favoured artists of the great periods. We believe that especially today, when in so many spheres the highest individual achievements are being manifested, in art also the highest value of personality will once again assert itself.

Hitler saw art as an expression of race. In his view the Aryan alone was capable of creating true art. The 'degenerate art' of the modern period was, therefore, a sign of racial degeneration. The racial and ideological 'renewal' of the German people on which he and his movement were engaged, the purging of the 'decadent Jewish-Liberal culture' of the Weimar period, would create the conditions for the flourishing of a new German art which would reject the weak and the ugly and glorify the healthy, the strong, and the heroic. Art would no longer be restricted to an arrogant and degenerate elite but would once more be rooted in the people, a true expression of the spirit of the *Volk*.

Some of these ideas—the hostility to modern forms of art, labelled 'cultural Bolshevism' by the nationalist middle class of the Weimar period, the desire to move away from an esoteric *avant garde* culture to a more popularly-based one, the aspiration to create a new national German culture in place of the international modern movement in the arts which had tended to dominate Weimar culture—had a strong resonance both among some of those professionally engaged in the arts and above all among ordinary people. The 20,000 visitors a day who flocked to see the exhibition of 'Degenerate Art' no doubt enjoyed finding their prejudices about modern art being officially approved by the new cultural establishment.

The first manifestation of the new cultural line occurred with the so-called 'Burning of the Books' on 10 May 1933. In fact, although it was attended by Goebbels, it had not been organized by the regime as such but by the main German student body, the *Deutsche Studentenschaft*. Influenced by the models of Luther and the Wartburg Festival of 1819, the students had decided on a symbolic 'act against the un-German spirit'. With the help of Dr Wolfgang Hermann, a Nazi who had been given the task of 'reorganizing the Berlin City and People's Libraries' by the Association of People's Librarians they drew up a list of arbitrarily chosen undesirable writers whose works were then burnt in Berlin and other university towns. Louis P. Lochner, head of the Associated Press Bureau in Berlin described the scene there:

282

The whole civilized world was shocked when on the evening of 10 May 1933 the books of authors displeasing to the Nazis, including even those of our own Helen Keller, were solemnly burned on the immense Franz Josef Platz between the University of Berlin and the State Opera on Unter den Linden. I was a witness to the scene.

All afternoon Nazi raiding parties had gone into public and private libraries, throwing on to the streets such books as Dr Goebbels in his supreme wisdom had decided were unfit for Nazi Germany.[53] From the streets Nazi columns of beer-hall fighters had picked up these discarded volumes and taken them to the square above referred to.

Here the heap grew higher and higher, and every few minutes another howling mob arrived, adding more books to the impressive pyre. Then, as night fell, students from the university, mobilized by the little doctor, performed veritable Indian dances and incantations as the flames began to soar skyward. When the orgy was at its height, a cavalcade of cars drove into sight. It was the Propaganda Minister himself, accompanied by his bodyguard and a number of fellow torchbearers of the new Nazi *Kultur*. 'Fellow students, German men and women!' he cried as he stepped before a microphone for all Germany to hear him. 'The age of extreme Jewish intellectualism has now ended, and the success of the German revolution has again given

---

[53] Goebbels was not in fact personally responsible.

the right of way to the German spirit. . . . You are doing the right thing in committing the evil spirit of the past to the flames at this late hour of the night. It is a strong, great and symbolic act, an act that is to bear witness before all the world to the fact that the spiritual foundation of the November Republic has disappeared. From these ashes there will arise the phoenix of a new spirit. . . . The past is lying in flames. The future will rise from the flames within our own hearts. . . . Brightened by these flames our vow shall be: The Reich and the Nation and our Führer Adolf Hitler: Heil! Heil! Heil!

While the books were being consigned to the flames the following 'fire incantations' were recited:

283

1. Against class struggle and materialism.
   For the national community and an idealistic outlook.
   Marx, Kautsky.
2. Against decadence and moral decay.
   For discipline and morality in family and state.
   H. Mann, Ernst Glaeser, E. Kästner.
3. Against cynicism (*Gesinnungslumperei*) and political treachery.
   For devotion to people and state.
   F. W. Förster.
4. Against the debasing exaggeration of man's animal nature.
   For the nobility of the human soul.
   Freudian school. The Journal *Imago*.
5. Against the falsification of our history and the denigration of its great figures.
   For awe for our past.
   Emil Ludwig, Werner Hegemann.
6. Against alien journalism of a democratic-Jewish stamp.
   For responsible participation in the work of national reconstruction.
   Theodor Wolff, Georg Bernhard.
7. Against literary betrayal of the soldiers of the World War.
   For the education of the nation in the spirit of military preparedness.
   E. M. Remarque.
8. Against the self-opinionated pollution of the German language.
   For the preservation of our nation's most precious possession.
   Alfred Kerr.
9. Against arrogance and presumption.
   For veneration and respect for the immortal German national spirit.
   Tucholsky, Ossietsky.

In fact it took time for the regime to develop an effective censorship operation and two years later not a single one of the books burnt had been systematically banned throughout Germany.[54] If a book could not be obtained in one state then it could in another. The reason for this was the lack of a single authoritative censorship office and the lack of a unified national police apparatus. Clause 1 of §7 of the Decree for the Protection of the German People of 4 February 1933 gave the police virtually unlimited powers for the confiscation and banning of undesirable literature: 'Printed matter whose content is calculated to endanger public order can be confiscated by the police'. The concept 'endanger public order' was in practice given a very wide definition. Nevertheless, it was clearly unsatisfactory that the decision over what should or should not be banned should be left in the hand of the police who found themselves under pressure from a whole variety of agencies to ban books. This was particularly true since the original target of 'treasonable literature' was soon enlarged to include 'damaging and undesirable literature'.

The years 1933–35 saw a struggle for the control of censorship between Rosenberg, who had established a Party agency, the 'Reich Office for the Encouragement of German Literature' with an enormous apparatus of censors, and Goebbels, who not only controlled the Reich Chamber of Literature but also established a Reich Office of Literature. Rosenberg's agency was at a crippling disadvantage compared with Goebbels in being purely a Party affair. Thus, whereas Rosenberg had no *official* authority to request the police to ban books, under §29 of the first supplementary regulation of the Reich Chamber of Culture Law, dated 1 November 1933, the police and administrative authorities were placed at the disposal of the Reich Chamber of Culture and of the individual chambers to implement their directives. Already, on 11 November 1933, Goebbels requested all state governments 'to instruct the competent authorities in future only to pronounce provisional bans on books and before reaching a final decision . . . to ascertain the position of the Reich Chamber of Literature.' However, this arrangement did not prove very satisfactory and so, on 25 April 1935 it was replaced by a regulation of the Chamber of Literature concerning 'damaging and undesirable literature' which finally established the supreme censorship authority of Goebbels' Reich Chamber of Literature:

284

§1. The Reich Chamber of Literature maintains a list of such books and writings which threaten the National Socialist cultural aspirations. The circulation of these

[54] The following section owes much to the excellent article by D. Aigner 'Die Indizierung "Schädlichen und unerwünschten Schrifttums" im Dritten Reich' (Frankfurt 1971) Sonderdruck aus dem Archiv für Geschichte des Buchwesens xi, pp. 934–1026.

books and writings by libraries to which the public have access and by the book trade in any form (publishers, bookshops, mail order, door to door sales, lending libraries etc.) is forbidden . . .
§3. Anyone who contravenes the regulations of §1 & 2[55] justifies the assumption that he lacks the requisite reliability and suitability . . . He must, therefore, expect his exclusion from the Reich Chamber of Literature . . .
§4. Requests for inclusion in the lists of §§1 & 2 are to be directed to the Reich Chamber of Literature. The decision concerning such requests will be taken by the President of the Reich Chamber of Literature in consultation with the Reich Minister of Popular Enlightenment and Propaganda.
§5. Purely academic literature is excluded from this regulation; however, purely academic works can also be included in the list referred to in §1 if the Reich Minister for Science and Education so desires or is in agreement . . .

From now onwards bans took the form of inclusion in this confidential index of 'damaging and undesirable literature' prepared by the Reich Chamber of Literature. In future, if the police wished to ban or confiscate a book they were obliged to request its inclusion in the index, reversing the previous practice. In 1936 with official lists of banned books now at their disposal the Gestapo and SD undertook a 'general purge of the German book market', beginning with second-hand bookshops and lending libraries. Private libraries were not normally affected. The following report from the Düsseldorf Gestapo office dated 15 February 1937 shows this process in operation:

285

Re: Raids on bookshops
Decree of 19.viii. 36
On the basis of the above-mentioned decree all bookshops and libraries in the district of Düsseldorf were subjected to examination between 8.ix and 14.xi.36 with reference to the list of harmful and undesirable literature. The SD West region [*Oberabschnitt*] was heavily involved in these actions. . . .
In the district of Düsseldorf thirty-eight searches for forbidden literature took place during the period of the report during which 898 firms in forty-two places were searched and 37,040 volumes confiscated.
All literature found in these actions was handed over to the SD West region responsible for the Düsseldorf district, which will pass on the books, after the sorting which is still going on, to the security office in Berlin. The sorted literature will then be pulped under the supervision of the State police.

The key factor in the decision whether or not to ban a book was not so much the content of the book itself as the personality of the author. In 1939

---

[55] §2 referred to a corresponding list for children's literature.

there were 576 authors on the index whose works were under a total ban. They came into the following categories;

Emigrés ('Traitors')	261 (45%)
Marxists and Soviet authors	178 (31%)
'Pornographers'	56 (10%)
Others (incl. 5% not identifiable)	81 (14%)
Total	576

The following topics prompted the bans on literature contained in the index in operation on 31 December 1938:

286

1. German-language Marxist literature of all categories (27%). 2. All literature directed against National Socialism and the Third Reich from abroad (11%). 3. German-language literature of foreign powers dealing with questions which in the Nazi view affected Germany's vital interests. 4. Literature from the Christian camp directed against the NS ideology and the ambitions of the totalitarian State. 5. The literature of the 'House of Ludendorff' (a cranky religious cult). 6. All literature of a pacifist-liberal tendency. 7. German-language literature in which the 'basic values' of the NS ideology were 'undermined' and 'falsified'. 8. Literature which contained criticism of legislative measures of the NS Government (e.g. Sterilization Law). 9. Literature of the 'traitors' round Ernst Röhm (former Chief of Staff of the SA) and Otto Strasser (pre-1933 Nazi rebel). 10. 'Nationalist-reactionary literature' (e.g. monarchist). 11. Literature which was inopportune for foreign policy reasons. 12. Literature which could be to the detriment of the military security and defence of Germany. 13. Literature which appeared liable to weaken racial strength (e.g. encouraging birth control). 14. The 'corrupting asphalt literature of the literati of a decadent civilization'. 15. Pornographic literature. 16. Quack and occult literature. 17. Kitsch and literature exploiting National Socialism for commercial advantage. 18. Jewish works of all kinds. Before the war, however, no book was put on the index purely on the grounds that the author was Jewish, although Jewish origin provided a powerful argument in addition to others.

Even before 1933 criticism of the arts *per se* had always been regarded in negative terms by the exponents of right-wing cultural values. This was partly because the dominant critics of the Weimar period had tended to be supporters of the modern movement in the arts and also politically in the liberal centre or on the Left. It was also partly because the very idea of criticism of artistic activity seemed sacriligious to a mentality which regarded art as something holy and edifying. Criticism of the arts, therefore was almost invariably linked with the adjective 'corrosive' (*zersetzend*). Now, the fact that the regime acquired increasing responsibility for cultural life through its various control mechanisms contributed to its increasing sensitivity to adverse criticism. The assumption was that if a work of art had been officially approved by the authorities then it was not the function of critics to criticize it. After a number of warnings to critics, on 27 November 1936, Goebbels finally issued an official ban on criticism of the arts:

287

In the context of the reconstruction of German cultural life, criticism of the arts is one of the most pressing but also one of the most difficult questions to solve. Since the seizure of power I have given German critics four years to conform to National Socialist principles. The increasing number of complaints about criticism both from the ranks of artists themselves as well as from other sections of the population prompted me to summon the critics to a conference. At this conference I gave the German critics the opportunity to discuss in depth with the most prominent German artists the problem of criticism, at the end of which I expounded my own views on criticism in unambiguous terms. . . .

Since the year 1936 did not bring any satisfactory improvement in criticism, I finally forbid from today the continuation of criticism of the arts as hitherto practised.

Criticism of the arts as hitherto practised had been turned into art judgment in the days of Jewish cultural infiltration and this was a complete distortion of the term criticism. From today criticism of the arts will be replaced by commentary on the arts. The place of the critic will be taken by the arts editor. Articles on the arts will describe rather than evaluate. They will give the public the opportunity to make their judgment, encourage them to form an opinion about works of art on the basis of their own intellectual and emotional responses.

Scholarly and technical publications were, however, unaffected by the ban.

This position was underlined by an official directive from the Propaganda Ministry of 2 December 1936 which laid down that:

The press has merely to encourage and describe the performance or the work of art in more or less warm words. A positive criticism is permitted and welcomed as before in all spheres.

In addition to the restrictive climate in which they were produced, the quality of the arts during the Third Reich was determined above all by the quality of the people producing them. The purge of Jewish, Socialist, and liberal artists and intellectuals forced into emigration or silence, for which the term 'inner emigration' was coined, many of the finest German writers, artists, and musicians: the Mann brothers, Brecht, Beckmann, Schwitters, Kokoschka, Gropius, Walter—The list is endless. Those who did not fall into any of the categories of 'undesirables' were faced with the decision of whether or not to cooperate with the new regime. One who did cooperate, though after protesting about Nazi cultural policy during the first phase, was the conductor, Wilhelm Furtwängler. His correspondence with Goebbels not only illuminates the position of one who stayed and worked but also the subtlety with which Goebbels was capable of dealing with the problem. On 12 April 1933 Furtwängler wrote to Goebbels:

288

Dear Reich Minister,

In view of my work over many years with the German public and my inner bond with German music I take liberty of drawing your attention to events within the world of music which in my opinion need not necessarily follow from the restoration of our national dignity which we all welcome with joy and gratitude. My feelings in this are purely those of an artist. The function of art and artists is to bring together, not to separate. In the final analysis, I recognize only one line of division—that between good and bad art. But while the line of division between Jews and non-Jews is being drawn with a relentless, even a doctrinaire, sharpness, even where the political attitude of the person concerned gives no grounds for complaint, the other line of division, extremely important, if not decisive, in the long run—that between good and bad—is being far too much neglected.

Musical life today, weakened anyway by the world crisis, radio, etc., cannot take any more experiments. One cannot fix the quota for music as with other things necessary for life like potatoes and bread. If nothing is offered in concerts, nobody goes to them. So that for music the question of quality is not simply an idealistic one, but a question of life and death. If the fight against Jews is mainly directed against those artists who, lacking roots themselves and being destructive, try to achieve an effect through kitsch, dry virtuosity and similar things, then this is quite all right. The fight against them and the spirit they embody cannot be pursued emphatically and consistently enough. But if this fight is directed against *real* artists as well, this will not be in the interests of cultural life, particularly because artists anywhere are much too rare for any country to be able to dispense with their work without loss to culture.

It should therefore be stated clearly that men like Walter, Klemperer, Reinhardt, etc. must be allowed in future to express their art in Germany.

Once again, then, let our fight be directed against the rootless, subversive, levelling, *destructive* spirit, but not against the real artist who is always creative and therefore constructive, however one may judge his art.

In this sense I appeal to you in the name of German art to prevent things from happening which it may not be possible to put right again.

Very respectfully yours,
[signed] WILHELM FURTWÄNGLER

Goebbels replied:

289

I am grateful for the opportunity given me by your letter to enlighten you about the attitude of the nationally-inclined forces in German life to art in general and to music in particular. In this connexion, I am particularly pleased that, right at the beginning of your letter, you emphasize in the name of German artists that you gladly and gratefully welcome the restoration of our national dignity.

I never assumed that this could by anything other than the case, for I believe that the struggle we wage for Germany's reconstruction concerns the German artist not only in a passive but in an active way. I refer to something the Reich Chancellor said publicly three years ago, before our seizure of power: 'If German artists knew what we shall do for them one day, they would not fight against us but with us.'

It is your right to feel as an artist and to see things from an artist's point of view. But that need not mean that you regard the whole development in Germany in an unpolitical way. Politics too is an art, perhaps the highest and most comprehensive there is, and we who shape modern German policy feel ourselves in this to be artists who have been given the responsible task of forming, out of the raw material of the mass, the firm concrete structure of a people. It is not only the task of art and the artist to bring together, but beyond this it is their task to form, to give shape, to remove the diseased and create freedom for the healthy. Thus, as a German politician, I am unable to recognize only the single line of division which you see—that between good and bad art. Art must not only be good, it must also appear to be connected with the people, or rather, only an art which draws on the people itself can in the final analysis be good and mean something to the people for whom it is created.

There must be no art in the absolute sense as known by liberal democracy. The attempt to serve it would result in the people no longer having any inner relationship to art and in the artist himself isolating and cutting himself off from the driving forces of the time in the vacuum of the 'l'art pour l'art' point of view. Art must be good; but beyond this it must be responsible, professional, popular [volksnah] and aggressive. I readily admit that it cannot take any more experiments. But it would have been more suitable to protest against artistic experiments at a time when the whole world of German art was almost exclusively dominated by the love of experiments on the part of elements alien to the people and of the race who tainted and compromised the reputation of German art.

I am sure you are quite right to say that for music quality is not only an idealistic question but a matter of life and death. You are even more right to join our struggle against the rootlessly destructive artistic style, corrupted by kitsch and dry virtuosity. I readily admit that even Germanic representatives took part in these evil goings-on, but that only proves how deeply the roots of these dangers had penetrated into the German people and how necessary it has seemed, therefore to oppose them. Real artists are rare. Accordingly they must be promoted and supported. But in that case they must be real artists.

You will always be able to express your art in Germany—in the future too. To complain about the fact that now and then men like Walter, Klemperer, Reinhardt etc. have had to cancel concerts seems to me to be particularly inappropriate at the moment, since on many occasions real German artists were condemned to silence during the past fourteen years; and the events of the past weeks, not approved of by us either, represent only a natural reaction to those facts. At any rate, I am of the opinion that *every real artist* should be given room for free creativity. But in that case, he must, as you say yourself, be a *constructive creative person* and must not be on the side of the rootlessly subversive, levelling, in most cases purely technical professionals whom you rightly criticize. . . .

Nazi attempts to create a 'people's culture' with new art forms to express their 'revolution' soon proved abortive. The new '*Thing*-Theatre', for example, a cross between a pageant and a cult spectacle, held in romantically-situated and specially designed open air theatres and intended to express the 'national community' in cult form proved a fiasco and was discontinued in 1936. In 1935 the Reich Minister of Education established a Schiller Prize for a play by a German playwright to be awarded on the 130th anniversary of Schiller's death on 9 May. Unfortunately, however, the committee set up to judge the competition was obliged to announce that 'a major playwright in the spirit of National Socialism' had not emerged and, therefore, they were unable to award the prize.[56] In fact, most of the authors writing during the Third Reich were basically conservative nationalists or *völkisch* reactionaries rather than militant Nazis. A few theatres such as the *Münchner Kammerspiele* continued to put on productions of merit. The Munich theatre benefited from Hitler's protection against local Party philistines. This protection was provided largely for reasons of local pride and was prompted by rivalry with Göring's *Staatstheater* in Berlin. After 1936, however, the general trend was to play safe with conventional productions of conventional plays, including some of the classics, just as the film industry played safe with escapist entertainment. In 1941 Goebbels was obliged to admit: 'The National Socialist State has given up the ambition of trying to produce art itself. It has wisely contented itself with encouraging art and gearing it spiritually and intellectually to its educative function for the people'.[57] Four years later, in January 1945, Hans Hinkel, the general secretary of the Reich Chamber of Culture summed up the state of German theatre after twelve years of Nazi rule as follows:

<hr>

290

<hr>

Even on the stages of numerous major theatres or even state theatres nowadays there is a surfeit of 'Blood and Soil', a Party art form which is necessarily bad and

[56] J. Wulf, *Literatur und Dichtung im Dritten Reich. Eine Dokumentation* (Gütersloh 1963) p. 255.
[57] E. Frölich, 'Die Kulturpolitische Pressekonferenz des Reichspropagandaministeriums' in *Vierteljahrshefte für Zeitgeschichte* 22.4.1974 pp. 358–9.

must be rejected in the interests of the high demands of artistic achievement. Quite apart from the fact that the characters in such super-Nordic plays and the actors portraying them must be rejected by anyone of sound instinct, no matter how National Socialist they put themselves over as! It does not matter whether we are dealing with the now famous Herr Hintertupfer or another new virtuoso. One day they will all crumble through their own dishonesty and their so-called coordination and will have to let more honest and more able artists take over. The results of this so-called purging of the stage must be rejected even by the most avid Party supporter.

Attempts were made to encourage new talent with competitions, exhibitions, subsidized instruction and so on. Simultaneously, efforts were made to bring art to the people, with an emphasis on the statistics of those attending the events regarded as more important than the quality of what was being produced. Nothing could disguise or change the all-pervading atmosphere of cultural mediocrity.

(v) Ritual and Social Conformity

In addition to propaganda and indoctrination via the media and the arts, the regime also imposed on the population the obligation to make repeated gestures of conformity. These involved the creation of a new set of rituals and symbols associated with the new regime and the transformation of old ones in accordance with the new values. By obliging people to make gestures of conformity the aim was gradually to undermine any will to resist the new order, to break people's spirit by the need repeatedly to compromise their principles, and in general to create a kind of symbolic framework through which people would be incorporated into the new 'national community'.

The regime insisted, for example, that all officials should replace the traditional German greetings of 'Good Day' and (in South Germany) 'God be with you' with the 'German greeting' of 'Heil Hitler'. When addressed with the German greeting, national comrades were expected to respond in kind. For example, on 7 February 1935, State Minister Jung of Hesse issued the following instruction to all state and local authorities:

291

The Law on the Head of State of the German Reich of 1.8.1934[58] and the Law on the Swearing In of Officials and Soldiers of the Wehrmacht of 20.8.1934[59] have turned the solidarity of the German Civil Service with the Führer and Reich Chancellor into a highly personal and indissoluble relationship of loyalty. I am convinced that the

---

[58] See above, p. 185.
[59] *Ibid.*

civil servants, employees, and workers in the public service are gladly willing to give expression to this in the special form of the German greeting. In an extension of the circular of the Reich Interior Minister of 27 November 1933, I therefore order officials, employees and workers employed in Government bodies from now onwards to give the German greeting while on duty and within official buildings and grounds by raising their right arm—or in the case of physical disability the left arm—while at the same time saying out loud 'Heil Hitler'. I expect civil servants, public employees and workers to greet one another in the same way outside working hours as well.

The regime also established a new series of public rituals to celebrate important days in the Nazi calendar, in effect in rivalry with the traditional religious days of celebration; 30 January to commemorate Hitler's appointment as Reich Chancellor; 24 February to commemorate the refounding of the Party in 1925; the National Day of Mourning in March to commemorate Germany's war dead was rechristened 'Heroes' Remembrance Day' and gradually transformed from a day of mourning into a day of celebration of heroism. In 1939 it was renamed the 'Day of the Restoration of Military Sovereignty' under the motto 'they have not died in vain'. April 20 Hitler's birthday; 1 May was transformed from a day traditionally celebrating working class solidarity in the cause of Socialism into the 'National Day of Labour', a celebration of the 'national community', in which employers and workers in all the various occupations and professions paraded side by side; Mothering Sunday, the second Sunday in May; the Day of the Summer Solstice; the Nuremberg Party Rally in September; Harvest Thanksgiving in which thousands of peasants from all over Germany paraded in their traditional costumes in a celebration of 'Blood and Soil' on the Bückeberg near Hamelin; and the ceremony at the Feldherrnhalle in Munich on 9 November to commemorate those who died in the abortive Hitler putsch of 1923.

National comrades would be expected to show respect for such rituals by hanging out flags and attending parades or speeches and their observance of these rituals would be monitored by the local Party Block Warden and their employers. Failure to conform would mark one down as 'politically unreliable' which in turn could lead to promotion blocks, exclusion from welfare or other state benefits, dismissal or worse.

The following official account of the filming of the celebration of Hitler's fiftieth birthday in 1939 for the weekly newsreel, the *Wochenschau*, describes the atmosphere of such rituals and illuminates Nazis propaganda film techniques:

292

The Führer's fiftieth birthday. Berlin puts on its finery, makes the last preparations for this twentieth of April 1939, which is to become a unique day of thanksgiving. The *Filmwochenschau* has a specific assignment in this. Transcending the present, it must create an historic document for the future, to capture in pictures the greatness of this day for all the future to see. This parade must become a paradigm of film reporting. It is not simply a matter of outward form—the spirit of the hour must be captured also, the whole atmosphere of discipline and of concentrated power. Every second of the action must be captured as it occurs. If something is missed, it cannot be repeated and is lost for ever.

The programme begins. The Führer drives between lines of troops from the park [*Lustgarten*] to the parade ground. Immediately on his arrival the march past begins. But in the meantime, unseen by most of the people despite the variety of events, the formation of the units of the parade takes place. Each unit, after first lining the street, is wheeled into a marching column; men on foot and men in vehicles are skilfully interspersed in a colourful order. A broad street, many kilometres long, is completely filled by soldiers of all the armed forces, which must now be ordered into a regular formation for the great moment when they are to march past Adolf Hitler. The twelve pairs of eyes of the twelve cameramen must see more than all the hundreds of thousands of onlookers. And so they do, as the success of this *Wochenschau* demonstrates. . . .

Under a bright, shining sky the birthday itself begins. Cheerful marching tunes resound: the SS *Leibstandarte*[60] give Hitler a birthday serenade. Surrounded by some of his co-workers, among whom Himmler stands out, Hitler receives the homage. The camera lingers lovingly on the Goebbels children, all clothed in white, who stand, curious but well behaved, next to Hitler, thus strengthening his reputation as a true lover of children—a special shot for the women in the audience. Now the picture turns to the crowd. A gigantic chorus in front of the Reich Chancellery swells in a song of jubilation for Hitler. Now Hitler appears on the balcony before the crowd, which breaks out into a repeated ovation.

In the second half of the film the scene shifts finally from the preparations to familiar close-ups, to mass demonstrations, and then at last to the sphere of the official, political, and military. With screaming engines the great automobiles leave the Wilhelmstrasse; Hitler and his entourage depart for the parade. Military orders and marching tunes introduce the second act of the spectacle. Jubilation breaks out: the film is focused, sight and sound, on the exact moment when Hitler passes the Brandenburg Gate between the troops. The Hitler who now, erect and poised, climbs the steps to the canopied platform and takes his place on a 'throne' (already significantly picked out by the camera) to await the parade—this Hitler is not only a 'statesman' but also clearly a field-commander-to-be, who intends to review his armed forces. This is the way the film has it.

---

[60] Hitler's bodyguard.

The most widespread and resented form of compulsory gesture of conformity was the continual collection for the Winter Relief Programme and other Nazi causes. The Winter Relief had been initiated in the early days of the regime as a programme for collecting money, food, and clothing for the assistance of distressed families during the period of mass unemployment. It was continued, however, long after unemployment had ceased to be a problem, partly as a means of soaking up consumer spending power with funds being diverted to pay for Nazi welfare activities or towards the rearmament programme. But, above all, these collections had a propaganda function as exemplary demonstrations of the 'national community' in action. Every winter from October to March special monthly badges were sold and displayed on front doors to show that a contribution had been made. However, since the collectors were goaded by their superiors into producing larger and larger receipts, these badges provided less and less immunity from the importunities of the collectors. 'Days of National Solidarity' were organized in which top Nazis and other leading figures went on the streets with collecting boxes to demonstrate their solidarity with their 'national comrades', who were expected to respond with a generous financial contribution. On 10 December 1935, the local paper in Neu-Isenburg near Frankfurt am Main reported:

293

The 7 December, the 'Day of National Solidarity', has vividly demonstrated to anyone who wants to see what a strong and decisive leadership filled with true Socialist spirit has made of the German people in whom previously class differences and pride in status flourished. This day represented the most vivid expression of our newly created national community, in which even high-ranking personalities did not regard themselves as too distinguished to go into the streets and collect for the alleviation of the distress of their poorer national comrades.

The leading members of the Party, the Reich, the state, and municipal authorities, the SA, SS, NSKK, and HJ, men of the free professions, of industry and trade etc. assembled in Neu-Isenburg for the collection as well. Eighty collectors in all produced the sum of RM 885. And so the second 'Day of National Solidarity' in Neu-Isenburg has once again been a complete success. It has provided the proof that the German people really do form a national community in which everyone gladly makes sacrifices for their fellows. The higher aim of the day has thereby been achieved over and above the concrete success. . . . The 'one pot' collection on Sunday produced the nice sum of RM 1465.70.

The reference to the 'one pot' collection concerned the practice of holding 'one pot Sundays', in which once a month during winter families were expected to have only one dish for their Sunday lunch and donate what they had saved to the collectors who came round to the door and even into the kitchen to make sure the ritual was being observed. On 11 March 1939 the *Neu-Isenburger Anzeigeblatt* reported:

294

The Last One-pot Sunday of the Winter Relief Programme. . . . For the last time in the Winter Relief Programme of 1938/39 the German people are observing their One-pot Sunday. Once more they will show the world that German Socialism involves not words or slogans but deeds. The German people has not become the community it is through money and riches, but rather crisis and a tragic fate shared in common have bonded the German people together in recent years. For the last time this winter the Winter Relief Programme is appealing to all national comrades and asking for a One-pot contribution. It goes without saying that every family will give a One-pot contribution. But since it is the last One-pot Sunday the German people expect from every national comrade that he will increase his contribution for the end of the Winter Relief Programme because it is the last time the One-pot collector will be calling and it would be a sign of gratitude to the Führer. For one should not show one's gratitude to the Führer for his great work with words but rather one must show through deeds that one wants to help the Führer make the German people great and strong. And so the motto for the coming One-pot Sunday is: 'Everyone should make as far as he can a bigger sacrifice for the One-pot and thereby show gratitude to the Führer for his great work'.

Despite all the propaganda, however, these collections met with increasing resentment and resistance to which the authorities responded with tough measures. According to a statement of the responsible Gau official in Gau Hessen–Nassau dated 28 November 1939: 'Contributions are voluntary but they are an expression of political reliability, they are proof of loyalty to the Führer.'[61] The following instructions from Gauleiter Jokob Sprenger of Gau Hessen–Nassau of 17 December 1935 indicated the tough line taken. Notorious backsliders faced public exposure in the press and even violence from Nazi mobs:

295

Despite all our education of the public, the Winter Relief Programme is still being to some extent covertly sabotaged. These attempts must be crushed with all means. Open sabotage must be dealt with immediately by the agencies of the Secret State

---

[61] See D. Rebentisch, 'Die "politische Beurteilung" als Herrschaftsinstrument der NSDAP' in D. Peukert and J. Reulecke, eds., *Die Reihen fast geschlossen. Beiträge zur Geschichte des Alltags unterm Nationalsozialismus* (Wuppertal 1981) p. 118.

Police, also the Secret State Police must be informed in the case of all covert attempts to damage the Winter Relief Programme. Furthermore, preventive measures must be taken to make it clear to those who maliciously refuse to make contributions to the WHW that through their refusal to support the WHW they are placing themselves outside the national community. Thus, for example, all businesses which receive State or municipal contracts will have these contracts revoked, and people of whom it is known that they do not support the WHW will be excluded from deliveries and contracts from official bodies.

The tax authorities will be instructed not to respond favourably to appeals for tax reductions from national comrades who sabotage the WHW.

In every sphere attempts to weaken the measures of the Winter Relief Programme must be suppressed with all available legal means.

CHAPTER 19

Youth and Education

The Nazi leadership appreciated the difficulty of indoctrinating the older generation which had already been socialised in accordance with the norms and values of a 'decadent' culture. They were all the more determined to mould the new generation along Nazi lines. As the leader of the Nazi Teachers' League, Hans Schemm, put it: 'Those who have youth on their side control the future.'[62] This was a theme which Hitler took up in two speeches: the first was on 14 September 1935 at the Nuremberg Party Rally where he stressed the new image of German youth; in the second on 4 December 1938 in Reichenberg he made clear the total claim of Nazism on young Germans.

296

(a) The ideal of manhood has not always been the same even for our own people. There were times which now seem to us very far off and almost incomprehensible when the ideal of the young man was the chap who could hold his beer and was good for a drink. But now his day is past and we like to see not the man who can hold his drink, but the young man who can stand all weathers, the hardened young man. Because what matters is not how many glasses of beer he can drink, but how many blows he can stand; not how many nights he can spend on the spree, but how many kilometres he can march. We no longer see in the boorish beer-drinker the ideal of the German people: we find it in men and girls who are sound to the core, and sturdy.

What we look for from our German youth is different from what people wanted in the past. In our eyes the German youth of the future must be slim and slender,

---

[62] Quoted in W. Feiten, *Der Nationalsozialistische Lehrerbund*, (Weinheim–Basel 1981), p 203.

swift as the greyhound, tough as leather, and hard as Krupp steel. We must educate
a new type of man so that our people is not ruined by the symptoms of degeneracy
of our day....

297

(b) These young people learn nothing else but to think as Germans and to act as
Germans; these boys join our organization at the age of ten and get a breath of fresh
air for the first time, then, four years later, they move from the *Jungvolk* to the Hitler
Youth and there we keep them for another four years. And then we are even less
prepared to give them back into the hands of those who create our class and status
barriers, rather we take them immediately into the Party, into the Labour Front, into
the SA or into the SS, into the NSKK and so on. And if they are there for eighteen
months or two years and have still not become real National Socialists, then they
go into the Labour Service and are polished there for six or seven months, and all
of this under a single symbol, the German spade. And if, after six or seven months,
there are still remnants of class consciousness or pride in status, then the Wehrmacht
will take over the further treatment for two years and when they return after two
or four years then, to prevent them from slipping back into old habits once again
we take them immediately into the SA, SS etc., and they will not be free again for
the rest of their lives. And, if someone says to me—there will still be some left out;
I reply: National Socialism is not at the end of its days but only at the beginning.

(i) The Hitler Youth (HJ)

Since the turn of the century, Germany had been remarkable for the degree
of its youth organization. At the beginning of 1933, between five and six
million young people were organized in a plethora of youth groups. Some
were attached to political parties or to religious denominations, while others
were geared to sports activites. Many, however, were independent, forming
the so-called *bündisch* or free youth movement. They were heirs of the
Wandervögel of the Wilhelmine era, middle-class young people who had
reacted against the materialism and philistinism, the stifling conventions and
moral hypocrisy of their parents' generation. The movement was characterized by a combination of contempt for conventional politics and an
emotional longing for a national renewal through a kind of alternative youth
culture which would act as a source of social, cultural, and spiritual
regeneration for Germany. It developed its own life-style with activities such
as hiking parties and the singing of folk songs round camp fires, all designed
to create a feeling of heightened experience through a sense of community
and comradeship with other young people. These forms of activity and
concepts such as 'the unity of youth' and 'the renewal of the nation' also
permeated the political and denominational youth groups, so that during the

Weimar Republic an alternative youth culture did indeed exist to a remarkable degree.

At the beginning of 1933, the Hitler Youth (HJ) had been a relatively small organization with a membership of 55,000, one per cent of the organized youth, who were largely drawn from the lower middle and working class. However, its leader, Baldur von Schirach, was determined to assert his organization's claim to total control over German youth. On 17 July 1933, Hitler appointed him 'Youth Leader of the German Reich' and gave him the responsibility of supervising all youth activities under the overall authority of the Reich Minister of the Interior. By the end of 1933, the HJ had 'coordinated' all youth organizations with the exception of the Catholic ones, which for a time were protected by the Reich Concordat. Moreover, increasing pressure was used on young people to join the HJ, particularly via the schools. Teachers were officially instructed to try and persuade their pupils, and even Catholic pupils were not exempt from this pressure, of which the following case in Trier is admittedly an extreme example. A local Catholic priest wrote to the Party district leader on 14 February 1934 complaining:

298

In the 5th Class which is taught by teacher A there are 10 members of the Youth Club W. These boys have been youth club members for years and remained when the Hitler Youth was founded. Because of this latter fact they have had to endure a good deal of chicanery from their teacher. Despite the fact that there is a Reich Concordat, despite the fact that the Supreme Youth Leadership of the Reich stresses again and again that no boy is to be forced into the Hitler Youth, teacher A exerts such pressure on the members of the Youth Club that it is almost unbearable for the boys. For example: last Saturday he set those boys concerned the essay: 'Why am I not in the Hitler Youth?', while all the other children in the class had no homework. On setting the essay he added: 'If you don't write the essay I shall beat you until you can't sit down.' Another case: a member of the HJ had rejoined the Catholic Youth Club. When Mr A heard of this he threatened he would set him forty sums every time he stayed away from the HJ parade. This was made even worse by his threat of a beating as well. After this, the boy who had voluntarily wanted to come back to us stayed in the Hitler Youth. The teacher's pressure on the Youth Club members even goes so far as to threaten the boys that he would 'muck up' their reports at Easter and would not move them up and so on. When Mr A was asked why he often punished only the members of the Youth Club, he said: 'It goes against the grain to beat a boy wearing the brown shirt of honour.'

From this one can figure out how unbearable the pressure of the teacher is on members of the Catholic Youth Club. It would be in the interest of the boys and of the whole class if this situation was changed and the Youth Club members were given the same freedom and just treatment as the other members of the class.

The reply from the Party district leader of 2 March makes it clear that, at this stage at least, the Party wished to avoid too much controversy by precipitate action:

I send the enclosed report of the Chaplain of W re treatment of the Catholic Youth Club of W in the primary school by Mr A for your information. It is advisable to suggest to the teacher concerned that he proceed more wisely, cautiously, and inconspicuously so that the other side has no occasion for complaint.

Additional pressures on young people to join the HJ came from the increasing restriction of eligibility for jobs in the State service and for apprenticeships in the private sector to members of the HJ, and from the agreement between Schirach and the Reich Sports leader in July 1936 granting the HJ a monopoly of youth sports activities up to the age of 14, later extended to 18. During 1936, the HJ concentrated on trying to recruit all the 10–14 age group into the *Deutsches Jungvolk* (DJ) and *Jungmädelbund* (*JM*) sections of the HJ. April 20 was designated as the official entry date for ten-year-olds and, by the end of the year, the HJ claimed that 95 per cent of those born in 1926 had joined.

Finally, on 1 December 1936, Hitler accepted Schirach's request, against the wishes of Frick and the ministerial bureaucracy, to remove his office from the overall authority of the Reich Ministry of the Interior and establish it as an independent 'Supreme Government Agency' directly subordinate to the Führer. The Law on the Hitler Youth also designated the HJ an official educational institution equivalent in status to home and school:

299

The future of the German nation depends upon its youth and German youth must therefore be prepared for its future duties. The Reich Government has accordingly decided on the following law which is published herewith:

1. The whole of German youth within the borders of the Reich is organized in the Hitler Youth.

2. All German young people, apart from being educated at home and at school, will be educated in the Hitler Youth physically, intellectually, and morally in the spirit of National Socialism to serve the nation and the community.

3. The task of educating German youth in the Hitler Youth is being entrusted to the Reich Leader of German Youth in the NSDAP. He therefore becomes the 'Youth Leader of the German Reich'. His office shall rank as a Supreme Governmental Agency with its headquarters in Berlin and he will be directly responsible to the Führer and Chancellor of the Reich.

4. All regulations necessary to execute and supplement this decree will be issued by the Führer and Reich Chancellor.

Despite the first clause, the Law did not in fact make the HJ compulsory. That only occurred with the Second Decree for Implementing the Hitler Youth Law of 25 March 1939, which introduced the so-called 'duty of youth service':

300

§1. *Length of service*
   (1) Service in the Hitler Youth is honorary service to the German people.
   (2) All young people are obliged from the age of 10 to their 19th birthday to serve in the Hitler Youth. In particular,
       1. the boys aged 10 to 14 in the German Young People (DJ).
       2. boys aged 14 to 18 in the Hitler Youth (HJ).
       3. girls aged 10 to 14 in the Young Girls League (JM).
       4. girls aged 14 to 18 in the League of German Girls (BDM).

§2. *Educational Authority*
   All boys and girls of the Hitler Youth are subject to a public and legally binding training according to the regulations to be laid down by the Führer and Reich Chancellor.
   . . .

§9. *Registration and Admission*
   (1) All young people must be registered for admission by the 15 March in the year they reach their 10th birthday with the HJ leader responsible. . . .
   (2) The legal guardian of the young person is responsible for registration.
   (3) Admission to the Hitler Youth follows on 20 April each year.
   . . .

§12. *Penalties*
   (1) A legal guardian will be liable to a fine of up to 150 RM or to imprisonment, if he deliberately contravenes the stipulation of §9 of this decree.
   (2) Anyone who maliciously prevents or attempts to prevent any young person from serving in the Hitler Youth will be punished by fine or imprisonment.
   (3) Prosecution will follow only at the request of the Youth Leader of the German Reich. The request can be withdrawn.
   (4) Young people can be required by the responsible local police authority to fulfil the duties which are imposed on them by this decree and the regulations for its implementation.

301

MEMBERSHIP FIGURES OF THE HITLER YOUTH

	HJ (boys aged 14–18)	DJ (boys aged 10–14)	BDM (girls aged 14–18)	JM (girls aged 10–14)	Total	Total population of 10–18 year olds
End 1932	55,365	28,691	19,244	4,656	107,956	
End 1933	568,288	1,130,521	243,750	349,482	2,292,041	7,529,000
End 1934	786,000	1,457,304	471,944	862,317	3,577,565	7,682,000
End 1935	829,361	1,498,209	569,599	1,046,134	3,943,303	8,172,000
End 1936	1,168,734	1,785,424	873,127	1,610,316	5,437,601	8,656,000
End 1937	1,237,078	1,884,883	1,035,804	1,722,190	5,879,955	9,060,000
End 1938	1,663,305	2,064,538	1,448,264	1,855,119	7,031,226	9,109,000
Beg. 1939	1,723,886	2,137,594	1,502,571	1,923,419	7,287,470	8,870,000

and the BDM Werk (girls aged 18–21): 440,189

ABBREVIATIONS. HJ, Hitler-Jugend (Hitler Youth); DJ, Deutsches Jungvolk (German Young People); BDM, Bund Deutscher Mädel (League of German Girls); JM, Jungmädelbund (League of Young Girls).

Members of the Hitler Youth were required to swear an oath to the Führer. The following ceremony for admission to the DJ was laid down on instructions of the Trier section of the Hitler Youth (dated April 1940):

302

It is of the greatest importance that the admissions are arranged in a solemn way. For everybody the hour of his induction must be a great experience. The cub [*Pimpf*] and young lass [*Jungmädel*] must regard this hour of their first vow to the Führer as the holiest of their whole life.

Text of the speech of the DJ leader, to be read in all branches:

Dear boy!/Dear girl,

This hour in which your are to be received into the great community of the Hitler Youth is a very happy one and at the same time will introduce you into a new period of your lives. Today for the first time you swear allegiance to the Führer which will bind you to him for all time.

And every one of you, my young comrades, enters at this moment into the community of all German boys and girls. With your vow and your commitment you now become a bearer of German spirit and German honour. Every one, every single one now becomes the foundation for an eternal Reich of all Germans.

When you too now march in step with the youngest soldiers, then bear in mind that this march is to train you to be a National Socialist conscious of the future and faithful to his duty.

And the Führer demands of you and of us all that we train ourselves to a life of service and duty, of loyalty and comradeship. You, ten-year-old cub, and you, lass, are not too young nor too small to practise obedience and discipline, to integrate yourself into the community and show yourself to be a comrade. Like you, millions of young Germans are today swearing allegiance to the Führer and it is a proud picture of unity which German youth today presents to the whole world. So today you make a vow to your Führer and here, before your parents, the Party and your comrades, we now receive you into our great community of loyalty. Your motto will always be:

'Fuhrer, command—we follow!'

303

Vow

You, Führer, are our commander!
We stand in your name.
The Reich is the object of our struggle,
It is the beginning and the Amen.

Your word is the heartbeat of our deeds;
Your faith builds cathedrals for us.
And even when death reaps the last harvest
The crown of the Reich never falls.

We are ready, your silent spell
Welds our ranks like iron,
Like a chain, man beside man,
Into a wall of loyalty round you.

You, Führer, are our commander!
We stand in your name.
The Reich is the object of our struggle,
It is the beginning and the Amen.

Although the HJ destroyed the previous youth organizations, it adopted some of the style and activities of the pre-1933 free youth movement and tried to create the impression that it was fulfilling their aspirations. The slogan 'youth must be led by youth', for example, was ritually echoed and to some extent followed in practice. But the spirit in which it was applied was very different from that of the pre-1933 youth movement. These young leaders were not representing an autonomous youth culture but were functionaries of an official bureaucracy regimented by rules and regulations and following set patterns of training. This was a point emphasized by a BDM leader, Melita Maschmann, in her memoirs, together with the typical Nazi stress on achievement and its restless dynamic:

304

Apart from its beginnings during the 'years of struggle', the Hitler Youth was not a youth movement at all: it became more and more the 'State youth organization', that is to say, it became more and more institutionalized, and finally became the instrument used by the National Socialist regime to run its ideological training of young people and the war work for certain age groups.

The reasons for this development can be found in the external pressure of events, since the increased membership which the Hitler Youth had to absorb after 1935 was such that any healthy growth was impossible....

And yet the Hitler Youth was a youth organization. Its members may have allowed themselves to be dressed in uniforms and regimented, but they were still young people and they behaved like young people. Their characteristic surplus of energy and thirst for action found great scope in their programme of activities, which constantly required great feats to be performed. It was part of the method of the National Socialist Youth leadership to arrange almost everything in the form of competitions. It was not only in sport and one's profession that one competed. Every unit wanted to have the best group 'home', the most interesting expedition log, the biggest collection for the Winter Relief Fund, and so forth—or at least they were supposed to want it. In the musical competitions Hitler Youth choirs, fife and drums bands, chamber orchestras and amateur theatrical groups competed as did young singers, instrumentalists, sculptors, painters and poets for the glory of the most brilliant performance. There were even story-telling competitions to see which boys and girls out of all their contemporaries were best at telling folk stories.

This constant competition introduced an element of unrest and forced activity into the life of the groups even in peacetime. It did not merely channel young people's drive for action; it also inflamed it, where it would have been wiser and better to give the individual within the group and the group as a whole periods when they could mature and develop in tranquillity.

There was certainly a great deal of good and ambitious education in the Hitler Youth. There were groups who learned to act in a masterly way. People told stories, danced and practised handicrafts, and in these fields the regimentation was fortunately often less strict. But the idea of a competition (behind which lay the glorification of the fighter and the heroic) often enough banished the element of meditation even from musical activities, and the playful development of the creative imagination, free of any purpose, was sadly stunted.

The leaders of a youth movement so drilled to activity and performance gradually created a style of their own as 'managers'. They were themselves driven from one activity to the next, and so they drove their charges on in the same manner. Even the young men and women in the Reich Youth Leadership who initiated all this activity were subject to the same restless compulsive drive. The constantly turning wheel of incessant activity continually created a fresh momentum and carried along everyone who came within its sphere of influence....

The following plan for a fortnight's camp outlined by the cultural office of the Reich Youth Leadership (1937 Handbook) illuminates the mentality which was being inculcated in young people;

305

What is outlined below is only to be regarded as an example of how various material should be evenly distributed. The 9th of July is used as the day of arrival, the 23rd of July as the day of departure.

Friday 10 July:
Password: Adolf Hitler
Motto for the day: Hitler is Germany and Germany is Hitler.
Words: We owe to our leader Adolf Hitler the fact that we can open our camp today.
Song: Onward, onward ...
Community hour: is omitted since the group is still very tired.

Saturday 11 July:
Password: Baldur von Schirach
Motto for the day: Anything that undermines our unity must go on the pyre!
Song: We are not civilians, peasants, workmen ...
Community hour: What do I want in the Hitler Youth? (Reich Youth Leadership folder)

Sunday 12 July:
Password: Germany
Motto for the day: Germany, Germany above all!
Words for the morning celebration: We are not in the Hitler Youth to be provided for life, to receive perhaps a position or office later on, but we want to serve Germany unselfishly, as is mentioned in the song: 'We carry in our beating hearts faith in Germany.'
Song: On, raise our flags ...
Community hour: is omitted on account of Sunday duties, e.g. sports contests etc.

Monday 13 July:
Password: Widukind[63]
Motto for the day: To be one nation is the religion of our time.
Words: If we fight to create a united youth organization and for all young men to be in it, we serve our nation, because the youth of today will become the nation of tomorrow.
Song: Holy fatherland ...
Community hour: We commit ourselves to the ideal of our ancestors. (Reich Youth Leadership folder)

Tuesday 14 July:
Password: Frederick the Great
Motto for the day: It is not necessary for me to live, but certainly necessary for me to do my duty!
Words: We speak of the principle of volunteering, on which basis we have met.
Song: The marching of the column sounds ...
Community hour: Prussianism, our ideal.

---

[63] Leader of the Saxons against Charlemagne.

Wednesday 15 July:
Password: Schill[64]
Motto for the day: Germany's defence—Germany's honour.
Words: Schill revolted against a Prussia without defences and therefore without honour. Adolf Hitler restored honour to Germany when he gave the German nation back its weapons. We want to make ourselves strong so that we never again lose our honour.
Song: Now we must march . . .
Community hour: The soldier protects German work. (Reich Youth Leadership folder)

Thursday 16 July:
Password: Langemarck[65]
Motto of the day: You have not fallen in vain!
Words: the camp leader speaks of the respect all young people should have for the two million dead who were killed in the World War. They died for Germany; we strengthen ourselves also for Germany. Therefore we are the heirs of the front. Once the soldiers of the Great War were dragged through the dirt (they were called murderers!); today the whole of German youth goes on a pilgrimage to the places where they were killed and lowers its flags in memory of their holy sacrifice.
Song: Wild geese rush through the night . . .
Community hour: Out of the World War grew the Third Reich. (Reich Youth Leadership folder)

Friday 17 July:
Password: Richthofen[66]
Motto for the day: Nation, fly again!
Words: The camp leader tells about the determined sacrifice which the few German combat aviators had to make during the World War. Names like Immelmann, Boelcke, Richthofen are not forgotten. Today we possess a strong air force which has continued the tradition of those few who accomplished the impossible with technically imperfect planes.
Song: Soldiers carry rifles . . .
Community hour: Letters and some excerpts are read from the numerous good books about aviation.

Saturday 18 July:
Password: Schlageter[67]
Motto for the day: Let struggle be the highest aim of youth!
Words: The camp leader speaks about the fact that we all have to become fighters, that we have to accept as mottoes for our life everything which requires from us

---

[64] Ferdinand von Schill was a Prussian Officer in the War of Liberation against Napoleon, killed in 1809.
[65] The site of a battle in the First World War in which a company of German students marched straight at British machine-gun posts, allegedly singing 'Deutschland, Deutschland über alles'.
[66] Manfred Baron von Richthofen was a German aviator in the First World War, credited with shooting down 80 aircraft.
[67] Albert Leo Schlageter, officer in the First World War and later member of the NSDAP, was shot for sabotage by the French during their reoccupation of the Ruhr in 1923. The Nazis made him one of their 'martyrs'.

a manly, heroic attitude: That which does not kill me makes me only the stronger!
One does not beg for a right, one fights for it! What is good?—To be brave is good!
He who fights has right on his side; he who does not fight has lost all rights! What
we can do ourselves, we must not leave to God. . . . Therefore pray, when we have
to pray: Lord, let us never be cowardly!
Song: Unroll the blood-red flags . . .
Community hour: Germans in the world—Versailles is a burden on us. (Reich Youth
  Leadership folders)

Sunday 19 July:
Password: Herbert Norkus[68]
Motto for the day: Our service to Germany is divine service!
Song: Now let the flags fly . . .
Morning celebration: On this morning a bigger morning celebration takes place.
Fundamental thought: We cannot be called heretics and pagans, if we have made
  Herbert Norkus's readiness for sacrifice the motto of our lives.
Community hour: is omitted because of Sunday duties, e.g. parents' day, contests,
  etc.

Monday 20 July:
Password: Blood
Motto for the day: To remain pure and become mature.
Words: The camp leader talks about this motto by Walker Flex and demands from
  the boys clean, decent thinking and action. The sentence, 'Service is service and
  liquor is liquor' is not valid for us; but: 'All or nothing!'
Song: Young nation, step forward, for your hour has come . . .
Community hour: Ideological examination for the Hitler Youth and German Young
  People efficiency medal.

Tuesday 21 July:
Password: Honour
Motto of the day: For a member of the youth organization his honour is the greatest
  thing!
Words: The camp leader speaks about this motto.
Song: Behind the flag we march . . .
Community hour: see 20 July.

Wednesday 22 July:
Password: Old Guard
Motto of the day: Germany must live, even if we have to die!
Song: Through Greater-Berlin we march . . .
Final celebration: On this evening the final celebration takes place, at which the camp
  leader speaks for the last time. Adolf Hitler, Baldur von Schirach, Widukind,
  Frederick the Great, Schill, Langemarck, Richthofen, Schlageter, Herbert Norkus,
  Blood, Honour, Old Guard have been the passwords. All commit themselves to
  the one word 'Germany' which shall also prevail over the whole life of the club
  [*Pimpf*].

---

[68] Herbert Norkus was a member of the Hitler Youth killed by Communists in 1932. He also became a Party
'martyr' and was held up as a hero to members of the HJ.

What then was the impact of the HJ on German youth? The evidence suggests that it was mixed and depended to a considerable extent both on the quality of the local HJ leadership and on the individual boy or girl's personality and home background. The following SPD reports from the early summer of 1934, however, suggest that, initially at any rate, it was quite successful in attracting the support of young people:

306

(a) Youth is still in favour of the system: the novelty, the drill, the uniform, the camp life, the fact that school and the parental home take a back seat compared to the community of young people—all that is marvellous. A great time without any danger. Many believe that they will find job opportunities through the persecution of Jews and Marxists. The more enthusiastic they get the easier are the exams and the sooner they will get a position, a job. For the first time, peasant youth is associated with the State through the SA and the HJ. Young workers also join in: one day Socialism may come; one is simply trying to achieve it in a new way; the others certainly did not manage to achieve it; the national community is better than being the lowest class. That is roughly what they are thinking. The new generation has never had much use for education and reading. Now nothing is demanded of them; on the contrary, knowledge is publicly condemned.

The parents experience all this too. One cannot forbid the child to do what all children are doing, cannot refuse him the uniform which the others have. One cannot ban it, that would be dangerous.

The children and young people then follow the instructions of the HJ and demand from their parents that they become good Nazis, that they give up Marxism, Reaction, and dealings with Jews.

(b) It is the young men who bring home enthusiasm for the Nazis. Old men make no impression nowadays. The new town clerk of our town, the deputy major, is 29 years old. I am almost inclined to say that the secret of National Socialism is the secret of its youth. The chaps are so fanaticized that they believe in nothing but their Hitler.

The HJ extended opportunities for participation in youth activities to groups which previously had not had easy access to them—notably those in country districts and to girls in general. Depending largely on the quality of the local leadership, its activities could have considerable appeal, as is clear from the post-war reminiscences of a Hitler Youth leader:

307

What I liked about the HJ was the comradeship. I was full of enthusiasm when I joined the *Jungvolk* at the age of ten. What boy isn't fired by being presented with high ideals such as comradeship, loyalty, and honour. I can still remember how deeply moved I was when we learned the cub mottoes: '*Jungvolk* boys are hard, they can keep a secret, they are loyal; *Jungvolk* boys are comrades; the highest value for a *Jungvolk* boy is honour'. They seemed to me to be holy. And then the trips! Is there anything nicer than enjoying the splendours of the homeland in the company of one's comrades. We often went off into the countryside round K to spend Sunday there. What joy we felt when we gathered at some blue lake, collected wood, made a fire, and then cooked pea soup on it. We found it marvellous that we could go on these trips despite the war . . . And it always makes a deep impression to sit of an evening round a fire outside in a circle and to have a sing song and tell stories. These were probably our happiest hours in the HJ. Here sat apprentices and school boys, the sons of workers and civil servants side by side and got to know and appreciate one another. In addition, I was pleased that sport also had its place in the *Jungvolk*. We never went on our trips without a ball or some other piece of sports equipment. It was a means of relaxation and of building us up physically to play handball or football on a meadow or to bathe in a lake far from the noisy city.

Later, however, when I became a leader in the *Jungvolk* the negative aspects became very obvious. I found the compulsion and the requirement of absolute obedience unpleasant. I appreciated that there must be order and discipline in such a large group of boys, but it was exaggerated. It was preferred that people should not have a will of their own and should totally subordinate themselves. But this approach could not educate the boys into becoming strong-willed men. Then, when I moved to Bann headquarters and acquired rather more insight I had the first serious doubts. The HJ was interfering everywhere in people's private lives. If one had private interests apart from the HJ people looked askance.

Some young people, however, were completely put off by the growing regimentation and militaristic emphasis in the HJ activities as is clear from the following reminiscence:

308

If other people rave about their time as cubs (*Pimpfen*) (as if the whole thing was only a scout pack under another name), I cannot share their enthusiasm. I have oppressive memories. In our troop the *Jungvolk* activities consisted almost entirely of stolid military drill. Even if sport or shooting practice or a sing song was scheduled, we always had to do drill first: endless marching with 'attention', 'at ease', 'left wheel', 'right wheel', 'about turn', commands which I can still reel off in my sleep. It was like Sergeant Himmelstoss on the parade ground: twelve-year-old horde leaders bawling out ten-year-old cubs and driving them all over the school play ground and meadows . . . The slightest signs of recalcitrance, the slightest faults with our uniforms, the slightest lateness on parade were punished with extra drill— powerless subleaders projected their rage onto us. But there was method in the madness: from childhood onwards we were drilled in toughness and blind obedience. At the command 'down', we had to throw ourselves with bare knees onto the gravel; when we were doing press ups our noses were pushed in the sand; anyone who got a stitch cross-country running was ridiculed as a weakling.

How did we put up with that for four years? How did we fight back our tears and grit our teeth at the pain? Why didn't we complain to parents and teachers about the unpleasant things that were happening to us? The only explanation I can find is that we were all in the grip of ambition; we wanted to impress our sub-leaders with exemplary discipline, with our powers of endurance, with our military bearing. For, those who did well were promoted, could put on stripes and braid, could give orders even if only for the five minutes when the leader disappeared behind the bushes. Youth must be led by youth was the motto. In practice that meant that those on top could put the boot in . . .

The Hitler Youth's success in indoctrinating young people in Nazi ideology as such was probably limited. Above all, the quality of its leadership was generally poor, particularly in the HJ section proper, because military and labour service removed many potential leaders, and middle-class pupils in the senior forms of secondary schools often proved unsuitable leaders of working class youths who were already in employment. Nevertheless, the HJ almost certainly reinforced certain values and stereotypes already influential in German culture—notably, the glorification of military or quasi-military virtues such as duty, obedience, honour, physical courage, endurance, strength, ruthlessness in achieving goals, and contempt for such values as peace, gentleness, moderation, intellect, moral courage, sensibility, and humanity. Certainly many parents and teachers complained about the brutalizing effects of the HJ on young people. It appealed to the desire of youth to be independent of the adult world and exploited the conflict of generations and the typical tendency for young people to challenge authority figures, whether parents or teachers. Teachers, in particular, were also concerned at the contempt for intellect cultivated by the HJ and at the arrogance displayed towards them by pupils who were leaders in the HJ. A report of the Nazi Teachers' League organization in the Mainfranken district of northern Bavaria of 1937 made the following typical complaint:

309

The extraordinary attitude displayed by large numbers of our young people to school in general and to intellectual achievement in the grammar schools in particular continually gives the comrades of Branch II cause for justified complaints and for concern for the future. There is widespread lack of any keenness or commitment. Many pupils believe they can simply drift through for eight years and secure their school leaving certificate even with minimal intellectual performance. The schools receive no support whatsoever from the HJ and DJ units; on the contrary, it is those pupils in particular who are in positions of leadership there who often display unmannerly behaviour and laziness at school. In general, it must be said that school discipline has declined to an alarming extent . . .

This situation prompted many teachers to opt out of cooperation with the HJ, which had serious repercussions for HJ organization in the countryside, as is clear from the monthly report of 22 June 1939, compiled by the Nazi local branch of Workerszell in Franconia:

310

In the countryside our biggest worry is youth education, which threatens to get out of control. The BDM has some quite good leaders but the DJ is going to the dogs more and more every day since the teachers have withdrawn their previous cooperation. They have even begun giving the pupils homework on the days when they have got DJ activities, with the result that they stay away. One main reason why the teachers no longer cooperate is the fact that the Reich Youth Leader continually attacks teachers both in his speeches and in the press. The teachers have good reason for their complaints and in the interests of our youth I request that you press with the greatest possible energy for an end to these attacks. It is inconceivable that the leaders of the DJ, let alone those of the HJ, will succeed in the countryside. The HJ survives only in name, since a HJ leader can only very rarely make his weight felt amongst louts of the same age . . .

(ii) Education: the Schools

For a regime bent on indoctrinating youth with a new set of values, education was clearly a vital area. The Nazis used various methods to try and control the education system and use it for their purposes.[69] In the first place, they tried to ensure that the teaching profession was both politically reliable and ideologically sound. The weeks following the Nazi take-over saw a number of ad hoc measures by the various states to purge the profession of unreliable teachers, which were then superseded by the application of the Law for the Re-establishment of a Professional Civil Service of 7 April 1933. The purge which followed continued well into 1934 and varied in its impact from state to state with Prussia among the strictest. Here the Nazi Gauleiter of Hanover–South-Brunswick, Bernhard Rust, a grammar school teacher from Hanover, was appointed Minister of Culture on 6 February 1933. He began by purging his Ministry: the State Secretary, the Under State Secretary, all four *Ministerialdirektoren*, both *Ministerialdirigenten*, and nine out of thirteen *Ministerialräte* were replaced, in several cases by Party comrades from his Gau. Committees were then established under the auspices of the *Oberpräsidenten* and *Regierungspräsidenten*—popularly known as 'Murder Committees'—consisting of three teachers, appointed by the local Gauleiter, to report on the political reliability of the local teachers.

---

[69] This section owes much to R. Eilers, *Die nationalsozialistische Schulpolitik* (Cologne 1963).

Adverse reports led to careful vetting of the teachers concerned.
By 29 July 1934, the following senior teachers in the secondary school
sector in Prussia had been purged:

	Male	Total	%	Female	Total	%
Head teachers	157	1065	15	23	68	32
Oberstudienräte	37	515	7	10	81	12
Studienräte	280	11348	2.5	75	1675	4

60 per cent of the lecturers in the Colleges of Education throughout
Germany were dismissed.

Party control over teachers' careers was also secured through the Führer
Decree of 24 September 1935, which gave the Führer's Deputy the duty of
providing a political reference for all Civil Service appointments and
promotions at the higher levels. This affected teachers of *Studienrat* rank and
above. Lower ranking teachers were also subject to political vetting by Party
offices. The effects of this system were, however, somewhat reduced by a
growing shortage of teachers. By 1936, for example, there were 1,335
vacancies for elementary school teachers in Germany, by 1937 2,038, by 1938
around 3,000. By 1938 the profession needed to recruit 8,000 new teachers
each year but only 2,500 were coming out of the Teacher Training Colleges.
The teaching profession was becoming increasingly less attractive as a career,
particularly in a full-employment economy. Its morale was being undermined by public vilification and constant interference from the HJ, by the
barely concealed contempt of leading figures of the regime, who took their
cue from the Führer himself, and finally by continuing relatively low rates
of pay. In this situation of shortage the political criteria imposed for the
appointment and promotion of teachers had to be increasingly watered
down.

Teachers were, however, also subject to control from their professional
association, the National Socialist Teachers' League (NSLB). This had been
established in April 1929 by Hans Schemm, an elementary school teacher
and the Gauleiter of the Bavarian *Ostmark* (Bamberg–Bayreuth). By
January 1933, it has acquired a membership of only some 6,000, but with
the Nazi take-over it grew rapidly. By the end of 1933 it had a membership
of 220,000 and, by 1937, it reached a figure of 320,000, comprising 97 per
cent of all teachers. Like other Nazi occupational organizations it expanded
through a mixture of propaganda and intimidation, concentrating on trying
to 'coordinate' the rival professional associations, a process which was not
completed until 1938. The main functions of the NSLB were, first, the
provision of reports on the political reliability of teachers for appointments
and promotions and, secondly, the ideological indoctrination of teachers. In
1937, an NSLB functionary provided the following definition of its role:

311

National Socialism is an ideology [*Weltanschauung*] whose claim to validity is total and does not wish to be subject to the random formation of opinion. The means of implementing this claim is through education. German youth must no longer—as in the Liberal era in the cause of so-called objectivity—be confronted with the choice of whether it wishes to grow up in a spirit of materialism or idealism, of racism or internationalism, of religion or godlessness, but it must be consciously shaped according to principles which are recognised as correct and which have shown themselves to be correct: according to the principles of the ideology of National Socialism.

Naturally, the German teacher must first be converted to this completely new task of German youth education. The real task of the NSLB is to create the new German educator in the spirit of National Socialism. It is being carried out with the same methods with which the movement has conquered the whole nation: indoctrination and propaganda.

Ideological indoctrination took the form of special courses and the provision of literature. On 6 May 1936, the Reich Minister of Education transferred to the NSLB the responsibility for the political indoctrination of the whole teaching profession. The courses, usually lasting 8–14 days, were held in special camps, of which the NSLB had 57 by 1938, and, by 1939, 215,000 or two thirds of its members had passed through them. These camps, which apart from indoctrination concentrated on sport, were intended to break down status differences and create a sense of community among teachers. A report on 'The teachers' Camps' in the Hamburg teachers' newspaper in December 1937 explained their function as follows:

312

Uniforms, field exercises, songs, lectures and discussions, sport, marching, eating and sleeping, when they take place in a camp, acquire a quality of team spirit. Only those who have experienced it, and those who have the experience ahead of them are capable of appreciating the HJ, only they can educate towards the educational goal of National Socialism.

Finally, the NSLB, which was dominated by elementary school teachers, tried to press for improvements in the position of the teaching profession—in pay and in the training and status of elementary school teachers.

How successful was the regime in winning over and indoctrinating the teaching profession? Initially, many teachers had been favourably disposed towards it. They had been alienated from the Weimar Republic by its failure to pursue effective educational policies as a result of federal, political, and religious divisions and, specifically, by the failure to improve the position of elementary school teachers. This was particularly true of the front generation. Then, the economic crisis of 1929–33 hit teachers very hard as state governments introduced cuts in salaries, pensions, and jobs. In July 1932 there were 22,959 young teachers without permanent appointments. The Nazis promised to improve the status and training of elementary school teachers and to grant teachers in general a key role in the shaping of the new Germany. Such propaganda bore fruit. Teachers were heavily over-represented both in the Party as a whole and in its leadership corps. By the end of 1934, some 84,000 teachers, roughly one quarter of the profession, were members, compared with only 10% of the population as a whole by the outbreak of war. In 1936, of 1.2 million members of the Reich Civil Servants League 206,000, or 17 per cent, were Party members, compared with 32 per cent of the NSLB, and 5.8 per cent of the civil servants were political leaders, compared with 14 per cent of the NSLB. Seven Gauleiters or deputy Gauleiters, 78 district leaders, and 2,000 branch or strong point leaders were teachers. In many rural areas the local teacher was a vital component of the Party machine. In the end, however, teachers were among the groups most disillusioned by the regime. Promises to improve the training and status of elementary school teachers were not kept and, although many gained status from their roles in the various Nazi organizations, this must have provided only partial compensation, particularly since their profession was subject to repeated vilification by leading Nazis and to constant interference by the HJ.

The NSLB itself appears to have had only limited success. Its political clout was too small to push through its demands against the indifference of the major power centres. Hitler, in particular, had no interest in improving the position of elementary school teachers, believing that retired NCOs would make the most suitable recruits. Secondly, many of its members, particularly teachers in secondary schools, were alienated by the crudity of its indoctrination. Some secondary school teachers also resented the dominance of the elementary school teachers within the organization. The *Philologenverband*, the association representing secondary school teachers of the humanities, had fought a long rearguard action against being 'coordinated' by the NSLB. The unity of the organization was indeed vitiated by the inadequate coordination of the various teachers' associations, encouraged in turn by its rather loose organization. The NSLB's empty rhetorical activism was typical of many of the Nazi occupational organizations. It did, however, function as a useful control mechanism.

Another method whereby the regime endeavoured to assert its control over the education system was through reorganization and centralization. Under the Weimar Constitution the Reich Government had been granted certain supervisory powers exercised by the Reich Ministry of the Interior, but basically education remained a matter for the individual state governments. With the destruction of the federal system in January 1934, the Reich Government acquired the opportunity to establish central control over education. On 1 May 1934, the Prussian Minister of Culture, Bernhard Rust, was appointed to the new post of Reich Minister of Science and Education and, on 1 January 1935, the two ministries were merged. The new Reich Ministry absorbed the educational responsibilities of the Reich Ministry of the Interior. From now onwards, the state ministries of culture functioned as field agencies for the Reich Ministry of Education. The Reich Ministry issued general decrees and the states then issued their own regulations to implement the Reich decrees. The Reich Ministry seized the opportunity to centralize the examination procedures for trainee teachers, establishing a Reich Examination Office in 1939, which reduced the state offices to a purely executive role. On 20 August 1937, the appointment of teachers of *Studienrat* rank and above was centralized in the Reich Ministry and the central control of teachers was taken still further when, on 5 July 1939, they all became Reich civil servants.

The school system was also reorganized. A reform of 20 March 1937 reduced the number of different types of secondary school from nearly seventy down to three basic models, with streams for those specializing in modern languages, science or—where it had a long tradition behind it—the traditional *Gymnasium* concentrating on the classics. The girls secondary schools had two streams for those specializing in languages and those concentrating on home economics. Private schools and denominational schools gradually succumbed to various pressures: the loss of government subsidies or tax concessions, regulations forbidding civil servants and members of the armed services to send their children to such schools, rigged local plebiscites and so on. Finally, the power structure within schools was also altered through the introduction of the leader principle during 1933–34 first by Prussia and then by the other states. The rights of the staff to participate in decision-making were removed and replaced by the sole responsibility of the head teacher.

The trend towards centralization and rationalization of the German education system in order to adapt it to the needs of a modern and increasingly mobile society had preceded the Nazi regime and some of these reforms were a logical extension of pre-1933 developments. The nature of the regime, however, ensured that countervailing forces disrupted this process of rationalisation, producing confusion rather than clarity. Above all, there was no clear guidance from the top, since Hitler failed to provide any consistent lines of policy, apart from a general contempt for intellect, a strong emphasis on sport, and the need for indoctrination in Nazi values. In this policy vacuum individual leaders and agencies were free to try and seize the initiative, while the Reich Minister of Education, Rust, was a weak figure who found it impossible to maintain control over education policy in the face of outside interference. Schirach, Bormann, Ley, Rosenberg, Bouhler, Himmler, and Goebbels all intervened in various aspects of education. This process is clear, for example, in the setting up of new elite schools. Rust was himself responsible for establishing the first of these. On 20 April 1933, Hitler's birthday, he established the first three National Political Educational Institutions (*Napolas*). These were boarding schools established on the sites of former Prussian military cadet schools and were intended to produce a new general elite for the regime. By the end of 1938 there were 21 Napolas. From 1936 onwards they came under the influence of the SS, although they remained nominally under State control. This was not the case, however, with another group of elite schools—the Adolf Hitler Schools and the *Ordensburgen* or Nazi colleges. On 15 January 1937, Schirach and Ley issued the following announcement:

313

The Führer has issued the above decree dated 15.1.1937 concerning the Adolf Hitler Schools of the NSDAP. The NSDAP and the HJ have thereby acquired a new and immense task which extends beyond our own time into the distant future. Details about the AHS will not be published today. To avoid uncertainty, however, we announce the following principles:
1. The Adolf Hitler Schools are institutions of the HJ, which is responsible for running them. Teaching materials, curriculum, and teaching staff will be determined by the undersigned Reichleiters for the Reich as a whole.
2. The Adolf Hitler Schools will contain six classes. Pupils will as a rule be admitted at the age of twelve.
3. Boys admitted to the Adolf Hitler Schools will have distinguished themselves in the DJ and have been recommended by the responsible Party cadre leader.
4. Instruction at the Adolf Hitler Schools will be free of charge.
5. Supervision of the schools is part of the responsibilities of the Gauleiter of the NSDAP. He will either exercise it himself or will delegate it to the Gau Indoctrination Office of the NSDAP.
6. After the successful completion of the school leaving examination the pupils of Adolf Hitler Schools may pursue any career in Party and State.

Rust was furious at this new challenge to his authority. Ley, however, was unrepentant in his reply to Rust's complaint on 22 January 1937:

314

1. Your task as Reich Minister of Education has never extended to the Party schools and thus the AHS as well as the *Ordensburgen* have nothing to do with you. Your

accusation of disloyalty, is, therefore, completely unfounded and I demand that you retract it.

2. The Führer has seen the memorandum on the AHS. He issued the decree only after he had perused it and therefore approved it. The points in the joint announcement issued by the Youth Leader of the German Reich and myself are in this memorandum approved by the Führer. Thus your most serious accusation, namely that we—the Youth Leader and myself—were guilty of an irresponsible misuse of the Führer's will, is equally unfounded and I demand that you formally retract this accusation as well ...

The first AHS and the first *Ordensburg* were founded at Crössinsee on 20 April 1937. Because of financial restrictions imposed by the Party treasurer, only ten AHS were established, with a total annual intake of some 600 pupils, and three *Ordensburgen*. The numbers involved, therefore, were not great. Nevertheless, the decision to establish a separate Party-controlled education system was significant.

These new educational institutions were not in fact successful in their goal of creating a new elite. The curriculum of the *Napolas*—apart from an even stronger emphasis on paramilitary-type sport and indoctrination—was based on that of the other German secondary schools and intellectual standards were satisfactory. They were in many respects similar to the old military cadet schools and indeed came under increasing military influence, with most of their *alumni* going into the armed forces and later the *Waffen* SS. The AHS and the *Ordensburgen*, on the other hand, provided an education so dominated by physical training and indoctrination as to be entirely inappropriate for the education of a modern elite. Above all, however, the ambitions focused on these new schools were largely thwarted by the fact that the traditional institutions of German education—the secondary schools and universities—remained popular among the traditional elites because they provided a satisfactory education and, since they were fee-paying, tended to reproduce those elites.

Finally, in addition to controlling and indoctrinating the teaching profession, reorganizing the education system and establishing new elite schools, the regime sought to influence youth through the content of what was taught in schools. On 18 December 1934, the Reich Minister of the Interior announced that 'the principal task of the school is the education of youth in the service of nationhood and State in the National Socialist spirit'. This made clear the Nazis' determination to shift the focus of education away from the needs of the individual and the development of his potential as a human being to the requirements of the community of nation and State, of which the individual was a member and to which he must subordinate himself. Nevertheless, the regime took time to establish guide lines on how the 'National Socialist spirit', whatever it was, should be inculcated. The years 1933–37 saw a series of sporadic and ad hoc measures by the various states affecting both the form and content of the curriculum and many pre-1933 text books remained in use, supplemented by booklets on such topics as the 'National Revolution' and race. Between 1938 and 1942, however, official guidelines were issued for the various levels and officially approved textbooks were published.

Hitler's own views on education as expressed in *Mein Kampf* and the occasional speech were vague and consisted of little more than statements such as 'a healthy man imbued with decisiveness and strength of will is more valuable for the national community than an intelligent weakling'. These views were then echoed by others in comments such as: 'Our goal is not the contemplative man but the man of action.' They found concrete expression in a vastly increased emphasis on the role of sport. Five hours per week or approximately 15 per cent of the total school time was devoted to it and pupils were required to reach the required standard in sport in order to move up to the next class. A serious physical handicap provided grounds for refusal of entry to secondary education.

As far as academic subjects were concerned, the regime's impact varied, depending on their relevance to the main objectives of inculcating a nationalist spirit and the principles of racism and eugenics. In the Colleges of Education new subjects were introduced: genetics, racial theory, folklore, military studies, and the study of the German borderlands. In the schools, German, biology, and history were the subjects most affected. The teaching of German aimed to encourage a 'consciousness of being German'. Teachers were expected to look at German language and literature under four aspects: the nation as 'a community of blood', 'a community of fate and struggle', 'a community of work' and 'a community of mind'. In the selection of teaching materials they should eschew those works which 'contradict German feelings or paralyze energies necessary for self-assertion' and only those modern works would be selected which 'have an affinity with the spirit of the new Germany, have helped to prepare the way for the new ideology, or have given exemplary form to its innermost aims'. In practice this meant an emphasis on folk-and blood-and-soil-type literature as well as works extolling nationalism and militarism. However, while the guidelines clearly ruled out a considerable number of works, they were sufficiently vague to give teachers some scope for an imaginative selection of works which, while politically innocuous, were nevertheless culturally distinguished. There is evidence that some teachers, at any rate, availed themselves of this opportunity.

In view of the racist and eugenist core of Nazi ideology, biology inevitably acquired a new importance in the curriculum. It was designed to emphasize the natural law of selection and the qualitative differences between the various races and also to encourage understanding for the regime's population policy—the selection of biologically sound marriage partners, the sterilization of 'inferiors', and the duty to have children.

History also received great emphasis. In 1938 the German Central
Institute of Education issued the following official guidelines for the teaching
of history in secondary schools:

315

The German nation in its essence and greatness, in its fateful struggle for internal
and external identity is the subject of the teaching of history. It is based on the
natural bond of the child with his nation and, by interpreting history as the fateful
struggle for existence between the nations, has the particular task of educating young
people to respect the great German past and to have faith in the mission and future
of their own nation and to respect the right of existence of other nations. The
teaching of history must bring the past alive for the young German in such a way
that it enables him to understand the present, makes him feel the responsibility of
every individual for the nation as a whole and gives him encouragement for his own
political activity. It will thereby awaken in the younger generation that sense of
responsibility towards ancestors and grandchildren which will enable it to let its life
be subsumed in eternal Germany ...
    A new understanding of the German past has emerged from the faith of the
National Socialist movement in the future of the German people. The teaching of
history must come from this vital faith, it must fill young people with the awareness
that they belong to a nation which of all the European nations had the longest and
most difficult path to its unification but now, at the beginning of a new epoch, can
look forward to what is coming full of confidence ...
    The certainty of a great national existence ... is for us based ... at the same time
on the clear recognition of the basic racial forces of the German nation which are
always active and indestructibly enduring. Insight into the permanence of the
hereditary characteristics and the merely contingent significance of environment
facilitates a new and deep understanding of historical personalities and contexts ...
    The course of history must not appear to our young people as a chronicle which
strings events together indiscriminately, but, as in a play, only the important events,
those which have a major impact on life, should be portrayed in history lessons. It
is not only the successful figures who are important and have an impact on life, but
also the tragic figures and periods, not only the victories, but also the defeats. But
it must always show greatness because in greatness, even when it intimidates, the
eternal law is visible. Only a sentient grasp of great deeds is the precondition for an
understanding of historial contexts; the powerless and insignificant have no history ...

Other subjects such as maths and foreign languages were less subject to
ideological contamination. Even here, however, Nazi ideology could enter
by the back door, as is clear from the following tests in two maths textbooks:

316

(a) *Question 95:* The construction of a lunatic asylum costs 6 million RM. How many houses at 15,000 RM each could have been built for that amount? *Question 97:* To keep a mentally ill person costs approx. 4 RM per day, a cripple 5.50 RM, a criminal 3.50 RM. Many civil servants receive only 4 RM per day, white collar employees barely 3.50 RM, unskilled workers not even 2 RM per head for their families. (a) Illustrate these figures with a diagram.—According to conservative estimates, there are 300,000 mentally ill, epileptics etc, in care. (b) How much do these people cost to keep in total, at a cost of 4 RM per head? (c) How many marriage loans at 1000 RM each . . . could be granted from this money?
(b) A modern night bomber can carry 1,800 incendiaries. How long (in kilometres) is the path along which it can distribute these bombs if it drops a bomb every second at a speed of 250 km per hour? How far apart are the craters from one another. . . ? How many kilometres can 10 such planes set alight if they fly 50 metres apart from one another? How many fires are caused if 1/3 of the bombs hit their targets and of these 1/3 ignite?

That the regime did not feel the need to introduce new guidelines and text books until the late 1930s and early 1940s suggests that many of the teaching methods and materials already used in schools were regarded as acceptable or could be easily adapted. Even before the Nazi take-over, for example, the teaching of German and history was strongly influenced by a nationalist bias. This reflected the mentality of a profession which had itself passed through a school and university system dominated by the *völkisch* nationalist ethos. The fact that the democratic values of Weimar had failed to have much impact on the teaching profession between 1919 and 1933 greatly facilitated the Nazi coordination of education.

(iii) Higher Education

In 1933, the Nazis had no specific plans for higher education other than the general aim of subordinating it to their goal of a radical transformation of German values in line with their ideology. They believed that this would require the creation of a new type of student, a new type of university teacher, and a new concept of scholarship.

In their objective of 'coordinating' the university system the Nazis benefited from the fact that under the Weimar Republic the universities had been dominated by right-wing nationalist and anti-democratic attitudes. The students, in particular, had tended to adopt a radical rightist stance and proved vulnerable to the appeal of Nazism. On the one hand, its combination of extreme nationalism and populist egalitarianism made it seem more relevant than the reactionary politics of the traditional student fraternities and tapped a strong vein of idealism. On the other hand, the new movement offered prospects of future employment at a time of massive graduate unemployment. At the student congress in Graz in 1931 the Nazi Student League (NSDSt.B) won a majority and took over the leadership of the main student body, the *Deutsche Studentenschaft*.

After the Nazi take-over, the regime took steps to create a new type of student. Under the Law against the Overcrowding of German Schools and Universities of 25 April 1933 student numbers were cut by revoking the automatic entitlement of possessors of the secondary school leaving certificate (the *Abitur*) to higher education. Subsequent measures assigned fixed quotas of new students to each state. This dealt with a genuine problem of overcrowding. However, it also meant that in future, access to higher education would be subject to criteria of political reliability, e.g. membership of the Hitler Youth, physical fitness, and racial origin—the number of Jewish students was reduced to their proportion within the population as a whole (1.5 per cent).

Three days earlier, on 22 April, membership of the *Deutsche Studentenschaft* (DS) was made compulsory for 'all full-time students at an institution of higher education who are of German origin and whose mother tongue is German . . . irrespective of nationality'. And, on 7 February 1934, a new constitution was issued for the DS:

317

The German Student Association (DS) represents the whole student body. It guarantees that students fulfil their duty towards the university, the nation, and the State. Above all—through the duty of SA service, labour service, and through political indoctrination—it is responsible for teaching students to become true and honourable German men and to be ready for selfless service in the cause of nation and State. Through lively cooperation in the tasks of the university it secures indissoluble solidarity between the university and the nation and a new generation of graduates who are rooted in the nation, strong in body and soul, as well as intellectually able . . . The military training is the responsibility of the SA University Office. The political education within the DS is entrusted to the National Socialist Students' League.

Students were obliged to do four months of labour service and two months in an SA camp as well as three hours a week of compulsory sport. The purpose of labour service was partly practical—to reduce overcrowding in the universities and provide a source of cheap labour—but mainly ideological. It was part of the cult of community (*Gemeinschaft*) current in the youth movement and elsewhere since the 1890s, but now manipulated by the Nazis for their own ends. Students would be confronted with Real

Life and, by being forced to mix with the less privileged sections of the community, would be reminded that they were all *Volksgenossen* (national comrades) together. An important aspect of Nazi education was the cult of 'Experience' (*Erlebnis*) as being more crucial to the development of the individual than the academic process of learning (*Wissenschaft*) with its stress on 'knowledge' (*Erkenntnis*). Unlike knowledge which involved the intellect, experience involved 'feeling' (*Gefühl*) which alone provided access to the deep truths of Nazism which were essentially 'based on blood' (*blutgebunden*), on a common racial heritage. Such an 'experience', normally envisaged in terms of a physical challenge in the company of a community of one's fellows, was regarded as essential to character-building. The concept clearly derived, first, from Romantic notions reworked through pre-war vitalist philosophy, which had found expression in the youth movement, and secondly, from the cult of the 'front line experience' of World War I, glorified by post-war writers such as Ernst Jünger, and continued in the Free Corps movement of 1919–21. Many members of the Nazi cadres had shared both these experiences.

The Nazi Prussian Minister of Education told a rally of the first batch of students from the University of Berlin who were going off to their Labour Service:

318

So now you are marching into the labour camps. There you will find training in other things than powers of historical and critical analysis, than pure intellect. There you will stand, you young academics, and will be confronted with the spade and a primitive camp and then it will emerge which of you has the will to follow in the steps of those whom the student leader welcoming me referred to, your predecessors of Langemarck.[70] He who fails in the camp has forfeited the right to lead Germany as a graduate. We cannot fight our way out of this deep crisis through intellectualism, rather an extraordinary test of character must come first to establish who in future has the right to bear the name of German citizen in Germany. The school for character that you are going through there and which is a practical test of true comradeship in work and living is irreplaceable. I will make no bones about it: the true, great, practical school is not over there (the University), and not in the grammar schools, it is in the labour camp, for here instruction and words cease and action begins . . .

The reality of such labour service under the Nazis was rather different as is indicated by the following post-war account by Professor Otto Roegele who attended such a camp as a student in 1939:

---

[70] See footnote 65 p. 425.

319

Apart from a few idealists who had survived from the old labour service movement, the leadership corps of the Reich Labour Service consisted predominantly of men who had failed in life and had been rejected by the Wehrmacht even during its reconstruction phase. Neither before nor since in my life have I ever experienced such a negative selection of men as in the leadership corps of the RAD, even in the Army you never come across such a despicable, corrupt, inhuman atmosphere with such spiteful terrorising of the school leavers. We expended much time and sweat on a strict but, as far as fighting a war was concerned, virtually useless basic military training which consisted mainly of formal drill in the style of Fredrick the Great; in addition, we completed the fortifications on the Upper Rhine...

Another means of shaping students was via the so-called 'Comradeship Houses'. They represented an attempt to continue the community experience of the labour service camps. Initially, students were supposed to spend their first three semesters in these houses, but resources proved inadequate to carry out the programme systematically. The model, which was by no means always realized, since some fraternities managed to continue a clandestine existence under the guise of a Comradeship House, was described by one student functionary as follows:

320

The Comradeship House is an instrument of struggle... It represents the transfer of the form of the labour camp to the University and originated in the Labour Service... The young student lives in the Comradeship House in straightforward, austere discipline. He sleeps together with his comrades, gets up with them, does early morning exercises, and eats lunch and supper with them... In addition, political education is arranged several times a week in the House, communal get-togethers are organized, SA duties are performed...

A set of 'Ten Laws for German Students' was published in 1934:

321

I. German student, it is not necessary that you live, but it is necessary that you fulfil your duty towards your nation! What you become, become as a German.
II. For a German man the highest principle and the supreme virtue is his honour. Offences against one's honour can only be atoned for with blood. Your honour is your loyalty to your nation and yourself.

III. To be a German means to have character. You too are called to do battle for the German spirit. Seek the truths which are contained in your nation.

IV. There is no freedom in unrestrained behaviour and a lack of ties. There is more freedom in serving than in being in command. The future of Germany depends on your faith, your enthusiasm, and your militant will.

V. He who does not possess the imagination to conceive something will achieve nothing. You cannot kindle a flame if no flame burns within you. Have the courage to show admiration and awe.

VI. One is a National Socialist by birth, even more by training, but most of all by training oneself.

VII. If anything is more powerful than fate then it is your courage to bear it fearlessly. Whatever does not kill you only makes you strong. Praise be to what makes you hard.

IX. As a leader be tough in your own fulfilment of your duty, decisive in doing the necessary, helpful and kind, never petty in the judgment of human weaknesses, generous in the recognition of the needs of others and modest in your own.

X. Be a comrade! Be chivalrous and modest. Be an example in your personal life. Your relationships with others are a sign of your maturity. Be consistent in thought and action. Model yourself on the Führer.

What evidence there is suggests that many students came to terms with the new regime relatively easily, fired by the nationalist rhetoric, blinded by the initial political and military successes of the regime and dazzled by the prospects of brilliant careers in a greater Germany. By the end of the 1930s, however, a growing number of students were coming to resent the regimentation, the pressures to conform, the anti-intellectual climate, the crudity of the regime's style and its moral duplicity.

To transform higher education in accordance with Nazi goals it was necessary not only to produce a new type of student but also a new type of university teacher. The years 1933–34 saw a purge of the German universities. It began during the first few months with actions of boycott and intimidation against racially and politically objectionable professors, carried out by the Nazi Student League. With the passage of the Law for the Re-establishment of the Professional Civil Service of 7 April 1933, however, the state governments took over the purge, carrying it out in a more orderly fashion. Between the winter semester of 1932–33 and 1933–34, 1145 out of the 7,758 established university teachers were replaced, nearly 15 per cent of the total. Of these approximately one third were dismissed on racial grounds and 56 per cent for racial or political reasons. Of those dismissed 313 were full professors. If one includes assistants, senior employees at research institutes, librarians, and museum directors there was a total of 1,684 dismissed scholars.

The impact of the purge varied from university to university: Berlin and Frankfurt Universities, with 32 per cent of their staff involved, were worst affected, Rostock (4 per cent) and Tübingen (1.6 per cent) least. It also varied from subject to subject. As far as the future of the regime was concerned, the most damaging effects were felt in the field of science. Eighteen per cent of those engaged in the natural sciences were dismissed—26 per cent in Physics, 13 per cent in Chemistry. Twenty past or future Nobel prizewinners were dismissed or resigned, all but one of whom emigrated. Eleven of these were physicists, including Einstein.

Those university teachers who were purged received little or no support from their colleagues. Indeed, to begin with the regime benefited from substantial support from university teachers. On 11 November 1933, 700 professors signed a 'Declaration of Professors at German Universities and Colleges in support of Adolf Hitler and the National Socialist State' intended as a 'Call to the Educated People of the World' to counteract hostile criticism from abroad. Famous scholars made individual declarations of support. Thus, the famous philosopher, Martin Heidegger, who had just been appointed Rector of the University of Freiburg, declared in his inaugural address: 'Your lives will no longer be regulated by dogmas and ideas! The Führer himself and he alone is the present and future reality for Germany and its law.' These scholars were caught up in the atmosphere of the 'national uprising' during the first phase of the regime.

In their determination to secure a new type of university teacher the authorities were anxious to establish tight controls both over the profession itself and over university government. The traditional pattern of democratic self-government based on the senate was replaced by the leadership principle with the Rector as leader appointing the deans. However, the State, in the shape of the Reich Minister of Education, was given the final say in all appointments. Proposals for appointments and promotions were made by the relevant faculty and then passed on to the Ministry together with the comments of the Rector and the political assessment of the National Socialist Lecturers' League.

The Nazi Party regarded the question of appointments as crucial. They realized they could do little with the existing professors if they outwardly conformed. They concentrated, therefore, on trying to transform the profession by controlling entry and promotion within it through a process of political indoctrination and vetting. Indoctrination was carried out in camps run by the SA and in so-called 'Lecturers' Academies', another form of camp run by Nazi professors. Attendance at these camps was compulsory and reports were made on the performance of lecturers. The political vetting process was carried out by the NS Lecturers' League which contained the committed Nazis among the univerisity teachers. It had been established by Hess's office in 1935 to act as the eyes and ears of the Party in the universities, to vet appointments, and to encourage every teacher to discover the Nazi 'idea' in his professional work.

There were, however, strict limits to the extent to which the Party could control appointments and promotions. First, the rectors and university faculties resented outside interference and even many members of the NS Lecturers' League felt inhibited about making adverse comments about colleagues which were unlikely to remain confidential. Secondly, the officials of the Reich Ministry of Education, many of whom were themselves Nazis of pre-1933 vintage, were determined to defend their authority over appointments against Party interference. The Nazi Security Service (SD) reported on this situation in 1938:

322

Problems of cooperation between the State and the Party authorities are apparent in the internal administration of the universities and are almost routinely attributable to violations of [each other's] authority . . . There are complaints within the internal administration concerning the conflict between the university leadership and that of the Lecturers' League which adversely affects the work [of the universities].

Finally, the growing shortage of young academics, especially in the technical and medical fields as a result of the low pay, low prestige, and political insecurity of university teachers, was causing growing concern. In the light of this situation the emphasis in the evaluation of candidates for appointment and promotion tended to become more and more academic and less and less political. This was strongly supported by the university authorities, as is clear from the following comment by Rector Hoppe of the University of Berlin at the Conference of University rectors in Marburg on 15 December 1937:

323

I must emphatically stress the need to establish that the candidate's academic ability is entirely adequate. I do not deny that the candidate's ideological and political attitude must be guaranteed, but if it is given priority and if academic knowledge is lacking, we may end up with problems none of us wants. Academic ability is undoubtedly above all the main requirement . . .

Most academics were either apolitical or approved of at least some aspects of the regime—the nationalist ones, for example. Those who did not, were either forced out or intimidated into silence. But, although it was possible to persuade academics to conform outwardly, it was much more difficult to persuade them to adjust their science and scholarship in accordance with Nazi ideas. The Nazi leadership, however, made it clear from the start that they wished the universities to operate according to principles very different from those which had governed their work hitherto. Thus, in 1933, Hans Schemm, leader of the NS Teachers' League and Bavarian Minister of Culture, told Munich professors: 'From now on it is not up to you to decide whether or not something is true but whether it is in the interests of the National Socialist Revolution.' Similarly, the Leader of the Nazi Students League declared on 19 April 1933:

324

We have no respect for the clever monks in their quiet cells when the future of the German universities is at stake... The university can no longer accommodate the private individual either in the shape of a lecturer or in the shape of a student. It is precisely in this shift against the private individual, against this emissary from bourgeois society, the breeding ground of liberalism, who is high on education (*bildungssüchtig*)—it is precisely in this shift that the new university distinguishes itself fundamentally from the 'autonomous' educational academies of a liberal Republic.

However, how was this shift to be achieved in academic terms? New courses were introduced in such fields as racial studies, eugenics, and defence studies and there was a new emphasis on pre-history. Racialist and eugenic ideas permeated other disciplines to a greater or lesser extent, notably medicine. Law and political science courses were adapted to fit in with the changes introduced by the regime. But Nazi ideology was so diffuse that over large areas it was totally incapable of replacing the traditional approach to learning. Moreover, so incoherent was the regime with its competing individuals and organizations that no one was ever quite sure who or what represented true National Socialism. Was it Rust or Rosenberg or Himmler? Finally, there was the danger that attempts to apply half-baked Nazi ideological concepts would threaten the science and technology vital to German industry and to the military effort.

The most notorious example of the attempt to apply Nazi ideology to German scholarship occurred in the field of physics. The Nobel prizewinner, Phillip Lenard—a fierce critic of the new theoretical physics based on Einstein's theory of relativity—published a book, *German Physics*, in which he claimed that even science was racially conditioned:

325

'*German* physics?' you will ask. I could have said 'Aryan physics' or 'physics of the Nordic type', physics of the explorers of reality, the truth-seekers, physics of those who founded scientific research. You will want to object: 'Science is international and always will be!' But that is based on an error. In reality, science like everything that people produce is racially conditioned. It can present an appearance of being international when from the general validity of the results of science one wrongly assumes their common origin or fails to see that the peoples of different countries who have produced science of the same or of a kindred nature to that of the German people could do so only because they also are or were of predominantly Nordic race. Nations of another racial composition have a different way of carrying out science.

Significantly, however, this view did not succeed in asserting itself as the new orthodoxy. Lenard and his fellow Nobel prizewinner, Johannes Stark, failed to win support for their ideas from major political figures who were in any case not interested in academic physics. Without such strong political backing they were unable to defeat the opposition from the German physics community containing intellectual heavyweights such as Werner Heisenberg.

CHAPTER 20

Women, The Family, and Population Policy

(i) The Nazi Attitude to Women

Women formed a crucial focus for Nazi policy because of their vital roles within the community as mothers, wives, and as an increasingly important source of labour. Nazi attitudes to women were in most respects extremely reactionary. They were strongly opposed to ideas of female emancipation which had formed part of the liberal ethos of the Weimar Republic if not the social and political practice. The Weimar Constitution had both given women the vote and proclaimed their equality of rights with men, although little had been achieved in that direction because the Civil Code of the Empire (1900) remained in operation. Nazi anti-feminism—a major component in their ideology—was an extreme version of an outlook shared by many Germans, particularly among traditional groups such as the rural population, and supported by the Churches and before 1933 by conservative and Catholic political parties which enjoyed particularly strong female backing. The Nazis insisted that men and women had distinct roles in life founded on their natural differences. Women were not inferior but they were different and as such should confine themselves to those 'natural occupations' which nature had ordained for them—above all as wives and mothers. In particular, politics was, in the Nazis' view, a male preserve and women were excluded from high positions in the Party except in their own organizations (all NSDAP Reichstag deputies were male, despite the fact that during the 1920s Germany had for a western country a record number of female parliamentary deputies). Hitler elaborated the official Nazi attitude to women in a speech to the National Socialist Women's section (NSF) on 8 September 1934:

326

... The slogan 'Emancipation of women' was invented by Jewish intellectuals and its content was formed by the same spirit. In the really good times of German life the German woman had no need to emancipate herself. She possessed exactly what nature had necessarily given her to administer and preserve; just as the man in his good times had no need to fear that he would be ousted from his position in relation to the woman.

In fact the woman was least likely to challenge his position. Only when he was not absolutely certain in his knowledge of his task did the eternal instinct of self and race-preservation begin to rebel in women. There then grew from this rebellion a state of affairs which was unnatural and which lasted until both sexes returned to the respective spheres which an eternally wise providence had preordained for them.

If the man's world is said to be the State, his struggle, his readiness to devote his powers to the service of the community, then it may perhaps be said that the woman's is a smaller world. For her world is her husband, her family, her children, and her home. But what would become of the greater world if there were no one to tend and care for the smaller one? How could the greater world survive if there were no one to make the cares of the smaller world the content of their lives? No, the greater world is built on the foundation of this smaller world. This great world cannot survive if the smaller world is not stable. Providence has entrusted to the woman the cares of that world which is her very own, and only on the basis of this smaller world can the man's world be formed and built up. The two worlds are not antagonistic. They complement each other, they belong together just as man and woman belong together.

We do not consider it correct for the woman to interfere in the world of the man, in his main sphere. We consider it natural if these two worlds remain distinct. To the one belongs the strength of feeling, the strength of the soul. To the other belongs the strength of vision, of toughness, of decision, and of the willingness to act. In the one case this strength demands the willingness of the woman to risk her life to preserve this important cell and to multiply it, and in the other case it demands from the man the readiness to safeguard life.

The sacrifices which the man makes in the struggle of his nation, the woman makes in the preservation of that nation in individual cases. What the man gives in courage on the battlefield, the woman gives in eternal self-sacrifice, in eternal pain and suffering. Every child that a woman brings into the world is a battle, a battle waged for the existence of her people. And both must therefore mutually value and respect each other when they see that each performs the task that Nature and Providence have ordained. And this mutual respect will necessarily result from this separation of the functions of each.

It is not true, as Jewish intellectuals assert, that respect depends on the overlapping of the spheres of activity of the sexes; this respect demands that neither sex should try to do that which belongs to the sphere of the other. It lies in the last resort in the fact that each knows that the other is doing everything necessary to maintain the whole community....

So our women's movement is for us not something which inscribes on its banner as its programme the fight against men, but something which has as its programme the common fight together with men. For the new National Socialist national community acquires a firm basis precisely because we have gained the trust of millions of women as fanatical fellow-combatants, women who have fought for the common life in the service of the common task of preserving life, who in that combat did not set their sights on the rights which a Jewish intellectualism put before their eyes, but rather on the duties imposed by nature on all of us in common.

Whereas previously the programmes of the liberal, intellectualist women's movements contained many points, the programme of our National Socialist Women's movement has in reality but one single point, and that point is the child, that tiny creature which must be born and grow strong and which alone gives meaning to the whole life-struggle. . . .

(ii) Population Policy

For the Nazis motherhood was a woman's most important role. This reflected a deep and widespread concern about the declining birthrate. This decline was common to all European countries in the 1920s and resulted from an expanding urban population which wished to raise its standard of living by reducing its number of offspring and now had the means to do so through the spread of contraception. However, largely as a result of the exceptional economic crises of the 1920s, Germany had the sharpest decline in the birthrate of any European country apart from Austria. Whereas Germany had over two million live births per annum at the turn of the century, this rate had declined to 1.3 million in 1925 and to 971,000 in 1933, and mean fertility had dropped even more sharply, from 128 live births per 1,000 women aged between 15 and 50 in 1910–11 to 80 in 1925 and 59 in 1933. Concern at this development had been growing during the 1920s and caused nightmares among the Right that, if the decline continued, Germany would not only be unable to regain her position as a great power but would be swamped by fecund hordes of Slavs from the East. The Nazis shared these fears and determined to launch a major and systematic campaign to reverse the trend.

This campaign took various forms. First, §218 of the Civil Code, prohibiting abortion, was rigorously enforced, with the result that between 1934 and 1938 convictions rose by 50 per cent. Birth control centres were closed down and attempts were made to restrict access to contraceptive information and devices. Secondly, financial incentives were given to parents to produce children. Maternity benefits were improved and income tax allowances for dependent children were virtually doubled in October 1934 at the expense of single people and childless couples. Concessions on such things as school fees and railway fares were introduced for large families. Family allowances were introduced: In 1935 penurious large families were given grants of up to 100 RM per child and, by March 1938, 560,000 families had received grants averaging 330 RM each. In April 1938, an allowance of 10 RM per month was introduced for the third and fourth child and 20 RM for all subsequent children for those whose incomes did not exceed 650 RM per month—2.5 million children were eligible. The most original single financial incentive, however, was the marriage loans scheme contained in Section 5 of the Law for the reduction of Unemployment of 1 June 1933 and the subsequent enforcement decree;

327

The Reich encourages marriages in accordance with the following regulations.

Marriage Loans, section I

1. People of German nationality who marry one another after this law has come into force can on application be granted a marriage loan of up to 1000 Reichsmarks. The application for the marriage loan can be made before marriage. The amount is paid only after the marriage. The conditions which must be fulfilled before the grant of a marriage loan are as follows:

(a) That the future wife has spent at least six months in employment in Germany between 11 June 1931 and 31 May 1933.

(b) That a banns has been issued by the Registry Office and that the future wife gives up her job at the latest at the time of the wedding or has already given it up at the time the application is made.

(c) That the future wife pledges herself not to take up employment so long as her future husband receives an income (within the meaning of the Income Tax Law) of more than 125 Reichsmarks a month and so long as the marriage loan has not been fully paid off. . . .

The marriage loan is paid in the form of vouchers. These entitle one to purchase furniture and household equipment in retail shops which are prepared to accept vouchers. The vouchers will be redeemed by the Finance Offices in cash. . . .

These interest-free loans had to be repaid at the rate of one per cent per month i.e. over a period of eight-and-a-quarter years. Section 5 was initially intended to improve the employment prospects of men by encouraging women to give up employment on marriage. On 20 June, however, the Law received a new emphasis with a supplementary decree which laid down that the sum to be repaid (on average 600 RM = four months' average industrial wage) would be cut by one-quarter for each child produced by the recipient couple and that the birth of a child would lead to a moratorium on further repayments of one year.

Between August 1933 and January 1937, some 700,000 couples, nearly a third of those who married during the period, received a loan. The revoking of the prohibition on employment in the autumn of 1937 resulted in a sharp rise in applications so that in 1939 42 per cent of all marriages were loan-assisted. However, as an instrument of population policy the scheme appears to have had only a limited success. In 1933–34 it almost certainly encouraged young working-class and lower middle-class people, many of whom had postponed marriage during the Depression. The number of marriages went up from 516,800 in 1932 to 638,000 in 1933 and to 740,200 in 1934, but it did not produce a marked increase in the numbers of children per family, since most couples preferred to have only one or two children, presumably believing that the extra expense of more children would outweigh the advantage of the cancellation of the remainder of the loan.

Another measure to increase the birth rate was a campaign to improve the facilities for expectant mothers. The Nazi umbrella organization for women, the *Deutsches Frauenwerk*, with a membership of at least six million, organized Mothers' Schools', which offered training courses in household management and the skills of motherhood as well as ideological indoctrination geared to women's role. Another source of maternity advice was the organization 'Mother and Child' within the Nazi welfare organization, the NSV. It was claimed that in mid-1938 the NSV had 25,000 advice centres in its 'Mother and Child' section and that more than 10 million women had attended them so far. In addition, the section arranged for job placement for unemployed husbands, education grants, home help, and holidays for mothers in need. The scheme was financed by public collections. Finally, the Labour Front pressed for protective measures for working mothers.

Lastly, the regime launched a massive propaganda campaign to raise the status of mothers and housewives within the community and to enhance their own perception of their role. For example the Reichsstatthalter of Hessen sent out the following circular to all schools in the state on 15 April 1935:

328

This year like last the German people will once more express their commitment to the German mother and to German family and national life . . . I expect schools to remind young people of their debt of gratitude to their mothers with dignified celebrations and that a large number of useful gifts will be handed over to the Reich Mothers' Service.

The most striking example of this was the introduction in May 1939 of the Mother's Cross in gold for those with eight children, in silver (six), and bronze (four), possibly in imitation of the French who had been distributing similar crosses since 1920. The cross was only issued on condition that the parents of the children were 'of German blood and hereditarily healthy' and the mother was worthy of the award. The cross bore the inscription: 'The child ennobles the Mother'.

How successful was this campaign in achieving its goal of increasing the birth rate? This is a difficult question to answer. The following figures indicate that the birth rate went up quite sharply after 1933, although it still remained below the level of the years 1922–26:

329

POPULATION STATISTICS

Year	Marriages	Marriages per 1,000 inhabitants	Divorces per 10,000 existing marriages	Live births	Deaths	Surplus of Births over deaths	Per 1000 inhabitants Births	Per 1000 inhabitants Deaths	Illegitimate Births per 100 births	Loans per 1,000 marriages	Loan remissions per 100 births
1929	589,600										
1931				1,047,775	734,165	313,610	16.0	4.8			
1932	516,793			993,126	707,642	285,484	15.1	4.3			
1933	638,573	9.7	29.7	971,174	737,877	233,297	14.7	3.5	10.7	33.0	8.7
1934	740,165	11.1	37.0	1,198,350	724,758	473,592	18.0	7.1	8.6		
1935	651,435	9.7	33.0	1,263,976	792,018	471,958	18.9	7.1	7.8	24.1	12.3
1936	609,631	9.1	32.6	1,277,052	795,203	481,849	19.0	7.2	7.8	28.1	14.6
1937	620,265	9.1	29.8	1,277,046	794,367	482,679	18.8	7.1	7.7	29.7	17.5
1938	645,062	9.4	31.1	1,348,534	799,220	549,314	19.6	7.9	7.7	35.2	19.0
1939	772,106	11.1	38.3	1,407,490	853,410[1]	554,080	20.3	8.0	7.8	33.0	20.5

[1] Deaths excluding those killed in action.

It is, however, debatable how far the increase in the birth rate can be attributed directly to Nazi population policies. In part, the rise may have been a result of increased confidence following the economic recovery. Secondly, there was a trend throughout the inter-war years for a growing proportion of people of marriageable age actually to marry and to do so at a younger age than before. Thus there were more married couples, and being younger they were fertile for longer. It is significant, however, that the couples who married after the Nazi take-over were considerably less fertile than those who married in the 1920s, which suggests that Nazi propaganda had little effect on them. On the other hand, there were a number of developments which must have tended to depress the birth rate. Inadequate Nazi housing policies, which took second place to the rearmament programme, and the priority given to prestige building projects produced a deficit of 1.5 million dwellings by 1939 as well as high rents for new homes In addition, there were labour service and conscription for young men, and the increase in female employment after 1936. The fact that, despite these disincentives, the birth rate went up suggests that, although Nazi population policies were probably not primarily responsible for the increase, they almost certainly contributed to it, helping to counteract these negative pressures.

It is important to grasp the instrumentality of all these measures. Mothers were not being encouraged to have babies for their own fulfilment as individuals or as members of a family but in order to provide future 'national comrades' (*Volksgenossen*). They were expected to see their role as mothers as essentially a public one, and in their roles as educators both parents were regarded essentially as agents of the state. Parents who failed in their duty of bringing up their children in accordance with the precepts of the regime—for example, by refusing to send them to the Hitler Youth after 1939—would have their children removed from them and transferred to a state home. The following excerpts from contemporary publications illustrate these points:

330

(a) *Marriage*:

Marriage is the lasting, life-long union of two genetically healthy persons of the same race and of different sexes, which has been approved by the national community, and is based on mutual ties of loyalty, love and respect. Its purpose is the maintenance and furtherance of the common good through harmonious cooperation, the procreation of genetically healthy children of the same race, and the education of them to become hard-working national comrades.

(b) *The function of sex*:

Sexual activity serves the purpose of procreation for the maintenance of the life of the nation and not the enjoyment of the individual . . . If, however, the desire to have a child has been fulfilled and the continuation and enlargement of the nation has been secured by the production of a sufficient number of children, then, from the point of view of the nation, there is no objection to further satisfaction of the sexual urge.

(c) *Motherhood*:

To be a mother means giving life to healthy children, bringing to fruition all the physical, mental, and spiritual faculties in these children and creating a home for them which represents a place where nationalist and racialist culture is nurtured. It means realizing in the community of the family a part of the ideal national community and giving to the nation, in the form of grown-up children, people who are physically and mentally developed to the fullest extent, who are able to cope with life and face it boldly, who are aware of their responsibility to the nation and race, and who will lead their nation onwards and upwards.

(d) *Parenthood*:

The rights of parents over the bringing-up of their children . . . have become a duty undertaken at the behest of the nation and under the supervision of the state and involving unlimited responsibility.

It is also important to grasp the fact that the welfare measures of the regime were invariably subject to political, racial, and eugenic criteria. Recipients of welfare were obliged to be politically reliable. The receipt of welfare was also confined to so-called Aryan Germans—Jews and other non-Aryans were excluded. Moreover, in the Law for the Protection of German Blood and German Honour of 15 September 1935 the regime banned marriages and any form of sexual relations between Germans and Jews.[71] Finally, the regime was not only concerned to increase the quantity of births, it also wished to improve their quality judged in terms of physical and mental health. Welfare benefits were, therefore, confined to those who were not suffering from congenital disease and were not considered 'asocial', a category which often merely reflected the petty bourgeois prejudices of the local Party leadership about the 'deserving' and 'undeserving' poor.

The supplementary decree to the Marriage Loans Scheme, dated 20 June 1933, defined the criteria for disqualification as follows:

331

(b) If one of the two spouses is not in possession of the rights of a citizen.

(c) If on the basis of the political attitude of one of the two spouses it can be assumed that he [or she] will not give unfailing support to the national(ist) State.

(d) If one of the two spouses suffers from hereditary mental or physical ailments which indicate that his [or her] marriage is not in the interest of the national community.

---

[71] See below pp. 535–6.

(e) If the previous way of life or reputation of one or both of the spouses suggests that they would not fulfill their obligation to repay the loan...

The instructions for investigating the political and moral life style of the applicant laid down the following practice to be followed:

332

The political attitude can be determined through questioning of the applicant himself and in addition of reliable persons who have knowledge of the intimate circumstances of the applicant, such as for example welfare officers, clergy, reliable neighbours. Careful observations during home visits may also provide indications, e.g. pictures, newspapers etc. Marriage loans are not to be granted to members of parties hostile to the State such as the KPD, SPD, and associated organizations. On the other hand, if the applicants were formerly members of such organizations—not as leaders but as people who were misled—and now definitely no longer belong to them, but rather support the National Socialist State, then there are no objections to granting them loans. However, previous convictions for political offences against the National Socialist State normally disqualify applications. Political reliability can be assumed in the case of members of the SS, SA, Stahlhelm, NSF, BdM, HJ.

Among the persons who are not to be granted a loan on the grounds of their previous way of life and their reputation are: alcoholics, habitual criminals, people known to be workshy, tramps, prostitutes etc.

A key role in the vetting of applicants for welfare benefits—indeed for any kind of official application—was played by the local Party leadershp which, through a system of Block Wardens in every block of flats or in every street kept a close watch on the inhabitants. The official approval of the local branch leader of the Party was required for marriage loan applications as in the following example from Neu-Isenburg, a small town near Frankfurt a.M. dated 7 October 1938.

333

The character and reputation of the above-mentioned person are unimpeachable. She comes from a well-ordered family background. Before the take-over of power, Miss A. was not politically active. She participates in collections and donations, is behind the constructive work of the Führer and supports the present state. Her political reliability is established. It may be assumed that she would support the National Socialist state on all occasions. There are, therefore, no objections to the granting of a marriage loan.

This vetting process for welfare benefits was part of a major campaign to 'improve the stock' of the nation by a process of selection. The assumption was that various categories of 'asocial' behaviour, for example, alcoholism and prostitution, were either wholly or partly genetically determined. The Nazis wished to prevent the 'unfit' (or in German 'inferiors' (*Minderwertigen*)) from breeding and to encourage the healthy. This reflected the ideas of the Eugenics movement, which had become extremely influential among medical, academic, and legal circles during the last years of the Weimar Republic. These eugenists were concerned about what they saw as a threat to the health of the German 'race' posed by the genetically diseased who, it was claimed, tended to breed faster than the healthy. By exploiting concern at the cost of maintaining the handicapped in asylums and special hospitals at a time of economic crisis, they won support from civil servants and other opinion leaders for the idea of encouraging voluntary sterilization of those who were considered congenitally ill. A draft law to that effect had been prepared by the Prussian government at the end of 1932. When the Nazis came to power they not only took the matter up with some urgency but, in the Law for the Prevention of Hereditarily Diseased Offspring which they issued on 14 July, they replaced the voluntary principle by compulsion (§12). Although this had been opposed by the majority of eugenists before 1933, this opposition had been largely based not on principle but on the feeling that public opinion was not yet ripe for such a drastic measure. After its introduction, however, most were happy to endorse it, with only the Roman Catholic Church making strong objections. The Law stated:

334

§1. (i) Anyone who has a hereditary illness can be rendered sterile by a surgical operation if, according to the experience of medical science, there is a strong probability that his/her offspring will suffer from serious hereditary defects of a physical or mental nature.
(ii) Anyone is hereditarily ill within the meaning of this law who suffers from one of the following illnesses: (*a*) Congenital feeblemindedness. (*b*) Schizophrenia. (*c*) Manic depression. (*d*) Hereditary epilepsy. (*e*) Huntington's chorea. (*f*) Hereditary blindness. (*g*) Hereditary deafness. (*h*) Serious physical deformities.
(iii) In addition, anyone who suffers from chronic alcoholism can be sterilized.
§2. An application for sterilization can legitimately be made by the person to be sterilized. In the case of persons who are either not legally responsible or have been certified because of mental deficiency or have not yet reached their nineteenth birthday, the legal guardian is so entitled.
§3. Sterilization can also be requested by (i) The Medical Officer. (ii) In the case of inmates of hospitals, or institutions of the incurably ill or penal institutions, the director . . .

§5. The responsibility for the decision lies with the Hereditary Health Court which has jurisdiction over the district where the person to be sterilized officially resides.
§6. The Hereditary Health Court is to be connected administratively to the Magistrates Court (*Amtsgericht*). It consists of a magistrate as chairman, a medical officer, and a further physician qualified to practise within the German Reich who is particularly familiar with the theory of hereditary health . . .
§12. If the Court had decided finally in favour of sterilization, the sterilization must be carried out even against the wishes of the person to be sterilized unless that person was solely responsible for the application. The medical officer is responsible for requesting the necessary measures to be taken by the police authority. In so far as other measures prove insufficient the use of force is permissible.
Reasons for the Law: Since the National Uprising public opinion has become increasingly preoccupied with questions of population policy and the continuing decline in the birthdate. However, it is not only the decline in population which is the cause of serious concern but equally the increasingly evident genetic make-up of our people. Whereas the hereditarily healthy families have for the most part adopted a policy of having only one or two children, countless numbers of inferiors and those suffering from hereditary ailments are reproducing unrestrainedly while their sick and asocial offspring are a burden on the community . . .

The compulsory aspect of the law was reinforced by the supplementary decree of 5 December 1933, which laid down that if, when treating a patient, a doctor or other medical personnel became aware that he or she was suffering from an hereditary illness or chronic alcoholism, it was their duty to inform the local medical officer. He would then, if necessary, request sterilization if he could not persuade the patient or his legal guardian to make the request himself. Despite attempts to introduce objective criteria for diagnosis, such as an intelligence test, the interpretation of the criteria of suitability for sterilization under several of the categories in §1 (ii), such as that of 'congenital feeblemindedness' proved very elastic. Moreover, it sometimes included social criteria (e.g. 'asocial') which merely reflected the social prejudices of the medical personnel involved. By 1937, almost 200,000 people had been sterilized, of whom 102,218 were men and 95,165 were women. The use of vasectomy or salpingectomy as a method of birth control by normal couples was strictly forbidden. Sterilization on eugenic grounds was not unique to Nazi Germany, but far more widespread there than anywhere else. In the United States, for example, there were only 12,145 such sterilizations for the period 1907–32, though admittedly this was a conservative estimate.

The Nazis did not only practise 'negative eugenics', they also tried to 'improve the stock' by positive measures. 'Advice Centres for the Improvement of Genetic and Racial Health' (*Erb-und Rassenpflege*) were established where engaged couples could be given advice, and in 1934 the following 'Ten Commandments for the Choice of a Spouse' were published:

<u>335</u>

1. Remember that you are a German.
2. If you are genetically healthy you should not remain unmarried.
3. Keep your body pure.
4. You should keep your mind and spirit pure.
5. As a German choose only a spouse of the same or Nordic blood.
6. In choosing a spouse ask about his ancestors.
7. Health is also a precondition for physical beauty.
8. Marry only for love.
9. Don't look for a playmate but for a companion for marriage.
10. You should want to have as many children as possible.

On 18 October 1935, the Law for the Protection of the Hereditary Health of the German People (Marriage Health Law) was issued which introduced a ban on the marriage of those with serious infectious diseases or hereditary illnesses. Under §2 engaged couples were obliged to produce 'Certificates of Suitability for Marriage' signed by a doctor, although until sufficient facilities could be provided the certificate had to be produced only when the registrar had doubts about the suitability of the marriage on health grounds. This clause guaranteed that couples went for marriage guidance and, even if they did not actually fall within the provisions of the Law, might still be persuaded not to marry. The more ambitious eugenists within the regime began to plan the drawing up of family trees for all citizens containing information about the racial, physical, mental, and moral characteristics of their families.

(iii) Nazi Women's Organizations

In its objective of indoctrinating women and training them for their roles as loyal housewives and mothers and supporting them in those occupations outside the home judged 'appropriate' to women, the regime relied mainly on the work of two women's organizations—the *Deutsches Frauenwerk* (German Women's Enterprise—DFW) and the *NS Frauenschaft* (NS Womanhood—NSF). The DFW was the umbrella organization established in September 1933 to absorb all the various women's organizations which had been 'coordinated' after the Nazi take-over. In May 1934 it established the Reich Mothers' Service (RMD) whose task was 'the training of physically and mentally able mothers to make them convinced of the important duties of motherhood, experienced in the care and education of their children and competent to carry out their domestic tasks.' It was based on the mothers' welfare organizations previously run by confessional women's groups which had now been co-ordinated. By March 1939, over 1.7

million women had attended almost 100,000 RMD courses despite the fact
that they were voluntary and a small fee was charged. In some cases
employers helped to finance RMD courses held on their premises to try and
reach women workers and in 1937 37 per cent of employed women attending
were workers. In addition to practical instruction, the courses also endeavoured to further the regime's population policies by persuading women
to have large families, but evidently with little success.

The other main section of the DFW was the domestic science department
which was set up in September 1934 on the ruins of the National Association
of Housewives which was coordinated. Its main function came to be
consumer guidance—the education of housewives in the most effective use
of those raw materials and foodstuffs left over for consumers after rearmament requirements had been met. By the end of 1938 1.8 million women had
attended its courses, predominantly in cooking. The courses contained
thrifty recipes, an emphasis on bottling and preserving, and encouragement
to people to gather wild nuts and fruits in the countryside. The impact of
the courses was reinforced by newspaper articles and radio programmes.

The DFW clearly had some success in attracting women to courses which
they felt were directly relevant to their daily lives, but its enormous
membership, consisting of four million corporate and 1.8 million individual
members, appears to have been largely inactive. It also failed to attract
working-class women in any numbers, partly because it was based on the
previous middle-class women's organizations, and partly because the
Labour Front successfully asserted its claim to organize working class
women. It also failed to have much impact on rural women, largely because
of their continuing adherence to the Churches and also because of competition from the Nazi agricultural organization.

While the DFW was intended to be the mass women's organization
carrying out practical tasks, the NSF was intended to be a kind of élite cadre
organization of Nazi women. In fact, however—like the Nazi Party as a
whole—it proved unable to decide whether it wanted to be an élite or a mass
organization and, by the end of 1938, it had a membership of 2.3 million,
the vast bulk of whom were inactive. The activists consisted of 3,500
full-time salaried staff, 40,000 women functionaries at Gau, district, and
local branch level as well as 280,000 cell and block leaders, the majority of
whom were part-time and unpaid. The goals of the NSF were ambitious, as
is clear from the following documents which convey the flavour of Nazi
women's ideas and rhetoric:

336

*Basic Principles and Organizational Guidelines of the National Socialist Womenhood
(NS Frauenschaft) Undated c.1932–33.*

I Basic Principles.
1. We desire the awakening, the training, and the renewal of women's role as the preservers of the nation's springs: the nation's love life, marriage, motherhood and the family, blood and race, youth and nationhood. The whole education, training, careers and position of women within the nation and state must be organized in terms of their physical and mental tasks as mothers.
2. We recognize the great transformation which has taken place in women's lives over the past 50 years as a necesstiy produced by the machine age, and approve of the education and official integration of women for the good of the nation in so far as they are not performing their most immediate service for society in the form of marriage the family and motherhood.
3. We regret, however, the false paths of the democratic-liberal-international women's movement because it has not found new paths for the female soul rooted in GOD and his nation, but, on the basis of maintaining the ability to compete with men, has raised temporary expedients to the level of basic demands and has thereby created a womanhood which has lost its deepest sources of female strength and which has not understood its female task in the German crisis.
4. We desire a women's movement of renewal which reawakens those deepest sources of female strength and strengthens women for their particular tasks in the freedom movement and in the future Germany.
5. We demand and therefore carry out the fight against the planned denigration and destruction of women's honour and women's dignity and against the moral corruption of youth.
6. We erect against it the will of German women which is rooted in GOD, nature, the family, the nation and fatherland, and our own *Women's Cultural Programme*, which will be organized in the 3. Reich.
7. We participate, therefore, with all our strength in the struggle of the freedom movement for the transformation of the domestic political situation and the establishement of the 3. Reich through the strongest possible propaganda on a small scale.

337

The Organization, Tasks, and Duties of the National Socialist Womanhood by Dr Krummacher, Reich Leader of the NSF and leader of the DFW 1.11.1933.

The German woman belongs in the first instance to her family either in the sense that as a mother she has to devote herself to her husband and children or as a working woman has contacts with the members of her family, her parents and relatives. Apart from that, the working woman must be offered a spiritual home in the NS Womanhood and be set special tasks of a female nature to a greater extent than the married woman and mother. The NS Womanhood will have to provide the working woman with protection and help vis-à-vis all the legislative and administrative agencies and introduce appropriate institutions at her place of work.

This responsibility determines the way in which our work is organized.

The main task of the NS Womanhood is and remains the National Socialist indoctrination of the German woman. This National Socialist indoctrination embraces practically all spheres of female life and will shape these in accordance with the National Socialist attitudes towards the state and duty. Working groups will be set up within the NSF which will be responsible for support and indoctrination in the following areas: the National Socialist idea of the state, racial studies, history, pre-history, children's upbringing and school, welfare, maternity services, maternity training, economics and legal advice, the protection and encouragement of the working woman, the cultural life of the home, poetry, music, art, home economics, health care for women and children, clothing, handicrafts. In the process all practical experience in the particular fields must be exploited irrespective of whether or not this experience of practical women comes from women who did not hitherto share the National Socialist ideology. There must, therefore, be cooperation with the existing women's organizations as they are now organically combined in the German Women's Enterprise ...

In practice, the NSF failed to have much impact, Its influence over policies affecting women was restricted by the male-dominated Government and Party organization, and even its organization of women was contested by rival bodies such as the BDM, the Labour Front, and the Reich Food Estate. Nevertheless, arguably both the DFW and the NSF succeeded in mobilizing the energies and idealism of a number of women and channelling them in directions which contributed marginally to the achievement of the regime's goals and to its stabilization.

(iv) Women in employment

Although the regime regarded women's maternal role as the most important, it could not ignore the fact that many women did not have children or even get married and were obliged to support themselves and often dependants as well. Nearly 1.7 million German soldiers had been killed during World War I, and throughout the inter-war years there were approximately 2 million more women than men, with 500,000 more widows in 1925 than in 1910. Moreover, of those women who did get married many desired to work or were obliged to for financial reasons both before getting married and afterwards. In 1925, there were 11.5 million 'economically active' women, over one-third of whom worked as family assistants on farms or in family businesses. Only 4.2 million women were normally engaged in regular paid employment. The rationalization movement of the late 1920s in industry, however, saw an increase in the demand of big firms for unskilled female labour which was both cheaper and allegedly more suited to repetitive mass production techniques than male labour. Above all, these years saw a considerable increase in the numbers of women in non-manual work as clerks, typists and shop assistants. In fact, the number of women in regular paid employment rose by 20 per cent between 1925 and 1929. Few women, however, succeeded in gaining positions of responsibility and high status during the Weimar years, although there was a gradual improvement. In this Germany was by no means exceptional.

The regime's policies towards female employment between 1933–39 were governed first, by the state of the labour market, secondly, by considerations of public morale, and finally, by Nazi ideology which was not totally inflexible. Thus, while wishing to encourage marriage and motherhood, the Nazis accepted women's employment provided it was concentrated in 'natural occupations' such as teaching and welfare services. During the first three years or so, these determinants of policy were all operating in the same direction. Widespread male unemployment, including many heads of households, appeared to provide powerful justification in terms of public conceptions of social justice for the idea that women in paid employment should, where possible, return home and be replaced by men. This applied particularly to married women in households where the husband also had a job—the so-called 'double earners'. A campaign to replace working women, and particularly the 'double earners', by unemployed men had in fact already begun in 1930 with support from the Brüning government. However, apart from a law affecting officials, it was limited to exhortation and advice to employers and labour exchanges to discriminate where possible in favour of men. The Nazi marriage loan scheme of June 1933 was the first piece of legislation designed to deal with precisely this category. The depression itself had however, already drastically reduced female employment by 31.6%, and it soon became clear that the problem of 'double earners' had been grossly exaggerated: most married women who worked did so out of necessity.

The level of women's employment did in fact remain low between 1933–36, increasing from 4.85 million in June 1933 to only 5.63 million in June 1936. This was the result not so much of Nazi policies as of the fact that the initial phase of economic recovery was largely restricted to the production goods sector of the economy, where rearmament investment had been concentrated, whereas women were predominantly employed in the consumer goods sector. By 1936–37, however, as the rearmament boom and the introduction of compulsory labour service and conscription in 1935 made themselves felt, a labour shortage began to develop, and it became clear that women provided the main untapped source of labour. In this situation the regime was forced to do an about turn: having previously discouraged women from going to work, it now had to encourage them to do so. From now onwards, its anti-feminist ideology and the requirements of the labour market worked at cross purposes. The first major indication of this change came with a series of decisions during 1936–37 which progressively abolished the provision in the marriage loans scheme requiring the wives of recipients to give up paid employment. One of these was embodied in the Decree on the Re-employment of Women in Receipt of Marriage Loans of 5 February 1937:

338

According to section 1 of the Family Benefits Law of 30 March 1936, the wife of a National Serviceman who is called up for the armed forces, or of a man liable for Labour Service who is called up to do his Labour Service, receives benefits to ensure her receiving the necessities of life. These benefits are . . . only to be granted if the wife cannot secure the necessities of life through her own efforts, in particular by working.

In these circumstances, the maintenance of the ban on the employment of wives who have received a marriage loan and whose husbands have been called up to the armed forces or to the Labour Service would not be in accord with the regulations of the Family Benefits Law which is intended to reduce the amount of benefits to the absolute minimum in order to relieve the Reich treasury.

On the basis of section 1 of the 6th Decree concerning Marriage Loans,[72] I permit wives who have received a marriage loan to take up employment, provided their husbands have been called up for the Labour Service or for training by the armed forces.

The regime's attempts to encourage women to take up employment had only a very limited success. Thus, although the number of women manual and non-manual workers who were in regular paid employment rose sharply in the late 1930s from 5.71 million in October 1936 to 7.14 million in July 1939, it still remained below the levels of the late 1920s—7.41 million in October 1928, despite the fact that the total number of women of working age had increased by some 2 million between 1928 and 1939. Tim Mason has suggested a number of reasons for this failure to mobilize women for work: first, more women were following the exhortations of the regime to get married and have children and, although the proportion of married working women increased from 29.9 per cent in 1933 to 33.6 per cent in 1939, most of these were family assistants. The younger women aged 20–29, however, who normally were the most likely to be in paid employment, were tending to leave work to get married and have babies in greater numbers than before. In 1939, 56 per cent of this age group were married compared with 41.6 per cent in 1933, a situation made worse by the fact that this group formed an exceptionally small cohort being the generation born during World War I. Further disincentives for women to work were the poor job prospects, low wages, and poor working conditions, particularly in industrial

---

[72] This decree of 28 July 1936 empowered the Reich Finance Minister to grant exceptions to the ban on the employment of women in receipt of marriage loans.

work. Middle class women were particularly liable to opt out of work when married.

The same kind of conflict between the anti-feminist ideology of the regime and the changing requirements of the labour market occurred in the case of the training and employment of professional women. Thus, at first, academic education for girls, particularly science and maths was deemphasized and a stress put on domestic science subjects such as needlework. Moreover, the proportion of female university students was reduced from 16.7 per cent of the total in 1933 to 12.5 per cent in 1934. After 1936, however, as shortages of professional and technical skills developed, girls were officially encouraged to develop their academic gifts, although the stress on the importance of domestic skills continued. Moreover, particularly after the outbreak of war, girls made up an increasingly large proportion of the student body.

The Nazis initially introduced tough measures against women in responsible positions in the Civil Service, primarily on political grounds but, particularly in the case of married women, also on the basis of sex discrimination. In effect, they were extending the policy of the Brüning government which, on 30 May 1932, had introduced a law which provided that married women in responsible positions in the civil service might be dismissed if 'their financial maintenance seemed from the size of the family income to be guaranteed in the long term'. This Brüning law had been confined to Reich agencies, and thus did not affect teachers, among others. In June 1933, however, the Nazi government extended it to state and local level, thus affecting women teachers, and included a paragraph permitting the payment of lower salaries to women and restricting the age of tenure for women to 35. During 1933, in the first flush of power, the dismissal of women civil servants and teachers had clearly got out of hand, provoking protests from women's organizations. On 5 October 1933, therefore, Frick felt obliged to issue the following official guidelines for the employment of women civil servants and teachers:

339

As I understand from numerous petitions, a strong sense of disquiet prevails among women civil servants, teachers and employees about the way in which they have been affected by measures of retrenchment carried out by different Reich, state and municipal authorities. It must be pointed out that different authorities evidently take action on the assumption that in the National Socialist State female officials and employees are on principle to be removed from the public service or to be forced from the posts they have held up to now into posts of lower rank and income or into employee status.

I must emphatically point out that the legal position governing such general action against women civil servants and teachers does not cover the handling of the question in this way. In particular, the stipulations of the Law for the Restoration of the Professional Civil Service, which according to the needs of the service make possible the transfer of officials to a lower rank or the retirement of officials who are not yet incapable of service, cannot be used in a general way against women civil servants as mentioned at the beginning.

I consider it fundamentally right that, in the event of males and females being equally qualified for employment in the public service, the male applicant should be given preference. On the other hand, I must point out that in certain fields, namely in the sphere of youth welfare and the care of youth, also to some extent in that of tuition, the needs of the service require the employment of female labour as civil servants and as employees.

A succession of complaints prompts me to call attention to married female civil servants and teachers, who according to the Law on the Legal Status of Female Civil Servants of 30 May 1932 in the form set out on 30 June 1933 (*Reichsgesetzblatt* Pt. I, p. 435), can be discharged only if their economic maintenance seems permanently secured. The relevant stipulations indicate a regulation with exceptions for women civil servants. These provisions must therefore be taken into consideration.

Hitler held strong views on the role of women, but the only sphere—apart from politics—from which he insisted that women should be totally excluded was the law courts. Significantly, he appears to have been prompted to do this by Bormann. On 24 August 1936 Bormann reported to the Reich Ministry of Justice:

340

Following the conference in your Ministry on 5.viii.1936 concerning the admission of women as lawyers, I have put the matter to the Führer, since, as the course of the meeting showed, the Party has a special interest in these things. He has decided that women cannot become either judges or lawyers. Women trained in law can therefore be employed only in the public service. I particularly request that trouble should be taken to find places there, where possible, for the existing female probationary lawyers.

Although they were largely excluded from the law, as Jill Stephenson has pointed out, the pressures of the labour market ensured that after an initial slump during 1933–34, women maintained or improved their positions in many other professions, particularly the caring ones. Thus, the number of female doctors and their proportion within the profession increased steadily during the 1930s from 2,455 (5 per cent) at the beginning of 1930 to 2,814 (6 per cent) at the beginning of 1934 and to 3,650 (7 per cent) at the beginning of 1939. Moreover, 42 per cent of all women doctors were married, of whom 70 per cent were mothers. As far as the teaching profession was concerned, between 1931 and 1939 women marginally increased their numbers in elementary schools and suffered a decline of 5 per cent in the middle schools and of 2 per cent in the secondary schools, though they retained a share of 68 per cent of staff posts in the the girls' secondary schools, despite the attempt by the Prussian government to set a 3:2 ratio in favour of male teachers for these schools in 1934. In the universities, however, the number of female academics declined from 74 in 1932–33 to 28 in 1934–35 but recovered to 46 (0.8 per cent) by 1936, when they were in fact better represented in the medical and science faculties than in Arts. On 4 September 1936, the leading Nazi paper, the *Völkischer Beobachter* summed up the new situation by stating unequivocally: 'we can no longer do without the woman doctor, lawyer, economist and teacher in our professional life.'

Nevertheless, it would be a mistake to read too much into this development. It was clearly a product of the priority being given to the rearmament programme, and the consequences of the resulting labour shortage were accepted as a temporary aberration. Nazis continued to believe in their anti-feminist programme and where possible wished women to be confined to their family roles or, in the field of employment, to the caring occupations. Moreover, in this it appears they had the support of most women. The evidence suggests that women approved of the regime's glorification of domesticity, since for most women employment in the circumstances of the 1930s was not a particularly attractive proposition. Moreover, men too seem to have approved of this emphasis, which reaffirmed traditional distinctions discriminating between men and women and flattered their male pride. Lastly, as Tim Mason has suggestively argued, in Nazi Germany, even more than in modern industrial society generally, the home provided men with a refuge from the pressures of the outside world. With the stresses of political intimidation—no less effective for being largely latent—of the constant barrage of duplicitous propaganda, of the 'achievement principle' at work, and of the sense of being subject to the arbitrary forces of an unpredictable regime, men could find in their home life a source of stability and emotional comfort, a rest from the struggle for survival in the world outside. Thus, in making a propaganda cult of the home—even while their other activities such as the HJ were undermining it—the Nazis were tapping a deep source of emotional support.

Finally, there was one area which involved all three aspects of Nazi policy towards women—the importance of the family, population policy, and female labour: the question of divorce. In 1938 the Nazis introduced a reform of the marriage law, parts of which appear on the surface quite progressive but which on closer examination provide an interesting insight into the regime's priorities in the treatment of women at that stage:

===
341
===

§53. (1) A marriage partner can seek a divorce if the other partner has become prematurely infertile after marriage.

(2) Divorce is impossible if the partners have produced hereditarily healthy offspring or an adopted child.

(3) The person who is infertile has no right to a divorce. The same is true for a partner who would not be permitted to enter another marriage on grounds of health or whom the Health Office would be obliged to discourage from so doing...

§55. (1) If the marriage partnership has been dissolved for three years and if the re-establishment of a life partnership corresponding to the essence of marriage is not anticipated on account of a fundamental and irretrievable breakdown of the marriage relationship either partner can seek a divorce.

(2) If the partner who seeks the divorce has been wholly or primarily responsible for the breakdown, the other partner can object to the divorce. The objection is to be disregarded if the maintenance of the marriage is not morally justified in the light of a proper appreciation of the essence of marriage and of the whole behaviour of the two partners.

Under the limited divorce facilities granted by the earlier German legislation the parties who wanted to separate usually had to come to a collusive agreement which was then registered by the Court under one of the existing legal categories. The new statute, though, abandoned the principle of guilt and replaced it with the concept of 'irretrievable breakdown' (§55 (1)). Typically, however, the law contained vague general concepts such as 'morally justified' and 'the essence of marriage 'which, in effect, delegated to the judge the responsibility not just for deciding the facts of breakdown but for whether or not a divorce was 'morally justified'. In the view of the Supreme Court, his decision was limited only by the need 'to apply the particular legal provision in the spirit which dominated the whole law'.[73] Thus, he had to bear in mind the definition of the 'essence of marriage', contained in the official justification of the law, as 'a sanctuary for the procreation of an abundance of children and the essential precondition for the healthy and orderly education of offspring'. In short, when deciding whether or not to grant a divorce, the courts were expected to interpret 'morally justified' (§55 (2)) in the light of the interest of the 'national community' in acquiring more healthy offspring. To require marriages which had broken down to continue would prevent the making of new marriages from which such offspring could come. Thus, according to the Supreme Court, an important point for the judges to bear in mind was 'the biological situation of the German people and the requirements stemming therefrom'.[74]

---

[73] See B. Rüthers, *Die unbegrenzte Auslegung. Zum Wandel der Privatrechtsordnung im Nationalsozialismus* (Frankfurt 1973) p. 417.
[74] *Ibid.* p. 409.

Two particular cases illustrate the practice of the courts. In the first, a woman had lost her fertility through an operation necessitated by an abdominal cavity pregnancy. The husband's request for a divorce was granted and a plea of duress was denied to the defendant mainly on the grounds that the State had an active interest in the plaintiff's getting children from a new marriage.[75] In the second, after numerous instances of adultery, the husband wanting a divorce infected his wife, who was resisting, with venereal disease, thus rendering her sterile. The Supreme Court decided that the wife's objection was in effect not 'morally justified' because the marriage had broken down and was damaging the nation as a whole.[76] Thus, the practice of the new divorce regulations meant that, as Otto Kirchheimer put it at the time; 'Marriage becomes a business relationship, the success or failure of which is measured in terms of the production of soldiers and future mothers who live up to the physical and intellectual standards of the Third Reich.'[77]

Furthermore, the official justification for the law indicated that even respect for women as housewives ceased where their alimony stood in the way of enabling husbands to start a new family with the prospect of producing more children for the Reich. They would be expected to swell the labour force and do their bit for the 'national community':

342

... The obligation of the wife to earn her keep through her own labour has been considerably increased compared with the previous regulation. In the light of the position which the gainfully employed woman now enjoys in economic life, indeed in the whole social structure of the nation, and in the light of the current view of work as a duty to the national community, when considering the question of whether a divorced wife who is entitled to maintenance should be expected to earn her keep through her own labour either in whole or in part, the answer can no longer depend on whether or not gainful employment was customary for the woman in the circumstances in which the partners lived during their marriage. It must depend on whether in the light of a just appreciation of all the circumstances gainful employment can be expected of the woman or not.

The claim to maintenance appropriate to the life situation of the partners cannot be realized in many cases because the partner on whom the responsibility for payment lies has other claims to satisfy apart from his obligations to his divorced partner...

---

[75]See O. Kirchheimer, 'The Legal Order of National Socialism' in *Studies in Philosophy and Social Science* 1941 p. 464.
[76]Cf. Rüthers *op. cit.* p. 419f n.111.
[77]Kirchheimer *op. cit.* p. 465.

The new divorce regulations were very popular: in 1939, the first full year of the law's operation, there were almost 62,000 divorces, 21.6 per cent of which were granted under §55—50 per cent of these marriages had been contracted twenty years or more earlier. In 1940 the number dropped to below 50,000 but still 15.5 per cent were granted under §55 and almost half of the marriages involved had been of long duration.[78]

---

[78] *Cf.* Kirchheimer *op. cit.* p. 465.

CHAPTER 21

Law and Order

Introduction

While the regime sought both to win the support and change the mentality of the German people through propaganda and indoctrination, the Nazi instruments and practice of law and order were designed to ensure that both those who failed in their duties as 'national comrades' and those who were ineligible for membership of the national community on the grounds of race or hereditary defect were either rendered harmless or eliminated 'one way or the other'.

Both Hitler personally and Nazism as an ideology and movement were fundamentally hostile to legal processes. The nature of the law as a set of rules regulating human activities with the aim of introducing rationality and predictability into social relationships was totally incompatible with the *Führerprinzip* which formed the basis of the Nazi concept of authority. For, since the Führer regarded himself and was regarded by his movement as a man of destiny, chosen to lead Germany and expressing the will of the nation, any body of laws was viewed with suspicion as a restriction on his freedom of action, particularly since their enforcement was the responsibility of a legal profession which was considered pedantic and tainted with liberalism. Point 19 of the Nazi Party programme of 1920 had demanded 'that Roman Law, which serves a materialistic world order, be replaced by a German common law'. In fact, however, just as Hitler avoided introducing a new constitution, preferring to leave the Weimar Constitution as a façade while undermining its substance, similarly attempts to formulate a new comprehensive corpus of National Socialist law came to naught. Thus, the attempt to replace the Civil Law Code with a so-called People's Law Code and, more important, the elaborate discussions about a new Nazi penal code were all eventually shelved. As in the constitutional sphere, this policy of adapting the legal system to suit the requirements of the regime by a series of *ad hoc* measures over a period of years rather than by speedy and systematic reform, reflected the nature of the Nazi take-over of power, with its quasi-legal emphasis on continuity, its anxiety to avoid serious economic or social disruption, and also its total lack of forward planning, the result of the Party's concern with immediate questions of power rather than with formal structures. Above all, however, it had the advantage of leaving the Nazis free to criticize the existing laws as products of a liberal era without at the same time binding them to new ones which would have had the authority of the regime behind them.

Instead of issuing new comprehensive legal codes, the Nazis used a variety of methods to subordinate the legal system to their ends. First, they introduced a few new laws specifically designed to deal with political offences and to reflect racial and eugenic goals. Secondly, they introduced new courts to deal with sensitive areas of particular concern to the regime such as political offences, hereditary farms, labour disputes, and compulsory sterilization. They also transferred responsibility for dealing with many offences to various administrative agencies with independent powers of their own. Thus, members of the Nazi Party, the SA and SS, the Labour Service, and the Army were all partially at least exempt from the competence of the ordinary courts. Moreover, various economic agencies had their own disciplinary procedures—for example, the various 'corporate' bodies in trade and industry—which had acquired official status and therefore effective penal powers. This process greatly diminished the scope of action of the regular criminal courts and undermined a unified system of law. Above all, it markedly increased the vulnerability of the individual whose freedom to have recourse to independent adjudication from the regular courts was drastically curtailed. Thirdly, they introduced new legal principles which judges were expected to apply in the interpretation and application of the law. Fourthly, they introduced a harsher penal practice and, in particular, they sharply increased the use of the death penalty, especially after the outbreak of war. And, finally, they introduced various mechanisms for controlling and influencing the legal profession in general and the judiciary in particular. This last point was vital. If the regime did not undertake a fundamental revision of the legal codes then it was essential to ensure that the judiciary interpreted the law in accordance with Nazi precepts and was responsive to the priorities of the executive.

As a result of these various measures, the basic legal principles which the Western legal tradition had evolved since the eighteenth century—the equality of all citizens before the law, the independence of the judiciary from the executive, the protection of the individual against arbitrary arrest and imprisonment without trial, the development of humane penal practice—all these were ruthlessly discarded by the Nazi regime as obstacles to the achievement of its goals. Furthermore, in place of the admittedly rather rigid but at least relatively clear-cut and objective approach of legal positivism, the law was increasingly applied in a highly subjective, arbitrary, and contradictory way. Its application was determined more and more by political and ideological criteria, and this, when combined with a judiciary largely subservient to the regime, resulted in the progressive undermining and perversion of the law.

Hitler and many Nazi leaders never really came to terms with the law and the legal system, despite its increasing subordination to the requirements of the regime. The fact that the Nazis increasingly viewed society in terms of a rigid dichotomy between those who were loyal members of the 'national community' and those who were either outside it *per se* on the grounds of racial origin or hereditary disability, or 'placed themselves outside it' either through overt resistance or through their failure to conform to its (often unclear) norms and values, ensured that all offenders tended to be increasingly regarded as 'enemies of the people' and, therefore, political offenders. In particular, criminal matters, especially during the war, came in greater degree to be considered as quasi-political offences since they were seen as directed against the 'national community' during its struggle for survival. There was also an increasing tendency to see criminality and even social non-conformity or deviance in biological terms, as being in many cases innate in the criminal or 'asocial'. This was an attitude by no means confined to Nazi Germany, but the Third Reich provided a very favourable climate for it. Moreover, as it became increasingly evident that the Nazis' utopian vision of an ideologically and racially homogeneous 'national community', united in fanatical allegiance to the Führer, bore little relation to reality, so the bureaucratic ambitions of the security services to expand their sphere of competence were reinforced by an increasingly paranoid search for subversive elements and for 'social aliens' (*Gemeinschaftsfremde*), a definition which was continually expanding to include almost any sign of nonconformity. The assumption was that if the regime could eradicate (*ausmerzen*) these negative forces, then the 'national community' would come into its own and Germany would finally triumph.

This trend towards the increasing politicization of life in the Third Reich benefited the institution whose key function was political control—the SS. The years 1933–36 saw the gradual extension of SS control over the police. With its powers of 'protective custody' for political offenders, under the decree of 28 February 1933, and of 'preventive custody' in the criminal and 'asocial' spheres, under an edict of the Interior Ministry of 14 December 1937, and with the establishement of its own independent prison network in the concentration camps, the SS developed a penal system parallel to the official system. Moreover, the SS-police began increasingly to interfere in the judicial process itself, ignoring verdicts and putting those acquitted in concentration camps, or intervening to have the verdicts changed. The two systems continued to coexist side by side just as the State administration continued to coexist side by side with the Party administration. The peculiarity of the Third Reich lay precisely in this coexistence of the two systems—on the one hand, the civil servants and lawyers trained to adhere to rational and legal norms, some indeed trying to retain some sort of rationality in the regime and thereby in effect helping to stabilize it; on the other hand, the representatives of arbitrary Führer authority who resisted any attempt to limit the exercise of this authority on legal or procedural grounds, although ironically within its own organization the SS endeavoured to operate according to bureaucratic principles. Well before the end of the war it had become only too clear which of the two systems had achieved dominance.

(i) The Nazi View of the Law

Hitler's view of the law was a cynical one: 'There is only one kind of law in this world', he told a meeting in 1928, 'and that lies in one's own strength'. He and the Nazi leadership saw the law and the legal system purely in instrumental terms as weapons for the achievement of their ends. The official view of the function of the law was outlined by Hans Frank, the head of the Nazi Lawyers' Association and of the Academy of German Law, in a statement in the Academy's journal in 1934:

343

In the National Socialist state the law can only be a means for the maintenance securing, and encouragement of the racial-*völkisch* community. The individual can be judged by the law only from the point of view of his value for the *völkisch* community.

Frick summed up this view succinctly in the phrase: 'Everything which is useful for the nation is lawful; everything which harms it is unlawful'.
This view had profound implications for the basic principles of the rule of law as they had come to be accepted by all nations within the European legal tradition during the previous one hundred and fifty years. Hitler wasted little time before spelling this out in unequivocal terms in a speech to the Reichstag on the occasion of the passage of the Enabling Law on 23 March 1933:

344

... The Government of the national revolution regards it as its duty on principle, in accordance with the nation's vote of confidence, to keep those elements from influencing the nation which consciously and intentionally act against its interests. The theory of equality before the law cannot be allowed to lead to the granting of equality to those who, on principle, treat the law with contempt, let alone to the surrendering of the freedom of the nation to these people on the grounds of democratic principles. But the Government will grant equality before the law to all those who, by taking part in the formation of a national front against this danger, back the national interest and do not fail to support the Government. . . .

Our legal system must, in the first place, serve to maintain this national community. The irremovability of the judges must, in the interests of society, be paralleled by an elasticity in sentencing. The nation rather than the individual must be regarded as the centre of legal concern. High treason must in future be ruthlessly exterminated. The basis of the existence of the judicial system cannot be other than the basis of the nation's existence. It should therefore always consider the difficult decisions which face those who, under the hard pressure of reality, are responsible for shaping the life of the nation. . . .

The Nazi view of the law was not some aberration from the lunatic fringe. It evoked a sympathetic response from a considerable number of academic lawyers and members of the legal profession. In the first place, it derived to some extent from a powerful school of German jurisprudence which argued that the Enlightenment tradition of Western Europe and the Anglo-Saxon world was wrong in regarding the function of law as the embodiment of fundamental principles of justice common to all humanity—the Rights of Man. Instead of this, the 'historical school' claimed that laws both should and did reflect the 'national spirit' of each particular nation within which they had their historical roots. It was a view shaped also by the massive influence of the nineteenth-century philosopher, Hegel.

Secondly, the Nazis could exploit the influential critique of the legal and constitutional ethos and arrangements of the Weimar Republic developed by the constitutional lawyer, Carl Schmitt and his followers. Schmitt attacked the 'normativism' which he saw as characteristic of the liberal approach to law, the attempt, that is, to define the relations between individuals themselves and individuals and the State in terms of a set of rules which proved less and less capable of containing the reality of those relationships. Above all, he objected to the idea of rules to which both rulers and ruled should be subordinated. Instead, he advocated 'decisionism' in which the source of law is the decision of the sovereign power which is capable of maintaining order. People should recognize the priority of politics over formal law and the essence of politics was the division between friends and enemies in which legal niceties could have no place. In the first phase of the Third Reich Schmitt threw the weight of his authority behind the concept of the 'Führer state'.

The most authoritative of the academic lawyers in Nazi Germany—though in view of the Nazis' contempt for lawyers that is not saying much!—was Ernst Rudolf Huber, Professor of Jurisprudence at Kiel. Huber expressed the following views on the law:

345

The law itself is nothing other than the expression of the communal order in which the people live and which derives from the Führer. The Führer Law makes concrete the unwritten principles of the *völkisch* communal life. It is therefore impossible to measure the laws of the Führer against a higher concept of the law because every Führer law is a direct expression of this *völkisch* concept of the law.

346

Formal equality [before the law] cannot be the deciding factor for the law-giver. Its place is taken by the material equality of *völkisch* law which grows out of the experience of the equality of a common *völkisch* nature. This new concept of equality enables us to distinguish in the legislative sphere as well the alien from our own character, the hostile from those loyal to the community, the subversive from the constructive forces, while the relativism of previous formalistic philosophy would have required equal treatment of these elements.

347

The National Socialist racial laws, the Law Against the Refounding of Political Parties, the Sterilization Law—all reject the formal concept of equality in order to bring about the victory of a real equality of those with a common nature.   The civil rights of the individual vis-à-vis the state are incompatible with the principle of *völkisch* law. There is no personal freedom of the individual prior to the state and outside the state which the state is obliged to respect.

(ii) The Legal Profession

Before 1933 German lawyers had been members of a free profession. Having passed their examinations, they were free to practise in a court and were not subordinate to the State in any way. After 1933 their independence was rapidly eroded. The provisions of the Civil Service Law of 7 April 1933 were applied to lawyers in a Law Concerning the Admission of Lawyers of the same date. Even more significant was a law of 13 December 1935, which established probationary periods for new lawyers and gave the Ministry of Justice authority over the admission of lawyers to practise. Decisions over admissions were to be made in consultation with the Reich Law Leader, Dr Hans Frank. In addition lawyers were required to swear an oath of loyalty to Hitler.

Before 1933 discipline within the profession had been exercised through district chambers which were self-governing bodies. In 1933 a new Reich Chamber of Lawyers was established whose officials were nominated by the Reich Minister of Justice in consultation with the Reich Law Leader and membership of which was compulsory. The new Chamber concentrated on ensuring that lawyers conducted themselves in the way expected of them by the National Socialist State and maintained discipline through a Court of Honour, as in the following case of 1 November 1937 concerning a lawyer who failed to give the Heil Hitler salute:

348

The Court of Honour regards the refusal to give the German greeting as a breach of professional etiquette which deserves severe punishment. The Appeal Court of Honour cannot share the assumption of the previous court that the accused acted from understandable indifference and not on purpose. Both the behaviour of the accused and the observations of the witness make it clear that the accused frequently failed to give or return the German greeting on purpose. This evidence and the fact that the behaviour of the accused caused annoyance and tended to degrade the German legal profession in the eyes of other citizens were bound to result in an increase in the sentence imposed by the lower Court of Honour. The sentence of reprimand seems an appropriate punishment, taking into account the extenuating circumstances already mentioned by the Court of Honour.

The training of lawyers was designed to include a generous dose of Nazi ideology, as is indicated by the following Decree on the Qualifications for the Offices of Judge, Public Prosecutor, Notary Public, and Lawyer of 4 January 1939:

349

1. A thorough, conscientious specialized training should be at the centre of the course of studies.
2. But it is desirable that the course should not be restricted to this. On the contrary, the candidate should as a student acquire such a general picture of the whole intellectual background of the nation as would be expected of an educated German. This should include a knowledge of German history and of the history of those

nations which have had a positive influence on the cultural development of the German people, above all the Greeks and the Romans. Furthermore, it must include a serious study of National Socialism and its ideological foundations, of the idea of the relationship between blood and soil and between race and nationality, of German community life and of the great men which the German nation has produced.

(iii) Nazi Legislation and Courts dealing with Political Offences

The crucial legislative act which provided the quasi-legal basis for political terror in the Third Reich was the Decree for the Protection of People and State of 28 February 1933, which suspended all the civil rights guaranteed under the Weimar Constitution.[79] This enabled the Secret State Police (Gestapo) to take any person into 'protective custody' and hold them indefinitely without any right to a trial or any form of appeal. Ostensibly designed to deal with Communist subversion, the decree was in fact used against any person suspected of resisting the regime from genuine Communists to Catholic priests.

This decree was supplemented by the Decree for the Protection of the Nationalist Movement against Malicious Attacks upon the Government of 21 March 1933. It represented one among a number of measures—e.g. the Civil Service Law of April 1933—through which the State administration responded to the arbitrary terror of the SA and SS during the first months of the regime, endeavouring to systematize and therefore establish some kind of control over political discrimination:

350

Paragraph 3
1. Whoever purposely makes or circulates a statement of a factual nature which is untrue or grossly exaggerated or which may seriously harm the welfare of the Reich or of a state, or the reputation of the National Government or of a state government or of the parties or organizations supporting these governments, is to be punished, provided that no more severe punishment is decreed in other regulations, with imprisonment of up to two years and, if he makes or spreads the statement publicly, with imprisonment of not less than three months.
2. If serious damage to the Reich or a state has resulted from this deed, penal servitude may be imposed.
3. Whoever commits an act through negligence will be punished with imprisonment of up to three months, or by a fine. . . .

The decree was replaced on 20 December 1934 by the Law against Malicious Attacks on State and Party and for the Protection of the Party

---
[79] See above, p. 142.

Uniforms, which strengthened the provisions of the decree by extending the impact of its original §3 (now §1) through the inclusion of a new clause (§2), according to which 'malicious, rabble-rousing remarks or those indicating a base mentality' concerning the Party or personalities of the State or of the NSDAP or its regulations or institutions were to be punished by imprisonment. This opened the way to the persecution of even relatively innocuous derogatory comments about the regime or its leaders.

In addition to legislative measures to deal with political subversion, on 21 March 1933, the regime also introduced a decree setting up so-called 'Special Courts' with jurisdiction over political crimes except for cases of high treason, which for the time being remained within the jurisdiction of the Supreme Court in Leipzig. These courts were staffed with loyal Nazi judges and there was no right of appeal from them. Originally intended to deal with cases of actual political resistance, between 1935 and 1939 they in fact dealt largely with cases brought under the Law against Malicious Attacks, whereas overtly political cases were dealt with by the higher state courts or by the new People's Court.[80]

The cases brought to the Special Courts under this law very largely concerned derogatory remarks about leading figures of the regime, its organizations or its policies. They sometimes took the form of the passing on of rumours which, in the absence of access to reliable and independent sources of information, flourished in the Third Reich, and also of political jokes. Most of these remarks were fundamentally unpolitical in the sense that the persons involved almost invariably had no particular axe to grind and were not trying to make a public or political statement. They were typically private grumbles about this or that aspect of life in the Third Reich which personally affected the persons concerned, discontents which were often expressed through criticism of the leaders, 'those up there'. The following are some typical examples which occurred in cases heard before the Munich Special Court:

351

The Reich Hunting Law serves Göring's private interest—Göring has transferred his property to Switzerland—Civil Servants get too high salaries—The peasants are crushed by high taxation—The Hitler Youth is ruining children—*Der Stürmer* is a cultural disgrace[81]—Hitler should get married then he can. . .—Hitler is a scoundrel —In Dachau concentration camp people get beaten.

---

[80] The following section owes much to P. Hüttenberger, 'Heimtückefälle vor dem Sondergericht München 1933–39' in M Broszat, E. Fröhlich, A. Grossmann eds., *Bayern in der NZ-Zeit*, Vol. IV (Munich/Vienna) 1981.
[81] For details on *Der Stürmer* see below pp. 541ff.

The regime was determined to crack down on comments which it felt might undermine popular morale and specifically people's trust in the political leadership. Moreover, its model of the harmonious 'national community' united behind its leadership prohibited it from tolerating any kind of dissent, whether or not it was publicly expressed and however harmless the individuals concerned. Thus, through its attitudes and behaviour, the regime itself politicized these basically innocuous remarks.

In practice, of course, whether or not a person was reported for such derogatory remarks and whether he escaped with a warning from the police or received a fine or a prison sentence depended on a large number of variables. Most denunciations came from private individuals, few from police informers. They often came through chance remarks overheard by zealous Nazis or loyal 'national comrades' or those who wished to ingratiate themselves with the authorities, as in the following case reported by an SPD contact man in Rhineland–Westphalia in July 1938:

352

In a café a 64 year old woman remarked to her companion at the table: 'Mussolini has more political sense in one of his boots than Hitler has in his brain.' The remark was overheard by other patrons and five minutes later the woman was arrested by the Gestapo who had been alerted by telephone.

Denunciations could also follow disputes between members of a family, neighbours, or colleagues at work. On the whole, strangers and those whose life style singled them out as odd or unpopular—tramps, beggars, alcoholics, and social misfits in general were more vulnerable to denunciation than those who were respected and popular members of a particular group or community, though these were by no means invulnerable. Where the community was close knit, as for example in a village, denunciations would tend to be limited to those who did not fit in.

The authorities too differentiated in their treatment of offenders. They were influenced by conventional social values and prejudices as well as Nazi ideological principles and tended to be tougher on social non-conformists, on the educated who allegedly should have known better, and also on those who stubbornly stuck to their statements and opinions. Prison sentences normally varied from one month to one year with occasional longer sentences, but the majority between one and six months—they were clearly intended to act as a kind of short sharp shock which would intimidate the culprit and his immediate circle without alienating them through excessive harshness. The Munich Special Court dealt with 4,453 cases between 1933 and 1939 involving 5,422 people, of whom 5,069 were accused under the Law for Malicious Attacks, the remainder under various criminal laws. Of these cases 1,861 came to trial of whom 1,522 were convicted and sentenced. The fact that only a relatively small proportion of the cases came to court indicates that the police and the courts were fairly cautious about prosecuting, no doubt a necessary attitude in view of the large number of malicious and mendacious denunciations. There was, however, a steady increase in the number of cases after 1936 with a marked jump in the years 1938–39, reflecting the growing pressures on the population of the pre-war period.

The fact that cases of high treason did not come under the Special Courts but were still tried by the Supreme Court proved to be a loophole, for the trial of those allegedly involved in the Reichstag Fire of 27 February 1933 ended in the acquittal of most of the alleged Communist accomplices of van der Lubbe. On 24 April, therefore, the following Law to Change the rules of Criminal Law and Criminal Procedure was issued, establishing a so-called 'People's Court' to try all cases of treason. It consisted of two professional judges, carefully selected for their loyalty to the regime and five Party officials as lay judges. Its most notorious trial was of those involved in the plot to assassinate Hitler on 20 July 1944:

353

III. 1. A People's Court shall be formed to try cases of high treason. When the People's Court sits for a trial, the judgements are to be made by five members, otherwise by three members, including the President. The President and one other member must be qualified judges. Several senates may be formed. The Supreme Reich Prosecutor is the prosecuting authority.
2. The Reich Chancellor appoints the members of the People's Court and their deputies for a period of five years, on the proposal of the Reich Minister of Justice....
5. There is no appeal from the decisions of the People's Court....

IV. 3. The appointment of defence council must be approved by the President of the People's Court....

The Reichstag Fire and its legal repercussions had not only been responsible for the creation of the People's Court for cases of high treason, it had also prompted one of the most fundamental changes in legal practice implemented by the regime: the abrogation of the principle of *nulla poene sine lege* basic to the Western legal tradition, namely the principle that no one should be tried for an act which was not an offence at the time he committed it or be given a punishment which was not stipulated for that offence at the time he committed it. The question first arose in the Cabinet meeting of 7 March 1933:

354

The Reich Minister of the Interior spoke about the Reichstag fire and the punishment of the culprits and stated that it was urgently necessary to hang van der Lubbe at once—and moreover, in the Königsplatz. To be sure, the law on arson provided for no more than a prison sentence, but it must be possible to impose with retroactive effect, the penalty of death by hanging for such a heinous crime. The principle of *nulla poena sine lege* should not have an unqualified application. Professor Dr Nagler (Breslau), Professor Dr von Weber (Jena), and Professor Dr Öttler (Würzburg) had delivered opinions along these lines.

The Reich Minister of Interior then reported on the substance of the opinions as enclosed.

The Chancellor stated emphatically that he also believed it to be urgently necessary to hang van der Lubbe. The German public demanded it. He could not recognize the doctrine that 'the law must be observed', if this constituted a threat to the life of the whole nation. . . .

State Secretary Schlegelberger stated that he agreed entirely with the view of the Reich Chancellor that the law must be adjusted to the circumstances. A preliminary investigation of van der Lubbe on charges of high treason and arson had been opened that day (7 March). He must strongly emphasize the doctrine of *nulla poena sine lege*. Only in Russia, China, and some of the minor Swiss cantons did that doctrine not apply. He would again study carefully the opinions mentioned by the Reich Minister of Interior. The Reich Ministry of Justice would itself then formulate an opinion and send both opinions to the Reich Ministers for their information.

State Secretary Dr Meissner stated that the arguments of the Chancellor were politically quite correct. The public was right in demanding a severe penalty for van der Lubbe.

The Reich President might, however, suffer severe twofold qualms of conscience, namely, if he were to sign an order prescribing the death penalty and so forth, and then later to decide on a petition for pardon of the condemned man. He asked that the Reich Chancellor, the Reich Minister of the Interior, and the Reich Ministry of Justice should submit the matter to the President before the Cabinet reached a final decision.

Reich Commissioner Dr Popitz[82] stated that he feared the Reich Supreme Court would not recognize the retroactive effect of an order prescribing the death penalty.

The Chancellor stated that he would get in touch with the President of the Reich Supreme Court about this.

It was expected that the Chancellor would first speak alone with the President on the matter. . . .

In fact a law introducing the death penalty for arson—a 'lex Lubbe'—was passed on 29 March 1933.

---

[82] Dr Johannes Popitz was Prussian Minister of Finance.

In place of the principle of *nulle poena sine lege* the regime introduced the principle of 'the analogy' which was enshrined in the Law to Change the Penal Code of 28 June 1935 and given an official interpretation by Gürtner:

355

...

(*a*) I. (2.) Any person who commits an act which the law declares to be punishable or which is deserving of punishment according to the idea of a penal law and sound feelings shall be punished. If there is no penal law directly covering an act it shall be punished under that law the basic idea of which fits it best. . . .

(*b*) *The Reich Minister of Justice on the principle of* nulla poena sine lege, *1935.*

A law which originates from the rule '*nulla poena sine lege*' regards as illegal only such action as violates an existing clause of a penal law. Whatever is not forbidden and threatened with punishment is considered to be permissible. Such a law follows from the conception of formal wrongdoing. National Socialism substitutes for the conception of formal wrong the idea of factual wrong: it considers every attack on the welfare of the national community, every violation of the requirements of the life of a nation as wrong. In future, therefore, wrong may be committed in Germany even in cases where there is no law against what is being done. Even without the threat of punishment, every violation of the goals towards which the community is striving is wrong *per se*. As a result, the law gives up all claim to be the sole source for determining right and wrong. What is right may be learned not only from the law but also from the concept of justice which lies behind the law and may not have found perfect expression in the law. The law certainly continues to be the most important source for the determination of right and wrong because the leaders of a nation express their will in the law. But the legislator is aware of the fact that he cannot give exhaustive regulations covering all the situations which may occur in life; he therefore entrusts the judge with filling in the remaining gaps. . . .

(iv) The Judiciary

In his commentary on the replacement of the principle of *nulla poena sine lege* by the analogy principle Gürtner had drawn attention to a crucial point—the vital role played by the judiciary under the new dispensation. Since the Nazi regime did not develop its own codes of law reflecting Nazi ideological principles, but instead continued to use the existing codes, modified by decrees and laws covering specific points, a crucial role would clearly have to be played by the judges who had to interpret the law. The regime was well aware of this and took steps to try and ensure that the judges intepreted the law in accordance both with its political imperatives and with Nazi ideological principles.

In their coordination of the legal system the Nazis were assisted by the fact that during the Weimar Republic the judiciary had remained a bastion of the Right. Its sentencing policy was notoriously biased in favour of extremists of the right and against those of the left. But there are also other factors which help to account for the relative ease with which the legal system was coordinated. The vast majority of judges were initially Nationalists rather than Nazis and it is doubtful whether the judiciary, despite its right-wing bias would have proved so vulnerable, had its position not already been relatively weak.

The status of the judiciary in Weimar Germany was not particularly high. The position of a judge did not carry the great prestige associated with that office in Britain. Apart from anything else, there were far more of them— between 8,000 and 10,000. In other words, the range of activity of the German judiciary embraced far lower courts than in Britain, where laymen have a more important role to play as magistrates. But more significant in their relative lack of prestige was the fact that they did not appear to have the same degree of independence. Judges were career civil servants. Furthermore, the judicial branch of the Civil Service was considered inferior to the administrative branch. The salary was modest and, for the majority, prospects of promotion were poor. The ablest law students therefore tended to go into the administrative branch or to become private lawyers. The fact that, unlike its British counterpart, the German judiciary did not form a powerful independent professional body with long traditions, highly conscious of its role as the guardian of the law, if necessary, against governments, and supported by the respect of the population, undoubtedly weakened its powers of resistance to Nazism.

Nevertheless before 1933 its independence was very real. For, although judges were civil servants, it would be wrong to suggest that German judges before 1933 allowed themselves to be influenced in reaching their decisions by any political pressures. Judicial independence was respected by the Government and backed by the law. Judges were appointed for life and could not be dismissed or transferred against their will except in very narrowly defined circumstances. This independence of the judiciary clearly represented a barrier which the new regime would have to remove or by-pass if it was to establish total political control. This point was soon underlined by the judgement of the Supreme Court in the Reichstag Fire trial, in which the charges against the majority of the Communist defendants were dismissed.

In the first place, the judiciary were subject to the Law Concerning the Reconstruction of the Professional Civil Service of 7 April 1933, which abolished the principle that judges could not be dismissed or demoted for political reasons and thus undermined the principle of the independence of the judiciary. But this law affected relatively few judges since the vast majority were right-wing. More important were other measures affecting the Civil Service in general. The 1935 decree involving the Party, through the

Office of the Deputy Führer, in the appointment of civil servants also applied
to judges. Finally Paragraph 71 of the German Civil Service Law of 26
January 1937 laid down that civil servants could be compulsorily retired if
they 'could not be relied upon to support the National Socialist State at all
times'. Although Hitler was persuaded to agree to a qualification in
Paragraph 171 by which Paragraph 71 did not apply to a judgement in court,
he removed it a year later in a confidential memorandum from Lammers to
the Reich Minister of Justice dated 12 July 1938.

Secondly, the judges' position was undermined by the progressive erosion
of judicial self-government after 1937. The various tasks within the court
were no longer assigned by the President of the Court in association with
the presidents of the various sections and with the highest ranking associate
judge, operating as independent organs of the court, but rather by the
President of the court acting alone as the representative of and under orders
from the Reich Ministry of Justice. In short, the judiciary was increasingly
reduced to the status of a mere administrative agency of the Ministry. This
weakening of the position of the judiciary was reinforced by another
important development—the growing influence of the role of the public
prosecutor in the court proceedings, a trend that was reflected in the fact that
the rate of acquittals in the regular criminal courts went down from 13 per
cent in 1932 to 7 per cent in the second quarter of 1940.

The most significant influence on the behaviour of the judges, however,
came from the pressure imposed by the new climate of opinion in Nazi
Germany and the expectations of the regime. This point was well put by an
academic lawyer, Stoll, in an article for *Die Deutsche Juristenzeitung* in 1933:

356

If the military commander is changed during an operation, then all the old orders,
the whole line of battle, can be retained but they acquire a completely new
significance through a brief, precisely targeted command from the new leader. The
German jurist is now in the same position with private law. The provisions of the
Civil Law Code are still valid, but they acquire a new direction through the 'central
legal concept' of the victorious movement.

The 'central legal concept' remained somewhat unclear, but judges were
frequently reminded of what was expected of them in statements issued by
persons in authority such as the following statement formulated by Professor
Karl Eckhardt, the editor of a legal journal, but issued on 14 January 1936
under the name of Dr Hans Frank:

357

1. The judge is not placed over the citizen as a representative of the State authority, but is a member of the living community of the German people. It is not his duty to help to enforce a law superior to the national community or to impose a system of universal values. His role is to safeguard the concrete order of the racial community, to eliminate dangerous elements, to prosecute all acts harmful to the community, and to arbitrate in disagreements between members of the community.
2. The National Socialist ideology, especially as expressed in the Party programme and in the speeches of our Führer, is the basis for interpreting legal sources.
3. The judge has no right to scrutinize decisions made by the Führer and issued in the form of a law or a decree. The judge is also bound by any other decisions of the Führer which clearly express the intention of establishing law.
4. Legal decrees issued before the National Socialist revolution are not to be applied if their application would violate the present sound feelings of the people. In the event of a judge suspending some legal regulation on these grounds, the decision of the highest court must be sought.
5. To carry out his duties effectively within the national community, the judge must be independent. He is not bound by instructions. The independence and dignity of the judge make it necessary to give him adequate protection against any attempt to influence him or against any unjustified attacks.

§1. summarized the philosophy of law dominant among academic lawyers in the Third Reich. The assumption behind §5 was that a true Nazi judge should not need to be told what judgments to pass. In fact, however, Nazi lawyers such as Frank were optimistic in imagining that the Nazi leadership would ever concede the principle of an independent judiciary. Their suspicion of and hostility towards the law was too great for that. §§2–4 indicated that judges were expected to use three other major sources for their judgments in addition to the statutes themselves: Nazi ideology as expressed in the Party programme and in the Führer's speeches, decisions of the Führer, and the sound feelings of the people. Of these only the decisions of the Führer provided a relatively unambiguous guide for the judges. In particular, the question of the use and interpretation of the 'sound feelings of the people', which formed part of the basis of the replacement of the principle of *nulla poena sine lege* by the analogy principle in §2 of the Law to Change the Penal Code of 1935, raised serious problems. For example, how much discretion should the judge have in interpreting the 'sound feelings of the people' or indeed the analogous statute?

In practice, the Supreme Court tried in its own judgments, which provided guidance for the lower courts, to retain as much rationality in the interpretation of the law as it could. It did this first, by preserving the statute as the main focus for the decisions of individual cases, and secondly, by insisting that the analogy principle should only be applied where two preconditions existed: the fundamental idea underlying the analogous statute *could* be applied to the case in question *and* the 'sound feelings of the people' required such application. Moreover, the judge himself was not supposed to act as an independent source of the 'people's feelings' but rather to deduce those feelings from the pronouncements of the leaders of the regime.

This attempt by the Supreme Court to retain a modicum of rationality in the application of the law was, however, limited by two developments. First, the Court showed little willingness to modify the application of the regime's racial and eugenic policies indeed, if anything, its judgments increasingly tended towards an extreme interpretation of the law in this field: an example is the interpretation of the Law for the Protection of German Blood and Honour.[83] Secondly, the influence of the Supreme Court itself tended to be increasingly undermined by direct interference from the Reich Ministry of Justice, the SS-police system, and the Führer himself in the form of a stream of decrees and decisions sometimes applying to specific cases.

The fact that the Nazi regime asserted a claim to influence and control virtually all aspects of German life ensured that the new climate of opinion influenced the interpretation of the law in almost every sphere. The application of labour law, for example, clearly came to function as a coercive weapon, as is clear from the following decision of a state Labour Court in Karlsruhe of 6 July 1934:

358

By absenting himself from the premises before the start of the singing of the national anthem and the Horst Wessel Song and by the failure to participate in parades, celebrations and other events put on for the staff, an employee intentionally places himself outside the national community and hereby demonstrates his anti-State attitude. This justifies instant dismissal.

Similarly, the interpretation of the new divorce regulations introduced in 1938 showed the extent to which the interpretation of family law had become subordinated to the regime's population policy. In part, this development merely demonstrated the fact that in any society the interpretation of the law by the judiciary tends to reflect the authoritative norms and values of that society. In part, however, it was a consequence of the weakening of the judiciary as a relatively autonomous institution. For, from being relatively independent agencies of society, capable of arbitrating freely between any of the contending social groups and deciding individual cases on the basis

---

[83] See below p. 541.

of a skilled and comparatively objective interpretation of the law, the courts in the Third Reich were (as a result of political and administrative pressures) increasingly reduced to the level of executive agencies of the Government whose main function was to reflect in their application of the law as accurately as possible the will and ideological principles of the leadership.

There were of course exceptions in which judges and courts resisted such pressure and endeavoured to give an objective hearing to a case. For obvious resons this happened more in civil matters. In the criminal courts, particularly where political issues were involved, the pressure was much greater. An instance of the latter is, however, worth recording;

359

On the day of the trial the cross-examination of the defendants took an unusually long time. . . . Appeal Judge —, who presided over the provincial Court of Appeal, had obviously already lost patience and only asked my defendant whether he wanted to plead guilty or not guilty. My client replied briefly that he denied the crime of which he was accused. Then Appeal Judge — said: 'In that case we can begin with the hearing of the evidence.' At that moment I intervened and asked permission to question the defendant, before the hearing of evidence, about the circumstances in which he had signed the statement quoted above,[84] and in particular as to whether he had been beaten by the officers of the Secret State Police in connexion with the signing of these statements.

I had hardly finished the question when the State prosecutor jumped up excitedly and asked the president of the court to protect the officers of the Secret State Police against such attacks by the defence.

Appeal Judge — rose from his chair, leant on his hands on the court table and said to me: 'Council for the defence, I must draw your attention to the fact that even though the trial here is conducted *in camera* a question such as you have asked can lead to your being arrested in the courtroom and taken into custody. Do you wish to sustain the question or not?'

These details are still fresh in my memory because they made an extraordinary impression on me. Also, subsequently I have repeatedly discussed this case because it seemed to me typical of National Socialist justice.

Suddenly, into the dead silence which followed the Appeal Judge's question came the words of the assistant judge, Dr —. I remember these words very clearly; they were: 'The defence need not sustain this question, I will take it over on behalf of the court.'

I do not know if I would personally have had the courage to stick to my question under the pressure of the situation and as a recently admitted lawyer. Dr — saved me this decision. I wholeheartedly admired such courage from a German judge. I also got the impression that only a judge who had been badly wounded in the 1914–18 war could get away with such courage.

---

[84] The defendant had signed a statement confessing his guilt after interrogation by the Gestapo.

In the course of the trial the question raised by me and taken over by Dr — was thoroughly examined. The trial lasted from 9 a.m. to 7.30 p.m. The cross-examination alone took about two hours. My client was released for lack of evidence.

Unfortunately, however, not only were such examples of civic courage rare but even in the event of the accused being acquitted, he was still liable to be rearrested outside the courtroom by the Gestapo and speedily conveyed to the nearest concentration camp. For Nazi Germany was essentially not a state under the rule of law, even Nazi law, but a police state in which the organs of terror ultimately held sway.

CHAPTER 22

The SS-Police System

However much the legal system was subservient to the regime, Hitler continued to regard it with great suspicion. He needed an organization which would not feel restrained by legal clauses or bureaucratic qualms, which would act with utter ruthlessness, and which would be dedicated to expressing his will and the ideology of the Nazi movement. He found what he needed in the SS. The SS established a separate organizational framework for the enforcement of the will of the regime. This organization was independent of the State and yet, through its control over the police, it was linked with the State. It could therefore operate either outside the legal system or in association with it, depending on circumstances. The characteristic political and administrative development in the Third Reich was for the traditional State authorities to become increasingly a façade, the substance of which was progressively being eaten away by the cancerous growth of new organizations under individuals appointed by Hitler. The old authorities were not abolished; they were left still in apparent control. But in reality, their power was being drained away to the new organizations which were untrammelled by traditional norms and bureucratic procedures, and whose leaders were directly dependent on Hitler. This development was reflected in the relationship between the SS and the police and legal system.

(i) The Character and Aims of Himmler: the SS as an Elite Order

The SS began as an elite bodyguard for the Party leaders, and it was only after it had been taken over by Heinrich Himmler in 1929, that it acquired its characteristic features. The SS was a paradox and in this it reflected the personality of its leader. Himmler was a bizarre combination of naive crank, pedantic schoolmaster, and coldly efficient bureaucrat, a master at accumulating power in the administrative jungle of the Third Reich. The following documents signed by him illustrate the various aspects of his personality:

360

(a) *How to make sure a boy is born*

SS Obersturmbannführer Dr Brandt to SS Standartenführer Max Sollman, Head of the *Lebensborn*[85], 14.ii.44:

I enclose a copy of the letter of a certain Artur Dombeck of Hamburg. I also add a minute dictated by the Reichsführer SS. The Reichsführer SS wishes the *Lebensborn* to start a research project on 'The question of the procreation of girls or boys'.

Enclosure: *12.ii.44 Minute of RF:*

SS Obergruppenführer Berger told me recently, when we were talking about the procreation of girls or boys, that it is the custom where he comes from in the Swabian Alps that if a family wants to have a boy at last they do the following:

The man, after keeping off alcohol for a week like his wife, sets off from home at 12 o'clock noon and walks the 20 kilometres to Ulm and back. He must not stop at an inn on the way. The wife does no work in the preceding week, eats very well, sleeps a lot, and does not exert herself in any way. After the man's return intercourse takes place. The result is said to be always the birth of a boy.

(b) *Himmler imposes a ban on smoking*

Himmler to SS Sturmbannführer Count Adalbert Kottulinsky, 16.ix.38:

You have been very ill and have had a lot of trouble with your heart. In the interests of your health I am imposing on you a total ban on smoking for two years.

Will you please provide a doctor's health certificate at the end of these two years. I will then decide whether the ban should be lifted or maintained.

(c) *'All agreements with the Army High Command require my personal approval'*

Reichsführer SS Himmler to SS Obergruppenführer August Heissmeyer, Inspector of the National Political Educational Establishments,[86] 7.v.40:

I have received your report of 29 April 1940 concerning the expansion of the National Political Educational Establishments. There can be no question of a division of responsibilities. I told Colonel Friessner this personally before the start of the parade of the 6000 officer cadets in front of the Führer.

Colonel Friessner's suggestion would result in the National Political Educational Establishments being entirely subordinated to the Army Cadet Corps and all their pupils would go into the Army.

---

[85] The *Lebensborn* (lit. 'Life Spring') was an SS organization for the care of illegitimate children who were 'of good racial stock'.

[86] The 'Napolas'—see above p. 435.

In addition, I strongly object to the particular emphasis placed on officer-type attitudes and behaviour in accordance with normal Army principles. I would be obliged if you would tell the gentlemen during your next discussion politely but firmly that I am the one who lays down the lines of policy on education for the National Political Education Establishments and not the Army.

All agreements with the Army High Command require my personal approval.

The SS reflected its leader's personality. On the one hand, it was the exponent and instrument of the most extreme ideological views of the Nazi movement. On the other hand, many of its officers—men such as Walter Schellenberg, the head of its foreign security service—tended to be the most unideological of men. They were often career men, young graduates who would today be business executives or bright young civil servants, men for whom administrative efficiency was the main criterion.

Heinrich Himmler had joined the Nazi Party as a young agricultural student in Munich in 1921. Even at that early stage he had acquired the basic views which he was to retain until his death: a biologically-oriented racism which regarded the struggle between the Aryans and the Jews as the key to world history; a belief in the ideology of 'blood and soil', i.e. the conviction that a healthy peasantry was the key to the biological and indeed moral health of the German people; a conviction that the Germans were a 'people without space' and that if Germany was ever to achieve the status in the world to which her racial superiority entitled her, then she would have to expand her agricultural area through a policy of peasant settlement in the East. Influenced by the activities of the German Free Corps units in the Baltic States in 1919–20, many of whose members moved to Bavaria after their disbandment, Himmler believed that Germany's future lay in her settlement of the Baltic States and Western Russia with German soldier peasants. As early as 22 November 1922, he noted in his diary:

361

I am more convinced than ever that if there is a campaign in the East I will go with it. The East is the most important thing for us. The West will die easily. In the East we must fight and settle.

A few years, later he joined a youth group, the *Artamanen*, who saw it as their mission to encourage German peasant settlement in the East.

On his appointment as Reichsführer SS on 6 January 1929, Himmler determined to turn the SS into the elite order of National Socialism. His models were, first, the Jesuit order in the role as he saw it of the spiritual police of the Roman Catholic Church, whose members subordinated themselves with total dedication to the service of the order and above all of the Pope, and secondly, the Teutonic Order—an order of knights who had used their role as Christian missionaries to carve out an empire in Eastern Europe. But Himmler intended his order to be imbued not with Christianity, which he saw as a 'plague', but with the ideology of National Socialism, and above all he intended it to be a racial elite. As he told an audience of SS Group Leaders on 8 November 1937:

362

In addition we have set ourselves the goal not of creating an association of men which, like all men's associations, will sooner or later disintegrate, but rather of letting an order develop gradually. The word 'order' is used too often. It does not become an order simply because we call it an order. I hope that in ten years' time we will be an order and not only an order of men but an order of clans (*Sippengemeinschaften*). An order to which the women are required to belong just as much as the men. Let us be clear about this: it would be stupid to collect together good blood from the whole of Germany and to conceive this good blood in theoretical terms, while at the same time allowing it to marry and form families just as it wants. On the contrary, we want for Germany an upper stratum, a new nobility continually selected over the centuries, which replenishes itself continually from the best sons and daughters of our nation, a nobility which never becomes senile, which taps tradition and the past in the darkest millenia wherever they are valuable and which eternally represents a youth for our nation.

To achieve this goal Himmler insisted that the wives of SS men should be racially pure and hereditarily sound in a SS Marriage Order issued on 31 December 1931:

363

1. The SS is a band of German men of strictly Nordic origin selected according to certain principles.
2. In accordance with the National Socialist ideology and with the realization that the future of our nation rests on the preservation of the race through selection and on the inheritance of good blood, I hereby institute from 1 January 1932 the 'Marriage Certificate' for all unmarried members of the SS.
3. The aim is to create a hereditarily healthy clan of a strictly Nordic German type.
4. The marriage certificate will be awarded or refused solely on the basis of racial health and heredity.
5. Every SS man intending to get married must procure for this purpose the marriage certificate of the Reichsführer SS.
6. SS members who marry despite having been denied marriage certificates will be removed from the SS; they will be given the chance of resignation.

7. It is the task of the SS 'Race Office' to work out the details of marriage petitions.
8. The SS Race Office is in charge of the 'Clan Book of the SS' in which the families of SS members will be entered after being awarded the marriage certificate or after acceptance of the petition to enter into marriage.
9. The Reichsführer SS, the director of the Race Office, and the specialists of this office are pledged to secrecy on their word of honour.
10. The SS is convinced that with this order it has taken a step of great significance. Derision, scorn, and incomprehension will not move us; the future is ours!

In fact, however, marriage certificate statistics for 1932–40 show that only 958 applicants out of 106,304 were turned down; but only 7,518 satisfied every requirement.[87]

Himmler was anxious to create a new Nazi elite based on criteria of race and personal qualitites (in fact he tended to regard personality as a product of race) rather than on the traditional criteria of birth, and property and education which had hitherto determined the German elites. Nevertheless, he was anxious to seek recruits among the traditional aristocracy, partly to raise the status of his organization, and partly because he believed that the aristocracy continued to contain some 'good blood' as he told a meeting of SS Group Leaders on 18 February 1937;

364

During the years 1919-20–1921-23, it was always the same—when we went to meetings in city pubs it was not done to wear a tie. Why not? Because one would be considered untrustworthy. One went as dirty and unwashed as possible. We wanted to win over the Communists and so had to adjust ourselves to their style of life. By doing that we did not become inwardly proletarians.

That made sense to us then. Now we must move the other way. I refer, for example to the Horse Show attended by the majority of the Prussian landed artistocracy. If one looks at the individuals there, one must admit that there is some damn good blood among them; and one must further admit that the Party has not won over this good blood. That is a sober statement of fact. The Party says they are reactionary. Fine, they may be, obviously in fact, no one knows better than I. I think that I as the Chief of the German Police am the man in Germany who knows that best. But I place the greatest importance on our succeeding in winning over these people. Because in saying that these people are reactionary, are opponents of the State, one does not wipe them off the face of the earth; on the contrary, they are here. If I win them over I will win a lot of good blood for the movement. And, speaking from the standpoint of the SS, I will win a lot of good blood which I would like to have for the SS.

---

[87] See H. P. Bleuel, *Strength through Joy. Sex and Society in Nazi Germany* (London 1973) p. 199.

We must try and fill the sons and daughters of people who are now opposed to us with our ideology which, after all, is not miles apart in its essence from the ideology of the nobility. . .

After the take-over of power the SS systematized its recruitment procedures. On 22 May 1936, Himmler told a Hitler Youth rally about the selection process for SS recuits.

365

The young SS candidate leaves the Hitler Youth at 18. That will mostly happen on 9 November. Up to 30 January he will do his probationary period with us and on 30 January, the anniversary of the take-over of power, will receive his provisional membership card. How then do we test him to see if we want him?

We require from him his personal medical certificate and his certificate of hereditary health, i.e. we investigate his whole family. If we discover any illness or defect in his family, he is regarded as unfit so that we do not notice only later, when he gets married, that someone is mentally ill or has tuberculosis. That is established right at the start. In addition, the Hitler Youth testimonial and that of the *Jungvolk* are required to be presented. Furthermore, a report on his parents is required: how and in what sort of a milieu has the boy been brought up? Then, in addition, there is the most important certificate—the family tree. It is compulsory for every SS man back to the year 1650 . . . I will not go any further back than that, at least not formally, because there is no point, for 1648, the end of the Thirty Years War, is mostly the limit. The parish records are largely missing from the earlier period i.e. the requisite documentation. Then comes as the last but perhaps most important test what we call the Racial Board, the Selection Board. It has been familiar in animal breeding for a long time . . .

Himmler summed up the principles of selection and the values of the SS order in a speech at the Reich Peasant Congress in Goslar on 12 November 1935 on 'The SS as an Anti-Bolshevist Combat Organization':

366

The first principle for us was and is the recognition of the values of blood and selection . . .

We went about it like a seedsman who, wanting to improve the strain of a good old variety which has become crossbred and lost its vigour, goes through the fields to pick the seeds of the best plants. We sorted out the people who we thought unsuitable for the formation of the SS simply on the basis of outward appearance.

The nature of the selection process was to concentrate on the choice of those who came physically closest to the ideal of nordic man. External features such as size and a racially appropriate appearance played and still play a role here . . .

The second principle and virtue which we tried to instil in the SS and to give to it as an indelible characteristic for the future is the will to freedom and a fighting spirit . . .

The third principle and virtue are the concepts of loyalty and honour . . .

We teach the SS man that many things on this earth can be forgiven but one thing can never be: disloyalty . . .

For loyalty is a matter of the heart, never of the intellect. The intellect may go astray. That is sometimes damaging but never irreparable. The heart must always beat at the same pulse rate . . . We mean by that loyalty of all kinds, loyalty to the Führer and thereby to the German, to the germanic people, to its knowledge and its own kind, loyalty to blood, to our ancestors and our grandchildren, loyalty to our clan, loyalty to our comrades and loyalty to the immutable laws of decency, clean living, and chivalry.

The fourth principle and virtue that is valid for us is obedience, which does not hesitate for a moment but unconditionally follows every order which comes from the Führer or is legitimately given by a superior, obedience . . . which obeys just as unconditionally and goes into the attack even when one might think in one's heart one could not bring oneself to do so.

I know there are some people in Germany who feel sick at the sight of this black uniform; we can understand their feelings and do not expect many people to love us. All those who have the interests of Germany at heart will and should respect us, and those who somehow some time have guilty consciences towards the Führer or the nation should fear us. To deal with these people we have built up an organization called the Security Service and also we as the SS provide the men for service in the Secret State Police [Gestapo]. We shall unremittingly fulfil our task of being the guarantors of Germany's internal security, just as the German *Wehrmacht* guarantees the security of the honour, the greatness, and the peace of the Reich externally. We shall ensure that never again will the Jewish-Bolshevist revolution of sub-humanity be unleashed in Germany, the heart of Europe, either from within or by emissaries from without. We shall be a merciless sword of judgment for all these forces, of whose existence and activities we are well aware, on the day they make the slightest attempt whether it happens today, or in years, decades, or centuries to come . . .

. . . Thus we have fallen in and march according to immutable laws, as a soldierly, National Socialist order of men of nordic origin and as a sworn community of their clans, along the road into a distant future and wish to believe that we may not be merely the grandchildren who fought better, but over and beyond that the ancestors of those later generations which are vital for the eternal life of the German, of the germanic people.

In this speech Himmler referred to the key values of the SS. The most important of these was loyalty. In 1931, after the SS had helped put down a revolt of a section of the SA led by Walter Stennes, chief of the Eastern SA region, Hitler had bestowed upon the SS its motto for the future: 'Your honour is loyalty'. Loyalty within the SS was interpreted as loyalty to the Führer. Members of the SS were obliged to swear the following oath:

We swear to you Adolf Hitler as Führer and Chancellor of the German Reich to be loyal and brave. We vow to you and the superiors appointed by you obedience unto death. So help us God.

In other words honour was equated with loyalty and loyalty with absolute obedience to the Führer. As Himmler told his Group Leaders on 8 November 1938: 'The Führer is always right whether about suits, or about bunkers, or about the Reich autobahns... I want to have such obedience that people do not even have critical thoughts'. This represented the final debasement of the military values associated with the Prussian tradition. The concepts of honour and loyalty had been in effect drained of all ethical content, all sense of personal responsibility. All that remained was the hollow shell of a concept of obedience which could be manipulated at will and used to perform the most inhumane acts.

The SS in fact aimed to replace the traditional Christian-based ethic of Western civilisation with a new morality based on a new form of religion. As the SS leadership put it in an undated plan of 1937:

367

We live in the age of the final confrontation with Christianity. It is part of the mission of the SS to give to the German people over the next fifty years the non-Christian ideological foundations for a way of life appropriate to their own character. This task cannot be carried out purely through the conquest of the ideological opponent but must be accompanied step by step by a positive advance: that is to say by tapping the germanic heritage understood in the widest and most comprehensive sense.

As part of this attempt to 'tap the germanic heritage' and establish a substitute for Christianity, the SS developed its own cults and rituals, including an SS wedding service:

368

The central point in the ceremonial was represented by the wedding table decorated by two conjoined runic[88] figures. On the table lay a yellow sun disc made of flowers on a blue background; to the left and right stood torchbearers and behind the table a bowl, containing fire, and the pulpit. The choir opened the ceremony with a chorus from *Lohengrin*. A representative of the new usage, SS Comrade Elling, gave the dedication—and address based upon the song from the Edda Helga and Sigrun. The

---

[88] Symbols in German mythology.

choir chanted both before and after the address. Then the bridal pair were offered bread (representing the germinating force of earth) and salt (the symbol of purity) on silver vessels. Finally, the pair thus married according to German custom received their wedding rings.

Himmler described his own religious beliefs in an address to the top leadership of the SS on 9 June 1942. His view of man as an 'insignificant part of this world', who only gains whatever significance he possesses as part of 'this eternal chain and eternal sequence' of ancestors and grandchildren within a 'clan', helps to explain the contempt for individual human beings which lay at the heart of Nazi ideology.

369

... We will have to deal with Christianity in a tougher way than hitherto. We must settle accounts with this Christianity, this greatest of plagues that could have happened to us in our history, which has weakened us in every conflict. If our generation does not do it then it would I think drag on for a long time. We must overcome it within ourselves. Today at Heydrich's funeral[89] I intentionally expressed in my oration from my deepest conviction a belief in God, a belief in fate, in the ancient one as I called him—that is the old germanic word: Wralda. We shall once again have to find a new scale of values for our people: the scale of the macrocosm and the microcosm, the starry sky above us and the world in us, the world that we see in the microscope. The essence of these megalomaniacs, these Christians who talk of men ruling this world, must stop and be put back in its proper proportion. Man is nothing special at all. He is an insignificant part of this earth. If a big thunderstorm comes, he can do nothing about it. He cannot even predict it. He has no idea how a fly is constructed—however unpleasant, it is a miracle—or how a blossom is constructed. He must once again look with deep reverence into this world. Then he will acquire the right sense of proportion about what is above us, about how we are woven into this cycle.

Then, on a different plane, something else must happen: we must once again be rooted in our ancestors and grandchildren, in this eternal chain and eternal sequence. By rooting our people in a deep ideological awareness of ancestors and grandchildren we must once more persuade them that they must have sons. We can do a very great deal. But everything that we do must be justifiable vis-à-vis the clan, our ancestors. If we do not secure this moral foundation which is the deepest and best because the most natural, we will not be able to overcome Christianity on this plane and create the germanic Reich which will be a blessing for the earth. That is our mission as a nation on this earth. For thousands of years it has been the mission of this blond race to rule the earth and again and again to bring it happiness and culture.

---

[89] Heydrich then Reich Protector of Bohemia–Moravia, had just been assassinated by Czech partisans. On Heydrich see below pp. 499–515.

(ii) The SS take-over of the Police 1933–36

Himmler envisaged the future role of his SS order as that of 'political soldiers'—a concept which derived from the Free Corps of 1919–21—who would deal with the enemies of the 'national community', initially those inside Germany but ultimately those outside it as well. For the SS, the world was divided into friends and enemies. As an article in the SS newspaper, *Das Schwarze Korps*, put it on 26 January 1939:

370

In politics there are only two possibilities: for Germany or not. Anyone who is not basically for Germany but against Germany does not belong to us and will be eliminated. If he does not emigrate on his own initiative, then he will have to be locked up. If that does not help then we will have to make him a head shorter.

The domestic enemies of the SS were divided into racial enemies—the non-Aryans, and above all the Jews, the embodiment of evil; the ideological enemies—Marxists, Liberals, 'Reactionaries', Christians, and Freemasons; and the moral enemies—habitual criminals, 'asocials', and homosexuals, who threatened to subvert the moral fibre of the 'national community'. The first were irredeemable and had to be 'eradicated' (*ausmerzen*); the second and third might be 're-educated' in concentration camps, although many of those in the third category were considered genetically 'inferior' and, therefore, would have to be prevented from reproducing through sterilization. To enable it to deal with these domestic enemies Himmler aimed for the SS to take over the police and establish a Reich police force or 'Reich Protection Corps', which would operate according to very different principles from the police force of the Weimar Republic. This was the task he set himself after the take-over of power in January 1933.

On 30 January 1933, the SS consisted of some 52,000 men. It was still technically subordinate to the SA and remained so until July 1934, although in practice Himmler, as Reichsführer SS, could operate largely independently of the SA. Since his appointment in 1929, apart from endeavouring to establish the SS's position as an elite corps by imposing strict—largely physical—criteria for selection and by adopting external marks of status such as the striking black uniform with the death's head insignia and by seeking recruits among the upper echelons of society, Himmler had concentrated on trying to develop for the SS a role as the Party's main intelligence section and internal police force. For this purpose he had founded a special Security Service (SD) in August 1931 and appointed as its head a young Naval officer cadet, Reinhard Heydrich, who had been forced to leave the Navy because of a case of breach of promise and needed a job badly. During

1932, Heydrich recruited a network of agents throughout Germany with a particular concentration on graduates. His wife later described his attitude as follows:

371

Himmler was obsessed by ideas, kept developing new ones, at first only in theory, but then he tried to realize them. My husband did not play with ideas. His tasks were concrete and clear and depended on the day-to-day events. Naturally, he identified himself with the ideological framework. This framework was, however, regarded as self-evident and hardly bothered my husband, at least in those days. When he joined the SS the order had not yet become what Himmler with his ideas was to turn it into. Each person interpreted National Socialism as it suited them. There were as many ideologies as there were members. As far as my husband was concerned, the idea of a greater Germany naturally played a decisive role—the rebirth of Germany. But that was really something obvious rather than being a matter of ideology. The German nation was for him more a geographical than a racial concept and his concrete tasks developed with the tasks of the Reich as Hitler projected it.

From the start he directed everything personally and on his own. Naturally, he did not think about the moral aspect of his activity. He would have considered thinking about human life as a thoroughly civilian mode of thought. If he had thought about it he could not have been a soldier.

Naturally he did not accept all orders from above without criticism. He treated them critically and fought to change them if he thought they were wrong from a practical point of view or impossible to carry out.

On 1 April 1933, Himmler was promoted from his first post as Police President of Munich to that of 'Political Police Commander of Bavaria', a new office which gave him responsibility for all political police organs, the auxiliary police,[90] and the concentration camp in Bavaria and made him directly responsible to the Bavarian Interior Ministry. He appointed Heydrich as his deputy with the task of implementing his ambition. Heydrich responded by claiming: 'Now we no longer need the Party. It has played its role and has opened the way to power. Now the SS must penetrate the police and create a new organization there.'[91]

Heydrich set about his task with characteristic pragmatism. He filled the new office with a blend of professional policemen and SS amateurs like himself. The two key figures were Heinrich Müller and Franz Josef Huber. Until 1933, Müller had been responsible for the Communist desk and Huber the Nazi desk within the Munich Police Department. Moreover, both men

---

[90] See above, p. 136
[91] See S. Aronson, *Reinhard Heydrich und die Frühgeschichte von Gestapo und SD* (Stuttgart 1971), p. 107. This section owes much to this book.

had advocated repelling the Nazis by force during their take-over on 9 March. Heydrich, however, recognized their professional skills and promoted them much to the disgust of more ideologically-minded members of the movement. The following political vetting report by the deputy Gauleiter of Munich–Upper Bavaria dated 4 January 1937 on Müller, who was by then chief of the Gestapo, is illuminating in this respect:

372

Criminal Police Chief Inspector Heinrich Müller is not a Party member. He has also never actively worked within the Party or in one of its ancillary organizations. He was presented with an SS *Obersturmbannführer's* uniform in honour of his employment in the Secret State Police; at the same time, he was permitted to wear the stripe (the sign of membership prior to the National Uprising).

Before the seizure of power Müller was employed in the political department of the Police Headquarters. He did his duty both under the direction of the notorious Police President Koch[92] and under Nortz and Mantel. His sphere of activity was to supervise and deal with the left-wing movement. It must be admitted that he fought against it very hard, sometimes in fact ignoring legal provisions and regulations in the process. But it is equally clear that, if it had been his task to do so, Müller would have acted against the Right in just the same way. With his enormous ambition and his marked pushiness he would have won the approval of his superiors under the System doing that too. In terms of his political opinions he belonged in the Nationalist camp and his standpoint varied between the German National People's Party and the Bavarian People's Party. But he was by no means a National Socialist.

As far as his qualities of character are concerned, these are regarded in an even poorer light than his political ones. He is ruthless, uses his elbows, and continually tries to demonstrate his efficiency, but claims all the glory for himself.

In his choice of officials for the Bavarian Political Police he was very concerned to propose either officials who were more junior than himself or only those who were inferior in ability to himself. In this way he could keep rivals at bay. In his choice of officials he did not take account of political considerations, he only had his own egoistical aims in view ...

The Gau leadership of Munich-Upper Bavaria cannot, therefore, recommend accelerated promotion for Müller because he has rendered no services to the National Uprising.

Heydrich had a much shrewder because ideologically unblinkered grasp of Müller's major contribution to the National Uprising and of his subsequent services as chief of the Gestapo.

---

[92] Julius Koch, Munich Police President 1929–33. Nortz and Mantel were also former police presidents.

The Nazi take-over in Bavaria enabled men like Müller to continue their work rooting out subversion but now freed from all previous legal and administrative restraints and, within days, hundreds of the Nazis' political and ideological opponents found themselves in 'protective custody'. This posed problems of accommodation, problems which were met by the establishment during March of a concentration camp in derelict factory buildings in Dachau near Munich with accommodation for 5,000 prisoners and manned by SS guards. The first commandant in Dachau, Hilmar Wäckerle, who was brutal but inefficient, was replaced at the end of June 1933 by an ex-Army pay-master and IG Farben security officer, Theodor Eicke, who was both brutal and efficient. Eicke introduced system and order into the camp, replacing the crude, haphazard individual brutality of Wäckerle's regime with a bureaucratised form of terror. He gave the SS guards both a paramilitary training, which was to make these 'death's head units' into the nucleus of the later Armed SS, and a training designed to destroy any feelings of humanity which they might have for their prisoners, a systematic process of brutalization which was to turn out men like Rudolf Hoess, the future Commandant of Auschwitz. On 1 October 1933 Eicke issued the following Regulations for Discipline and Punishment, which were extended to all concentration camps on 1 August 1934:

373

Introduction. The following regulations on punishment are issued for the maintenance of discipline and order within the area of the Dachau Concentration Camp as part of the existing camp regulations.

All internees of the Dachau Concentration Camp are subject to these regulations from the time of their imprisonment to the hour of their release.

Authority for ordering punishments lies in the hands of the camp commander, who is personally responsible to the political police commander for the carrying out of the camp regulations.

Tolerance means weakness. In the light of this conception, punishment will be mercilessly handed out whenever the interests of the fatherland warrant it. The fellow countryman who is decent but misled will never be affected by these regulations. But let it be a warning both to the inciting politicians and to intellectual agitators, no matter which: watch out that you are not caught, for otherwise it will be your neck and you will be dealt with according to your own methods.

§1. The following are punishable with three days' solitary confinement:
1. Anyone who after reveille does not leave his sleeping quarters at once or does not put his bed or room in proper order.
2. Anyone who in serving his food takes a second helping without the permission of his company leader or allows the cook to give him two portions.

§2. The following are punishable with five days' solitary confinement . . .
9. Anyone who sits or lies on his bed during the day without the permission of his company leader . . .

§6. The following are punishable with eight days' solitary confinement, and twenty-five strokes to be administered before and after the serving of the sentence:
1. Anyone making derogatory or ironical remarks to a member of the SS, deliberately omitting the prescribed marks of respect, or in any other way demonstrating unwillingness to submit himself to disciplinary measures.
2. Prisoner-sergeants and prisoner squad leaders or foremen who exceed their authority as orderlies, assume the privileges of a superior over other prisoners, accord likeminded prisoners special privileges in work or in any other way, tyrannize over fellow prisoners who have political views different from their own, make false reports on them, or prejudice them in any other way.

§7. The following are punishable with two weeks' solitary confinement:
1. Anyone exchanging by his own volition, without being authorized by the company commander, the quarters to which he is assigned, or instigating or inducing his fellow prisoners to do so.
2. Anyone enclosing or hiding forbidden articles or articles produced in the camp in outgoing laundry bundles, or sewing them into pieces of laundry, etc.
3. Anyone entering or leaving barracks, shelters, or other buildings by other than authorized entrances, or creeping through windows or other openings.
4. Anyone smoking in shelters, toilets and places which are fire hazards, or keeping or depositing inflammable objects in such places. If a fire results from neglect of this prohibition, it will be considered as an act of sabotage.

§8. The following are punishable with two weeks' solitary confinement and twenty-five strokes to be administered before and after the serving of the sentence:
1. Anyone leaving or entering the internment camp without an escort or who joins an outgoing work detail without proper authority.
2. Anyone making derogatory remarks in letters or other documents about National Socialist leaders, the State and Government, authorities and institutions, glorifying Marxist or liberal leaders or November [Weimar] parties, or reporting on occurrences in the concentration camp.
3. Anyone keeping forbidden articles, tools, or weapons in his quarters or in palliasses. . . .

§11. In accordance with the law on revolutionaries, the following offenders, considered as agitators, will be hanged. Anyone who, for the purpose of agitating, does the following in the camp, at work, in the sleeping quarters, in the kitchens and workshops, toilets and places of rest: discusses politics, carries on controversial talks and meetings, forms cliques, loiters around with others; who, for the purpose of supplying the propaganda of the opposition with atrocity stories, collects true or false information about the concentration camp; receives such information, buries it, talks about it to others, smuggles it out of the camp into the hands of foreign visitors or others by clandestine or other means, passes it on in writing or by word of mouth to released prisoners or prisoners who are placed over them, conceals it in clothing or other articles, throws stones and other objects over the camp wall containing such information; or produces secret documents; or, for the purpose of agitating, climbs on barrack roofs or trees, seeks contact with the outside world by giving light or other signals, or induces others to escape or commit a crime, gives them advice to that effect or supports such undertakings in any way whatsoever.

§12. Anyone who physically attacks a guard or SS man, refuses obedience or declines to work at his place of work, encourages or induces others to do the same for the purposes of mutiny, leaves a marching column or a place of work, howls, shouts, agitates, or holds speeches on the march or during work will be shot on the spot as a mutineer or subsequently hanged...

§19. Confinement will be in a cell, with a hard bed, and with bread and water. The prisoner will receive warm food every four days. Punitive work consists of severe physical or particularly dirty work, performed under close supervision. Incidental punishments are: drilling, beatings, withholding of mail and food, hard rest, tying to stakes, reprimands and warnings.
All punishments will be recorded on files.
Confinement and punitive labour prolong the term of internment by at least eight weeks, an incidental punishment by four weeks. Prisoners in solitary confinement will not be released for a considerable time.

I.X.33

Service Regulations for Prisoner
Escorts and Guards

Anyone letting a prisoner escape will be arrested and handed over to the Bavarian Political Police for liberating prisoners through negligence.

If a prisoner attempts to escape, he is to be shot without warning. The guard who has shot an escaping prisoner in the line of duty will not be punished.

If a prisoner attacks a guard, the latter is to resist the attack not by physical force but by the use of his weapons. A guard disregarding this regulation must expect his immediate dismissal. In any case anyone who keeps his back covered will seldom have to worry about an attack.

If a unit of prisoners mutinies or revolts, it is to be shot at by all supervising guards. Warning shots are forbidden on principle.

The work time is determined by the camp commander. A guard who brings his prisoners back too early is guilty of serious dereliction of duty and can be dismissed.

Should a work detachment be obliged to stop its work prematurely for some reason or other, then the work detachment leader must have the reason certified on the back of the work service slip [*Arbeitsdienstzettel*] by either the construction division or the requisitioning office.

Eicke turned Dachau into the model for all SS concentration camps of which he was appointed Inspector on 1 July 1934, directly subordinate to Himmler.

Himmler's later comments on the concentration camps in a radio broadcast of 21 September 1939 throw an interesting light on his own mentality and that of his SS.

374

I know how mendaciously and foolishly people abroad write and tell tales about and run down this institution. Concentration camp is certainly, like any form of deprivation of liberty, a tough and strict measure. Hard productive labour, a regular life, exceptional cleanliness in matters of daily life and personal hygiene, splendid food, strict but fair treatment, instruction in learning how to work again and how to learn the necessary crafts—these are the methods of education. The motto which stands above these camps reads: there is a path to freedom.[93] Its milestones are: obedience, hard work, honesty, orderliness, cleanliness, sobriety, truthfulness, self-sacrifice and love of the Fatherland.

The commandants were masters over life and death within the concentration camps. However, decisions over who was to be imprisoned and who was to be released were the responsibility of Heydrich and the political police who exercised their authority through the 'political department' within the concentration camp. In making these decisions, Heydrich and his officials replaced the traditional objective criteria of an actual offence having been committed which was punishable under a specific law. Instead, they substituted subjective criteria of racial origin, 'mentality' (*Gesinnung*), and qualities of character assumed to pertain to particular individuals or groups. People had to be punished for these attitudes or racial or behavioural characteristics which placed them outside the 'national community'. Thus people were put into 'protective custody' and kept there on the grounds of being Jewish, of having a 'mentality hostile to the state', or for being 'asocial'. Himmler later summed up the changes he introduced in police methods in Bavaria in a speech to the session of the Committee for Police Law of the Academy of German Law on 11 October 1936:

375

. . . When we, the National Socialists, came to power in 1933, some of us were given the task of taking over the police. I can speak here from personal experience: in March 1933 I took over the post of Police-President of Munich, and later of Munich and Nuremberg. We National Socialists found a police force which had originally been formed as an instrument of power, blindly obedient to an absolutist State; its main and most important legacy from that period, however, was the dislike, indeed the hatred, of the population for it; yet it had lost the absolute power which distinguishes the police of an absolutist State. It was still called 'a power structure' but in reality it was not; it was a helpless organization, tied hand and foot. Whenever police officers arrested a criminal they had to watch out that they did not get into

---

[93] The motto above the gates of concentration camps was 'Work liberates' (*Arbeit macht frei*).

trouble themselves while the criminal got away scotfree. We National Socialists then set to work—it may sound odd that I should say this in the Academy of German Law but you will understand what I mean—not without justice behind us since we had that within ourselves, but possibly outside the law. Right from the start I took the view that it did not matter in the least if our actions were contrary to some clause in the law; in my work for the Führer and the nation, I do what my conscience and common sense tells me is right. During those months and years when the life and death of the German people were at stake, I was completely indifferent about the fact that others were bemoaning 'violations of the law'. There was of course talk abroad—to a large extent inspired by elements within Germany—about the police, and therefore the State, being in a condition of lawlessness. They called it lawless because it did not correspond to their conception of law. It was in reality through our work that we laid the foundations for a new code of law, the law governing the life of the German people. . . .

During 1933, through their authority over the political police and Dachau concentration camp, the SS managed to establish complete control over the security apparatus in Bavaria. Attempts by the *Reichsstatthalter*, General von Epp, and the Bavarian Prime Minister, Siebert, to support the few brave attempts by the legal authorities to resist the SS regime of terror were defeated since Himmler could rely on the support of his immediate superior, the Bavarian Interior Minister and hardline Gauleiter of Munich, Adolf Wagner, and ultimately of Hitler himself. However, although Himmler and the SS had acquired control of security in Bavaria, they regarded this as merely the springboard for control over the police throughout the Reich. During the Winter of 1933-34, with the help of Heydrich's SD apparatus, Himmler succeeded in getting himself appointed chief of the political police in all the German states except for by far the most important one, Prussia.

During the Weimar Republic political police functions in Prussia were in the hands of Department Ia of the Berlin Police Praesidium. It was the centre for political intelligence for the whole state, indeed informally for the whole Reich, and prepared reports on those extreme movements of Left and Right hostile to the State. It did not, however, have any executive functions of its own and was fully integrated into and subordinated to the administrative apparatus of the Prussian Interior Ministry. With the Nazi take-over this was to change radically. In February 1933, Göring, as acting Prussian Interior Minister, appointed a civil servant from the Ministry, Rudolf Diels, to head Department Ia. Diels had previously been responsible for dealing with the extreme Left and had assisted Papen in the Nationalist coup in Prussia in July 1932,[94] later establishing contact with the Nazis. Then, on 20 April 1933, Göring removed Department Ia from the Police Praesidium to form a new office which was named the Secret State Police Office (*Gestapa*)

---

[94] See above, p. 103.

and was given the status of a separate 'state agency' (*Landesbehörde*), though still subordinate to the Ministry. The *Gestapa*, unlike the old Weimar Department Ia, officially had executive powers and its chief, Diels, who had already acted unofficially, could now officially take into protective custody those suspected of opposition to the new regime.

However, the Prussian *Gestapa* was in many respects weaker than its Bavarian counterpart. It had a smaller number of officials despite Prussia's much greater size. Unlike Heydrich, Diels had no Party status and nor did most of his colleagues. The *Gestapa* did not have field offices directly subordinate to it, but had to 'request' the district police authorities to take action and these remained subordinate to the local *Regierungs präsidenten*. Finally, it was faced with competition from the SA which, with its 'auxiliary police' and its own 'wild' concentration camps, operated as a rival security apparatus to a much greater extent than in Bavaria.

In the Autumn of 1933, the *Gestapa* suddenly faced a new threat in the shape of a plan of the Reich Interior Ministry to absorb the state police forces into a new Reich police force and to abolish the political police as a separate agency. Göring responded with a law of 30 November which created the Secret State Police (Gestapo). The *Gestapa* was removed from the supervision of the Prussian Interior Ministry and subordinated to the Prussian Prime Minister (Göring). It acquired its own field offices (*Stapostellen*), formed from the political police sections at district level, which were now removed from their police departments and established as independent agencies subordinate to the *Gestapa* in Berlin. In effect the political police (*Gestapo*) had become an independent branch of the internal administration. However, this process took time and was opposed in a rearguard action by the Prussian internal administration (*Regierungspräsidenten*), which from 1 May 1934 was under Frick, who was now both Reich and Prussian Minister of the Interior, and by SA police presidents who resented the loss of their political police arm.

This was the context in which the SS sought to complete their take-over of the political police by acquiring the Prussian Gestapo. Their first attempts failed as Diels recalled in his memoirs:

376

The SS prepared their *coups* long in advance and in a more consistent way than the careless SA. The net of the Security Service of the SS led by Heydrich from Munich had already been thrown across Prussia. In the areas ruled by the SA the SD confined itself to the completion of their card files of Jews, Freemasons, 'Catholic Action' and Communists. The SS, in the states in which their leaders had taken charge, were already putting into practice their slogan against the 'cosmopolitical powers'.[95] In Prussia they gave a hint of their future development in only a few areas. Their concentration camps in Papenburg, Esterwegen and Stettin were, following the example of Dachau, no longer haphazard *ad hoc* foundations, they were already organized systematically. When Heydrich had been careless enough to make Göring even more suspicious of SS competition by arresting people in Bavaria who were close to him, I was able to counter Himmler's vanguard in Berlin. I forbade the SD 'actions' which had been directed almost exclusively against the lodges, particularly the Jewish ones, and against Catholic Action. When Göring told me one day to arrest Heydrich when he next entered Berlin, I replied that I could not carry out an order which I knew would be cancelled an hour later by pressure from Himmler; but at that moment of anger he had really made up his mind to put him out of business. I told him I knew that he would not protect me from Himmler's revenge once Heydrich had finally taken over the Berlin political police despite his resistance. At that time he still replied cuttingly and with determination, 'Himmler and Heydrich will never come to Berlin.' Yet with this vain man there was always a restless insecurity undermining his lust for power. He was by no means stupid. He knew Hitler and the upstarts seeking his favour. 'Everything is like cottonwool', he once said to me when he talked about the future, the State and his aims.

However, the desire to have the increasingly powerful Himmler as an ally against Frick and the SA rather than as an enemy finally persuaded Göring, on 20 April 1934, to agree to replace Diels with Himmler as 'Inspector of the Gestapo'. Heydrich took on the day-to-day executive authority as head of the *Gestapa* and Himmler's chief of staff. But this still did not give the SS complete control. As Inspector, Himmler remained subordinate to Göring as Prime Minister of Prussia and the conflicts with the Prussian internal administration and the SA were still not resolved.

Himmler's hands were greatly strengthened by the purge of the SA in the 'Night of the Long Knives' and the SS's crucial role in that affair.[96] It had once more demonstrated its importance to Hitler as both an absolutely loyal and a completely ruthless weapon of power. Its reward was to be granted its final independence from the SA and, more important it almost certainly received Hitler's support in the final stage of its fight to acquire absolute control of the Gestapo. This struggle was fought out with the officials of the Reich/Prussian Interior Ministry and of Göring's Prussian Prime Minister's Office (*Staatsministerium*). Himmler had the advantage of being able to play the two off against each other. Thus, when Frick endeavoured to assert the authority of his *Regierungspräsidenten* over the *Stapostellen* and to prevent the SS from appointing SS amateurs to the Gestapo, it was Göring who put him firmly in his place in a letter dated 5 July 1934:

---

[95] The Nazi term for Jews, Freemasons and Catholics.
[96] See above, pp. 176ff.

377

Your ... letter of 2.7.34 ... re: official communication between government bodies contradicts the instructions which I have received from the Reich Chancellor for the administration of the political police. In recognition of the special services which the political police have rendered in the past few days [i.e. during the SA purge] the Reich Chancellor has given me and the Reichsführer SS Himmler a free hand to run the political police and to decide on the means with which it should operate within the framework which he himself has laid down. In the present situation the cooperation of unofficial persons and the involvement of the SD of the Reichsführer SS cannot be dispensed with in individual cases. I, therefore, request that you withdraw the regulation referred to insofar as it effects the political police and the SD.

It was not long, however, before Göring's officials were complaining about the impossibility of exercising any control over the activities of the SS. They responded by issuing an instruction on 15 October 1934 reasserting the authority of the Prussian Prime Minister over the Gestapo and stating that concentration camps were subject to Himmler in his role as Inspector of the Gestapo (rather than as Reichsführer SS) i.e. ultimately were subject to Göring's overall supervision. A month later, however, one of Göring's officials gave vent to his frustration in the following minute dated 20 November:

378

The enclosed disciplinary and punishment regulations for the prison camp at Esterwegen, dated 1 August 1934, came into the hands of the State Prosecutor's Office in connexion with the Reichling case[97] and were brought to the attention of the Prime Minister's Office in mid-September via the Prussian Ministry of Justice. The content of the regulations prompted a decision to inform the State Secretary [Körner of the Prime Minister's Office] at once of these contents. Furthermore, the regulations were passed on to the Prime Minister ... The Prime Minister indicated that [he wished] to discuss the matter with the Führer and show him the camp regulations as well. The preparation of alterations to the camp regulations was begun immediately ... The conclusion of the matter kept being delayed because it was impossible to procure from the Secret State Police Office documentation concerning the organization of the concentration camps. Also à propos the pending budget discussions for ... 1935, in the budget of the Secret State Police the Inspector simply requested a round sum for the concentration camps. There was no detailed breakdown of the budget ... The issuing of new camp regulations was closely connected to the question of the organization of the concentration camps in general.

---

[97] Clearly a case of an atrocity.

The measures which were necessary to make the Secret State Police dependent on the supervisory authority [i.e. the Prime Minister's Office] as was legally envisaged encountered extraordinary difficulties, despite the issuing of the instruction of 15 October. In particular, reports concerning important matters which had been requested were not presented despite reminders. It was, therefore, impossible to exercise the necessary influence on the measures of the Secret State Police, although to all outward appearances the co-responsibility of the... Prime Minister and the responsibility of the desk officers of the Prime Minister's Office remained intact since most of the correspondence of the Secret State Police went under the rubric of 'The Prussian Prime Minister—Chief of the Secret State Police'... Since the preparations for the new camp regulations could not be completed by then, according to the edict of 20 November 1934, the responsibility of the Prime Minister's Office for dealing with matters concerning the Secret State Police ceases from now onwards...

The final sentence referred to the following edict, of the same date as the minute, in which Göring effectively capitulated to Himmler, recognising his inability to exercise proper supervision over the Gestapo:

379

I have been prompted for organizational reasons to request the Inspector of the Secret State Police, Reichsführer SS Himmler, to deputize for me in the affairs of the Secret State Police which have hitherto involved the Prime Minister's Office. In those matters which I have reserved to myself the correspondence will be carried on under the rubric 'Prussian Secret State Police. The Deputy Head and Inspector'. I hereby give notice of this and request that the correspondence in all matters of the Prussian Secret State Police should from now onwards be directed exclusively to the Secret State Police Office. Signed Göring.

Although Göring had capitulated, Frick had not and complained about the situation as it developed during 1935–36 in the following undated memorandum (c. end of 1935), presumably intended for Lammers and Hitler:

380

As head of the police department in the Reich and Prussian Ministry of the Interior, I have noticed recently an increase in tension in domestic politics which clearly requires, as a matter of urgency, the clarification of authority both as regards the general police and, more especially, the political police.
1. *The Fight against the Church.* The Reich Minister of the Interior is the competent authority for general regulations on denominational policy. The leaders of the various denominational groups therefore address their petitions to our office.

Recently, half the political police reports have concerned religious matters. We have no end of petitions from all sorts of cardinals, bishops, and dignitaries of the Church. Most of these complaints concern matters under the jurisdiction of the Reich Ministry of the Interior, although the relevant regulations were not drawn up by it. Frequently, in our capacity as a court of appeal, we have to settle incidents about which we know nothing at all until we receive the complaint. There no longer appears to be any coordination between our principles regarding matters of ecclesiastical politics and the way in which these are carried out in the states. It is an inexcusable state of affairs that advice should be given to complainants and promises made to ecclesiastical leaders without there being any guarantee that they will be carried out in the states. I regard it, therefore, as absolutely essential that this matter should be fully clarified, not only as regards the *principles but also the way in which they are to be enforced.*

I should like to point out that, in my opinion, when these principles are being considered and carried out, account should be taken not only of domestic but also of foreign policy. I enclose a papal encyclical which was submitted to me today. In this instance, the question arises as to whether the treatment meted out to young Catholics returning to Germany in front of Swiss Customs guards has something to do with the unfavourable foreign reactions evoked by this action on the part of the political police.

This concerns not only the political police; the whole police force as such will be involved in the consequences resulting from the political struggle. The number of blatant disturbances of congregations has recently been greatly on the increase, often necessitating the intervention of the emergency squad. I cannot carry the responsibility in the long run; officials will become involved and will be compelled to support one party or the other. The struggle for power is so recent that we know from our own experience that in the end the police official will quite often be blamed for everything by both warring parties. Now that the rubber truncheon has been discarded, it is intolerable that police officials should be exposed to situations in which, during the disturbance of meetings, they may be forced to use cold steel.

In my opinion, everything must be done to prevent an uncalled-for religious struggle exhausting the police force as well as general State authority.

Nor do I believe it is desirable for the lower ranks of the police to handle and report on these religious matters in a somewhat one-sided manner.

2. There has been of late a marked increase in cases of protective custody.[98] I urgently demand that in this matter also final directives be given concerning *methods, proof, length of time,* and manner of *execution.* The decree on protective custody issued by the Reich Ministry of the Interior[99] has long ago been rendered invalid by the actions of the political police. It is almost impossible to get an adequate report on a case of protective custody. The petitions addressed to us on this matter all stress the same point, which I too regard as important. The persons concerned and their relatives accept the fact of protective custody, but not the utter uncertainty of the principles and methods of its imposition. This definite *lawlessness* fosters unrest and

---

[98] Between October 1935 and May 1936, the Gestapo took into protective custody 7,266 people 'on account of activity in support of the Communist and Socialist parties'.
[99] 11 March 1934.

antagonism. It is intolerable for the Reich Ministry of the Interior that any uniform application of the law should be prevented by the variety of its interpretation and application in the various states. The question must also be settled whether, in cases of protective custody, a person is to be allowed a lawyer, as approved by the NS Lawyers' Association in conjunction with the Reich Ministry of Justice, or, following the present practice of the Gestapo, to be refused one. I refer in this connexion to the case of the lawyer, Pünder. He was confined in protective custody with his colleagues for bringing an action, being obliged to do this by a Reich law, after duly informing the Reich Ministry of Justice and our Ministry. This complaint could not involve any complications, since the legal proceedings could be immediately quashed by us.

3. *For official political reasons*, I must object on principle to the fact that once again recently, and without the previous knowledge of their superiors, civil servants have been taken into protective custody or have been subjected to Gestapo investigations. I can cite here the case of my teacher, who is the *Kreisleiter* at Esterwegen, and who was kept in custody for eight days, because he had sent a report, proved afterwards to be correct, to his district councillor on abuses by the SS. I recall the investigations by detectives of the Gestapo in Kottbus which lasted two weeks, on the chief of police who was, by the way, an SS *Brigadeführer*. Likewise, I have already presented today a complaint by *Oberpräsident* Lohse[100] concerning the order, given by officers of the political police to an official of the gendarmerie, to spy on superior officials.

It is intolerable from the point of view of the National Socialist authoritarian form of State leadership that subordinate offices should procure information on officials in this manner over the heads of a superior office. This will create a great deal of trouble quite apart from the fact that information thus obtained must be prejudiced and very often even actually false.

4. Abductions by officers of the political police on *foreign territory* have lately created serious incidents in the sphere of foreign affairs. I cite the cases of Berthold Jakob (Switzerland), Gutzeit (Holland) and the latest incident at the Czech frontier. In my opinion, in view of possible diplomatic complications, the police office should receive orders for such measures only from the Reich officer responsible, and not from subordinate offices.

5. On several occasions the Reich Ministry of Economics has pointed out to me the disturbing effect on the economy which must result from the various political incidents caused by the police, the atmosphere of insecurity caused by cases of protective custody (particularly in the case of leading businessmen), and also in the latest cases of a boycott of the Jews (Cologne, Düsseldorf).

6. I can only undertake the protection of the Führer through my police department if I am entirely responsible for the officials working there, their service, capabilities, and their cooperation with the other sections of the Crime Department.

7. I propose that it be settled once and for all, not only who is to carry the responsibility for orders, but also who shall bear the responsibility for the execution of those orders in all matters that concern the political police.

Either this responsibility rests with the Reich Minister of the Interior, in which case he must be vested with altogether different powers to give orders in political matters concerning the police;

---

[100] Oberpräsident and Gauleiter of Schleswig-Holstein.

or this responsibility with all its implications rests with the Reichsführer SS, who is already actually claiming the control of the political police in the Reich. In that case I would propose that the law proposed for Prussia by Reichsführer SS Himmler becomes a Reich law immediately, elevating the Office of the Secret State Police [*Gestapa*] to the status of a ministry and enabling the Chief of the Office of the Secret State Police to undertake the tasks which he, in the words of the draft law, 'determines'.

This and similar complaints from the Ministry of the Interior and its regional authorities, the *Oberpräsidenten* and *Regierungspräsidenten*, eventually obliged Himmler and Heydrich to agree to a new Gestapo law. This law of 10 February 1936 represented merely a token concession on the part of the SS, for it did not give the Ministry of the Interior effective control of the Gestapo. For whereas Paragraph 5 subordinated the regional offices of the Gestapo (*Stapostellen*) to the regional offices of the Ministry of the Interior (*Regierungspräsidenten*), Paragraph 3 laid down that the Gestapo head office in Berlin (*Gestapa*) was the highest Gestapo authority, to which the *Stapostellen* were therefore also subordinate. No provision was made by the law for dealing with conflicting orders from the two authorities and in fact the Gestapo continued to go its own way regardless of the Ministry of the Interior. Moreover, Paragraph 7 confirmed the independence of the Gestapo by freeing its actions from review by the administrative courts. This was important because it meant that there was no possibility of appeal against actions of the Gestapo except to a higher authority within the Gestapo itself. The law of 30 November 1933 had limited this exemption to the actions of the *Gestapa*. The Prussian Gestapo Law of 10 February 1936 was as follows.

381

The State Ministry has determined on the following law:

1(i). The task of the Gestapo is to investigate and combat all activity throughout Prussia which poses a threat to the State, to collect and assess the results of these investigations, to keep the State government informed, to keep other authorities posted about any conclusions that concern them and to make suggestions. The Chief of the Gestapo, in agreement with the Minister of the Interior, will decide in detail what duties are to be transferred to the Gestapo.

1(ii). The responsibilities of the constituted legal authorities remain unaffected.

2(i). The Chief of the Gestapo is the Prime Minister.

2(ii). Current business will be transacted on his behalf by a Deputy Chief of Gestapo nominated by him.

3(i). The highest Gestapo authority in the state is the *Gestapa*. It has the prerogatives of a *Land* Police authority.

3(ii). The *Gestapa* is located in Berlin.

4. The functions of the Gestapo will be carried out at intermediate level by *Stapostellen* in the individual state Police districts [*Landespolizeibezirke*]. Gestapo duties on the frontier will be the responsibility of special frontier commissions. Apart from this, Gestapo duties will be carried out by the *Kreis* [district] and *Ort* [local] Police authorities acting as agents for the *Stapostellen*.

5. *Stapostellen* are at the same time subordinate to the competent *Regierungspräsident*, will follow his instructions and will keep him informed of all political police matters. The Head of the *Stapostelle* is at the same time the *Regierungspräsident*'s expert political adviser.

6. The appointment and dismissal of Gestapo officials will be the responsibility of the Chief of the Gestapo in agreement with the Minister of the Interior in accordance with the general legal provisions of the Reich concerning the appointment and dismissal of state officials.

7. Neither the instructions nor the affairs of the Gestapo will be open to review by the administrative courts.

8. The Chief of the Gestapo will issue executive instructions for the present law in agreement with the Minister of the Interior....

Finally, on 17 June 1936, Hitler at last went some way towards answering Frick's plea for a regulation on who was to control the police. But he did not decide in favour of the Ministry of the Interior. Instead, he unified all police powers in the hands of Himmler, who was made Chief of the German Police. Himmler was still nominally subordinate to Frick as Reich Minister of the Interior, but in practice he now exercised sole authority over the police forces throughout Germany.

382

I. To unify the control of police duties in the Reich, a chief of the German Police shall be appointed within the Reich Ministry of the Interior, to whom is assigned the direction and executive authority for all police matters within the jurisdiction of the Reich and Prussian Ministries of the Interior.

II. 1. The Deputy Chief of the Prussian Gestapo, Reichsführer SS Himmler, is hereby nominated Chief of the German Police in the Reich Ministry of the Interior.

2. He is personally and directly subordinate to the Reich and Prussian Ministers of the Interior.

3. For matters within his jurisdiction he represents the Reich and Prussian Ministers of the Interior in the absence of the latter.

4. He carries the service title: Reichsführer SS and Chief of the German Police within the Reich Ministry of the Interior.

III. The Chief of the German Police in the Reich Ministry of the Interior will take part in the meetings of the Reich Cabinet in so far as matters within his jurisdiction are concerned.

IV. I hereby charge the Reich and the Prussian Ministers of the Interior with the execution of this decree.

On 26 June 1936, following on from this law, Himmler brought together the Gestapo and the Criminal Police to form separate sections of a new Security Police (*Sicherheitspolizei*) which was placed under the command of Heydrich, who also continued to direct the Security Service (SD) of the SS. The uniformed police (*Ordnungspolizei*) remained a separate branch under Karl Daluege, an SS leader. From now onwards SS men were increasingly drafted into the police and police officers joined the SS. Although remaining part of the State apparatus in purely organizational terms, the police became increasingly removed from the State in terms of their ethos and mode of operation. They became an instrument of 'Führer power'. Himmler had succeeded in his goal of creating a 'Reich Protection Corps'. Himmler defined the future task of the SS-police in a lecture to Wehrmacht officers in January 1937 on 'The Nature and Task of the SS and the Police':

383

In this context I now come to the main question: security at home and the task of the Police during a war. In a future war we shall not only have the Army's front on land, the Navy's front at sea, and the Air Force's front in the skies over Germany, but we shall have a fourth theatre of war: the home front! There are the grass roots which we must keep healthy by hook or by crook because otherwise the three others, the fighting parts of Germany, would once more be stabbed in the back.

We must be clear about the fact that our opponent in this war is not only an opponent in a military sense, but also an ideological opponent. If I speak of an opponent I mean of course our natural enemy, international Bolshevism, led by Jews and Freemasons ... We must be clear about the fact that Bolshevism is the organization of subhumanity, is the absolute underpinning of Jewish rule, is the absolute opposite of everything worthwhile, valuable, and dear to an Aryan nation. It is a diabolical doctrine because it appeals to the meanest and lowest instincts of mankind and turns them into a religion. Make no mistake: Bolshevism with its Lenin lying in state in the Kremlin only needs a few more decades and then this diabolical religion of destruction, based in Asia, will be the religion for the destruction of the whole world. One must also remember that this Bolshevism is planning the Bolshevization of other nations and in fact this destruction is aimed at the white man
...

(iii) The Organs of Terror—Security Police, SD, and Concentration Camps

The Security Police and the SD had a rather awkward relationship in which it was not always easy to disentangle their respective tasks. The SD developed a broad conception of its role, as is indicated in the following undated memorandum (December 1934?) by SS *Hauptscharführer* Paul Bigga with the title 'The Tasks of the Security Service in Relation to the Task of the State Police':

384

Opponents of all shades of opinion. . . now try and fight against the State with illegal means and to water down the National Socialist ideology. There are not only opposition currents in the purely political sphere, but also in a broader context away from day-to-day politics, e.g., in the sphere of art, scholarship, literature, etc., bent on watering down National Socialism, falsifying it in the various sectors of life, disparaging it in the eyes of the population, carrying Government measures too far and twisting them into the opposite of what was intended. The Security Service (SD) was created on the basis of a correct assessment of the situation, namely that this behaviour of the opposition has a damaging effect on the nation. It is the task of the SD to provide the higher authorities with a comprehensive mosaic picture of the real political, economic, and cultural situation by means of a widely spread and smoothly operating intelligence network. The appropriate State agencies will thereby be enabled to adjust their measures to the real needs of the nation . . . Furthermore, the SD is intended to assess the operations of the opposition and keep them under observation and facilitate and supplement the work of the Gestapo.

The relationship between the two organizations was formally defined by Himmler in an order of 4 July 1934, referred to in a circular of the Bavarian police dated 7 December 1934:

385

Through a regulation of the Political Police Commander and Inspector of the Gestapo of 4 July 1934, the SD has been recognized by the Gestapo as the sole political intelligence service and the police have been ordered to ban intelligence activities by other agencies [e.g. the SA]. The SD thereby participates in the fulfilment of all the tasks of the State Security and represents a significant supplement to the State agencies to which these tasks have been delegated. To ensure cooperation between the State police authorities and the SD, the following regulation is to provide the basis for a clear separation of respective spheres of operation: (*a*) the State police authorities ward off and combat the enemies of the NS State; (*b*) the SD investigates the enemies of the NS ideology and proposes intervention by the State police authorities to combat them. From this follows that: (*a*) every act of enforcement (executive action) is the task of the State enforcement agencies, whereas: (*b*) the SD is forbidden to take any executive action, but is permitted to deal with the intelligence side and is responsible for informing the political police . . . In addition, it is laid down that the offices of the SD and the State enforcement agencies stand side by side and independent of one another.

This order remained in force until the reorganization of the whole security apparatus in 1939 to form the Reich Security Main Office. It did not, however, prevent friction. One of the key differences between the two organizations was that the Gestapo was a State organization staffed by officials, most of whom—like its chief Heinrich Müller—though nominally SS men were basically professional police men, albeit operating in a new climate. The SD, on the other hand, was staffed with amateurs and the atmosphere there was less bureaucratic and more ideologically saturated. Its ethos was formed by its conception of its role as an intelligence organization responsible for the ideological struggle and free from restraints, a conception encouraged by a continuing process of indoctrination. It had a heterogeneous staff. The four senior SD officials during the 1930s—Professor Reinhard Höhn, Otto Ohlendorf, Walter Schellenberg, and Professor Franz Six were all young graduates, the first three being lawyers, and all but Schellenberg had joined the Party before 1933. On the other hand, other SD officials such as Adolf Eichmann in the Jewish section II/112, a former commercial traveller, had more humble backgrounds and like Eichmann were products of Eicke's Dachau school.

The Gestapo proved exceptionally efficient at its task of rooting out all opposition activity. The following document indicates the thoroughness of its surveillance:

386

A message to all Gestapo Offices and to the Political Police of the State
No. 33590   *Berlin, 22 April 1936*
Re: Prominent personalities of the Weimar period [Systemzeit]
A list must be sent in by return of post of those people in your area who were prominent in opposing and slandering the National Socialist movement before the take-over of power. The following details are requested concerning the prominent leaders in politics and business from the camp of the former DNVP,[101] DVP,[102] and Democratic Party [*Staatspartei*]:[103] the first name and surname, the date and place of birth, whether or not a Jew, present domicile, profession, including all offices held by the person concerned, whether the person is in receipt of a pension etc. and whether the person had his citizenship revoked or whether an application has been made for the revocation of his citizenship. Furthermore, his present occupation must be reported. At the same time, a detailed report must be made about the incidents in which the individual was involved, particularly hostile activity towards the NSDAP, and whether or not the person in question is still a clandestine opponent

---

[101] *Deutschnationale Volkspartei*: the German National People's Party.
[102] *Deutsche Volkspartei*: the German People's Party.
[103] The *Deutsche Demokratische Partei* (DDP) adopted the title of '*Staatspartei*' in 1930 after merging with another organization, the *Jungdeutscher Orden*.

of the National Socialist State or has drawn attention to himself by acting in a hostile way towards the State and the Party.

In addition to its own agents, the Gestapo could also rely on information from the enormous network of Party informers—the Block Wardens (*Blockwarte*) who were on every staircase, in every block of flats, and on every street, and whose job it was to keep a close eye on the tenants of their block. An SPD agent in Berlin reported in May 1937 as follows

387

The supervision is now so well-organized that members of the illegal movement can hardly meet in people's flats any more. Every staircase now has an informer. This 'staircase ruler', as one might call him, collects the Winter-Aid contributions, runs around with all sorts of forms, inquires about family matters, and tries to find out about everything under the sun. He is supposed to talk to the housewives about prices and food shortages, he pushes into people's homes, he is supposed to find out what newspapers people read, what their lifestyle is like etc. Even old Party members have taken their protests about this snooping up to the Gau headquarters. Effectively, every tenant is visited at least once a week by one of these block wardens and is pumped by him. These block wardens then have to send in regular reports on their investigations to their Party office.

The Gestapo proceeded with increasing contempt for the law. Even where an individual had been tried by a court of law and had been found innocent, or had served his sentence, he was still not immune from the Gestapo. The following circular to the Gestapo offices by the Gestapo chief, Heinrich Müller, dated 5 August 1937, indicates the sense of powerlessness felt by the legal system in regard to the Gestapo. They were now merely concerned to preserve appearances:

388

Reference: Protective Custody for Jehovah's Witnesses
The Reich Minister of Justice has informed me that he does not share the opinion expressed by subordinate departments on various occasions, according to which the arrest of Jehovah's Witnesses after they have served a sentence is supposed to jeopardize the authority of the Law Courts. He is fully aware of the necessity for measures by the Gestapo after the sentence has been served. He requests, however, that Jehovah's Witnesses should not be taken into protective custody under circumstances that may harm the reputation of the Law Courts.

The Reich Minister of Justice has instructed his subordinate departments in this connexion that protective custody for Jehovah's Witnesses, when this has been decreed after the serving of sentence or after the cancellation of an order of arrest, will no longer be carried out in convict prisons under the administration of the courts. At the same time, at my suggestion he has instructed the departments concerned with the carrying out of the sentences to notify the appropriate Gestapo department of the impending discharge of Jehovah's Witnesses one month before they are discharged.

Accordingly, I issue the following order:

1. If a Jehovah's Witness has been acquitted as the result of a trial, or if part of the sentence is remitted because of the period spent on remand, an arrest in court under my circular decree dated 22 April 1937 will not, for the time being, be carried out.

2. If information regarding the impending release of a Jehovah's Witness from arrest is received from the authorities carrying out the sentence, my decision regarding the ordering of measures by the State Police shall be requested in accordance with my circular decree dated 22 April 1937, so that transfer to a concentration camp can take place immediately after the sentence has been served. If it is impossible to transfer Jehovah's Witnesses to a concentration camp immediately after the serving of the sentence, they will be detained in police prisons.

In each case an immediate report must be made.

The Gestapo could rely on Heydrich's deputy as Chief of the Security Police, Dr Werner Best, a trained lawyer, to provide a 'positivist' legal rationalization for their practice as in the following statement on the relationship between the police and the law.

389

... The police never act in a lawless or illegal manner so long as they act in accordance with the rule laid down by their superiors—up to the highest authority. The High Administrative Court of Hamburg rightly states in its judgement of 10 November 1937:

It is the function of the police to deal only with what the Government wishes to have dealt with.

What the Goverment wants to be dealt with by the police is the essence of police law and is what guides and restricts the actions of the police. So long as the police carries out the will of the Government, it is acting legally; should it overstep the will of the Government, then it is no longer a case of police action, but a breach of duty by a member of the police.

Whether the will of the Government it 'right', i.e. whether it lays down rules that are practical and needed for police action, is no longer a question of law, but one of destiny. If the leadership of the nation misuses the 'right to lay down the law' (through excess either of severity or of weakness) it will be punished more inexorably by fate, because of its violation of the 'laws of existence', than by any State court. It will be punished with disaster, upheaval and ruin....

Those who were arrested by the Gestapo ended up either—if they were lucky—in prison, or in a concentration camp. Between March 1933 and November 1937, 27,512 people had been taken into protective custody in Bavaria alone, and of these 23,100 cases occurred between March 1933 and August 1935, the vast majority during 1933 and most only for short periods. The purge of the SA and the appointment of Himmler as Inspector of the Gestapo enabled the SS to take over the SA concentration camps and rationalize the whole system. The reduction in the number of prisoners by 1937 enabled the concentration camps to be reduced to three main ones: Dachau for the prisoners from South Germany, Sachsenhausen north of Berlin for prisoners from the east, north, and central Germany, and Buchenwald on the edge of Weimar for prisoners from the West and for those from Saxony, Thuringia, Hessen and the northern parts of Bavaria. At the end of June 1937, Dachau contained 1,146 prisoners in protective custody from Bavaria, 349 from outside Bavaria, 92 from the Palatinate, 330 professional criminals from all over Germany, 230 who were obliged to do compulsory labour under welfare regulations, and 93 persons who had been arrested under the action against beggars and tramps launched by the Bavarian Interior Ministry on 22 June 1936. In September 1939 there were some 25,000 prisoners in the concentration camps, which now included three new ones, Flossenbürg in the Upper Palatinate, Mauthausen near Linz, and a women's camp, Ravensbrück in Mecklenburg.

Even if a person were fortunate enough to be let out of a concentration camp, he was still subjected to further police supervision as is clear from the following police reports:

390

Naumburg (Saale), 5.ix.36

Walther P., commercial traveller, formerly in protective custody, now of no fixed address, appears voluntarily and makes the following statement:

I hereby submit my certificate of release from Lichtenburg concentration camp and report to the competent local police authority.

I am bound to report to the local police authority, criminal department, room 114, every Wednesday and Saturday at 11 o'clock. I shall fulfil this obligation punctually.

Naumburg (Saale), 28.iv.37

Walther P. has punctually obeyed the police order to report twice a week. P. finds this measure extremely unpleasant and embarrassing. He has repeatedly expressed the wish to be released from this obligation to report. P. performs his job regularly and lives a very secluded life. He has no contact with people who are suspected of an attitude hostile to the State. P. is a member of the German Labour Front and is obviously trying to integrate himself into the national community. Further strict observation of P. no longer appears necessary.

CHAPTER 23

Antisemitism 1933–39

Antisemitism was at the core of Nazi ideology in general and of Hitler's own 'world view' in particular.[104] It expressed a vision of a cosmic racial struggle in which the Jews, representing the forces of darkness, were pitted against the Aryan forces of light, of whom the German people were the standard-bearers. For most Nazis, apart from those for whom the Jews were actual business or professional competitors, the Jew figured largely as a propaganda stereotype, a collection of negative attributes representing the antithesis of the qualities of the true German. He was an abstraction, a myth, a focus for anxieties about modern developments in the economy, in society, and in the cultural field which seemed to threaten people's sense of identity. There was little knowledge or awareness of the reality of Jews and of the actual role they played in German society.

The Nazis had made little attempt to prepare a detailed programme of anti-Jewish measures which could be implemented on their coming to power. They were determined to exclude the Jews from German life, but little thought had been given to how this was to be achieved. A few draft bills had been drawn up by the Legal and Domestic Political sections of the Reich Party headquarters, but these departments lacked political weight and their drafts were to have no impact on future legislation. The fact that the Jew was regarded as a figure of total evil, as an abstraction, meant that partial measures excluding Jews from this or that sphere of German life were in a sense irrelevant. The totality of his iniquity implied from the start a total solution, though there is no real evidence that the Nazis had any clear idea what form such a total solution should take until very much later. At the take-over of power, the decisive fact was that among the hard-core

---

[104]See above, pp. 1–4

membership of the Party and its paramilitary organizations, the SA and SS, antisemitism was an article of faith. The Jews were the arch-enemy who must be removed—one way or the other.

What then did this enemy really amount to? How many Jews were there in Germany in 1933? Where did they live? And what did they do for a living? According to figures issued by the Reich Statistical Office in 1933, there were 503,000 Jews in Germany in 1933 comprising 0.76 per cent of the population. Of these 355,000 or 70.7 per cent lived in big cities of over 100,000 people, forming 1.78 per cent of the total population of these cities. The largest concentrations were in Frankfurt (4.71 per cent), Berlin (3.78 per cent), and Breslau (3.23 per cent). Their occupations were distributed as follows:

391

Jewish Occupations in 1933

	Total Population in thousands	%	Jews in thousands	%	% of Jews in total population
Agriculture and Forestry	9343	24.5	4.2	1.4	0.04
Industry and Handicrafts	13053	34.2	55.7	18.5	0.43
Commerce and Trade	5932	15.6	147.3	48.9	2.48
Public Service and the[1] Free Professions	2699	7.1	30.0	9.9	1.11
Domestic Service	1270	3.3	3.4	1.1	0.27
Self-employed without a Profession	5822	15.3	61.0	20.2	1.05

Column 4 represents the percentage of those employed within the Jewish population; Column 5 represents the percentage of Jews employed as a proportion of the total population.

[1] The census was taken on 16 June 1933 i.e. after the Laws discriminating against Jews in the Civil Service and the free professions had come into effect. This figure is therefore an underestimate of the figure on 30 January 1933. However, the corresponding figures for Prussia in 1925 were 8.7 per cent and 1.6 per cent.

392

Occupations in which the Jews composed more than Five Per Cent of the Total in 1933

	Total	%
Lawyers and Public Notaries	3030	16.6
Brokers and Commission Agents	1722	15.05
Patent Lawyers	79	13.28
Doctors	5557	10.88
Travelling Salesmen and Commercial Agents	24386	9.20

Dentists	1041	8.59
House Managers	297	8.53
Furriers	1198	6.33
Theatre and Film Directors	60	5.61
Legal advisors (without a law degree)	165	5.40
Other types of Property Owners and Lessees	66891	5.05
Editors and Writers	872	5.05

(i) 1933—Terror, Boycott, and Discriminatory Legislation

In the light of the strong commitment of the Party's rank and file to antisemitism, it was not surprising that the 'revolution from below' which followed the election of 5 March saw a wave of attacks against the Jews. The American consul in Leipzig, Ralph Busser, reported on 5 April:

393

In Dresden several weeks ago uniformed 'Nazis' raided the Jewish Prayer House, interrupted the evening religious service, arrested twenty-five worshippers, and tore the holy insignia or emblems from their head-covering worn while praying.

Eighteen Jewish shops, including a bakery, mostly in Chemnitz, had their windows broken by rioters led by uniformed 'Nazis'.

Five of the Polish Jews arrested in Dresden were each compelled to drink one-half litre of castor oil. As most of the victims of assault are threatened with worse violence if they report the attacks, it is not known to what extent fanatical 'Nazis' are still terrorizing Jews, Communists, and Social Democrats, who are considered as favouring the old parliamentary regime in Germany.

Some of the Jewish men assaulted had to submit to the shearing of their beards, or to the clipping of their hair in the shape of steps. One Polish Jew in Chemnitz had his hair torn out by the roots.

The involvement of foreign Jews brought protests from diplomatic representatives in Germany.

These attacks were largely spontaneous, initiated at local or regional level and not coordinated from the top. Although Hitler sympathized with the sentiments of his rank and file, such attacks of Jewish businesses and on foreign Jews threatened to get out of hand, thereby jeopardizing his alliance with the conservative elites. He decided, therefore, to give the Party radicals a controlled outlet for their energies by getting the Party to organize a nation-wide boycott of Jewish business and professionals. The boycott would be justified on the grounds that the Jews had allegedly organized a propaganda campaign abroad, accusing the Nazis of atrocities. The boycott was run by a committee of Nazi hardliners headed by Julius Streicher, the rabidly antisemitic Gauleiter of Franconia. On 29 March, they issued the following order:

394

1. Action committees in every local branch and subdivision of the NSDAP organization are to be formed for putting into effect the planned boycott of Jewish shops, Jewish goods, Jewish doctors and Jewish lawyers. The action committees are responsible for making sure that the boycott affects those who are guilty and not those who are innocent.

2. The action committees are responsible for the maximum protection of all foreigners without regard to confession, background or race. The boycott is purely a defensive measure aimed exclusively against German Jewry.

3. The action committees must at once popularize the boycott by means of propaganda and enlightenment. The principle is: No German must any longer buy from a Jew or let him and his backers promote their goods. The boycott must be general. It must be supported by the whole German people and must hit Jewry where it is most vulnerable. . . .

8. The boycott must be coordinated and set in motion everywhere at the same time, so that all preparations must be carried out immediately. Orders are being sent to the SA and SS so that from the moment of the boycott the population will be warned by guards not to enter Jewish shops. The start of the boycott is to be announced by posters, through the press and leaflets, etc. The boycott will commence on Saturday, 1 April on the stroke of 10 o'clock. It will be continued until an order comes from the Party leadership for it to stop.

9. The action committees are to organize tens of thousands of mass meetings, which are to extend to the smallest villages for the purpose of demanding that in all professions the number of Jews shall correspond respectively to their proportion of the whole German population. To increase the impact made by this action, this demand is limited first of all to three fields: (a) attendance at German schools and universities; (b) the medical profession; (c) the legal profession. . . .

Originally, the boycott had been intended to be indefinite, but concern about its negative impact on the economy and opposition to it from the Reich President and the Foreign Minister persuaded Hitler to limit it to one day—1 April—in the first instance, with the intention of reviving it if, as he put it, international Jewry did not cease its anti-German activities. The police had been instructed 'not to hinder the boycott action in any way and only to intervene where there was a threat to life or property'. Its effects varied up and down the country. There were excesses in Frankfurt, Kiel and elsewhere. The Nazis were disappointed with its effects. The public was generally apathetic and some people even ignored the SA men stationed outside Jewish shops to warn off intending customers and insisted on going in. The American consul in Leipzig noted that the boycott was 'unpopular with the working classes and the educated circles of the middle classes'.[105] Finally, problems arose over defining what was and what was not a Jewish shop since ownership was often unclear. In the light of all this, the Nazi leadership decided to call it off completely after only one day.

The boycott had demonstrated the damaging repercussions for the economy which would result from a frontal assault on Jewish business interests. It had, however, also been aimed at Jewish professionals and, although its impact on them had been no greater than on Jewish business, they were altogether a much softer target. Jewish lawyers in particular had in fact already been a major focus for the SA attacks during March. SA troops, for example, had invaded the law courts in Berlin, Breslau and a number of other cities, had brought legal proceedings involving Jewish judges, prosecutors, and lawyers to a halt, and in some cases had given vent to their feelings of class or cultural antagonism by forcing them to disrobe in the street. Similar incidents occurred involving doctors and university teachers. The authorities responded by advising those Jewish professionals in public employment to go on leave and then by officially suspending them. Clearly, however, this situation in which the initiative was in the hands of local SA units and the local authorities was unsatisfactory. The German establishment in general and the Reich President in particular were becoming disturbed by these excesses. Thus, while the *objective* of the militants—the exclusion of Jewish professionals was correct from the point of view of the Nazi leadership, the *means*—terror and arbitrary suspension—were not. A more orderly and systematic approach was necessary and this could only come through legislation.

This, however, raised the question of the attitude of the traditional civil servants who would be obliged to draft such legislation. Would they be prepared to discriminate officially against the Jews? Some insight into Civil Service attitudes towards Jews is provided by the way in which the apparently innocuous question of the alteration of surnames was dealt with by the Prussian Ministry of the Interior between November 1932 and March 1933. Already, on 23 December 1932, i.e. before the Nazi takeover, the Ministry had issued the following 'Guidelines for dealing with Requests for a Change of Surname':

395

I *General*

(1) The existing law, in particular, the Civil Law Code, assumes that surnames denote descent from a particular family. They thereby serve to indicate an individual's bloodline. Every change of name through administrative process impairs the

---

[105] ND PS 2705.

discernibility of family origins, conceals the bloodline, and thereby facilitates the obscuring of a person's status . . .

VI *Jewish Names*
(1) The view that it is dishonourable for a person of Jewish origin to bear a Jewish name is unacceptable. Attempts by Jewish persons to conceal their Jewish descent by giving up or changing their Jewish names cannot, therefore, be supported. Conversion to Christianity provides no reason for altering their names. There is just as little ground to justify a change of name through reference to antisemitic attitudes or to the desire for career advancement.
(2) On the other hand, offensive Jewish names which experience shows give rise to mockery (such as Itzig, Schmul) or which may provoke dislike of the bearer (Nachtschweiss, Totenkopf) may be altered in the same way as offensive German names, but normally only by permitting the use of *another Jewish name* (e.g. Cohn, Levy, Issaksohn), the name of a near relative, or an imaginary name, not by permitting the use of a normally occurring name.

The desk officer responsible, Dr. Hans Globke, a keen supporter of the Catholic Centre Party, specified further in an internal minute dated 30 November 1932:

396

. . . in the case of typical Jewish names it will be necessary in addition for documents to be produced which show the religion of the applicant's ancestors back to approximately the first two decades of the nineteenth century. Aryan descent must be proved in all cases in which an application for a change of name is made; the reason for the application is immaterial . . .

On 1 March 1933, the German Nationalist Party district branch of Lower Silesia wrote to the Prussian government requesting, first, a ban on the use of pseudonyms by public figures, particularly in the cultural field, and secondly, the revocation of all name changes since the Revolution of 1918. This first request was directed at the biographer, Emil Ludwig Cohn, who had recently published a biography of Bismarck under his normal pen name, Emil Ludwig. While the responsible desk officer, Schütze, reacted negatively, significantly, the State Secretary, Herbert von Bismarck, a leading member of the German Nationalist Party, took a rather different view in a minute for the minister dated 4 April 1933:

397

. . . 1) The idea of banning the use of confusing pseudonyms by personalities in public life is a demand which follows logically from the fundamental change in the

relationship between the individual and the community which has occurred. The preceding liberal epoch was concerned with the protection of the anonymous individual and his individual views and aspirations however perverse. According to the modern view, the individual only has a claim to the protection of his individual opinion in so far as it coincides with the will of the community. In view of the flooding of present day public life with individual opinions, those which do not come from well-known or important persons or from particular groups are of no public interest. It is a different matter with the opinions of leading figures or particular groups which are ideologically or otherwise committed. The collective, i.e the State, must insist that a large number of similar opinions are not expressed by a number of people who conceal their real names from the public and produce an impact among the public, which is contrary to the general interest, without the mass of the readership being aware of which side these opinions are coming from . . . Even if there have only been a few cases in which Jews with Jewish names have written under a Christian-sounding pseudonym, in my view it is not so much a question of the number of cases as of the extent of the effect produced. In the case of the writer, Emil Ludwig Kohn, for example, this is extremely large. However, the matter can only be regulated through Reich legislation, although in my view the attention of the Reich should be drawn to it.
(2) The revocation of all changes of name which have occurred since the revolution would also in my view be going too far. Among such changes there are many cases in which Polish, Lithuanian, or other foreign-sounding names have been replaced by German ones which can only be welcomed in so far as their bearers are not of foreign racial origin and belong culturally and ethnically to the German nation. On the other hand, national pride is deeply wounded by those cases in which Jews with eastern Jewish names have adopted particularly nice Germanic surnames such as, for example, Harden, Olden, Hinrichsen etc. I consider a review of name changes urgently necessary with the aim of revoking changes of this kind. The legal basis for this would also have to be created through Reich legislation. I request that you order the preparation of a suitable draft.

In fact, on 10 April 1933, Bismarck was replaced as State Secretary by a former official of an employers' organization, Ludwig Grauert, since as a leading German Nationalist, however cooperative, he was still suspect in such a politically sensitive post.

Thus, with such a mentality in the higher ranks of the Civil Service, discriminatory legislation against the Jews was unlikely to meet with much opposition inside the ministries. Indeed, most civil servants welcomed what they saw as a transition from the excesses of the SA to 'law and order' and eagerly cooperated with the drafting. The first antisemitic legislative measure, which was hurriedly prepared, was the Law for the Restoration of the Professional Civil Service of 7 April.[106] Article 3, the so-called 'Aryan Clause', laid down that officials of non-Aryan descent were to be retired.

---

[106] See above p. 233–5.

However, Reich President Hindenburg had insisted on the incorporation of a clause exempting those who had already been in office on 1 August 1914, who had fought at the front during World War I, or whose fathers or sons had been killed in the war. On the same day, the Cabinet approved a parallel Law Concerning the Admission to the Legal Profession, published on 11 April, which imposed the 'Aryan Clause' on lawyers. In fact, however, blinded by their own propaganda, the Nazis had underestimated the number of civil servants and lawyers who were exempted from dismissal. Thus, of 717 non-Aryan judges and public prosecutors only 336 (47 per cent) were dismissed and only 1,418 Jewish lawyers (around 30 per cent) could be removed from their profession.[107]

At the Cabinet meeting of 7 April, Hitler had specifically excluded Jewish doctors from the application of the Aryan Clause. His subordinates, however, simply ignored his wishes. Nazi local authorities banned Jewish doctors from the health insurance panels on their own initiative so that, on 22 April, the Reich Minister of Labour felt obliged to issue a Reich regulation to that effect, which was extended to Jewish dentists and dental technicians in June. This is an example of the way in which Nazi anti-Semitic policy, far from being planned and coordinated from the top, in fact developed in a largely incoherent and *ad hoc* fashion. The Reich Government was often forced to adopt measures which had been introduced by local militants, issuing a Reich regulation in an endeavour to produce some kind of order. It was not that the Government did not sympathize with these measures, but it found that the pace was being dictated to it by the lower levels of the administration and the Party.

The same process occurred with the final major piece of antisemitic legislation of 1933. During March–April, individual states had begun to try and solve a genuine problem of overcrowding in schools and colleges by simply excluding Jews from the more popular subjects. On 25 April, therefore, the Reich Government passed the Law Against the Overcrowding of German Schools, whose first implementing decree of the same date restricted Jewish pupils and students to a maximum of 5 per cent of any one school or university and 1.5% in total. In fact, exceptions were permitted whereby Aryan children could where necessary be given priority, exceptions which were made full use of by the state and local authorities when implementing the law. This exploitation by the lower levels of the administration of loopholes in laws, which were in any case left intentionally vague, was a characteristic feature of Nazi antisemitic legislation which invariably increased the harshness of its application.

In the autumn of 1933 several other pieces of legislation facilitated discrimination against the Jews, most notably the establishment of the Reich

---

[107] Cf. K. A. Schlennes, *The Twisted Road to Auschwitz. Nazi Policy toward German Jews 1933–39* (London 1970) p. 109.

Chambers of Culture on 29 September and the Editors' Law of 4 October, which paved the way for the exclusion of Jews from the cultural sphere and from journalism.[108] By this time, however, the regime had become increasingly concerned about the economic repercussions of antisemitism, particularly the negative impact on foreign opinion. However, its attempts to control the dynamic of the Party militants, which was fuelled by a combination of economic rivalry and ideological fanaticism, were continually thwarted, as the following announcement by Gauleiter Bürckel of the Rhineland Palatinate on 3 October 1933 indicates:

398

I am continually receiving queries about our attitude on the department store question and the treatment of Jewish business. People refer to various decrees which can lead to misunderstanding. The following may help everybody:
1. Before the seizure of power we regarded department stores as junk shops which ruined the small businessman. This assessment will remain valid for the future. It seems odd that anyone bothers to waste time discussing it. The same is true of our treatment of the Jewish question.
2. We old Nazis don't give a damn about the remarks of some Nazi bigwig. As far as we are concerned, all we have to do is fulfil the Programme as the Führer wishes.

On 14 January 1934, a Nazi 'bigwig', the Reich Minister of the Interior, issued the following circular to national and regional Government authorities:

399

German Aryan legislation is necessary for racial and political reasons. On the other hand, the Reich Government has set itself certain limits which must likewise be observed. German Aryan legislation will be correctly judged at home and abroad if these limits are everywhere heeded. It is especially improper and even open to objection for the principles of Para. 3 BBG [Civil Service Law of April 1933], the so-called 'Aryan paragraph' (which has become the model for numerous other laws and orders), to be extended to other fields to which they by no means apply. This is particularly true of the economic sphere as the National Socialist Government has always declared.

I therefore repeat my request that infringements of this kind shall be decisively opposed and also that subordinate authorities shall be emphatically instructed that they are to base their measures and decisions only on the valid laws.... Any

---

[108] See above pp. 388 and 397.

annulment or extension of Reich laws which are valid can be carried out only by the Reich Government itself according to the Enabling Law, and not by the bodies which administer these laws. They must, on the contrary, apply these laws so long as they are in force and are not to contradict them because they appear not to accord completely with National Socialism.

(ii) 1935—The Revival of Terror and the Nuremberg Laws

The year 1934 was in fact a period of relative calm for the Jews, although they continued to suffer discrimination and sporadic harassment at local level. At the end of March 1935, however, there were reports of Jewish boycotts from various parts of Germany, prompting Hess to issue the following order to Party members on 11 April:

400

... While I can understand that all decent National Socialists oppose these new attempts by Jewry with utter indignation, I must warn them most urgently not to vent their feelings by acts of terror against individual Jews, as this can only result in bringing Party members into conflict with the political police, who consist largely of Party members, and this will be welcomed by Jewry. The political police can in such cases only follow the strict instructions of the Führer in carrying out all measures for maintaining peace and order, so making it possible for the Führer to rebuke at any time allegations of atrocities and boycotts made by Jews abroad.

The situation calmed down briefly, but in May a major campaign of boycotts and violence against Jews began which continued off and on till the end of August and affected all parts of Germany. It was organized by the local Party organizations and affiliates and had some support from local authorities. The source of the initiative for the campaign is not entirely clear. It appears to have come from leading Nazis at the regional and local levels with the support of individual national figures, notably Goebbels. It seems to have derived partly from the frustration of men such as Julius Streicher, the Gauleiter of Franconia, at the lack of progress in the persecution of the Jews and also from a desire to divert the attention of the rank and file. Many of the local Nazi activists had become disillusioned with the regime. First, they resented what they saw as its alliance with Reaction in the shape of the traditional German elites, represented by the strong positions held by such figures as Schacht and Field-Marshal von Blomberg; secondly, they had not forgotten the emasculation of the SA in the Night of the Long Knives; and finally, they were discontented at their own failure to receive adequate material rewards for their past support for the Party. In attacking the Jews they could feel that they were achieving at least something.

The following report by the Bavarian Political Police of 1 August 1935 of one such incident demonstrates how such local harassment eroded the rights of Jews in a piecemeal fashion:

401

... On the same day (14.7.1935), there were anti-Jewish demonstrations in the swimming pool in Heigenbrüken, *Bezirksamt* Aschaffenburg. Approximately 15–20 young bathers had demanded the removal of the Jews from the swimming bath by chanting in the park which adjoins the baths. The chant went: 'These are German baths, Jews are not allowed in, out with them' and such like. A considerable number of other bathers joined in the chanting so that probably the majority of visitors were demanding the removal of the Jews. In view of the general indignation and the danger of disturbances, the district leader of the NSDAP, Lord Mayor Wohlgemuth of Aschaffenburg who happened to be in the swimming baths, went to the supervisor of the baths and demanded that he remove the Jews. The supervisor refused the request on the grounds that he was obliged to follow only the instructions of the baths' administration and moreover, could not easily distinguish the Jews as such. As a result of the supervisor's statement, there was a slight altercation between him and the Lord Mayor, which was later settled by the baths' administration. In view of this incident, the Spa Association today placed a notice at the entrance to the baths with the inscription: 'Entry forbidden to Jews'.

More serious attacks on Jewish businesses were disrupting the economy and a meeting of Ministers was summoned on Schacht's initiative to discuss the treatment of the Jews. It took place on 20 August:

402

President [of the Reichsbank] Schacht gave a detailed review of the serious damage to the German economy produced by the exaggeration and excesses of the antisemitic propaganda and pointed out that the drift into lawlessness among other things is putting the economic basis of rearmament at risk ... His statement culminated in the assertion that the NSDAP's programme must be carried out but solely on the basis of legal regulations.

State Minister Wagner[109] also disapproved of the excesses. He explained them in terms of the fact that there was a divergence in the treatment of the Jewish question both between Party and State as well as within particular Reich Government departments ... It was not necessary for everything to happen at once; to start with, it would be sufficient if at least some steps forward were taken, e.g., if bans were to be issued on the opening of new businesses and on the granting of public supplies

---

[109] Adolf Wagner, Bavarian Interior Minister and Gauleiter of Munich—Upper Bavaria.

to Jews. Also to begin with, they should restrict themselves to measures against full Jews so that the question of whether or not to include the half-castes (*Mischlinge*) in this or that regulation would not hold up the legislation again. President Schacht agreed with this last point . . .

Reich Minister Gürtner emphasized that every order from the State or the Party must remain ineffective so long as the nation was encouraged to believe that the authorities were not unhappy when their restrictions were infringed because it was only on account of political considerations that they were unable to act as they would like to. The basic principle of the Führer State must be asserted against that view. It was particularly reprehensible when local authorities ignored orders from the Government . . .

After several representatives of other departments and offices had expressed their views, the chairman of the meeting Schacht summed up the result of the meeting as follows: the meeting was important in the first instance in providing the opportunity for an initial discussion—there was unanimity about the goal but not yet about the ways to achieve it. It was necessary: (1) to carry out the particular measures that were planned as soon as possible and (2) for there to be close collaboration between the Party and the State in such a way that the Party did not just drive the nation forwards with propaganda, but above all passed on suggestions for desirable measures to the Reich Government.

Clearly, the pressure was now on the Government to produce anti-Jewish legislation if it wished to prevent further acts of Party terror. One demand, which was contained in the Party's programme (§4), was to revoke the citizenship of Jews. The Reich Interior Ministry had in fact been considering alterations to the regulations governing Reich citizenship through the introduction of racial criteria ever since the beginning of 1933. It had not, however, proceeded very far, partly because of the desire not to aggravate the economic situation, partly because of the complexity of the issues involved, in particular the problem of establishing a satisfactory definition of a Jew and, last but not least, because of bureaucratic inertia. On 26 April 1935, Frick had publicly announced plans for a change in the Reich Citizenship Law involving the use of racial criteria. But the law which finally appeared on 15 May dealt only with the question of the adoption of German nationality by foreigners and was totally inadequate from the point of view of the Nazi militants.

Another piece of legislation which had been a major demand of anti-semites from the late nineteenth century onwards was a ban on mixed marriages between Germans and Jews. This was clearly essential from their point of view given the assumption that the Jews were a race distinguished from the Germans by their blood. Sexual relations between Germans and Jews was in fact a highly emotive subject for Nazi militants. The issue had been raised in connexion with plans for a reform of the Penal Code in 1933–34, with the Nazi jurist, Roland Freisler, State Secretary in the Reich Justice Ministry, demanding the prosecution of sexual relations between

Aryans and Jews. However, other legal experts on the committee had succeeded in putting forward plausible objections and in any case the planned new Code was not introduced. During 1934, the Government adopted a strict interpretation of the Aryan clause; in a judgment of 12 July 1934 the Supreme Court declined to annul a marriage of an Aryan petitioner who had married a Jew in 1930 and now wanted a divorce on the grounds that only now, thanks to his enlightenment through Nazi ideology, had he become aware of the importance of racial differences.

Meanwhile, however, pressure had begun to build up from the Party on the Government for action on this issue, pressure which was deflected by reference to the undesirable repercussions abroad of such discriminatory legislation. With the growth of Party terror during 1935, however, the local Nazis began to take matters into their own hands. Individual Jews suspected or known to be having sexual relations with Aryans were sometimes pursued by lynch mobs and then taken into protective custody. Pressure was put on registrars not to issue banns for marriages between Jews and Aryans. When those affected appealed to the courts, the judges gave differing responses, but many supported the prevention of such marriages on the grounds that the Party's principle of the maintenance of the purity of German blood was a 'binding legal principle'. The Gestapo also intervened requesting the registrars to inform them of such proposed marriages so that they could 'enlighten' the Aryan partner. As a result of the legal confusion produced by these arbitrary actions at local level, the Reich Justice Ministry began preparing a draft law and on 16 July 1935 Frick issued a circular to the registrars in which they were informed that the Reich Government intended 'presently to regulate the question of marriage between Aryans and Non-Aryans through a general law'.[110] Until then the registrars should postpone indefinitely 'the banns or marriage in all those cases in which it was known to them or proven that one of the participants was a full Aryan and the other a full Jew'. At the same time, at the end of July, Heydrich pressed in the name of the *Gestapa* that 'in view of the disturbance among the population [i.e. the Nazi militants] by the racial miscegenation of German women' not only should the Ministry ensure that 'the prevention of mixed marriages be legally fixed but also extramarital sexual relations between Aryans and Jews should be punished'.[111]

By the end of August, the antisemitic campaign had died down. At a meeting with Hitler at the beginning of September, Schacht appeared to have convinced him of the dangers to the economy posed by antisemitic terror and tough orders had already gone out to the Party to cease such actions.

---

[110] Cf. L. Gruchmann,'"Blutschutzgesetz" und Justiz. Zur Entstehung des Nürnberger Gesetzes vom 15. September 1935' in *Vierteljahrshefte für Zeitgeschichte* 1983.
[111] *Ibid.* p. 430.

At the same time, this period of calm seems to have encouraged the Reich Interior Ministry to return to its state of bureaucratic inertia: with one exception—a law to prohibit Jews from raising the swastika flag—it had no immediate plans to introduce anti-Jewish legislation.

The Party's annual Nuremberg rally was scheduled to take place from 9–15 September and, on the final day, the Reichstag was due to meet there in a special session to pass the Flag Law and to hear Hitler deliver a foreign policy speech which was subsequently cancelled. The Party's racial 'experts', led by the Reich Doctors' Leader, Gerhard Wagner, evidently decided to use the presence of massed ranks of Party activists to press for further action on the Jewish question. On 12 September, Wagner announced in a speech that a 'Law for the Protection of German Blood', banning mixed marriages, would soon be issued to prevent the further 'bastardization' of the German People. It seems plausible to assume that Hitler had promised him that such a measure would be introduced. On the following day, Hitler apparently decided that, to fill the gap left by the cancellation of his foreign policy speech, the Reichstag could pass the law on mixed marriages in addition to the rather unimportant Flag Law. He, therefore, informed Frick that he wished to have a 'Law for the Protection of German Blood 'passed on 15 September, which would ban the marriage of Jews and Aryans, forbid them to have sexual relations outside marriage, and limit the employment of Aryan housemaids in Jewish homes.

The Interior Ministry's desk officer for Jewish questions, Bernhard Lösener, now had to be hurriedly flown from Berlin, and he and four top civil servants struggled overnight to produce an acceptable law. It is unclear to what extent they used the preliminary draft of the Ministry of Justice as a basis. As far as Lösener was concerned, the crucial point was to try and ensure that distinctions between different degrees of Jewishness should be defined by the law and that its application should be limited as far as possible to full Jews. It is uncertain how far this was merely to simplify matters for the sake of administrative convenience or how far Lösener was inspired with a genuine concern to protect the part-Jews. The drafting team included Walter Sommer from Hess's staff (though he spent most of his time playing with a toy tank) and the final draft had to be vetted by both Frick, who was not very interested, and Gerhard Wagner who was, and who unlike Frick formed part of Hitler's immediate entourage. Wagner kept insisting on tougher formulations with the result that eventually four drafts—A-D— were presented to Hitler, with the Ministry team recommending the weakest draft, D. At this point—midnight on the 14 September—Hitler suddenly requested another law to deal with Reich Citizenship which he thought was necessary to 'round off the legislation'. The exhausted officials spent only half an hour drafting a brief vague law on the back of a menu which Hitler finally accepted at 2.30 am. Later that morning, Hitler adopted the D version of the draft Law for the Protection of German Blood but struck out the crucial sentence 'This law is only valid for full Jews'. The result was that the extent of the law's application was left to be defined by a supplementary decree, whose details would have to be negotiated between the Party and the Ministry.

In his speech announcing the new laws to the Reichstag Hitler referred to the new Reich Citizenship Law as 'the attempt to achieve the legislative regulation of a problem which, if it breaks down again will then have to be transferred by law to the National Socialist Party for final solution.' This statement echoed the threat continued in his speech to the rally.[112] Both statements suggest that he had come to Nuremberg disgruntled at the lack of enthusiasm of the bureaucracy to introduce anti-Jewish legislation and then, perhaps encouraged by racial hardliners such as Wagner and by the atomosphere created by the mass of the Party's rank and file and the desire to win their applause, he had suddenly decided to use the opportunity of the special session of the Reichstag in effect to 'bounce' the bureaucracy into producing the desired legislation. His decision to accept the softest of the four drafts was calculated to confirm his position in the eyes of the bureacracy as a moderate, while it was also a reminder to the party militants that he would decide the pace of Jewish persecution. On the other hand, his decision to strike out the crucial sentence reflected his gut feelings and also ensured that the position remained fluid, open to future adjustment in a changing situation.

403

Law for the Protection of German Blood and German Honour,
15 September 1935
Entirely convinced that the purity of German blood is essential to the further existence of the German people, and inspired by the uncompromising determination to safeguard the future of the German nation, the Reichstag has unanimously adopted the following law, which is promulgated herewith:

I. 1. Marriages between Jews and citizens of German or kindred blood are forbidden. Marriages concluded in defiance of this law are void, even if, for the purpose of evading this law, they were concluded abroad.
2. Proceedings for annulment may be initiated only by the Public Prosecutor.

II. Sexual relations outside marriage between Jews and nationals of German or kindred blood are forbidden.

---

[112] See above p. 237.

III. Jews will not be permitted to employ female citizens of German or kindred blood under 45 years of age as domestic servants.

IV. 1. Jews are forbidden to display the Reich and national flag or the national colours.
2. On the other hand they are permitted to display the Jewish colours. The exercise of this right is protected by the State.

V. 1. A person who acts contrary to the prohibition of Section I will be punished with hard labour.
2. A person who acts contrary to the prohibition of Section II will be punished with imprisonment or with hard labour.
3. A person who acts contrary to the provisions of Sections III or IV will be punished with imprisonment up to a year and with a fine, or with one of these penalties.

VI. The Reich Minister of the Interior in agreement with the Deputy Führer and the Reich Minister of Justice will issue the legal and administrative regulations required for the enforcement and supplementing of this law.

VII. The law will become effective on the day after its promulgation; Section III, however, not until 1 January 1936.

The Reich Citizenship Law of 15 September redefined the Jews as 'subjects' without, however, at this stage removing any concrete rights from them, apart from political rights which were restricted to 'Reich Citizens'—not a very significant privilege in the Third Reich! Certificates of Reich citizenship were in fact never introduced, and all Germans other than Jews were until 1945 provisionally classified as Reich citizens. Many Jews were initially relieved by the law, which appeared to bring an end to three years of uncertainty. Now at least they knew where they were and they did have some rights. However, the fact remained that they were now officially second-class citizens and the vagueness of the law played into the Nazis' hands by enabling Jewish rights to be stripped away piecemeal in a series of supplementary decrees over the following years:

404

Reich Citizenship Law of 15 September 1935
I. 1. A subject of the State is a person who belongs to the protective union of the German Reich, and who therefore has particular obligations towards the Reich.
2. The status of subject is acquired in accordance with the provisions of the Reich and State Law of Citizenship.

II. 1. A citizen of the Reich is that subject only who is of German or kindred blood and who, through his conduct, shows that he is both desirous and fit to serve the German people and Reich faithfully.

2. The right to citizenship is acquired by the granting of Reich citizenship papers.
3. Only the citizen of the Reich enjoys full political rights in accordance with the provision of the laws.
III. The Reich Minister of the Interior in conjunction with the Deputy of the Führer will issue the necessary legal and administrative decrees for carrying out and supplementing this law.

In their official commentary on the Nuremberg Laws Dr Wilhelm Stuckart and Dr Hans Globke of the Reich Ministry of the Interior justified the inequality of treatment of Jews and 'Aryan' Germans in terms of a critique of (a simplistic view of) the Western liberal position as follows:

405

National Socialism opposes to the theories of the equality of all men and of the fundamentally unlimited freedom of the individual vis-à-vis the State, the harsh but necessary recognition of the inequality of men and of the differences between them based on the laws of nature. Inevitably, differences in the rights and duties of the individual derive from the differences in character between races, nations and people.

The idea that the Reich Citizenship Law had somehow stabilized the Jewish situation was soon shown to be an illusion. On 30 September, only a fortnight after the Nuremberg Rally, Frick ordered the dismissal of all civil servants who were descended from three or four grandparents who were 'full Jews', thereby removing the exceptions which had been written in to the Civil Service Law of 7 April 1933.[113] However, the question of the definition of a Jew remained a major outstanding problem.

Hitler had pencilled out the sentence 'This law applies only to full-blooded Jews'; so clearly the Reich Citizenship Law must also apply to those who were partly Jewish. The question was how Jewish did one have to be to be a Jew and how exactly did one define 'Jewishness'? The issue was discussed intensely by Party and State offices in the weeks following Nuremberg. The key agencies involved were the Reich Ministry of the Interior, represented by Lösener, and Hess's office represented by Gerhard Wagner. Lösener wished to restrict the definition of a Jew to non-Aryans with more than two non-Aryan grandparents. Wagner, on the other hand, wished all half Jews, i.e. those with two Jewish grandparents to be included. Lösener countered Wagner's arguments in terms of Nazi ideology. Thus, he pointed out that if half Jews were classified with full Jews it would mean that the Jews would acquire 200,000 allies who, with 50 per cent Aryan 'genetic material' would be even more dangerous. Moreover, since they did not belong to either group

---

[113] See above p. 224.

they would be liable to become outcasts and therefore criminal, an argument calculated to influence the Gestapo. The discussions continued throughout October with the Interior Ministry insisting on the half-Jews being generally accepted as Reich citizens with only a few exceptions, while the Party, although it had conceded that quarter-Jews should be Reich citizens, still insisted that most half-Jews should be categorized as Jews with only a few exceptions. The Interior Ministry mobilized Schacht and Foreign Minister Neurath in support of their case for a speedy decision in their favour.

The problem was, however, that Hitler typically did not wish to get involved. He was supposed to give his verdict at a conference on 29 September, but, in the event, simply talked in general terms about the history of the Jews in Germany and then concluded by saying that the remaining points would have to be cleared up by negotiations between Party and State officials. Finally, when it became clear that Party and State were at loggerheads, he cancelled a second conference, scheduled for 5 November, in order not to be obliged to take sides. As a result the Party and Ministry were forced to reach a compromise acceptable to Hitler.

The First Supplementary Decree of the Reich Citizenship Law of 14 November 1935 was based on Wagner's draft with the crucial exception of the definition of a Jew, which followed Lösener's proposals, and the dropping of the demand for the divorce of mixed marriages. This was to be of absolutely vital importance for the future, saving thousands of half-Jews from death:

406

I. 1. Until further regulations regarding citizenship papers are issued, all subjects of German or kindred blood, who possessed the right to vote in the Reichstag elections at the time the Citizenship Law came into effect, shall for the time being possess the rights of Reich citizens. The same shall be true of those to whom the Reich Minister of the Interior, in conjunction with the Deputy of the Führer, has given provisional citizenship.
2. The Reich Minister of the Interior, in conjunction with the Deputy of the Führer, can withdraw the provisional citizenship.

II. 1. The regulations in Article I are also valid for Reich subjects of mixed Jewish blood (*Mischlinge*).
2. An individual of mixed Jewish blood is one who is descended from one or two grandparents who were racially full Jews, in so far as he or she does not count as a Jew according to Article V, paragraph 2. A grandparent shall be considered as full-blooded if he or she belonged to the Jewish religious community.

III. Only the Reich citizen, as bearer of full political rights, exercises the right to vote in political affairs or can hold public office. The Reich Minister of the Interior, or any agency empowered by him, can make exceptions during the transition period, with regard to occupation of public office. The affairs of religious organizations will not be affected.

IV. 1. A Jew cannot be a citizen of the Reich. He has no right to vote in political affairs and he cannot accupy public office.
2. Jewish officials will retire as of 31 December 1935. If these officials served at the front in the world war, either for Germany or her allies, they will receive in full, until they reach the age limit, the pension to which they were entitled according to the salary they last received; they will, however, not advance in seniority. After reaching the age limit, their pensions will be calculated anew, according to the salary last received, on the basis of which their pension was computed.
3. The affairs of religious organizations will not be affected.
4. The conditions of service of teachers in Jewish public schools remain unchanged until new regulations for the Jewish school systems are issued.

V. 1. A Jew is anyone who is descended from at least three grandparents who are racially full Jews. Article II, para. 2, second sentence will apply.
2. A Jew is also one who is descended from two full Jewish grandparents, if (a) he belonged to the Jewish religious community at the time this law was issued, or joins the community later, (b) he was married to a Jewish person, at the time the law was issued, or marries one subsequently, (c) he is the offspring of a marriage with a Jew, in the sense of Section 1, which was contracted after the Law for the Protection of German Blood and German Honour became effective, (d) he is the offspring of an extramarital relationship with a Jew, according to Section 1, and will be born out of wedlock after 31 July 1936.

VI. 1. Requirements for the pureness of blood as laid down in Reich Law or in orders of the NSDAP and its echelons—not covered in Article 5—will not be affected.
2. Any other requirements for the pureness of blood, not covered in Article V, can be made only by permission of the Reich Minister of the Interior and the Deputy Führer. If any such demands have been made, they will be void as of 1 January 1936, if they have not been requested by the Reich Minister of the Interior in agreement with the Deputy Führer. These requests must be made by the Reich Minister of the Interior.

VII. The Führer and Reich Chancellor can grant exemptions from the regulations laid down in the law.

The administration of this regulation proved complicated because the necessary evidence on family background was not always readily available for distinguishing between the various categories of Jews. Part-Jews were divided into *Mischlinge* (part-Jews) 'of the first degree' with two Jewish grandparents, who did not fall under the category of V.2, and *Mischlinge* 'of the second degree' with one Jewish grandparent. Each of these categories was subject to varying degrees of discrimination. Large numbers of 'family researchers' were employed to scour parish records but selection was often arbitrary. Moreover, it was ironical that a movement which prided itself on the scientific basis of its racism was in the end obliged to fall back on a religious definition of race, which was merely supplemented by physical examination of doubtful cases by 'racial experts'. Nevertheless, possession of proof of one's Aryan identity was to become a matter of life and death.

The Law for the Protection of German Blood and Honour was administered by the existing criminal court apparatus and not by special courts. Only the male partner was put on trial, partly because the female partner could then be used as a witness against him and partly because Hitler believed that the man invariably initiated the sexual activity. Between 1935 and 1940, 1,911 people were convicted of miscegenation (*Rassenschande* = lit. racial disgrace): 11 in 1935, 358 in 1936, 512 in 1937, 434 in 1938, 365 in 1939, and 231 in 1940[114]. The number of prosecutions varied widely from place to place. In Hamburg, for example, 429 men were put on trial between 1936 and 1943 for alleged contravention of §2, of whom 270 were Jews. Of these 391 were convicted and 36 found not guilty. In Frankfurt only 92 were convicted during the same period, despite a larger population of Jews.[115] Courts could impose sentences of from one day to fifteen years. Initially, ordinary prison sentences were normally imposed, but in March 1936, the *Gestapa* complained to the Justice Ministry that 'the punishments imposed by the Courts hitherto, which in most cases were only between six weeks and one-and-a-half years' imprisonment, had hitherto failed to have a deterrent effect' and were not appropriate for 'ensuring the purity of German blood as the precondition for the continued existence of the German people.'[116] Heydrich demanded that the prosecutors should request penal servitude on principle. The result of this intervention was that sentences of penal servitude did increase, particularly of Jews. In Hamburg roughly half of those convicted were given prison sentences of 1–2 years and half sentences of penal servitude of 2–4 years, though on occasion sentences were of up to six years or more.[117] The following is an example of a typical judgment from the Hamburg Court, which sentenced a Jew to two-and-a-half years of penal servitude in November 1937:

407

The Court based its judgment on the fact that it was a serious case of miscegnation (*Rassenschande*). The fact that the accused and the witness had known one another

---

[114] Cf. Gruchmann, op. cit., p. 434.
[115] H. Robinsohn, *Justiz als politische Verfolgung. Die Rechtsprechung in Rassenschande—Fällen beim Landgericht Hamburg 1936–1943* (Stuttgart 1977) p. 18.
[116] Cf. Gruchmann, op. cit., p. 435
[117] Cf. Robinsohn, op. cit., p. 52

since 1920 and that they had had a lasting relationship since 1927 could not be regarded as a mitigating circumstance, since the relationship continued for one-and-a-half years after the passage of the Nuremberg Laws and was only terminated through the arrest of the accused. The Law for the Protection of German Blood and German Honour is one of the basic laws of the new Germany and this law must be implemented with harsh measures.[118] It may be true that it was difficult for the accused to part from the witness; however, he should have found the strength to carry out this step at all costs and the Court was obliged to base its judgment on the fact that he was fully conscious of contravening the Law until his arrest in June 1937. . .

In the following judgment of 9 December 1936, the Reich Supreme Court gave a wide interpretation of the concept of 'miscegenation' on the grounds that 'the regulations of the Law serve not only to protect German blood but also to protect German honour' and because 'it would confront the courts with almost insuperable difficulties of proof and would necessitate the discussion of the most embarrassing questions':

408

The concept of sexual intercourse within the meaning of the Law for the Protection of Blood does not include every indecent act, but is not confined to actual intercourse. It includes all natural and unnatural intercourse, i.e. apart from intercourse itself, all sexual activities with a member of the opposite sex which are intended in place of actual intercourse to satisfy the sexual urges of at least one of the partners.

In practice, the application of the law varied between Jews, for whom a kiss or a hug would often be regarded as sufficient grounds for prosecution, and Aryan Germans who would normally only be prosecuted for more extensive sexual activity. The law of course laid Jews wide open to denunciation and even framing by those with a grudge against them. The sexual aspect was undoubtedly an important feature of Nazi antisemitism. Thus, it is significant that the loudest applause of the Party's rank and file at Nuremberg in September 1935 was reserved for the Law for the Protection of German Blood and Honour. It was also a feature of Nazi antisemitic propaganda.

(iii). Nazi Antisemitic Propaganda and the Popular Response

The most notorious Nazi antisemite was the Gauleiter of Franconia, Julius Streicher. Since the early 1920s, Streicher had published a scandal sheet, *Der*

---

[118]In fact the concept of a 'basic law' was hitherto unknown in German law

Stürmer, which specialised in denunciations of alleged Jewish moral corruption and vice, including the use of age-old libels about Jewish sacrificial rites. The following is a typical example:

409

The murder of the 10-year-old Gertrud Lenhoff in Quirschied (Saarpfalz). . . . The Jews are our MISFORTUNE!

Moreover, the numerous confessions made by Jews show that to the devout Jew the carrying out of ritual murders is an ordinance. The former Chief Rabbi (and later monk) Teofiti declares that the ritual murders take place especially on the Jewish Purim (in memory of the Persian murders) and Passover (in memory of the murder of Christ).

The instructions are as follows:

The blood of the victims is to be forcibly tapped. On Passover, it is to be used in wine and matzos; thus, a small part of the blood is to be poured into the dough of the matzos and into the wine. The mixing is done by the Jewish head of the family.

The procedure is as follows: The head of the family empties a few drops of the fresh and powdered blood into the glass, wets the fingers of the left hand, then says: 'Dam Izzardia chynim heroff dever Isyn porech harbe hossen maschus pohorus' (Exodus VI, 12) ('Thus we ask God to send the ten plagues to all enemies of the Jewish faith'). Then they eat and at the end the head of the family cries: 'Sfach, chaba, moscho kol hagoym!' ('May all Gentiles perish, as the child whose blood is contained in the bread and wine!')

The fresh (or dried or powdered) blood of the slaughtered child is further used by young married Jewish couples, by pregnant Jewesses, for circumcision and so forth. Ritual murder is recognized by all devout Jews. The Jew believes he thereby absolves himself of his sins.[119]

Before 1933, the paper's circulation was largely restricted to Bavaria. After the Nazi take-over of power, however, it acquired a semi-official character and soon *Der Stürmer* was being publicly displayed in showcases in town and villages up and down the country. Streicher had a vivid sexual imagination to which he gave free rein in his paper and the impact of the stories of alleged Jewish sexual scandals was heightened by the drawings of his crude but effective cartoonist, Philipp Rupprecht. In 1938 *Der Stürmer* published a book for older schoolchildren called *Der Giftpilz* ('The Poisonous Mushroom'). It was written by Ernst Hiemer, edition of Streicher's

---

[119] This extract, misrepresenting as it does the character of the two festivals of Purim and the Passover, which do not commemorate murders but deliverance from oppression, and embodying alleged quotations from Jewish sacred writings which are not to be found there and are moreover expressed in a tongue that cannot be identified, is a characteristic example of the falsehoods by which Nazi propagandists sought to work upon the ignorance of their readers.

paper and contained coloured illustrations drawn by Rupprecht. The book began with a mother telling her son Franz during a walk in the forest that there were good and bad people in the world just as there were good and poisonous mushrooms. The latter were of course the Jews. The following excerpts convey the flavour of the book:

410

'It is almost noon,' says the teacher. 'Now we must summarize what we have learned in this lesson. What did we discuss?'

All the children raise their hands. The teacher calls on Karl Scholz, a little boy on the front bench. 'We talked about how to recognize a Jew'.

'Good! Now tell us about it!'

Little Karl takes the pointer, goes to the blackboard and points to the sketches. 'A Jew is usually recognized by his nose. The Jewish nose is crooked at the end. It looks like the figure 6. So it is called the "Jewish Six", Many non-Jews have crooked noses too. But their noses are bent, not at the end, but further up. Such a nose is called a hook nose or eagle's beak. It has nothing to do with a Jewish nose.'

'Right!' says the teacher. 'But the Jew is recognized not only by his nose . . .', the boy continues. 'The Jew is also recognized by his lips. His lips are usually thick. Often the lower lip hangs down. That is called "sloppy". And the Jew is also recognized by his eyes. His eyelids are usually thicker and more fleshy than ours. The look of the Jew is sly and sharp. . . .'

Then the teacher goes to the desk and turns over the blackboard, on its back is a verse. The children recite it in chorus:

From a Jew's countenance/the evil devil talks to us,
The devil, who in every land/is known as evil plague .
If we are to be free from the Jew/and to be happy and glad again,
Then youth must join our struggle/to overcome the Jew devil. . . .

Inge sits in the Jew doctor's reception room. She has to wait a long time. She looks through the magazines on the table. But she is much to nervous even to read a few sentences. Again and again she remembers her talk with her mother. And again and again her mind dwells on the warnings of her BDM leader: 'A German must not consult a Jew doctor! And particularly not a German *girl!* Many a girl who has gone to a Jew doctor to be cured has found disease and disgrace!'

After entering the waiting-room, Inge had an extraordinary experience. From the doctor's consulting-room she could hear the sound of crying. She heard the voice of a young girl: 'Doctor, doctor, leave me alone!'

Then she heard a man laughing scornfully. And then all of a sudden, absolute silence. Inge held her breath and listened. 'What can this mean?' she asked herself and her heart was pounding. Once again she thought of her BDM leader's warning.

Inge has now been waiting for an hour. She takes up the magazines again and tries to read. The door opens. Inge looks up. There stands the Jew. She screams. She's so frightened, she drops the magazine. She jumps up in terror. Her eyes stare into the Jewish doctor's face. His face is the face of a devil. In the middle of this devil's face is a huge crooked nose. Behind the spectacles two criminal eyes. And the thick lips are grinning. A grin that says: 'Now I've got you at last, little German girl!' The Jew approaches her. His fleshy fingers stretch out for her. But now Inge has recovered her wits. Before the Jew can grab hold of her, she slaps the Jew doctor's fat face. Then a jump to the door, and Inge runs breathlessly down the stairs. She escapes breathlessly from the Jew house. . . .

Streicher and *Der Stürmer* were the most extreme and the most degraded examples of Nazi antisemitism and even some of the senior members of the regime found his material hard to stomach, though Hitler protected him. However, the propaganda apparatus of the regime ensured that a consistently negative image of the Jews was conveyed by the mass media. In particular, Goebbels endeavoured to create an impression of the Jews as foreigners by substituting in people's minds a stereotype of the ghetto Jew of Eastern Europe—with (for Germans) a strange appearance and peculiar customs—for the norm of the assimilated Jew who was more or less an average German in all but his religion.

How successful was this propaganda? Evidence from the reports of Nazi agencies and those of SPD contact men suggest that it had some impact, but that the impact was limited to reinforcing the existing generally negative image of the Jews, which produced a widespread passive antisemitism, without, however, succeeding in winning over many Germans to the dynamic racism characteristic of Nazi ideology. For most people the Jews were not a subject of much interest, and the evidence suggests that where they had a concrete reason for dealing with Jews, such as material self-interest, they were happy, indeed anxious, to do so. On the other hand, there was not a great deal of sympathy for them. People often distinguished between individual Jews whom they knew and liked and Jews in general, a point made by Melita Maschmann in her *Memoirs*:

411

I had learned from the example of my parents [who were German Nationalist supporters] that one could have antisemitic opinions without this interfering in one's personal relations with individual Jews. There may appear to be a vestige of tolerance in this attitude, but it is really just this confusion which I blame for the fact that I later contrived to dedicate body and soul to an inhuman political system, without this giving me doubts about my own individual decency. In preaching that all the misery of the nations was due to the Jews or that the Jewish spirit was seditious and Jewish blood was corrupting, I was not compelled to think of you or old Herr Lewy or Rosel Cohn: I thought only of the bogy-man, 'The Jew'. And when I heard that the Jews were being driven from their professions and homes and imprisoned in

ghettos, the points switched automatically in my mind to steer me round the thought
that such a fate could also overtake you or old Lewy. It was only *the* Jew who was
being persecuted and 'made harmless'.

An SPD contact man in Munich reported:

412

On the night of 1 May [1935] large stones were thrown from a car at the windows
of the shop belonging to the Jew Pappenheim in Weisenburgplatz and smashed the
panes. The following day a large crowd gathered outside the store and openly
opposed these excesses. One heard comments such as 'incredible goings-on', 'cheek',
'vandalism' etc. Thus, it was clear that the population had no sympathy with the
tricks of the Nazis. In the end, the police had to disperse the crowd which was getting
bigger and bigger. It was clear to the observer that this incident was not the result
of mass discontent but an act planned by a few criminals. National Socialists also
appeared in front of the Jew Schwarz's shop and warned customers not to enter the
shop. But it was noticeable that no one let themselves be put off; in fact, one could
see that some customers demonstratively carried the goods they had bought with
hardly any wrappings.

Another SPD contact man in Saxony reported in September 1935:

413

The Jewish laws are not taken very seriously because the population has other
problems on its mind and is mostly of the opinion that the whole fuss about the Jews
is only being made to divert people's attention from other things and to provide the
SA with something to do. But one must not imagine that the anti-Jewish agitation
does not have the desired effect on many people. On the contrary, there are enough
people who are influenced by the defamation of the Jews and regard the Jews as the
originators of many bad things. They have become fanatical opponents of the Jews.
This enmity often finds expression in the form of spying on people and denouncing
them for having dealings with Jews, probably in the hope of winning recognition and
advantages from the Party. But the vast majority of the population ignore this
defamation of the Jews; they even demonstratively prefer to buy in Jewish department stores and adopt a really, unfriendly attitude to the SA men on duty there,
particularly if they try and take photographs of people going in.

In February 1936 a local police report from the Rhineland noted:

414

Unfortunately, many people still regard the Jew as a friend whom they do not want
to abandon yet. But enlightenment is progressing in this field also, albeit very slowly

with the country population. On 21 February of this year the funeral of a Jewess took place. The population held back and did not take part. A few women who wanted to attend were dissuaded from doing so by the other inhabitants. It was striking that the Jews from all the surrounding areas had come together to show their unity.

On 1 August 1937 the Munich Gestapo Office reported as follows:

415

Investigations were made in several government districts with the aim of finding out which peasants still have business contacts with Jewish dealers, particularly cattle dealers. These investigations produced shocking results. They showed that a large percentage of peasants still have business dealings with Jews. Thus, it was established that in *Regierungsbezirk* Schwaben-Neuburg alone over 1,500 peasants had had commercial contacts with Jewish cattle dealers over the years 1936–37. It is suggested that the reason for this deplorable state of affairs is the fact that there is a lack of trustworthy Aryan cattle dealers with capital in the countryside so that the peasants are compelled to do business with the Jews. Thus, for example, 80–90 per cent of the cattle trade at the Nördlingen market is in Jewish hands. This is only partly true because, as a result of the regulations of the Reich and Prussian Ministry of Food and Agriculture, the Gestapo cannot do anything to control this evil. The deeper reason for it, however, lies in the attitude of the peasantry who show a complete lack of awareness of race. The investigations which are not yet completed already demonstrate that, particularly in those districts where political Catholicism is still in control, the peasants are so infected by the teachings of an aggressive political Catholicism that they are deaf to any discussion of the racial problem. This situation indicates further that the majority of the peasants are completely immune to the ideological teachings of National Socialism and that only material disadvantages will compel them to enter into a business relationship with Aryan dealers. The Bavarian state peasant organization in the Reich Food Estate was, therefore, informed of all those peasants who are known to buy from Jews so that all the privileges of the Reich Food Estate can be denied them.

An SPD contact man reported from South-West Germany in June 1935:

416

The owners of pubs are compelled—with the threat of boycotts and 'other consequences'—to put up notices with the inscription: 'Jews are not welcome here'. The majority of pubs already have these notices. Many hang them up in inconspicuous places. One day a Jew found one of these notices up in a café where he was a regular customer. He asked the manageress why she had not told him that he was not welcome. The manageress kept apologising and told the customer that he should stay and that she had been made to put up the notice.

(iv) Jewish Policy 1936–37—the 'Quiet Years'

Fear of a foreign boycott of the Olympic Games, held in Germany during 1936, and concern to avoid disruption of the economy before rearmament had made sufficient progress ensured that the years 1936–37 were relatively speaking the quietest period for Jews in the Third Reich. This did not mean that Jews were free from further discrimination and harassment. On 9 October 1936, for example, a decree was issued which banned civil servants from consulting Jewish doctors, pharmacists, hospitals and nursing homes and in the event of non-compliance, denied them all benefits and refused to accept sickness certificates signed by Jewish doctors. Similarly, sporadic harassment of local Jewish businesses continued. However, by comparison with what had been and above all what was to come these were quiet years.

Perhaps the most significant development was the successful assertion by the SS of its claim to a major role in the formation of Jewish policy: by 1938 it had established its right to participate in Jewish legislation. As the high priesthood of Nazi ideology the SS was bound to be interested in playing a role in the Jewish question. However, it applied to it that same cool professional rationality which distinguished its activities from the crude and amateur excesses of the SA and Party fanatics such as Streicher. In May/June 1934, the SD issued a 'Situation Report—Jewish Question' which, having analyzed the nature of the problem, proposed a solution in terms of mass emigration. Moreover, it went on to draw the logical conclusion from this, namely that, in its treatment of the Jews, the regime should distinguish between the Zionists, who should be encouraged, and the assimilationists who should be persecuted. Heydrich summed up this policy in an article published in the official SS journal, *Das Schwarze Korps*, on 15 May 1935:

417

After the Nazi seizure of power our racial laws did in fact curtail considerably the immediate influence of the Jews. But the Jew in his tenacity has seen this merely as a temporary restriction. The question as he sees it is still: How can we win back our old position and once again work to the detriment of Germany?

But we must separate Jewry into two categories according to the way in which they operate: those who work openly as Jews and those who hide behind international Jewish welfare agencies and the like.

The Jews in Germany fall into two groups: the Zionists and those who favour being assimilated. The Zionists adhere to a strict racial position and by emigrating to Palestine they are helping to build their own Jewish state. The assimilation-minded

Jews deny their race and insist on their loyalty to Germany or claim to be Christians, because they have been baptized, in order to overthrow National Socialist principles.

The SS, therefore, encouraged those organizations which asserted their Jewish identity and aimed to strengthen Jewish self-awareness, At the same time, the SS set about establishing detailed records of Jews and their organizations. In the Autumn of 1936, the SD established a separate section—II 112—for Jewish affairs, of which the deputy head was a young man who had already established something of a reputation for himself as an 'expert' on Jewish matters—Adolf Eichmann. On 7 December 1937, the section summed up its objective as 'the centralization of the entire work on the Jewish question in the hands of the SD and Gestapo'.[120] Ten days later, on 18 December, it defined the aims of Jewish policy as follows:

418

The provisional objective of National Socialist Jewish policy must be:
1. The pushing back of Jewish influence in all spheres of public life (including the economy).
2. The encouragement of Jewish emigration.
The future work of the SD must move in this direction. The SD must become an effective instrument of the RFSS in this sphere too, which can periodically propose necessary draft laws to the Government.

There were, however, serious obstacles in the way of Jewish emigration. First, it was in the hands of the Reich Office of Emigration attached to the Interior Ministry which operated according to bureaucratic rules, i.e. slowly. More important was the fact that foreign countries were not anxious to receive impoverished Jews and yet the regime had introduced various measures which stripped the Jews of most of their possessions on departure. Thirdly, Germany was not alone in trying to get rid of its Jews. There were also waves of Jewish emigration from antisemitic regimes in Eastern Europe. Partly in consequence, many countries had begun to raise barriers to Jewish immigration. Even Palestine could only receive a limited number, partly because of British concern at growing Arab hostility to mass Jewish immigration, and partly because Palestine—at that stage an undeveloped agricultural region—was more appropriate for younger Jews and those with practical skills. Unfortunately, however, the age and skill distribution within German Jewry was weighted towards the old and towards intellectual and specialised commercial skills. This posed problems for emigration in general. Finally, many Jews, particularly the older generation, felt themselves to be

---

[120] Cf. Schleunes op. cit., p. 204.

Germans and had no wish to emigrate if they could help it. They were encouraged by the relative peace of the years 1936–37. The confusion within the Jewish community about what to do is indicated in the following police report of January 1936, referring to meetings of Jews in the Rhineland:

419

Meetings of Jewish associations have decreased. Apart from the Zionist movement, the Association of Jewish Culture and the Association of Jewish Front Soldiers hold meetings. The meetings gave no cause for complaint, apart from one meeting held by the provincial association of synagogues. At this meeting the lawyer Stern from Berlin spoke to the synagogue congregation in Neuwied. He encouraged people to stay in Germany and warned against hasty emigration. In contrast to the words of the lawyer Stern, Superintendent Dr Kurt Singer from Berlin spoke at a meeting in Koblenz held by the Association of Jewish Culture. In his speech he emphasized that the Nuremberg Laws were beyond discussion; the Jews, especially the young ones, must emigrate.

The following figures illustrate the development of Jewish emigration during the Third Reich:

420

Year	Jewish Population (in thousands)	Emigrés (in thousands)	Deportees (in thousands)	Surplus of Deaths (in thousand)
16.6.1933	503[1]	38		5.5
1934		22		5.5
1935		21		5.5
1936		24.5		6
1937		23.5		6
1. big wave of aryanization				
1938		40		8
	214			
17.5.1939		78		10
	234			
1940		15	10	8
1.5.1941	169	8	25	4
1.10.1941	164			
1942	139		73	7.5
1943	51	0.5	25	5
1944	14.5		1	1
1945	20–25[2]			
		ca. 270	135	72

[1] Religious Jews. All other figures apply to racial Jews.
[2] In the 'Old Reich' 14,000 Jews were living legally, ca. 5,000 illegally. This together with the return of survivors from Theresienstadt camp, explains the apparent increase in the number of Jews from 1944–45.

The fact that one office of the regime—the SD—was trying to encourage Jews to emigrate, while other agencies were complicating that process by stripping them of their capital is indicative of the confusion that reigned in the sphere of Jewish policy. Although in theory the Interior Ministry was responsible for Jewish policy, its loss of power to the SS and other bodies meant that in practice it was unable to assert that responsibility. Hitler declined to set clear guide lines probably because he himself was uncertain exactly how to proceed. He intervened only occasionally and unwillingly, sometimes to insist on economic priorities, as in his temporary support for Schacht, but at other times to insist on a hard line in relation to some particular act or piece of legislation that was in dispute. In April 1937 he explained his position to a meeting of Party district leaders. After emphasizing that the final aim of Jewish policy was 'crystal clear to all of us', he went on:

421

All that concerns me is never to take a step that I might later have to retrace and never to take a step which could damage us in any way. You must understand that I always go as far as I dare and never further. It is vital to have a sixth sense which tells you broadly what you can and cannot do. [Hearty laughter and applause]. Even in a struggle with an adversary it is not my way to issue a direct challenge to a trial of strength. I do not say, 'Come and fight because I want a fight'; instead I shout at him, and I shout louder and louder, 'I mean to destroy you'. Then I use my intelligence to help me to manoeuvre him into a tight corner so that he cannot strike back, and then I deliver the fatal blow. That is how it is [shouts of Bravo].

Although his listeners presumably understood his final aim as the elimination of the Jews from German life, unfortunately he did not indicate how this was to be achieved in practice. This lack of clear guidance from the top produced a vacuum in which the various power centres within the regime competed to assert their own Jewish policy. Moreover, since anti-semitism was recognized as the core component of Nazi ideology to which the Führer was totally committed, there was strong pressure to take a tough line on Jewish policy in order to establish the credentials of oneself and one's office in the struggle for influence over policy. And, although there were a few individual civil servants such as Lösener who tried to act as a brake, this process operated within the State bureaucracy itself. For example, in the case of the 1936 decree banning civil servants from consulting Jewish doctors etc., the original Interior Ministry draft had confined itself to doctors, but the Justice Ministry had then insisted on including pharmacists and hospitals, and the War Ministry had then demanded the extension of its application to civil servants' widows and dependants—a concrete example of 'cumulative radicalization'.[121]

(v) The Radicalizing of Antisemitism—Autumn 1937–Autumn 1938

The turning point towards a new and much more radical phase of Nazi antisemitism came in the Autumn of 1937 and was part of a more general radicalizing of the regime. Hitler appears to have come to the conclusion that the regime was becoming bogged down. It had had no major foreign policy success since the reoccupation of the Rhineland in March 1936 and the SD was reporting growing resistance from the Churches and from the Conservatives as in the following report of January 1938. Such reports or the substance of them appear to have reached Hitler:

In the course of the development of the regime two main opponents of the NS ideology and the NS State have emerged: the political Churches and Reaction ... The plan of the higher clergy, both on the Protestant and on the Catholic side, is to call for resistance to the State ... At the same time, the reactionary forces have developed a hitherto unsuspected degree of activity and are trying with all their power to deprive the Party and its formations, particularly the SS, of their influence, and in their place to transfer all power to the Wehrmacht and the spiritual-ideological indoctrination to the Churches ... The pro-Jewish attitude of the Churches, which renders all anti-Jewish propaganda by the Party ineffective as far as the mass of the Church faithful are concerned ... is having an effect such as has not been felt since the take-over of power. Thus a considerable reduction in Jewish emigration is certainly to be expected.

By the end of 1937 Germany's economic position had become much stronger and Hitler decided that he could now afford to dispense with Schacht, the first victim of a major purge of Conservatives in the administration, the Armed Forces, and the diplomatic corps during the winter of 1937–38. It represented virtually a second 'seizure of power', ending the delicate balance between the Nazis and the traditional elites which had lasted since 1934. The elites had in effect fallen victim to the internal dynamic within the regime.

On 5 September, Schacht was sent on leave and, on 27 November, he was finally dismissed from his post as Reich Minister of Economics. He owed his dismissal to his vocal and persistent objections to what he saw as an economically irresponsible form of rearmament programme. He was replaced by Göring, who integrated the Ministry into his Four Year Plan organization and then appointed Walther Funk, a pliable figure, as Minister on 15 February 1938.

---

[121] See above p. 206.

Schacht had been the main barrier to radical antisemitism in the economic field. But, just as his contribution to Germany's economic recovery had rendered his further employment unnecessary, so this economic recovery had removed the major restraint on Nazi antisemitism in the economic sphere. In his speech to the Nuremberg Party rally in September 1937 Hitler launched a major attack on the Jews for the first time since 1935. In the following months pressure increased on Jewish businesses 'voluntarily' to sell out at a price well below market value to Aryan German firms, which were now eager to cooperate in this process of 'Aryanization'. Economic recovery had given them the incentive and the capital with which to expand, and they welcomed the opportunity to eliminate Jewish competitors and secure their allocations of raw materials. This process was encouraged by decrees issued by Göring on 15 December 1937, reducing the foreign exchange and raw material quotas for Jewish firms, and, on 1 March 1938, banning the granting of public contracts to Jewish businesses.

The occupation of Austria in March 1938 brought about a marked acceleration of the economic campaign against the Jews. The Nazi take-over in Austria saw an orgy of confiscations of Jewish businesses by local Party officials. This seems to have had the effect of galvanizing Göring into action both through the example of what could be achieved in terms of seizing Jewish property but also as an example of how it should not be done. Göring was determined to ensure that Jewish expropriation should be carried out in an orderly fashion and that his organization should be in control. On 26 April 1938, therefore, he issued a Decree for the Registration of Jewish Property and two days later announced at a ministerial meeting that the Jewish question would have to be solved and that he envisaged the final exclusion of Jews from German economic life. His decree laid down that every Jew had to value and register his entire property at home and abroad with the higher administrative authorities of his domicile. Only property valued at less than 5,000 RM and articles of personal use and household utensils were exempt, provided they were not luxuries. In future, permission would be required to sell or lease such property. This was clearly intended as a preliminary move to pave the way for the confiscation of all Jewish property. At the same time, the regime moved against Jews in the professions. On 14 June 1938, the Fourth Decree of the Reich Citizenship Law banned Jewish doctors from treating Aryan patients from 30 September. Similar measures soon followed against Jewish lawyers, dentists, and veterinary surgeons, while a law of 16 July excluded Jews from specified commercial occupations. An estimated 30,000 Jewish travelling salesmen were dismissed during the remainder of the summer. Finally, on 17 July, a decree was introduced, for which the Staff of the Führer's Deputy had been pressing for over a year, aimed at facilitating the identification of Jews as well as humiliating them:

422

I. 1. Jews must be given only such first names as are specified in the directives issued by the Reich Minister of the Interior concerning the bearing the first names.[122]
2. Section I does not apply to Jews of foreign nationality.
II. 1. If Jews bear first names other than those authorized for Jews by Section I, they must, from 1 January 1939, adopt another additional first name, namely 'Israel' for men and 'Sarah' for women.

(vi) The Reichskristallnacht of 9–10 November 1938 and its Repercussions

Just as the repercussions of the Nazi take-over of Austria in March 1938 helped to precipitate a further radicalization of antisemitism, so that process was accelerated by an unforeseen incident which occurred in November—the so-called 'Night of Broken Glass' (*Reichskristallnacht*), named after the glass from the shattered windows of Jewish premises which littered the streets of the morning of 10 November. It began when, on 7 November 1938, Ernst von Rath, a minor official in the German Embassy in Paris, was shot dead by a young Polish Jew, Herschel Grünspan, in revenge for the mistreatment of his parents by the Nazis. Goebbels, who was in bad odour with Hitler because of his affair with the Czech actress, Lida Baarova, decided to try and rehabilitate himself with the Führer. A hardliner on the Jewish question, he seized the opportunity of an 'old fighters' reunion in commemoration of the Munich putsch of 9 November 1923, attended by Hitler, to propose a radical initiative which would satisfy the pent-up resentment among the Nazi rank and file at the gradual nature of the regime's antisemitic measures. Later the Nazi Party Supreme Court prepared a secret report on the incidents of that night:

423

On the evening of 9 November 1938, Reich Propaganda Director and Party Member Dr Goebbels told the Party leaders assembled at a social evening in the old town hall in Munich that in the districts of Kurhessen and Magdeburg-Anhalt there had been anti-Jewish demonstrations, during which Jewish shops were demolished and synagogues were set on fire. The Führer at Goebbels' suggestion had decided that such demonstrations were not to be prepared or organized by the Party, but neither were they to be discouraged if they originated spontaneously....

---

[122] These contained a list of Jewish names.

The oral instructions of the Reich Propaganda Director were probably understood by all the Party leaders present to mean that the Party should not appear outwardly as the originator of the demonstrations but that in reality it should organize them and carry them out. Instructions in this sense were telephoned immediately (and therefore a considerable time before transmission of the first teletype) to the bureaux of their districts by a large number of the Party members present. . . . The first known case of the killing of a Jew, a Polish citizen, was reported to Reich Propaganda Leader and Party Member Dr Goebbels on 10 November 1938 at about 2 o'clock and in this connexion the opinion was expressed that something would have to be done in order to prevent the whole action from taking a dangerous turn. According to the statement by the deputy Gauleiter of Munich–Upper Bavaria, Party Member Dr Goebbels replied that the informant should not get excited about one dead Jew, and that in the next few days thousands of Jews would see the point. At that time, most of the killings could still have been prevented by a supplementary order. Since this did not happen, it must be deduced from that fact as well as from the remark itself that the final result was intended or at least was considered possible and desirable. In which case, the individual agent carried out not simply the assumed, but the correctly understood, wishes of the leaders, however vaguely expressed. For that he could not be punished.

This report estimated the number of Jewish dead at 91. Over 20,000 Jewish men were arrested and taken to concentration camps. Nazi propaganda dressed the affair up as a spontaneous uprising of the German people against the Jews. In fact, the reaction of the public was apparently one of shock. The British *chargé d'affaires* in Berlin claimed that he had not met 'a single German from any walk of life who does not disapprove to some degree of what has occurred'. Most people objected to the lawlessness, vandalism and destruction of property involved. There were few complaints about the discriminatory legislation that followed.

The American Consul in Leipzig, David Buffum, prepared a detailed report (21 November) on the events of the *Kristallnacht* in Leipzig. His account of the violence demolishes any question of strong popular backing for what happened and draws attention to the powerlessness of the public and the refusal of the police to intervene against the outrages:

424

The shattering of shop windows, looting of stores and dwellings of Jews which began in the early hours of 10 November 1938, was hailed subsequently in the Nazi press as a 'spontaneous wave of righteous indignation throughout Germany, as a result of the cowardly Jewish murder of Third Secretary von Rath in the German Embassy at Paris'. So far as a very high percentage of the German populace is concerned, a state of popular indignation that would spontaneously lead to such excesses, can be considered as nonexistent. On the contrary, in viewing the ruins and attendant measures employed, all of the local crowds observed were obviously benumbed over what had happened and aghast over the unprecedented fury of Nazi acts that had been or were taking place with bewildering rapidity throughout their city. . . .

At 3 a.m. on 10 November 1938 was unleashed a barrage of Nazi ferocity as had had no equal hitherto in Germany, or very likely anywhere else in the world since savagery began. Jewish buildings were smashed into and contents demolished or looted. In one of the Jewish sections an eighteen-year-old boy was hurled from a three-storey window to land with both legs broken on a street littered with burning beds and other household furniture and effects from his family's and other apartments. This information was supplied by an attending physician. It is reported from another quarter that among domestic effects thrown out of a Jewish building, a small dog descended four flights on to a cluttered street with a broken spine. Although apparently centred in poorer districts, the raid was not confined to the humble classes. One apartment of exceptionally refined occupants known to this office was violently ransacked, presumably in a search for valuables which was not in vain, and one of the marauders thrust a cane through a priceless medieval painting portraying a biblical scene. Another apartment of the same category is known to have been turned upside down in the frenzied pursuit of whatever the invaders were after. Reported loss by looting of cash, silver, jewellery, and otherwise easily convertible articles, has been apparent.

Jewish shop windows by the hundreds were systematically and wantonly smashed throughout the entire city at a loss estimated at several millions of marks. There are reports that substantial losses have been sustained on the famous Leipzig 'Grühl', as many of the shop windows at the time of the demolition were filled with costly furs that were seized before the windows could be boarded up. In proportion to the general destruction of real estate, however, losses of goods are felt to have been relatively small. The spectators who viewed the wreckage when daylight had arrived were mostly in such a bewildered mood that there was no danger of impulsive acts, and the perpetrators probably were too busy in carrying out their schedule to take off a whole lot of time for personal profit. At all events, the main streets of the city were a positive litter of shattered plate glass. According to reliable testimony, the debacle was executed by SS men and Stormtroopers not in uniform, each group having been provided with hammers, axes, crowbars and incendiary bombs.

Three synagogues in Leipzig were fired simultaneously by incendiary bombs and all sacred objects and records desecrated or destroyed, in most cases hurled through the windows and burned in the streets. No attempts whatsoever were made to quench the fires, the activity of the fire brigade being confined to playing water on adjoining buildings. All of the synagogues were irreparably gutted by flames, and the walls of the two that are close to the consulate are now being razed. The blackened frames have been centres of attraction during the past week of terror for eloquently silent and bewildered crowds. One of the largest clothing stores in the heart of the city was destroyed by flames from incendiary bombs, only the charred walls and gutted roof having been left standing. As was the case with the synagogues, no attempts on the part of the fire brigade were made to extinguish the fire, although apparently there was a certain amount of apprehension for adjacent property, for the walls of a coffee house next door were covered with asbestos and sprayed by the doughty firemen. It is extremely difficult to believe, but the owners of the clothing store were actually charged with setting the fire and on that basis were dragged from their beds at 6 a.m. and clapped into prison.

Tactics which closely approached the ghoulish took place at the Jewish cemetery where the temple was fired together with a building occupied by caretakers, tombstones uprooted and graves violated. Eyewitnesses considered reliable the report that ten corpses were left unburied at this cemetery for a whole week because all gravediggers and cemetery attendants had been arrested.

Ferocious as was the violation of property, the most hideous phase of the so-called 'spontaneous' action has been the wholesale arrest and transportation to concentration camps of male German Jews between the ages of sixteen and sixty, as well as Jewish men without citizenship. This has been taking place daily since the night of horror. This office has no way of accurately checking the numbers of such arrests, but there is very little question that they have run to several thousands in Leipzig alone. Having demolished dwellings and hurled most of the movable effects onto the streets, the insatiably sadistic perpetrators threw many of the trembling inmates into a small stream that flows through the Zoological Park, commanding horrified spectators to spit at them, defile them with mud and jeer at their plight. The latter incident has been repeatedly corroborated by German witnesses who were nauseated in telling the tale. The slightest manifestation of sympathy evoked a positive fury on the part of the perpetrators, and the crowd was powerless to do anything but turn horror-stricken eyes from the scene of abuse, or leave the vicinity. These tactics were carried out the entire morning of 10 November without police intervention and they were applied to men, women and children.

There is much evidence of physical violence, including several deaths. At least half-a-dozen cases have been personally observed, victims with bloody, badly bruised faces having fled to this office, believing that as refugees their desire to emigrate could be expedited here. As a matter of fact this consulate has been a bedlam of humanity for the past ten days, most of these visitors being desperate women, as their husbands and sons had been taken off to concentration camps.

Similarly violent procedure was applied throughout this consular district, the amount of havoc wrought depending upon the number of Jewish establishments or persons involved. It is understood that in many of the smaller communities even more relentless methods were employed than was the case in the cities. Reports have been received from Weissenfels to the effect that the few Jewish families there are experiencing great difficulty in purchasing food. It is reported that three Aryan professors of the University of Jena have been arrested and taken off to concentration camps because they had voiced disapproval of this insidious drive against mankind.

Sources of information: Personal observation and interviews.

The diary entry of a seventeen-year-old schoolboy, Hermann Bremser:

425

9/10.11.1938. Reply of the German 'people' to the murder of the Embassy Councillor von Rath by a Jew. Throughout Germany synagogues, Jewish children's homes and Jewish houses as well as furniture and possessions are being destroyed. Culture in the Third Reich! Foreign opinion everywhere is disgusted. History will remember the day as one of barbaric behaviour by the German population. The order for the destruction and manslaughter came from official circles.

Melita Maschmann analysed her own reactions to the events of that night in Berlin and referred to the effect of Party indoctrination in blunting human feelings:

426

Next morning—I had slept well and heard no disturbance—I went into Berlin very early to go to the Reich Youth Leadership office. I noticed nothing unusual on the way. I alighted at the Alexanderplatz. In order to get to the Lothringerstrasse I had to go down a rather gloomy alley containing many small shops and inns. To my surprise almost all the shop windows here were smashed in. The pavement was covered with pieces of glass and fragments of broken furniture.

I asked a patrolling policeman what on earth had been going on there. He replied: 'In this street they're almost all Jews.'

'Well?'

'You don't read the papers. Last night the National Soul boiled over.'

I can remember only the sense but not the actual wording of this remark, which had an undertone of hidden anger. I went on my way shaking my head. For the space of a second I was clearly aware that something terrible had happened there. Something frighteningly brutal. But almost at once I switched over to accepting what had happened as over and done with and avoiding critical reflection. I said to myself: The Jews are the enemies of the New Germany. Last night they had a taste of what this means. Let us hope that World Jewry, which has resolved to hinder Germany's 'new steps towards greatness', will take the events of last night as a warning. If the Jews sow hatred against us all over the world, they must learn that we have hostages for them in our hands.

With these or similar thoughts I constructed for myself a justification of the pogrom. But in any case I forced the memory of it out of my consciousness as quickly as possible. As the years went by I grew better and better at switching off quickly in this manner on similar occasions. It was the only way, whatever the circumstances, to prevent the onset of doubts about the rightness of what had happened. I probably knew, beneath the level of daily consciousness, that serious doubts would have torn away the basis of my existence from under me. Not in the economic but in the existential sense. I had totally identified myself with National Socialism. The moment of horror became more and more dangerous to me as the years went by. For this reason it had to become shorter and shorter. But now I am anticipating. On the 'Night of Broken Glass' our feelings were not yet hardened to the sight of human suffering as they were later during the war. Perhaps if I had met one of the persecuted and oppressed, an old man with the fear of death in his face, perhaps, . . .

Goebbel's action in initiating the pogrom had caused extreme irritation to certain other Nazi leaders, especially Göring, whose responsibilities for the economy caused him to see the events of the *Kristallnacht* in a different light, and Himmler and the SS who, though disapproving, cooperated fully in the arrests of Jews. Reactions abroad were highly unfavourable and resulted in a stricter boycott of German goods. The total damage to property was estimated at around 25 million marks, but much of this was inflicted on property not owned by Jews (Jewish shopkeepers were often the tenants of German house-owners).[123] It was a typical example of the policy chaos which had hitherto characterized Nazi measures towards the Jews. Hitler, however, who continued to consult with Goebbels, had evidently decided to use this opportunity for a marked radicalization of Jewish policy, with the aim of driving them out of German economic life altogether and as quickly as possible. On the afternoon of 10 November, Göring joined Hitler and Goebbels to discuss the technicalities for which he would be responsible. The aim was also to exploit the situation in order to restore 'the critical situation of the Reich's finances' at the expense of the Jews. Two days later, on 12 November, Göring summoned a conference to discuss the issue. Apart from Göring and Goebbels, those present at the conference included Walther Funk (Economics Minister), Schwerin von Krosigk (Finance Minister), Heydrich (Chief of Security Police), Daluege (Head of the Uniformed Police) and representatives of the Foreign Ministry and insurance companies.

427

Göring: Gentlemen! Today's meeting is of a decisive character. I have received a letter written on the Führer's orders by Bormann, the chief of staff of the Führer's deputy, requesting that the Jewish question be now, once and for all, coordinated and solved one way or another. And yesterday once again the Führer requested me on the phone to take coordinated action in the matter.

Since the problem is mainly an economic one, it is from the economic angle that it will have to be tackled. Naturally a number of legal measures will have to be taken

---

[123] According to provisional figures prepared for Heydrich, 815 shops were destroyed, 29 department stores and 171 houses set on fire or otherwise destroyed, 191 synagogues set on fire and a further 76 completely demolished. In addition 11 Jewish community halls chapels of rest etc. were set on fire and 3 more completely destroyed. But the report noted that 'the true figures must be several times greater than those reported'. Heydrich to Göring 11 November 1938 ND 3058-PS.

which fall within the sphere of the Minister of Justice and within that of the Minister of the Interior; and certain propaganda measures will be taken care of by the Minister of Propaganda. The Minister of Finance and the Minister for Economic Affairs will take care of problems which fall into their respective fields. . . .

Now we have had his affair in Paris, followed by more demonstrations, and this time something decisive must be done! Because, gentlemen, I have had enough of these demonstrations! It is not the Jew they harm but myself, as the final authority for coordinating the German economy. If today a Jewish shop is destroyed and goods are thrown into the street, the insurance company will pay for the damage, which does not even touch the Jew; and furthermore, the goods destroyed come from the consumer goods belonging to the people. . . .

I would not wish there to remain any doubt, gentlemen, as to the purpose of today's meeting. We have not come together simply for more talk, but to make decisions, and I implore the competent agencies to take all measures to eliminate the Jew from the German economy and to submit the measures to me, so far as it is necessary. . . .

Goebbels: . . . Furthermore, my advice is that the Jew should be eliminated from any position in public life in which he may prove to be a provocation. It is still possible today for a Jew to share a compartment in a sleeping car with a German. Therefore, we need a decree by the Reich Ministry of Transport stating that separate compartments shall be available to Jews; in cases where compartments are full up, Jews cannot claim a seat. They will be given a separate compartment only after all Germans have secured seats. They are not to mix with Germans, and if there is no more room, they will have to stand in the corridor.

Göring: In that case, I think it would be more sensible to give them separate compartments.

Goebbels: Not if the train is overcrowded!

Göring: Just a moment. There will be only one Jewish coach. If that is full up, the other Jews will have to stay at home.

Goebbels: Suppose, though, there aren't many Jews going to the express train to Munich, suppose there are two Jews in the train and the other compartments are overcrowded. These two Jews would then have a compartment all to themselves. Therefore, Jews may claim a seat only after all Germans have secured one.

Göring: I'd give the Jews one coach or one compartment. And should such a case as you mention arise and the train be overcrowded, believe me, we won't need a law. We'll kick him out and he'll have to sit all alone in the lavatory all the way!

Goebbels: I don't agree. I don't believe in that. There ought to be a law. Furthermore, there ought to be a decree barring Jews from German beaches and resorts . . . Jews should not be allowed to sit around in German parks. I am thinking of the whispering campaign on the part of Jewish women in the public gardens on the Fehrbelliner Platz. They go and sit with German mothers and their children and begin to gossip and work upon their feelings. I see here a particularly grave danger. I think it is imperative to give the Jews certain public parks, not the best ones, and tell them: 'You may sit on these benches.' These benches shall be marked 'For Jews only'. Besides that they have no business in German parks. Furthermore, Jewish children are still allowed in German schools. That's impossible. It is out of the question that any boy should sit beside a Jewish boy in a German grammar school and take lessons in German history. Jews ought to be eliminated completely from German schools. They ought to take care of their own education in their own communities....

The cost of the damage of the *Kristallnacht* was borne partly by the insurance companies (who compensated for the losses suffered by non-Jewish property owners) and partly by the Jews themselves. For, on 12 November, Göring issued the following decree with the cynical title: Decree for the Restoration of the Street Scene in relation to Jewish Business Premises (!):

428

§1. All damage which was inflicted on Jewish businesses and dwellings on 9 and 10 November 1938 as a result of the national indignation about the rabble-rousing propaganda of international Jewry against National Socialist Germany must at once be repaired by the Jewish proprietors or Jewish traders.
§2. (1) The costs of the repairs will be met by the proprietors of the Jewish business and dwellings affected.
(2) Insurance claims by Jews of German nationality will be confiscated for the benefit of the Reich.

Despite his disapproval of the *Kristallnacht*, Göring was quick to seize the opportunity to assist the rearmament programme by using Jewish funds to top up the Reich's depleted finances. On 12 November he issued the following Decree concerning Reparations from Jews of German nationality:

429

The hostile attitude of the Jews towards the German people and Reich which does not shrink even from cowardly murders, demands decisive resistance and heavy reparation. On the basis of the Decree for the Implementation of the Four Year Plan of 18 October 1936 ... I therefore announce the following:
§1. The Jews of German nationality are required communally to pay a contribution of RM 1 billion to the German Reich ...
§2. A Jew can no longer be an employer within the meaning of the Law for the Ordering of National Labour of 20 January 1934 ...

The most decisive measure taken on 12 November, however, was Göring's Decree excluding Jews from German Economic Life, formalizing the extensive 'Aryanization' of Jewish-owned property which had begun in the autumn of 1937:

430

On the basis of the Decree of 18 October 1936 for the Implementing of the Four-Year Plan the following is decreed:
I 1. From 1 January 1939 the running of retail shops, mail order houses and the practice of independent trades are forbidden to Jews.
2. Moreover, Jews are forbidden from the same date to offer goods or services in markets of all kinds, fairs or exhibitions or to advertise them or accept orders for them.
3. Jewish shops which operate in violation of this order will be closed by the police.

II 1. No Jew can any longer be manager of an establishment as defined by the Law on the Organization of National Labour, of 20 January 1934.
2. If a Jew is a leading employee in a business concern he may be dismissed at six weeks' notice. After the expiration of this period, all claims of the employees derived from the denounced contract become invalid, especially claims for retirement or redundancy pay.

III 1. No Jew can be a member of a cooperative society.
2. Jewish members of cooperatives lose their membership from 21 December 1938. No special notice is necessary.

IV The Minister of Economics is empowered to issue regulations necessary for the enforcement of this decree with the approval of the Reich ministers concerned. He may allow exceptions in the case of the transfer of Jewish business establishments into non-Jewish hands, or of the liquidation of Jewish business establishments, or in special cases.

The process of Aryanization, a new phase of which had begun in the Autumn of 1937, now accelerated dramatically. In April 1938 there were still 39,532 Jewish businesses in operation. By 1 April 1939, of these 14,803 had been liquidated, 5,976 'dejewified', 4,136 were in the process of being 'dejewified', and 7,127 were being investigated.[124] Göring's measures had been designed to systematize the process and assert State control, thereby avoiding the arbitrary plunder which had occurred in Austria. In practice, however, things turned out rather differently. The Party, both as an organization and as a collection of ambitious individuals, was determined to take full advantage of the rich pickings available and, since permission from its local officials was required before decisions were taken concerning

---

[124] Cf. H. Genschel, *Die Verdrängung der Juden aus der Wirtschaft im Dritten Reich* (Göttingen 1966), p. 206.

the disposal of the property, it had the opportunity to do so. The following report of 5 January 1939 to the Reich Minister of Economics by the Office of the City President of Berlin on the Aryanization programme during the final three months of 1938 provides a good insight into the moral corruption, the arbitrary methods, the contempt for legal process which combined to ensure that the law of the jungle, so characteristic of Nazi practice, predominated. And, since victory went to the strong, this meant that overall the results of Aryanization benefited big business rather than the small men whose resentment of Jewish competition had fuelled their antisemitism and encouraged their commitment to the Nazi movement in the early years. For the fact that a few Nazi retailers and craftsmen benefited from the elimination or acquisition of their Jewish rivals could not disguise the reality that Aryanization had in effect furthered the process of business concentration already in operation:

431

Egoism in economic life

The confused weeks after the new decrees of November 1938 concerning the Jews reflected a coarsening of business methods, perhaps also as a result of the September crisis. Not only in the retail trade, in the competition of applicants for the Jewish retail shops, but in general the impression prevails of an increasingly ruthless exploitation of positions of power. This begins with the fight for the allocation of raw materials, continues with the fight for labour and leads to the ruthless exploitation by people of their own, sometimes merely apparent, financial power, in order to attract workers with wage increases. It sometimes leads to agreements to ignore the wage freeze announced by the Trustee and not even to make an application. The number of interventions on the ground of an alleged acquaintanceship with me of the most superficial kind has increased in influential quarters, despite the fact that such interventions were already criticized by the Party authorities in September 1938 at the beginning of Aryanization. Every group has its favourite for whom it would like to procure, let us say, the plant just ripe for Aryanization. . . .

Such drastic actions as those initiated by the Decree on the Exclusion of Jews from German Economic Life, of 12.xi.38, easily tend to 'get out of hand' at the lower levels of the executive authorities. With the first newspaper announcement or the first announcement by an influential figure on the radio, forces are set in motion which claim the right to carry out such measures themselves, whereas in reality their function is at best advisory. Thus the illegal use of private 'commissioners' has developed, with Jewish owners of plants giving them extensive plenary powers in order to get rid of the factory as quickly as possible (since they hope for the biggest advantage thereby); also, there are attempts at notarial transfers of properties on the basis of such plenary powers, etc. This can be prevented by the issuing, when possible, of executive regulations simultaneously with the basic decree. The main task of my office in the context of Aryanization in retail trade has been to mitigate the uncontrollable actions of such forces.

Arbitrary interpretation of the law

In the same way I have noticed in connexion with the Aryanization programme that legal regulations and decrees are supplemented by a somewhat arbitrary interpretation not only on the part of organizations affiliated to the Party but also on the part of State authorities. Thus, in the process of drawing up the registry of Jewish businesses, a factory was declared Jewish simply because the Aryan proprietress was married to a Jew, although, according to the instructions for the drawing up of this register, there is no such regulation. In fact, according to the edict of the Minister of the Interior of 14.vii.38, the decision is to be made in the light of individual circumstances and according to whether or not the Jewish partner had a dominant influence over the business. The other regulation may even have been avoided on purpose. The further development of legal regulations on the basis of a progressive refinement of the sense of legality within the community is certainly a supplement to legislation which must not be underestimated. It becomes dangerous only if in this sphere, away from the legislator and without knowledge of his motives, the varying strength and power of penetration of the organizations taking part, and of the State and non-State authorities, begin to get out hand. This happened when the Jews were prohibited from being landlords. Pressure was exerted that Jews should be forced to interpose German administrators over their own house property; basically this was certainly an aim worth striving for, but it was something which had not yet been expressed in legislation (Law for the Alteration of the Industrial Code of 6.vii.38). Thus, letters were written to Jews stating that an administrator had been appointed for their house property and that the owner had to appear at the office so that the 'take-over of administration' might be effected; he was also to bring along any managers who had been appointed by other agencies. He was threatened with 'further measures' if he did not appear. Subsequently, for such measures the explanation was given 'that it was found necessary to keep various Jewish managements under observation during the critical days of November'. Moreover, this procedure was justified since another authority had also given orders for the same property to be supervised. In this way, through the simultaneous actions of two different organizations, several representatives appeared without authority and sometimes even tried to collect the rent. . . .

At the conference on 12 November there had been some discussion about the need to separate Jews and Germans in the sphere of housing, transport, places of public entertainment etc. Himmler had issued a tough police decree on 28 November, enabling regional and local authorities to impose strict regulations on the appearance of Jews in public. Police authorities soon took advantage of this, with the result that there was a danger of a great lack of uniformity in the treatment of Jews in various parts of the Reich. At the conference on 12 November, Heydrich had raised the question of epidemics breaking out if ghettos were established. He had also doubted whether his police could regularly supervise daily life in such ghettos. After consulting Hitler, Göring responded in a decree of 28 December by concentrating the Jews in houses instead of areas. Another outstanding matter was the intermarriages which had existed before the Blood Protection Law of 1935. That measure had applied only to marriages contracted after it came into effect. In the same decree Göring introduced a new classification in the case of such marriages based on the criterion of the children's religious affiliation. Another determining factor was which spouse was the Jewish partner in the marriage. The Jewish wife was given better treatment than the Jewish husband, presumably because her German husband was assumed to be the owner of the family house:

432

At my suggestion the Führer has made the following decisions concerning the Jewish problem:

SECTION A

I. *Housing of Jews*
1(a). The law for the protection of tenants is not, as a rule, to be abrogated for the Jews. On the contrary, it is desired, if possible, to proceed in particular cases in such a way that the Jews are quartered together in separate houses in so far as the housing conditions allow.
1(b). For this reason the Aryanization of house ownership *is to be postponed until the end of the total Aryanization*, that is to say, for the present the Aryanization of houses has to be carried out only in those individual cases where urgent reasons exist. The Aryanizing of industries, businesses, agricultural estates, forests, etc., is to be considered as urgent.
2. Use of sleeping and dining cars is to be forbidden to the Jews. At the same time, no special Jewish compartments are to be established. In addition, the use of trains, street cars, suburban railways, underground railways, buses, and ships cannot be prohibited to Jews.
3. Only the use of certain public establishments, etc., is to be prohibited to Jews. In this category belong the hotels and restaurants visited especially by Party members (for instance: Hotel Kaiserhof, Berlin; Hotel Vierjahreszeiten, Munich; Hotel Deutscher Hof, Nuremberg; Hotel Drei Mohren, Augsburg; etc.). The use of bathing establishments, certain public places, bathing resorts, etc., can be prohibited to Jews; also health baths particularly prescribed by doctors may be used by Jews, but only in such ways that no offence is caused.
II. Jews who were officials and have been pensioned are not to be denied their pensions. Investigations must be made, however, as to whether these Jews can manage with a reduced allowance.
III. The Jewish welfare organizations are not to be Aryanized or abolished, for otherwise the Jews will only become a public charge; but they may be supported by Jewish welfare organizations.
IV Jewish patents are property, and as such must be Aryanized. (A similar procedure towards Germany was carried out by the USA and other countries during World War I.)

Mixed Marriages
I. 1. *With children* (part-Jews, 1st degree)
(a) Where the father is a German and the mother a Jewess, the family may stay in future in its present lodging. The regulations for the exclusion of Jews are not to be applied to such families as far as their housing is concerned.

In these cases, the property of the Jewish mother can be transferred to the German husband or to the mixed children.
(b) Where the father is a Jew and the mother a German, these families are also not to be moved for the present into Jewish quarters, because the children (part-Jew, 1st degree) must serve in the labour service and the armed forces in the future and must not be exposed to Jewish propaganda. As far as the property is concerned, one must for the present proceed in such a way that it can be completely or partly transferred to the children.
I. 2. *Without children*
(a) If the husband is a German and the wife a Jewess, the provisions of 1(a) are valid accordingly.
(b) If the husband is a Jew, and the wife a German, these childless couples are to be proceeded against as if they were full-blooded Jews. The husband's property cannot be transferred to the wife. Both husband and wife can be moved into Jewish houses or Jewish quarters.

Especially in case of emigration, such married couples are to be treated as Jews, as soon as increased emigration is begun.
II. If a German wife divorces a Jew, she re-enters the German racial community and all disadvantages for her discontinue.

(vii) SS Jewish Policy 1938–39

At his conference on the Jewish question on 12 November 1938, Göring had insisted that 'since the problem is mainly an economic one, it is from the economic angle that it will have to be tackled'. In this he was asserting his own claim to sole competence for the Jewish question, a claim which Hitler had evidently approved. Then, prompted by the problems caused by Himmler's Police Decree of 28 November and the flood of subsequent local police regulations restricting the Jews, he officially confirmed his claim in a letter to all Government departments on 14 December:

433

To secure the necessary unity in the handling of the Jewish question, upon which rests the handling of economic matters, I am asking that all decrees and other important orders touching upon Jewish matters be cleared through my office and have my approval. Remind all the officials under your authority that absolutely no independent initiatives on the Jewish question are to be undertaken.

Göring's competence for the Jewish question was, however, being increasingly, though not overtly, challenged by the SS. At the 12 November conference, the SS representative, Reinhard Heydrich, had pointed out that 'the main problem, namely to kick the Jew out of Germany, remains'.

434

Heydrich: . . . As another means of getting the Jews out, measures for emigration ought to be taken in the rest of the Reich for the next eight to ten years. The highest number of Jews we can possibly get out during one year is 8,000–10,000. A great number of Jews will therefore remain. Because of the Aryanizing and other restrictions, Jewry will become unemployed. The remaining Jews will gradually become proletarians. I shall therefore have to take steps to isolate the Jew so that he won't enter into the normal German routine of life. On the other hand, I shall have to restrict the Jew to a small circle of consumers, but I shall have to permit them certain activities within the professions: lawyers, doctors, barbers, etc. This question will also have to be examined. As for the question of isolation, I'd like to make a few proposals regarding police measures which are important also because of their psychological effect on public opinion. For example, anyone who is Jewish according to the Nuremberg Laws will have to wear a certain badge. That is a possibility which will simplify many other things. I don't see any danger of excuses, and it will make our relationship with the foreign Jews easier.

Göring: A uniform?

Heydrich: A badge. This way we would also put an end to the molesting of foreign Jews who don't look different from ours.[125]

Göring: But, my dear Heydrich, you won't be able to avoid the creation of ghettos on a very large scale in all the cities. They will have to be created.

Just as the experience of the Anschluss had given an impetus to Aryanization in the 'old Reich' so it also had a marked impact on SS emigration policy. Indeed, Austria became a kind of laboratory for SS policy because, as a conquered territory, it did not present the same legal and bureaucratic obstacles as existed in Germany itself. Immediately after the German occupation, Eichmann established a 'Central Office for Jewish Emigration' and exploited the disorganization of the first few months to pursue a ruthless policy of forced emigration. Jewish property was illegally confiscated and partly used to finance the emigration of poor Jews. Six months later, in November, Eichmann could claim to have forced the emigration of 45,000 Jews, one quarter of Austrian Jewry. He had succeeded by giving priority to emigration over economic considerations—for example, permitting Jews

---

[125] Such a badge was finally introduced by a police regulation of 1 September 1941.

to transfer some of their assets abroad, a policy not entirely popular with Göring and his officials. Its success, however, could not be denied and, on 24 January 1939, following a proposal from the Jewish Section II 112 of the SD, Göring ordered the establishment of a 'Reich Central Office for Jewish Emigration' in the Reich Ministry of the Interior to promote the emigration of Jews 'by every possible means'. Göring delegated reponsibility for this new office to the Chief of the Security Police and SD and on 11 February it held its first session under Heydrich's chairmanship. This was a crucial development. For, with the Jews now effectively excluded from economic life, emigration remained the only logical solution to the Jewish question. In short, the plans which the SD had been following since 1934 had now born fruit: Jewish emigration with Palestine as the favoured destination—despite opposition from the Foreign Ministry—had now become official policy and the SS was now officially responsible for implementing it.

In his directive of 24 January Göring had requested that 'an appropriate Jewish organisation for the uniform preparation of emigration applications' be established. In his programme of forced emigration in Austria Eichmann had used the main Austrian Jewish organization, the 'Jewish Religious Community', to assist him. Now, the SD proposed the amalgamation of all German Jewish organizations to form a single Jewish body. This proposal was implemented through the creation of a 'Reich Association of the Jews in Germany' to which was assigned the responsibility of preparing Jews for emigration and financing them. In addition, it was made responsible for the education and welfare of those Jews remaining in Germany. Supervision of the Reich Association was placed in the hands of Heydrich. Thus, by the outbreak of war, the SS had established effective control both over the main sphere of Jewish policy—emigration—and over the Jews themselves through their organisation, the Reich Association.

CHAPTER 24

Popular Opinion—Consent, Dissent, Opposition and Resistance

Introduction: the problem of sources

Through propaganda, indoctrination, and terror—always in the background as a threat and ruthlessly applied when necessary—the Nazis endeavoured to create a 'militarized national community'. How successful was their attempt and how did the German people respond to the regime?

The image of German society conveyed by Nazi propaganda in newsreels and the press was of mass enthusiasm and commitment. However, in trying to understand what Germans really felt during these years the historian is faced with serious problems. Not only were there no opinion polls but it was impossible for people to express their views in public with any freedom: the results of elections and plebiscites were rigged; the media were strictly controlled. Newspapers are of limited value as a source, since the editors were subject to detailed instructions from the Propaganda Ministry on what to print and were severely disciplined if they stepped out of line. In short, an independent public opinion did not exist in the Third Reich. Even in liberal democratic countries public opinion is to some extent a creation of the media themselves; in Nazi Germany it was almost entirely a product of the Reich Ministry of Popular Enlightenment and Propaganda.

This situation posed problems for the regime itself which, for obvious reasons, was anxious to know what the German population were thinking and feeling. In his monthly report of 11 November 1935, for example, the *Regierungspräsident* of Upper Bavaria complained:

435

A true assessment of the barometer of popular opinion is faced with difficulties at the present time. Because of denunciations, which are still regrettably numerous, and in view of the fanaticism of some subordinate offices, it can be observed that large sections of the population and, in particular, those who are loyal to the State only give vent to their true opinion about public and especially local conditions in their most intimate circle. Otherwise, they simply keep their mouths shut because of completely unjustified fears.

A number of agencies made it their business to find out the state of popular opinion. The SD, the Gestapo, the Party, regional government offices, the judicial authorities—all, at various stages, prepared regular reports on the factors affecting public morale and the popular response: food shortages, price increases, fear of war, the employment situation and so on. Such reports were understandably particularly concerned about active opposition. These reports were based on information from informers scattered throughout the population who reported on conversations with 'national comrades' or on what they had overheard. It has been estimated that just before the war the SD alone had some 3,000 full-time officials and some 50,000 part-time agents. An indication of the mode of operations of this network is provided by the instructions of the Stuttgart branch of the SD to its agents. They were ordered on 12 October 1940:

436

To ensure that the attitudes of all sections of the population are under continuous observation every agent must seize every opportunity through casual conversation within his family, in his circle of friends and acquaintances, and above all at his place of work to ascertain the concrete effects on morale of all important domestic and foreign events and measures. In addition, conversations with national comrades in trains, particularly commuter trains, in trams, in shops, in hairdressers, at newspaper kiosks, at government offices such as the places where ration books are issued, employment exchanges, town halls etc., at markets, in pubs, in canteens, all these offer numerous opportunities for this task, opportunities which are too often neglected.

Despite the obvious problems of interpretation, the reports of these agencies provide an important source.

The second major source on popular opinion is provided by the reports of the Social Democratic Party's contact men in Germany. These were former SPD members who supplied regular information about various aspects of life in the Third Reich which provided the basis for monthly reports prepared by the SOPADE, the SPD in exile. Again, despite problems of interpretation, these provide a remarkable source for attitudes to the regime among various sections of the population and their response to its policies.

(i) The Elements of Consent

Although the regime deployed a formidable apparatus of terror, it is clear that it was also based on a large measure of consent from broad sections of the population. First, the Nazis' success in creating a positive image of Hitler as 'Führer' and in identifying the regime with that Führer image was of crucial importance. In part, this was the result of skilful propaganda by Goebbels and his Ministry who portrayed Hitler as a national leader distinct from the Party, above politics, selfless in his dedication to the service of the German people, a master politician and a great statesman. However, their success also derived from the fact that many Germans were hungry for leadership. After the collapse of the monarchy in 1918, the Weimar Republic had failed to win widespread acceptance let alone emotional loyalty; there emerged a vacuum of authority which could only be deeply disturbing to a nation accustomed to authoritarian modes of behaviour in its social and political life. During his time as Reich President, the old World War I hero, Field Marshall von Hindenberg, functioned as a kind of *ersatz* Kaiser. By 1933, however, he was too old and infirm to satisfy the craving for effective leadership. This feeling was intensified by the disastrous economic crisis which began in 1929 and which the Weimar governments proved incapable of solving. Moreover, a more dynamic concept of leadership, providing a model of authority and social organization, had achieved a major impact in many spheres during the Weimar period. This had occurred through the influence of the youth movement and of military models which were perpetuated during the post-war period in the Free Corps and the numerous paramilitary organizations. In place of a model of equal citizens co-operating within a framework of, on the one hand, voluntary bodies operating according to democratic principles of decision-making, and, on the other hand, bureaucratic hierarchies operating according to rational-legal norms, one had the ideal of a leader and his followers bound together by irrational ties of loyalty, honour, obedience and hero-worship. In short, the climate of opinion was highly receptive to the projection by the Nazis of their leader as the 'Führer' of the German people. Nevertheless, without concrete successes Hitler could not have sustained his positive image as Führer. The fact that he was associated with the solving of the unemployment problem and with the restoration of Germany's position as a European power appeared to confirm the message of Goebbels's propaganda.

Within the first two months of the regime Hitler had succeeded in achieving a remarkable position of personal authority in the eyes of large sections of the German people. This was in the context of the campaign of the 'national uprising' during February–March 1933 which culminated in the Day of Potsdam on 21 March.[126] His prestige was then confirmed by the impression of ruthless firmness which he created with the purge of the SA in June–July 1934. The first SOPADE report on popular attitudes to Hitler followed his purge of the SA in the Summer of 1934:

437

Our reports have shown that the events of 30 June have not shaken the authority of Hitler in the SA and the Party but that his authority among the people has, if anything, grown. He's got guts; he takes tough action; he does not spare the bigwigs—those were the remarks made even by outsiders. Wherever in Germany people grumble about the maladministration, about the brown big shots, Hitler is normally excepted. He does not want all that and is simply badly advised and informed. This effect of Hitler on the indifferent masses also extends to the workers insofar as they are not politically educated. Our factory reports record cases in which during factory visits Hitler undoubtedly has an effect on workers as well.

If one wishes to assess Hitler's importance to the present regime one must bear in mind the position which he now holds within the NSDAP and in the eyes of large section of the population. Hitler has sustained a mass basis for the regime which the 'movement' as such has long since forfeited.

For some Germans, such as the authors of the following pieces Hitler became a quasi-religious figure of worship. The first is virtually a parody of the Lord's Prayer, the second a kindergarten prayer:

438

Adolf Hitler, you are our great leader,
Your name makes our enemies shudder,
May your Third Reich come,
Your will alone be law on earth,
Let us daily hear your voice.
And command us through your leaders
Whom we wish to obey even at the risk
Of our own lives.
We swear this,
Heil Hitler!

---

[126] See above, pp. 153–4.

439

Dear Führer,
We love you like
Our fathers and mothers.
Just as we belong to them
So we belong to you.
Take unto yourself
Our Love and trust
O Führer!

This pseudo-religious element also emerges in the following letters from ordinary people to the press:

440

(a) Just as in my youth the dear Lord used to appear in my dreams, so now the Führer appears. We have had hundreds of dream conversations—funnily enough never about politics, but always about day-to-day, human, family matters. These nights are times of celebration.

(b) As my 'creator', his portrait hangs both in my work room and in the parlour at home. A look at him has often produced in me what 'pious people' allegedly feel when deep in prayer.

(c) He is the creator and preserver, the protector of our magnificent, great German Reich and, therefore, also the preserver of my little bit of soil, my garden. Every flower which blooms here blooms in gratitude to him, every apple which ripens, ripens in gratitude to him.

(d) Lead us!
In your hands lies the fate of millions
who dwell in your heart
for whom you are a faith.

(e) He who serves the Führer serves Germany and he who serves Germany serves God.

By the Spring of 1939 Hitler's position appeared even more impregnable, as is clear from the following SOPADE reports, the first from Danzig, the second from South-West Germany:

441

One may well assert that the whole nation is convinced that Hitler is a great politician. That is solely attributable to his foreign policy successes, which no one —not even the most confirmed Nazis—would have thought possible before. It is conceivable that this respect for Hitler as a politician will soon disappear when he has the first obvious diplomatic failure. Up till now the nation does not have the feeling that he has already had such a failure. Only the most convinced opposition people already to some extent believe that Hitler has got bogged down and that his decline will now begin. Until now, however, both his supporters and his enemies have been convinced that as a politician Hitler is greater than all his opponents.

442

As far as the attitude to Hitler is concerned, one must admit that now more than in past years when abuses occur, people keep saying: 'Hitler does not want that, but all the small fry do what they want.' If anyone has any dealings either with the Welfare Office or the Finance Office or with some other government office and comes into conflict with this office, then he immediately says: 'I will write to Hitler'. And, as far as I can see, an incredible number of letters must pour into the Reich Chancellery addressed personally to Hitler. The result of such a complaint is in most cases that the complainant receives a pre-printed card on which he is informed that his letter has been passed on to the appropriate authority. Most people then hear nothing more about it. This mass-processing has opened many people's eyes to the fact that there is no point in writing to Hitler.

Popular consent to Nazism was, however, based on more than simple respect or adulation for Hitler as Führer. In the Autumn of 1936, a half-Jewish teacher explained to an SPD contact man some of the bases of this popular consent:

443

... The anti-Bolshevik agitation is making a deep and powerful impact. The teacher denied my repeated and precise query whether this fuss did not have the opposite effect, although he does live in a largely peasant and petty bourgeois district. On the other hand, there are naturally also groups who, out of their bitterness and hatred, tend towards the Communists. Of the vast majority of the population, however, one can say that—looking at Bolshevism—they declare: 'Well, I'd rather have Hitler'. The reduction in the standard of food is being widely felt, but although rearmament is mainly to blame, according to his observations, there is no bitterness towards the Army or even towards the officers who enjoy much more sympathy among the general population than in the old days. The two year military service was an unpleasant surprise, but he does not believe that large numbers of people are basically against general military service; it is welcomed on educational grounds even by many Social Democrats. He does not believe the National Socialist mood has penetrated very deeply. However, Hitler has understood how to appeal to nationalist instincts and emotional needs which were already there before. Even the workers have become more nationalist. That has nothing to do with complaints about the

Government and the distress. It is more a nationalist feeling such as Naumann preached in his writings.[127]

Hitler is still outside the line of fire of criticism, generally speaking at least, but the messianic belief in him has more or less died out. People do not criticize him, whereas, for example, Goebbels is almost universally loathed even among the Nazis. As far as the economic future is concerned, everyone is feeling uncertain, although the large numbers of people who have got work through rearmament regard this work creation as a great feat. In general, one can say that almost everybody blames the previous system for failing to get the unemployed, and particularly youth, off the streets. The reduction in unemployment, rearmament, and the drive it shows in its foreign policy are the big points in favour of Hitler's policy and, on the basis of his own observations, he personally believes that only a tenth of the population does not recognize these facts. People feel that the previous governments were weak-willed and the parties as well. He assured me that that was not his own view because he knew the great feats of the Republic very well, but it was the almost unanimous view of public opinion. Hitler knew how to handle the popular mood and continually to win over the masses. No previous Reich Chancellor had understood anything of that.

A crucial element in popular consent to the regime was the fact that Nazism embodied, albeit in an extreme form, many of the basic attitudes of a very large section of the German people. Apart from the obvious nationalism and militarism, people also approved of its cultural conservatism, its hostility to modern movements in the arts, the so-called 'asphalt culture', which had appeared to play such a prominent part in the Weimar Republic, an image reinforced by the sexual licence characteristic of Berlin's entertainment quarter. To conservative Germans in the provinces Berlin under Weimar appeared as a modern Sodom, an impression confirmed by the fact that it was controlled by the 'Reds', the Social Democrats. Such people also approved of the regime's hostility towards unpopular minorities, not just Jews but also gypsies, and of its harsh attitude towards deviant groups—homosexuals, tramps, habitual criminals, the so-called asocials and the 'workshy'. They welcomed the fact that such people were now being locked up in concentration camps, just as they welcomed the strict line being taken towards youth through the introduction of labour service, military service, and harsh measures against juvenile delinquents. In short, the regime confirmed and enforced the values and prejudices of a substantial section of the population, giving them official status as 'sound popular feelings'.

(ii) Organization, Atomization, and Depoliticization

The Nazis grasped the significance of the vast numbers of clubs and associations charateristic of German social life, which had traditionally

---

[127] Friedrich Naumann was a politician at the turn of the century who established a 'National Social Association' with the aim of trying to win over the working class to support the monarchy and nationalism by carrying out political and social reforms. His ideas were influential among young Liberal intellectuals.

functioned as one of the main links between the private individual and the public arena and in some cases as a kind of infrastructure for political mobilization. The regime endeavoured, therefore, to control the population not only in their occupational roles through its network of occupational organizations such as the NS Teachers' League and the German Labour Front, in which membership was more or less compulsory, but also in their activities as private individuals by 'coordinating' private associations and clubs, putting them under the control of reliable Party members and replacing democratic procedures with the leadership principle. On 4 August 1933, for example the local newspaper in Neu-Isenburg reported the coordination of the local tennis clubs:

444

After the coordination of the 1. Neu-Isenburg Tennis Club e.V. and the nomination of Bank Manager Heinz Schmidt as leader, the first combined membership meeting of the two previously existing tennis clubs, which have been amalgamated to form the tennis club "Red-White" Neu-Isenburg, took place in the upper hall of the Gymnastics Club 1861. The numerous members who attended warmly approved the minutes of the combined committee meeting of 27 July and declared themselves to be in agreement with the proposed renaming of the club. The leader, Heinz Schmidt, then nominated the new committee . . .

In November 1935, the SOPADE reported on the significance of these compulsory organizations and the process of coordination as follows:

445

The purpose of all National Socialist mass organizations is the same. Whether one thinks of the Labour Front or of Strength through Joy, of the Hitler Youth or the *Arbeitsdank*, everywhere these organizations serve the same purpose: to 'involve' (*erfassen*) or to 'look after' (*betreuen*) the 'national comrades', not to leave them to themselves and if possible not to let them think at all. Just as someone forfeits any possibility of doing serious work by a vacuous activism, so the National Socialists display everywhere an overzealous bustle with the admitted intention of preventing any real common ground, any voluntary combinations from coming about. Ley has recently admitted it with complete frankness: the 'national comrade' is to have no private life and above all he must give up his private skittles club. This monopoly of organizations is intended to make the man in the street completely dependent, to stifle in him every initiative of any kind towards forming even the most primitive voluntary association, to keep him apart from all like-minded people, even from people on the same wave length, to isolate him and at the same time to bind him to the State organization. This has had an effect. Occasionally one hears from workers a word of approval about Strength through Joy, with the additional comment: in the old days nobody bothered about us. The point is that previously the State did not regard it as its task to send the workers one after the other to the theatre for free. In the old days the workers had their own pride in doing these things for themselves. But there are many who prefer the amusement and 'relaxation' organized by the State because it is less demanding ... The essence of fascist control of the masses is compulsory organization on the one hand, atomization on the other ...

The effect of this Nazi technique of organization and atomization was a process of depoliticization which affected large sections of the population as the following SOPADE reports indicate.

An SPD contact man in Westphalia reported in June 1936:

446

Here all public life seems to have died out. We have no idea what is going on in the world and most of the time not even what is going on in our town or in the neighbouring district. A large section of the population no longer reads a newspaper. Basically, the population are indifferent to what is in the papers. It is not only always the same but, in people's opinion, it is often untrue. The Nazi newspapers are no longer read because in the long run one cannot force people and because one cannot deny the fact that people lack the means to subscribe to a paper. Finally, 80 per cent have no inward connection with the National Socialists. Wherever one goes one can see that people accept National Socialism as something inevitable. The new State with all its institutions and with its compulsion is there, one cannot get rid of it. The great mass has come to terms with this situation to such an extent that it no longer thinks about how the situation could be changed.

The Nazi movement is scarcely visible any more in daily life. The SA and the other formations only appear for the big occasions. Basically, the same situation prevails in Nazi circles as it does among the nation in general. An enormous number of hopes and expectations have been destroyed. But people put up with everything like a fate which they cannot escape.

I know that this is a gloomy picture which I am giving. It is particularly gloomy because it shows that up to now the Nazis have succeeded in achieving one thing: the depoliticization of the German people, who after the war appeared to participate so passionately in political life ...

There can be no doubt that the Nazis have succeeded in persuading the masses to leave politics to the men at the top. The Nazis try as they say to turn everybody into committed National Socialists. They will never succeed in that. People tend rather to turn inwardly away from Nazism. But they are ensuring that people are no longer interested in anything. And that is at least as bad from our point of view. Only really major events can rouse people. Up to now it looks as though for the time being these will not occur. And, therefore, those people in Germany who think for themselves are awaiting events ...

From a small town in Württemberg in August 1937 an SPD contact man reported:

447

The whole of social life which in the old days was very rich and varied in our town has dwindled to the few associations which have been completely coordinated. Everyone tries to get out of attending events such as those on 1 May or similar occasions unless he absolutely has to attend. If one did not continually bump into a uniformed big wig in the street—the DAF alone has 10 officials here, whereas in the old days the trade unions had only honorary officials—one would hardly imagine one was living in a town in the Third Reich. One can walk the streets for days without seeing a Hitler salute . . .

Whereas in previous years when people grumbled it was mostly some personal annoyance that was the cause of this discontent, in the past year a certain change has taken place. Again and again one can hear from an artisan or a peasant that there is no longer any point in taking part in meetings. One is not allowed to say anything anyway. Everything is decreed from above and whether it is a case of having to pay up or something else, one is only allowed to say yea and amen to it. This opinion is not the expression of a momentary bitterness, it has sunk in deep and paralyzes all social contacts. Even solid bourgeois organizations are being affected. When recently in the course of the reorganization of the sports associations, the cycling association, which had always been more or less pro-Nazi, was going to be integrated into the new amalgamated sports organizations, the membership distributed all the association's property amongst themselves beforehand because they did not want it to seep away somewhere and only very few transferred their membership to the new organization.

The people who are most embittered against the Nazis are the numerous pub landlords in our town. They have good reasons for being so. Nowadays, only the landlords who are in with the Party do fairly reasonable business. They have the Party events and the meetings of the other NS organizations. In all other pubs it is as silent as the grave even on Sundays. 'If one cannot say what one thinks in public it is better to stay within one's own four walls. Then at least one does not run the risk of letting rip and ending up in Dachau . . .' That is the comment of a retired civil servant who previously had the reputation of being a very sociable man who liked his beer. People creep away to their homes and are afraid that someone might speak to them . . . However, more people go to Church these days.

At the beginning of 1938 an SPD contact man in Saxony reported:

448

Never since the overthrow [of the Republic] has participation in day-to-day political events been so limited as it is now. It seems to us that the indifference which has gripped large sections of the population has become the second pillar supporting the system. For these indifferent groups simply want to get by and to know nothing about what is going on around them. And that suits the Nazis fine. Only the continual collections for the WHV and the periodic shortages of various foodstuffs give these groups cause for slight grumbling. It is extremely rare to hear a critical word from workers who are laid off because of raw material shortages. On the other hand, one cannot speak of popular enthusiasm for National Socialism. Only the school children and the majority of those young men who have not yet done their military service are definitely enthusiastic about Hitler.

(iii) Dissent, Opposition, and Resistance

The categories used by historians to describe degrees of non-conformist behavior towards the regime—'dissent', 'opposition', and 'resistance' are not water-tight: the margins are porous and it is not always easy to see where one begins and the other ends or achieve agreement on definitions. It was in the nature of Nazism, with its claim to total conformity, to politicize all actions or statements which did not conform to official doctrine or practice irrespective of the intent behind such action and despite the fact that such doctrine and practice was often ambiguous or contradictory. Thus, innocuous non-political dissent from some policy could be transformed by the response of the regime into active opposition to that policy, which then in a few cases could provoke resistance to the regime itself. There is also a category of institutional resistance in which the members of a particular organization—for example, a Government department—defended their autonomy or sphere of responsibility from Nazi infiltration or control. Since it was in the nature of Nazi organizations to try and expand their sphere of influence at the expense of others and particularly non-Nazi ones, such institutional resistance represented in a sense resistance to the regime itself. On the other hand, it might not involve opposition to Nazi policy or values. It often merely expressed a determination on the part of the particular organization to carry out those policies itself—hardly a sign of resistance!

We have seen that dissent based on material grievances was quite widespread among various sections of the population—for example, among peasants, artisans, and small retailers. However, most of this dissent was limited to specific grievances and basically non-political. Indeed, the very fact that people dared to give vent to their discontent showed that they did not intend such criticism to be hostile to the regime as such. Moreover, the diversity of the complaints, which reflected the specific interests of a variety of groups, ensured that the dissent remained fragmented. This fragmentation was also encouraged by the fact that Nazism as an ideology was diffuse and many of its ideas were simply extreme variations of traditional German middle-class norms and values. Secondly, the effects of the regime not only varied from group to group but even within groups. This meant that most people could approve of and support certain aspects of it even if they disapproved of others. Even the Churches, although they might disapprove of interference in their affairs and attacks on Christianity, nevertheless thoroughly approved of the regime's nationalism and its attacks on Bolshevism. Similarly, the working class, though it had lost its independent voice, benefited from economic revival and the ending of unemployment. There were few people who were willing or able to see the regime as a whole, who could see that the attack on Christianity and on Bolshevism were parts of one and the same ideology and could not be treated separately, or that the economic revival was largely a consequence of rearmament, and that foreign policy successes were part of a programme in which war was seen as an integral element. This failure to see the regime as a whole was partly because few people possessed a strongly-held counter-ideology of their own which could enable them to see the flaws and horrors of the regime as intrinsic to it. It was also partly because people were isolated from one another and deprived of access to reliable information, let alone alternative views, by the systems of terror and propaganda. Moreover, the fact that the regime had destroyed rival political parties and prevented the formation of new ones meant that there was no organization which could aggregate the various discontents and mount a broad critique of the system. Finally, the complexity and opacity of the regime itself with its ever-shifting locations of power and influence made it difficult even for those on the inside to orientate themselves politically let alone for those without access behind the scenes. This too complicated the task of opposition.

Some of these points were made in the following SOPADE reports. The first was from the summer of 1934:

449

1. The regime still controls important instruments of power: the comprehensive propaganda apparatus, hundreds of thousands of supporters whose posts and prosperity depend on the continuation of the regime. At the top of the regime are men who have no scruples in the exercise of power and who in the hour of danger will not shrink from the greatest crimes.
2. No system of rule collapses by itself. The weakness of the opposition is the strength of the regime. Its opponents are ideologically and organizationally weak. They are ideologically weak because the great mass are only discontented, they are merely grumblers whose discontent springs simply from economic motives. That is particularly true of the *Mittelstand* and of the peasantry. The loudest and strongest criticism comes from these groups, but the criticism springs mostly from narrow selfish interest. These groups are least prepared to fight seriously against the regime because they have the least idea of what they should be fighting for. Their minds are still not yet governed by the idea that change can only come about through a

transition to other economic methods, to another form of society. On the contrary: fear of Bolshevism, of chaos, which, in the view particularly of the vast majority of the *Mittelstand* and peasantry, would follow Hitler's fall, is still the negative basis of the regime as far as the masses are concerned.

Its opponents are organizationally weak because it is of the essence of a fascist system that it does not allow its opponents to organize collectively. The forces of 'Reaction' are extraordinarily fragmented. In informed circles people register no fewer than five monarchist tendencies. The labour movement 'is still split into Socialist and Communists and, within the two movements, there are numerous factions. However, if the terror was reduced and the pressure towards atomization slackened it would become apparent that these factions would very soon merge into a great mass movement which, as an idea and a concept, may already be further developed in the minds of the workers than is evident.

The attitude of the Church opponents of the regime is not uniform. Their struggle is evidently not least directed towards improving the position of the Churches *within* the regime . . .

In the Spring of 1937, an SPD report from South-West Germany commented as follows:

450

The number of those who consciously criticize the political objectives of the regime is very small, quite apart from the fact that they cannot give expression to this criticism. And the fact that discontent [about other matters] makes itself loudly felt on numerous occasions also confirms the 'good conscience' of these people in terms of the National Socialist regime. They do not want to return to the past and if anyone told them that their complaints about this or that aspect threaten the foundations of the Third Reich they would probably be very astonished and horrified. The mood of 'opposition' consists of an absolute conglomeration of wishes and complaints. The remarks of a low-ranking official of the administration concerning the Jewish question are a good example of this. In response to an attempt to explain to him the mendacity of the antisemitic propaganda he replied: 'You don't imagine that I am a National Socialist! Not at all. I have many doubts about what is happening. But I must say one thing: It's quite right that nowadays it is no longer the interest of the individual but that of the community that matters. And on the racial question, although I used to reject the loud clamours of the Antisemites and even now do not like Streicher's excesses, after a thorough study of the question I have become convinced that it would be good for Germany to get rid of the Jews'. And yet the man was quite prepared to recognize how dangerous Hitler's policy was in many areas, e.g. rearmament. Conversations with workers and with members of Church circles demonstrate how varied are the causes of the anti-National Socialist mood. Some were and still are very much up in arms about the development of National Socialist Church policy and look at everything in terms of that. However, in conversations with workers the reply to the question of what they thought about the

Church dispute was almost invariably: 'That doesn't interest us'. And if one probed deeper there was hardly a trace of any feeling for the inner connection between the struggle of the workers and the other internal tensions of the regime. 'It suits us fine if the Nazis make short work of the Church. Both denominations have deserved it.' In other sections of society, e.g. among the self-employed and the peasantry things are not very different. Their discontent focuses superficially on matters which they find unpleasant and it can sometimes go as far as open sabotage of official measures. But in this sphere they mostly stop at the point where the peasant used to rebel against all restrictions of his freedom of action in the old days—with his dislike of bureaucracy.

It becomes increasingly evident that the majority of people have two faces: one which they show to their good and reliable acquaintances; and the other for the authorities, the Party offices, keen Nazis, and for strangers. The private face shows the sharpest criticism of everything that is going on now; the official one beams with optimism and contentment.

In July 1938 this picture was confirmed by an SPD contact man in North Germany:

451

The general mood in Germany is characterized by a widespread political indifference. The great mass of the people is completely dulled and does not want to hear anything more about politics. Thus, for example, the *Anschluss* with Austria did not produce anything like the enthusiasm and lasting effect as the reintroduction of conscription three years before. One should not be misled by the general grumbling. Nowadays people grumble everywhere about everything but nobody intends this grumbling to represent a hostile attitude to the regime. One can now experience grumbling in public: in trams, in restaurants etc. and in general nobody is prepared to defend the regime. But it is also generally true that no one regards the grumbling as an attack on the regime itself, as a political statement against the dictatorship. People and regime do not identify themselves with one another. People feel themselves to be objects of the present form of government and no longer have the idea that one day they could again be subjects. The attitude of the Western powers has made a decisive contribution to this general depoliticisation ...

The most shocking thing is the ignorance of wide circles about what is actually going on in Germany ... They are completely convinced that there are no longer concentration camps; they simply do not want to believe that the Nazis treat their opponents with ruthless brutality. They do not want to believe it because that would be too terrible for them and because they would prefer to shut their eyes to it. The moral front against National Socialism could be much broader if people really knew what things are really like in Germany. But this front is now very small even among the workers. It is always happening that even in the case of arrests of opponents of the regime only a few families hear about it and even the neighbourhood remains completely in the dark ...

(a) *The Churches*

The churches were the only institution which both had an alternative 'ideology' to that of the regime and were permitted to retain their own organizational autonomy. This made them a major obstacle to the Nazi attempt to establish total control over German life. Both the ideological independence and the organizational autonomy were, however, in a sense flawed. For, although in theory both the theology and the ethics of Christianity should have represented a total contradiction to the ideology of Nazism, in practice this was to some extent vitiated by the existence of common ideological ground between them. The fact that German Protestantism had long been identified with German nationalism and—particularly in the case of Lutheranism—with ultra-Conservative political views—made it vulnerable to the appeal of the Nazis' nationalism and their hostility to the liberal and Marxist Left. Similarly, the fact that the Roman Catholic Church regarded Bolshevism as its arch-enemy between the wars, and the fact that the national loyalties of German Catholics had been somewhat suspect since Bismarck's *Kulturkampf* of the 1870s, encouraged them to seek an accommodation with the new regime. Also, although the racist aspect of Nazi antisemitism was in principle unacceptable to the churches, in practice antisemitic prejudice within both churches helped to undermine their defence of this principle, particularly since this prejudice was shared by many of their parishioners. Finally, the fact, that they were permitted to retain an autonomous organization proved a doubled-edged weapon. For the principle of 'rendering unto Ceasar' was reinforced by anxiety to protect the churches' organization which, moreover, received important benefits from the State, notably the official collection of church taxes.

The response of the churches to the regime was thus complex and ambiguous. It varied among individual priests and pastors and individual bishops from outright opposition to particular policies of the regime and eventually, in the case of a few, even resistance through conformity to collaboration. The majority of churchmen concentrated on trying to maintain the churches' own functions as far as possible, including the pastoral sphere such as youth activities, and to resist the regime's attempt to restrict the churches' activities to performing purely a spiritual role, with their functions being limited to holding Church services.

The Protestant Church was weakened by serious divisions. Not only had it long been divided into two main branches—the Lutheran and the Reformed—but with the rise of Nazism there had emerged a movement within the church, known as the 'German Christians', which saw itself as the 'SA of the Church'. They professed a theology which combined evangelical piety and *völkisch* nationalism, identifying the Church with the *Volk* and claiming that the German nation had a divinely-ordained destiny. The movement had some support from academic theologians but above all attracted the support of young pastors and theology students who felt that during the previous fifty years the Church had lost touch with the people and had become too established and bureaucratic. They wanted a new 'people's church' and they saw the Nazis' 'national uprising' as the chance for a religious as well as a national renewal. They adopted the Nazi paramilitary forms and style—the uniforms, the marches, the salutes, and the slogan 'the swastika on our breasts and the cross in our hearts'.

The various state churches into which the Protestant Church was divided responded to the German Christian theme of a national church, a theme by no means confined to them, by establishing, on 27 May 1933, a centralized constitution with a gesture to the *Führerprinzip* in the form of a Reich Bishop. But the existing Church establishment endeavoured to retain some independence from the regime by electing as the new Reich bishop the respected Pastor von Bodelschwingh, the director of Bethel, a famous asylum for the handicapped. On 24 June, however, Bodelschwingh was obliged to resign and, in the elections to the Church synod of 23 July, the German Christians used the Nazi propaganda machine to win a substantial majority, enabling them to make a bid for power in the Church. A military chaplain, Ludwig Müller, who was a personal acquaintance of Hitler's became Reich Bishop and a group of young German Christians were appointed to posts as state bishops and high Church functionaries.

Meanwhile, however, a reaction had set in based on a defence of the Protestant 'Confession'. The more extreme wing of the German Christians wished to downgrade the Old Testament or remove it altogether from religious practice as a 'Jewish book'. At a German Christian rally in the Berlin Sports Palace on 13 November 1933, a speaker denounced 'its Jewish morality of rewards, and its stories of cattle dealers and concubines' and insisted that Christ should be presented heroically not as the broken figure of the Crucifixion to demonstrate that 'the completion of the Reformation of Martin Luther means the final victory of the nordic spirit over oriental materialism'.[128] The theology and activities of the German Christians provoked an essentially conservative response from a substantial section of the Protestant Church led by the Swiss theologian, Karl Barth. His treatise 'Theological Existence Today', in which he took issue with the new developments in the name of Lutheran orthodoxy, had sold 30,000 copies by the end of 1933. And a group of pastors, led by Martin Niemöller, the pastor of the Berlin suburb of Dahlem, joined together to form the 'Pastors' Emergency League' (*Pfarrernotbund*) with which to resist the German Christians and defend orthodox Lutheranism. The official German Christian-dominated Church authorities tried to crack down on the opposition, reprimanding pastors and even having them arrested. In the

---

[128] See J. Conway, *The Nazi Persecution of the Churches 1933–45* (London 1968) pp. 52–3.

Autumn of 1934, two politically conservative and orthodox Lutheran state bishops, Hans Meiser of Bavaria and Theophil Wurm of Württemberg, were arrested. The result was mass demonstrations by the Protestant faithful in defence of their bishops. A circular sent to pastors on 24 September commented on the remarkable events in the Protestant part of northern Bavaria, a Nazi heartland until this event:

452

We witnessed a miracle here in Nuremberg. There was enormous commotion going on in the town, at its strongest on the Wednesday. We only gave out hand notices at twelve o'clock and in the evening sixteen churches were full to bursting. Similar favourable news is coming in everywhere from the preaching trips which our brethren are carrying out throughout the Franconian countryside. Everywhere, often at the most inconvenient times, churches are full. The Gunzenhausen meeting was one single exultant profession of faith in Meiser by thousands of Franconian peasants.

These developments led to a formal schism. On 21 October 1934, the members of the Pastors' Emergency League formally rejected the Reich Church and created their own 'Confessional Church' government in a declaration proclaimed in Dahlem Parish Church:

453

1. We declare that the Constitution of the German Evangelical Church has been destroyed. Its legally constituted organs no longer exist. The men who have seized the Church leadership in the Reich and the states have divorced themselves from the Christian Church.
2. In virtue of the right of Churches, religious communities and holders of ecclesiastical office, bound by scripture and confession, to act in an emergency, the Confessional Synod of the German Evangelical Church establishes new organs of leadership. It appoints as leader and representative of the German Evangelical Church, as an association of confessionally determined Churches, the Fraternal Council of the German Evangelical Church and from among it the Council of the German Evangelical Church to the management leadership. Both organs are composed and organized in accordance with the confessions.
3. We summon the Christian communities, their pastors and elders, to accept no directives from the present Church Government and its authorities and to decline cooperation with those who wish to remain obedient to this ecclesiastical governance. We summon them to observe the directives of the Confessional Synod of the German Evangelical Church and its recognized organs.

Meanwhile, Hitler had become concerned about the dissension which the 'Church struggle' was causing and decided to drop the attempt to control the Church directly through Reich Bishop Müller and official support for the German Christians. Meiser and Wurm were reinstated and the German Christian domination was replaced by that of cautious, fairly orthodox bishops and Church officials. Thus, the Protestant Church was divided into three groups: the German Christians, declining in importance, the Confessional Church, which had strong support in some parishes but was subject to harassment from Church and State authorities, and the official Church establishment which cooperated with the regime while trying to maintain the remnants of Church autonomy.

After 1934, the main problem for the Protestant Church was not direct persecution but various pressures designed to impede its activities, notably the attempt to exclude it from influencing youth through such actions as the abolition of the confessional schools and the activities of the Hitler Youth.

A report on Protestant Church visitations in largely rural parts of Bavaria during 1937–38 indicates some of the problems facing the Church in an area in which the Protestant faith tended to be particularly strong because of rivalry with the much more numerous Catholics:

454

The conditions of the period 1936–39 have had more of an impact on the inner life of the individual parish than even the years 1932–35. Whereas the major struggles within the Church were not apparent to everyone in the majority of the Bavarian village parishes, now the decisions are having an impact even in the smallest village. People keep emphasizing how the situation in general and in respect of the Church in particular has changed, especially during the last four years, and that this phase represents a much bigger test for Church life than even the eventful year of 1934. Above all, the year 1938 seems to have brought a series of difficulties which have a negative impact on the general attitude of the parish. A dean felt obliged to sum up his impressions at the time of the Visitation in the Spring of 1939 as follows: 'The general impression was heavily determined by the catastrophic changes in the school sphere and in that of religious instruction'. . . The work of the pastors has become much more difficult than before and places increased demands on character and pastoral wisdom.

The problem of the German Christians is already a matter of history as far as the general situation is concerned. A few German Christian clergy have returned to the Confession. Others must at least restrain themselves in their own parishes in order to maintain their position at all . . .

The last few years are much more characterized by the fact that after the defensive victory against the German Christians, they find themselves confronted by a new enemy, who is difficult to get to grips with and yet is clearly fighting everywhere against Christianity. . .

The danger which threatens our parishes is of being ground down, of becoming dispirited, atrophied. The vast majority of the parishes will not be voluntarily unfaithful to their Christian beliefs, but they continue to believe that 'one cannot do anything' against the new forces and give up. People do not forget so easily any more, but they also do not dare to act so easily. The lack of concern shown by the churches and pastors in some parishes has suddenly swung round to become a certain disheartenment. The school question has had a particularly deep impact in many parishes: they have felt the dangers instinctively but believe they are faced with an 'inevitable' development.

In a number of reports from various districts the Church question appears in village parishes as a partial aspect of the internal transformation of peasant life. The flight from the land, overwork, child poverty produce a serious shortage of labour. Overwork also oppresses the peasant population mentally and makes them tired and resigned even for Church matters. People sense in the new conditions and the spiritual transformation of the village, the disappearance of familiar ways of life and customs, old traditions decay and the internal unity of the village disintegrates. Church and school separate from one another. The pastor's house and the teacher's house become the visible embodiments of two worlds where a few years ago there was unity. People see the crisis even if they do not all grasp it intellectually. But they feel too weak to hold up this new development . . .

The situation becomes difficult when villages with a peasant population come under the influence of large cities . . . Despite all these differences [between areas], however, there are the same difficulties which, fundamentally at least, affect all Church districts: the trend towards a slight reduction in Church-going and participation in Communion, the prevention of young people, and often the men too, from taking part in parish life because of other events, the putting of obstacles in the way of religious instruction, anti-Christian influence and clandestine pressure on certain groups to keep a low profile vis-à-vis the Church.

In many areas the events put on by the State youth organization take less and less account of the Parish Church services and what would have been inconceivable in 1935 has become the norm in some places in 1939. Above all, youth is losing the habit of going to Church regularly. One need not fear that the village youth will be influenced by the German Faith Movement[129] but rather will lose the habit of going to Church through being intentionally kept from Church services which will be followed by an inner estrangement.

The conscious renunciation of the Christian Church mainly involves small groups. However, the reserved attitude of the men, who out of consideration or fear outwardly stay away from the Church, is making itself noticeable to a marked extent. The real problem, however, is—as with youth—the timing of services and bible hours imposed by the various events. Also, the fact that the peasants are overworked has a negative effect. This slackening of Christian custom and discipline should not be underestimated particularly as it affects the family men . . .

The problem of youth and its religious instruction . . . is the focus of many discussions at visitations. The problems involve all age groups of the young . . .

As far as the younger ones are concerned, school is the central problem. While at the time of the visitation in 1936 the confessional school was still in existence, the questionnaire for 1939 reports on the community school, the reduction in religious

---

[129] An anti-Christian nordic cult movement associated with the philosphy of Alfred Rosenberg.

instruction, the obstruction of such instruction for technical college pupils, the giving up of religious instruction on the part of most teachers. The removal of religious instruction from the core curriculum . . .

The consequences which the separation of the teaching profession from the Church have had for the villages have been referred to above. The young teachers, in particular some of whom come from their training colleges with German Faith ideas, represent a foreign body in the villages, which produces quite a bit of unrest and division. However one should not forget the teachers who still faithfully carry out religious instruction and have a very beneficial effect . . .

In the future, it will be a matter of life and death for the Church how far parents can provide children with a Christian education and instruction . . .

Church-going is normally satisfactory. Of the 200 reports 2/3 describe church-going as good, 2/9 as moderate, and 1/9 as poor and unsatisfactory. However, in contrast to this subjective assessment, it must be said that in comparison with the situation in 1932 a moderate reduction in church-going is the general rule even in village and small town parishes. A small group of people have been inwardly alienated from the Church in the last few years, certain sections remain 'neutral' through timidity, many are prevented by lack of time, young people are being alienated from the Church and its services by obstacles being put in their way and by mental conditioning. Several deacons complain that a reduction in Church-going as in the whole of Church life had occurred, particularly in 1938 . . .

The Catholic Church was in a stronger position in Germany because it was more united and also more cosmopolitan. In 1933 it had decided to come to terms with the new regime in a Concordat along the lines of that with Fascist Italy.[130] The history of relations between the regime and the Catholic Church during 1933–1939 is the history of the attempt by the Church to assert the privileges granted to it by the Concordat and the attempt by the regime to erode them. On 13 December 1936, the Bavarian bishops had expressed their disillusionment with the Government in a pastoral letter which, however also indicates areas of agreement:

455

After the deplorable fight carried on by Marxists, Communists, Free Thinkers and Freemasons against Christianity and the Church we welcomed with gratitude the National Socialist profession of positive Christianity. We are convinced that many hundreds of thousands are still loyal to this profession of faith and, indeed, we observe with sorrow how others tend to remove themselves from Christian belief and from the programme of the Führer, and by this means put the Third Reich on a new basis, a *Weltanschauung* standing in open contradiction to the commandments of Christianity. This formation of National Socialism into a *Weltanschauung* which cuts

---

[130] See above, p. 166.

it away from any foundation in religion is developing more and more into a full-scale attack on the Christian faith and the Catholic Church. All this bodes ill for the future of our people and our fatherland. Our Führer and Chancellor in a most impressive demonstration acknowledged the importance of the two Christian confessions to State and society, and promised the two confessions his protection.[131] Unfortunately, men with considerable influence and power are operating in direct opposition to those promises and both confessions are being systematically attacked. Certain of those who lead the attack on the Churches wish to promote a united church in which the confession of faith will become meaningless. Most especially they seek to rid Germany of the Catholic Church and declare it to be a body foreign to our country and its people. These folk lack all real understanding of our holy faith and of the Christian religion in any form.

In 1933 a Concordat was signed between the Holy Father and the German Reich. This was done, as is said in the preamble, out of a 'common desire to consolidate and enhance the friendly relations existing between the Holy See and the German State'. But instead of the much wished-for friendship, there has developed an ever-growing struggle against the Papacy, a struggle carried out in writings and speeches, in books and study courses, in organizations, schools and camps. A hate for 'Rome' has been engendered even in the ears of children. . . . Under the Concordat, Catholic organizations and societies were promised protection for their continued existence. But instead of this continued protection, the exact reverse has taken place until by gradual means the continuation of these organizations has been made impossible. . . . According to the Concordat, insults to the clergy were to be punished. But where is the protection against the kind of insults which come in speeches, writings, broadsheets and pictures? Where is the State protection of the honour of clergy when it comes to cartoons and posters which are set before the eyes of children even in the remotest villages? It has been reported to us that an anticlerical cartoon was exhibited in a class-room. When the parish priest urged the teacher to remove it, he refused. . . .

Nothing could be further from our intentions than to adopt a hostile attitude toward, or a renunciation of, the present form taken by our Government. For us, respect for authority, love of Fatherland, and the fulfilment of our duty to the State are matters not only of conscience but of divine ordinance. This command we will always require our faithful to follow. But we will never regard as an infringement of this duty our defence of God's laws and of His Church, or of ourselves against attacks on the Faith and the Church. The Führer can be certain that we Bishops are prepared to give all moral support to his historic struggle against Bolshevism. We will not criticize things which are purely political. What we do ask is that our holy Church be permitted to enjoy her God-given rights and her freedom.

As with the Protestant Church, a particular bone of contention was influence over youth. The replacement of the traditional confessional schools, in which Protestant and Catholic children were taught separately by 'community schools' where they only received separate religious in-

---

[131] A reference to Hitler's speech in the Reichstag at the time of the passage of the Enabling Law on 23 March 1933. See above, pp. 156–70.

struction, which was also downgraded as a subject, was a serious blow. Nevertheless, the attempt by the Nazi authorities to remove crucifixes from Catholic schools in Oldenburg in November 1936, which produced such a storm of protest that they had to back down and replace them, demonstrated that there were limits which the regime could not afford to overstep in its policy over religion. The loyalty of Catholics to their Church remained very strong, particularly in rural areas such as Bavaria and southern Oldenburg. This is clear from the following monthly report of the district police in Ebermannstadt in northern Bavaria dated 29 June 1939:

456

The uncertainty of the diplomatic situation, the harsh taxation, certain economic difficulties, in particular, however, the pressure against the Church are at the moment producing increasing apathy among the rural population as far as nationalist issues are concerned. The Catholic Church is reaping the profit from these burdens. The more attempts are made to keep a watch on the Church or such attempts are even suspected, the more the peasantry support their priests. Catholic church-going, participation in various events such as processions, the blessing of the fields, pilgrimages, attendance at services during weekdays, and confession remain strong. For the time being the Party's propaganda is helpless in trying to resist this development. The mood is directed less against the State and much more against the Party. There are many peasants who make no bones about publicly declaring that their attitude to the Party is dependent on the Party's measures towards the Church. The question of the attitude adopted towards these ideological disputes by the Catholic priesthood cannot be definitely answered. Outwardly, the priests attempt not only to save their faces but also to do justice to national requirements; in purely confessional questions, however, they work all the harder behind the scenes to keep their parishes stubbornly to the faith. The influence of the Protestant clergy like the Church life of the Protestant parishes in general is much smaller. The relationship between the pastor and his flock is mostly very loose here and the circle of committed supporters mostly very small.

Finally, the attitude of the religious sects varied. The Jehovah's Witnesses, unlike the established churches, refused to compromise with the regime and gloried in their martyrdom in the concentration camps.

(b) Resistance from the Left

Between 1933 and 1939 the main resistance to the regime was mounted by organizations of the Left—the remnants of the Socialist and Communist parties and their offshoots which had been banned in 1933.[132] One of the

---

[132] The military-dominated conspiracy against the regime, which began in 1938–39, will be dealt with in Vol. 2.

major problems facing the resistance of the Left was precisely the fact that their forces were divided and at loggerheads. The Communists regarded the Social Democrats as 'Social Fascists' and the Socialists rejected the Moscow alignment and totalitarian aims of the Communists. Only in the concentration camps and occasionally at local level did a measure of cooperation and fraternity develop.

The Socialists and Free Trade Unions were unprepared for illegal activity and for the degree and effectiveness of Nazi terror. After the wave of arrests during 1933 had devastated the organization, there were divisions among the Socialists as to how to proceed, particularly between those in exile and those who remained in Germany. Soon, the remaining functionaries and members concentrated on trying to remain in loose contact with one another, forming small groups who engaged in innocuous occupations such as card-playing or hiking in order to have the opportunity to swop views and reinforce their Socialist faith through mutual encouragement. Illegal propaganda was restricted to a few local initiatives and the limited distribution of material provided by their emigré organization by means of frontier-based agencies. The Socialists had quickly come to the conclusion that active resistance would not seriously damage the regime and would be suicidal for those who took part. They would have to wait until the regime collapsed from its own internal contradictions or, more likely, was destroyed from outside. In the meantime, they must concentrate on ensuring that a cadre of dedicated Social Democrats survived to fill the vacuum left by the regime's collapse. The Gestapo summed up this policy in the following report:

457

... the expected change will come from outside. But preparations have to be made for this event so that past activities can be resumed in a pre-arranged form. This inner conviction and the wish of the SPD leaders that there should be no rigid organizations is reflected in the behaviour and solidarity of the country's illegal workers. After work they join each other over a glass of beer, meet former kindred spirits near their homes, or keep in touch by means of family visits; they avoid all forms of organizations, and seek in the manner described to help their friends remain steadfast. During these meetings, of course, there is talk about the political situation and news is exchanged. They promote energetically the so-called whispering campaign which, for the time being, represents the most effective illegal work against the State, against its institutions and activities, and against the Party. The main subjects of discussion are price increases, low wages, economic exploitation of the people, freedom, shortage of raw materials, corruption, nepotism, gifts at the nation's expense and so on. Since many former SPD and trade union officials are now commercial representatives and travelling salesmen, such catchwords will spread comparatively quickly into the furthest parts of the Reich. Despite the extent of these subversive activities it has not yet been possible to catch a single one of these persons in the act and bring him to trial.

The Communist organization was also devastated by arrests during 1933, but they continued to try to carry out an active campaign of subversion with the result that successive waves of Communist activists found their way into prison and concentration camp. Of the approximately 300,000 members of the KPD in 1933 around 150,000 were affected by Nazi persecution and thousands of these were murdered. Unfortunately, however, there was little to show for this self-sacrifice. The Communists had assumed that the Nazi take-over was the death knell of capitalism and that one final push would destroy it. In fact, the regime was soon too well-entrenched for either Communist or Socialist resistance to have any effect. An SPD report from central Germany in February 1936 indicated one of the main problems:

458

The average worker is primarily interested in work and not in democracy. People who previously enthusiastically supported democracy show no interest at all in politics. One must be clear about the fact that in the first instance men are fathers of families and have jobs, and that for them politics take second place and even then only when they expect to get something out of it.

Many people reject participation in illegal activity on account of this basic attitude. They consider it pointless and that one only ends up in jail because of it. But that does not by any means imply that they are going over to the Nazis.

An important point—it even seems to me the crucial point for our policy—is the fact that our people are averse to any unpatriotic attitudes. While it is true that they are in favour of an international understanding they feel that in the first instance they are Germans. One cannot drive it out of them.

A report by the Gestapo office in Düsseldorf for the year 1937 gives an idea of the kind of resistance activities undertaken by the Communists and Socialists and indicates how well-informed the Gestapo were:

459

A. The Communist movement
During the first years after the take-over of power, until about 1936, the Communists tried to expand their party and its various subsidiary organizations. But later they saw clearly that they only endangered those members illegally active inside the country and made it easy for the police to break up the illegal organizations, particularly since the distribution route of a pamphlet could be followed and traced fairly easily. In the high treason trials carried out in recent years it has already been

noted that those engaged in illegal activities refused to distribute literature because of the danger involved in it. So this may have been one of the reasons that prompted the Central Committee of the Communist Party of Germany based in Paris under the leadership of the former Communist Reichstag deputy, Wilhelm Pieck, to publish new guidelines for illegal activity in Germany at the beginning of 1937. Whereas until 1936 the main propaganda emphasis was on distributing lots of pamphlets, at the beginning of 1936 they switched to propaganda by word of mouth setting up bases in factories and advocated the so-called Popular Front on the French pattern....

It became apparent that the Communist propaganda described above was already having some success in various factories. After factory meetings at which speakers of the Labour Front had spoken, some of whom were in fact rather clumsy in their statements, the mood of discontent among the workers was apparent in subsequent discussions. In one fairly large factory the speaker from the Labour Front greeted the workers with the German [Nazi] salute: but in reply the workers only mumbled. When the speaker ended the factory parade with the German salute, it was returned loudly and clearly, but they made it clear that they had only used the German salute because it brought the factory parade to an end. The shifting about of workers within the various factories, necessitated by the scarceness of raw materials, creates more fertile soil for the subversion of the workers by the KPD. Furthermore, the transfer of workers who were shortly due for leave to a different factory with the result that the leave due to them was cancelled contributes to the discontent of the workers. The Christmas bonuses produced more discontent among the workers. Some factories paid Christmas bonuses to their workers with the result that workers from other factories who received nothing were annoyed. Here too a uniform method would help to remove fertile soil for KPD propaganda.

The 'Rote Hilfe' ['Red Aid] must be regarded by now as the only subsidiary organization of the KPD still in existence. Political prisoners and their families are still supported by the Rote Hilfe to a considerable extent. It has been noted that money collections and food parcels have arrived at the relevant departments of the courts, the senders of which could not be traced. Grocery parcels have also been sent from Holland to families of political prisoners by the Communist Party. These parcels are sometimes handed over to the State police by the recipients and transferred to the NSV....

C. Social Democratic Party

In the period covered by the report the SPD has worked mainly by means of the dissemination of news. The information that reaches the leadership of the illegal SPD from their news service in Germany is collected there and distributed as information material in Gothic type. The information material that is smuggled into Germany is produced in postcard size editions in small print. The articles appearing in these information leaflets are biased criticisms of Government measures. They are sent only to reliable old SPD people....

Apart from this, the illegal activity of the SPD is the same as that outlined in the newly published guidelines for the conspiratorial work of the KPD: the setting up of cells in factories, sports clubs and other organizations. Since the former SPD members carry on propaganda only by word of mouth, it is very difficult to get hold of proof of their illegal activities which would be usable in court.

One thing, however, appears to be certain: Even if former members of the SPD and its subsidiary organizations have always more or less refused to form organizations, or to distribute leaflets in larger numbers etc., the solidarity among them appears even now to be extremely strong owing to the fact that most of them have known each other for years, if not decades. They are too clever and have been trained for too long to be proved guilty of illegal activity.

Before the take-over of power the works' councils consisted mainly of old officials of the SPD workers' movement. These people who were removed or dismissed from their functions in the factories have been largely accommodated in other factories. As old and trained officials, they are well known in the workers' movement and are well versed in the workers' fight against the employers over questions of wages, hours of work, etc.

It is often noticed that workers, instead of approaching the representatives of the Labour Front with wage questions, go instead to trained people who are known to them and ask them for their advice. Not infrequently these people have been re-elected to the works council. Then through their skilful propaganda they get their former comrades on to the works council and into leading positions in the factories. The illegal SPD leadership places the greatest emphasis on these people and relies on them to stand up for their former ideals at the right moment and to influence the workers by their own spirit.

On 10.xi.37 we succeeded in arresting a Dutch sailor called Gert Dooyes from Rotterdam. . . . Dooyes admits to having smuggled pamphlets into Germany for two Dutchmen who were members of the SPD centre in Amsterdam and to having passed them on to SPD officials in Duisburg and Oberhausen. Furthermore, Dooyes has confessed to importing nearly thirty food parcels into Germany by water between 1936 and his arrest in November 1937 and to passing these on to SPD functionaries who sent the parcels on to the families of political prisoners. . . . During the course of these investigations another thirty-four people were arrested who were under strong suspicion of working for the illegal SPD. . . .

The top brain and leading official in the SPD is the *émigré* Ernst Schumacher. He works in accordance with the instructions of the SPD leadership in Prague. At Schumacher's request reading circles were formed in Duisburg and Oberhausen in which the material referred to above was passed on from hand to hand. It was hoped to increase the number of supporters through these reading circles. The people who have been arrested also belonged to the news service described above. . . .

In 1938 we will have to devote particular attention to illegal activity in the factories. Trusted agents have been infiltrated into several big factories in my district who have already provided proof that the KPD and the SPD are carrying out conspiratorial work jointly. In one factory the KPD, KPO and SPD work hand in hand. In another factory the KPD is deviating from its prescribed rules and is forming a factory group according to previous guidelines of the RGO. Here too it is noticeable that no pamphlets whatsoever are distributed; information is only passed on orally.

(iv) Plebiscites and the Mobilization of Popular Acclaim

Because of the lack of a genuine public opinion the regime needed periodically to reassure both itself and foreign opinion that it had the whole-hearted support of the population. This was the function of the elections and plebiscites which were held from time to time. However, since it was basically unsure of itself, it felt it had to rig the tests of opinion to ensure that they appeared as demonstrations of acclamation for the regime. The SOPADE outlined the various mechanisms which had been used to ensure the success of the plebiscite of 18 August 1934 to confirm Hitler's assumption of the office of 'Führer and Reich Chancellor' after the death of Hindenburg:

460

1. *Before the Election.*
(a) The pressure of the ubiquitous propaganda: there was only the "Yes"; Hitler's portrait hanging from every window, every car; public loudspeakers to broadcast the speeches on the radio etc.
(b) The moral pressure: those who said 'No' were branded as traitors, rogues, saboteurs of national reconstruction.
2. *During the Voting.*
(a) The uniformed SA people and Party members in the polling stations created an atmosphere of terror in the polling room right from the start, which did not fail to have an effect even where terror was not directly used.
(b) In many cases there were no polling booths at all, in others it was made virtually impossible to enter them. Either the booth was put in a far corner, or SA men barred the way to it or there were posters to put people off (e.g. 'Every German votes publicly, who votes otherwise?' or 'Only traitors go in here').
(c) In various parts of the country the yes was already crossed on the ballot paper.
(d) Veterans of other associations were marched en bloc to the polls and had to vote in public.
(e) Voting by ineligible people was encouraged: in Munich one could vote 'on one's honour', in the Palatinate for friends and acquaintances. Members of labour camps were allowed to vote en bloc without their eligibility being checked.
3. *During the Counting.*
(a) The counting mostly took place only in the presence of SA and Party members.
(b) Invalid votes were simply counted as yes votes. Polling officers crossed the yes on empty ballot papers.
(c) No votes were replaced by yes votes 'in the requisite amount', sometimes in excessive enthusiasm even beyond that, so that in the end more votes were counted than there were people entitled to vote.
(d) The result announced was simply falsified (discovered in many small places where a number of SPD comrades had sworn to each other to vote no) or the result was simply not published.

These various method of pressurizing voters and falsifying the vote were employed to a very varied extent in particular parts of the country, not according to general instructions and a rigid scheme, but adapted to local possibilities and requirements. It is an experience of the last year and a half that terror does not occur everywhere to the same extent but in different ways in different places. In Hamburg at the beginning of fascist rule conditions were almost normal, whereas in Saxony the most fearful persecution was going on. This observation explains some of the big differences in the voting results. In the Palatinate, for example, 94.8% of all those eligible to vote voted yes, more than in any other electoral district. In the immediately adjacent district of Koblenz-Trier, which has essentially the same economic and denominational structure, on the other hand, the vote was only 82.4%. The result confirms what all reports from the Palatinate have noted, namely that their terror and falsification reached a record level evidently because the Gauleiter Bürckel, the new plenipotentiary for the Saar, needed a particularly good result, in view of the neighbouring Saar territory.

The following police report on the plebiscite of 10 April 1938 to approve the *Anschluß* with Austria confirms that a secret ballot did not exist at any rate in some parts of Germany:

461

Subject: Plebiscite of 10 April 1938
Copy of a schedule is attached herewith enumerating the persons who cast 'No' votes or invalid votes at Kappel, district of Simmern. The invalid votes are listed first, ending with —; thereafter come the 'No' votes.

The control was effected in the following way: some members of the election committee marked all the ballot papers with numbers. During the ballot itself, a voters' list was made up. The ballot papers were handed out in numerical order, therefore it was possible afterwards with the aid of this list to find out the persons who cast 'No' votes or invalid votes. One sample of these marked ballot papers is enclosed. The marking was done on the back of the ballot papers with skimmed milk.

The ballot cast by the Protestant parson Alfred Wolferts is also enclosed.

The identification of two persons was impossible because there are several persons of the same name in the village and it was impossible to ascertain the actual voter.

Although in one sense the process of depoliticization suited the regime by ensuring political passivity, at the same time it felt a continual need both to try and win popularity and confirm this popularity in its own eyes and in the eyes of the people through a constant stream of 'events', 'occasions', and 'successes'. In January 1938 an SPD contact man in Bavaria reported as follows:

462

It cannot be denied that the regime is lacking obvious political successes with which to influence public opinion such as, for example, the Saar plebiscite and the

Rhineland occupation. The current of criticism which can be observed now has lasted longer than all those hitherto. A propaganda 'victory' has been necessary for a long time. They have not had one and the National Socialists clearly feel this lack. However, the regime has by no means lost the means to maintain itself. It is already very evident that the regime has succeeded in replacing declining trust with respect for its police power. This respect is not only for the force of arms but also for the increasing organizational achievements. Mussolini's visit was a good example of this. There was no sympathy for Mussolini among the Munich population. Apart from compulsion, what drove people onto the streets was in the first instance curiosity. But it is interesting how people are then simply knocked out by the force of the occasions . . . One of our reporters has described this mood in the following apt sentence: 'People grumble, stand and marvel.' The drive which the Nazis put into their activities impresses people. And even if one has got used to many things and much has lost its pulling power, the Propaganda Ministry is skilled in always coming up with something new and great; it can always pull off successes.

After it had restored full employment, the regime sought such successes increasingly in the field of foreign affairs. At the same time, however, these successes and the plebiscites associated with them tended to produce diminishing returns as the SOPADE report for April/May 1938 pointed out:

463

In these reports we have often expressed the view that Hitler can count on the support of the majority of the people in two essential respects: (1) He has created work and (2) He has made Germany strong. The further the crisis recedes into the past the more the first point will lose its attraction and the more the dictatorship will have to rely on support for its foreign policy line. The regime simply could not let slip such a favourable opportunity as the annexation of Austria for a general attempt to justify its policy.

Undoubtedly the great majority of the German people was prepared to approve the question posed in the plebiscite about the 'Reunification of Austria with the German Reich'. But the dictatorship cannot rest content with a majority, not even with a large majority. After the result of the last plebiscite was announced as 98.8 per cent, this time it could not be any less; it had to be more. The dictatorship feels itself to be so weak that it could not bear it if it was only 97 per cent. Thus the dictatorship becomes a prisoner of its own methods. It could not dispense with the propaganda excesses, terror, and fraud which it employed in previous 'elections'. It had to attempt to outdo even these excesses. It is part of the conditions of life of this dictatorship that it has to keep running flat out and that it cannot afford any loss of tempo.

The plebiscite of 10 April shows clearly how the methods which the dictatorship has to keep employing lose their impact. To have won eighty per cent in a free vote for the Anschluß of Austria could have been a tremendous demonstration of trust for the dictatorship. To have achieved 99 per cent with the full power of the regime is only a demonstration of the fact that its power is still crushing. Eighty per cent would have made a strong impression on the regime's opponents, 99 per cent cannot even be taken seriously by its supporters. The regime's propaganda no longer supports its policies; it already devalues them.

As the threat of war increased, so it became increasingly clear that, while the Nazis had succeeded both in creating a docile population and in marginally increasing nationalist and militarist tendencies among this population, particularly the young, it had failed in its attempt to create a 'militarized national community' ready and eager for war. The following reports by the Army's Economic Staff at the time of the Munich crisis indicate that there was no enthusiasm whatever for a war to gain the Sudetenland or Czechoslovakia.

The monthly report of the Military Economic Inspectorate VII/Munich of 9 September 1938 stated:

464

... There is full employment right down the line and, what is more, rising wages which are welcome on social grounds but economically dubious. The theatres are fully booked, the cinemas full, and the cafés are overflowing into the early hours with music and dancing; there are record numbers of outings on Sundays. And yet despite all these signs of a favourable economic situation the mood among large numbers of people is not one appropriate to a boom. It is in many cases depressed about the future ...
There is serious concern among the broadest sections of the nation that a war will sooner or later put an end to the economic revival and have terrible consequences for Germany. Members of the older generation, including those among the working class, are reminded of the obvious comparison with the period before the war. At that time, everything was going fine economically: production, foreign trade, consumption, savings deposits—everywhere things were going onwards and upwards ... until finally, in August 1914 the fearful catastrophe broke over Germany ...

A composite report of the Military Economic Inspectorates dated 1 October 1938 pointed out;

465

There is no enthusiasm for military entanglements on account of the Sudeten German question. The uncertainty of the political situation is making the population depressed. Nobody wants to contemplate a war with England and France. The education of the whole nation in the tasks required by a total war with all its burdens of various kinds is by no means adequate.

The mood is in many cases depressed, mainly on account of the serious concern that sooner or later a war would put an end to the economic boom and would end in disaster for Germany.

In view of the diplomatic situation and the prospects for war which are often discussed without inhibition the mood can generally be described as depressed, serious and worried; there is a 'general war psychosis'.

A month later they reported on reactions to the Munich crisis:

466

There was great tension and concern everywhere and people expressed the wish that there should be no war. This was put particularly firmly by the front-line fighters of the World War. . . . Listening in to foreign broadcasts has produced confusion and fickleness on the part of the great mass of the politically uneducated. Political indoctrination and education, particularly to prepare people for war, is still completely inadequate. Only very few of the lower-ranking Party leaders at present in office have achieved success with this education. One can only regard it as an almost total failure.

This final sentence is a remarkable declaration of the bankruptcy of the regime's attempt to mobilize the German nation for war, the key objective of its domestic political strategy, which in turn was to provide the basis for its central goals in the fields of foreign policy and war. Nevertheless, the regime had secured a kind of passive acceptance for its policies, a sense of resignation in the face of the outbreak of war, a mood of what one historian who lived through the period, Helmut Krausnick, has described as 'reluctant loyalty'.

List of Sources for Part II

137. a) P. Diehl-Thiele, *Partei und Staat im Dritten Reich* (Munich 1969) p.246.
   b) *The Memoirs of Ernst von Weizsäcker* (London 1951) pp.164–5.
138. E.R. Huber, *Verfassungsrecht des Grossdeutschen Reiches* (Hamburg 1939) p.142.
139. H. Frank, *Im Angesicht des Galgens* (Neuhaus bei Schliersee 1955) pp.466–7.
140. Ibid. pp.122-3.
141. Bundesarchiv Koblenz (BAK) NS 10/550.
142. Otto Dietrich, *12 Jahre mit Hitler* (Munich 1955) pp.127–132.
143. Krogmann Tagebuch 1.11.1937 Hamburger Staats und Parteipolitik 1937. Forschungsstelle für die Geschichte des Nationalsozialismus, Hamburg.
144. Niedersächsiches Staatsarchiv Oldenburg 131 I-3-22A
145. F Wiedemann, *Der Mann der Feldherr werden wollte* (Kettwig 1965) pp.69–70, 77, 90.
146. Killy Vernehmung BAK Kleine Erwerbung 234-3.
147. *Freude und Arbeit* November 1938 BAK R 43 II/ 1036.
148. Kritzinger Vernehmung BAK Kleine Erwerbung.
149. Killy Vernehmung op. cit.
150. BAK R 43 II/143.
151. *Reichsgesetzblatt* (RGBl. I) (1933) p.175.
152. H. Mommsen, *Beamtentum im Dritten Reich* (Stuttgart 1966) pp.160ff.
153. Ibid. pp.171–3.
154. Ibid. pp.138–142.
155. Ibid. pp.146ff.
156. RGBl. I (1933) p.1016.
157. Hans-Adolf Jacobson und Werner Jochmann (eds.), *Ausgewählte Dokumente zur Geschichte des Nationalsozialismus 1933–1945* (Bielefeld 1961), Bd.II.
158. *Deutsche Verwaltung* November 1934 p.325.
159. N.H. Baynes, (ed.) *The Speeches of Adolf Hitler 1922–1939* (Oxford 1942) Vol. I, pp.449–51.
160. *Deutschland-Berichte der Sozialdemokratische Partei Deutschlands 1934–1940 (SOPADE Berichte)* (Frankfurt 1979) 1935 p.764.
161. Nuremberg Trial document (ND) 138-D.
162. RGBl. I (1935) p.1203.
163. BAK NS 6/217.
164. a) BAK Slg. Schumacher 368.
   b) Ibid.

165. W. Sommer, 'Partei und Staat' in *Deutsche Juristenzeitung* 19.5 1936 BAK R2/31095.
166. BAK NS 10/25.
167. BAK R 43 II/707a.
168. BAK NS 22/713.
169. BAK R 43 II/1345.
170. RGBl. I (1934) p.75.
171. BAK R 43 II/1376.
172. M. Broszat, *Der Staat Hitlers* (Stuttgart 1969) p.153.
173. BAK R 43 II/494.
174. F. Heyen, *Nationalsozialismus im Alltag: Quellen zur Geschichte des Nationalsozialismus vornehmlich im Raum Main-Koblenz-Trier* (Boppard am Rhein 1967) pp.263ff.
175. W. Runge & W. Schumann (eds.), *Dokumente zur deutschen Politik* 1933-35 op. cit. pp.118-9.
176. Gregor Strasser, *Kampf um Deutschland* (Munich 1932) pp.347-8, 357-8.
177. *Documents on German Foreign Policy* (DGFP) Series C, vol. I, p.35.
178. H. von Kotze & H. Krausnick (eds.), *"Es spricht der Führer. 7 exemplarische Hitler-Reden* (Gütersloh 1966) pp.200-202.
179. ND 436-EC.
180. Ibid.
181. Bundesarchiv-Militärarchiv, Freiburg Wi/F 5/406.
182. DGFP, Series C, vol. III pp.344ff.
183. DGFP, Series C, vol. III pp.356ff.
184. ND 611-EC.
185. DGFP, Series C, vol V, No. 490 (modified translation).
186. ND 46-EC.
187. Ibid.
188. D. Petzina, *Autarkiepolitick im Dritten Reich: Der nationalsozialistische Vierjahresplan* (Stuttgart 1968) p.182.
189. SOPADE-Berichte 1938 pp.799-805.
190. SOPADE-Berichte 1939 p.950.
191. Ibid. p.951-2.
192. B.A. Carroll, *Design for Total War: Arms and Economics in the Third Reich* (The Hague/Paris 1968) p.188.
193. Ibid. p.184.
194. *Statistisches Handbuch von Deutschland 1928-1944* (Munich 1949) pp.392-4
195. *Ursachen und Folgen: Vom Deutschen Zusammenbruch 1918 und 1945 bis zur staatlichen Neuordnung Deutschlands in der Gegenwart*, ed. H. Michaelis *et al.* (Berlin, undated Vol. ix) p.666.
196. H.Uhlig, *Die Warenhäuser im Dritten Reich* (Cologne 1956) p.105.
197. Ibid. p.111.
198. Ibid. p.128.
199. *SOPADE-Berichte* 1939 p.877.
200. A.von Saldern, *Mittelstand im Dritten Reich* (Frankfurt 1979) p.279.
201. W. Abelshauser & A. Faust, *Wirtschafts-und Sozialpolitik: Eine nationalsozialistische Sozialrevolution?* (Nationalsozialismus im Unterricht. Studieneinheit 4. Deutsches Institut für Fernstudien an der Universität Tübingen 1983).
202. R. Neebe, *Grossindustrie, Staat und NSDAP 1930-1933* (Göttingen 1981) pp.181-2.
203. RGBl. I (1934) p.185.
204. Ibid. pp.1194ff.
205. W. Runge & W. Schumann (eds.) *Dokumente zur Deutschen Geschichte 1936-39* (Frankfurt 1973) pp.46-7.
206. Ibid p.82.

207. Ibid. p.141.
208. Ibid. p.59.
209. RGBl. I (1933) p.392.
210. M.Broszat & E. Fröhlich, (eds.) *Bayern im Dritten Reich* Bd.I (Munich/Vienna 1978) p.343–344.
211. *SOPADE-Berichte* 1934 p.232.
212. Ibid. p.737.
213. Ibid. 1937 p.1104.
214. D. Petzina, *Autarkiepolitik* op. cit., p.95.
215. SOPADE-Berichte 1939 p.955.
216. *Statistisches Jahrbuch* 1939/40 p.585.
217. A. Hanau & R. Plate, *Die deutsche landwirtschaftliche Preis und Marktpolitik im Zweiten Weltkrieg* (Stuttgart 1974) p.24.
218. T. W. Mason, *Arbeiterklasse und Volksgemeinschaft* (Opladen 1975), p.154.
219. *Ursachen und Folgen* op. cit. Bd. IX pp.430-1.
220. ND-2283-PS
221. *Dokumente der Deutschen Politik* Bd.I ed. P. Meier-Benneckenstein (Berlin 1939/40) pp.151–3.
222. *Völkischer Beobachter* 5.v.1933.
223. RGBl. I (1933) p.45.
224. BAK R 43 II/532.
225. *Dokumente der Deutschen Politik* op. cit. Bd. V pp.366–9.
226. M. Broszat, *Der Staat Hitlers* (Munich 1969) p.192.
227. RGBl. I (1934) pp.45ff.
228. ND 1814-PS.
229. *Fundamente des Sieges: Des Gesamtarbeit der deutschen Arbeitsfront von 1933 bis 1940*, ed. Otto Marrenbach (Berlin 1941) p.325.
230. Ibid. pp.334–5.
231. Ibid. p.350.
232. Ibid. p.355.
233. G. Starcke, *Die Deutsche Arbeitsfront* (Berlin 1940) p.124.
234. Ibid. p.143.
235. Willy Müller, *Das soziale Leben im neuen Deutschland* (Berlin 1938) pp.189–190.
236. *SOPADE Berichte* 1938 p.175.
237. Ibid. 1939 p.474.
238. Ibid. 1938 p.172.
239. Ibid. 1939 p.472.
240. Ibid. 1939 pp.488–489.
241. N.H. Baynes, (ed.) *The Speeches of Adolf Hitler 1922–1939* (Oxford 1942) vol. I, pp.893–4.
242. *SOPADE-Berichte* 1938. pp.480–1.
243. Ibid. pp.481–2.
244. A. Barkai, *Das Wirtschaftssystem des Nationalsozialismus. Der historische und ideologischer Hintergrund 1933–1936* (Cologne 1977) p.181.
245. *SOPADE-Berichte* 1934 p.22.
246. Ibid. p.129.
247. Ibid.
248. *Dokumente der deutschen Politik* op. cit. Bd. V p. 355; *Statistisches Handbuch von Deutschland 1928–1944* (Munich 1949) p.484.
249. Mason, *Arbeiterklasse* op. cit. pp.198-203.
250. *Fundamente des Sieges* op. cit. p.326.
251. Mason, *Arbeiterklasse* op. cit. p.479.
252. Ibid. pp.624.

253. Ibid. pp.463–464.
254. Ibid. p.453.
255. Ibid. pp.779-780.
256. H-E. Volkmann, 'Die NS-Wirtschaft in Vorbereitung des Krieges' in W. Deist *et. al.*, *Das Deutsche Reich und der Zweite Weltkrieg* Bd. I *Ursachen und Voraussetzungen der deutschen Kriegspolitik* (Stuttgart 1979) p.297.
257. *SOPADE-Berichte* 1939 p.46.
258. Mason, *Arbeiterklasse* op. cit. pp.669–670.
259. Ibid. pp.847ff.
260. *SOPADE-Berichte* 1938 p.981-2.
261. Ibid. 1936 p.482.
262. Ibid. p.568.
263. Ibid. 1938 p.980–981.
264. W. Hofer (ed.) *Der Nationalsozialismus: Dokumente 1933-1945* (Frankfurt/M 1957) p.82.
265. J. Sywottek, *Mobilmachung für den totalen Krieg. Die propagandistische Vorbereitung der deutschen Bevölkerung auf den Zweiten Weltkrieg* (Opladen 1976) p.21.
266. *Dokumente der deutschen Politik* op. cit. Bd. I pp.289ff.
267. H. Heiber (ed.) *Goebbels Reden Bd. I 1932-1939* (Düsseldorf 1971) p.90.
268. A Diller, *Rundfunkpolitik im Dritten Reich* (Munich 1980) p.89.
269. J. Klepper, *Unter den Schatten deiner Flügel. Aus den Tagebüchern der Jahre 1932-1942* (Stuttgart 1956) pp.46, 59–60, 65.
270. H. Heiber (ed.) *Goebbels Reden* op. cit. pp.87, 91, 94–5.
271. D. Rebentisch and A. Raab, Neu-Isenburg op. cit. p.110.
272. RGBl. I (1933) p.713.
273. O.J. Hale, *The Captive Press in the Third Reich* (Princeton, NJ 1973) pp. 154–7.
274. J. Wulf, *Press und Funk im Dritten Reich* (Gütersloh 1964) *p.*79.
275. See f.n. 266.
276. J. Wulf, *Presse und Funk* op. cit. pp.87ff.
277. W. Runge & W. Schumann (eds.) *Dokumente zur Deutschen Geschichte 1936–39* op. cit. pp.76–8.
278. J. Wulf (ed.) *Presse und Funk* op. cit. p.111.
279. Ibid. p.146.
280. RGBl. I (1933) p.661.
281. N.H. Baynes, (ed.), *The Speeches of Adolf Hitler* op. cit. pp.589–92.
282. Louis P. Lochner, (ed.) *The Goebbels Diaries 1942-3* (Washington D.C. 1948), pp.177–80.
283. H. Brenner, *Die Kunstpolitik des Nationalsozialismus* (Hamburg 1963) p.186.
284. D. Aigner, *Die Indizierung "schädlichen und unerwünschten Schrifttums" im Dritten Reich* (Frankfurt 1971). Sonderdruck aus dem Archiv für Geschichte des Buchwesens XI p.1026.
285. H. Brenner, *Die Kunstpolitik* op. cit. p.183.
286. D. Aigner, *Die Indizierung* op. cit. pp.992ff.
287. W. Runge & W. Schumann (eds.) *Dokumente 1936–39* op. cit. p.28.
288. *Dokumente der Deutschen Politik* Bd. I op. cit. pp.296ff
289. Ibid.
290. E. Fröhlich, 'Die Kulturpolitische Pressekonferenz des Reichspropagandaministeriums' in *Vierteljahrshefte für Zeitgeschichte* 22.4.1974 p.357.
291. D. Rebentisch & A. Raab, *Neu-Isenburg* op. cit. p.110.
292. E.K. Bramstedt, *Goebbels and National Socialist Propaganda 1925–1945* (East Lansing, Mich. 1965) pp.217–18.
293. D. Rebentisch & A. Raab, *Neu-Isenburg* op. cit. p.123.
294. Ibid. p.124.
295. Ibid. p.123–4.

296. *Völkischer Beobachter* 15.IX.1935.
297. A. Klönne, *Jugend im Dritten Reich. Die Hitler-Jugend und ihre Gegner* (Düsseldorf 1982) p.80.
298. F.J. Heyen (ed.) *Nationalsozialismus im Alltag* op. cit. p.213.
299. RGBl. I (1936) p.993.
300. A. Klönne, *Jugend im Dritten Reich* op. cit. p.35.
301. ND 2435-PS.
302. F. J. Heyen, op. cit. p.690.
303. Ibid. pp.228–9.
304. M. Maschmann, *Account Rendered* (London 1964) pp.35–6.
305. ND 2436-PS.
306. a) SOPADE-Bericht 1934 p.117-118.
    b) Ibid.
307. A. Klönne, *Jugend im Dritten Reich* op. cit. pp.136–7.
308. ibid. pp.138–139.
309. M. Broszat *et al. Bayern in der NS-Zeit* op. cit. Bd. I pp.542–543.
310. Ibid. p.524.
311. R. Eilers, *Die nationalsozialistische Schulpolitik* (Cologne 1963) p.3.
312. W. Feiten, *Der nationalsozialistische Lehrerbund* (Weinheim & Basel 1981) p.177.
313. R. Eilers, *Die nationalsozialistische Schulpolitik* op. cit. p.118.
314. Ibid.
315. K-I. Flessau, *Schule der Diktatur. Lehrpläne und Schulbücher des Nationalsozialismus* (Frankfurt/M1982) pp.82ff.
316. a) W. Wuttke-Groneberg, *Medizin im Nationalsozialismus. Ein Arbeitsbuch* (Rottenburg 1982) p.20.
    b) K-I. Flessau, op. cit. p.198.
317. O.B. Roegele, 'Student im Dritten Reich' in *Die deutsche Universität im Dritten Reich* (Munich 1966) p.144.
318. *Dokumente der deutschen Politik* op. cit. pp.279ff.
319. O.B. Roegele, 'Student im Dritten Reich' op. cit. pp.154–5.
320. Ibid. p.159.
321. Ibid. pp.147–8.
322. R.C. Kelly, National Socialism and German University Teachers. Diss. University of Washington 1973 p.321.
323. Ibid. pp.360–361.
324. D. Sauberzweig, 'Die Hochschulen im Dritten Reich' Die Zeit 15.1.1961.
325. W. Hofer, *Der Nationalsozialismus.* op. cit. p.98.
326. *Frankfurter Zeitung* 9.ix.1934
327. RGBl. I (1933) pp.326–7.
328. D. Rebentisch & A. Raab, *Neu-Isenburg* op. cit. p.111.
329. D. Klinksiek, *Die Frau im NS-Staat* (Stuttgart 1982) p.158.
330. a) Ibid. p.69.
    b) Ibid.
    c) Ibid. p.84.
    d) Ibid. p.82.
331. A. Grafin zu Castell Rüdenhausen, "Nicht mitzuleiden, mitzukämpfen sind wir da!" Nationalsozialistische Volkswohlfahrt im Gau Westfalen-Nord in D. Peukert & J. Reulecke, *Die Reihen fast geschlossen, Beiträge zur Geschichte des Alltags unterm Nationalsozialismus* (Wuppertal 1981) p.234.
332. Ibid. p.235.
333. D. Rebentisch & A. Raab, *Neu-Isenburg* op. cit. pp.125–126.
334. RGBl. I (1933) p.529.
335. D. Klinksiek, *Die Frau im NS-Staat* op. cit. p.150.

336. Ibid. p.151.
337. Ibid. p.152.
338. RGBl. I (1937) p.24.
339. BAK R 43 II/427.
340. U. von Gersdorff, *Frauen im Kriegsdienst 1914-1945* (Stuttgart 1969) p.292.
341. RGBl. I (1938) p.807.
342. *Deutsche Reichsanzeiger und Preussische Staatsanzeiger* Nr. 157 vom 9.7.38.
343. B. Rüthers, *Die unbegrenzte Auslegung. Zum Wandel der Privatrechtsordnung im Nationalsozialismus* (Frankfurt 1973) p.119.
344. M. Domarus, *Hitler: Reden und Proklamationen 1932-1945* Bd.I (Würzburg 1962) pp.229ff.
345. *SOPADE-Bericht* 1938 p.527.
346. Ibid.
347. Ibid.
348. I. Staff (ed), *Justiz im Dritten Reich* (Frankfurt 1964) pp.69ff.
349. Ibid. p.140.
350. RGBl. I (1933) p.135.
351. P. Hüttenberger, 'Heimtückefälle vor dem Sondergericht München 1933-1939 'in M. Broszat *et al.* *Bayern in der NS-Zeit* Bd. IV (Munich-Vienna 1981) p.455.
352. SOPADE-Bericht 1938 pp.784-5.
353. RGBL. I (1934) pp.345ff.
354. *Documents on German Foreign Policy*, series C, vol. I, pp.113ff.
355. a) RGBl. I (1935), p.839.
     b) ND2549-PS.
356. B. Rüthers, *Die unbegrenzte Auslegung.* op. cit. p.176.
357. *Dokumente der deutschen Politik* op. cit. Bd. IV p.337.
358. SOPADE-Bericht 1934 p.671.
359. I. Staff, *Justiz im Dritten Reich* op. cit. pp.72ff.
360. a) H. Heiber (ed) *Reichsführer! Briefe an und von Himmler* (Stuttgart 1968) p.317.
     b) Ibid. p.75.
     c) Ibid. p.98.
361. J. Ackermann, *Heinrich Himmler als Ideologe* (Göttingen 1970) p.198.
362. B.F. Smith and A.E. Peterson, *Heinrich Himmler. Geheimreden 1933 bis 1945* (Frankfurt 1974) p.61.
363. ND 2284-PS.
364. B.F. Smith & A.E. Peterson, *Heinrich Himmler* op. cit. p.74.
365. Ibid. pp.61-2.
366. W. Runge & W. Schumann, *Dokumente zur deutschen Geschichte*, op. cit. *1936-1939* pp.124-5.
367. J. Ackermann, *Heinrich Himmler als Ideologe* op. cit. p.253f.
368. J. Conway, *The Nazi Persecution of the Churches 1933-1945* (London 1968) pp.153-4.
369. B.F. Smith & A.E. Peterson, *Heinrich Himmler* op. cit. pp.160-1.
370. *Schwarze Korps* 26.1.1939
371. S.Aronson, *Reinhard Heydrich und die Frühgeschichte von Gestapo und SD* (Stuttgart 1971) p.63.
372. Ibid. p.321.
373. ND 778-PS.
374. B.F. Smith & A.E. Peterson, *Heinrich Himmler* op. cit. *p.*111.
375. H.-A. Jacobsen & W. Jochmann, *Ausgewählte Dokumente* op. cit.
376. R. Diels, *Lucifer ante portas* (Stuttgart 1950) p.236.
377. S. Aronson, *Reinhard Heydrich* op. cit. p.218.
378. Ibid. pp.223-4.

379. Ibid.
380. ND 775-PS.
381. ND 2107-PS.
382. RGBl. I (1936) p.487.
383. *Dokumente zur deutschen Politik 1936–39* op. cit. pp.44–45.
384. S. Aronson, *Reinhard Heydrich* op. cit. p.199.
385. Ibid. p.196.
386. H. Michaelis *et al.* (eds.) *Ursachen und Folgen* op. cit. Bd. XI p.6.
387. *SOPADE-Berichte* 1937 p.677.
388. ND 84-D.
389. ND 1852-PS.
390. T. Mason, *Arbeiterklasse und Volksgemeinschaft* op. cit. pp.329–330.
391. H. Genschel, *Die Verdrängung der Juden aus der Wirtschaft im Dritten Reich* (Göttingen 1966) p.279.
392. Ibid. p.287.
393. ND 2709-PS.
394. *Völkischer Beobachter* 29.iii.1933.
395. R-M. Strecker (ed.) *Dr. Hans Globke. Aktenauszüge. Dokumente* (Hamburg undated) p.24.
396. Ibid. p.20.
397. Ibid. pp.27–28.
398. H. Genschel, *Die Verdrängung der Juden* op. cit. p.82.
399. *Ursachen und Folgen* op. cit. Bd. IX p.397.
400. Ibid. Bd. XI p.159.
401. M. Brozat et al. (eds.), *Bayern in der NS-Zeit* op. cit. Vol. I, p.450.
402. W. Runge & W. Schumann (eds.) *Dokumente zur Deutschen Politik 1933-1935* op. cit. p.116.
403. RGBl. I (1935) pp.1146ff.
404. Ibid.
405. *'Reichsbürgergesetz-Blutschutzgesetz-Ehegesundheitsgesetz'* nebst allen Ausführungs-vorschriften und den einschlägigen Gesetzen und Verordnungen. Erläutert von Staatssekretär Dr. Stuckart und ORR Dr. Globke. Kommentare zur deutschen Rassengesetz-gebung Bd. I (Munich-Berlin 1936) p.25.
406. RGBl. I (1935) p.1333.
407. H. Robinsohn, *Justiz als politische Verfolgung. Die Rechtsprechung in "Rassenschande-fällen" beim Landgericht Hamburg 1936–1943* (Stuttgart 1977) p.58.
408. R-M. Strecker, *Dr. Hans Globke* op. cit. p.115.
409. ND PS-2699.
410. ND PS-1778.
411. M. Maschmann, op. cit. pp.56–7.
412. *SOPADE-Berichte* 1935 p.813.
413. Ibid. p.1043.
414. F.J. Heyen, *Nationalsozialismus im Alltag* op. cit. p.146.
415. M. Brozat et al. (eds.) *Bayern in der NS-Zeit* op. cit. Vol. I, pp.466-7.
416. *SOPADE-Berichte* 1935 p.814.
417. K.A. Schleunes, *The Twisted Road to Auschwitz. Nazi Policy Toward German Jews 1933–39* (London 1972) pp.193–4.
418. U.D. Adam, *Judenpolitik im Dritten Reich* (Düsseldorf 1972) p.157.
419. Heyen, *Nationalsozialismus im Alltag* p.139.
420. H. Genschel, *Die Verdrängung der Juden* op. cit. p.291.
421. H. von Kotze & H. Krausnick, *"Es Spricht der Führer"* op. cit. pp.147–8.
422. RGBl.I (1938) p.1044.
423. ND PS-3063.

424. ND L-202.
425. D. Rebentisch & A. Raab, *Neu-Isenburg* op. cit. p.259.
426. M. Maschmann, *Account Settled* op. cit. pp.56–7.
427. ND PS-1816.
428. W. Hofer (ed.), *Der Nationalsozialismus* op. cit. p.295.
429. RGBl I (1938) p.1579.
430. RGBl. I (1938), p.1580.
431. T.W. Mason, *Arbeiterklasse* op. cit. pp.890ff.
432. ND PS-841.
433. Landesarchiv Berlin AVfK DGT 1-2-6/1.
434. ND PS-1816.
435. Bayerisches Hauptstaatsarchiv MA 106/670.
436. M. Steinert, *Hitlers Krieg und die Deutschen* (Düsseldorf-Vienna 1970) p.44.
437. *SOPADE-Berichte* 1934 p.471.
438. D. Klinksiek, *Die Frau im NS-Staat* op. cit. p.145.
439. Ibid. p.144.
440. a) *SOPADE-Berichte* 1939 p.446.
     b) Ibid. p.447.
     c) Ibid.
     d) D. Klinksiek, *Die Frau im NS-Staat* op. cit. p.145.
     e) Ibid.
441. *SOPADE-Berichte* 1939 p.52.
442. Ibid. pp.450–1.
443. *SOPADE-Berichte* 1936 pp.1249.
444. D. Rebentisch & A. Raab, *Neu-Isenburg* op. cit. pp.84–5.
445. *SOPADE-Berichte* 1935 pp.1375–6.
446. *SOPADE-Berichte* 1936 pp.683–4.
447. *SOPADE-Berichte* 1937 p.1084.
448. *SOPADE-Berichte* 1938 pp.26–27.
449. *SOPADE-Berichte* 1934 p.172.
450 *SOPADE-Berichte* 1937 pp.481–2.
451. *SOPADE-Berichte* 1938 p.697.
452. I. Kershaw, *Political Opinion & Political Dissent in the Third Reich. Bavaria 1933-1945* (Oxford 1983) pp.166–7.
453. *Kirchliches Jahrbuch 1933–1944* (Gütersloh 1948) p.70.
454. M. Broszat et al. (eds.), *Bayern in der NS-Zeit*, op. cit. vol. I, pp.412–416.
455. *The Persecution of the Catholic Church in the Third Reich* (London 1940) p.170.
456. M. Broszat et al. (eds.), *Bayern in der NS-Zeit* op. cit. vol. I, pp.130–1.
457. G. Weisenborn, *Der lautlose Aufstand: Bericht über die Widerstandsbewegung des deutschen Volkes 1933–45* (Hamburg 1954) pp.153–4.
458. *SOPADE-Berichte* 1936 p.157.
459. T.W. Mason, *Arbeiterklasse* op. cit. pp.379ff.
460. *SOPADE-Berichte* 1934 p.347.
461. ND R-152.
462. *SOPADE-Berichte* 1938 p.256.
463. Ibid. pp.394–5.
464. Bundesarchiv-militärarchiv Freiburg RW 19/87.
465. Ibid.
466. Ibid.

A Selective Bibliography for Part II

P. Aycoberry, *The Nazi Question. An Essay on the Interpretations of National Socialism*, New York 1981.

R. Bessel, ed., *Life in the Third Reich*, Oxford 1987.

A.D. Beyerchen, *Scientists under Hitler. Politics and the Physics Community, under the Third Reich*, New Haven 1977.

K.D. Bracher, *The German Dictatorship*, London 1970.

E.K. Bramstedt, *Goebbels and National Socialist Propaganda 1925–1945*, East Lansing, Mich. 1965.

R. Bridenthal et al., *When Biology Became Destiny. Women in Weimar and Nazi Germany*, New York 1984.

M. Broszat, *The Hitler State. The foundation and development of the internal structure of the Third Reich*, London 1981.

J. Caplan, 'The politics of administration. The Reich Interior Ministry and the German Civil Service', *Historical Journal*, 20.3.1977.

W. Carr, *Hitler. A Study in Personality and Politics*, London 1978.

J. Conway, *The Nazi Persecution of the Churches 1933–45*, London 1968.

R. Dahrendorf, *Society and Democracy in Germany*, London 1967.

J.E. Farquarson, *The Plough and the Swastika*, London 1978.

J. Fest, *The Face of the Third Reich*. London 1970. *Hitler*, London 1974.

E. Fraenkel, *The Dual State*, London 1941.

M. Freeman, *Atlas of Nazi Germany*, Beckenham 1987.

S. Gordon, *Hitler, Germans, and the 'Jewish Question'*, Princeton N.J., 1984.

J. H. Grill, *The Nazi Movement in Baden 1920–1945*, Chapel Hill 1983.

R. Grunberger, *A Social History of the Third Reich*, London 1971.

O.J. Hale, *Captive Press in the Third Reich*, Princeton N.J., 1964.

P. Hayes, *Industry and Ideology. I. G. Farben in the Nazi Era*, Cambridge 1987.

H. Heiber, *Joseph Goebbels*, London 1973.

E. C. Helmreich, *The German Churches under Hitler*, Detroit 1979.

J. Herf, *Reactionary Modernism. Technology, Culture and Politics in Weimar and the Third Reich*, Cambridge 1984.

K. Hildebrand, *The Third Reich*, London 1984.

B. Hinz, *Art in the Third Reich*, Oxford 1980.

H. Höhne, *The Order of the Death's Head*, London 1969.

H. James, *The German Slump*. Politics and Economics 1924–1936. Oxford 1986.

M. Kater, *The Nazi Party. A Social Profile of Members and Leaders 1919–1945*, Oxford 1963.

H. Kehr & J. Langmaid, *The Nazi Era 1919–1945*, London 1982.

I. Kershaw, *Popular Opinion and Political Dissent in the Third Reich: Bavaria 1933–1945*, Oxford 1983.

I. Kershaw, *The Nazi Dictatorship*, London 1984.

I. Kershaw, *The Hitler Myth: Image and Reality in the Third Reich*, Oxford 1986.

H.W. Koch, ed. *Aspects of the Third Reich*, London 1985.

L. Kochan, *Progrom. 10 November 1938*, London 1957.

R. Koehl, 'Feudal Aspects of National Socialism' *American Political Science Review*, LIV 1960.

R.L. Koehl, *The Black Corps; the Structure and Power Struggles of the Nazi SS*, Wisconsin 1983.

C. Koonz, *Mothers in the Fatherland. Women, the Family and Nazi Politics*, London 1987.

R. Koshar, *Social Life, Local Politics and Nazism*, Chapel Hill 1986.

H. Krausnick *et al.*, *Anatomy of the SS State*, London 1968.

G. Lewy, *The Catholic Church and Nazi Germany*, London 1964.

A. Maschmann, *Account Rendered*, London 1963.

T. Mason, 'Labour in the Third Reich 1933-1939', *Past and Present*, *XXXIII* 1966. 'The Primacy of Politics' in S.J. Woolf (ed.), *The Nature of Fascism*, New York 1969. 'Women in Germany 1925-1940: Family, Welfare and Work' Parts I & II in *History Workshop* 1976 1 & 2. 'Intention and Explanation: A Current Controversy about the Interpretation of National Socialism', in G. Hirschfeld and L. Ketternocker, eds. *Der 'Führerstaat': Mythos und Realität*, Stuttgart 1981.

H. Mommsen, 'National Socialism: Continuity and Change' in W. Laqueur' (ed.) *Fascism. A Reader's Guide*, London 1976.

F. Neumann, *Behemoth: The Structure and Practice of National Socialism 1933-1944*, London 1974.

J. Noakes (ed.) *Government, Party and People in Nazi Germany*, Exeter 1980.

D. Orlow, *A History of the Nazi Party 1933-1945* (Newton Abbot 1973).

R. Overy, *The Nazi Economic Recovery 1932-1938*, London 1982.

R.J. Overy, *Goering. The 'Iron Man'*, London 1984.

D. Penkart, *Inside Nazi Germany*, London 1987.

E.N. Peterson, *The Limits of Hitler's Power*, Princeton N.J., 1969.

D. Peukert, *Inside Nazi Germany. Conformity, Opposition and Racism in Everyday Life*, London 1987.

R. A. Pois, *National Socialism and the Religion of Nature*, London 1986.

H. Rauschning, *The Revolution of Nihilism: Warning to the West*, New York 1939.

J.M. Ritchie, *German Literature Under National Socialism*, London 1983.

W. Sauer, 'National Socialism: Totalitarianism or Fascism?' *American Historical Review* LXXIII 1967.

K. Schleunes, *The Twisted Road to Auschwitz: Nazi Policy towards German Jews 1933-1939*, Urbana, Ill., 1970.

D. Schoenbaum, *Hitler's Social Revolution: Class and Status in Nazi Germany 1933-1939*, London 1967.

A. Schweitzer, *Big Business in the Third Reich*, Bloomington, Ind./London 1964.

R. Smelser, *Robert Ley. Hitler's Labour Front Leader*, Oxford 1988.

A. Speer, *Inside the Third Reich: Memoirs*, London 1970.

P. Stachura (ed.) *The Shaping of the Nazi State*, London 1978.

M.S. Steinberg, *Sabers and Brownshirts. The German Students' Path and National Socialism 1918-1935*, Chicago 1977.

J. Stephenson, *Women In Nazi Society*, London 1976. *The Nazi Organisation of Women*, London 1981

J.P. Stern, *Hitler: The Führer and his People*, London 1975.

R. Taylor, *The Word in Stone: the role of architecture in the National Socialist ideology*, Berkeley 1974.

H. A. Turner, ed., *Nazism and the Third Reich*, New York 1972.

A.L. Unger, *The Totalitarian Party: party and people in Nazi Germany and Soviet Russia*, Cambridge 1974.

P.L.D. Walker, *Hitler Youth and Catholic Youth*, Washington DC 1970.

D. Welch, *Propaganda and the German Cinema 1933-1945 Nazi Propaganda. The Power and the Limitations*, Oxford 1983. (ed.) London 1983.

About the Authors

Jeremy Noakes was educated at Oxford University and is currently a Reader in Modern European History at Exeter University. He is the author of *The Nazi Party in Lower Saxony 1921–1933* and of many articles on various aspects of Nazi Germany.

Geoffrey Pridham was educated at Cambridge University and is now a Reader in European Politics at Bristol University. He is the author of *Hitler's Rise to Power: The Nazi Party in Bavaria 1925–1933*.